PREHISTORIC NEW MEXICO

PREHISTORIC NEW MEXICO

Background for Survey

by

David E. Stuart, Rory P. Gauthier

with contributions by

Thomas W. Merlan

University of New Mexico Press
Albuquerque

Library of Congress Cataloging-in-Publication Data

Stuart, David E.
    Prehistoric New Mexico.

    Reprint. Originally published: Albuquerque: New Mexico Archeological Council, 1984.
    Bibliography: p.
    1. Indians of North America—New Mexico—Antiquities. 2. New Mexico—Antiquities.
I. Gauthier, Rory P. II. Merlan, Thomas W. III. Title.
E78.N65S85 1988   978.9'01 88-20450
ISBN 0-8263-1066-4

First published 1981 by the State of New Mexico, Office of Cultural Affairs, Historic Preservation
Division. Reprinted 1984 by the New Mexico Archeological Council. © 1984 NM/HPD. University
of New Mexico Press edition reprinted 1988 and 1996 by arrangement with the authors and the state
of New Mexico. All rights reserved.

Frontispiece: Kana's banded olla, ca. A.D. 800.
by Scott Andrae, La Plata, New Mexico.

MARK WIMBERLY

1947-1981

Pasó por Aquí

TABLE OF CONTENTS

LIST OF ILLUSTRATIONS

List of Illustrations (Continued)

Page

List of Illustrations (Continued)

LIST OF TABLES

ACKNOWLEDGMENTS

Many people were helpful to us in the course of preparation of this volume.

First and foremost, Mr. Stewart Peckham of the Laboratory of Anthropology, Museum of New Mexico, gave us his advice throughout and provided site descriptions for sites on the State and National Registers. While Mr. Peckham is the original author of most of the site descriptions and site maps that appear in this volume, others had contributed to these materials over the years. These are: Dr. S. LeBlanc, M. Marshall, Dr. F. Levine, P. Schaafsma, C. Schaafsma, D. Snow, J. Stein, D. Lang, F. Broilo, P. Beckett, L. Flynn, A. Schroeder, C. Smith, Dr. W.J. Judge and personnel of the National Park Service and Lea County Archeological Society. While a few of the site descriptions which appear in this volume are in nearly original format, we have added commentary to many in order to relate sites to issues raised in the text. Rosemary Talley, Marsha Jackson, Barbara Mauldin and Marina Ochoa, all of the Laboratory of Anthropology staff, were also quite helpful.

Others permitted us to cite their material verbatim at length. These are: P. Beckett, New Mexico State University and R. Wiseman, Laboratory of Anthropology, Museum of New Mexico, in Chapter V and M. Wimberly and P. Eidenbach, Human Systems Research, Tularosa, in Chapter IV. In other cases we abstracted and tabulated data from major works which characterized the archeology of a given area in some detail. These appear throughout the volume. The authors of the original material are cited in each. Citations of lesser extent are credited in the customary way, in text.

A number of other archeologists also provided us with review copies of reports and other supporting materials. Dr. D. Green, U.S. Forest Service, Dr. M. Harlan, University of New Mexico, and L. Flynn provided the series of Bureau of Land Management — United States Department of Agriculture Forest Service overviews to which much of our commentary is directed. J. Beardsley, Bureau of Land Management (Colorado) provided sources from his personal library. Dr. F. Levine, Bureau of Land Management, gave us survey reports for Southeastern New Mexico and researched photo archives for us. L. Flynn and Drs. T. Birkedal and W. Wait of the National Park Service provided data and overviews from the northern tier of New Mexico. We have also been afforded the luxury of citing copious data from the National Park Service' SJBRUS File (San Juan Data Base).

A number of representatives of archeological contracting institutions/research foundations gave us survey reports for review. These are: D. Snow, Laboratory of Anthropology, Santa Fe, J. Beal, School of American Research, Santa Fe, Dr. M. Kemrer, San Juan County Museum, Bloomfield, B. Naylor, New Mexico State University — Farmington Branch Campus, T.J. Ferguson, Zuni Archeological Program, S. Schermer, Eastern New Mexico University, Portales, C. Carroll and R. Loose, Public Service Company, New Mexico — Albuquerque, Dr. M. Harlan, University of New Mexico, M. Wimberly and P. Eidenbach, Human Systems Research, Tularosa, P. Beckett, New Mexico State University, Las Cruces.

Other colleagues reviewed early versions of draft manuscript in detail and made editorial suggestions. These are: Dr. J. Tainter, Forest Service, M. Marshall, R. Farwell, Museum of New Mexico, and Dr. S. Beckerman, Southern Methodist University, Dallas.

There is also a category of persons with whom one consults as ideas are formed, and data are assembled. In a way, some of these persons are hidden authors of the volume, since other's suggestions often become inextricably interwoven with ones own ideas. These are: Dr. Beckerman (an important contributor, specifically, on ideas about power and efficiency — see Chapter II), Dr. W. J. Judge (Chaco Center — National Park Service), M. Marshall, J. Stein, P. Eidenbach, M. Wimberly, G. Cleveland (Pullman, Washington), Dr. M. Harlan, S. Peckham, W. Allan (Bureau of Indian Affairs), S. Andrae and D. Ford (La Plata, New Mexico) and Dr. L. Cordell (University of New Mexico).

Some colleagues insist on offering support that knows no limit and comes to be very special. Though these friends invariably played roles cited above, we want these to know we remember. John Broster listened to the senior author's every theoretical idea and scheme for organizing the chapter material for 21 months; his patience, range of suggestions and support make him a technical consultant to the volume. Gail Wimberly (Composing Services, Tularosa) typed draft after draft of this manuscript, and when the senior author had eye trouble she transcribed material from tape. When a chapter came out badly (and several early pieces of manuscript were very badly conceived) or when the reference materials needing to be covered seemed so extensive that we despaired of ever reading and analyzing them, she would tell us that we could do it. How well we did it is for the reader to decide. We reviewed data on some 5,000 archeological sites and seven to eight hundred reports and publications, and are now rather surprised to have gotten so far.

The frontispiece was drawn by Scott Andrae. Chapter II illustrations were drafted by Emily K. Abbink and all the many others by Ernest Shearin. We thank each for lending their talents to our effort.

Mark Wimberly and Peter Eidenbach of Human Systems Research, Inc. provided the administrative and technical support that made the project possible. Although they represented the contract institution and were in a position to demand editorial control of the project, they aid nothing of the sort, but gave us the liberty to exercise professional judgment in every aspect of the work. At the same time, they never failed to give us whatever support was needed. We feel privileged to have been selected for this project.

We especially thank Dr. Carol J. Condie, President of the New Mexico Archeological Council, for her efforts in arranging to publish the second edition of this work.

D.E. Stuart
R.P. Gauthier

Chapter I
INTRODUCTION

This report comes at the end of ten years in which the New Mexico Historic Preservation Program has attempted to evaluate and identify the state's prehistoric resources. Federal and State laws, which are considered in detail in Chapter VIII, require such identification and evaluation.

This report is delinquent. It could be argued that it should have been done first, before the program attempted to do anything else. Earlier plans have been written, particularly the one which was published in 1973. All these plans, however, were conventional histories, or lists of sites, or short-term administrative proposals. None of them attempted to summarize our knowledge of the state's prehistory, to make a theoretical reconstruction of prehistoric processes out of that knowledge, to contrive a theoretical basis broad enough to explain the processes being reported, and to recommend future work in detail. These are the things that the present volume tries to do.

We suppose that this report was not written earlier because the relationship between administrative requirements and research problems was not fully recognized. We were led to write this report by severely practical concerns. How, for example, does one apportion limited funds for the required survey of resources? The question is more complicated than it at first appears. You cannot describe an archeological site without establishing categories of data to be recorded, and you cannot establish data categories without setting forth some sort of theory about the processes that created the site. The significance of an archeological site, as we will point out later on, is a relationship between the physical attributes of the site and the state of our knowledge of the nature of the site. We found that we could not answer the administrative questions without attempting the theoretical problems. So we applied ourselves to both.

We had problems from the start with colleagues who said that any report in the nature of a statewide research design was bound to ignore or exclude some research interests. The state historic preservation program, in cooperation with agencies of the federal government, defines significance in prehistoric sites. Such definitions have the eventual effect of excluding some sites or resources from further consideration or investigation. Our critics knew this. They told us that it made a statewide research design undesirable, invidious.

They were forgetting the circumstances behind our program. The Congress passed a law providing for the identification, evaluation and protection of sites because an alarming number of sites was being destroyed. Now when sites are destroyed *in the manner permitted by the federal law*, they are first investigated by a principal investigator who deals with them in one way and no other. No one else will have an opportunity to investigate them on another theoretical basis. The state historic preservation programs are parties to the formulation of the program of research to be undertaken in these cases. It follows that the state programs must have some theoretical basis for their proposals about survey and data recovery. We do not propose to dictate anyone's research interests, but we cannot comply with our legal responsibilities without having a research design of our own. We have tried, through consultation with colleagues and review of publications, to make the design as broad as possible.

We are not aware of any circumstance which will prohibit the application of various theories and points of view to sites which are to be preserved rather than salvaged. The opponents of this project told us in substance that the state historic preservation program should be willing to pay for whatever they chose to do. They forgot that the preservation programs are not research programs. Research designs are a means, not an end, in the state programs. Our interests are mainly managerial, which means among other things that we will inevitably pursue some lines of inquiry and exclude others.

Remember that the problem of significance in cultural resources is an administrative problem in more ways than one. Some agencies and interests involved in land modification figured in the Congressional discussion of the Historic Preservation Act of 1966. The law was to a great extent an answer to those agencies, and an attempt at a solution of the problems they typified. These agencies and interests have watched us work since then. They want to know when we will be finished identifying significant resources. They tell us that there must be a limit to the number of such resources. They say and imply often that we may have already passed that limit. And more and more they want to know what significance in cultural resources is. They insist on a definition.

Here, then, in this report, is a definition of significance in prehistoric resources in New Mexico. The definition is fragmentary, obscure and provisional, and very complicated. It is not the short, neat, objective definition we have often been asked for, in which the sites themselves never figure as terms. It is not permanent. We calculate that it will need revision in five years at most. Perhaps it doesn't read like a definition at all, but it is.

We began this project knowing it needed to be done, but without a clear idea of its nature and extent. We thought we could write a state plan for National Register surveys in New Mexico. We believed it would be a dull straightforward job requiring us to summarize regional archeological data, compile a list of areas surveyed and not surveyed, and translate these into a plan that was administratively feasible and would represent a consensus of contemporary research interests in the state.

First we wanted to read a statewide research design and survey plan from another state, to get an idea of the proper form. There was no such document. Then we determined to poll our colleagues for opinions as to how we might divide New Mexico up into appropriate archeological subareas for research purposes. We suggested culture areas, drainage basins, major vegetation zones, and political subdivisions (e.g. counties) as possible subareas. We waited for some sort of consensus to emerge. None did! We sought a consensus, too, on research priorities. We found none. The territorial and theoretical problems seemed to be getting more and more tangled, so we dropped it for awhile and started to collect data. More problems emerged. We went ahead finally and addressed them here without a satisfactory consensus. We would like to say something about our approach.

It might seem simple to divide New Mexico up into appropriate archeological subareas. This is far from being the case. While it is easy to identify the core area of a major cultural tradition (Anasazi vs. Mogollon, for example), the boundaries are hard to define. There is also the fact that the geographic limits of major archeological developments change noticeably over time. A set of core areas for A.D. 800 is inappropriate and misleading at A.D. 1200. Of course, the concept of an archeological phase was intended to describe these space-time correlates and so overcome the problem. However, there are two particular problems with drawing a picture of the archeological record entirely in these terms. One is theoretical, the other practical. Many archeologists now argue that the *phase* is an inappropriate classification, since it gives too much attention to *trait lists*, or superficial similarities and differences in material assemblages. We will come back to this point in a moment. Secondly, many archeological phases in New Mexico have been defined on the basis of the attributes of only one or two sites in a small area. The Black Mountain Phase in the Mimbres district and the Late McKenzie Phase in the middle Pecos Valley are examples. Phases so defined are no sound basis for broad generalizations.

In attempting to overcome these problems, many archeologists have come to emphasize the study of regional systems and have rejected systems based on traits, phases and core areas as not conforming to scientific practice. This argument might be funny if it were not made so seriously. Systems orientation is based on an idea of how populations behaved adaptively. The systems theory concepts travelled into the archeological literature from disciplines, among them ecology, economics, psychology and sociology, in which living systems were the primary units of study. The system, then, was defined by the interactive behavior either of living organisms, or the components of such organisms (e.g. molecules). The interactive context of an archeological system ended, of course, when the people who participated in it died or moved on.

A field archeologist observes neither a system nor adaptive behavior when he records archeological sites. Only material and spatial attributes are observed. The archeologist makes an inference as to what constitutes a system or adaptation. The phase-oriented archeologist does about the same thing, except that he infers a culture rather than a system. Since both schools of thought have essentially the same problem, it is unfortunate that so many have declined to join forces and to give their attention to the major unresolved issue: methodology. It is usually methodology which resolves the problems of observation in the long run.

Circumstances saved us from having to propose a solution to the culture area vs. adaptive system problem. When we got to work, the Bureau of Land Management and the U.S. Forest Service had just begun to commission a series of cultural resource overviews of New Mexico. Eight areas of the state had been identified for review, largely on the basis of agency landholdings, but designed also not to partition generally accepted core areas. The BLM and the Forest Service asked us to cooperate, basing our subareas on theirs to produce a coordinated set of reports. Except for Torrance County, the woebegone stepchild generally referred to at the time as *central New Mexico*, the federal overview areas were not hard to bring into line with our own general ideas about how to organize the discussion. So, we agreed. The map of federal overview areas appears as Map I.1. The federal overviews are cited in each chapter and are meant to be read as companions to this volume. Many data contained in these regional summaries are not repeated here.

In adapting the federal subareas (see Map I.2), we joined the San Juan Basin and Upper Rio Grande areas to emphasize post-Chacoan (P-III — A.D. 1100+) population shifts to the east (Chapter III). We also thought it would be useful to discuss the Mt. Taylor and Socorro districts together (Chapter IV), with one adjustment so as to include only areas south of Interstate 40. Southwestern and south-central New Mexico also belonged together, in our view, since we wanted to focus on the relationships between the Mimbres and Jornada branches of Mogollon development (Chapter V). Southeastern New Mexico and the Northeast Plains underwent a minor revision, based on our judgment of differing assemblage attributes. These two areas appear in Chapters VI and VII, respectively. Orphaned Torrance County we treated with the Northeast Plains, as the best practical solution to a problem with various possible solutions.

Our version and discussion of these federal agency overview areas is the basic structure of the book. The reader ought not to forget that the borders of these areas were marked to follow an administrative decision. They do not generally reflect the verifiable discontinuities between regions in the archeological record. Early in the project Mr. Stewart Peckham of the Laboratory of Anthropology of the Museum of New Mexico advised us to consider organizing our discussion by *natural areas* (based on vegetation, soils, physiography and hydrology) that a multidisciplinary panel had arrived at a few years earlier. We would have followed this

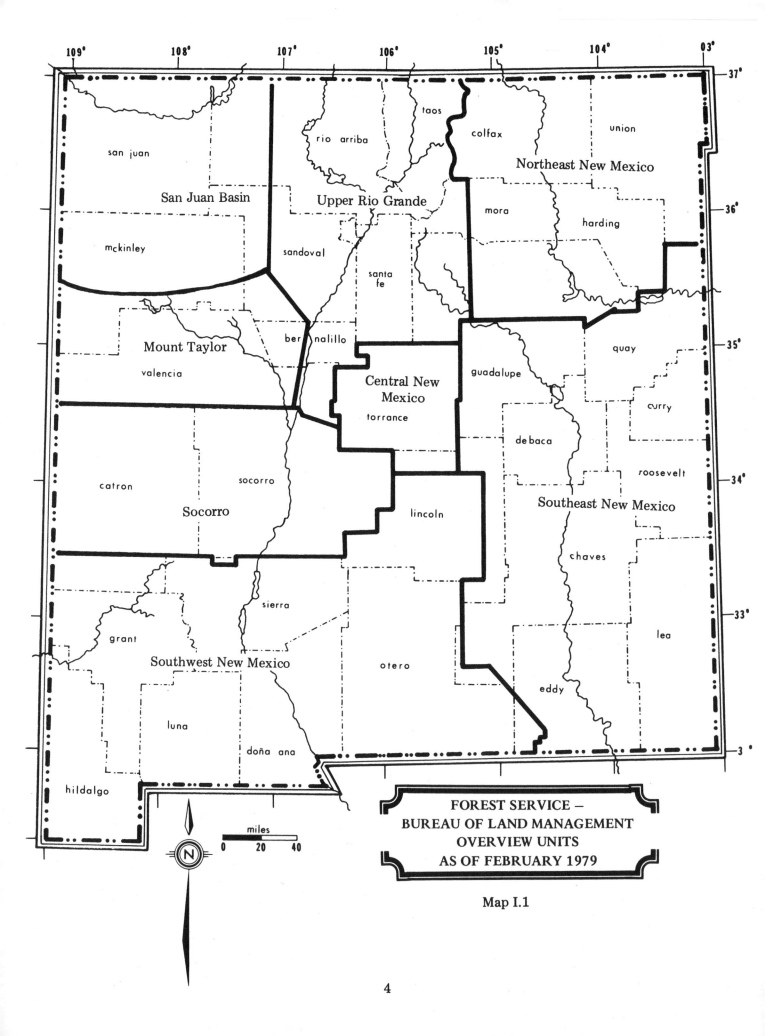

109° 108° 107° 106° 105° 104° 03°

san juan

rio arriba

taos

colfax

union

Northeast New Mexico

San Juan Basin

Upper Rio Grande

mora

harding

mckinley

sandoval

santa fe

Mount Taylor

bernalillo

quay

Central New Mexico

guadalupe

valencia

curry

torrance

debaca

catron

socorro

roosevelt

Socorro

lincoln

Southeast New Mexico

sierra

chaves

grant

Southwest New Mexico

lea

otero

eddy

luna

doña ana

hildalgo

miles

0   20   40

N

FOREST SERVICE —
BUREAU OF LAND MANAGEMENT
OVERVIEW UNITS
AS OF FEBRUARY 1979

Map I.1

37°

36°

35°

34°

33°

3°

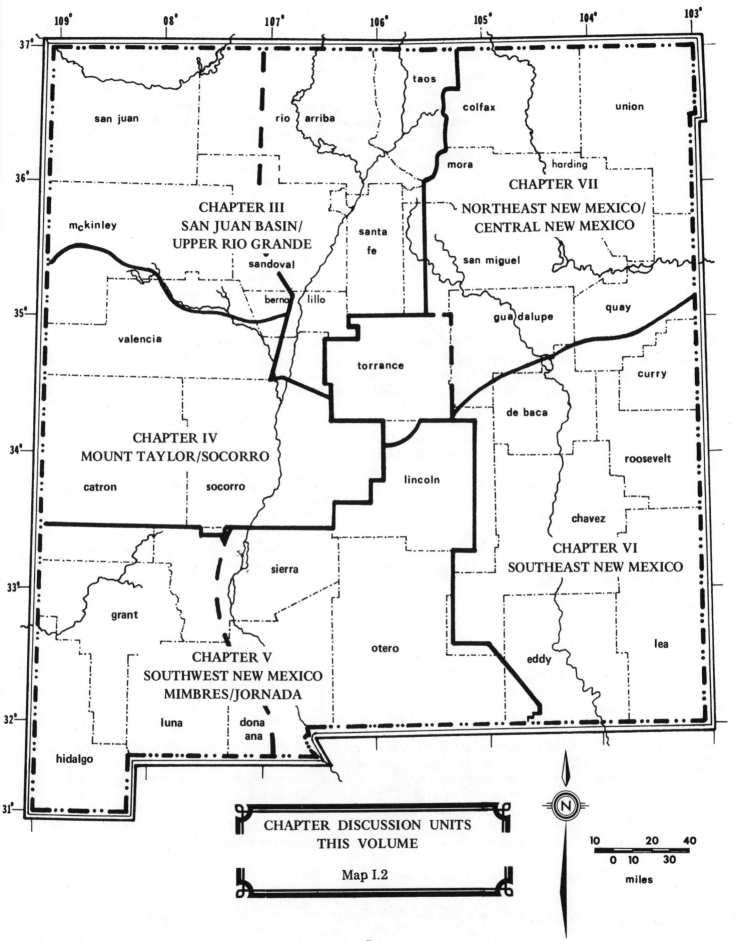

109°   08°   107°   106°   105°   104°   103°

37°

san juan

rio arriba   taos   colfax   union

36°

mckinley

**CHAPTER III
SAN JUAN BASIN/
UPPER RIO GRANDE**

sandoval

santa fe

mora   harding

**CHAPTER VII
NORTHEAST NEW MEXICO/
CENTRAL NEW MEXICO**

san miguel

35°

valencia

bern⌐   lillo

torrance

gua dalupe   quay

curry

**CHAPTER IV
MOUNT TAYLOR/SOCORRO**

de baca

34°

catron   socorro

lincoln

roosevelt

chavez

**CHAPTER VI
SOUTHEAST NEW MEXICO**

33°

grant

sierra

otero

eddy   lea

**CHAPTER V
SOUTHWEST NEW MEXICO
MIMBRES/JORNADA**

32°

luna   dona ana

hidalgo

31°

**CHAPTER DISCUSSION UNITS
THIS VOLUME**

Map I.2

N

10   20   40
0   10   30
miles

5

sensible advice but for the evident advantages of making our report conform generally to the federal agency organization. We lost something by not following the natural area concept. Logically distinct subareas in the archeological record should have emerged. We would have been focusing on presumed adaptive similarities, and appropriate research strategies and priorities could have been proposed to bring essential adaptive characteristics into more detail. In short, Mr. Peckham's suggestion, if we had followed it up, might have opened a way for the eventual resolution of the phase-core area vs. systems problem — no small achievement. But this, as we have said, was not to be.

We did derive unexpected gains from the method we adopted. Perhaps because of the seeming illogical juxtaposition of data from sites which should have been discussed separately, certain contrasts began to impress us. At first we found patterns of site placement and assemblage characteristics that we had not expected and did not understand. Then slowly, very slowly, what we had learned and been taught to expect faded into the background, and a new pattern of temporally asymmetrical development in different altitude zones emerged. At first we thought we had made a case in only two regions, but as the work went on our evidence grew for a surprising symmetry in the timing of major settlement changes throughout New Mexico.

As we became more accustomed to searching out patterns in site placement, size and subsistence remains, a picture of New Mexico's archeology began to form. Our recognition of some fundamental problems grew with it. As each new question was raised, the data were found inadequate to the task of a satisfactory solution.

At one point we wanted to make a computation based on the elevations of five hundred sites in each overview area. We could not do it. Another time we wanted to separate early P-III sites in one region (P-III being traditionally the period A.D. 1100-1300) from late P-III sites in another. We could not do it. The scale of the new picture of archeological development in New Mexico which we have adumbrated is several times larger than the comparability of site data. So we reviewed many contract survey reports, and elected to discuss these problems and their possible solutions in Chapter IX.

We hope that as you read, you will learn, not only some things about archeology in New Mexico, but some things about what *we know* about archeology in New Mexico. Did you know that there are only twenty-nine archeological sites which have been dated by absolute means in the eastern 45% of the state? This is equivalent to one dated site per 450 years of total occupation in nearly sixty thousand square miles. No wonder we have some problems of regional interpretation! Did you know that the early (A.D. 1100-1200) P-III period is characterized by pithouse occupations throughout the highlands of New Mexico — two to three hundred years out of phase, by Pecos Classification standards? You no doubt know that there is no single comprehensive source for the number of recorded sites or excavated sites in the state. We put these in where we could throughout the volume. The result is pretty unsatisfactory, but the job is Homeric.

The research conducted for this report proceeded from recorded site characteristics to local phase definitions, and back to patterns of regional development. At first we did not expect to put much emphasis on development as described by local phase sequences. Then, as we constructed our *new* picture of shifts in settlement, we discovered that it was largely an old picture, but a picture that had existed in dozens of fragments which were the descriptions of local phase sequences. We discovered that archeologists had given many good portraits of change and development in local areas, but had shown less ability in creating regional perspectives.

We also found that problems of classification grew with the geographic expansion of the classificatory framework. In the Anasazi area the Pecos Classification presents problems that may never be entirely overcome, but the scheme has benefits that may keep it alive indefinitely.

The theoretical reconstruction presented in this volume is summarized in Chapter X. There we take the site records and local phase sequences discussed in each chapter and put these into the Pecos Classification. We use the classification as a series of temporal horizons. We have removed much of the detail from the Pecos Classification (architecture, ceramics, etc.), but have left those details in the local phase sequences. So we have used the Pecos Classification to describe major reorganizations in settlement and subsistence throughout New Mexico, but we are impressed by the possibilities for use of detailed local phase sequences for the foreseeable future. Archeologists should resist the temptation to carelessly create local phase designations and to confuse the terminology, but judicious use of local phase sequences will give us a picture of unexampled clarity and detail.

Finally, we have created a theoretical framework which addresses fundamental issues of evolutionary process and the divergence of homogeneous systems into separate entities. It is our argument that evolution does not proceed in stages, but in episodes of such divergence. We suggest an explanation for the cycles of change in human society that have been observed and commented on through 2500 years of written history.

Though we begin and end the report with these ideas, one thing seems to us more important. A useful archeological field survey report is guided by theory but is, first and foremost, descriptively precise. In order for it to achieve descriptive excellence it must be based on excellence in method. Whatever the force or value of the theory, a survey report that is not an impeccable record of observations and method is nothing but an essay. We discovered that there are very few survey reports in the literature, and altogether too many essays.

This volume, then, is a background to future archeological survey and analysis. We have tried to be fair to various schools of thought. We do not know if our portrayal of prehistoric development in New Mexico will be generally accepted. We hope that this report will encourage its readers to think over their own positions and to see new patterns in the archeological record as a prelude to future research.

D.E.S. — Amizette, September 1980
T.W.M. — Arroyo del Tajo, October 1980
R.P.G. — La Plata, September 1980

Photo 1: An aerial photograph of Chaco Canyon. Barely visible at the top of the photograph is the ruin of Pueblo del Arroyo (Judd 1959), followed by Pueblo Bonito (Judd 1954), Chetro Ketl (Hawley 1934, Hewett 1936), and the Chetro Ketl agriculture field (Loose and Lyons 1976). Most of the modern buildings around Pueblo Bonito were constructed by Richard Wetherill along with the large dam located immediately to the southeast of Pueblo Bonito (McNitt 1957). The Chaco wash is on the left side of the photograph. View is to the west. Photograph by Charles Lindbergh, courtesy of the Museum of New Mexico.

Chapter II

RESEARCH PERSPECTIVE: POWER AND EFFICIENCY

INTRODUCTION

A century of theorizing about cultural development has offered anthropologists only explanatory frameworks which remain rather incomplete. While the specific subject of this volume is the prehistory of New Mexico, it is not the only subject, for, at the same time, it is necessary to rephrase general questions about the way the human world operates. This is, after all, the real subject of anthropology. Cultural evolutionary theories suffer their particular incompleteness because, in focusing on general evolutionary consequences, they have not focused sufficiently on individual human behavior. Such theories are only imperfectly anthropological in perspective.

In other words, we are secure only in our knowledge that the general direction of cultural evolution has been towards larger and more complex systems. As Lotka (1922) phrased it: "evolution proceeds such that systems flux greater and greater quantities of energy over time". The idea of energy flow in cultural systems is an important theme in ecology (Odum 1971) and in cultural evolution (White 1959; Sahlins and Service 1966). We attach great importance to it also, for it is, of course, irrefutable that larger and more complex systems process more energy than smaller, less stratified ones, but the traditional attention has been placed on the *products* of cultural evolution rather than the evolutionary processes themselves. Since many cultural systems have not evolved into more complex forms, anthropology has, for example, faced the acute difficulty of explaining the continued existence of hunters and gatherers or modest-scale agriculturalists.

This issue more than any other has shaped the general development of anthropological enquiry. With the failure of the late 19th century's unilinear evolutionists to explain satisfactorily why many cultural systems did not undergo broad transformational stages, attention turned to the particulars of history to account for cultural diversity. Though historical method substantially enriched the *style* of anthropological interpretation, it inevitably lacked authenticity when specifically applied to prehistoric subjects. To our mind, this uneasiness about authenticity, coupled with the recent self-conscious quest for the status of scientists, accounted more for the gradual shift away from historical method in archeology than did the underlying theoretical issues, which remain unresolved.

The more recent ecological-processual school of thought in archeology is only off-handedly evolutionary. True, Dr. Steward (1955) presented cultural ecology and multilinear evolution together as parts of the same construct, but ecology and adaptation have provided us only a model of parallel evolution. When the ecological model does become explicitly evolutionary in its application, ecological possibilism inevitably must be transformed into environmental determinism. It is for this reason that environmental determinism and climatic reconstructions are so highly related. Such models are not able to cope with the coexistence of several fundamentally different types of cultural adaptations in the same locale. Nor are they able to account for complex development in a given eco-type and the lack of it in a similar one elsewhere. Why, for instance, did agriculture not develop in the semiarid zones of Australia or North America's Great Basin? Invariably, the climatic reconstructions necessary to resolve these and similar problems require such detail that they become histories of a sort themselves. The explanation given depends on events. That such events are *climatic* rather than *historical* does not obscure the fact that they are events, not processes.

Any really plausible theory of cultural evolution must account for the transformation of some, but not all, hunters and gatherers into agriculturalists. It must account for the continued growth and complexity of some cultural systems and the fact that others continue to be much the same. Further, it must account for the observed relationship between post-Pleistocene population growth and evolutionary process. Finally, authenticity requires that real people behaving in their own self-interest can have set major and irreversible long-term evolutionary process into motion. What is lacking, then, in cultural theory is a model of divergent evolution. When one stops to think about it, this is nothing less than a spectacular omission.

We will begin by providing a model of divergence between hunter-gatherer and agricultural systems, and suggesting a general theoretical framework within which such a model can be put into operation.

The arguments presented here are tentative and unorthodox. For instance, it is argued that agriculture was initially a very fragile strategy employed by the unsuccessful in hunter-gatherer society and that initial population increase during the shift to agriculture was generated by hunters-gatherers, not agriculturalists. As a response to demographic stress and social practices which created an unstable environment, incipient agriculturalists increased rates of population production to reestablish stability, or homeostasis. Such a strategy has been demonstrated elsewhere (Stuart 1980) as a response to periodic catastrophe among hunters-gatherers. Finally, when early agriculturalists learned to act in their own interest by stabilizing their losses demographically and economically, the homeostatic fabric of the surrounding hunter-gatherer society was torn asunder. That is, unable technologically to stabilize the uncertainties of agriculture during its early stage, they stabilized its effects through *social* behavior.

POWER AND EFFICIENCY

We suggest that cultural evolution can be viewed as the consequence of opposition between two selective forces: Power and Efficiency* (see Odum 1971 for formal definitions, especially Chapter 2). Cultural systems create a power drive when they increase rates of population growth, rates of production, or rates of energy expenditure. Colloquially, such systems *pump up*. They also burn out. An efficient system is rather the opposite, so that energy in and energy out are more nearly equal, and the efficiency drive is characterized by decreased rates of population growth, production or energy expenditure. If one conceives of two great trajectories in cultural evolution, then hunters-gatherers fall on the efficiency trajectory, while we in the U.S. as a system fall near the top of the power trajectory. Obviously, the majority of existing cultural systems fall somewhere in between.

More to the point is that cultural systems continually oscillate between these two extremes. In an unstratified cultural system, the whole system *appears* to oscillate in relative internal harmony even when in mild disequilibrium, but we are not so easily fooled with a complex stratified system. For instance, we note in our daily lives that some segments of our society actively seek (and achieve) zero population growth while other segments seek (and achieve) active population increase. If we assume that population rises to the *limits of available energy*, then we must take note of the paradox that the bottom stratum of our society (having less per capita energy) produces population increase at a greater rate than upper strata (access

---

*Dr. S. Beckerman (SMU) and David E. Stuart discussed these ideas in marathon late night coffee sessions during 1975. Over the years Dr. Beckerman has contributed substantially to these ideas, though he is not, of course, accountable for the specific form of the argument presented here.

to more energy — *more powerful*). More accurately, those in the economically more *stable* stratum of society are more homeostatic (efficient) when compared with those in the less stable economic stratum. Since mortality is higher and life span is shorter in the lowest economic stratum, the judgment of instability is both perceived culturally and demonstrable objectively.

We view the shift from hunting-gathering systems, that conferred the benefits of differential reproduction through polygyny upon successful hunters (competitors), to contemporary systems that confer differential reproductive benefits to the economically unsuccessful, as a significant evolutionary change. Obviously, by segmenting or stratifying its behavior, a complex system can be simultaneously powerful and efficient.

It is argued here, as in biology (Eldredge and Gould 1972; Gould 1977, 1977a), that the maintenance of homeostasis is the *goal* and more usual state of living systems. A homeostatic system is an *efficient* system (rates of energy input and output, gross size, complexity, etc.) when compared with one in disequilibrium. A system which is expanding rapidly is not only in a power drive, it is in disequilibrium. Thus, the shift in cultural evolution from a social system which couples economic and demographic power (hunters-gatherers) to a (industrial society) system which reverses this relationship and couples economic power with biological efficiency is an important evolutionary process.

Figure II.1

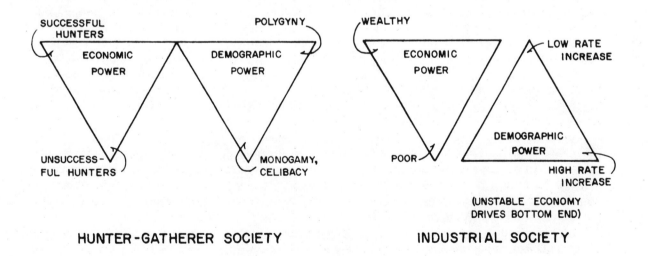

DEMOGRAPHIC V.S. ECONOMIC POWER

HUNTER-GATHERER SOCIETY   INDUSTRIAL SOCIETY

In the course of cultural evolution, then, systems which display demographic power have diverged from those which display demographic efficiency. Obviously, cultural evolution operates to create the divergence of the powerful and the efficient. In biological evolution, speciation can be understood as the divergence between organisms having different thermodynamic properties. The separation of the powerful from the efficient *is* the fundamental process of evolution. When a complex, stratified system fragments under stress, it fragments along lines of differential power and efficiency. In social theory this phenomenon has long been observed at one level as class struggle and the Marxist dialectic. At this point, however, it is premature to rank a given cultural system's components on a scale of power/efficiency, since the energetic costs of stored structure and maintenance are beyond the scope of this inquiry.

In anthropology, we have tended to focus on cultural evolution as the study of successively more complex form. That is, our observations have gone from the material and organizational products of one peak in the power trajectory to the next. In focusing on succession of the large, we have overlooked the role of the small, and the interaction between the two. Hunter-gatherer cultural systems are small, efficient and, having a long history, are vastly durable. The *great* systems (early Egypt, Classic Maya, Rome, etc.) were large and powerful but had shorter histories. Though an uncontrolled drive towards either extreme generates extinction, we argue, in general, that power favors short-term competition while efficiency favors durability in evolutionary terms. The need of a system to be successful in both generates a *balancing act* between immediate and longer term risks, which results in the oscillation we mentioned earlier.

In the San Juan Basin, for example, these oscillations are visible on the ground, archeologically, as small scattered communities aggregate, create a power drive (*pump up* in size and complexity) and then disperse again without clear evidence of corresponding changes in population size (Cordell and Plog 1979). The life cycle of locusts is a useful example of such phases. Locusts and cicadas lie dormant in the ground for years and suddenly emerge (usually triggered by moisture) to fly in vast swarms. The swarming stage is characterized by voracious eating, when competitors for food are literally overwhelmed as the locusts consume everything in their path. Predators (birds) are so overwhelmed by the numbers of locusts that they cannot eat fast enough to dispose of them all. After a few weeks, the members of the swarm breed and die. The offspring develop in the ground, then remain for years as near dormant pupae. These are cycles of power and efficiency. The power drive is characterized by remarkable metabolism, complex anatomical structure, voracious energy intake, and exclusion of competitors for foodstuffs. The power drive is short and dramatic. It burns out quickly and is replaced by the much longer efficiency phase. This phase is characterized by low metabolism, low (or no) energy intake, and simplified anatomical structure. The price of power is compensating efficiency and loss of structural complexity. We refer to the exclusion of competitors by voracious use of resources as creating a *calorie vacuum*. As we shall see, humans do it as well.

We ordinarily think of creatures such as elephants and lions as powerful. They are not, thermodynamically — they are merely large. In fact, they are thermodynamically efficient. In the natural world, large is ordinarily efficient and small is ordinarily powerful. A mass of locusts equal to the body weight of an elephant is a horror of thermodynamic power by comparison. The elephant metabolizes more slowly, eats less, lives longer. Its structure degrades only slowly until death. It is efficient.

This balancing among homeostatic hunters-gatherers such as the Ona of Tierra del Fuego (Stuart 1980) was ordinarily conducted as ever-fluctuating demographic oscillations between local groups. When confronted with an unmanageable catastrophe, the loss of half their territory to European influx, a regionwide efficiency response was induced. In this case, unable to compete, the Ona, a density-dependent system, adjusted itself to fit into an ever

12

shrinking world until it was extinguished by a second catastrophe — disease (Stuart 1972, 1977, 1980). Among hunters-gatherers in general, then, subsistence stress (or the signals which raise its spectre) is reduced quickly, for, whether through conflict or dispersal, the relationship of human biomass to space (population density) is dramatically lowered. Survivors are forced into a dramatic longer-term drive for population regulation (slow birth rates, etc.) if the environmental problem continues.

If the environment returns to normal, a demographic power drive to reestablish the old homeostasis will be induced. It seems to us that long term climatic cyclicity during the earlier glaciations in Northern Europe (Clark 1969:77, 83-84) for example, did not generate a phenomenon like sedentism and agriculture, because the hunter-gatherer systems either dispersed widely or were demographically flattened by such climatic change. In short, the variables of available space, food resources and population were all pulled back into the bottom end of the hunter-gatherer range. It would not have mattered whether cultigens were available or not — after such an occurrence, population would be low and there would be no pressure or advantage for intensification and sedentism. Such flattening just makes surviving populations more like classic hunters-gatherers.

We argue that too much stress simply stalls a homogeneous system, in evolutionary terms. Fundamental evolutionary change takes place primarily in relatively homogeneous cultural systems under very mild stress. In other words, great stress generates extinction or requires efficiency (conservatism), while minimum stress generates diversity and permits inefficiency.

The evolution of the large, stratified systems is also curious. We observe that, with the Classic Maya and in early Egypt, substantial local populations continue to exist, indicating that when such systems failed a substantial portion of the gene pool survived. It is also notable that *fellahin* still practice agriculture much as it was before the disappearance of the pharoahs. Contemporary lowland Maya continue to plant *milpa* as well. In discussing prehistoric New Mexico, it now appears more useful to suggest that substantial population survived the decline of the Chacoan and Mimbres systems.

On the other hand, no one can tell you locally how a pharoah was mummified or how certain Maya astronomical observations were made. In addition, the surviving lineages of kings are scarce in the world today when compared to the surviving lineages of peasants. Large, stratified systems have substantial amounts of energy invested in non-human structure and information. When such systems fail they tend to leave behind surprisingly little evidence of massive die-offs. We argue that in such systems, the complex cultural structures at the top end fail first and reduce the risks of actual population loss. In the archeological remains that we most concern ourselves with we have, we suggest, focused heavily on precisely those features of the archeological record that the population in such a system apparently considers most expendable in a crisis. We argue that the structure of complex cultural systems mimics or reflects the evolutionary principles of power vs. efficiency, since the most power-specialized structures are lost first.

How are the processes of cultural evolution played out, as viewed here? In the tarot, there is a card known as the *tower*. Its message is that *pride goeth before the fall*. Our message is that the fall is proportional to the height of the tower, as is the time left before the fall. The point of a stratified system is that there are organizationally, for instance, three towers, each larger and more complex than the last. Number three, the most complex, suffers the greatest failure and endures the least, and so forth. If, as archeologists, we identify a system by the material or artifactual attributes associated with the most complex cultural structures (tower number three), we are likely to pronounce its demise upon evidence of collapse from the top. We risk obscuring the fact that, organizationally, towers 1 and 2 are still largely intact.

The least complex organizations will include the greatest percentage of the population. In archeology, the difference between a *classic* and *postclassic* phase of a system illustrates this phenomenon. We also have failed to focus on the fact that after a fall, a great system is more nearly equal to a small one — the disparity in the power to compete is dramatically reduced. These relationships are the heart of the *principle of stratification of risks* that has been outlined elsewhere (Stuart n.d.).

EMERGENT EVOLUTIONARY TRAJECTORIES

In order to argue the course of cultural evolution, it is necessary to focus on the differing characteristics of large-complex agricultural systems and hunter-gatherer systems as we know them. The complex agricultural system is characterized by intensive use of the landscape, high rates of population production, high labor investments and increasing size and complexity over time. The hunter-gatherer system is characterized by extensive use of the landscape, low rates of population production (under relatively stable circumstances), very low labor investments and relative stability in size and complexity over time.

That each of these systems has a long observed constellation of differing characteristics comes as no surprise, for the former is a model of power and the latter a model of efficiency. In the former we see substantial complex heterogeneous structure, susceptible to high rates of social/technological change and to disequilibrium. In the latter we see a system with little visible structure, largely homogeneous and egalitarian, characterized by tremendous cultural conservatism, and often homeostatic over time. These types of systems are evolutionarily different, in part, because they occupy powerful as opposed to efficient niches.

Those who exploit large game as a preferred resource are exploiting thermodynamically efficient creatures which may be obtained with comparatively little labor. Whenever smaller creatures and vegetable resources are exploited, humans are pushing down into the broad base of a great pyramid of biomass. Like locusts, small game (rodents, for instance) and grains have short life cycles and high metabolic rates. At its base, the world's pyramid of biomass contains the thermodynamically powerful. The powerful are more numerous per unit of earth's surface where they are found, and since they are small, more work is inevitably required to secure the equivalent of calories obtainable from larger species. When a hunter-gatherer collects wild grains on a given day, a more powerful resource is collected. Since more subsistence labor is required over the course of time than when large game are hunted, the rate of labor input, i.e. the power input, is increased. Wild stands of collectable vegetable resources represent an aggregation or focalization of biomass, and the rate of calorie production per square meter of surface is higher than in the animal production of an equal area. Since the rate of calorie production is higher, the vegetable acreage can be characterized as more powerful from the consumer's viewpoint. These basic ecological relationships are, of course, known to every anthropologist, but intensification of production, increased labor and exploitation of resources which are individually small have not typically been characterized as powerful responses. Colloquially, or in specific terms, they are often referred to as the reverse.

These characterizations of powerful and efficient subsistence foci help make clear the relationships between potential human population size, labor investment and intensification, which are so different between hunter-gatherer and agricultural systems, but they alone do not explain the transformation of hunter-gatherer society.

Most hunters-gatherers, by definition, collect as well as hunt; that is, they exploit both powerful and efficient resources. Simply because of differences in timing and location of available resources, there are periodic (usually seasonal) shifts in dependence. One could argue that simply separating hunting from collecting strategies could create the evolutionary process

14

towards separation of developmental trajectories. In point of fact, some recently surviving hunters-gatherers (the Tasaday, for instance) are highly dependent on collected foodstuffs but are not good candidates for rapid evolution. A focus on collecting behavior doesn't by itself appear to provide the stimulus to create an evolutionary power drive. It is most logical to argue that heterogeneous behavior, a mixed subsistence strategy (which oscillates between powerful and efficient resources), coupled with cyclical instability, is necessary to generate high rates of population growth. This constitutes the missing characteristic of the evolutionary powerful system. One must then argue that the system fragments eventually under stress, such that the power niche and the demographic power drive remain connected as a new system.

Let us turn, then, to a model of the shift to agriculture based on this discussion.

Figure II.2

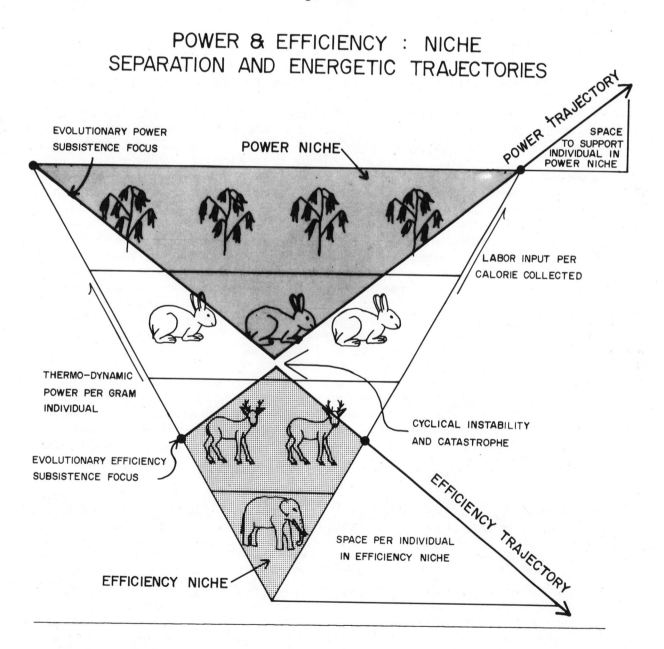

POWER & EFFICIENCY : NICHE SEPARATION AND ENERGETIC TRAJECTORIES

EVOLUTIONARY POWER SUBSISTENCE FOCUS

POWER NICHE

POWER TRAJECTORY

SPACE TO SUPPORT INDIVIDUAL IN POWER NICHE

LABOR INPUT PER CALORIE COLLECTED

THERMO-DYNAMIC POWER PER GRAM INDIVIDUAL

CYCLICAL INSTABILITY AND CATASTROPHE

EVOLUTIONARY EFFICIENCY SUBSISTENCE FOCUS

EFFICIENCY TRAJECTORY

SPACE PER INDIVIDUAL IN EFFICIENCY NICHE

EFFICIENCY NICHE

A MODEL OF DIFFERENTIAL POPULATION REGULATION
THE SHIFT TO SEDENTISM

It is clear to us that, in the archeological record, the initial evolutionary events (partial sedentism, differential population regulation and storage) leading to agriculture came long before the more complex archeological remains ordinarily associated with the shift to cultigens (Flannery 1969).

We further suggest that seasonal scarcity in semiarid environments favored such events because 1) R-selected population behavior (*exponential population growth) is biologically more likely; 2) in systems with pronounced productive lows, population regulating behavior can be more easily altered; 3) given a number of isolated pockets suitable for agriculture, the statistics of unpredictable rainfall preserved a deviating and, initially, fragile behavior; and 4) pockets of different productive potential create local population imbalances, naturally (see Binford 1968; Flannery 1969).

We have elected to focus briefly on the shift to sedentism in early Mesopotamia because it is both a familiar case and, climatically and geographically, an appropriate analogy to the San Juan Basin, with which we will begin our discussion of New Mexico.

In discussing the transition to agriculture and sedentism in the Zagros, Flannery argues for a deviation-amplifying device which was based on a preadaptive stage of broad spectrum collecting, knowledge of cereals and storage facilities and, "a series of responses to disturbances of density equilibrium in human populations around the margins of the favored areas caused by the fact that those areas were the zones of population growth and emigration" (1969:95). He provides a population chart (p. 93) which indicates population growth *prior to* the beginning of dry-farming and archeologically observable villages about 7500 B.C.

An annually cyclical environment does contain pockets of unequal productive capacity. That is, *favored areas*, in Flannery's (1969) terms. The point is that such environments convey substantial information to hunters-gatherers — the times and places of greatest stress (scarcity) are in a general way predictable enough that hunters-gatherers know when and where to direct competitive behavior when resources are scarce. In a stable (generalized) ecosystem (Harris 1969) the environment conveys less information, since one place is rather like another. Obviously, disruption of seasonal transhumance would have more serious consequences in a cyclical, specialized environment.

What was reached in the Zagros by about 10,000 B.C. was a situation in which 1) population was high relative to earlier periods, 2) space in which to disperse was at a premium over a wide geographic area, and 3) no catastrophism intervened to bring the regional balance back to lower limits. In essence, the world was full, as Cohen (1977) has argued, but not bursting — a combination of factors which can be reasonably argued not to have occurred earlier in human history.

---

* In reading this chapter it is necessary to grasp the contrast between the R-selected and K-selected population models used in biology. The K-selected system self-limits at or below carrying capacity; growth is slow (sigmoidal growth curve) once the carrying capacity is attained and tends to fluctuate only moderately in response to ordinary environmental changes. We associate such a population pattern with homeostasis, generally, and with human hunting-gathering populations in particular. The R-selected (exponential growth curve) population model is one of dramatic population surge which is not very responsive to local environmental limits. Cycles of population crash follow the explosive surge. The population cycles of many insects or rabbits, for instance, follow this second pattern. Here we need to discover how human populations might have changed from the K-selected (classic hunter-gatherer or "efficiency" model) to the R-selected (current world population explosion—a "power" model). See Stuart 1980 for contrasts between the two patterns, or see any introductory text in ecology.

Under such circumstances, we would have expected hunters-gatherers to reduce the rate of population growth gradually (long nursing period, female infanticide, polygyny with elder males, etc.), and in the short-term to have made local use of dispersal tactics during yearly lows (*using up* the landscape and creating unproductive zones or calorie vacuums, making it useless for others to encroach on territory).

The dispersal mechanism is an exquisitely delicate stress sensor among hunters-gatherers and, in the vast space needs of a bone-dry *summer* regime (Van Zeist 1969), its ability to predict population pressure should have brought self-regulating social behavior into play. Yet the long-term population trend was distinctly upward. There was apparently not enough general stress to actuate the efficiency (homeostatic) drive. How could the summer dispersal mechanism have failed to regulate the system?

We argue that the most reasonable explanation is one in which summer season sedentism pulled population off the landscape. The effects of even a few nuclear families or extended families collecting and storing just enough wild grain to sit out the summer season would have had a dramatic effect on population dynamics in a local area. Such a local population would no longer be regulated by food which was collectable during summer lows (Leibig's minimum). Thus, any segment of the population consistently storing cereals for summer use would be regulated by food available during the next most limited season — in Iran's summer-dry regime the next worst season might have been only half as limiting. Such a circumstance could have permitted a dramatic increase in population locally. Additionally, one group's strategy of staying off the landscape would have dramatically affected neighboring groups, since it would have made available new space for summer dispersal. This increase in dispersal space would have prevented the summer mechanism from activating *normal* population regulating behavior. In other words, it would instantly, if temporarily, have de-stressed the system where it occurred.

The effects of this initial change in a few local areas would have had additional implications as well. While any population, or segment, practicing summer sedentism could potentially increase to the extent limited by resources available in the next lowest season, any summer mobile segments could also increase population to fill up each new unit of summer space over which they had gained access. But all they would have gained is summer space — they would continue to be regulated by the summer lows. In short, it is possible to argue that populations living side by side could be differentially regulated. We argue that this is the initial mechanism which created disequilibrium. Or, in Flannery's terms, "the former rule which held human population in check was off" (1969:95). The effect at this stage is arguably more local than regional.

Once such a mechanism was in motion, how would it have been maintained? What would be its long range effects? Let us create a hypothetical case to illustrate. Initially, a local area might contain 100 people (divided into two groups for purposes of illustration). Let us assume they each require equal space. Group A stores enough for one season and is summer-sedentary (50 people), while Group B (50 people) is not. Group A can, in theory, double its population if the resources available during the next most limited season are only half as poor as those of summer. If Group A no longer uses its summer space, Group B can increase population to equal A, though still regulated by summer lows. However, in a bad year, when A's native cereal stands receive no rain, A's population (over time) has doubled but is again temporarily regulated by the summer low — Group A now has easily twice the population stress as has B, because it lost its summer dispersal space. Since B is still regulated by the same summer low, its population is at little risk in a bad year *if* it continues to have access to all of A's summer space.

Figure II.3

STATES OF POPULATION DISEQUILIBRIUM

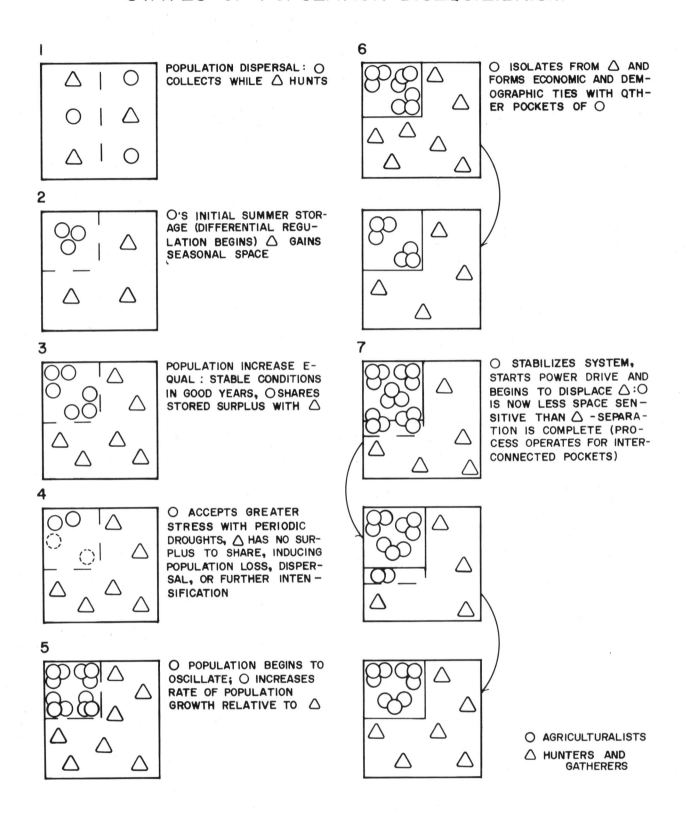

1 POPULATION DISPERSAL: ○ COLLECTS WHILE △ HUNTS

2 ○'S INITIAL SUMMER STORAGE (DIFFERENTIAL REGULATION BEGINS) △ GAINS SEASONAL SPACE

3 POPULATION INCREASE EQUAL: STABLE CONDITIONS IN GOOD YEARS, ○ SHARES STORED SURPLUS WITH △

4 ○ ACCEPTS GREATER STRESS WITH PERIODIC DROUGHTS, △ HAS NO SURPLUS TO SHARE, INDUCING POPULATION LOSS, DISPERSAL, OR FURTHER INTENSIFICATION

5 ○ POPULATION BEGINS TO OSCILLATE; ○ INCREASES RATE OF POPULATION GROWTH RELATIVE TO △

6 ○ ISOLATES FROM △ AND FORMS ECONOMIC AND DEMOGRAPHIC TIES WITH OTHER POCKETS OF ○

7 ○ STABILIZES SYSTEM, STARTS POWER DRIVE AND BEGINS TO DISPLACE △: ○ IS NOW LESS SPACE SENSITIVE THAN △ - SEPARATION IS COMPLETE (PROCESS OPERATES FOR INTERCONNECTED POCKETS)

○ AGRICULTURALISTS
△ HUNTERS AND GATHERERS

This is a stylized case, because we argue against a complete initial separation of strategies, but it illustrates several major points: 1) In A's case, the disequilibrium device oscillates between regulation at the second worst low and the summer low, while B's regulatory device is consistent; 2) *Group A accepts greater risk under cyclical stress than B.* Under such circumstances, one would expect intense competition for space at the local level in occasional bad periods, combined with heavy selective force against Group A's population and subsistence behavior, as environmental factors kept forcing it back to the summer dispersal regulatory device.

This perspective questions Flannery's assertion that the changes leading to intensive food production should be viewed as responses to population pressure moving *outward* from favored areas. In order to argue that this was so *initially*, one would have to demonstrate that any selective forces vastly favored the sedentary population. This might be possible if one could demonstrate that environment and rainfall were so stable during the initial phase of semi-sedentism that the summer-sedentary group did not suffer bad crop years, and that an unbroken population curve was set into motion which exceeded that of surrounding groups. Had this been the case, one would expect to have seen a far more rapid rise of the agricultural sequence in evidence in the archeological record.

On the other hand, one must also be able to argue that the seasonally-sedentary behavior was not just quickly eliminated either. Any initial move to seasonal sedentism over a wide area would have created pockets of land available to others for summer dispersal before population had time to increase biologically. And even under circumstances where summer sedentary groups exercised substantial control over their former summer foraging space, any cyclicity in production from year to year would still militate against them. The basic problem of such groups would have been to keep part of their population dispersed on the landscape, while maintaining the rest near grain crops. A one-season storage strategy would still have been vulnerable, though, because every few years a bad crop year would create severe problems.

Had it not been for the fact that bad years tend to be localized in a semi-arid environment, any initial seasonal-sedentism could have been eliminated fairly quickly. It is logical to argue that if a number of local areas practiced summer sedentism simultaneously, randomized rainfall would probably prevent all from experiencing either a crash at the same time or such success that a regional population curb was triggered. This, we believe, characterized the first stage of the evolutionary change. Its initial adaptive benefit locally was dramatic in a series of good years, but its longer term benefit, locally, was periodically unstable. This instability benefited the *regional* system — hunter-gatherer population increased and was directed inward. Once a local group indulged in sedentism during a season of maximum population dispersal, it was hard to get out — regional populations exerted continual pressure to use less space, or intensify, or suffer loss. Inequality in localized rainfall conditions likely prevented the seasonally sedentary behavior from being eliminated entirely or stylized too quickly, and preserved the benefit for hunters-gatherers over a larger region. Had the move to summer sedentism failed everywhere at once, a regionwide climatic catastrophe would have been necessary to cause it. Again, in such a circumstance, the ordinary hunter-gatherer pattern would have been triggered, to bring population down regionally and abort the evolutionary process — ensuing population pressure being harshly eliminated.

Since it is a process that created the initial deviation in population regulation, it cannot be observed archeologically in a direct way. And, as suggested, labor both to tend cereal stands and to disperse some population to maintain subsistence territory from encroachment can be logically argued to have prevented much early labor investment in archeologically observable features. After a local crop failure, everyone in a semi-sedentary group would have to move out on the landscape to survive. Clues like the appearances of storage facilities prior to the beginning of settled communities, site density evidence for generally increasing population, and a shift to broad spectrum foraging strategies before agricultural communities appear, are all to be expected. The actual evolutionary disruption of the hunting-gathering system far precedes in time the archeological evidence we ordinarily associate with it. Though we do not care to speculate here about the full range of environmental conditions under which such an initial event can occur, we suggest that major climatic disruption over a general region would abort the deviation-amplifying device by triggering hunter-gatherer regulatory behavior, that is, create either dispersal over a wide geographic front, or population reduction techniques. Finally, we conceive of too rapid an initial increase in regional or local population as triggering these same devices. The initial agricultural adaptation survived because it was adaptively advantageous to hunter-gatherers, being neither eliminated too quickly nor initially too successful.

Let us look at the second stage of these changes. A continuing population drive, directed inward toward the most favorable zones in the environment, would have exerted continual pressure on those at the center to be space efficient, or to intensify energy extraction. Here a dramatic adaptive shift would have been induced when storage of grains was extended over a yearly basis. The sedentary population would then have been regulated by an energy flow which began to approach a yearly mean. Short-term fluctuation in seasonally available food would be evened out, population potential would still have fluctuated between that supportable by the crops in average years and that of failed crop years (summer low). Loss of access to space would become far more serious than under a seasonally sedentary regime, since more of the population was off the landscape more of the year. That is, the more fully mobile population would continue to grow, since it would have more access to foraging space at other seasons as well. But the shift to a yearly storage meant there were often temporary surpluses of grain, for at other seasons, the increasingly sedentary group would have continued to try to preserve access to foraging space (and subsistence options) by living off the land and limiting encroachment. This might continue to create an intense labor shortage that could be reflected in modest investment in structural facilities. Storage facilities, however, should be well-formed and of significant capacity.

At this stage the more sedentary group would buy its way out of potential conflict with the still numerically superior (and probably related) *nomadic* population. In so doing (the greatest need comes in summer under a winter rainfall regime), the population limits of the surrounding hunter-gatherer trade partners would no *longer depend on foraging space available during the summer lows*. Their vulnerability to local fluctuations would now increase -- and, however slowly, hunter-gatherer ability to dominate dispersal season space would erode as they aggregated temporarily near the camps of more sedentary groups. An evolutionary *dependency*, albiet a highly volatile one, would be created between the two groups. At this stage the more sedentary group stores for itself as well as for others -- the storage cycle in good years allows surplus to be put aside for bad years. The population regulation cycle would have lengthened -- from a regular seasonal cycle to a periodic drought year stress cycle. The sedentary population would have been much less vulnerable, with increased storage capacity, to short-term cyclicity. In flattening out its yearly food cycle, it would have been better able to control fluctuations in the number of people deployed on the landscape at other seasons. The population dynamics of two groups who trade are markedly different from those of other nearby populations who do not have access to cereals during seasons of low productivity. Between the two groups, they can still keep a good number of people on the summer landscape to prevent further encroachment, and in normal years their collective potential to generate population is greater than that of surrounding groups regulated only by annual low seasons. To the extent that a given pair might be able to withstand a bad year with stored surplus, they would temporarily be in a more stable situation than would nearby fully nomadic groups. At this point in the evolution of things, such a number of local areas might be able to withstand further external population pressures. The net effect in a single bad year following a series of good ones would be to trigger the summer density mechanisms that operate in outlying populations rather than in the trading pair, since they would disperse outward as their storage subsidy evaporated.

At any given year in early Mesopotamia, for example, a few local sedentary populations must have been able to generate outward pressure and induce foraging stress against the original hunter-gatherers, rather than having to absorb it in their evolving system. But the fact remains that, in evolutionary terms, trade of goods between evolutionarily unequal systems is inherently unequal. If a largely sedentary crop-harvesting population trades with hunters-gatherers in good years, it only increases its opponent's population. In bad years, hunters-gatherers have nothing to trade except space, and that space is so unproductive, compared to a sedentary population's needs, that it cannot keep population stress from occurring. Agricultural food products traded represent the equivalent of vast space in the hunter-gatherer world, while a trade of hunted meat represents small productive space in the agricultural system. In essence, cereal foods traded to hunter-gatherers would alleviate their foraging space problem to a degree, but wild foods traded to agriculturalists would not ordinarily solve the storage, or time, problem. The net effect over long periods of time and substantial space would be to hold the two subsistence systems more closely in balance because, however infrequently, when an agricultural population's storage failed, the two systems were both regulated by foraging space available during the least productive season. Because the spacing mechanism of hunters-gatherers is so delicate when compared to that of agriculturalists, the net effect at this later evolutionary stage would have been an increasingly intense population pressure directed outwards. This, we believe, eventually brought pressure to the margins of the higher density areas and forced outlying groups to remove population from the dispersal season (summer) landscape and to intensify.

The margins of a highly productive area are *particularly* vulnerable to pressure if such low population density areas are between contemporaneously expanding systems. Thus, we agree with Flannery (1969) and Binford (1968) if one rephrases them as follows: the changes leading to intensive food production in marginal environments are induced when population disequilibrium of an evolutionary nature is generated from earlier events in favorable areas. In essence, we have argued that without an evolutionary event which deregulates one of the major variables (available food energy, storage over time, foraging space or population), a basically hunting-gathering system which could generate enough population pressure to force evolutionary change around it would probably have triggered repeated population regulatory devices and de-stressed itself *first*, thus aborting the process. It is easier to escape a mob if you are at its edge rather than trapped in its middle. Secondly, evolution is possibilistic, and we argue that it is simply more possible to change the values of energy (ex: Maize or Emmer wheat), time (longer collecting season, storable surplus), space (high energy return per unit of land), and population in a favorable area. After all, does anyone argue that the complex stratified hunter-gatherer system in the U.S. northwest coast originated outside a favored area? But then, of course, it is not the evolutionary equivalent of an agricultural system, for the amount of energy flowing into the system yearly is not manipulated.

Why, then, do we not find rich *in situ* archeological records *late* in any evolutionary sequence which occurred in favored areas? This, we believe, has to do with human nature. Let us refer to it as the *target effect*. Early intensification primarily increased hunter-gatherer population by opening up additional space seasonally. In good years this might be fine. But, how comfortable do you suppose it would be for 200 incipient agriculturalists to have stored surplus in bad years while surrounded by a sea of 2,000 hunter-gatherers?

The irony in the biblical allegory of the Garden of Eden is that if there were such a place

21

no one could live in it, for it would be a continual combat zone. There are many ethnographic accounts of highly productive environments which are not continuously occupied because they are too hotly contested. So, let us look at human behavior.

ACTING IN SELF-INTEREST: DIVERGING TRAJECTORIES

We have presented a tentative model of population disequilibrium and the shift to agriculture, which we think offers certain bridges between opposing sides of the population increase — cultural development argument. We have accepted, with several reservations, Cohen's (1977) notion that the world had become saturated with hunters-gatherers prior to sedentism. In the most favored area of a given region, the *inward* press of a biologically homeostatic population alone could have created a local drive for intensification in its center. Those in the center would simply have been in the situation of having to break through surrounding population to find some *elbow room*. In essence, those first in line have both the biggest potential payoff in good years and are at greatest risk in bad ones.

General drought or episodes of catastrophe in such a region would likely have aborted any process enhancing separation of (hunting-gathering from cereal or cultigen oriented) subsistence strategies by temporarily *demagnetizing* a favored area. Population would simply drift away. Thus, continual cycles or shifts, first toward, and then away from, intensification, could have been a pattern in some portions of the globe. This might account for staggered shifts to agriculture even after cultigens had been introduced in some areas.

In the shift to agriculture in the Near East, population appears to have increased biologically over too broad a geographical front for hunters-gatherers to indulge in their classic response to a problem — simply to walk away from it. Merely because the evidence favors it, we have argued that no substantial catastrophe intervened to eliminate the mechanism generating evolutionary divergence.

Occasional episodes of drought or seasonal shifts in rainfall undoubtedly occurred, and such events likely did slow the shift to agriculture substantially. But they did not abort it. We believe this was due only in part to the survival of substantial population. If one focuses on the egalitarian aspects of hunter-gatherer behavior, as has generally been done in the literature (Lee and DeVore 1968), it would be reasonable to argue that everyone shared equally (or nearly so) in the collection of wild cereals or casually tended cultigens. Yearly spottiness in rainfall could have had its effects evened out over a broad region, while periodic regional droughts would have created occasional cycles of population loss and replacement. One is then required to ask why a new long-term homeostasis, at slightly higher than previous population levels, was not achieved in the context of generalized semi-sedentism.

It is precisely this kind of question that, we suspect, has created Cowgill's caution (1975) against use of the argument that population increase is a prime mover in cultural evolution. The answer suggested here is one in which minor differences in subsistence, social and population behaviors are differently acted upon in similar climatic circumstances. In the first place, an undercurrent of R-selected population behavior (incipient agriculturalists) existed in a sea of more homeostatic behavior (nomadic hunters-gatherers-K-selected).

In order to suggest how this came to be, one has also to consider the potential for stratified and heterogeneous behavior among hunters-gatherers. Here we shall pursue the argument in terms of reasonable individual behavior based on self interest, which might suit Cowgill.

If one accepts Flannery's suggestion that cereals were initially a less preferred resource and big game a more preferred resource, it is easy to suppose that there was little initial competition for wild cereals. One has only to accept the idea that hunters of lesser skill relied more heavily on their wives for collected cereal resources than did highly successful hunters. We view the generalized dry season scarcity of resources as likely to have placed less successful hunters (or merely those more isolated family units) in a situation of greater dependency on summer storage. It may be argued that such behavior favored those successful hunters who did not practice it, by creating less competition for preferred animal resources and space in which they are found. Summer sedentism and partial disruption in patterns of transhumance confused judgments about the relationship of resources to population. That is, the system failed to regulate itself. This resulted in a general population increase.

Significantly, highly successful hunters are generally awarded the benefits of differential reproduction through polygyny in hunter-gatherer society. In other words, unsuccessful hunting, an emphasis on collecting, lower reproductive potential and seasonal storage are argued to have formed one pattern in early Mesopotamian hunter-gatherer society, while successful hunting, lesser dependence on cereals and enhanced reproductive potential formed another.

The need of those with an unusual dependence on summer storage for the labor of women is also in conflict with the hunter-gatherer tendency to award wives to others first. Such families in a local group were, it may be suggested, the least likely to practice female infanticide and other forms of reproductive restriction during episodes of scarcity. They would also have been unable to hold onto their women at maturity. At least some local groups would eventually have fragmented along such lines. As population drifted upward, general competition would have enhanced any tendency for fragmentation. If population partially fragmented along these lines, some individuals living in the center of favored areas and relying on stored vegetable resources would have found themselves the repeated subjects of periodic stress cycles which would have created a less stable effective environment than that enjoyed by neighbors. This relative instability would generate higher risks. Coupled with the demand for female labor, such factors would have created a differentially intense need, on the part of some, to replace population. Biologists would argue that a less stable situation and R-selected population behavior go together.

Rephrasing this argument into Jorde's (1977) style, we may say that the generalized hunter-gatherer system buffered the effects of low frequency stress cycles (initially periodic cereal failures — not annual lows) by placing only a portion of the population *at risk*, thereby minimizing periodic system-wide crashes. On the other hand, buffered crashes and pockets of R-selected population behavior might hinder a return to homeostasis in human cultural evolution, but would not ultimately have prevented it.

Earlier, we suggested that change in the net risks of a system's adaptive behavior over time could be reduced, in theory, to zero, if one portion accepted more risk and an equal portion accepted less. This is obviously the relationship argued throughout between summer-sedentists and the more mobile, very early in the shift to agriculture in Mesopotamia. In general terms, we have characterized the increased rate of population growth as power, and a drive to decrease it as efficiency. What happened in Mesopotamia, then, was an initially modest population increase by mobile hunters-gatherers, subsidized by the increased risks of semi-sedentists. Those risks induced greater population loss (probably higher infant mortality) on the partially sedentary portion of the population. To compensate, summer-sedentists increased their *rate* of population production relative to others of their own kind.

When they later (or also) learned to reduce risk by partially closing their system socially,

23

through trade in food with other cereal collectors, retained their own women or exchanged daughters with their own kind (thereby increasing their fertility ratio) and increased storage, they were first able to stabilize their numbers and then to generate their own competitive power drive. This drive induced population reduction, compensating efficiency behavior, in more mobile (density-sensitive) populations. Even a few summer-sedentists moving back on the summmer landscape to regain subsistence options would have been sufficient. The slightly heterogeneous population as a whole could not, in theory, have returned to regional homeostasis unless hunters-gatherers could equally induce self-regulatory population behavior in semi-sedentists. They could not, of course, if semi-sedentists did not react equally to density signals. The technique of inducing stress or driving competitors from the landscape merely by crowding them would not have worked. Semi-sedentists had repeatedly been forced by circumstances to judge population and subsistence risk on factors other than population density and seasonal dispersion. Eventually, density — dependent population regulation was blunted among semi-sedentists. Because hunter-gatherer population exerted continual pressure on the subsistence options and space once available during scarcity, we argue that later, incipient agriculturalists continued to accept greater population risk than hunters-gatherers in episodes of periodic stress.

In essence, we have questioned whether a system can be both in homeostasis and disequilibrium at the same time. Technically, we do not know. But it is argued that if portions of a system are in disequilibrium, it can still have much of the advantage of homeostasis if deviation requiring power is compensated equally by deviation requiring efficiency. More to the point is that such a system can *appear* to be in homeostasis. It may even *appear* homogeneous, but is in fact stratified by risk (and behavior) if even in only a miniscule way. Thus, both Cowgill's cases (1975) of local population increase with regional conservatism in population growth and Cohen's (1977) competitive population increase are problems more of observation than of theory.

The position advanced here is that demographic and social behavior to compensate for risk, rather than advances in pre-agricultural technology, closed the pathway to homeostasis and created practical irreversibility. It is heterogeneous behavior in the face of potential catastrophe, not a single mode of production, which has separated powerful from efficient systems and created stratified society.

While the ideas of power and efficiency provide a general theoretical framework for the rest of this volume, specific questions are raised as well. The possible *in situ* divergence of hunting-gathering populations is only one which will be pursued.

INTRODUCTION

The subject of this Chapter is not anthropological theory *per se*. Rather it is a more practical application of theory to on-the-ground archeological survey and to mundane, but important, administrative matters.

The geographic focus is the San Juan Basin of New Mexico and the Middle and Upper Rio Grande Valley. These geographic areas are defined as the U.S. Forest Service — Bureau of Land Management joint Cultural Resources Overview Units IIINM and IINM (see Maps III.1 and III.2).

The two archeological overviews that these federal agencies have commissioned for this portion of New Mexico are available as of this writing, and the reader will wish to refer to them in detail. The overview of the San Juan Basin is entitled *Class I Cultural Resources Inventory of the Chaco, San Juan and Portions of the Cabezon Planning Units* (Magers, n.d.) and is available from New Mexico State University, Las Cruces. The second overview is entitled *Cultural Resources Overview, Middle Rio Grande Valley, New Mexico* (Cordell 1979) and is available from the U.S. Superintendent of Documents. Since the Cordell volume has been formally published, it is reasonable to suppose that it is in final form, but the San Juan overview is currently obtainable only in the format in which it was presented to the Bureau of Land Management by the preparer. Thus we may assume the possibility of future revision.

The geographic units presented here, then, do not proceed from the authors' own notions of ecological features which defined effective environment for former cultural systems. Rather, they derive generally from the planning requirements of several federal agencies. This is just as well, for arbitrary boundaries can be created in a thousand ways to serve specific research purposes, while in this report, research and practical concerns are accorded roughly equal merit.

If one draws a line west to east through Gallup, New Mexico to Cabezon Peak, then northward through Cuba and Dulce, New Mexico to the Colorado state line, the San Juan Basin is curcumscribed as defined here. The Middle and Upper Rio Grande is circumscribed by a diagonal which proceeds roughly from northwest to southeast along (and to the west of) New Mexico Hwy. 44 at Bernalillo, thence in a southwesterly direction along the west side of I-25, south to its junction with New Mexico Hwy. 60. It then proceeds in a southeasterly direction to the western boundary of the Cibola National Forest (in the Manzano Mountains). From there, it proceeds through a series of dog-legs, northward to the Torrance County line near Interstate 40. The boundary then proceeds westward again, along the Torrance County boundary, then northward along the western boundary, then east along the northern boundary of Guadalupe County to its intersection with New Mexico Hwy. 84. The eastern boundary of the study area then proceeds north from the village of Dalia to the Colorado state line.

We have included these two areas as one chapter because, collectively, they include the heartland of the Eastern Anasazi. Secondly, we shall shortly present the argument that, together, they constitute the geographic theater in which a fascinating series of cultural-evolutionary developments was played out.

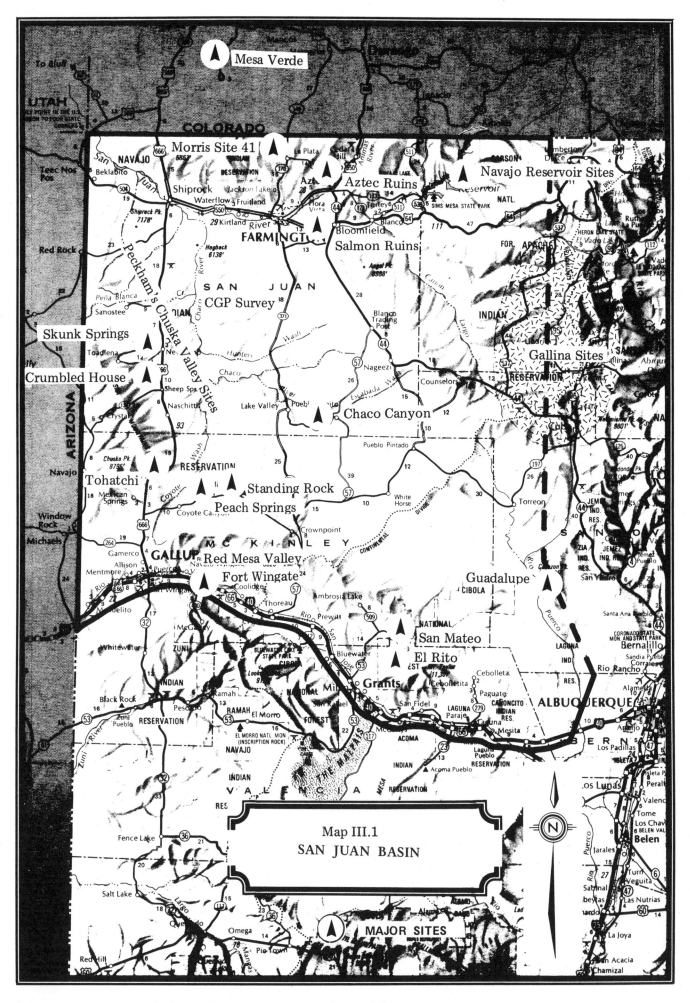

Map III.1
SAN JUAN BASIN

MAJOR SITES

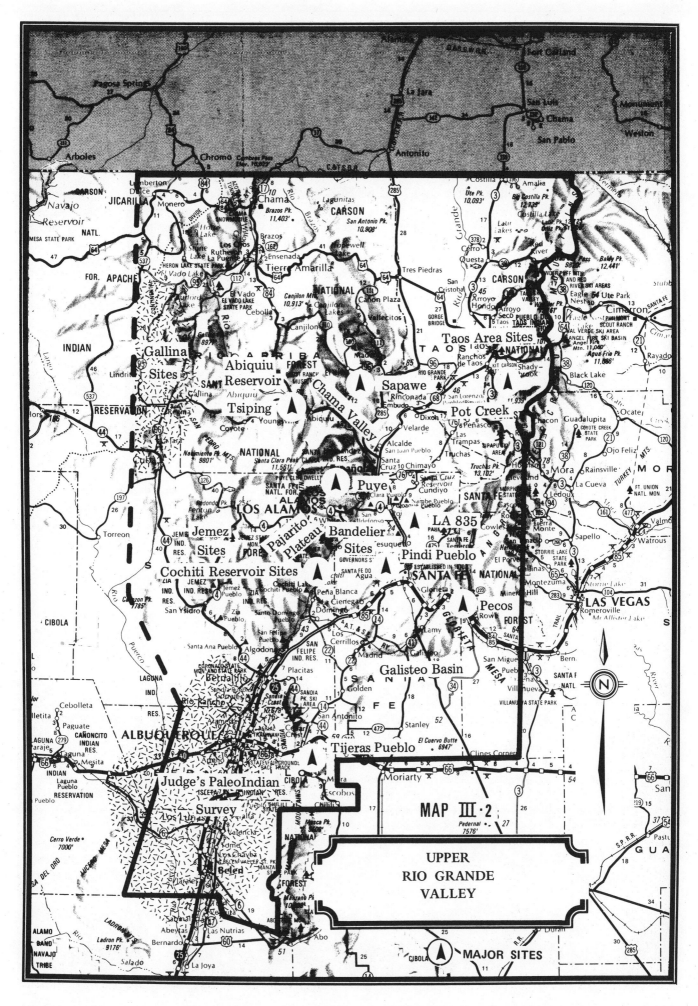

MAP III·2

UPPER
RIO GRANDE
VALLEY

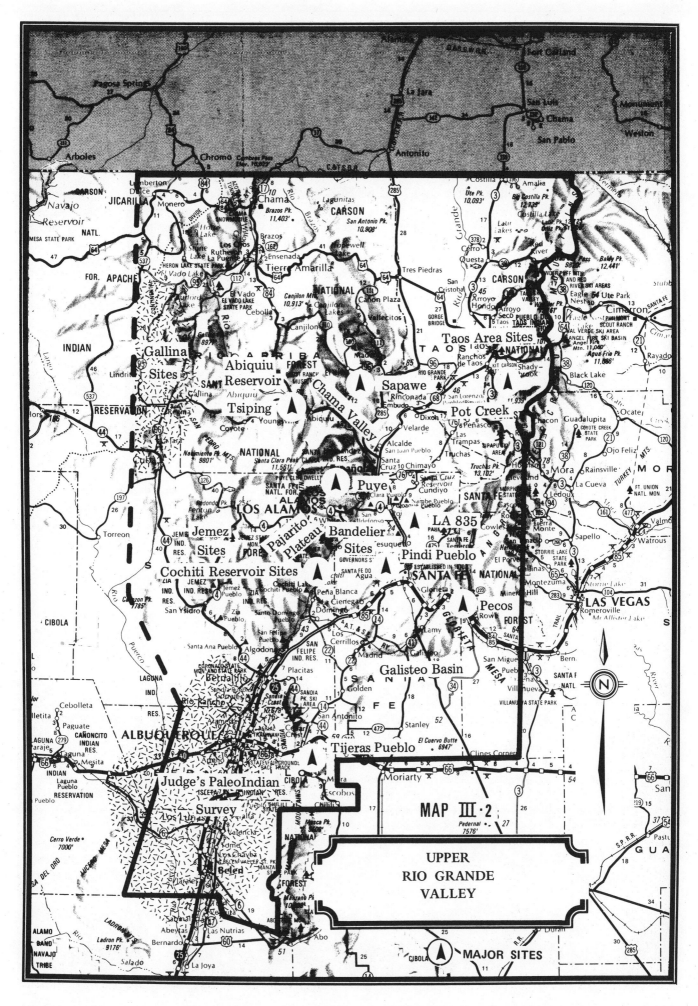 MAJOR SITES

PREHISTORY IN THE SAN JUAN BASIN — AN EVOLUTIONARY PERSPECTIVE

BACKGROUND

The purpose of this section is to suggest ways in which a macroscopic view of the archeological record might contribute to productive research questions which make fundamental comparisons among different archeological systems. The points to bear in mind here are first: Cultural evolution does not proceed primarily in discrete stages. That is, behavioral shifts within a population system are quite distinct from displacement by other cultural systems. The distinction is between the evolution of systems and succession of systems. Second, it is the interaction of diverse systems which largely defines the evolutionary trajectory of each. Third, competition between cultural systems is not simply between the large and the small, it is between those systems most closely competing for the same niche. Fourth, the apparent size and complexity of a system are not necessarily equivalent to its energetic or thermodynamic size and complexity. That is, a *small* cultural system may be energetically more powerful than a large, as well as the reverse. The *rate* of energy input/output is more important to understanding a system's behavior than is the sheer *quantity* of energy influx.

Let us turn, then, to a short discussion of the archeological record.

PALEO-INDIAN ADAPTATIONS AND THE SHIFT TO THE ARCHAIC

Dr. Cordell (1979) has provided a general and excellent overview of the literature on Paleo-Indian adaptation as it relates to northern New Mexico. In addition, the reader will want to consult both Dr. Judge's (n.d.) and Irwin-Williams' (1979) articles in the new *Handbook of North American Indians.*

As Dr. Cordell points out, problems of chronology, of identifying the full range of subsistence behavior, and the generally few Paleo-Indian remains in the study area, create a difficult situation regarding interpretation. In addition, we would like to reemphasize that most of the Paleo-Indian remains recorded in New Mexico have been located in areas of significant erosion. There are few recorded remains in the San Juan Basin, but this could be due (Cordell 1979:134) to lack of substantial erosion. That is, many Paleo-Indian deposits may simply be buried.

Paleo-Indian remains have been recorded in the central Rio Grande Valley (Judge and Dawson 1972; Judge 1973). In the far northern Rio Grande, the Cimarron area and in scattered locations elsewhere, Bussey (in Magers, n.d.) reports Broilo's site near Peach Springs as Folsom-Midland, and states that in the San Juan unit, "all of the known sites are Folsom or Folsom-Midland" (62). But when the senior author visited that site with Mr. Broilo in 1975, he took great joy in offering a lesson in Paleo-Indian archeology. Broilo pointed out *both* Folsom-Midland and Eden (Cody Complex) components, evidence of earlier and later occupation. He remarked that the Folsom-Midland was preponderant. In a current survey being conducted by the Bureau of Indian Affairs on Acoma Tribal lands south of Grants, New Mexico (moderately eroded — again, see Cordell 1979:134), a number of Paleo-Indian points and fragments have been recorded during survey at altitudes of 7,500-8,000 feet. These point types include Clovis, a preponderance of Folsom-Midland, and Eden (Cody), while several other fragments have not yet been classified. Though the facts of deposition may be problematic, early Clovis remains have been found at very high elevations (11,000 feet) (Wendorf and Miller 1959; Husted 1965:494), while at the end of the Paleo-Indian period, Judge (1973) also notes that Cody complexes in the Rio Grande Valley are in areas of substantially greater topographic relief than are sites of earlier periods. Though these are not at notably higher altitude, they represent a clear break from earlier patterns.

If one takes a broad perspective on Paleo-Indian problems, several patterns emerge. To the north, in Rocky Mountain National Park (Husted 1965), remains of Clovis, Meserve, Jimmy Allen, Agate Basin and Cody Complex have been found, though Folsom is absent. To the south, Mark Wimberly (personal communication), who has surveyed for many years in the Tularosa Basin-Sierra Blanca region, indicates that he has never found Paleo-Indian remains above 5,500 feet in elevation. The recent BIA survey of substantial acreage on the Mescalero Reservation, at altitudes of 7,200—10,000 feet, does not alter Wimberly's findings, for no Paleo-Indian remains were found (Broster, personal communication). Preliminary surveys of the BIA timber sale conducted earlier by the senior author and Mr. Broster (Stuart, *et al.* 1978), also failed to note Paleo-Indian remains, though Archaic remains were found at high altitudes. Many surveys have recorded Archaic remains at higher elevations, and Cordell is correct in saying that the Archaic Upper Rio Grande Culture (Renaud 1942, 1946, Honea 1969), artifacts from Garrapata Ridge (Hume 1974) and Steen's (1955) excavations in the Cimarron area (dated to 8282 ± 1,000 years ago) merit more attention than is generally given.

Focusing on Judge's (n.d., and outlined in Cordell 1979:15) distinction between generalized (fluted and laterally-thinned) series and specialized (constricted base and indented base) series, it is immediately apparent that Husted's data indicate the presence of both series, though Folsom is absent. If one looks at Cordell's summary of radiocarbon dates (though she herself cares to draw no firm conclusions), it will be seen that there is an early and late generalized point represented (Meserve and Jimmy Allen) and an earlier and later (though overlapping) specialized series (Agate Basin and Cody). At Blackwater Draw (Agogino 1968: see also Cordell 1979:15) Folsom (generalized) and Agate Basin (specialized) are considered contemporary, and the point types which are argued to have endured to the end of the period include the Cody Complex (specialized) and the Frederick, Lusk complex (generalized).

Though the sequence proposed for the Hell Gap Site may ultimately prove contradictory, we feel it reasonable to argue that the evolutionary trajectory for the Paleo-Indian period in point technology is from generalized and nondivergent (Clovis) to two distinct and divergent lines of generalized and specialized types. Whether these represent populations with differing subsistence strategies (as Judge implies) or different aspects of a total assemblage, is an important question that should be addressed. If these do represent distinct strategies, then the proportion of the types unrelated to bison hunting should decrease as altitude increases, since bison don't occur at higher elevations. The case is currently unclear.

In the study area there is thought to be a hiatus of Paleo-Indian occupation between 8,000 B.C. (Folsom-Midland) and 6,600 B.C. (Cody Complex). This is because the Southern Plains complex (Firstview) is not found — nor are the northern plains points like the Alberta (we return to this point shortly). As we view it, there are three things *missing* from the study area: a specialized series of points chronologically between Agate Basin and Cody, a generalized series between them, and a terminal generalized series to *balance* the Cody.

As Judge has suggested, the Belen points may be evidence of occupation during this period. Significantly, they are laterally thinned, and are therefore a candidate for the missing generalized point/knife. If one agrees with Honea (1969) that the Jay are quite similar to Hell Gap points, then one may assume the *Jay* point to be the missing specialized type. Again, the radiocarbon date that Steen reports for the Clayton horizon, plus further radiocarbon studies, could support this interpretation. Others have pointed out that the distinction between *Jay* and Hell Gap may ultimately prove to be based largely on the differing material of manufacture (Judge, comments in SAR Symposium: San Juan Basin Archeology; Broster, personal communication). Judge (in press) also reminds us that the resemblance may only be superficial — though still unresolved. The interpretation of early *Jay* material and its chronological place are extremely important in understanding the Paleo-Indian—Archaic transition.

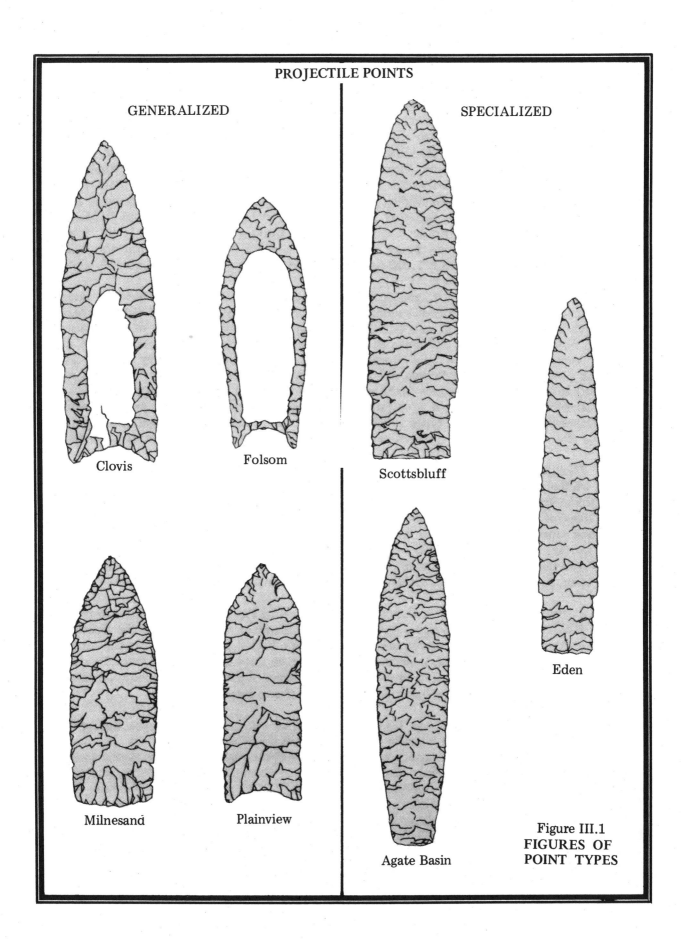

PROJECTILE POINTS

GENERALIZED

SPECIALIZED

Clovis

Folsom

Scottsbluff

Eden

Milnesand

Plainview

Agate Basin

Figure III.1
FIGURES OF
POINT TYPES

The *problem* of the missing generalized terminal series may be no problem at all, since the suggestion that in most localities there will be a generalized and specialized type may be disproven. On the other hand, it would be interesting to know whether the incidence of Cody knives is higher, the same, or lower in areas where the late (Scottsbluff) Frederick complex is also found, and whether the proportion of Cody knives to points is in the same proportion at various altitudes. One problem here is that the Cody Complex is more broadly defined than some of the others. One tentative expectation is that the generalized series will be, in general, more highly represented in the higher altitude zones. In the BIA surveys, Broster indicates sixteen generalized points (Clovis, Folsom, Midland and possible Belen) and only five specialized, which, tentatively, includes *Jay* points. These finds were recorded in only 360 acres. The scarcity of Cody knives in Judge's survey and from upland localities also requires further clarification.

Though these data are very tentative, we will sketch an evolutionary picture of the general dynamics of the Paleo-Indian adaptation to direct attention to future research problems. The current evidence suggests Paleo-Indian occupation at high altitude at 9,000—10,000 B.C. in the study area, though none much further south. The evidence suggests more continual high altitude occupation to the north (Colorado) and again around 7,000—8,000 B.C. in the study area (the question being whether this represents a continuation of the trend during Cody times or a distinct break to the Archaic—the interpretation of *Jay* being the key). It is significant that Judge views few Clovis sites to be kill sites, placing emphasis on the scavenging of mammoths and other megafauna. The trend from an average fifteen bison per kill in Folsom times to 128 in Cody times is significant, as is the development of a spatially distinct northern and southern plains complex (Alberta and Firstview) in specialized points (piercing). The increase in numbers of bison per episodal kill indicates increased power input. Is technological specialization, therefore, generally diagnostic of such *power surges*?

It is reasonable to portray the Clovis people as generalized hunters and collectors, both on the basis of the range of faunal remains in Clovis occupations, their poor success in kills, and their manipulation of variation in altitude to increase subsistence options. The manipulation of climatic variation through altitude, rather than through major movement north and south, if substantiated through continued finds during high altitude survey, will suggest that Clovis populations in the study area were fairly localized. The faunal remains from Clovis sites near mountain areas where there is no evidence of their occupation need to be compared to those where there is also evidence of nearby high altitude occupation. We need to know whether such behavior is due to geographic constriction (more likely if there are no differences in food remains) or has temporal-subsistence implications for gradual loss of megafauna.

With the loss of Pleistocene megafauna and decreasing climatic equability, the Folsom and later adaptations directed themselves, increasingly, to the hunting of migratory game. The migratory tendency of certain herding animals likely also became more marked during this period. Unlike the Clovis period, the broad mechanics of this adaptation are reasonably clear, and the potential for future research is fascinating.

One's point of vantage affects the apparent behavior of migratory game. The greatest aggregations of bison occur at the northern and southern termini of their journey, and they remain there longer than at any given point in transit. If you are at an end point, the bison *come* but once a year and are present for a substantial period of time. However, if you are at the center point of their migration, they pass in great numbers, but rather quickly AND twice yearly. We need to know if the average number of bison per kill varies with latitude. In the 1,500 miles from the Pecos to Wyoming, the bison hunt was segmented into three major parts. We refer to these as the northern and southern nodes, and the center, or focus. Additionally, we argue that the tendency in hunting them was to press them against the eastern spine of the

Rockies. Reher's (1977) excellent paper on adaptations to buffalo hunting supports this interpretation. In order to pursue game, the southern node followed them to the north, and the northern node followed them to the south. Annually, those in the center alternated in pursuing them north, then south. This resulted in several distinctive patterns of population movement. Population movement was directed northwest by the southern populations and southwest by northern groups. As population increased over time, segmentation became more pronounced. Human populations could not pursue over as great distances as previously, and those in the center had two potential episodes of encroachment yearly.

Let us argue that population pressure focused on the center and in the intermontane areas of the higher elevations. The archeological record supports this interpretation. The early generalized Folsom-Midland is followed by increasing specialization and number of animals per kill. There is great *mixing* of assemblages in the geographic center (population movement back and forth?). Ultimately, the northern and southern nodes became separated enough that we are able to speak of northern and southern plains archeological complexes. High altitude occupation of the central Rockies appears to have been continual — a function of being the focal point of population movement. As one moves south, the evidence for high altitude occupation and population pressure decreases until it disappears. This suggests that surveys in high altitudes of the northern Rockies should also show decreasing evidence for Paleo-Indian occupations as one moves into Canada in the extreme north. The early (7-9,000 B.C.?) shift to the Archaic to the south and west suggests that population pressure existed in that area and that Paleo-Indian populations could not easily disperse in that direction either.

Julian Steward (1955) has argued that those who hunt large game in large migratory herds consist of composite bands. Such groups generally practice bilateral descent and are endogamous. The patrilineal band which hunts small, nonmigratory herds is patrilineal, patri-local and exogamous. We have shown elsewhere (Stuart 1980) that the composite band is a response to situations of high risk in mortality, uncertainty of locating or reaching food supplies, dramatic long-term cyclicity in environment, and/or social isolation. More to the point, it has been demonstrated that the composite band is able to produce population at great rates to offset mortality in highly cyclical systems (R-selected population growth), and that it is not density-dependent. Again, Reher (1977) summarizes evidence for the dramatic cyclicity of buffalo populations. Temporary composite groups can also be surprisingly large. In addition to Reher's (1977) data from the historic period, we find that among the Yahgan (Stuart 1972), groups of 200 are documented at whale feasts and, among the Ona (Stuart 1977), 150 at seal hunts. This is *after* dramatic population decline at contact (perhaps, someone will someday excavate 200-500 yards upwind from a bison kill and find 30-50 temporary hearths and post molds from drying racks).

The more restricted valleys of the higher intermontane areas undoubtedly reduce bison herd size and, in areas, blunt the migratory tendency when compared to the vaster herds and unrestricted movement on the open plains. Smaller, intermontane herds of bison, you see, could achieve the same degree of climatic buffering by *manipulating* the altitude of grasslands, as could larger herds by latitudinal movement. This is the kind of pattern that leads to local population-resource imbalance and suggests the localized, more homeostatic *patrilineal* band model. Such groups do respond delicately to simple crowding. The patrilineal band is a response to conditions of regional population saturation and regulates local population-resource imbalances. It is the model of homeostatic hunters (K-selected)-gatherers most current in the literature.

The point is not to offer a lesson on social organizational features. The point is that, over time, those Paleo-Indian peoples who moved into the intermontane regions would have become populationally conservative compared to northern and southern plains groups who bordered the Rockies. In short, it is logical to argue that it became simpler for plains groups to push their way in than for intermontane groups to push their way out. Since the northern plains were more dramatically cyclic than the southern, it is reasonable to suppose that the northern node created the most dramatic episodes of population increase or cycles of loss and replacement (Reher 1977a).

At the end of the Paleo-Indian period we have groups that manipulated higher life zones, were fairly broad spectrum, and eventually intensified food production. We refer to them as Archaic. Our argument is that the Archaic could easily have developed *in situ* from the Paleo-Indian. If it is conceived that *Jay* points are Paleo-Indian, then it is possible to suppose that people having Paleo-Indian points were pressured to adopt broad spectrum techniques already in practice to the south and west. Thus, Irwin-Williams' (1973) view that the *assemblage* which goes with Jay points is like Archaic assemblages to the south and west, is likely correct. If *Jay* points were of pink chert and found in association with 125 bison in eastern Colorado, they would clearly be Paleo-Indian. But when they are of black basalt and found in the higher elevations of central New Mexico, we have doubts.

Survey of higher altitudes and pockets of eroded areas in northern New Mexico could prove critical to the interpretation of the Paleo-Indian adaptation and the shift to the Archaic. If we are able to date more late Paleo-Indian and early Archaic sites by obsidian hydration or C-14, we may find that the Early Jay and Cody complexes, for instance, are contemporaneous in New Mexico. If, as Cordell suggests (1979:21), size of kill, frequency of generalized versus specialized, time periods and geographical foci of the various Paleo-Indian complexes can be tied down in more detail, we may yet unlock new details about this adaptation. We might even discover how population growth and appearance of new tool kits were related geographically and temporally. If we knew this we might know, for instance, why the Cody complex seems to be more widely distributed than its specialized predecessors. In any case, since Paleo-Indian remains occur at elevations which exceed the range of large herding animals, we shall surely be able to make further refinements in our notions about generalized and specialized tool types with reference to hunting strategies. That is, do they have more to do with *size* of episodal kills or *frequency* of kills? We must pursue the identification of flake and debitage attributes that are associated with the generalized as opposed to specialized point series. Where such differences can be identified, field surveyors may be able to characterize a Paleo-Indian locality as to class (generalized, specialized, mixed) even where diagnostic points are not present and even where such distinctions otherwise impose little chronological control.

ARCHAIC ADAPTATION AND THE SHIFT TO AGRICULTURE

The shift to agriculture occupies a central role in anthropological inquiry, and while many problems have been clarified, there remain fundamental questions which are unresolved. The most frustrating of these involve the role of changing climate/ecological productivity and the role of population increase. We focused on population behavior in the last chapter, because, whatever else is eventually determined, one must account for a preagricultural world generally evidencing relatively slow rates of population increase (the homeostatic or carrying capacity, K-selected) view of hunter-gatherer behavior as opposed to a postagricultural world evidencing exponential population growth (R-selected population behavior).

In our judgement, the basic flaw in most arguments proceeds from over-stereotyping hunter-gatherer behavior. As we suggested earlier (Paleo-Indian discussion), hunters-gatherers may be either markedly homeostatic or population producers (Stuart 1980), depending upon circumstances.

In short, there are several basic ways to induce population pressure. A generally homeostatic population system can be confronted with long-term decrease in environmental productivity, or such a population can be confronted with increasing modulation or oscillation in environmental productivity. Following such events, a homeostatic population can respond by using the resource base in ways that upset timing, or regulation. The consequences of such changed circumstances likely depend rather highly on the degree to which the changes are predictable and within the population's experiential repertoire. If fluctuations are short-term and predictable, then population will likely respond by more conservatism and the density of such a population will go up. On the other hand, anthropology knows little about responses to totally unpredictable circumstances. How long does it take a cultural system to perceive that the *world is going to hell; that it not only won't return to normal, but will, in all probability, continue to go to hell?* Judging from the contemporary world, it takes repeated crises that are not too far apart in time to get the message across.

In the last chapter, a slightly different model was selected — that of gradually increased productivity which allowed population to drift upward, then the onset of disarray in regulatory mechanisms as differential dependence on cereals increased.

If one is assuming hunter-gatherer conservatism in population behavior, then a gradual increase in productivity, followed by a short, sharp dip in productivity and a slow return to normal, would be a critical series of events if labor could be intensified to offset the loss of preferred foods. Cordell (1979:30) cites Irwin-Williams as suggesting that the period between 2500 B.C. and 300 B.C. was characterized by greater effective moisture than at present, with a minor unconformity, indicating less effective moisture at about 500 B.C. This sequence would have created risk for those forced to rely more heavily on already introduced cultigens, nor would self-regulation of population have occurred if storage was practiced. The most critical evidence to obtain in this portion of New Mexico is a series of C-14 dates for early storage facilities. This timing is important, for on it hinges a possible answer to whether the Archaic shift to cultigens in the Arroyo Cuervo area (Oshara tradition) was internally generated or induced by external forces.

Without storage through poorer seasons, on at least the part of some, the later Archaic in the San Juan Basin would simply have offset resource pressure by one of two responses. First, dispersal, if possible; and second, population regulation, if not.

Several points need to be considered. This portion of the northern Southwest was generally more conservative technologically than other areas. The Paleo-Indian adaptation reportedly lingered on to 6000 B.C. (Irwin-Williams). It was generally a more favorable area, in terms of rainfall, than other more southern and western districts (Cordell), and the Archaic came fairly late, cultigens having been adopted earlier elsewhere. Cordell's (1979:23-33) discussion of the Archaic is very well done, but she is overly modest about the speculative nature of the suggestions she offers (on page 33), for those are essential speculations.

In the last chapter, we suggested a heirarchy of responses based on space, time and energy. These suggest the following sequence of responses, dispersal/aggregation; manipulation of energy over time; manipulation of total energy available. Thus, it is argued that as long as the Archaic populations in the San Juan Basin could disperse, they would have aborted the drive to intensify. The early shift to the Archaic in the south; the evidence for San Pedro Cochise in the Galisteo Basin (Lang 1977a), in the Rio Grande (Reinhart 1968), and in northeastern Arizona, suggests that by 800—1500 B.C. the dispersal option had been at least partially eliminated for populations in the San Juan Basin and adjacent areas. A second level of response should have been to alter the timing of things, or to budget the usage of energy over time (this is actually an efficiency variable). In a homeostatic hunter-gatherer population, responses generally have to do with lowering the birth rate, lowering population or increasing the rate of food production. But if such a group drastically reduces population while other groups are expanding, it loses territory.

Thus, if the adoption of maize among the Archaic populations of the San Juan Basin were due primarily to external population pressures, the San Jose Complex should have a broader geographic distribution than the Armijo, for the presumably more conservative Armijo population would have been pressured inward and regulated downward.

If the process was due primarily to gradual internal population buildup, there should be an equal or greater geographic extent for the *Armijo* lithic materials than for the San Jose, and the evidence for storage facilities should be late, since the shift to a broad spectrum subsistence strategy, including casual use of cultigens, might support higher population but would not prevent population regulation. Irwin-Williams' minor climatic perturbation at 500 B.C., if documentable elsewhere in the San Juan Basin, is a likely time period for the appearance of storage facilities. Moreover, if internal population dynamics generated the shift to active use of cultigens, population pressure should have been greatest in the center, and cultigen-bearing sites nearer the edges of the San Juan Basin should be slightly later in time period. In this case, general evidence suggests it may be the reverse.

On the other hand, it is not reasonable to assume that hunters-gatherers are necessarily homeostatic in population. Human groups generate population at high rates under circumstances of cyclical risk or catastrophe. Our American 1944-49 post-War *baby boom* is a classic response to catastrophe, mortality and uncertainty. So is contemporary India's birthrate. In the Southwest, the terminal Pleistocene was stable by comparison with ensuing periods [M. Wimberly and Rogers (1977) summarized the evidence in chart form in the recent Three Rivers Survey report] and, at least in southern New Mexico, rainfall began to fluctuate rather dramatically shortly before 2000 B.C., after a dramatic general decline which began about 6000 B.C. The first great bottoming-out came between 3000 and 4000 B.C., roughly the period during which evidence of cultigens appears at Bat Cave. This levelling out appears to have been followed by an increase in moisture, which peaked between 1800 and 2000 B.C., followed by another downturn.

It is also possible, in theory, that the general decrease in precipitation from 6000 B.C. to 3500 B.C. created a certain mortality, which was compensated for by increased birth rates. If so, the increased moisture from roughly 3000 B.C. to 1800 B.C. could have reduced mortality and led to rapid population increase. Alternatively, increased moisture and shifting seasonality of rainfall may be highly correlated. Thus, the timing of the population/dispersal mechanism may have been generally disrupted.

In short, hunter-gatherers can initially be generally homeostatic and, if a subsistence strategy which destroys regulatory mechanisms is pursued, a portion of the population may increase relative to the whole and generate population increase. On the other hand, a hunter-gatherer population can be demographically volatile if, due to high mortality, it has no tradition of homeostatic behavior and the causes of high mortality are reduced. That is, such a system only appears to have been homeostatic, or self-regulated, on account of high mortality (usually infant).

If studies of previous climates can ever be worked out to a satisfactory degree of reliability and agreement among them, it would be possible to create models of stress cycles as explicit as Jorde's (1977) for the late Puebloan periods. Until then, we can only state that the essential precondition for the adoption of agriculture seems to be prevention of the dispersal mechanism among hunter-gatherers.

A final series of insights must await more study of the archeological record, and the

Archaic assemblages in the San Juan Basin offer substantial opportunity for further research. It must be determined whether the chronology that Dr. Irwin-Williams has outlined prevails elsewhere. It is possible, since distinct seasonality in canyon-head sites during the Jay, Bajada and San Jose phases is not seen by Irwin-Williams (1979), that the canyon-head assemblages and seasonal collecting sites in slightly lower altitude settings represent more than merely different segments of a subsistence system of a single population. Perhaps these assemblages in different settings also represent small but growing traditions of internal heterogeneity in dependence on collected vegetable products as opposed to larger game. What, for instance, is the range of morphological variance in projectile points from all *hunting camps* as compared to those from collecting areas in the same Archaic phase?

It is not necessary to reiterate the lengthy arguments made in the last chapter about internal population regulation, cyclicity, partial separation of subsistence subsystems by risk, and finally, full separation by social and economic means. Those arguments are meant to apply here as well. They are altered only by the introduction of cultigens in relatively developed form — hence, the shortened period from adoption to sedentism and the Basketmaker adaptation. Here also, until a more refined picture is available, it is useful to suppose that there was a general increase in rainfall, followed by some interruption about 500 B.C.

At any rate, it is argued that in the San Juan Basin, the dispersal mechanism was limited, and those who collected enough to stay off the landscape during a season of high population dispersal were under strong pressure to intensify. The Archaic adaptation would only have given way gradually to a more sedentary existence on the part of some. Because of local variance in rainfall, such pockets of increased sedentism would not likely create archeological sites anywhere evidencing a long continuous history of development to full sedentism, since drives toward sedentism in a particular locale would periodically be aborted. We are in essential agreement with Irwin-Williams (1973) and Reinhart (1968) about *in situ* development of the Basketmaker from local Archaic populations.

THE BASKETMAKER AND PUEBLOAN: MULTIPLE EVOLUTIONARY TRAJECTORIES

We view it as quite likely that the first ephemeral pithouses were created by families who also created *Archaic* lithic scatters at other places, for this is a pattern in southern New Mexico. Later, under circumstances of increasing population, we view the need to be first to exploit casually tended stands of corn as a likely condition requiring one to locate near maturing crops to maintain ones claim. But ripening corn and the fall hunt coincide in a summer rainfall regime. Establishing a claim to the corn risked losing a claim to prime hunting territory. The placement of Basketmaker sites in generally higher elevations, dominating access to both agricultural and foraging/hunting lands, is the inevitable logistic response (maximization of options) (see Breternitz 1973 and Birkedal 1976).

A few horticulturalists in an unstable environment and surrounded by a sea of foragers, however, have several problems if they do not wish chance to eliminate their population. They must generate population increase and they must reestablish dominance over space which contains variable resources; that is, create a power drive. In the elevated perimeters of the San Juan Basin sometime between A.D. 100 and 400, the Basketmaker and Archaic foraging systems permanently separated (their economic/demographic interdependence weakens) to the extent that the Basketmaker generated a population drive first intended to stabilize the effects of infant mortality, and later intended to drive the Archaic system out of undominated open landscape. One directional force of this drive was directed northward and eastward, foraging populations being pressed into the Jemez, the Gallina, the northern Rio Grande and into southern Utah and Colorado. Another force pushed south and eastward, leaving hunting populations in the San Mateo district and Zuni highlands. The drive to dominate space culminated

36

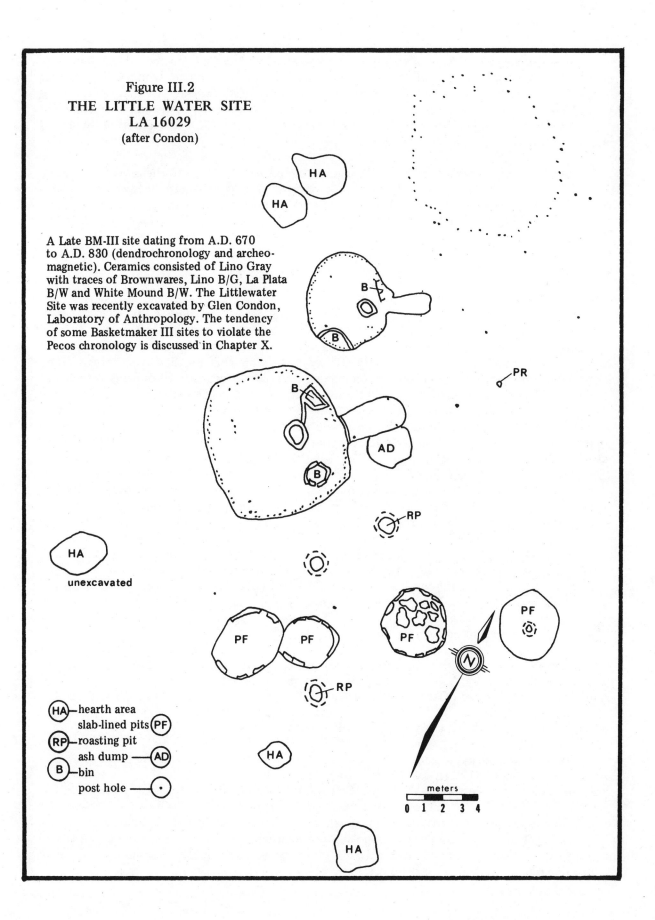

Figure III.2
THE LITTLE WATER SITE
LA 16029
(after Condon)

A Late BM-III site dating from A.D. 670
to A.D. 830 (dendrochronology and archeomagnetic). Ceramics consisted of Lino Gray
with traces of Brownwares, Lino B/G, La Plata
B/W and White Mound B/W. The Littlewater
Site was recently excavated by Glen Condon,
Laboratory of Anthropology. The tendency
of some Basketmaker III sites to violate the
Pecos chronology is discussed in Chapter X.

unexcavated

HA — hearth area
slab-lined pits PF
RP — roasting pit
ash dump — AD
B — bin
post hole — ●

meters
0 1 2 3 4

in the late Basketmaker III — a widely dispersed settlement pattern dotted with a few large (and increasingly defensive) villages. Systems generally overdo it, however, and quickly enough favored site locations would have been used up. In short, Basketmaker site placement likely proceeded systematically from primary to more ephemeral ecotones. This could be analyzed quite simply by arranging Basketmaker sites chronologically (one first has to obtain the dates) and evaluating ecological data.

By A.D. 700, pressure to utilize additional niches had built up to the extent that some population shifted its horticultural adaptation to open spaces in generally lower elevations, that is, to extensive space that had been partly opened up by displacement of foragers. Most archeologists term this shift in adaptation the Pueblo I period — it undoubtedly required slightly new agricultural techniques. Interestingly, the San Juan Data Base records 1,036 Basketmaker sites of all kinds and 986 P-I sites, exclusive of those transitional to P-II. This suggests that Cordell and Plog (1979) may be correct in pointing out evidence for only moderate population growth.

Let us quickly summarize the theoretical state of affairs. Basketmaker-like adaptations emerged from Archaic. Initially, this took pressure off the Archaic system and favored its continued survival. The emerging Basketmaker adaptation initially assumed high risk. It offset this risk by dispersing more widely into pockets somewhat protected from regionwide disaster by randomized rainfall, and by enhancing its hold on subsistence options (site placement). Risks were then further reduced by separating from its antecedent population (group identity allows you to direct competitive behavior outward to a target) and treating it as would any hunter-gatherer faced with local group competition. The population drive it generated to offset the history of its early losses, and to provide for the effects of notable rainfall cycles longer than a generation (Jorde 1977; Allan 1977:135-136), induced, (a) local conflict, (b) self-regulatory behavior, and (c) partial displacement in foraging populations. As a response to both environmental and social conditions, the rate of hunter-gatherer population growth was aborted, and that system was forced by stress to be stalled in evolutionary terms, i.e. hide in the *cracks* or space not utilizable (calorie vacuum) by the more intensive system. We equate this with a kind of niche separation which reinforced the efficiency drive (homeostatic population behavior) of hunter-gatherers. As trade increased to insulate the Basketmaker system against short-term local agricultural losses, it could no longer be destressed by local population regulation, and population drifted upward, encouraging a drive for yet increased agricultural intensification. Settlement size increasingly diverged between large and small. The total number of pithouses in each need to be compared, and again, there were distinct ecological settings between the two.

The P-I period was the response, and, in broad outline, the earlier processual sequence was repeated. Thus, by A.D. 700-800, the Basketmaker adaptation was also displaced from some areas such as Chaco Canyon (Vivian and Mathews 1964; Bannister 1964) and frozen or stalled elsewhere, such as in the Gobernador and Navajo Reservoir Districts (Eddy 1966). Our point is not so much that history repeats itself as that process does.

We view the period from roughly A.D. 900-950 as very instructive in the chain of events. According to Hayes (1964), the Mesa Verdean occupation was at its peak — a concentrated zone of population pressure to the north. Chaco Canyon had entered its classic period and was *gearing up* in size and dominance over vast space. Characteristics of the Late Rosa/Piedra Phases in Navajo Reservoir are notable: stockades, evidence of violent deaths, etc. Here we see the riptide effects of geographically opposing power drives from systems at the highest tier of complexity — power directed outward and probably exerted, in part, indirectly by semi-Nomadic populations under extreme pressure.

Table III.A

WETHERILL MESA – MESA VERDE PHASE CHARACTERISTICS*

Phase Name	Pecos Classification	Site Location	Pop. Size	Comments
La Plata	BM-III (500-700)	no information		very few sites, not enough evidence
Piedra Phase	P-I (700-900)	83% near dry farming areas	high	147 sites with 1,176 surface rooms; average of 8 rooms per site
Ackmen Phase	Early P-II (900-1000)	68% near dry farming areas	highest	208 sites w/1,248 rooms, average 6 rooms per site. Similar to Red Mesa Phase of Chaco. Sites smaller than preceeding phase & more dispersed.
Mancos Phase	P-II (975-1075) (975/1000 to 1050/1075)	32% in dry farming areas. More in caves and talus	decreasing	166 sites w/966 rooms average 6 rooms per site; further dispersal, reduction in number of sites; development of terrace farming. Sites shifting to caves & talus slopes
McElmo Phase	Late P-II (1050-1150)	10% in dry farming area. Caves or canyon bottoms	lowest	60 sites w/540 rooms; sites average 9 rooms. Most popular site location. Shift away from dry farming area of Piedra Phase (only 10% located there).
Mesa Verde Phase	P-III (1150-1300)	9% in dry farming areas. Caves are favored	higher than McElmo — lower than Piedra/Ackmen	168 sites w/1,512 rooms average 9 rooms per site. More sites & rooms than any other phase, but Hayes believes a drop in population.

* Source (Hayes 1964)

The Chaco phenomenon itself was the highest tier (four levels of adaptation, in our view: hunter-gatherer; mixed strategy Basketmaker, local agricultural networks, low level state system) that ever developed in the San Juan. We conceive of Chaco Canyon and its 80 or more (Judge, personal communication; Marshall, Stein, Loose & Novotny 1979) outliers as a vast wheel. The hub at Chaco Canyon, its spokes, or roads, directed outward to the rim, its outliers. In a cyclical environment, the beauty of such a system is several-fold. The effects of uneven crop years are spread over a vast area. By managing surplus, a momentarily failed outlier can be subsidized by supplies sent down a *spoke* with little information passage between outliers. One can also close the spokes and let an outlier fend for itself. The possibilities for manipulation or obscuring the true state of the system are spectacular. By dominating huge areas of relatively open space, one also puts intense pressure on foragers or small scale systems. As long as they remain in the *cracks* around such aggregated communities, they return to make life unpleasant when regional crop failures rob a system of its power and enhance the need to maximize options. We agree with others (Lister, personal communication; Lipe 1978; Cordell and Plog 1979) that the Chaco phenomenon was, in scale, a departure from the mainstream of Anasazi development. Moreover, such a system, like our own, operates on very small true margins of reserve. Analysis of assemblages, burials, pollen profiles and salinity of soils is bound to show several regional failures at Chacoan outliers just prior to the system's disintegration.

Our points are these. When Chaco fell, it left few bodies, and we argue that it acted like a proper stratified system — an umbrella of protection (erected in structure and organization) over the general populace's head. In accord with the notion of stratified risks, the fall of the system was in proportion to the mass of energy contained in it. It came quickly and much high-level information was lost. The smaller, more self-contained subsystems of Anasazi adaptation (and associated population), however, largely survived and moved on. If our views are correct, the height of Chacoan complexity was impossible to sustain in such an environment and was, in part, induced by earlier population stress. Since no primary agricultural dependence was ever stabilized there again, we suggest specifically that the long-term practice of agriculture there *depended* on such Chacoan organization. We predict that if archeologists look for it, they will find osteological evidence for an episode of increased infant mortality, disease, malnutrition, reduced age at death, etc. in the settlements surrounding the Chacoan outliers at roughly A.D. 900-1000. Additionally, we need to ask whether the Chacoan system gradually developed inward from its outliers, or outward from the center. The awesome but pleasurable task of excavation and precise dating at a number of outliers and surrounding communities should permit resolution of these issues.

One final vignette. For a time prior to Chaco Canyon's last big building projects (ca. A.D. 1125), it probably required vast labor demands. We view it as likely that this reduced stress on outlying areas, and incorporated individuals of diverse ethnic and linguistic groups. But as it began to lose its magnet effect, it released substantial population pressure outward. The oft cited backwardness of the Largo-Gallina is more easily understood if it is considered essentially a Basketmaker adaptation (see also, Cordell 1979) — partially frozen in its evolutionary trajectory by strata of development above it (Pueblo-Chaco) and below it (Northern Rio Grande Cultures?). That is, the evolutionary trajectory of a cultural system is confined by coexistence with diverse systems of different complexity. More complex systems *above* it prevent utilization of newly created niches, and it cannot collapse downward into the hunter-gatherer niche, since it is occupied and that would create population crisis. Because of the principle of competitive exclusion (Gause's Law), it would be Basketmaker-like adaptations (substantial *foraging*) who were in conflict most closely with remaining nomads. More to the point, the Largo-Gallina populations were shoved up against the Gallina highlands by Anasazi development in the San Juan Basin and Mesa Verde and, backed by both a geographic barrier to agriculture (the Jemez) and hunter-gatherers in the Jemez and Rio Grande areas, they took the force of a dispersing Chaco phenomenon, not directly, of course, but delivered by the archeologically subtle drive of foragers caught in the no-man's land between the two

Table III.B
NOTES ON NAVAJO RESERVOIR*

Phase Name	Pecos Classification	Site Size	Population Size	Comments
Los Pinos	BM-II A.D. 1-400	mostly single units (15) villages (4) multiple (2)	300 (considerably fewer per generation)	Houses consist of shallow depressions, cobble aprons, walls of jacal or cribbed logs. Floors space average: 300-500 ft², possible kivas at villages. Pottery (brownware) appears at about A.D. 300. Projectile points more common than in later periods. Evidence only of corn.
Sambrito	BM-III A.D. 400-700	single units (2) multiple (2) village (1)	56-63?	About A.D. 400 true pithouses appear, increase in brown ceramics & appearance of graywares from Mesa Verde, less projectile points, trade in shell ornaments.
Rosa	Early P-I A.D. 700-850	single units (115) villages (6) multiple (15)	1,129 (226/generation)	Late Rosa-Arboles trend toward larger villages. Population increases greatly over preceeding phases, at approx. A.D. 750. Gray pottery, neckbanded, Mesa Verde Redwares, decorated pottery, fewer projectile points, increase in grinding stones.
Piedra	Late P-I A.D. 850-950	single units (90+) multiple (45) villages (10?)	583 (233/generation)	Stockades A.D. 850-1000. Most from Piedra Phase. Enclosed from 1-3 pithouses. Population shifting upstream, large kivas at villages. High frequency of burned houses, cannabilization, burned bodies in pithouses. Decorated pottery, projectile points continue to decrease, increase continues of ground stone, larger numbers & varieties of exotic goods (stone, ceramic, shell) at villages.
Arboles	Early P-II A.D. 950-1050		357 (143 at anytime)	After population high during Rosa & Piedra Phases, population decreases. Continued shift upstream, decrease in projectile points.
			3.5 people /habitation	After A.D. 1000 population has drifted out, to the north. By A.D. 1050, area abandoned.

*Source (Eddy 1966)
Note: 6 depressions = village; 2-5 depressions = multiple unit.

41

systems. Exit the Chaco building boom ca. A.D. 1125, and enter palisades, bodies, burned sites, etc., in the Gallina.

When the Chaco system failed, population collapsed outward (Rio Grande, Zuni highlands, east Chuska slope and, perhaps, Mesa Verde as well) and left behind a comparative vacuum. Some Mesa Verdean occupation filtered in, and P-III should be distinguished from Chacoan populations, but we suggest that the late 1100's to the 1300's were a time when nomads and seminomads were again drawn to the central basin. The evidence for early Navajo dental remains from Trinidad Lake, Colorado, which date between A.D. 1148 and 1189, should not be taken lightly. It is worthwhile to ask again, just who emerged from this period into the historic? Anasazi development, of course, shifted eastward to the Rio Grande and the San Juan Basin later was filled again with nomads — people of lesser complexity traded places with those of more. A sustained agricultural adaptation could not be supported without the expansive economic/redistributive network.

Table III.C

NOTES ON CHACO CANYON**

* Bonito Phase	1030-1130 clusters between 900-1124	Large Pueblos, public architecture — cored veneer masonry. Long-term, in place development.
* Hosta Butte Phase	1040's+	Small villages, irregular plan. Long-term, in place development.
* McElmo Phase	1050-1124+	Large, compact pueblos; McElmo B/W ceramics; no *in place development*.

* The *Chacoan phenomena*, all phases are contemporaneous. The outliers also date within the same period. Outliers in the Red Mesa Valley appear to have been abandoned earlier (fewer ceramics were imported to Chaco) than those along the Chuska slope and San Juan. Marshall, Stein, Loose & Novotny (1979 and personal communication) have found that at outlying Chacoan communities the great kiva preceeded the Bonito House as a form of public architecture.

- -

Chaco Canyon Chronology
(Bannister 1964:200; Vivian and Mathews 1964:108-115)

1. Pithouse sites — A.D. 644-777 — earlier sites present (Hayes 1975)
2. Classic Chaco Sites — A.D. 828-1178 — best clustering is between 900-1124. The 1178 date is from a hearth at Kin Kletso. All major building activity had ceased by 1124.
3. Mesa Verde Reoccupation — A.D. 1250-1275, mid 1200's — reoccupation of several sites by makers of Mesa Verde B/W. This is also apparent at many of the outliers (the Bonito houses).
4. A.D. 1275-1300 — small scattered occupation on mesa tops south of the canyon. Defensive locations. Also occupation on the Chacra Mesa to the east. Ceramics are Mesa Verde B/W, Heshotauthla Polychrome, St. Johns Polychrome, Klagetoh Polychrome.
5. A.D. 1300-1350 — small occupation within Chaco Canyon. Ceramics include Mesa Verde B/W, Pinnawa G/W, Klagetoh B/W and B/O and Heshotauthla.

**This chronology is becoming outdated as research proceeds at the Chaco Center. Hosta Butte and McElmo Phase terms have been dropped and building activity may continue to A.D. 1140 or later at some sites (see Judge 1979, Schelberg 1980, and Toll, Windes and McKenna 1980).

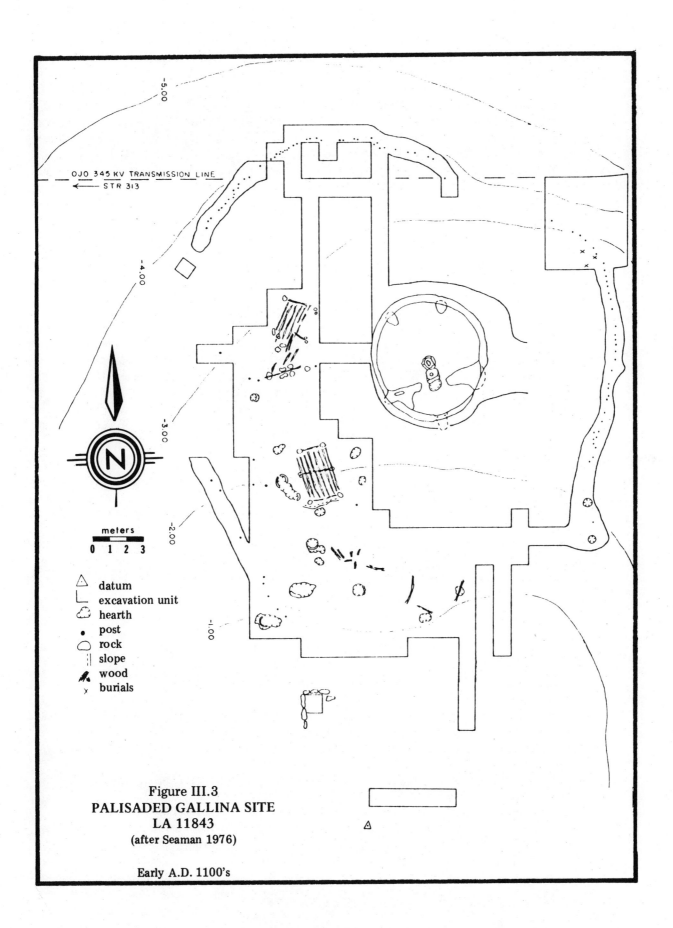

OJO 345 KV TRANSMISSION LINE
← STR 313

-5.00

-4.00

-3.00

-2.00

-1.00

meters
0 1 2 3

△ datum
∟ excavation unit
☁ hearth
• post
◯ rock
⫴ slope
🪵 wood
x burials

Figure III.3
PALISADED GALLINA SITE
LA 11843
(after Seaman 1976)

Early A.D. 1100's

OVERVIEW

In practical terms, much archeological work remains if we are to refine notions regarding the shift to agriculture. If, as we suggest, demographic homeostasis is first destroyed in the center of favored areas, the archeological record should yield evidence of changed tool kits or changed frequencies of tools in the same assemblage over time. More continuity, however subtle, is to be expected in the more homogeneous areas surrounding such favored pockets and, as Flannery (1969) and others have noted, evolutionary displacement at the edges. We predict that in the San Juan, as more archeologists scratch the surface around the edges of Archaic lithic scatters, they will find pithouses. Further, if more unknown lithic scatters can be dated through C-14, thermoluminescence of hearth stones, obsidian hydration or archeomagnetic techniques, a surprising range of dates should emerge. We suggest that so-called backward archeological populations such as the Largo-Gallina, or the Fremont in Utah, are no less mysterious in the context of more complex Anasazi development than is the continued existence of conservative Rio Grande pueblos in the industrial world.

In theoretical terms, we have argued that homeostasis is generally efficient and generally safe. Deviation from it comes at the price of increased risks and is generally inefficient. Power is the requisite for successful competition. With the shift to investment of energy in non-human structures and information, a system could buffer population loss during catastrophe. The worldwide population trend and increased rates of cultural succession in the last 10,000 years have resulted. The interactions between cultural systems which have diverged, and a given system's pattern of oscillations between power and efficiency, are fascinating, complex and a subject for a separate monograph. In this section, we have only focused on the idea that a diverging system can confer advantage on its progenitor by accepting differential risk.

THE UPPER RIO GRANDE

BACKGROUND

The upper Rio Grande portion of the region deserves some particular mention. When one excludes the southern extension of Dr. Cordell's overview area (roughly Bernalillo, New Mexico, southward — see Map III.2), the cultural sequences begin to assume very distinctive characteristics. As one moves north out of the Albuquerque district and into the Santa Fe district, the evidence for intensive occupation prior to the 12th century becomes increasingly scarce.

Unlike the San Juan Basin and its peripheral borders, the evidence for a long *in situ* evolutionary development, from at least Archaic to Late P-II/Early P-III times, evaporates as one moves into the northern uplands. For these reasons a distinct regional chronology is generally employed.

Table III.1
*GENERAL CULTURAL SEQUENCE -- NORTHERN RIO GRANDE

Archaic/Lithic Period — A.D. 600?
    Most currently use Irwin-Williams' Oshara sequence here, but there is still
    little direct evidence for its applicability in the northern Rio Grande.
Early Developmental — A.D. 600-900
Late Developmental — A.D. 900-1200
Coalition — A.D. 1200-1325
P-IV *Rio Grande Classic* — A.D. 1325-1600
P-V Historic Pueblo — A.D. 1600-Present

---

* Note: Sources (Wendorf 1954; Wendorf and Reed 1955; Irwin-Williams 1973)

In this volume we follow Warren's (1977) suggestion that the Santa Fe B/W ceramics appear at A.D. 1175, and also break the P-IV/P-V at A.D. 1540. We use the 1540 date because data from many site files use that to separate P-IV from P-V. The chronology we use as related to the Pecos Classification appears below.

Figure III.4
COMPARATIVE CHRONOLOGY: PECOS — UPPER RIO GRANDE

	Pecos Phase	Upper Rio Grande — Typical Ceramics*		
A.D. 1600	P-V	P-V Historic	VI	Tewa Polychromes
1540	P-IV	Rio Grande Classic (P-IV)	Glaze E (Early) I Rio Grande Glazes Los Padillas Glaze	Sankawi B/C Biscuit B Biscuit A Wiyo B/W
1325 1300		Coalition (P-III)	Santa Fe B/W, often Mesa Verde B/W, St. Johns Polychrome	
1175	P-III			
1100	P-II	Late Developmental (P-II)	Kwahee B/W often Chaco II B/W, some Wingate B/R (Late)	
900	P-I	Early Developmental (BM-III/P-I)	Primarily Plainwares, some Brownwares	
700				
600	BM-III	Lithic/Archaic	None	
400	BM-II			

* In addition to sources noted in Table III.1, see Smiley, Stubbs and Bannister (1953), Ford, Schroeder and Peckham (1972), and Warren (1979) for fuller details on ceramic assemblages. See especially Bibliography of Smiley, Stubbs and Bannister for important pre 1950 sources.

The ceramics of the region display a high degree of local specialization during and after the Coalition period. For instance, Taos B/W occurs in the Taos district during the Late Developmental-Early Coalition period transition (P-II to P-III shift), while the P-III/P-IV shift is marked throughout the region by specialization both in the glazewares and in black-on-white varieties, such as Galisteo B/W, Wiyo, Poge B/W, Pindi B/W and Jemez B/W (which endures as a type until the mid-1600's). For the moment, let us concentrate on a very brief overview of developmental trends. The following sketch is based largely on data presented in the monumental four-volume study of the Cochiti Reservoir project (herein referred to as Biella and Chapman 1977-79). The focus is thus on the western Santa Fe and Pajarito districts.

A BRIEF SKETCH: THE COCHITI-PAJARITO AREA

We should first point out that we are not herein duplicating Dr. Cordell's (1979) discussion of the upper Rio Grande, in general, or of the Cochiti-Pajarito area in particular. Rather, we have abstracted a large body of general data from roughly 1,200 sites in this 600 square mile area. Our object is to focus on site location, site size and shifts in settlement pattern as a prelude to our discussion on survey.

LITHIC/ARCHAIC PERIOD (2000 or 3000? B.C. to A.D. 400 or 600)

A few isolated Paleo Indian points have been located as scattered finds in the upper Rio Grande, but no major loci of Paleo-Indian activity have been recorded north of La Bajada hill. Later, a number of presumed Archaic lithic scatters are known, but are little studied. Most of these contain no diagnostic projectile points and are seldom datable, since few hearth features have been recorded and obsidians are only inconsistently found.

In the Cochiti study, Chapman and Biella (1979:386) conclude that "Archaic campsites within the project area were abysmally lacking in charcoal due to their generally deflated state of preservation. . . obsidian hydration analyses from the Archaic sites . . . seemed quite fruitful and indicated a late Armijo-En Medio Archaic occupation. The few projectile point fragments which were recovered were consistent with an Armijo-En Medio occupation and morphologically fit into the Oshara tradition" (1979:386). This places the occupation between 1800 B.C. and A.D. 400, though the Cochiti material fell primarily in the latter portion of these periods.

Significantly, the Archaic remains in the study area may differ from those in the San Juan Basin in two important respects. First, the most common, or numerous, Archaic components (based on projectile points) in the San Juan Basin are consistently the earlier San Jose phase materials (Judge, in press). In this portion of the Rio Grande, later materials are more common.

Secondly, Chapman (1979:75-102) has demonstrated that Archaic site placement was *not* conditioned in the Cochiti area by selection for areas of high vegetative diversity. His conclusions limit our ability to generalize from the earlier conclusions of Reher and Witter (1977) which clearly related Archaic site settings to areas of high vegetative diversity along the lower Chaco River (about 150 miles northwest of Cochiti). Reher's and Witter's work had been independently confirmed (Allan, *et al.* 1975) in the San Juan Basin, and field archeologists had begun to generalize the phenomenon. The attraction of the Reher-Witter hypothesis has, of course, been enhanced by ethnographic observations which also suggested that hunters-gatherers preferred to camp in ecotonal situations. Chapman's (1979:102) concluding comments are quite to the point:

"The Reservoir locale, as noted in the analysis, is situated in one of the most vegetatively diverse areas of the North American continent. Given this knowledge, we must consider whether variation in relative diversity within such a highly diverse setting is significant as a control of Archaic settlement within the reservoir or are better used as comparative data for evaluating other patterns of settlement in other less diverse environmental settings".

In essence, Chapman suggests that one must ask if, lost in a sea of high diversity, access to vegetative diversity in specific site location matters at all. We suggest that one must also ask why, then, the Cochiti Reservoir area did not become an intense magnet for early *in situ* Archaic development, in view of the high diversity of resources. In view of little evidence, locally, for an early *in situ* shift to an agricultural strategy, we should focus on two possibilities.

First, is Chapman's evidence against the Archaic-vegetative diversity model broadly valid? If so, how would we account for the paradox of its demonstration elsewhere? Could we propose, for instance, that areas of high vegetative diversity in generally desertic settings are essential in the process of stabilized sand dune formation? If so, perhaps we are monitoring the placement of Archaic sites as an artifact of the geological preservation of earlier habitation surfaces. This, of course, influences site visibility.

Secondly, we might propose that the high vegetative diversity of Cochiti Reservoir was productive enough to make it possible for hunters-gatherers under general population pressure to avoid the labor intensification of early horticulture. We might then propose that early agriculture takes place in less diverse settings where alternative options cannot be maintained. In a sense, this is in line with earlier arguments about agriculture taking place on the margins of favored areas, and contrary to our thesis in Chapter II that hunter-gatherer populations are drawn to favored areas — thus inducing intensifying strategies in the center. The paradox could be resolved if a favored area is defined as one in which *year-round subsistence is possible in a fairly restricted locale.*

Since Chapman suggests that the Cochiti Reservoir area evidences only one part of the hunter-gatherer seasonal round, it may not qualify on that basis as an area where local population pressure could induce the demographic and labor changes required for the agricultural transformation. In any case, the comparative studies he proposes are to the point and essential.

In our summary of data for 1,168 site components (see Tables III.2, 3 and 4) from a 500-600 square mile region surrounding (but not including) the Cochiti Reservoir project area, only 78 sites (7%) are attributable to the period from roughly 2000 B.C. to A.D. 400 or 600. This is a stunning scarcity of these components when compared to the several thousand lithic sites recorded in the San Juan Basin. It may be that there has been generally less interest in recording such sites in the upper Rio Grande, or that visibility in the more heavily wooded higher elevations is impossibly poor when compared to the arid settings at lower elevations. In either case, we know too little about Archaic occupations of the upper Rio Grande to be comfortable with any generalizations.

THE EARLY DEVELOPMENT PERIOD (A.D. 600-900)

Again, very little is known of the local BM-III/P-I occupation in the upper Rio Grande. Reinhart's (1967) work with the Rio Rancho phase sites (see last section) lies well to the south of the area we are focusing on here, and Lang's (1977) in the Galisteo Basin is just to the east. In our sample of sites from the region, there are 15 such components, or 1.5% in the data summary. To these, some of the 12 sites having pithouse depressions and few artifacts in the Cochiti Reservoir study should be added. Since many of the sites in our data summary overlap the Cochiti Reservoir area, we may suppose about 20 components in a 600 square mile area (we think survey coverage for this *control* region is between 10 and 20 percent).

47

During this period there is increasing investment in architectural features at sites, most having a few pithouse depressions, and some having small scatters of plain gray or brown sherds. During the Cochiti survey, ten sites were recorded which suggested a Basketmaker occupation from apparent pithouse depressions. Five of these (Hunter-Anderson 1979:208-216) were tested during the excavation phase, and none was found to be Baketmaker, all recovered ceramic materials were P-IV (though several are thought to be P-III, on other evidence). None of the excavated depressions proved to be demonstrable pithouses with floor features, etc.

The point, of course, is that sites of this period are generally ephemeral, and some depressions, on excavation, will not be conclusively a classic pithouse at all. LA 9140, LA 272, LA 6173, and a few others are listed as having pithouse components. Most similar sites in the area have been cross-dated ceramically at roughly A.D. 750-950. Unlike pithouse occupations which are well documented from Albuquerque's west mesa, the Navajo Reservoir district, the *White Mound phase* sites in the western periphery of the San Juan Basin and the extensive documentation of Late Georgetown through Early Three Circle phase occupations in the Mogollon area of southwestern New Mexico, there are few comparative data from the upper Rio Grande.

Sites of this period range from 1-3 pithouses, on average, and are located near permanent sources of water in the lowest elevations of the district. Thus, no structured sites of this period are reported from the uplands of the Pajarito Plateau at all. In this respect, the area is rather like the Zuni highlands discussed in the next chapter.

LATE DEVELOPMENTAL (A.D. 900-1175)

The P-II occupations in this region are also little studied. As Biella and Chapman (1977: 303) point out, only 34 P-II occupations are recorded in the area. That is 3% of our component sample. No additional P-II occupations were recorded during the survey in Cochiti Reservoir itself, only one sherd of Kwahee B/W was recorded from the sample at LA 5014, a P-III pueblo on the Rio Grande in White Rock Canyon (Biella and Chapman 1977:126, 251). Such sites range in size from either one or two surface rooms (or pithouses) to components of sites ranging up to 500 rooms. Almost all known P-II sites are multicomponent — being associated either with BM-III/P-I occupations or with later P-III components. The larger ones are associated with the P-III sites.

These are said to be found "intermittently throughout the study area, predominantly on mesa tops in the Pajarito Plateau and along the banks of the Santa Fe and Rio Grande Rivers" (Biella and Chapman 1977:303). Elsewhere, Hunter-Anderson (1979a:169) characterized P-II and P-III sites as evidencing occupation in the upland areas of high rainfall, a pattern interrupted during the terminal P-III period (about A.D. 1300) with a shift to occupation of zones of lower rainfall (both upland and lowland). Since Hunter-Anderson's statement conflicted, to a degree, with Biella and Chapman's characterization of site setting, we looked further into the matter and arrived at a most interesting pattern. Exactly half (17) of the P-II occupations also had a P-III occupation, but no other earlier or later components. Only three of these sites were below 6,000 feet in elevation. The average elevation of these 17 sites is 6,262 feet, including LA 6461 and 6462, which were at elevations which did not pattern with the rest (5,280 feet and 5,300 feet).

Only four sites were either BM-III or P-I and P-II occupations. These averaged 5,310 feet in elevation, and none was over 5,400 feet. Six P-II sites had three or four components, that is P-II and BM-III, P-I or P-IV or P-V. These averaged 5,538 feet in elevation. Six P-II sites were, so far as we can determine, single component occupations. The average elevation of these was 5,770 feet, though they ranged in elevation from 5,250-6,200 feet — very evenly spaced. These data are summarized below.

48

Table III.2

P-II COMPONENT ASSOCIATION AND ELEVATION

Association	No.	Avg. Elev.	Min. — Max.
P-II + P-III	17	6,262 ft.	5,280 — 6,530 ft*
P-II + BM-III and/or P-I	4	5,310 ft.	5,240 — 5,400 ft.
P-II + either above and/or P-IV, P-V	6	5,538 ft.	5,290 — 5,870 ft.
P-II single component	6	5,770 ft.	5,250 — 6,200 ft.***
TOTAL	33**		

* 14 of 17 clustered tightly between 6,160 ft. and 6,530 ft.

** 1 site (LA 3818) had no elevational data recorded.

*** very evenly distributed.

Now, we may reconcile Biella and Chapman's statements with Hunter-Anderson's (1979a) and add some comments of our own. Hunter-Anderson's statement should read, *one-half of the known P-II components in the Cochiti overview area are in high rainfall settings (higher elevation) and associated with similar P-III settings (to A.D. 1300).* Though these data are modest, we can contrive several rules that may be useful in future research. First, and obviously, those P-II components associated with earlier components (BM-III/P-I) are found in lower, drier elevational settings. Second, P-II components associated with multiple occupations (three or more phases) occur only below 5,870 feet, while P-II occupations above 5,880 feet occur with a later P-III occupation 90% of the time, the remainder being single component and spread evenly through altitude zones.

Since P-II occupations in low elevations tend to be associated with early components, and in upper elevations with later components, it becomes obvious to ask about the chronological relationship between P-II sites in each elevation zone. Cordell (1979:56) discusses Lang's (1977a) suggestion that the P-III period should be considered to begin at A.D. 1050 or 1100 with the production of Kwahee B/W. It therefore seems really important to review the ceramic assemblages from each of these 34 P-II components, even if it requires additional field survey to do so. We need to know if there is an earlier *in situ* P-II occupation and a later *in-migrated* P-II occupation, and therefore the occurrence of Kwahee B/W and its associations with tradewares is important.

That is, we might want to consider sites with Red Mesa B/W, Kwahee B/W and tradewares such as Wingate B/R separately. The ceramic assemblage at LA 114 (Arroyo Negro) strikes us as worth reviewing in detail. Of the 137 dates published for the site (Smiley, Stubbs and Bannister 1953:22) all but one fall between A.D. 1045 and 1145, and there are good clusters for separate excavation units, some around A.D. 1050 and others at A.D. 1125-45 (LA 191; LA 672, Forked Lightning; and LA 742 should be useful to review, as well). We think the period to control is A.D. 1125-1150, based on the collapse of the Chacoan system.

It may, of course, be the case that the P-II occupation of the area has little to do with later population influx from the San Juan Basin (or Mesa Verde and the Cebolleta Mesa area — see next chapter). At the moment it seems quite plausible for early P-II (BM-III/P-I multi-component pattern) occupations to represent some Chacoan expansion into lowland areas, while later P-II occupation (P-II/P-III multicomponent pattern) may represent the first infusion of population from the San Juan Basin after Chacoan collapse.

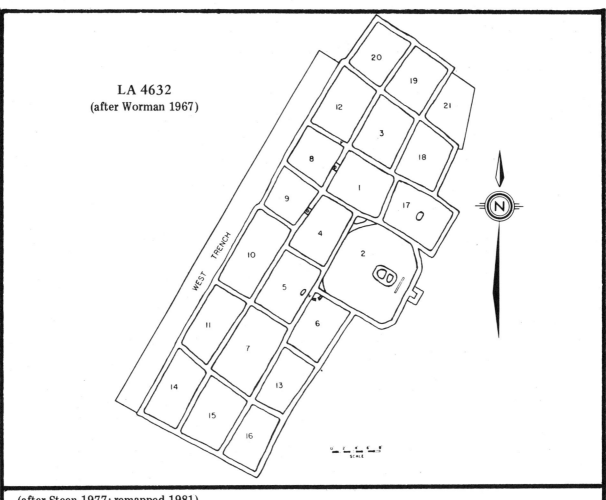

LA 4632
(after Worman 1967)

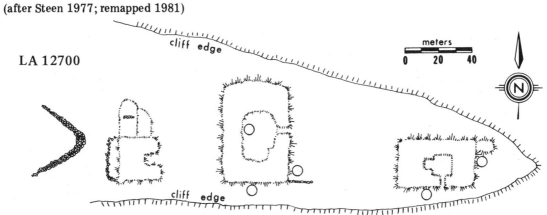

(after Steen 1977; remapped 1981)

LA 12700

Figure III.5
EXAMPLES OF COALITION PERIOD SITES ON THE PAJARITO PLATEAU

This portion of LA 12700 (bottom) has over 400 ground floor rooms.
Two hundred is often cited as the maximum for this period.

COALITION PERIOD (P-III) — (A.D. 1175-1325)

Coalition period occupation of the region is represented by 380 components in our sample. Ceramically, the co-occurrence of Santa Fe B/W (typically 50-80% of painted wares) with modest proportions of Kwahee B/W and tradewares such as St. Johns Polychrome, sometimes Springerville Polychrome and Mesa Verde B/W (sometimes alleged intrusive and sometimes alleged indigenous) is generally taken as a designator of the Early Coalition period.

P-III sites range in size from one or two rooms to over 200. The most common site size is 13-30 rooms. The majority of these are small linear or L-shaped roomblocks (often two tiers of rooms) and are generally taken to be earlier in the sequence. The largest of these generally occur in the northern Pajarito Plateau, and many are arranged in an enclosed plaza (quite similar to some contemporaneous site arrangements in the Cebolleta Mesa region and Gila Forest areas of west central New Mexico).

It is during this period that the Pajarito Plateau experiences major occupation, with hundreds of *Santa Fe B/W* sites known, though few are completely mapped and recorded (Steen 1977). Surprisingly, very few sites of the period have been dated independently of ceramic seriations.

In the wetter highlands of the Pajarito Plateau construction is masonry, while in the drier areas around Tesuque and Santa Fe, thin walled adobe was common in construction (though some adobe construction is also dated to the P-II period).

Terminal Coalition period sites are generally characterized by increasing percentages of Wiyo B/W, and in particular areas, Pindi, Poge, etc. Tradewares during the transition to Early P-IV will often include Heshotauthla Polychrome. The appearance of small quantities of Los Padillas Glaze-Polychrome and/or Arenal and Aqua Fria Glaze A wares is widely accepted as the P-IV horizon marker, though as one moves north of Santa Fe the introduction of Wiyo B/W and Biscuit A is considered the P-IV horizon marker. The best known excavation report for a Coalition period site is likely *The Excavation of Pindi Pueblo, New Mexico* (Stubbs and Stallings 1953). This brings us to major research interests in the region.

Most researchers in the northern Rio Grande have focused on the rapid influx of population just prior to A.D. 1200. A major concern has been with the identity of the migrants, most scholars arguing both Mesa Verdean and Chacoan influence and some, influx of population from west central New Mexico at the terminus of the phase. A second, and increasingly important emphasis has been on shifting patterns of subsistence and social complexity (Biella and Chapman 1977-79).

We are able to contribute in a small way here by focusing again on survey data. Pueblo III components increase to 380 from 34 P-II components. As Biella (1979) points out, this is on the order of a ten-fold increase. Room count for the period is 2,972 (Biella and Chapman 1977), again a ten-fold increase. That is, somewhere between A.D. 1150 and 1250 *population* increases by ten-fold in a 600 square mile area. Such population increase in a century, or thereabouts, is certainly possible, though not common. The Navajo, for instance, have increased ten-fold since 1870; Mexico will probably close out this century at 130-150 million persons, an eight-fold increase since 1900. Nonetheless, these kinds of sustained population increases are genuinely impossible where infant mortality is high. In Tainter and Gillio's (1980a) overview of the Mt. Taylor area, Tainter presents data that suggest that a woman would have had to have six children during her reproductive career *just* to maintain population levels at A.D. 1100. Though Tainter argues against in-migration in the western Mt. Taylor district as accounting for changing cultural patterns during late P-II times, such an argument cannot plausibly be made for the northern Rio Grande (it may prove not to be a supportable argument for the Mt. Taylor district either).

The collapse of the Chacoan system, the rapid development of the early Santa Fe B/W sites, and generally high infant mortality throughout the Puebloan Southwest about A.D. 1100, all preclude any argument for Rio Grande development which does not accept substantial in-migrating population. On the other hand, just how impressive are 380 sites comprising 3,000 (rounded) rooms, as an occupational base in 600 square miles?

Let us assume that not less than 10% of the region has been intensively surveyed (Biella and Chapman 1977 suggest 10%). Assuming also that a disproportionate number of the larger sites have attracted attention, we may safely suppose that we have a solid 20% room count (if not 30+%) for the entire region. That is, we have 380 sites in 150 years (A.D. 1175-1325) in 600 square miles. Though we suspect many to be narrowly contemporaneous, our knowledge is largely derived from ancedote. Nonetheless, the construction of 2.5 sites per year averaging 8 rooms each, or 20 rooms in total, would have to be constructed to account for the entire P-III occupation as we now know it. Not very impressive, is it? How about one site per 240 square miles per year, or one room per 30 square miles?

But, if one multiplied the room and site counts by ten-fold to approach total survey coverage, that is 25 sites per year or 200 rooms per year (one site per 24 square miles or one room per three square miles), it would slightly *exceed* construction rates for the P-II period in the San Juan Basin.

In the period from A.D. 950-1100, the San Juan Data Base lists 3,200 sites (P-II and P-II/P-III transitional), that is, 22.5 sites per year (also a 600 square mile survey base). In the Mimbres (see Chapter V) the number of recorded classic sites (÷ 150 — the number of years of the period) is identical to that in the San Juan Basin. Given that survey coverage in the area that Chapman and Biella overview is about 60 square miles (10% of 600 square miles), P-III occupation at 380 components is equivalent to or slightly higher than P-II/Chacoan occupation. About 600 square miles of the San Juan Basin have been intensively surveyed. Given the 3,200 Chacoan period sites, they average 5.4 sites per square mile surveyed, while P-III components in the Cochiti area average 6.3 per square mile surveyed. Overall site density is actually higher per surveyed square mile in the Cochiti control area than in the surveyed areas of the San Juan Basin as a whole (20+ sites/square mile compared to 12.5).

This brings us to Hunter-Anderson's (1979a) paper on competition-reduction as an explanation for the changed settlement pattern which led to the P-IV (or Rio Grande Classic), a period of higher aggregation into fewer large sites. Basically, Hunter-Anderson argues that the cost of maintaining access to better watered uplands was reduced under competition by relocating into lower elevations and using uplands for hunting and occasional foraging. In view of the generally dense local population, her argument may have some merit. But it is not *upland* population density which compels her to seek an explanation for the Late P-III/-Early P-IV relocation. Rather, she cites increased rainfall (1979a:171) during the 1300's, which would have permitted a return to agriculture in the higher elevations. But it did not occur.

We do not wish to dismiss her argument, but we must also consider the actual level of P-IV occupation.

THE P-III/P-IV TRANSITION

The P-IV period in the Rio Grande is characterized by aggregation into larger sites. Many of these are in excess of 100 rooms, and a few are in the range of 300-500 rooms (see Warren 1979:194-195 for a list of well-known glaze sites; the P-IV are Glaze A through E or *Early E*. By the way, this is an outstandingly useful paper).

Nonetheless, the distribution of site size is highly bimodal. One to four rooms are common, as are sites having over 50 rooms, while the 13-30 room count common for the P-III is nearly absent. Biella and Chapman (1977:305) cite 2,587 rooms for the period in their 500 square mile study. Total components for the period number 240, an average of 10.5 rooms per site (though few of that size really exist) compared to an average of eight rooms for the P-III (where many of that size exist). Thus, there is a drop of between 35 and 40% in the number of sites, but only about a 15% drop in room count.

More to the point, Hunter-Anderson (1979b:181) demonstrates a drop in room size from P-III to P-IV that varies from 25% to 75%, depending on site size and locale. It would be safe to suggest a 50% reduction in room size across the board for at least the Early P-IV period. In other words, the drop in total floor space between the periods is remarkable. The correct comparison then, we believe, is between 2,972 P-III sized rooms and 1,293 P-IV rooms or fewer that are equivalent in floor space. Further, P-IV occupations span 240 years, while the P-III spans 150. That is, only one-fourth as much floor space is created per year for the entire occupation as for the P-III. Two to five meter square rooms are impossibly small to house many persons. However one counts population to room numbers, there was already substantial population decrease by A.D. 1325-1350. Had not competition for space and resources already been reduced substantially by P-IV times? Then why the need for a stress-reduction model?

Hunter-Anderson (1979b:180) also provides an analysis of storage facilities between P-III and P-IV sites. While this is an important subject, her data from larger sites are too few to be convincing. Secondly, it has long struck us that the upland *Great Kivas* found in the Mogollon-Reserve area and kivas in the highlands of the upper Rio Grande were natural winter habitation sites.

It is, we think, a shade difficult to accept the labor investment in a kiva only for ceremonial purposes at a four or five room P-III site, where surface rooms are quite small and often without hearths. Clearly one must suppose there is substantial function beyond ceremonial integration of a *community* of perhaps 10-15 people, who probably are an extended family. One may either propose that such Pajarito Plateau sites were occupied seasonally (a common proposition in the literature, but under the competition Hunter-Anderson proposes, where would they go?) or that people in smaller sites commonly wintered in the kiva.

During the P-IV period, the number of rooms per kiva increases to 12.5 from an average of 5 or 6 rooms per kiva in the P-III period. But also during the P-IV period, sites are in lower elevational settings (average of 5,825 feet compared to 6,127 feet for the P-III period). Since Hunter-Anderson defines storage facilities on the absence of hearth features, one could propose that the P-IV increase in percent of storage facilities was due to more moderate site setting, or merely that it became warmer between A.D. 1250 and 1325. In addition, many isolated one and two room structures probably were either P-IV field houses or seasonal occupations. The absence of a hearth cannot be taken as the sole evidence for a system-wide increase in storage, when the possibility exists that the structures were used only in warm weather, or were not used to prepare food.

Hunter-Anderson's data are, however, very clear on the general decrease in room size and increasing variance (or standard deviation, as you wish) in room size as one enters the Classic period. This phenomenon, like the increasing divergence between generalized and specialized Paleo-Indian points, which are succeeded by smaller Archaic forms, is a fundamental evolutionary pattern. We discuss this further in the overview of this chapter. Whether we are talking about the replacment of *Bison antiquus* by *Bison bison* or the disappearance of great kivas, we are talking about cycles of power and efficiency. Suffice it here to say that rapidly decreasing room size is the harbinger everywhere in New Mexico of classic archeological periods as they have been traditionally defined.

PUEBLO V (1540-Present)

P-V occupation in the Rio Grande centered in the lower elevations along major drainages. There are 60 P-V components in the area of our sample. Almost all of these sites lie within the 5,500-6,000 feet elevations. Room size again increases, and population underwent episodes of substantial movement. As Biella (1979) notes, population was probably already moving out of the Cochiti overview area at contact.

At this point, however, the method of the historian/ethnohistorian blends with that of the archeologist. This period is not the major subject of this volume. We refer the reader to such general reconstructions as Wendorf and Reed (1955), Ford, Schroeder and Peckham (1972); and that in Volume 9 of the recently published *Handbook of North American Indians* (Ortiz 1979). The articles by Simmons (1979, 1979a) and by Schroeder (1979) are quite useful for the early historic period.

GENERAL DISCUSSION

In this discussion, we want to present some of the Cochiti survey data which we have combined with our own. Since there is much attention in the literature to altitude shifts during the A.D. 1100-1300 period, it seems appropriate to look at the evidence in some detail (see Table III.3).

Tabulated are 1,168 components of the Lithic-P-V period, plus historic and unidentified components. When site locations are plotted by elevational ranges, the pattern of occupation becomes much clearer than when average elevations are computed.

Lithic period occupations, though poorly dated, are found only in the lower half of the elevational range. It may be, of course, that poor surface visibility in the wooded uplands contributes to this pattern. The few Basketmaker III occupations are found in the lowest settings within a narrow occupational range, as are P-I occupations. Frankly, BM-III and P-I occupations in the area are so poorly dated that they may be considered together as one phenomenon. P-II occupation shows a distinct increase in the elevational range, but, as noted previously, falls into distinct higher (5,800-6,500 feet) and lower (5,300-5,600 feet) clusters, each associated with occupations of different temporal periods. The P-II occupation is the *only* one with a majority of sites in the 6,000 to 6,500 feet range.

P-III occupation is indeed split between a higher and lower elevational clustering — one at 6,500 feet to 7,000 feet and a lower one at 5,500 to 6,000 feet. The bulk of occupation is divided by nearly 1,000 feet in elevation. Of the 34 P-III sites at 6,000-6,500 feet, half also have a P-II occupation. May we presume this to be an early attempt at maximizing access to both uplands and lowlands under changing climatic conditions? A few of the other P-III sites in the 6,000-6,500 feet range have also a P-IV, but no P-II, occupation. These clustered tightly at 6,250-6,350 feet. We may then suggest that the majority of these sites are Early P-III, while a few are late. Practically none of the P-III sites over 6,500 feet had a P-IV occupation. These are primarily the Santa Fe B/W sites of the upper Pajarito Plateau, and were abandoned no later than A.D. 1275 to 1290 (see dendro dates in Cordell 1979:60-63). Hunter-Anderson (1979a) suggests that many P-III sites in the lower elevations (the 5,500-6,000 foot cluster?) were late and often associated with P-IV occupation. For the moment, we accept that judgment, though we would like to see a formal ceramic seriation and more dendro dates for the 159 P-III components that lie between 5,500 and 6,000 feet. Unlike any other class of sites (except *unknown Anasazi and unknown cultural affiliation* — we'll return to this in a moment), nearly 20% or 69 P-III components are actually in the Ponderosa zone.

Table III.3
CULTURAL PHASE AND COMPONENT DISTRIBUTION BY ELEVATION* – UPPER RIO GRANDE

Phase / Elevation in Feet	Lithic (Archaic-BM-II)	(BM-III)	P-I	P-II	P-III	P-IV	P-V	Other Historic	Unknown Anasazi	Unknown Cul.Affil.	Total Sample of Compon.
No. in Sample	78	8	7	34	380	240	60	72	97	192	1,168
7000	X	X	X	X	36	7	0	0	18	51	
6500	X	X	X	2	125	26	3	2	39	52	361
6000	2	X	X	15	34	23	2	4	9	31	120
5500	69	1	X	10	159	161	47	37	21	52	697
5000	7	7	7	7	26	23	8	29	10	16	
No. in Ponderosa (Transition) Zone	0	0	0	0	69	13	0	1	26	61	Transition Zone

TOTAL NUMBER OF ROOMS

	P-III	P-IV
	2,972	2,587
	Avg. 8	Avg. 10.5

Chronology:

Lithic	Archaic/BM-II — 3000 B.C. — A.D. 600	
Developmental	BM-III — A.D. 600	
	P-I →	
	P-II — to app. Santa Fe B/W — A.D. 1175	
Coalition	P-III — A.D. 1175-1325?	
Rio Grande Classic	P-IV — A.D. 1325-1540	
Historic	P-V — A.D. 1540-Present	

* Sources (Laboratory of Anthropology Survey Files; Biella and Chapman 1977-79:V.1:105-151, 301-309; Cordell 1979).

P-IV occupation is heavily concentrated in the 5,500-6,000 feet range (that is, lower elevational settings, generally near permanent water courses). Given the more modest P-IV occupation, there is a striking similarity in the number of P-III and P-IV sites in the 5,000-5,500 feet range (25 versus 23) and in the 5,500-6,500 feet range (159 versus 161). There is therefore a distinct downhill collapse prior to P-IV occupation, a few larger P-IV sites over 6,000 feet notwithstanding. Only 13 P-IV sites are in the Ponderosa zone. These are primarily LA 12646 — LA 12719 [in Biella and Chapman 1977-79(1):137]. The nature of, and chronological relationship between, P-III and P-IV components at these sites is currently unclear and merits very close scrutiny.[1]

There is an accentuation of the downhill settlement trend by P-IV times. No Early P-IV sites occur in the Transition zone, and none occurs above 6,580 feet. Over 90% of P-V occupation is below 6,000 feet, though several large sites are above (LA 82, LA 84, LA 295). LA 82 is Tyuoni, and LA 295 is Old Kotyiti (Cochiti). Tyuoni also has a P-III occupation, though the only published dates range from A.D. 1383-1466 (Smiley, Stubbs and Bannister 1953:21; see also, Hendron 1940 and Hewett 1938). Other historic period sites generally conform to the P-V pattern of occupation in the lower riverine settings.

We now arrive at the really interesting material. Undated Anasazi sites show generally the same distribution as P-III sites, though proportionally more components are in the Ponderosa zone. Those sites of Unknown Cultural Affiliations follow the same general pattern. Several complex issues are raised. Several years ago, in preparing a research design for survey at high altitude (Stuart 1978), we proposed that sites would tend to lose their phase identity as altitude extremes were reached. We based this proposition on two assumptions. As occupation became more specialized, seasonally, architecture would be less typical due to lower labor investments. Secondly, painted wares would become scarce in atypically high settings for a given phase occupation. This latter idea was based on the notion that people tend *not* to take *fancy* tradewares to temporary settings, and/or that those isolated from the mainstream of their phase's occupational pattern would be less likely to possess tradewares. The percentages of unidentified components for each altitude zone are tabulated below. These data tend to confirm loss of phase identity with increasing elevation.

Table III.4

LOSS OF PHASE IDENTITY AT HIGH ELEVATION

Elevation Zone	No. Components	No. Unidentified	% Unidentified	Grouped No. & % Unidentified
7,000-7,500 ft.	112	69	62% }	361/45%
6,500-7,000 ft.	249	91	37%	
6,000-6,500 ft.	120	40	33% –	120/33%
5,500-6,000 ft.	547	73	13% }	697/14%
5,000-5,500 ft.	140	26	19%	
TOTAL	1,168	299	26%	

1 A recent review of data on P-IV sites from a wider area (includes Jemez, Chama and Albuquerque districts) indicates yet another episode of aggregation in the highlands at *roughly* A.D. 1500.

In Tables III.5 and III.6, average elevations are computed for each phase and elevational ranges are given.

Table III.5
AVERAGE ELEVATION OF COMPONENT BY PHASE: UPPER RIO GRANDE

Phase	Elevation	No. in Sample
Lithic Periods	5,580 ft.	n.78
BM-III	5,374 ft.	n.8
P-I	5,316 ft.	n.7
P-II	5,970 ft.	n.33
P-III	6,127 ft.	n.380
P-IV	5,825 ft.	n.200
P-V	5,904 ft.	n.60
Unknown Anasazi	6,228 ft.	n.97
ALL PHASES	5,950 ft.	n.863*

* about 75% of sites in Table III.3

On the basis of these data, P-II, P-IV and P-V generally fall into one occupational pattern, while Lithic Periods and *Other Historic* fall into a second (with not much real information content considering technological differences between them). BM-III and P-I components are distinctive as a set, but the data are few. Again, P-III, Unknown Anasazi and Unknown Cultural Affiliation are strikingly similar.

Table III.6
MINIMUM AND MAXIMUM ELEVATIONS BY PHASE – UPPER RIO GRANDE

Phase	Minimum		Maximum		Range	Less Highest Site
1. Lithic	5,240		6,180		940 ft.	Same
2. BM-III	5,240		5,820		580 ft.	⎰ Samples too
3. P-I	5,240		5,450		210 ft.	⎱ small
4. P-II	5,240		6,880		1,640 ft.	1,210 ft. (6,450)
5. P-III	5,245		7,401		2,156 ft.	2,115 ft. (7,360)
6. P-IV	5,200		7,200		2,000 ft.	1,920 ft. (7,120)
7. P-V	5,245		6,580	(500 rooms)	1,335 ft.	1,275 ft. (6,520)
8. Unknown* Anasazi	5,220	(pithouses)	7,200		2,080 ft.	2,040 ft. (7,260)
	5,320	(rooms)	7,300			
9. Other Historic	5,240		6,860	(20th century wall feature)	1,620 ft.	920 ft. (6,160)
10. Unknown Affiliation	5,260		7,375	(rubble mound *Torreon*, LA 12722)	2,115 ft.	2,100 ft. (7,350)

* *Torreon-like* sites — all over 7,000 ft. — are mentioned. Are those like tower granaries in the Gallina area?

In Table III.7, we have made a hypothetical conversion of data for illustrative purposes. These data are arranged to illustrate the proportions of sites in each altitude zone as if all component samples were equal to the P-III data base. This is not a statistical procedure (do not use these data to conduct research), merely an arithmetic proportion.

Table III.7
HYPOTHETICAL SITE DISTRIBUTION BY PHASE AND ELEVATION*

P-II 34 (380) 11.176	P-III 380 ∅	P-IV 240 (380) 1.583	P-V 60 (380) 6.333	Anasazi Unknown 97 (380) 3.917	Unknown Affiliation 192 (380) 1.979	
0	36	11.08	0	70.50	100.92	7,000
22.35	125	41.58	18.99	152.76	102.90	6,500
167.64	34	36.40	12.66	35.25	61.34	6,000
111.76	159	254.86	297.65	82.25	102.90	5,500
78.23	26	41.58	50.66	39.17	31.66	
	Actual Sample					

*Note: Conversions done by simple arithmetic proportion to P-III sample of 380 sites. Multipliers noted below figures in parentheses.

On the basis of these data, and the fact that many unidentified sites are structural, we tentatively conclude that many of these are either P-II/P-III transitional or, P-III/P-IV transitional. We argue as follows. With the decline of the Chacoan trade system and characteristic ceramics, both new local B/W types and new trade networks were established everywhere in northwestern New Mexico. In the Cebolleta Mesa area (see next chapter) Dittert (1959) argues that sometime during the Pilares phase (A.D. 1100-1200) external trade relationships in ceramics broke down prior to the development of local B/W varieties. Population was also highest during that period in the Zuni highlands. We suggest the same phenomenon here.

In short, we suggest that perhaps one-third of the unidentified components (by phase or affiliation) could be demonstrated either by re-examination, in survey or excavation, to fall in either the A.D. 1125-75 period or the A.D. 1275-1325 period, the greater proportion falling in the first. Another third, we suggest, are difficult to identify from structural features because they fall outside the optimum occupation zone for their phase. These latter, whether high or low, are often small, ephemeral and have few tradewares. The excavations in Cochiti Reservoir tend also to suggest that sites *below* the elevation of optimum occupation are likewise hard to identify; this tendency is also suggested by Table III.3 for the 5,000-5,500 foot zone.

In other words, some sites cannot be identified because they represent the transformation between clearly recognized phases -- they are literally *out of phase* in the normative sense. Others suffer the same fate because they are literally *out of place* in the same sense. We should like to be proven wrong, if only someone will take the uncommon strategy of pursuing research into *unidentified* components. The final third? These are probably attributable to incomplete data for otherwise easily identified assemblages.

As a final line of suggestion before turning to other matters, we *create* a pattern of altitude shifts with the original Table III.3.

Table III.8
ALTITUDE SHIFTS OVER TIME: A SUGGESTION*

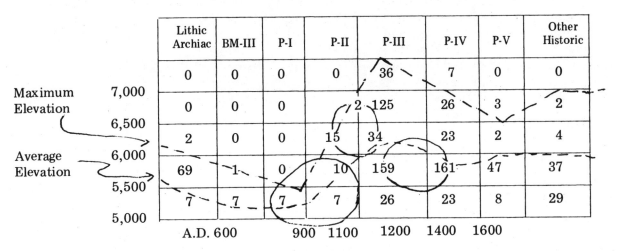

	Lithic Archiac	BM-III	P-I	P-II	P-III	P-IV	P-V	Other Historic
	0	0	0	0	36	7	0	0
Maximum Elevation 7,000	0	0	0	2	125	26	3	2
6,500	2	0	0	15	34	23	2	4
Average Elevation 6,000	69	1	0	10	159	161	47	37
5,500 / 5,000	7	7	7	7	26	23	8	29

A.D. 600   900 1100   1200 1400 1600

*Multicomponent clusters are circled.

Better temporal control would yield a much clearer picture, as would more detailed analysis of the locations of multicomponent occupations. The general pattern, however, is clear. Between A.D. 1100 and 1200 there is a striking uphill shift in population, while from A.D. 1200 to 1300 there is a notable downhill shift, with some population still in higher elevations.

You will notice in reading Cordell (1979:34-64) that a number of dated occupations in upland settings seem to involve dual building episodes. That is, dates typically cluster at about A.D. 1150-70 for an early construction phase, and have also a later occupation at 1240-1280. Saltbush Pueblo (LA 4997), at 6,120 feet in elevation, was excavated by Snow (1974) and exemplifies this pattern. On the other hand, Pindi Pueblo (Stubbs and Stallings 1953) is described as evidencing *three* building phases, as are a number of P-III/P-IV sites, excavated in the Cochiti Reservoir (Biella and Chapman 1977-79:2, 3, 4). LA 191 is another clear example of the latter pattern, with clustered dates around A.D. 1120, 1185 and 1192-1194 (Smiley, Stubbs and Bannister 1953:26).

We, clearly, need to assemble all the dated material for the period from A.D. 1100-1350 if we are to make sense of Rio Grande occupation. If it turned out that sites in higher and wetter settings generally had two building episodes, while those in drier and/or lower had three, we might discover that clusters of dates for building episodes were staggered, temporally, for the two kinds of sites. It takes little genius to propose that two uphill shifts, followed by downhill shifts, would create such a pattern. Yet it appears unlikely that this

        0   0
A.D. 1100   0   A.D. 1300

is the case, for the A.D. 1260-1290 occupations appear fairly well dated throughout several major ecozones, as are sites of the late A.D. 1100's.

59

What is curious is that, of the 1,108 tree-ring dates published by Smiley, Stubbs and Bannister (1953) for sites in the upper Rio Grande area, only 26 fall within the A.D. 1195-1230 period. If dates were evenly distributed for the entire 350 years from A.D. 1100-1450, there should be about three dates per year, or roughly 105 dates between A.D. 1195 and 1230. Why the scarcity of construction at A.D. 1195-1230? Is there anything common to the sites where these (A.D. 1195-1230) dates are found (LA 1, LA 8, LA 27, LA 296, LA 309, LA 742 and LA 1892)? Yes, these are in the lower/drier settings that Hunter-Anderson (1979) has characterized as the settings of the P-III/P-IV transition, yet none survived past the introduction of Rio Grande Glaze 1 wares. They are also on secondary streams and/or arroyos rather than on the primary drainage locations of most surviving P-IV sites. All but one contain Chupadero B/W as a tradeware. Where are there concentrations of sites in the upper Rio Grande having A.D. 1200 construction dates? We need to know.

CONSIDERATIONS FOR SURVEY

BACKGROUND AND PRIORITIES

Collectively, the San Juan Basin and Upper Rio Grande areas have been more intensively surveyed than any other general region of the state. Nonetheless, it is a vast area and much survey work remains. Taken as a whole, the area includes nearly 17,000,000 acres, or 27,000 square miles. That is, we are speaking of an area larger than that of Rhode Island, Delaware, Connecticut, New Jersey and Massachusetts *combined*.

Table III.9
LAND STATUS AND ACREAGE
SAN JUAN BASIN, NEW MEXICO

Access	Ownership/Administration	San Juan	McKinley	TOTAL ACREAGE	Percent
1	BLM	975,774	266,262	1,242,036	19.04
	NPS	21,176	0	21,176	.32
	Bureau of Reclamation	82	0	82	.0012
	BIA	36,266	186,862	223,128	3.42
	Forest Service[1]	0	0	0	0
	State	168,416	183,974	352,390	5.404
2 or 3	Indian[2]	2,110,692	1,834,974	3,945,666	60.51
3	Private and Misc.	217,834	518,361	736,195	11.29
	TOTAL ACRES	3,530,240	2,990,433	6,520,673	

[1] Forest Service lands transferred to Mount Taylor
[2] Zuni Pueblo and Ramah Navajo lands transferred to Mount Taylor

Table III.10

**LAND STATUS AND ACREAGE
UPPER RIO GRANDE, NEW MEXICO**

Access	Ownership/Administration	Santa Fe	Los Alamos	Taos	Rio Arriba	San-doval	Ber-nalillo	TOTAL ACREAGE	Percent
1	BLM	79,662	0	185,719	544,703	541,063	15,288	1,376,395	13.52
	NPS	826	6,483	0	0	22,352	0	29,661	.29
	Corps. of Eng.	0	0	0	0	0	20,702	20,702	.203
	ERDA	3,847	24,575	0	0	0	4,595	33,017	.32
	BIA	0	0	0	0	480	0	480	.004
	Forest Service[1]	250,474	30,174	484,220	1,411,734	397,998	74,119	3,103,346	30.48
	State	85,857	0	97,144	108,530	80,192	32,201	403,924	3.96
2 or 3	Indian[2]	79,224	0	110,281	646,143	596,455	166,030	1,695,434	16.65
3	Private and Misc.	712,870	7,888	557,116	1,054,010	740,340	435,225	3,507,449	34.54
	TOTAL ACRES	1,221,760	69,120	1,444,480	3,765,120	2,378,880	748,160	10,179,448	

[1] Additional Forest Service lands from San Miguel, Mora and Colfax Counties
[2] Includes Isleta Pueblo lands from Valencia County

These acreages are under diverse ownership or stewardship, which affects the conduct of archeological survey (see Tables III.9 and III.10). These tables rank ease of access from good to difficult (1-3). Access to federal land in the area is generally not problematic, given acquisition of federal antiquities permits. The same can be said of state lands. Ease of access to Indian lands varies from tribe to tribe and council to council. Navajo, Zuni, Acoma and Laguna have fairly regular and formal procedures for obtaining tribal permission to conduct survey. The Navajo Nation and the Zuni both have active cultural resource management programs of their own. Taos, Jicarilla, and several of the Rio Grande pueblos are generally more cautious in permitting archeological survey. Access to all these lands depends highly on the merits of the individual case. It is fair to say that most Indian groups in New Mexico are becoming more sensitive about land-use and sovereignty over tribal lands. Six million acres, or 35% of the study area, is Indian or BIA controlled. About 5% of these lands are under state ownership. Another 35% (six million acres) are federally owned, while just over four million acres, or 25%, are privately owned. This is the only region of New Mexico with such high percentages of Indian lands.

We have rated private lands most difficult of access on the practical basis that far fewer federal projects requiring archeological survey are conducted on such lands. Survey coverage is therefore lower than for most federal and Indian lands, and no ongoing funded programs provide for archeological survey. Thus, northwestern New Mexico is about evenly divided into lands difficult of access and easy of access. Federal lands that are often closed to outsiders include portions of Los Alamos and Kirtland and Manzano Bases in Albuquerque. These latter are all involved in defense programs and maintain secured areas.

The Bureau of Indian Affairs, Albuquerque area office, has been conducting extensive survey in the higher elevations of the Jicarilla Reservation, and future surveys are planned for timbered portions on several of the Rio Grande pueblos. This is indeed fortunate, since most of these areas are essentially unsurveyed and access can be difficult. Mr. Broster (personal communication) advises us that substantial numbers of Rosa and Piedra pithouse occupations are being recorded on the Jicarilla Reservation. We anxiously await these data to augment the Navajo Reservoir study (Dittert, Hester and Eddy 1961).

As a generality, the higher elevations of the region are substantially undersurveyed. These regions are mixed between the Navajo tribe (Chuskas; see Harris, Schoenwetter and Warren 1967), the Jicarilla (Largo — lower Gobernador) to the west and Forest Service lands (Carson and Santa Fe Forests) in the upper Rio Grande. Substantial research needs to be conducted in the higher elevations. The site inventory for these regions is disproportionately low, and the general dictum that few archeological remains are to be found over 7,000 feet is contrary to survey evidence in most areas actually investigated. Also undersurveyed are the southeastern and northwestern quadrats of the San Juan Basin proper. Survey in the upper Puerco drainage (work of Peckham 1971, Irwin-Williams 1977, 1978, Pippin 1978) has been extensive (though most is unpublished) but, surprisingly, Albuquerque's west mesa is only partially surveyed, and substantial portions of the Sangre de Cristos have only been subjected to general thematic reconnaissance. The canyon country along the San Juan River is only incompletely known, in spite of extensive survey in certain areas (NIIP to the west; Navajo Reservoir to the east).

In the upper Rio Grande (see Maps III.3 and III.4), the areas best known archeologically are the Rio Grande drainage from about Velarde, New Mexico, south to Albuquerque, including the southern Pajarito Plateau and the Galisteo Basin. In the San Juan Basin, the southern tier along Interstate 40, the central basin around Chaco Canyon and the environs along Route 666 from Gallup to Shiprock are comparatively well surveyed.

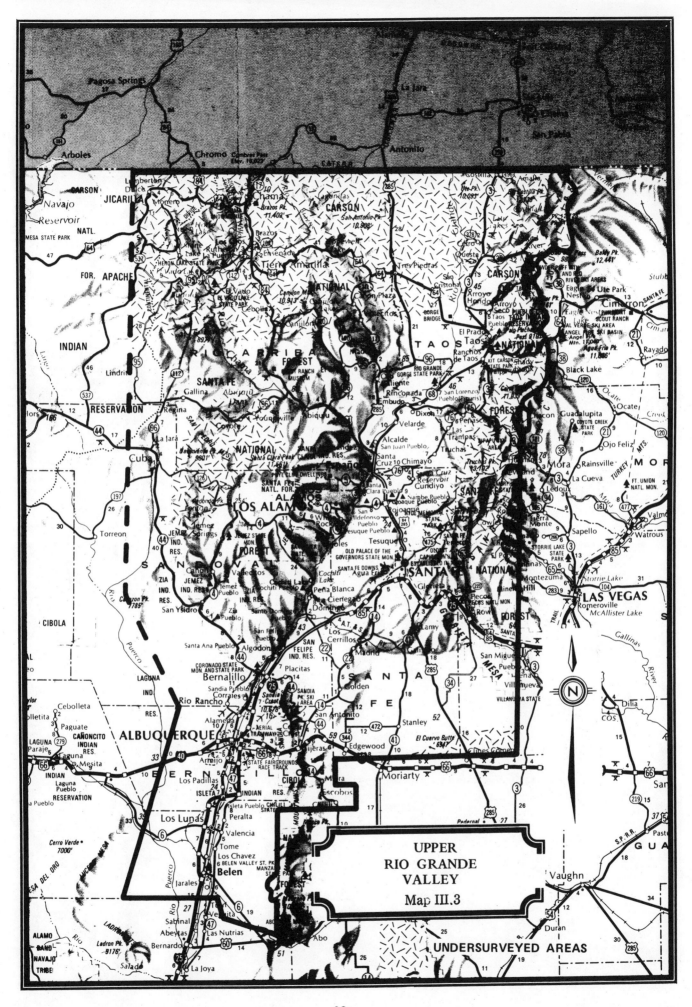

UPPER
RIO GRANDE
VALLEY
Map III.3

UNDERSURVEYED AREAS

SAN JUAN BASIN

Map III.4

UNDERSURVEYED AREAS

Impacts in the area are primarily of four kinds: 1) population growth and development; 2) intensive mining activity; 3) timbering operations, and 4) pothunting. A corridor along Interstate 25 from Algodones, New Mexico, south through Albuquerque to Belen will sustain the greatest population increase and urban expansion over the next 25 years. Since the area has yielded Paleo-Indian, Archaic and Early Basketmaker (II and III) remains, as well as later Puebloan occupation (primarily Late P-III/P-V), any survey work should be conducted soon, else one housing project or another will forever preclude restudy. A Basketmaker-Late Archaic thematic survey would be very appropriate.

Substantial population expansion will take place around Gallup, Grants, Farmington-Bloomfield, Shiprock and the Crownpoint areas. In each case, population projections are based on expected mining operations, so the extent of one will condition the other. Because most of the mining development is under federal control, archeological work will continue to be conducted in these areas, and while this does not lessen the extent of impacts, it lessens the finality of consequences where archeological data are retrieved. For this reason, thematic surveys such as conducted for the *Chacoan outlier* project (Marshall, Stein, Loose and No-votny 1979) are probably more appropriate than commissioning additional and massive block surveys to generate National Register nominations.

Timbering activities create relatively few archeological impacts where the erosional effects of clear-cutting are avoided and where logging roads are monitored during the earth-moving phase. Nonetheless, old logging roads often create the access that invites vandalism. The severity of pothunting increases with proximity to all-weather roads and population centers. It is widespread in the Gallup-Grants mineral belt and, as in the Mimbres area, assumes to be a business in the region surrounding Farmington, New Mexico. In the upper Rio Grande, pothunting decreases as altitude increases, and generally decreases as one moves north from Santa Fe. However, several large biscuitware pueblos north of Santa Fe are badly vandalized.

Since the eastward radiation of Anasazi population into the uplands of the northern Rio Grande, and finally to the margin of the Plains, is not well understood, further survey is essential. Additional survey is required along the Chama drainage, in the northern Pajarito Plateau and in the upland corridor from Pecos to Red River. Such survey appears essential to understanding adaptive process which runs through the Rio Grande Classic (A.D. 1100-1500). There are also many *known* but unrecorded large Pueblo sites in the Chama drainage and northern Pajarito Plateau. A *thematic* survey should be commissioned to record these. Finally, previously unfundable research in the highlands and lower forests of the upper Rio Grande, the highland periphery of the San Juan Basin, and in the specific areas of major residential/urban construction, should be given priority.

THE DATA

Creation of the SJBRUS file (the San Juan Basin Regional Uranium Study archeological file; see Wait, in press) by the National Park Service (Santa Fe) is a major event in southwestern archeological research.

Though we list acreage in the San Juan Basin as primarily in San Juan and McKinley Counties, the actual data file includes portions of Valencia County (south of I-40 West in the Zuni to Acoma area) and portions of Rio Arriba, Sandoval and Bernalillo Counties that are considered the upper Rio Grande. Roughly, the data base proceeds north from I-40, where the Puerco River crosses the Interstate, to Dulce, New Mexico (along the Continental Divide) to the Colorado state line. Thus, we use 15,000 square miles as comprising the data base for the San Juan Basin. Archeologically this means that most of the Largo-Gallina subarea is included in the data file.

Table III.11
SAN JUAN BASIN ARCHAEOLOGICAL DATA BASE: FEBRUARY 1979

Period/File No.	Frequency	Cum Frequency	Percent	Cum Percent
PALEO INDIAN (F1)				
Blank	8348	---	---	—
Present	13	13	92.857	92.857
Transitional	1	14	7.143	100.000
ARCHAIC (F2)				
Blank	7643	—	—	—
Present	700	700	97.357	97.357
Transitional	19	719	2.643	100.000
BM-II (F3)				
Blank	8260	—	—	—
Present	94	94	92.157	92.157
Transitional	8	102	7.843	100.000
BM-III (F4)				
Blank	7428	---	---	—
Present	769	769	82.334	82.334
Transitional	165	934	17.666	100.000
PUEBLO I (F5)				
Blank	7188	—	---	—
Present	986	986	83.986	83.986
Transitional	188	1174	16.014	100.000
PUEBLO II (F6)				
Blank	5162	---	---	---
Present	2533	2533	79.156	79.156
Transitional	667	3200	20.844	100.000
PUEBLO III (F7)				
Blank	6119	—	—	---
Present	2164	2164	96.478	96.478
Transitional	79	2243	3.522	100.000
PUEBLO IV (F8)				
Blank	8318	—	---.	---
Present	37	37	84.091	84.091
Transitional	7	44	15.909	100.000
PUEBLO V (F9)				
Blank	8274	---	—	---
Present	30	30	34.091	34.091
Transitional	58	88	65.909	100.000
UNKNOWN ANASAZI (F10)				
Blank	6921	---	—	—
Present	1440	1440	99.931	99.931
Transitional	1	1441	0.069	100.000

Period/File No.	Frequency	Cum Frequency	Percent	Cum Percent
NAVAJO PRIOR 1868 (F11)				
Blank	8274	—	—	—
Present	84	84	95.455	95.455
Transitional	4	88	4.545	100.000
NAVAJO AFTER 1868 (F12)				
Blank	8176	—	—	—
Present	156	156	83.871	83.871
Transitional	30	186	16.129	100.000
UNKNOWN NAVAJO (F13)				
Blank	7901	—	—	—
Present	458	458	99.349	99.349
Transitional	3	461	0.651	100.000
UTE (F14)				
Blank	8362	—	—	—
SPANISH (F15)				
Blank	8333	—	—	—
Present	29	29	100.000	100.000
ANGLO (F16)				
Blank	8352	—	—	—
Present	9	9	90.000	90.000
Transitional	1	10	10.000	100.000
UNKNOWN LITHIC (F17)				
Blank	8360	—	—	—
Present	2	2	100.000	100.000
UNKNOWN CERAMIC (F18)				
Blank	8362	—	—	—
OTHER (F19)				
Blank	8357	—	—	—
Present	5	5	100.000	100.000
UNKNOWN (F20)				
Blank	8299	—	—	—
Present	62	62	98.413	98.413
Transitional	1	63	1.587	100.000

Wait (in press) states that data from 5.9% of the sections in the San Juan Basin was obtained for the study. We have collapsed that figure here, and throughout the volume count *thematic* or reconnaissance surveys as 10% surface coverage. Thus, if we are in error, we are consistently in error. We calculate 4% surface coverage of 15,000 square miles for the data base, or 600 square miles of intensive ground coverage (in 1979).

As our figure for total number of sites we use the total of 8,348 *components* (Table III.11) which were provided us in April 1979 by Dr. Wait. To these someday will be added the 2,000 (give or take a hundred) additional *site* forms that NPS had received but not yet processed at that time. The SJBRUS file data will undoubtedly change by the time this is published. Be advised that these are working figures only. From these figures we then subtracted the multicomponents that we could readily identify. Thus, we use 8,254 as the number of sites in 600 square miles of 15,000. As the total number of sites in the San Juan Basin, we use the 8,254 + 2,000 (rounded) less 640 sites we calculate as south of I-40 in the Mount Taylor district. For management purposes we use a total of 9,614 sites in the San Juan Basin with 5% ground coverage (2,000 sites being roughly one-quarter the first figure, hence an additional one percent ground coverage). For comparing site densities to other areas, we use only the more firmly established 8,254 figure at 4% survey coverage.

Table III.12
SAN JUAN BASIN SURVEY DATA*

SJBRUS Data

    Square miles total = 15,000
    Square miles @ 100% survey = 600
    Percent survey coverage = 4%
    No. sites in Data Base = 8,254
    Site density/square mile = 13.5

    No. Sites A.D. 200 -1400 = 7,521 (excludes Archaic)
    No. Sites *Chacoan* = P-II + P-II/P-III (A.D. 900-1050 or 950-1100?) = 3,200
    Above as percent of Total in Data Base = 39% (less Archaic = 43% of 7,521)
    No. excavated sites = 194
    No. tested sites = 94
    No. *dated* sites = 100 (estimate)

    Additionally known sites = 1,360 (2,000 less 640 south of I-40)
    Survey coverage/square mile (estimate) = 150

    TOTAL SITES = 9,614 @ 5% survey = 750 square miles

*North of I-40 only

The upper Rio Grande, then, consists of 12,000 square miles for data purposes. Our figures are not nearly so well controlled, so we will provide both our controlled sample from the Cochiti region, and our broader estimates.

Table III.13

UPPER RIO GRANDE SURVEY DATA

---

* COCHITI CONTROL AREA
  Square Miles Total: 600
  **Square Miles = 100% survey: 75 [120]
  **Percent Survey Coverage: 10-20%
  No. Sites in Data Base: 1,390
  Site Density/Square Mile = 18+ [13+]
  No. Identified Sites to 1600: 1,051 [excludes *Unknown* P-V and *Other Historic*]

  No. Sites in P-III (A.D. 1175-1325): 391
  Above as Percent of Total in Data Base: 28%
  Above as Percent of A.D. 400-1600: 42% [less lithic sites = 42% of 970]

  No. Sites in P-IV Classic: 250
  Above as Percent of Total in Data Base: 18% [as percent of 970 above = 27%]

  No. Excavated Sites: 80 (est.) [excludes Santa Fe east of river]
  No. Dated Sites: 40 < (est.)

UPPER RIO GRANDE [Estimated]
  Square Miles Total: 12,000
  Square Miles @ 100% Survey: 300
  Percent Survey Coverage: 2.5%
  No. Sites Recorded: 3,600-3,800
  Site Density/Square Mile Surveyed: 12-13 [estimate]
  No. Excavated Sites: Unknown but over 100 and 200 <
  No. Dated Sites: ca. 100

---

* Data from Biella and Chapman (1977-79) and Laboratory of Anthropology Site Files
** Biella and Chapman (1977-79, Volume 1) give 10% (of 500 square miles); we think (based on San Juan Basin data) that close to 15% may be more accurate.

In the total region, then, we believe that approximately 13,300 sites have been recorded in the equivalent of 1,050 square miles of intensive survey. This represents just under 4% intensive survey coverage for northwestern New Mexico and a density of 12.5 sites per surveyed square mile.

These figures, of course, do not reflect true site densities regionwide. The Chama area and far northern Rio Grande do not have such high densities, nor do the substantial acreages over 7,000 feet in elevation. Archeologists also actively seek out high concentrations of sites when conducting most pure research projects. Nonetheless, there will certainly not be fewer than 75,000 sites recorded, should the day ever come when the region has been completely surveyed.

While a 3.5-4% survey coverage for northwestern New Mexico will seem impossibly small to many archeologists, no other general portion of New Mexico is so well surveyed.

What is interesting in these data is the remarkable scarcity of BM-II components (110 perhaps) for over 13,000 sites. They are far fewer than Archaic period sites. Additionally (see Table III.11), BM-III and P-I components are remarkably similar numerically (934 BM-III and transitional and 986 pure P-I). There is little evidence for growth if these are viewed as following one another (BM-III, A.D. 500-700 and P-I, A.D. 700-900) in the traditional time frames.

Because the two data bases are asymetrical temporally, and proportionally few *unknown components* appear in the San Juan Data Base (unlike Rio Grande site files), we introduced some control by calculating site occurrences from A.D. 200 (BM-II) to A.D. 1400 for the San Juan Basin (to abandonment). For the Rio Grande we suggest a similar span from A.D. 400 (BM-III/P-I) to A.D. 1600 (Late P-IV). Though the chronological basis for the early Rio Grande sequence is poor, we wished to compare a similar time period from each. Hence, we also calculated percentages of sites for the Chacoan period as consisting of P-II and P-III transitional, a 150-year span roughly terminating with Chacoan decline. We then isolated the P-III Rio Grande occupation as comparable. It was surprising to discover that the Chacoan sites represented such a high percentage of the A.D. 200-1400 site total (43%). To make the same comparison with the Rio Grande, we eliminated the lithic period sites, all *unknown* sites and the P-V—Historic sequence. P-III Rio Grande sites equalled 42% of that total (970 sites)!*

We felt justified in removing the *unknown cultural affiliation* sites, since few of such forms were filled out for the San Juan Data Base. We left the *unknown Anasazi* in the figure, since that category also occurs in the San Juan Data Base.

The P-IV period, however, did not compare numerically or percentage-wise in occupation, even when the *controlled* group of 970 sites was used for comparison. For a *Classic* period occupation, it may be considered modest.

In other respects these survey data are instructive. Many *Archaic* sites are not identified temporally at all, and are merely lithic sites conveniently designated *Archaic*.

In addition, professional attitudes are readily apparent in site recording. In the following four figures (Figs. III.6-9) discovery dates are plotted for Archaic-BM-II, Lithic, P-II and Navajo sites. Figures III.6, 8 and 9 show curves decadally from 1925. Figure III.9 shows Archaic-BM-II discovery dates quadriennally from 1959.

The 1963-65 period was heavily influenced in site recording by large surveys such as the Navajo Reservoir and in the Chuskas (Harris, Schoenwetter and Warren 1967). Notwithstanding the periodic results of a few large surveys (the 1975-76 peaks area also partly attributable to the 740-odd sites registered by the CGP survey — see Reher 1977b), the general trend is quite clear. Following the survey slump of the World War II years, Navajo sites were substantially less often recorded than the P-II sites and were not heavily (or regularly) recorded by many investigators prior to 1958 or 1960. General survey activities had declined by 1970 and again increased dramatically with the growth of the recent contract archeology *boom* which began about 1972-73. There is currently a continuing emphasis on recording Navajo sites, but it is clear that, whereas our interest in the P-II—P-IV occupation of the San Juan Basin spans nearly a century, our general interest in Navajo archeology spans but a third of that time.

---

* Note: See Chapter V (Survey Considerations). After completing Chapter V, we returned to these data. Both Classic Mimbres and Chacoan sites = 43% of the site series. So also does the P-III Rio Grande. Further Classic Mimbres site output/year from A.D. 1000-1150 was 5.5; Chacoan is 22 sites per year, and the P-III Rio Grande is 2.6 sites per year. When the surveyed areas (600 m^2, 150 m^2, 75 m^2) are equalized, so are the figures for site output; i.e. made equal to Mimbres surface coverage they are: Chaco, 5.5 sites per year; Mimbres, 5.5 sites per year; Rio Grande P-III, 5.2 sites per year. How does one account for this? We propose an explanation in Chapter V, but are open. How then do we consider the Rio Grande P-IV Classic where site output per year is one, and when converted by acreage to equal Mimbres surveys, is only 2 per year?

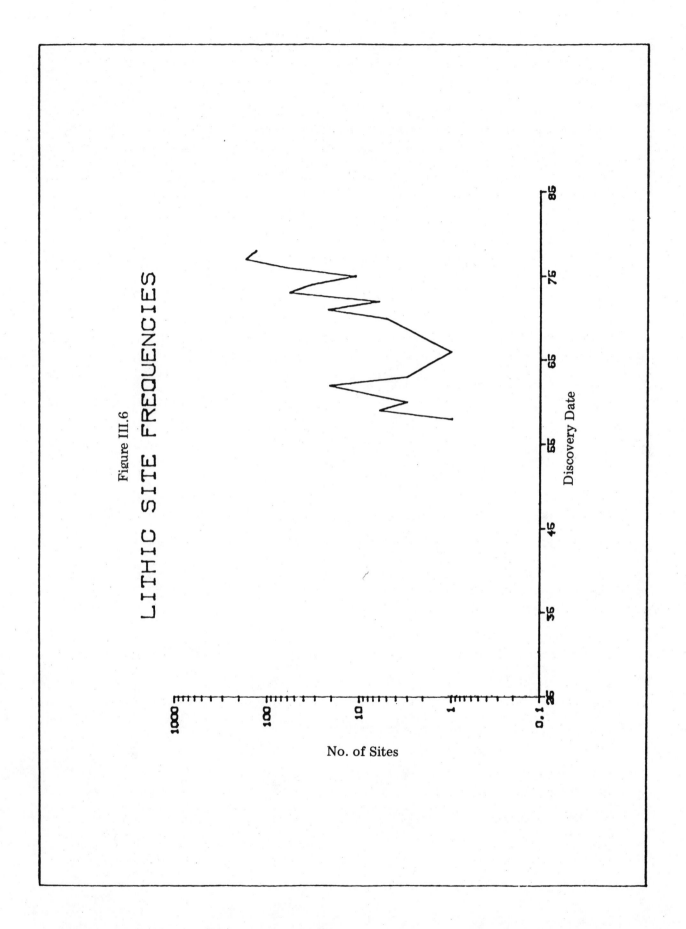

Figure III.6

LITHIC SITE FREQUENCIES

No. of Sites

Discovery Date

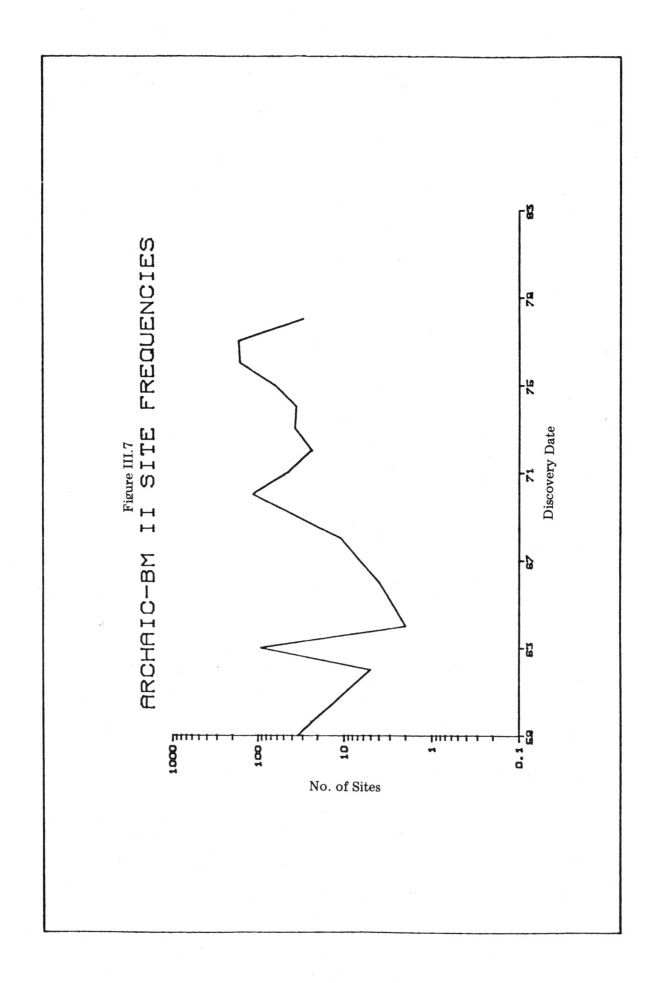

Figure III.7

ARCHAIC-BM II SITE FREQUENCIES

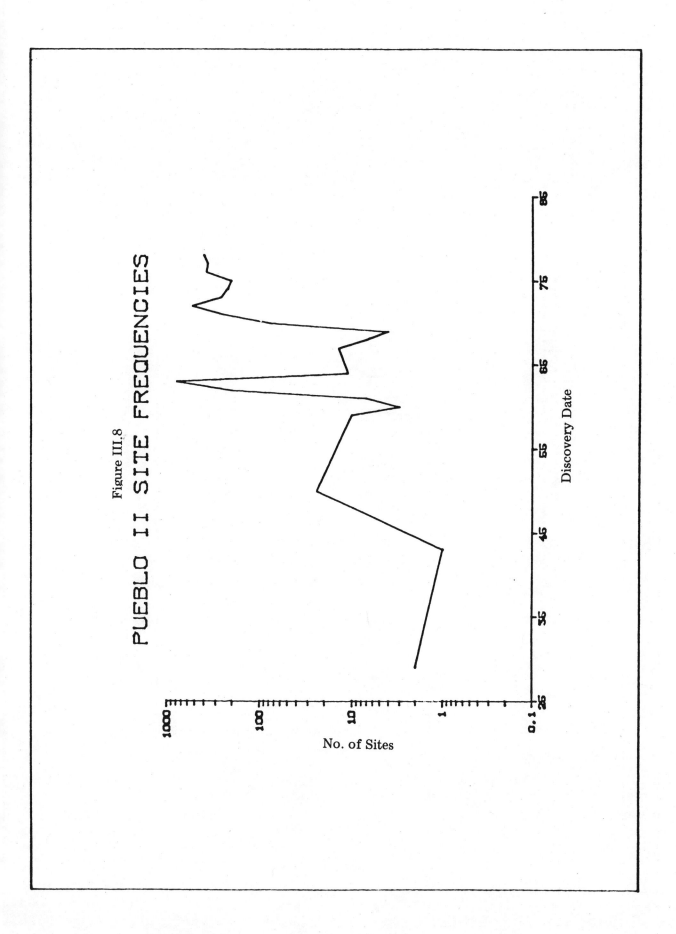

Figure III.8

PUEBLO II SITE FREQUENCIES

No. of Sites

Discovery Date

73

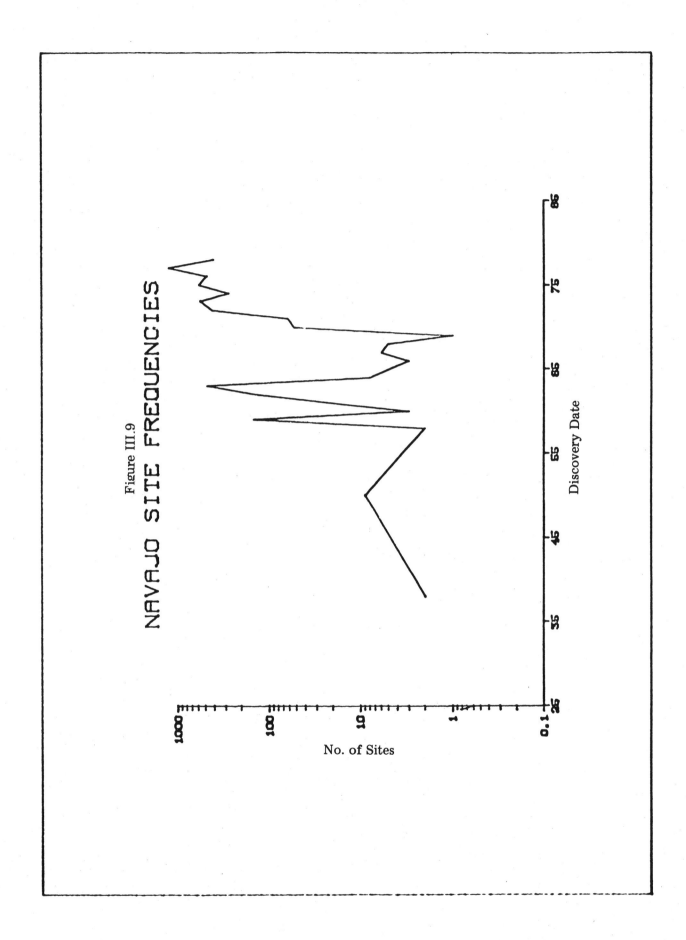

Figure III.9

NAVAJO SITE FREQUENCIES

No. of Sites

Discovery Date

It is also notable that sites termed *Archaic* and *Lithic unknown* were virtually unrecorded prior to 1955-57. It is even more notable that the recording of lithic sites fell well below general site recording output during the resurgence of contract archeology in the 1972-76 period. That is, until perhaps four years ago, many contract archeology surveys were still subtly *thematic*, though they purported to record all the resources in a given area. This is water under the dam, for currently most surveys are attempting full coverage. What this does mean, however, research-wise, is that we have the least investment methodologically in, and the least temporal control over, precisely that portion of the archeological record which ushers in the agricultural era. We must learn to control the lithic periods temporally even where *diagnostic* points are not present.

Finally, only one Ute and no Apachean sites were recorded in the San Juan Basin as of 1979. We have literally no record of this occupation, and given only 84 Navajo sites prior to 1868, we may state confidently that our archeological knowledge of the 1550-1850 period rests on 1% of the recorded sites in the San Juan Basin. Many of the early Navajo sites that are known can be attributed to Keur (1941), Hall (1944), Carlson (1965), Van Valkenburgh (1965), and the continuing interest of a handfull of investigators such as Kemrer (1974), Brugge (1977, 1977a), and Schaafsma (1976). Early Navajo origins, ethnically, geographically and temporally, are by no means a closed case. The literature on the Navajo *refugee* period and temporary amalgamation with Pueblo groups such as the Jemez is fascinating. The traditional thought was that such groups sought refuge in the Gobernador district during the Pueblo Revolt (1680-98), but, in fact, dated remains in the Gobernador postdate (1720-1740) the Spanish reoccupation. These are all open issues.

Let us turn now to State and National Register considerations.

STATE AND NATIONAL REGISTER PROPERTIES IN NORTHWESTERN NEW MEXICO

Our records indicate that there are 48 State Register nominations in the San Juan Basin. Of these, 7 also appear on the National Register of Historic Places. There are 39 nominations to the State Register in the upper Rio Grande. Of these, 12 also appear on the National Register of Historic Places. These do not represent actual numbers of sites, since several nominations are for archeological districts containing many individual components.

These sites are listed below in Tables III.14 and III.15. They are first enumerated by temporal phase, then listed by location.

DISCUSSION

Though 86 nominations appear on the State Register and 20 also appear on the National Register, the pattern of nominations is quite uneven, both geographically and temporally.

In the San Juan Basin, only the Gallegos Wash district nomination, containing some Paleo-Indian, Early Archaic-Late Archaic materials and the Chaco Canyon National Monument, represents 10,000 years of prehistory. No Paleo-Indian materials from other localities have been nominated. The Basketmaker II components known (100+) are only accidentally represented in the Chaco Canyon acreage. The type sites contributing to the Oshara sequence are not represented.

Basketmaker III occupations number over 700, but apart from Chaco Canyon components only three additional localities have been nominated. There are many BM-III sites of over 10 pithouses listed in the SJBRUS file. The file records should be gone through and early components nominated in several distinct areas. A thematic survey and literature research to

Table III.14
ARCHEOLOGICAL PHASES OF NATIONAL AND STATE REGISTER SITES
SAN JUAN BASIN AND UPPER RIO GRANDE

Phase	No. Nominations (may equal more sites)[1]
SAN JUAN BASIN	
Paleo-Indian	1 (components as isolated points in Gallegos Wash No. 341)
Archaic	2 (Gallegos Wash, some components Chaco Can.)
BM-II	1 (components at Chaco Canyon)
BM-III	4 (LA 7979, Chaco Canyon/several; Crow Canyon components, Tohatchi Village)
P-I	Chaco Canyon, Skunk Springs (Late P-I)
P-II/P-III	37 (all not identified separately)
P-III (Mesa Verdean)	6 (components at several Chacoan outliers and pure occupation at Crumbled House, CGP-56, CGP-54)
P-IV	[None — but the San Juan Data Base lists 42 P-IV occupations]
Navajo (Gobernador Phase)	4 (Crow Canyon, Christmas Tree, Simon Canyon, CGP-605)
Other	2 (Pictured Cliffs, Indian Racetrack)
Nominations = to Sites	48
UPPER RIO GRANDE	
Paleo-Indian	1 (Sandia Cave)
Archaic	1 (Boca Negra Cave)
BM-II	None
BM-III	None
P-I	None
P-II	None
P-III	? (LA 3444 components in Bandelier National Monument + several late components at P-IV sites)
& Gallina Phase	6 (LA 9053, 10641, Red Hill, Nogales Cliffs, LA 12062, LA 14318)
P-IV P-V	22 (all those not listed separately)
Navajo (Refugee - 1700-1760)	8 (LA 9072, LA 2298 and 5663, LA 5651, Largo School, LA 1869, LA 1871, Big Bead Mesa)
Nominations = to Sites	36

---

[1] In Upper Rio Grande, two archeological districts (Nambe and Red Hill) in addition to Bandelier are multisite.

nominate BM-II and III occupations is in order. There are fewer recorded pre A.D. 900 pit-house adaptations in the Reserve-Mimbres (Mogollon) districts of New Mexico than in the San Juan Data Base alone. Why, then, is the literature of early Southwestern pithouse occupation so heavily dominated by one region? When will archeologists in the Anasazi area create a body of literature on the pre A.D. 900 period which permits genuine comparison of cultural development between the two regions? Why is the Los Pinos-Piedra sequence (Navajo Reservoir) treated so differently as a developmental phenomenon, when, in fact, it closely parallels pithouse occupations to the southwest?

The Pueblo I period is not adequately represented either. We mentioned earlier that these occupations are suspiciously modest numerically, when compared to the more robust BM-III occupation of the San Juan Basin that allegedly precedes.

The P-II to P-II/P-III transition periods are well represented from nominations. The recent *Chacoan outlier* project has been very important in that respect. We hope that the sizeable communities around these *Bonito Phase* sites will also find their way to the State and National Registers. In general, more of the *district* nominations need to find their way to the National Register.

Late period sites are only represented accidentally, so to speak, because of Mesa Verdean reoccupation at a number of Chacoan outliers, except at Crumbled House, CGP-56 and CGP-54. The nature of Mesa Verdean reoccupation is not well known at all, in any but a rough temporal sense. More single component Mesa Verdean sites should be sought out and nominated. P-IV occupations (over 40) are listed in the SJBRUS file. However modest the occupation, it is not represented among protected sites.

Finally, only four Navajo components appear on the State Register, and these are Gobernador or refugee phase. There are no post 1760 Navajo sites on either Register — the majority of protected forked stick hogans are in these Gobernador sites. Again, some Navajo remains are preserved in Chaco Canyon. Why should there not be a *Dinetah National Archeological District*, particularly when that district, if located in the Gobernador or southern portions of the Carson Forest's northwest unit, could also include earlier pithouse occupations? The Carson National Forest is hardly represented in recorded site files.

In the upper Rio Grande, the pattern of nominations is singularly focused on the period 1325-1600. Though components of all the periods prior to 1200 are known and published, there is only one nomination prior to the P-III period. Most of the Paleo-Indian to BM-II remains have been recorded in the Albuquerque district (Judge 1973), but they are known more widely. BM-III occupations are known from the Cochiti-Santa Fe district, and BM-II from the Albuquerque-Bernalillo west mesa and from the Galisteo Basin. Known site files should be reviewed.

P-I and P-II components are also known, and several P-II sites are published — such as the Tesuque Valley Ruin (LA 742) and Arroyo Negro (LA 114). Dates from these sites range from A.D. 963 to 1145 for the P-II components (Smiley, Stubbs and Bannister 1953:22-23; 35-36).These dates are analogous to the period of Chacoan occupation in the San Juan Basin. These *Kwahee B/W* sites should be reviewed for State and National Register nominations.

The P-III period is also underrepresented, some sites in Bandelier aside. Sites from Steen's study (1977) on the Pajarito Plateau should be reviewed, and a good mix of *pure* P-III (Santa Fe B/W) and P-III/P-IV transitional sites from the Northern Plateau should be mapped and nominated. The largest of these sites are spectacular, and the reservoir features, mesa top setting, and smaller outlying occupation units remind one of sites in Arizona like Carter Ranch, which are closely contemporaneous. Since there are more than 300 of these sites to choose among, it should not be difficult to create thematic and district nominations.

The post 1300 period is well represented except in the Chama area, though smaller sites, an important component of the settlement system, have been neglected. It would seem reasonable to create a small district around one or two P-IV—P-V sites which included the *field house* occupations.

Geographically, Taos and Los Alamos (Bandelier) Counties have only one nomination apiece. The P-III nominations suggested above would certainly improve the balance in Los Alamos County (the very best, but probably least feasible idea, would be either to extend Bandelier National Monument or to create an additional archeological district for it to administer).

The Taos area clearly requires both additional survey and a complete review of site records from the area. The same holds for the entire eastern flank of the upper Rio Grande study area. These areas, again, are largely in the Carson and Santa Fe National Forests.

Table III.15 below lists the State and National Register properties in northwestern New Mexico. Descriptions of each with site sketches follow.

Table III.15
STATE AND NATIONAL REGISTER OF CULTURAL PROPERTIES
NORTHWESTERN NEW MEXICO
(National Register Properties are starred)

Reg. No.	Name	LA No.	County	Time Period (Approx.)	Phase
No. 55*	Aztec Ruin	45	San Juan	A.D. 1050-1300	Chaco— Mesa Verde
No. 361	Christmas Tree Ruin	11097	San Juan	1700-1750	Gobernador— Navajo
No. 370	Simon Canyon Ruin	—	San Juan	1700-1750	Gobernador— Navajo
No. 057*	Chaco Canyon National Mon.	—	San Juan	3000 B.C. — A.D. 1400	Archaic— Mesa Verde
Chaco Canyon Outliers Nominations:					
No. 686	Halfway House	15191	San Juan	950 or 1000- 1125?	Chaco-Bonito
No. 684	Bisa'ani Archeological District	—	San Juan	,,	,,
No. 690	Pierre's Archeological District	16508-535	San Juan	,,	,,
No. 669	Grey Hill Springs Arch. District	18244, *et al.*	San Juan	,,	,,
No. 676	Great Bend Community	6419	San Juan	,,	,,
No. 678	Willow Canyon	8235	San Juan	,,	,,
No. 668	Lake Valley Archeological District	18755	San Juan	,,	,,
No. 689	Twin Angels Pueblo	5642	San Juan	,,	,,

Table III.15 (Continued)

Reg. No.	Name	LA No.	County	Time Period (Approx.)	Phase
Chaco Canyon Outliers Nominations (Continued):					
No. 670	Hogback Archeological District	—	San Juan	"	"
No. 674	Whirlwind Lake Arch. District	18237	San Juan	"	"
No. 693*	Morris Site 41	—	San Juan	"	"
No. 276	Crow Canyon Arch. District	20219 *et al.*	San Juan	500-800/ 1700-1950	BM-III/ Gobernador Navajo
No. 341*	Gallegos Wash District	—	San Juan	pre-A.D. 500	Paleo-Archaic
No. 513	Old Indian Racetrack	9040	San Juan	?	?
No. 021*	Salmon Ruin	8846	San Juan	1090-1290	P-II & P-III (Chaco—Mesa Verde)
No. 428*	CGP-56	19290	San Juan	1200-1300	Mesa Verde
No. 429*	CGP-54-1	19305	San Juan	1200-1300	Mesa Verde
No. 430*	CGP-605	19794	San Juan	1700-1750	Gobernador Navajo
No. 105	Pictured Cliffs Archeological Site	8970	San Juan	900-1300?	P-II—P-III?
No. 251	Mitten Rock Archeological District	—	San Juan	500-1100	BM-III to Early P-III
No. 031	Two Grey Hills Arch. District	7979 7070 7080 *et al.*	San Juan	(Includes Yellow Adobe, Skunk Springs & Crumbled House, which follow)	
No. 120	Skunk Springs Arch. District	7000 *et al.*	San Juan	875-1125?	Late P-I-Chaco
No. 127	Yellow Adobe Site	7979	San Juan	600-800	BM-III/P-I
No. 098	Crumbled House	7070 & 7080	San Juan	1100-1300	P-III
No. 123	Tohatchi Village	3098	McKinley	500-750	BM-III
Chacoan Thematic Group****:**					
No. 679	Coolidge Archeological Site	17280	McKinley	A.D. 950 or 1000-1125?	Chaco Outlier P-II—P-II/P-III
No. 667	Casa de Estrella Arch. Site	—	McKinley	"	Transition
No. 677	Indian Creek Arch. District	17081	McKinley	"	"
No. 675	Muddy Water Community	10717 *et al.*	McKinley	"	"
No. 665	Peach Springs Arch. District	10770	McKinley	"	"
No. 681	Standing Rock Arch. District	18232 *et al.*	McKinley	"	"

Table III.15 (Continued)

Reg. No.	Name	LA No.	County	Time Period (Approx.)	Phase
Chacoan Thematic Group** (Continued):					
No. 682	Dalton Pass	—	McKinley	,,	,,
No. 685	Fort Wingate Ruin	2690	McKinley	,,	,,
No. 672	Haystack Arch. District	6022 *et al.*	McKinley	,,	,,
No. 688	Casamero Arch. District	18756	McKinley	,,	,,
No. 688	Casamero Ruin	8779	McKinley	,,	,,
No. 680	Coyotes Sing Here Arch. District	18754	McKinley	,,	,,
No. 687	Kin Nizhoni Arch. District	18166	McKinley	,,	,,
No. 666	Bee Burrow Arch. District	13163 *et al.*	McKinley	,,	,,
No. 671	Greenlee Arch. Sites	908, 909	McKinley	,,	,,
No. 683	Upper Kin Klizhin	—	McKinley	,,	,,
No. 760	Guadalupe Ruin	2757	Sandoval	A.D. 900-1300	P-II—P-III
Upper Rio Grande:					
No. 229*	Picuris Pueblo	127	Taos	post A.D. 1250	P-V
No. 124*	Tsiping	301	Rio Arriba	,,	P-III
No. 275*	Turkey Springs Arch. Site	10641	Rio Arriba	1100-1300	Gallina
No. 274	Red Hill Archeological Sites	10644	Rio Arriba	1100-1300	Gallina
No. 094	Castle of the Chama	9053	Rio Arriba	1100-1300	Gallina
No. 532*	La Jara Site	14318	Rio Arriba	1100-1300	Gallina
No. 348	LA 12062	12062	Rio Arriba	1100-1300	Gallina
No. 252	Nogales Cliff House Ruin	649	Rio Arriba	1100-1300	Gallina
No. 019*	Puye	47	Rio Arriba	post A.D. 1250	Late P-III—P-V
No. 025*	San Gabriel del Yugue-Yunque	—	Rio Arriba	,,	,,
No. 100	Frances Canyon Ruin	9072	Rio Arriba	1700-1750	Navajo
No. 364	Hooded Fireplace Site	5651	Rio Arriba	1700-1750	Navajo-Gobernador
No. 365	Largo School Ruin	8962	Rio Arriba	1700-1750	Navajo-Gobernador
No. 372	Split Rock Ruin	5664	Rio Arriba	1700-1750	Navajo-Gobernador
No. 262	Tapicito Ruin	2298 & 5663	Rio Arriba	1700-1750	Navajo-Gobernador

Table III.15 (Continued)

Reg. No.	Name	LA No.	County	Time Period (Approx.)	Phase
Upper Rio Grande (Continued):					
No. 015	Old Fort Ruin and Three Corn Ruin	1869 & 1871	Rio Arriba	1700-1750	Navajo-Gobernador
No. 005*	Big Bead Mesa	15231	Sandoval	1700-1800	Navajo
No. 225*	Kuaua Ruins (Coronado Mon.)	187	Sandoval	Post A.D. 1250	Late P-III— P-V
No. 281	Old Cochiti (Kotyiti)	295	Sandoval	"	"
No. 104	Kuapa Ruin	3443 & 3445	Sandoval	"	"
No. 278	Astialkwa	1825	Sandoval	"	"
No. 048*	Guisewa (Jemez Monument)	679	Sandoval	"	"
No. 279	Patokwa	96	Sandoval	"	"
No. 117*	San Juan Mesa Ruin	303	Sandoval	"	"
No. 347	Ko-ah'-sai-ya Ruin	384	Sandoval	"	"
No. 074*	Pecos	625	Sandoval	"	"
No. 056*	Bandelier National Monument	82 et al.	Los Alamos	"	"
No. 327	Nambe Archeological District	—	Santa Fe	"	"
No. 106	Pueblo Blanco	40	Santa Fe	"	"
No. 107	Pueblo Colorado	62	Santa Fe	"	"
No. 384	La Bajada Ruin	7	Santa Fe	"	"
No. 111	Galisteo Pueblo	26	Santa Fe	"	"
No. 112	San Cristobal	80	Santa Fe	"	"
No. 097	Colina Verde	309	Santa Fe	"	"
No. 110	Pueblo Largo	183	Santa Fe	"	"
No. 115	Pueblo of She	239	Santa Fe	"	"
No. 114	San Marcos	98	Santa Fe	"	"
No. 199	Cieneguilla	16	Santa Fe	"	"
No. 113*	San Lazaro	91 & 92	Santa Fe	"	"
No. 381	Boca Negra Cave	—	Bernalillo	5000-500 B.C.	Archaic
No. 284	Indian Petroglyph S. Park	—	Bernalillo	?	Pueblo
No. 22*	Sandia Cave	—	Sandoval	9000 B.C.(?); A.D. 1300 (?)	Paleo-Indian; Pueblo

**(see Marshall, Stein, Loose and Novotny 1979) Some of these sites lie just south of I-40, but are included here rather than in the following chapter for thematic reasons.

Note: These lists do not include historic period sites.

SHORT DESCRIPTIONS OF STATE AND NATIONAL REGISTER SITES
SAN JUAN BASIN
(National Register Properties are Starred)

No. 021* SALMON RUIN

The Salmon Ruin is the remains of a large Chacoan outlier constructed at approximately A.D. 1089. The ruin itself is 500 feet long and contains approximately 500 rooms which are arranged in a large C-shape. A great kiva is also present within the plaza.

There are two occupations evident at Salmon Ruin. The first consisted of a Chacoan group which constructed most of the pueblo and then abandoned the area in the A.D. 1130's. The second occupation was nearly one hundred years later by people of the Mesa Verde culture. Many individuals were trapped in one of the kivas when the burning roof fell in. This occupation lasted until A.D. 1300, when the region was abandoned. As yet, no definitive report is available concerning the recent investigations at Salmon Ruin, conducted by Irwin-Williams of Eastern New Mexico State University. The San Juan County Museum lies on the hill above the Ruin on the Bloomfield-Farmington highway.

Salmon Ruin is situated on the north bank of the San Juan River at an elevation of 5,400 feet.

No. 031 TWO GRAY HILLS ARCHEOLOGICAL DISTRICT

This district consists of the Yellow Adobe Site LA7979; Skunk Springs LA7000, 7007 and others; Crumbled House Ruin LA 7070 and 7080. Descriptions follow.

No. 127 YELLOW ADOBE SITE (LA 7979)

The Yellow Adobe site consists of approximately eleven linear and arced slab-lined surface roomblocks, fifteen or more pithouses and a scattering of small slab-lined structures. The architectural features and ceramic types indicate an occupation during Basketmaker III times, circa A.D. 600-800.

The site is situated on a gentle slope at about 6,000 feet in elevation, within a pinyon and juniper parkland.

No. 120 SKUNK SPRINGS ARCHEOLOGICAL DISTRICT

This dense cluster of sites is located within a grassland area at about 5,600 feet in elevation. There are over 100 individual *sites* within an area of one square mile. Some are Late P-I, with the great majority dating to the Pueblo II period (circa A.D. 875 to 1100).

This large cluster is dominated by two sites: LA 7000, *Black House* and LA 7007. Both sites have great kivas located nearby and may represent a local religious or administrative center (Marshall, Stein, Loose and Novotny 1979:109). This district is one of the highest density site localities in the Southwest.

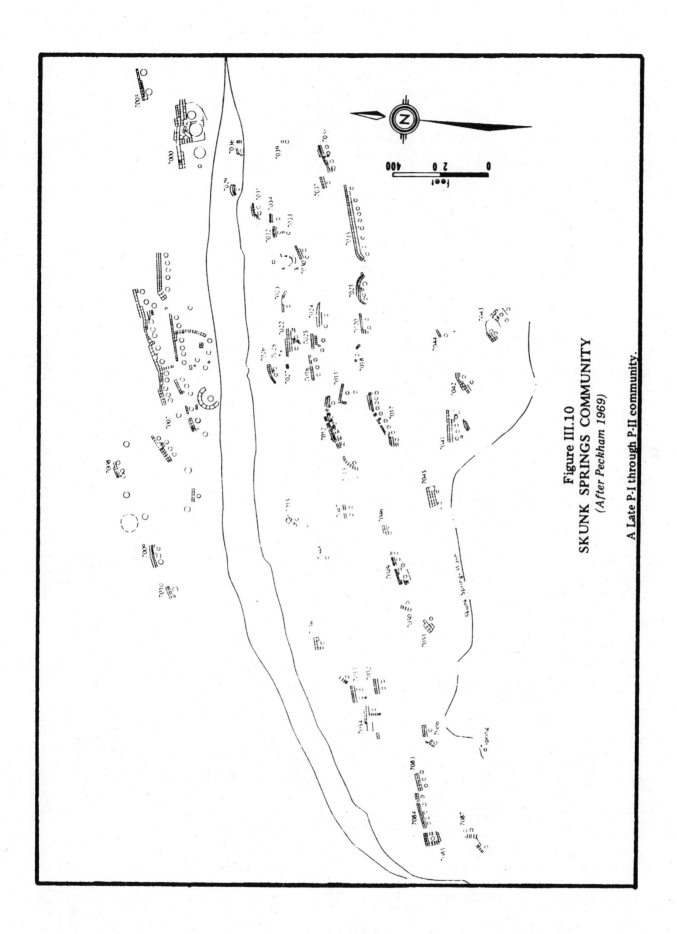

Figure III.10
SKUNK SPRINGS COMMUNITY
(After Peckham 1969)

A Late P-I through P-II community.

No. 098 CRUMBLED HOUSE (LA 7070 and LA 7080)

This site consists of two major proveniences. The first provenience, LA 7070, occupies a narrow, triangular portion of a mesa top. There are approximately 100 to 125 ground floor rooms and 14 to 15 kivas in this provenience. At the eastern end of this site there are a thick masonry wall and a broad ditch, or moat, possibly indicating a defensive function. In addition, there are three masonry towers at this portion of the site.

The second provenience of Crumbled House, LA 7080, occupies the steep talus slope immediately below the south side of LA 7070. There are an estimated 200 rooms and 15 kivas in this portion of the site. Crumbled House is the largest site known in the Chuska Valley and was occupied in the 12th and 13th centuries.

The elevation at Crumbled House is 5,880 feet. It is situated on the east slope of the Chuska Mountains and is sometimes known as the *Castle of the Chuskas* (Marshall, Stein, Loose and Novotny 1979:97). Marshall, et al. suggest a P-III affinity (A.D. 1150-1250) but the presence of some Wingate Black-on-Red also suggests a modest Late P-II occupation, perhaps around A.D. 1100.

No. 055* AZTEC RUINS

These are the remains of an excavated Chacoan outlier and several unexcavated pueblos dating to the Mesa Verde phase.

The excavated portion of Aztec Ruins consists of a large, C-shaped pueblo, containing over 500 rooms, kivas and a great kiva. Like Salmon Ruin, Aztec was first constructed and occupied by a group displaying Chacoan affinities, and then abandoned. Later reoccupation in the 1200's was by people of the Mesa Verde culture. The site was excavated by Earl Morris (Lister and Lister 1968).

Aztec Ruins are located on the banks of the Animas River at 5,600 feet in elevation.

No. 057* CHACO CANYON NATIONAL MONUMENT

Situated near the geographic center of the San Juan Basin, at an elevation of 6,100 feet, are the remains of numerous Anasazi ruins dating from Basketmaker III times to Pueblo III times (A.D. 700 to 1300). There are also Archaic and BM-II components in the monument area. Some of the most spectacular architecture in the American Southwest is found in and around the monument. Well known sites in the central canyon group include Pueblo Bonito (Judd 1954), Pueblo Alto and Casa Rinconada (Vivian and Reiter 1960). The earlier BM-III occupation at Shabikeschee (Roberts 1929) is a well known BM-III site dating to the A.D. 500's (Robinson, Harrill and Warren 1974). An early P-II occupation is typified by the well-known 3-C Site (Vivian 1965). Current research focuses on the continuing programs of the National Park Service, Chaco Center, located at the University of New Mexico campus and directed by W.J. Judge. Additionally, the recent *Chacoan outliers* thematic surveys conducted by Marshall and Stein (Marshall, Stein, Loose and Novotny 1979) represent a major compilation of data regarding the broader extent of the Chacoan system.

No. 105 PICTURED CLIFFS (LA 8970)

The Pictured Cliffs site is an area of sandstone cliffs, approximately one and one-half miles long, containing numerous petroglyphs and a few pictographs. There are abstract designs present, but most examples consist of human figures, deer, antelope, lizards, hand prints, etc.

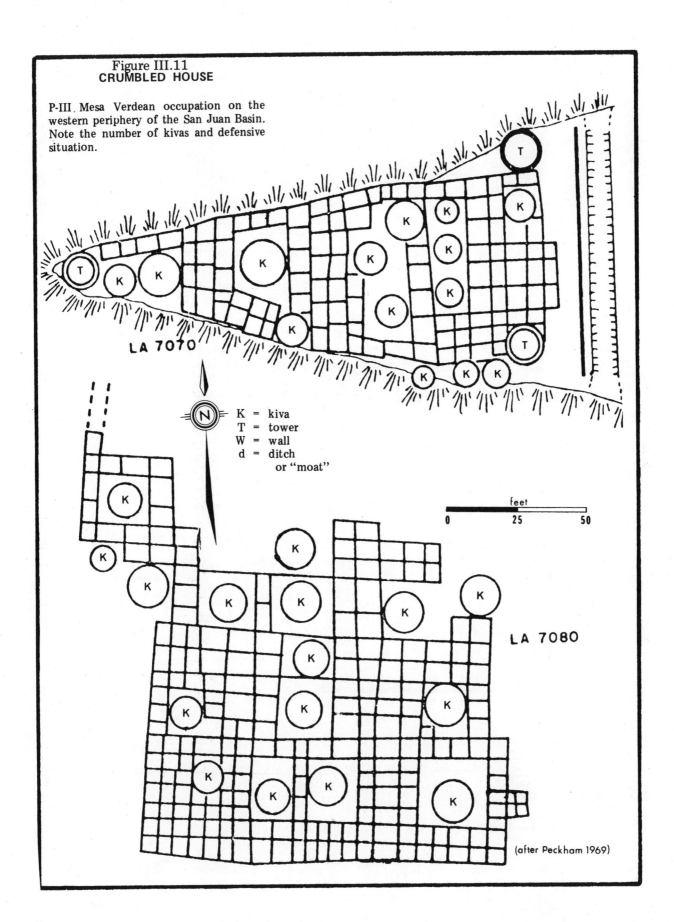

Figure III.11
CRUMBLED HOUSE

P-III. Mesa Verdean occupation on the western periphery of the San Juan Basin. Note the number of kivas and defensive situation.

LA 7070

K = kiva
T = tower
W = wall
d = ditch
    or "moat"

feet
0   25   50

LA 7080

(after Peckham 1969)

85

It is not known when most of the petroglyphs were drawn, but it is assumed that they fall into the period of A.D. 950-1300, when the San Juan Valley also experienced a large Anasazi occupation. This site has been extensively studied by Fallon (1979).

The site is located in the San Juan Valley, north of Waterflow, New Mexico, at an elevation of 5,200 feet.

No. 760 GUADALUPE RUIN (LA 2757)

The Guadalupe Ruin consists of the remains of a Chacoan outlier situated on the top of a high mesa, within the Rio Puerco (east) Valley. Excavations conducted by Eastern New Mexico University, under the direction of Lonnie Pippin, have revealed the presence of at least 15 rooms and 8 kivas. The site exhibits Chacoan masonry and ceramics. Like several other Chacoan outliers (i.e. Aztec Ruins and Salmon Ruin), Guadalupe was later reoccupied by peoples of the Mesa Verde culture following the Chacoan abandonment.

The architecture (single story, with large rooms and probably high ceilings) and the site location indicate that the original Chacoan construction was probably for a special purpose other than habitation. Again, like at other Chacoan outliers, this site is surrounded by numerous, smaller, domicillary structures, where most of the population lived.

No. 251 MITTEN ROCK ARCHEOLOGICAL DISTRICT

This district contains the remains of a cluster of 20 to 25 Anasazi ruins dating from the Basketmaker III to early Pueblo III periods (circa A.D. 500 to 1100). Structures present at this site include pithouses, surface granaries, masonry roomblocks (from one room up to 90 rooms), kivas, and one great kiva.

No. 276 CROW CANYON ARCHEOLOGICAL DISTRICT

This archeological district consists of five major ruins dating between A.D. 1700 and 1750, and several pithouse sites dating at roughly A.D. 700. In addition, there are several rock shelter storage bins and numerous examples of rock art panels, both dating to the early historic period.

The major ruins, or pueblitos, belong to the Gobernador Phase, also referred to as the Navajo Refugee period. The pithouse sites are thought to pertain to the Rosa Phase. Elevations in the general area are around 6,400 feet.

No. 314* GALLEGOS WASH ARCHEOLOGICAL DISTRICT

This archeological district includes the remains of an extremely extensive scatter of lithic tools and debris located along the Gallegos Wash. There are also numerous examples of hearths, manos and metates. Diagnostic artifacts found here indicate a date prior to A.D. 500 to the Paleo-Indian period. The major utilization of this site, however, was during the Archaic period. Some of these materials are discussed in the first part of this chapter (Elyea, Abbink and Eschman 1979).

Elevation ranges from 5,600 feet to 5,700 feet. Hadlock (1962) reported earlier surveys in *El Palacio*.

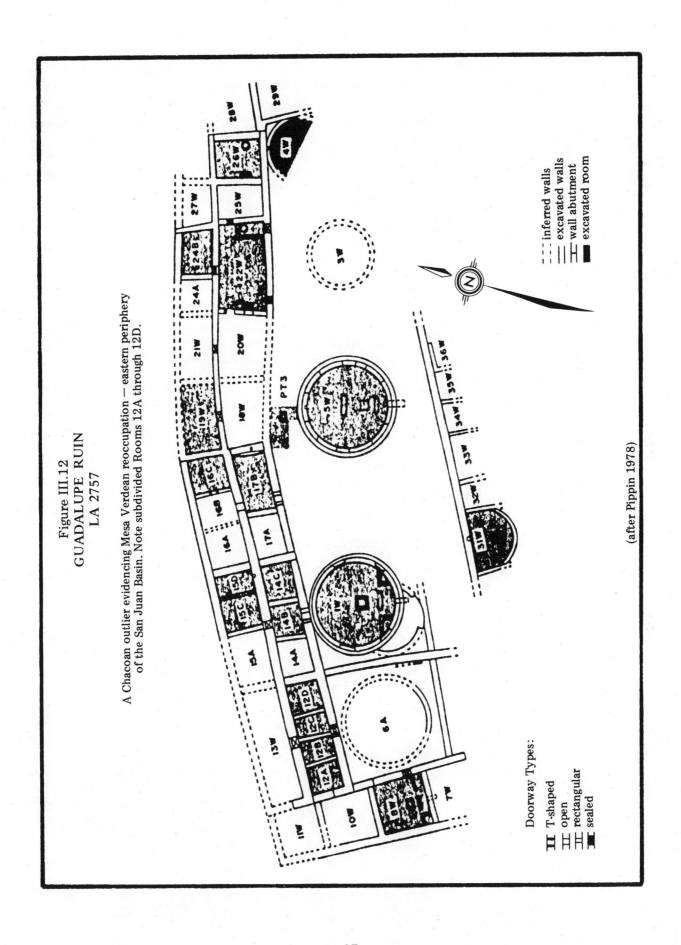

Figure III.12
GUADALUPE RUIN
LA 2757

A Chacoan outlier evidencing Mesa Verdean reoccupation — eastern periphery
of the San Juan Basin. Note subdivided Rooms 12A through 12D.

(after Pippin 1978)

Doorway Types:
T-shaped
open
rectangular
sealed

- - - inferred walls
· · · excavated walls
wall abutment
■ excavated room

No. 361 CHRISTMAS TREE RUIN

This site consists of a highly defensive Gobernador Phase occupation (1700 to 1775) near Navajo Reservoir. This site differs from most other Gobernador Phase pueblitos in that it is situated within a rock shelter and is not a free-standing pueblito constructed on a large boulder or promontory.

Christmas Tree Ruin consists of a large single room, occupying a rock shelter. The original inhabitants simply walled off the opening with adobe and masonry to enclose the room. The same strategy was employed for many smaller sites of the Gallina Phase, 500 years prior. The site is situated at approximately 6,100 feet elevation in Gobernador Canyon.

No. 370 SIMON CANYON RUIN

This site consists of a single room situated on a large boulder which was occupied during the Gobernador Phase (Navajo Refugee). The room is well preserved, with much of the roof still intact.

The Simon Canyon site lies further to the northwest than any other known Gobernador Phase pueblito. It is located on the north side of the San Juan River at an elevation of approximately 5,800 feet. As with other sites of the period, Gobernador Polychromes are considered diagnostic (along with Dinetah utility wares and Ashiwi polychromes), though ceramic assemblages tend to be very modest in size.

No. 428* CGP-56

This site consists of 15 sandstone masonry rooms located on the top of a small butte. The occupation of this site occurred during the Mesa Verde Phase (ca. A.D. 1200-1300).

The site suggests a defensive orientation, as access is possible only by scaling a cliff by hand and toe holds. More information on CGP-56 can be found in Reher (1977a).

The elevation at CGP-56 is 5,200 feet. It was one of three sites nominated to the National Register of Historic Places following the CGP surveys. It is believed to represent a *pure* P-III or Mesa Verdean occupation, while the more common pattern in the San Juan Basin seems to have been reuse of earlier Chacoan sites. Typically, such reoccupied Chacoan sites show evidence of the larger rooms having been subdivided into smaller living units. These dividing walls are strikingly non-Chacoan (*not* well-laid, coursed masonry, pebble chinked) in character. Significantly, P-III occupation in the Rio Grande is characterized by larger room size than that documented for the Mesa Verdean reoccupation of the San Juan Basin.

No. 429* CGP-54-1

This site consists of five circular rooms and five rectangular structures of sandstone masonry. The site was occupied during the Mesa Verde phase (A.D. 1200-1300) and is situated defensively on top of an isolated butte. A complete description is found in Reher (1977a). There were no White Mountain Redwares (St. Johns Polychrome, Pinedale, etc.) found at this site — a ceramic feature of the P-III period in general and often occurring with Mesa Verdean occupation. The site is located east of the Chaco River at an elevation of 5,200 feet.

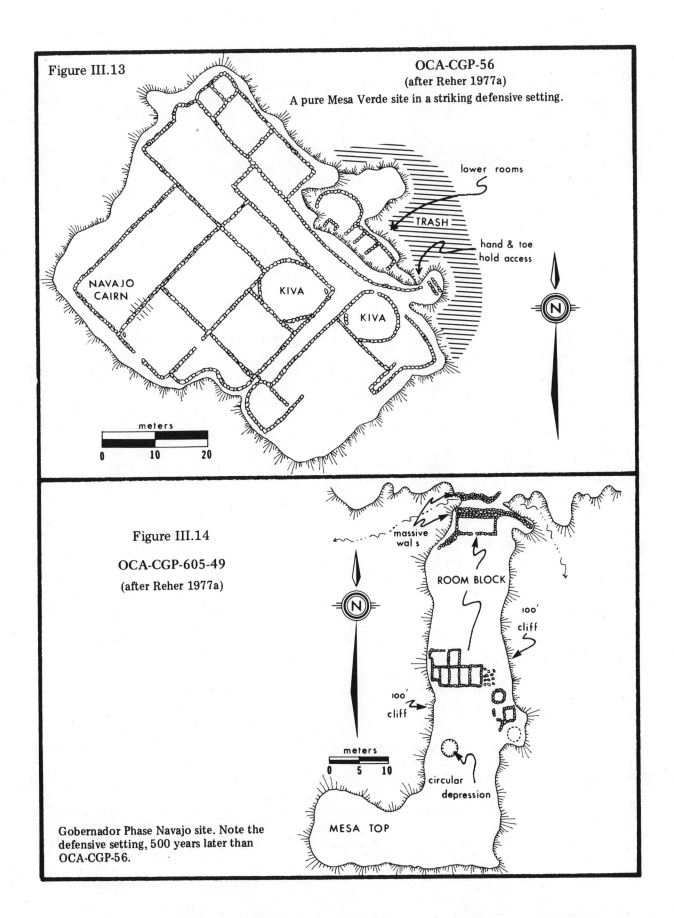

Figure III.13

OCA-CGP-56
(after Reher 1977a)
A pure Mesa Verde site in a striking defensive setting.

lower rooms

TRASH

hand & toe
hold access

NAVAJO
CAIRN

KIVA

KIVA

N

meters
0   10   20

Figure III.14

OCA-CGP-605-49

(after Reher 1977a)

N

massive walls

ROOM BLOCK

100'
cliff

100'
cliff

circular
depression

meters
0   5   10

MESA TOP

Gobernador Phase Navajo site. Note the
defensive setting, 500 years later than
OCA-CGP-56.

No. 430* CGP-605

This site consists of a Gobernador Phase pueblito situated on a defensive promontory. There is a defensive wall, two meters thick, on the west side of the site, and 100 foot high cliffs protect the other sides of the site. This site is also reported in Reher (1977a).

Approximately nine rooms and three hogans are present at this site. Most of the known pueblitos are located in the Gobernador area, over 75 miles to the east. This site is 5,450 feet in elevation.

No. 513 OLD INDIAN RACETRACK (LA 9040)

This site consists of four rows of arcs, constructed of cobbles, on a terrace overlooking the Animas River. The arcs are approximately 250 meters long and are generally oriented north-south, opening to the east. Two cobble mounds are located 133 meters to the east of the arcs. One meter west of the cobble mound is a group of five cobbles which is the center point for the radius of the arcs. The arcs are constructed of cobbles, probably laid on the ground surface.

It is assumed that this feature may represent a calendar of some type. It is currently under study.

No. 123 TOHATCHI VILLAGE (LA 3098)

This Basketmaker III site is situated on top of an isolated mesa in the southern Chuska Valley at an elevation of 6,460 feet. The elevation is similar to that of the Pine Lawn Valley of the Mogollon area. The site consists of 35 pithouses, 41 surface structures, or granaries, and one large kiva. The kiva (unexcavated) may be *rectangular with rounded corners* (Marshall, Stein, Loose and Novotny 1979:286). Such a kiva configuration is more commonly associated with Mogollon sites of the same period. Nearly the entire mesa top was utilized for these structures.

Ceramics at this site indicate a date from A.D. 500 to 700 or 750. The ceramics are exclusively Lino Gray and La Plata B/W, considered Anasazi and not Mogollon in character.

THE CHACOAN OUTLIERS THEMATIC NOMINATION

This group of sites, located within the San Juan Basin, was intensively studied and reported by Marshall and Stein (Marshall, Stein, Loose and Novotny 1979). Those which occur within the central and northern San Juan Basin are listed below. The remainder (Table III.12) occur along the southern periphery of the basin. A number of these were first recorded many years ago (Morris Site 41 on La Plata River is an example) but many of those had not been mapped. Others are newly discovered.

Halfway House
Bisa'ani Archeological District
Pierre's Archeological District
Grey Hill Springs Archeological District
Great Bend Community
Willow Canyon
Lake Valley Archeological District
Twin Angels Pueblo
Hogback Archeological District
Whirlwind Lake Archeological District
*Morris Site 41

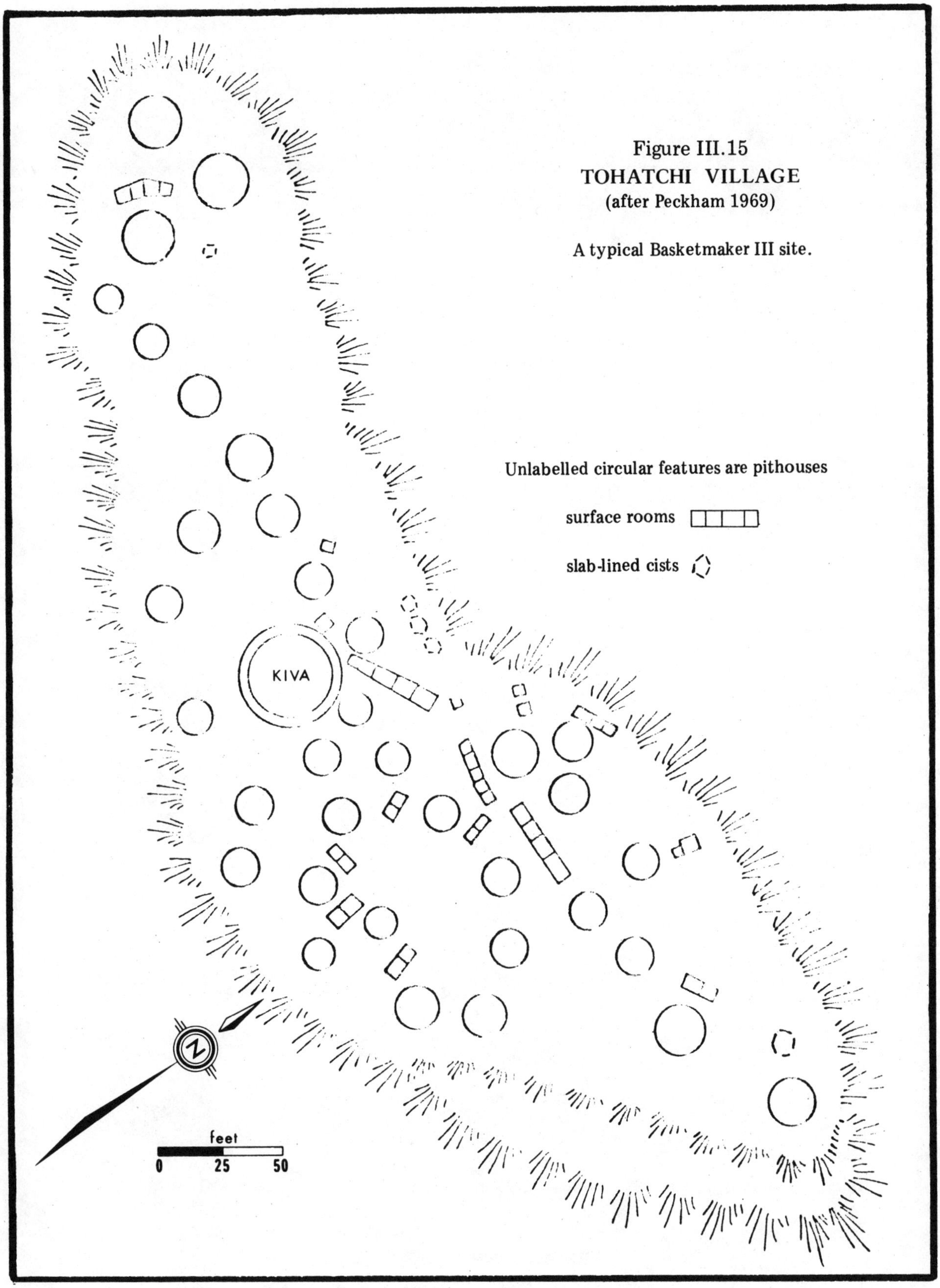

Figure III.15
TOHATCHI VILLAGE
(after Peckham 1969)

A typical Basketmaker III site.

Unlabelled circular features are pithouses

surface rooms

slab-lined cists

KIVA

feet
0   25   50

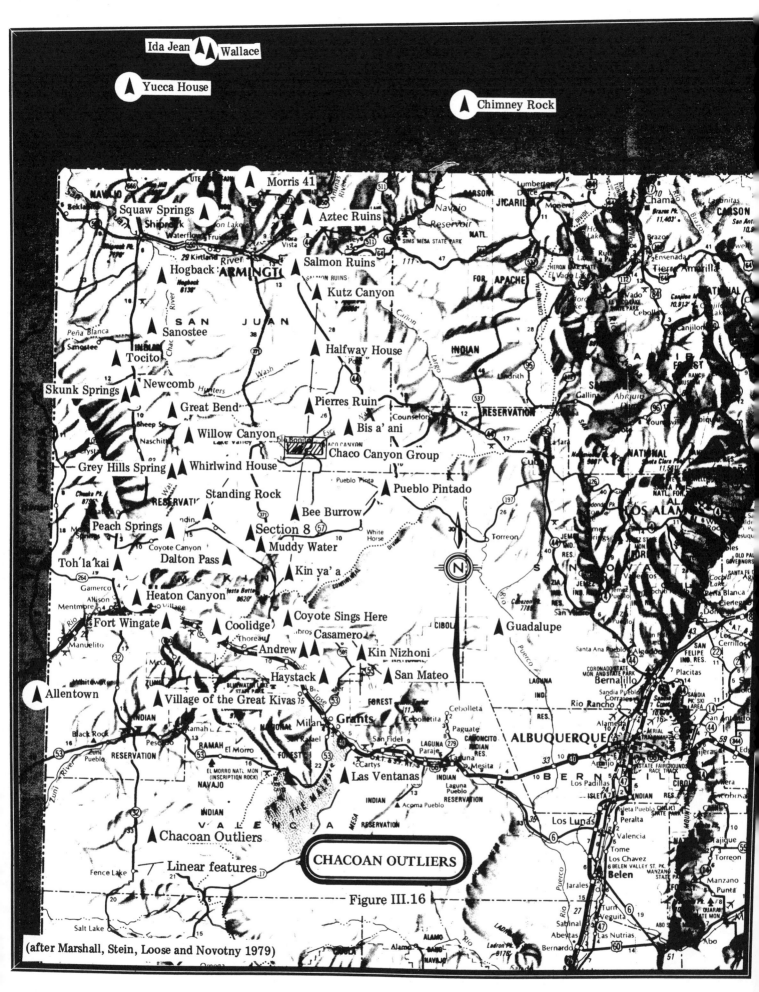

Ida Jean ▲▲ Wallace

▲ Yucca House

● Chimney Rock

Morris 41

Squaw Springs
Shiprock
Waterflow Fruit
29 Kirtland River
Hogback
ARMINGTON

▲ Aztec Ruins

▲ Salmon Ruins

▲ Kutz Canyon

SAN   JUAN

Peña Blanca
Sanostee
Sanostee
▲ Sanostee
▲ Tocito

▲ Halfway House

INDIAN

Skunk Springs
▲ Newcomb
▲ Great Bend

▲ Pierres Ruin

Counselor

▲ Willow Canyon

▲ Bis a' ani

RESERVATION

Chaco Canyon Group

Grey Hills Spring
▲ Whirlwind House

Pueblo Pinta

▲ Pueblo Pintado

Chuska Pk.
8795'
RESERVATION
▲ Standing Rock

▲ Bee Burrow

▲ Peach Springs
Coyote Canyon
Dalton Pass ▲

Section 8 ⑤⑦
▲ Muddy Water

White Horse

Toh'la'kai
Gamerco
Allison
Mentmore

▲ Heaton Canyon
Iesta Butte
8620'

▲ Kin ya' a

CONTINENTAL

N

▲ Coyote Sings Here

Fort Wingate
Manuelito
McGaffey

▲ Coolidge
Thoreau

Casamero

▲ Guadalupe

CIBOLA

Andrew

▲ Kin Nizhoni

Allentown
Black Rock
Zuni
Pueblo
RESERVATION
Pescado

Haystack
▲ Village of the Great Kivas

▲ San Mateo

FOREST

Cebolleta

Milan Grants
RAMAH
El Morro
FOREST
EL MORRO NATL. MON.
(INSCRIPTION ROCK)
NAVAJO

San Rafael
San Fidel
McCartys

LAGUNA
Paraje
Laguna

Paguate

INDIAN
Laguna
Pueblo
RESERVATION

ALBUQUERQUE

▲ Las Ventanas

Acoma Pueblo

INDIAN

BERN

Los Lunas

VALENCIA

MESA   RESERVATION

▲ Chacoan Outliers

Belen

── Linear features

CHACOAN OUTLIERS

Figure III.16

(after Marshall, Stein, Loose and Novotny 1979)

92

For the most part, these sites consist of a large specialized structure (Bonito Phase Pueblo), a host of smaller domiciliary structures (Hosta Butte Phase pueblos) and numerous other structures (great kivas, roads, etc.). An example of this type of site is described herein under Skunk Springs. For a full description of the character of these sites, the reader is referred to *Anasazi Communities of the San Juan Basin* (Marshall, Stein, Loose and Novotny 1979).

In the first part of this chapter, we likened the Chacoan roads and outlying sites to the *spokes of a great wheel*. Tainter and Gillio (1980a) have accepted this analogy, and pursue it in their overview of the Mt. Taylor District (discussed in Chapter IV).

THE RIO GRANDE

GALLINA CULTURE GROUP

The Gallina culture has attracted the attention of many scholars for nearly fifty years. Published interpretations of the Gallina culture have ranged from conservative to speculative, much attention once being placed on its isolation and backwardness. Its defensive fortifications and burned structures have been romanticized, at times.

The Gallina culture is assumed to have its origins in the general Puebloan culture which occupied the region around the Navajo Reservoir and Gobernador Canyon districts. That is, its origins lie in the Los Pinos-Sambrito-Rosa-Piedra-Arboles phase sequence. Early Gallina architecture consisted of pithouse villages surrounded by stockades. Later sites consist of pithouses, unit surface structures, massive towers and stockades. It does indeed appear that one major site selection factor in the placement and structure of Gallina sites was defense. Many Gallina sites are burned and numerous skeletal materials indicate violent death.

The earlier Rosa-Piedra sequence terminates about A.D. 950, while the Gallina sequence begins just after A.D. 1100 and terminates in the late A.D. 1200's. Though some scholars prefer not to accept the idea, the evidence heavily favors a hiatus in occupation between roughly A.D. 950 and 1150. It should also be pointed out that the bulk of the Rosa-Piedra pithouses lie to the north of the bulk of Gallina occupation. An overlapping area lies roughly at the latitude of La Jara, New Mexico (the La Jara site description follows). While the relationship between the Rosa-Piedra and the Gallina is assumed, it is still inadequately demonstrated. Similarly, the relationship between the A.D. 1100+ pithouse settlements of the Gallina and the masonry structures of the A.D. 1200-1275 period are presumed (Seaman 1976). Since less emphasis has been placed on the excavation and survey of Gallina pithouses, the evidence for this is not evenly balanced.

No. 094 CASTLE OF THE CHAMA (LA 9053)

This site consists of a concentration of pithouses, unit houses and towers located on the crest of a narrow ridge. Occupation was probably from A.D. 1100 to 1200. The site lies between 7,700 feet and 7,900 feet in elevation.

No. 275* TURKEY SPRINGS ARCHEOLOGICAL SITE (LA 10641)

This site consists of several Gallina phase dwellings, which are shelters built in and near lava flows. Many small caves within the lava flows were also utilized as shelters. In addition, several garden plots are also present in the immediate area (Ellis 1975; descriptions of nearby sites in Cordell 1979:48).

No. 274 RED HILL ARCHEOLOGICAL SITES (LA 10644)

This is a possible Gallina site locality, although no pottery has been found. It is uhusual in that it is located at 9,600 feet in elevation. From surface indications there appear to be from one to four pithouses, roughly six feet in diameter.

This site and with the nearby Turkey Springs Site are currently under investigation by Dr. F.H. Ellis and the Ghost Ranch Museum. Several dwellings have been excavated and should be reported in the near future.

Together, the Red Hill Site and Turkey Springs Site contain many features not commonly reported at Gallina sites. Various house types, storage units, caves, roasting pits and garden plots are present at these sites.

No. 252 NOGALES CLIFF HOUSE

This Gallina cliff dwelling consists of 20-25 adobe rooms located in a natural cave at approximately 7,800 feet in elevation. There are at least five unit houses located nearby. Tree-ring dates suggest an occupation from A.D. 1239 to A.D. 1267 (Pattison 1968). Numerous storage cists are also present at Nogales Cliff House.

Gallina Cliff dwellings are uncommon house types. Only five other examples are known. N.B. Pattison (1968) reported on excavations at this site.

No. 348 LA 12062

This Gallina site consists of a double unit house with one associated pithouse, dating from A.D. 1100 to 1300. The site is at approximately 7,400 feet in elevation.

S. Holbrook and J. Mackey (University of California) excavated this site as part of their Gallina studies. The architecture and floor plan of LA 12062 are typical of most Gallina surface structures. The presence of a central hearth, flanked on each side by storage cists, and a general southern orientation of the features, commonly occurs in most Gallina houses. The occurrence of similar features in Pueblo IV and Pueblo V sites in the Jemez area led Reiter (1938:69) to suggest a connection between the Gallina and Jemez cultures, which today is still held to be true (Ford, Schroeder and Peckham 1972:25).

No. 532* LA JARA SITE (LA 14318)

This large Gallina site consists of a unit pueblo, pithouses, kivas, towers, post holes from a wooden stockade and a masonry defensive wall. Portions of this site are currently being excavated and reconstructed by New Mexico State University and the Jicarilla Tribe for an interpretive exhibition. The site has been tentatively dated at A.D. 1050 to 1200. Elevation at the La Jara Site is around 7,400 feet.

During a recent visit by the authors, Scott Andrae and Dabney Ford of La Plata, New Mexico pointed out numerous other unit houses and towers in the immediate area, indicating an extremely high density of sites. Occupation extends along the adjacent mesa tongues for a substantial distance. The masonry roomblocks are, in fact, situated below the stockaded pithouse occupation at the base of a 50-70 foot promontory. J. Broster (personal communication) has questioned whether the reconstructed pithouses might not be a late Rosa phase occupation. He points out greater similarity in site setting to other Rosa phase occupations than to other Gallina sites currently being recorded a few miles to the north. We should be careful to point out that he raises this issue as a question, rather than a conclusion.

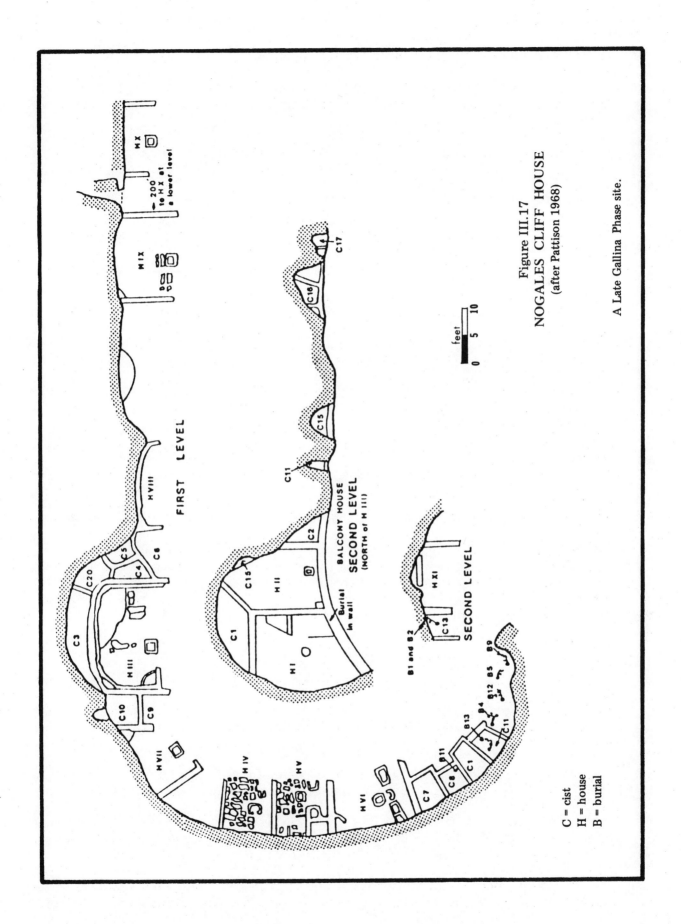

Figure III.17
NOGALES CLIFF HOUSE
(after Pattison 1968)

A Late Gallina Phase site.

C = cist
H = house
B = burial

95

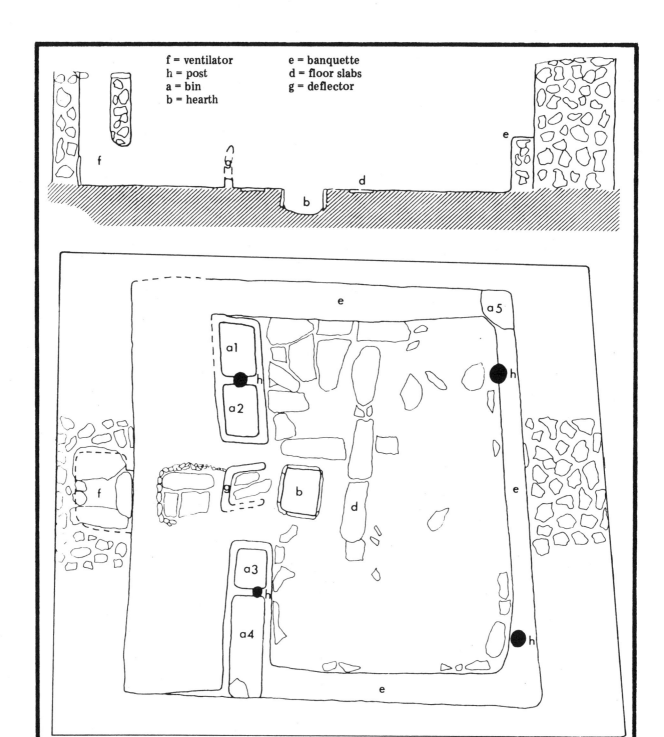

f = ventilator   e = banquette
h = post   d = floor slabs
a = bin   g = deflector
b = hearth

Figure III.18
A GALLINA STRUCTURE
(after Dick 1976)

A typical Gallina surface structure. Note the massive walls and the layout of floor features. This pattern of floor features is also present in Gallina pithouses and a similar pattern is found in Late Jemez sites.

A district nomination should be created around the La Jara Site, perhaps including a major portion of one projecting mesa and associated drainage. More excavation in the area to substantiate chronology is definitely indicated. There were no satisfactorily dated materials obtained from this site.

Allan Rorex has reconstructed and retimbered the primary pithouse. The amount of labor investment in a small surface pueblo would be no greater, and probably much less, than for such a pithouse. We must ask why a population would create such structures at all after the techniques of surface construction had become known.

JEMEZ GROUP

The Jemez area contains many important archeological sites. These sites, unfortunately, have not been systematically studied since Reiter (1938) and Alexander and Reiter (1935) excavated and tested several sites during the University of New Mexico field seasons in the Jemez area. One exception is a study of agricultural features conducted by Fleidner (1974). The early roots of Jemez Pueblo are generally agreed to be found in the Gallina culture area to the northwest (Ford, Schroeder and Peckham 1972; Cordell 1979). We believe this is one of the best ethnoarcheological cases documented (Sando 1979). It is also thought to be the Jemez populations that retreated to the Gobernador with Navajo groups during the Refugee (or Gobernador) period.

No. 117* SAN JUAN MESA RUIN (LA 303)

This pueblo ruin is located on a high mesa at an elevation of 7,900 feet. The site consists of masonry roomblocks arranged around five plaza areas. Four kivas are present within the plazas. Ceramic types found at this ruin indicate a date of circa A.D. 1600 to 1675, that is, a P-V occupation.

No. 279 PATOKWA PUEBLO (LA 96)

Patokwa Pueblo consists of masonry roomblocks surrounding two plaza areas. Two kivas are present within the plaza areas. The main feature at this pueblo are the remains of a Spanish mission built in 1694. The pueblo was abandoned in 1696. It is not known when Patokwa was founded.

The site is located at the junction of Guadalupe and San Diego Canyons at an elevation of 5,800 feet.

No. 278 PUEBLO OF ASTIALKWA (LA 1825)

This pueblo ruin is located in an extremely isolated position, on the top of an unusually high and rugged mesa. The site may be termed a *refugee* site, since the Jemez fled to Astialkwa in 1692 and 1694. The pueblo is at 6,750 feet in elevation.

No. 048* GUISEWA (JEMEZ STATE MONUMENT)

The remains of a Spanish mission and a Jemez pueblo are at Guisewa. The mission was founded around 1617 and deserted in 1622 due to Indian raids. The pueblo was then resettled and occupied until 1680. It is primarily the mission which is visible today. Portions of the pueblo itself lie under the Jemez Spring highway.

Photo 2: The Spanish mission at Guisewa. The mission was constructed around 1626 at the Jemez Pueblo of Guisewa and then shortly thereafter abandoned in the late 1630's. The mission is constructed of local stone, with walls six to eight feet thick. Photograph courtesy of C.M. Stuart.

No. 347 KO-AH'-SAI-YA (LA 384)

Although this site is actually claimed by Zia Pueblo as an ancestral site, it is included with the Jemez group due to its proximity with the Jemez area. The site is constructed of adobe, and consists of four roomblocks with perhaps 700 rooms. Four plazas and two kivas are also present. The site was occupied episodally from the 13th to 18th centuries and is at 5,440 feet in elevation, on the Jemez River. Schroeder (1979) discusses this site and its relationship to Zia Pueblo in the early historic period.

GALISTEO BASIN ARCHEOLOGICAL DISTRICT

This large basin is well known for its spectacular pueblo ruins. Extensive pueblo occupation of the Galisteo Basin began in the early A.D. 1200's and continued through the early historic period (ca. 1790's). Most of these pueblos were tested or excavated by N.C. Nelson in the early part of this century (Nelson 1914, 1916). Work in this area is being continued by R.W. Lang of the School of American Research, among others. Several sites summarized in Smiley, Stubbs and Bannister (1953) are in the Galisteo Basin. Though some P-II components are known in the area, they have not received much attention. Most sites were established between A.D. 1280-1320. The late A.D. 1400's saw a substantial decline in P-IV occupation. This general trend is reflected in the drop from 240 P-IV to 68 P-V components in the Cochiti area site sample (Table III.5).

No. 384 LA BAJADA RUINS (LA 7)

La Bajada Ruins consist of a large adobe pueblo arranged around numerous plaza areas. The major occupation of this site occurred during the early Pueblo IV period, or from circa A.D. 1325 to 1450. A later historic occupation also occurred. The site is at 5,520 feet elevation. Glazes A-C and F are present.

No. 199 CIENEGUILLA (LA 16)

The Cieneguilla Ruins were probably occupied from the late A.D. 1200's to the 1600's, based on ceramic evidence. Following the reconquest of New Mexico in A.D. 1693, the inhabitants of Cieneguilla joined other groups of Indians to form the Pueblo of Laguna. Glazes A-C and F are present. The site is P-III/P-IV transitional to P-V.

No. 097 COLINA VERDE (a.k.a. Galisteo Basin) (LA 309)

This ruin is one of a few pueblo sites in the Galisteo drainage that are dated to a pre-P-IV period. It is smaller in size than others in the locale, and was only briefly occupied. The occupation of this site dates to the late 1200's and early 1300's. Dendro dates are from A.D. 1260 to 1332. The site is a P-III/ P-IV transitional (Smiley, Stubbs and Bannister 1953:30-31). The dates cluster at A.D. 1270-72 and, again, just after A.D. 1300. This suggests two distinct occupation episodes, with an indistinct earlier one, since Wingate B/R is present. Wingate B/R terminates about A.D. 1200. Thus, as at Pindi Pueblo, three occupation episodes are apparent.

No. 112* PUEBLO SAN CRISTOBAL (LA 80)

San Cristobal is another extremely large pueblo ruin in the Galisteo Basin. Construction is primarily masonry, although several areas of adobe construction are also present. In addition to the pueblo ruin, there are also the remains of a chapel constructed about 1630, an extensive petroglyph area, and tipi rings of Apachean origin. San Cristobal was occupied from about A.D. 1300 to 1680-1692. Glazes A-F are present. Twenty-three tree-ring dates fall between

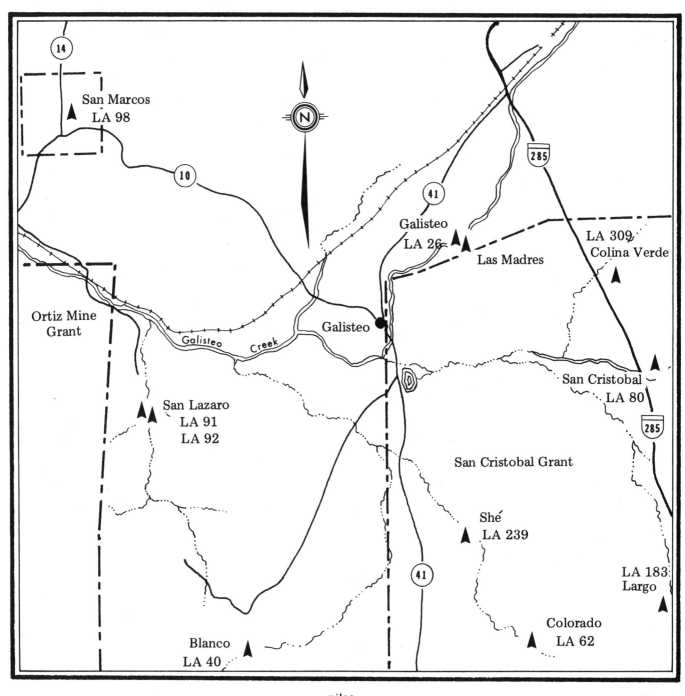

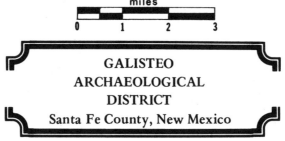

**GALISTEO
ARCHAEOLOGICAL
DISTRICT**
Santa Fe County, New Mexico

Map III.5

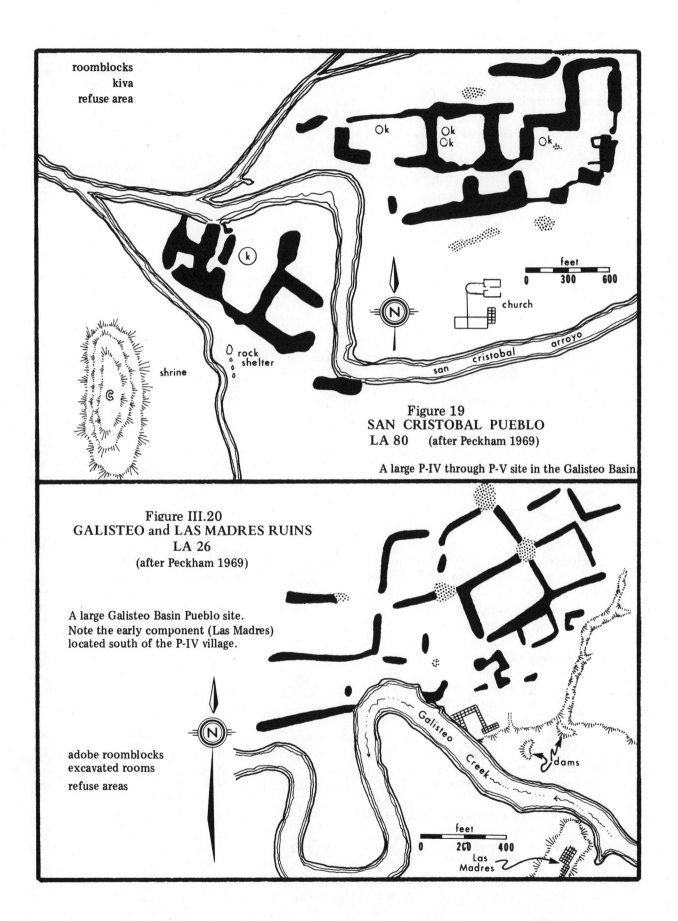

roomblocks
kiva
refuse area

Ok
Ok
Ok
Ok

feet
0   300   600

church

N

rock
shelter

shrine

san   cristobal   arroyo

Figure 19
SAN CRISTOBAL PUEBLO
LA 80   (after Peckham 1969)

A large P-IV through P-V site in the Galisteo Basin

Figure III.20
GALISTEO and LAS MADRES RUINS
LA 26
(after Peckham 1969)

A large Galisteo Basin Pueblo site.
Note the early component (Las Madres)
located south of the P-IV village.

N

adobe roomblocks
excavated rooms

refuse areas

Galisteo   Creek

dams

feet
0   200   400

Las
Madres

101

A.D. 1376 and 1437, with a cluster at A.D. 1428. Since these all come from one major construction unit, they do not represent the full range of occupation. No White Mountain Redwares are reported, so we may assume a P-IV—P-V occupation, rather than a P-III/P-IV transitional founding.

No. 113* PUEBLO OF SAN LAZARO (LA 91 and LA 92)

San Lazaro consists of a large masonry pueblo which is divided into two parts by an arroyo. Ceramic evidence indicates that parts of San Lazaro were occupied from the late A.D. 1200's until A.D. 1680-1692. As with other sites in the area, various portions of the pueblo indicate successive abandonments and reoccupations. In addition to the pueblo ruins, there are also the remains of a chapel. Glazeware ceramics at LA 91 (historic portion) include Glazes A-F, while at LA 92 the Glaze sequence terminates with the D complex (San Lazaro Glaze-Polychrome, of course) indicating termination by roughly A.D. 1515.

No. 106 PUEBLO BLANCO (LA 40)

Pueblo Blanco is a huge masonry ruin which contains an estimated 1,450 rooms. There are 16 roomblocks arranged around seven or eight plazas. Ceramic remains indicate a date from A.D. 1400 to 1600+. It was founded in the mid P-IV period. Site size apparently peaked about A.D. 1400-1425.

No. 107 PUEBLO COLORADO (LA 62)

This site consists of a large masonry pueblo constructed of red sandstone, hence the name. Approximately 881 ground floor rooms are present, arranged in eleven roomblocks around six or seven plaza areas. Ceramic material at Pueblo Colorado indicates successive occupations from the late A.D. 1200's to perhaps A.D. 1600.

No. 110 PUEBLO LARGO (LA 183)

Pueblo Largo is the smallest of the Galisteo Basin ruins of the Pueblo IV period. Approximately 489 ground floor rooms are present. The occupation period of Pueblo Largo apparently was shorter than that of most other P-IV Galisteo Basin pueblos. Published tree-ring dates are from A.D. 1275 to 1457. Glazes A-D are present. This pueblo was abandoned about the time many others were deserted in the Galisteo Basin. Its short occupation is a symptom of substantial instability in the late P-IV period.

No. 111 PUEBLO GALISTEO (LA 26)

Galisteo is an extremely large pueblo, consisting of 26 roomblocks with an estimated 1,640 rooms. To the south of Pueblo Galisteo, across the Galisteo Creek in a defensive location, is the site of Las Madres. This was excavated by Dr. B. Dutton in 1962 (Dutton 1964). It dates to the A.D. 1300's. Ceramic remains from Pueblo Galisteo indicate a date from the late A.D. 1200's to the 1700's. Galisteo also is an extremely important historical site. Its location on the Plains led to a situation such as that at Pecos Pueblo — economic interaction with Plains groups. See our discussion of that interaction in Chapter VII.

No. 114 PUEBLO OF SAN MARCOS (LA 98)

This pueblo ruin consists of approximately 22 adobe roomblocks arranged around eight to ten plaza areas. There are also the remains of a Spanish period mission. San Marcos was probably occupied from A.D. 1300 to 1680-1692. Glazes A-F are present. Warren (1979:190) says, "several villages in the Galisteo were producing pots at this time, BUT THE MAIN ceramic industry was at San Marcos Pueblo (LA 98). . . " That time period is the Glaze A Yellow from A.D. 1325-1450. This pueblo seems to be the source for most Glaze B, or *Largo Glaze-on-Yellow*.

No. 115 PUEBLO SHE' (LA 239)

This ruin is a large masonry pueblo, consisting of 14 roomblocks, 11 plaza areas and an estimated 1,543 ground floor rooms. The ceramic evidence for Pueblo She' indicates a period of occupation ranging from the A.D. 1300's to 1600, that is, the P-IV–P-V periods.

GENERAL RIO GRANDE

No. 281 KOTYITI (OLD COCHITI) (LA 295)

This site, located in a highly defensive location on top of Horn Mesa, was briefly occupied between 1680 and 1696. The site is a masonry pueblo with two plazas and two kivas. Only Glaze F of the Rio Grande Glaze sequence is found in association. The Glaze F period is known as the Kotyiti period. During the early 1600's the Cochiti area was completely abandoned. Glaze F wares have been found at both modern Cochiti and old Cochiti. Old Cochiti, then, was the occupation site of the Cochiti people during the period of the Pueblo Revolt.

No. 125* TSIPING (LA 301)

This pueblo ruin is located on the top of a volcanic tuff mesa, which is at least 800 feet above the surrounding valleys. Tree-ring samples and ceramics from Tsiping indicate a date of occupation from roughly A.D. 1200 or 1300 to 1325.

The pueblo itself is constructed of cut and shaped tuff blocks. Up to 300 rooms and 16 to 18 kivas are present. Tsiping was occupied during a period of stress for Anasazi populations. At that time, the entire San Juan Anasazi area had already been abandoned by Chacoan populations, and the area was in the midst of substantial drought. The highly defensive and fortified position of Tsiping may be related to these events. At this time period, A.D. 1250-1300, fortified sites are widespread throughout the Southwest (Smiley, Stubbs and Bannister 1953:30).

No. 104 KUAPA (LA 3443 and LA 3444)

Kuapa is an extremely large adobe pueblo located at the southern end of the Pajarito Plateau. Pottery from this site indicates that Kuapa I (LA 3444) was occupied during the A.D. 1200's and early 1300's. Kuapa II contains ceramics that date from the A.D. 1300's up to the 1600's.

The earliest portion of the site (Kuapa I) consists of three large adobe roomblocks and two smaller ones. Kuapa II contains approximately 25 roomblocks, eight kivas, and nine plaza areas. This portion of the site is almost entirely constructed of coursed adobe, although a few areas of masonry construction are present. By A.D. 1525 Kuapa was the only site on the southern Pajarito Plateau still occupied. Tyuoni on the Northern Plateau was the major contemporaneous population center to the north (Warren 1979). An early historic occupation (ca. 1700) is also present at this site. These may be outlying structures from the Spanish village of Cañada.

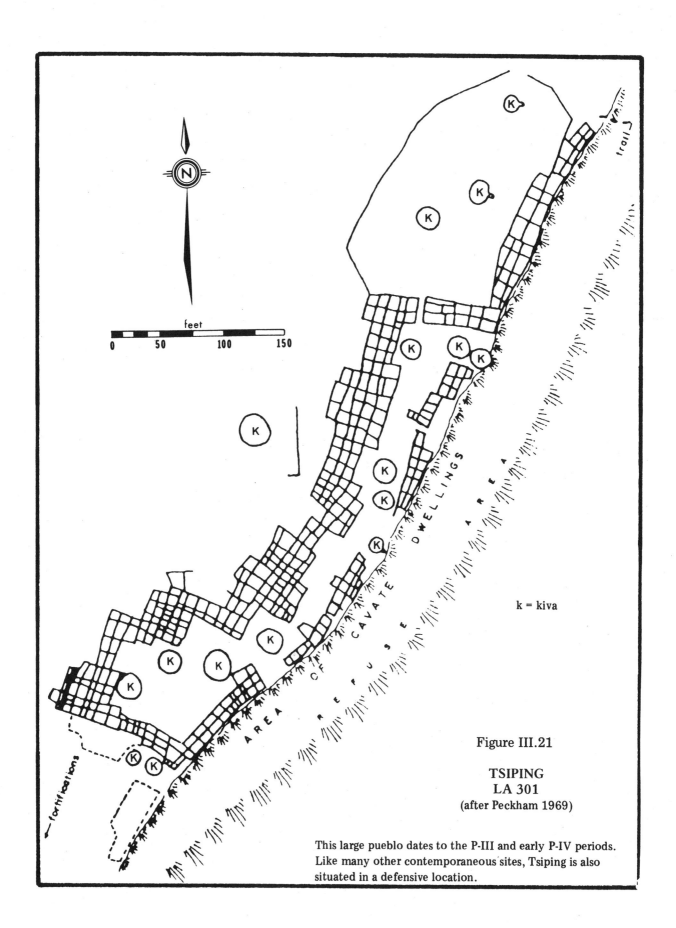

feet

0   50   100   150

N

K

K

K

K

K K K

K

K

K

K

K

A R E A   O F   C A V A T E   D W E L L I N G S

A R E A   O F   R E F U S E   A R E A

trail

k = kiva

K

K

K

K

K

K K

fortifications

Figure III.21

**TSIPING
LA 301**
(after Peckham 1969)

This large pueblo dates to the P-III and early P-IV periods.
Like many other contemporaneous sites, Tsiping is also
situated in a defensive location.

No. 225 KUAUA RUINS (CORONADO STATE MONUMENT) (LA 187)*

This site consists of the remains of an excavated adobe pueblo. Up to 1200 rooms were excavated, along with six kivas. Ceramic remains indicate that Kuaua was occupied from approximately A.D. 1300 to 1600. Kuaua is located on the west bank of the Rio Grande at an elevation of 5,100 feet. It is generally agreed that Coronado camped here with his men the winter of 1540 (Bolton 1949:192-200). This place is called *Alcanfor* in the Bolton account. This site is also on the National Register, and there is a small state-supported museum there.

No. 56 BANDELIER NATIONAL MONUMENT*

Within the confines of Bandelier National Monument are found literally hundreds of pueblo sites. The major occupation dates from A.D. 1200 to 1550. Numerous small pueblos are present during the early periods, and there is a gradual trend toward aggregation and settlement in lower elevations.

No. 74* PECOS NATIONAL MONUMENT

Pecos National Monument contains the remains of several Spanish missions and extensive pueblo ruins. The pueblo itself was originally founded in the 1200's and was occupied until 1838. The position of Pecos, on the gateway to the Plains, led to the establishment of an important economic trading system with Plains Indians. This proved to be a mixed blessing, since numerous raids by Plains Indians also occurred.

Pecos Pueblo is also a site important to the history of southwestern archeology. It was here that A.V. Kidder used the method of stratigraphy, while excavating the extensive middens, to develop a ceramic sequence based upon the sequential placement of deposits. It was also here that the idea for a conference (later known as the Pecos Conference) to classify by traits and time period was born. Excavated by A.V. Kidder (1932, 1958), it is one of the best known and most cited occupations outside of the *Chacoan Interaction System* (see also, Schroeder 1979a).

No. 5* BIG BEAD MESA (LA 15231)

This site consists of a large, early historic Navajo settlement situated on top of Big Bead Mesa at an elevation of 6,900 feet. The site is basically six groups of hogans and associated features (ash dumps, sweat lodges, and petroglyphs). Tree-ring dates indicate an occupation from 1745 to 1812. The site is reported in Keur (1941). Recently, a similar occupation was recorded in the Laguna area (Carrol, et al. 1979).

No. 19* PUYE RUINS (LA 47)

Puye Ruins consist of the remains of a large pueblo and associated cliff ruins. The pueblo is constructed of tuff blocks, and consists of a large rectangle of roomblocks arranged around a central plaza. The cliff ruins consist of cavate dwellings and talus pueblos built against the cliff. Puye is at an elevation of 7,000 feet. Ceramics and tree-ring dates indicate an occupation from A.D. 1250 to the late 1500's. Again, these occupations are in different components of the site, the earlier occupation being in the cavate rooms of the cliff face. Interestingly, only the E-F Glazewares appear in ceramic assemblage from the primary mounds below the cliff face. The precise episodes of occupation are only partly documented.

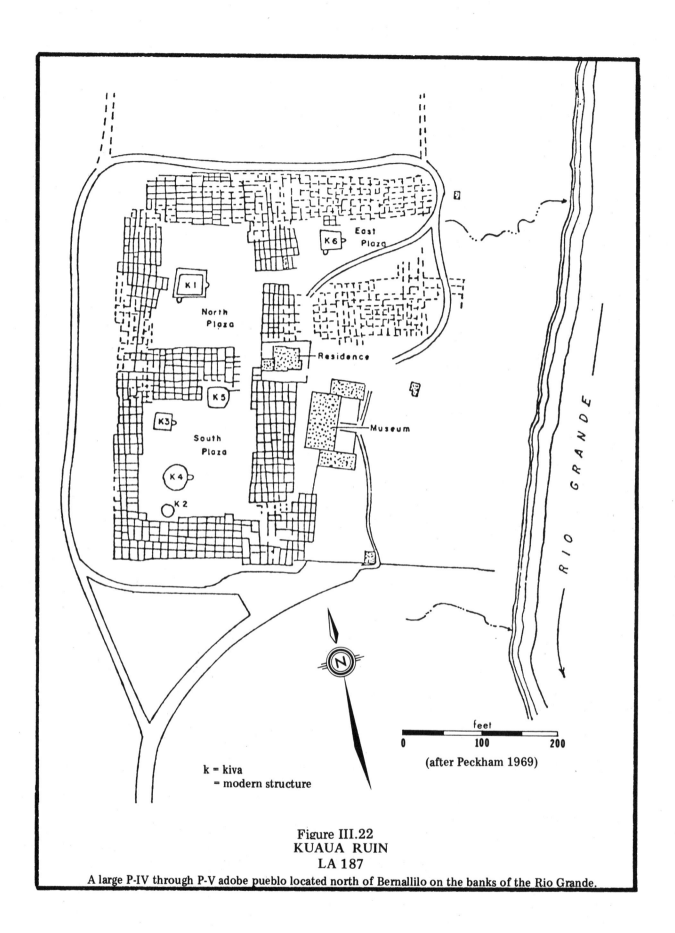

Figure III.22
KUAUA RUIN
LA 187

A large P-IV through P-V adobe pueblo located north of Bernallilo on the banks of the Rio Grande.

106

No. 284 INDIAN PETROGLYPH STATE PARK

This site is located on Albuquerque's west mesa in the surrounds of black volcanic lava formations. Many pictograph panels are present, primarily attributed to the Puebloan period. The area, once isolated from Albuquerque proper, is now being encroached on by urban sprawl.

No. 381 BOCA NEGRA CAVE SITE

The Boca Negra Cave consists of a volcanic cave west of Albuquerque. Occupation of this cave began approximately 4,000 years ago and continued until historic times.

The cave was excavated by Dr. T. Reinhart in the late 1960's (Reinhart 1968). Evidence recovered during excavation indicated that the first occupation consisted of the Atrisco Phase — an Archaic hunting and gathering stage. Following this occupation, the next habitation consisted of Basketmaker II and Basketmaker III groups. From these levels, the cave yielded dates of A.D. 370 ± 168 and a new variety of corn (Maiz de Ocho). This is the earliest date known for this type of corn.

Pueblo groups from A.D. 600 to 1600 also utilized Boca Negra Cave. In addition, the surrounding area contains evidence for early Archaic cultures and the Paleo-Indian period (ca. 8000 B.C.).

No. 22 SANDIA CAVE

Sandia Cave, located in Las Huertas Canyon, at the northern end of the Sandia Mountains, has produced evidence of Paleo-Indian and Pueblo remains. Excavated by Frank Hibben in the 1930's, two Paleo-Indian levels and one pueblo level were found. The Paleo-Indian levels consisted of a Folsom occupation and an earlier occupation referred to as Sandia. Artifacts from the Sandia level consisted of distinctive, single-shouldered projectile points, bone artifacts and scrapers (Hibben 1941).

Considerable controversy surrounds the reported stratigraphy and dating of the Sandia Cave material. The age of the Sandia material was originally believed to be approximately 19,000 years old. This has been modified and it is believed that the Sandia material may be associated with the Clovis horizon.

The distinctive Sandia points have a wide distribution, and have been reported from New Mexico, Texas, Oklahoma, Missouri and Iowa (Wormington 1957:90).

NAVAJO REFUGEE GROUP

The spectacular settings of these highly defensive pueblitos have long attracted archeological interest and speculation. Many of these sites are situated in virtually inaccessible locations and are very well preserved. A number still have intact roofs and several have forked-stick hogans which are still standing. These sites were primarily constructed in the early 1700's, during a period referred to as the Navajo Refugee period or the Gobernador phase. It was first believed that these pueblitos were constructed by Pueblo Indians fleeing from the violence of the Pueblo Revolt. However, many scholars now feel that these structures were constructed by Navajos for protection against raiding Ute and Comanche groups. Tree-ring evidence would support the second contention, since nearly all tree-ring dates indicate a post-1700 occupation, or long after the Pueblo Revolt and subsequent reconquest.

No. 100* FRANCES CANYON RUIN (LA 9072)
(We also have LA 2135, as published in Carlson 1965:109)

Frances Canyon Ruin is one of the largest known refugee sites. There are about 40 masonry rooms, a plaza area and a tower which was once three stories tall. Tree-ring dates indicate an occupation from 1716 to 1742. Whatever the LA number, this is, indeed, Earl Morris' Site No. 6, described in Carlson (1965:31-44). Ceramics included Gobernador Polychrome, Dinetah Scored, Jemez B/W, Puname Polychrome, Biscuit B and Hawikuh Polychrome.

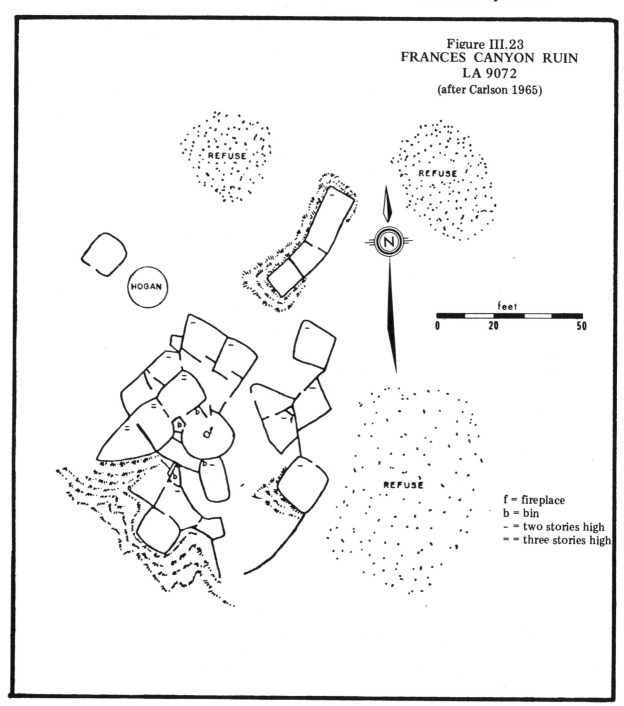

Figure III.23
FRANCES CANYON RUIN
LA 9072
(after Carlson 1965)

f = fireplace
b = bin
- = two stories high
= = three stories high

Earl H. Morris was perhaps the first to study these ruins intensively — later, other investigators followed (Keur 1941, Hester 1962 and Carlson 1965). Carlson compiled the results of Morris' early investigations.

Several of these sites (Crow Canyon Archaeological District, Christmas Tree Ruin, Simon Canyon Ruin, and CGP-605) are discussed with the State Register sites in the San Juan Basin.

Photo 3: A forked stick hogan at Old Fort, LA 1869. This Navajo Refugee site contains both unit houses and forked stick hogans within a walled compound. Photograph by D.E. Stuart.

No. 262   TAPACITO RUIN (LA 2298 and LA 5663)

This site consists of four well-preserved rooms and the remains of three others. This site differs from other *refugee* sites in that it is not located in a highly defensible location. Anthony Lutonsky mapped many of these sites for the Bureau of Land Management in 1974.

No. 372   SPLIT ROCK RUIN (LA 5664)

As the name implies, this site was constructed on the top of a large, cracked boulder. There are approximately four first-story rooms at this site, although some second-story rooms may have been present at one time.

No. 365   LARGO SCHOOL RUIN

This site is a small pueblito containing two or three rooms. No second story is evident at this site, and only a small portion of a roof is present.

No. 364   HOODED FIREPLACE SITE (LA 5651)

The site name is attributed to a well-preserved hooded fireplace located within a room at this site. There were originally eleven rooms in this pueblito, and one stone hogan. Portions of the roof are still present at this site. A hooded corner fireplace is also present at Morris' Site No. 6 (Frances Canyon; Carlson 1965:41, Plate D).

No. 015   OLD FORT (LA 1869) AND THREE CORN RUINS (LA 1871)

These sites are considered together due to their proximity. Three Corn Ruin is situated on the top of a sandstone pinnacle. Many masonry rooms with intact roofs are present. The name is derived from a petroglyph at the base of the sandstone pinnacle which consists of three corn plants. See plates in Carlson (1965:22-24). The site was found to be more reduced than in the 1953 photos when the authors visited it during this project.

Old Fort Ruin is situated about two-thirds of a mile from Three Corn Ruin, but is separated by a canyon. Old Fort Ruin is a walled pueblito, with rooms built along the enclosing wall and some rooms built in the compound. Several forked-stick hogans are also located within the compound. Compare the photograph of hogan three taken by the senior author in the fall of 1979 with those in Carlson (1965:14 top). Incredibly, the hogans are less disturbed than are portions of Rooms 14 and 15.

The purpose of the New Mexico State Register of Cultural Properties is to ". . . select for preservation examples which best represent the themes which are dominant in our history. We expect that these examples will provide a sense of continuity and serve as points of orientation in a rapidly changing world, that they will illustrate in a tangible, three dimensional way the story of New Mexico" (State Planning Office 1973:58). Excluding late historic period buildings, the New Mexico State Register of Cultural Properties is, as of December 1979, largely composed of large, late masonry pueblos in the San Juan Basin and Rio Grande areas. Exceptions include the Gallegos Canyon area and Sandia Cave (Archaic and Paleo-Indian periods) and the Tohatchi Village and Yellow Adobe Site (Basketmaker III period). Other early sites are also on the State Register, but are listed as components with later sites (i.e. T.G. and E. Route, Crow Canyon District). Generally, early archeological sites which lack large rubble mounds or standing walls are underrepresented on the New Mexico State Register of Cultural Properties. With the several exceptions, the same pattern holds for the National Register.

In addition to certain classes of sites missing from the Registers of Cultural Properties, certain areas, or culture areas, are also underrepresented. Not one large Pueblo IV ruin in the Chama drainage is represented, with the exception of Tsiping, which dates just prior to the major Pueblo occupation of the Chama Valley. Probably the largest Pueblo site in the Southwest, Sapawe, is also located within the Chama drainage, but is not listed on either State or National Registers of Cultural Properties.

Another area which has received little emphasis is the Taos area, despite a wealth of archeological materials and investigations since the early 1900's. The Pajarito Plateau, until recently, was also in this category. Charlie Steen, consulting archeologist for Los Alamos Scientific Laboratory, recently nominated to the National Register of Historic Places the following large and well known sites of Tsirege, Otowi, Little Otowi, and several cavate ruins, including a cave kiva in Mortandad Canyon (Steen 1977). Puye and Bandelier National Monument are currently listed on the State Register of Cultural Properties. Other areas in the Middle Rio Grande Valley which are generally underrepresented (excluding the Pueblo IV period) are the Jemez and Albuquerque areas.

The recent Chacoan outlier survey is a good model for nominations, in that it added numerous sites to the State Register which included roads, great kivas, small pueblos and agricultural features, as well as the large pueblos. Such thematic listings on the State Register give a clear picture of the total range of features surrounding a major occupation node.

Archaic sites in the far northern Rio Grande Valley are virtually unknown, save those recorded by Renaud (1946). Their existence is common knowledge among investigators, but relatively few sites have been formally reported. One focus of research might be on areas such as the Chama Valley or Pajarito Plateau, where Pueblo occupation begins fairly late, ca. A.D. 1250, even though other pueblo sites are nearby. Is this late occupation a function of other groups (hunters and gatherers) occupying these areas? Certainly, we suggest this possibility in our discussion of the San Juan Basin. In the Cebolleta Mesa-Mt. Taylor area the archeological record suggests a similar possibility, and this is discussed in the following chapter (Chapter IV).

A recent BLM inventory survey conducted by Texas Tech University recorded several Archaic sites in the Chama area. Several of these are quite extensive and one, located near the Pueblo of Tewi'i, has several well preserved hearths and an abundance of lithic material. These hearths can be easily dated by C-14 methods, and should be, to inform on ideas concerning the age of Archaic adaptations (hunting and gathering) and interactions with agriculturalists presented in this volume.

The archeological site files maintained by the Laboratory of Anthropology in Santa Fe mirror some of the biases in the State and National Registers. That is, there has been a general bias towards filing site forms for large pueblos, and some cultural and temporal gaps are present. In other cases, large tracts of land remain unsurveyed, and therefore little information is available. Also, many of the site information forms lack certain data such as elevation, site maps, ceramic and artifact types, etc. In some instances areas have been surveyed but site data forms have not been deposited in the site files.

In spite of these difficulties, the survey files of the Laboratory of Anthropology represent one of the nation's most remarkable repositories of archeological data. Presently, the archeological site files are being updated and computerized at the Laboratory of Anthropology. The professional archeological community needs to support the Laboratory's goal of maintaining the best and most complete data file possible. This support must be provided in every possible way: in supplying missing data on site forms, in supplying good data on *every* new site recorded, and in supporting the disposition of financial resources to meet these goals. We also owe an enormous debt of gratitude to those who have maintained, and added to, these files over the years. This task was, for many years, accomplished with few resources and even less acclaim. It is time for this situation to be reversed.

OVERVIEW – NORTHWESTERN NEW MEXICO

THE AGRICULTURAL TRANSITION

In general terms, we have suggested that the demographic imbalances leading away from the hunter-gatherer strategy are best understood as an interaction between population segments that collect and *store* seasonally and those that do not. In the archeological record, then, it is the appearance of well-formed storage facilities which indicates that an evolutionary transition is already in motion.

In New Mexico these facilities are well-documented from about 500 B.C. onwards. Significantly, the Talus Village BM-II occupation near Durango, Colorado indicates that storage facilities, rather than ceramics, are the critical artifact of an increasing sedentism. The late Archaic/BM-II period requires substantially more investigation than it has received, as do the distribution of *Oshara* tradition lithic assemblages when compared to the Cochise. Since both the space requirements and the logistic demands of the two systems are eventually so different, we are required to know whether the greater space demands of the hunting-gathering regime were met primarily in highland, more heavily wooded areas. Tentative evidence from the Rio Grande and Zuni highlands suggests this to be the case.

The Basketmaker III period is still not well understood. Why, for instance, have we fairly large villages dated to the A.D. 400-600 period, followed by more modest village size, or suspected lacunae, in occupational sequences? In Chapter V it is obvious that this pattern also occurs in the Mogollon area. Moreover, why has the *Rosa* sequence received so little widespread attention? Even accepting the difficulties in establishing clearly isolated phase dates from Los Pinos through Piedra/Arboles, it is most striking to us that the sequence is quite like that generally accepted for the Mogollon tradition.

Table III.16

THE NAVAJO RESERVOIR SEQUENCE
(All data from Dittert, Hester and Eddy 1961)

1. LOS PINOS PHASE: A.D. 1-400
[Contemporaneous with BM-II occupation at Talus Village, Durango]

[Pine Lawn?] *   This phase is characterized by cobble ringed, shallow depression houses, *larger* than those of Talus Village. Jacal surface units are associated. The period is largely *pre-ceramic* (Dittert, Hester and Eddy 1961:213-220).

[Georgetown?] *   Dendro dates for Talus Village range from A.D. 46 to A.D. 330, the majority falling in the late A.D. 200's to early 300's. The Los Pinos Phase is thought to fall into the latter Talus Village period, A.D. 300-500. Occupational evidence is not apparent again until about A.D. 700.

2. ROSA PHASE: A.D. 700 to about 900

[San Francisco?] *   Use of large, deep pithouses, 15-40 feet in diameter, associated with surface or subterranean jacal structures (smaller). One to seventeen pithouses are known per settlement. There is high variability in internal architectural features (presence/absence of hearths, benches, etc.). An unusually large house depression appears in villages. Local Brown and Gray wares are present.

3. PIEDRA PHASE: A.D. 900-?950

[Three Circle?] *   Semi-surficial pithouses, cobble or slab-based walls, more *village* occupations (over six units). Pithouses become *smaller* and *shallower*. At each village there is an unusually large depression. There is an *upstream* settlement shift during this phase. These pithouses are increasingly rectangular.

4. ARBOLES PHASE: A.D. 950?-1050

[Mimbres?] *   Surface masonry pueblos; most occupation *had moved away from* the Navajo Reservoir district proper. (Is this like the suggested Mangus Phase dispersal?)

* Mogollon cultural phases are suggested as comparable. See Chapter V.

As one reads Chapter V (Mimbres), recall this brief sketch and compare it to the Mogollon data. Bear in mind the difficulty of agreeing on dates for the Mogollon sequence, the inconsistent presence of ceramics at early pithouse (Pine-Lawn) occupations, similar trends in pithouse size, and the proposed population decline of the A.D. 500-700 period (Martin and Plog 1973). Perhaps we should continue to pursue basic comparisons between these two areas of occupation as a major theme in southwestern prehistory.

THE CHACOAN SYSTEM

The Chacoan system has been characterized as an *in situ* expansion from the late Basketmaker III/P-I period, when movement into open basin settings, away from the highland periphery, took place. It has been argued that agriculture was so unstable as an adaptation that many different pockets of productive activity had to become interconnected in order to overcome localized crop/rainfall failures. We suggest also that this economic network began to develop over a wide area in the basin between A.D. 850 and 900. By the advent of the P-II period, a number of major productive nodes began to expand. Such a system probably operated on an increasingly small margin of surplus, as the sheer rate of increase in size outstripped increased production regionally. As the system collapsed sometime after A.D. 1100, much population moved outward to the periphery of the basin, causing dislocations in highland areas. We point out again that the peaks of Mesa Verdean development (Hayes 1964) came both *before* and *after* the apex of Chacoan development. In a classificatory sense we believe the Chaco system could be characterized as Terminal P-II or P-II *Classic* to distinguish it from later Mesa Verdean reoccupation, or P-III.

POST CHACO

In the highlands surrounding the basin, including the Rio Grande and Cebolleta Mesa areas, there are abrupt population peaks at A.D. 1150-1200. Associated with these is an interesting sequence of events. Pithouse occupations reappear in the Gallina highlands, the Rio Grande and the Cebolleta Mesa area. In Chapter IV, the reader will note, they also appear in the Reserve area (Apache Creek Phase) and (Chapter V) in the Sierra Blanca region (Late Glencoe/Early Lincoln Phases). This *late* pithouse phenomenon is a prelude to the P-III masonry Pueblo occupation *in every major highland area of New Mexico*. It is, in fact, at least as good a *horizon marker* for the A.D. 1125-1175 period as are ceramic seriations which, in any case, become controversial for the period about A.D. 1150.

But why? Is it as we have proposed? Are remaining highland populations stressed under the space requirements of semi-nomadic basin populations moving outward? If so, why the apparent A.D. 1000-1100 occupational hiatus in the highlands? Are these truly highland hunters-gatherers under space pressure to become more sedentary, hence the pithouses? Or, are they lowland populations returning to the highlands? If so, why would there be a 50-75 year time lag before masonry construction is taken up again? At the moment, it can be argued either way.

Finally, it was suggested that hunter-gatherer populations moved into the San Juan Basin at this time (A.D. 1100-1300) because agriculturalists could not maintain a stable adaptive base without the economically widely-connected Chacoan network, or one similar. That is, agriculture was dependent itself on the organizational structure. Some scholars will counter that it was Mesa Verdean population that moved in. We respond: not immediately, not for long (about 50 years *at most*) and, judging from their site locations, they were very nervous folks. Since the Chacoan population was at least three generations gone, just who were Mesa Verdean people watching over their shoulders? Other Mesa Verdeans? Not likely, since A.D. 1200-1300 masonry sites along the tier of heaviest Mesa Verdean occupation (the San Juan River) show no such defensive locations. Some who style themselves theoreticians might care to argue that one must *prove* independently that a site is defensively located. In view of the nearly 100 foot climb up a free-standing butte to CGP-54 (Reher 1977a) and other similar localities, we merely invoke the principle or *theorem of least effort (or cost)* which is currently in vogue.

We specifically suggest Athabaskan movement into the basin as early as A.D. 1150-1250, although we do not necessarily argue that the distinctive ethnic or material attributes of Navajo society emerge for yet another century or two.

GENERAL PATTERNS

In the Rio Grande we have pointed out the altitude (and ecozonal) shifts apparent in the Cochiti/Pajarito region from BM-II to P-V times. The data prior to P-II occupation are too modest to be more than suggestive. From A.D. 1100 onward, the general pattern is reasonably clear. The P-III period is largely an upland adaptation with a late downhill P-III/P-IV shift. Though the P-III site setting data could be interpreted to indicate an occupation split between higher and lower elevation at some given point within the phase, we are disinclined to that viewpoint, because of the greater tendency of multiple occupations of P-III and P-IV components to cluster in settings under 6,000 feet. The theme of elevational shifts recurs throughout the volume, primarily because it is a recurring topic in the vast literature on New Mexico archeology. While the A.D. 1100-1300 period is of a complexity no one has yet completely penetrated, a general uphill shift, followed by either complete or near abandonment of *forest* settings by P-IV (A.D. 1300-1325) times, is a general feature of the archeological record.

Changes in room size are systematic, and, in their totality, form a striking pattern. Changes between major phases are *always* associated with changing room size. Dramatically decreasing room size signals the onset of a new *Classic* period, whether in the Rio Grande or in the Mimbres. Increasing diversity between large and small in room size signals the *power phase* of a rapidly developing system. Increasing room size with little differentiation (low coefficient of variation, if you like) signals a *survivor* pattern, or more properly this is an *efficiency* phase. In this sense the Mesa Verdean reoccupation (small rooms) of the San Juan Basin is distinct from the P-III occupation of the Rio Grande.

While the specific reasons for changes in room size are not yet understood by us, these general characterizations seem useful and, because they are still speculative, will attract additional attention to the subject. Martin and Plog (1973) suggest that decreasing room size over time has to do with a shift to nuclear family organization. We do not deny the logic of this statement and, in fact, pursue it in the overview in Chapter V. Nonetheless, we point out that decreasing room size may also inform highly on the adaptive *health* of a system. Specifically, we propose that room size will be inversely proportional to the rate of infant mortality, as derived from burial data, in a general time period. That is, the systemic stress of maintaining equilibrium in population levels ultimately *drives* the system to stabilize its adaptive strategem. Since small room size is the harbinger of a *Classic* period, we argue that the increased adaptive complexity (technologically or economically) that archeologists recognize anecdotally in such *Classic* assemblages is the result of such stress reduction strategies. This pattern, we argue, forms the very basis of the *power drive*. Reread Chapter II if you are unsure of the form of the argument. We realize that the argument is unorthodox, yet we wish to make clear that we are not talking about changes in room size in any one site [though we can cite evidence for general progress from small to large rooms, followed by increasing diversity in size within a single site (McGimsey 1980:184, Sketches A-H)].

The practical difficulty in working with a variable like changing room size is that we do not know, in many cases, precisely which archeological remains in a region belong together temporally, ethnically or economically. In spite of these difficulties, the patterns appear strong enough between major time periods to permit further research. We hope someone will accept our suggestion to determine how percentage of infant burials covaries with room sizes in some reasonable sample of sites.

Again, we point out (as have others over the years — Wimberly, Eidenbach and Betancourt 1979, among others) that most occupations in the Southwest are not continual. Rather, they are periodic at a given site. The patterns of tree-ring dates have never been properly studied as a single body of literature. We pointed out in the Rio Grande, for instance, that triple episodes of construction seemed a common pattern. We further point out that clusters from many well-dated sites seem to fall either 20-30 years apart or 50-60 years apart [Smiley, Stubbs and Bannister 1953; see p. 22, LA 114 (30 and 60 year); 18, LA 27 (30 year); p. 16, LA 5 (30 year), and so on]. How does one account for such patterns? Are these evidence in the archeological record of some deeper rhythm in the scheme of things? Are we observing something like the *long economic cycles* first described by the Russian, Kondratieff? These are usually characterized in textbooks as *50 year cycles*, whereas the mean of the three documented is actually 51.6 years, with variance from 44-58 years. Is this mean close enough to the Meso-American calendric cycle of 52 years to evoke interest (Rostow 1980)?

In the San Juan Basin (Marshall, Stein, Loose and Novotny 1979), sites such as Pueblo Pintado (A.D. 1060-61), Kin Klizhin (A.D. 1087), etc. may have been constructed within an extremely short period of time. These contrast with sites such as Kin Bineola (A.D. 942-43 and A.D. 1111-1120), Aztec West (A.D. 1111-1120), Una Vida (A.D. 850-950 and A.D. 1050). Clearly, sites constructed at once, with no prior occupation, and those having the multiple construction episodes, should be analyzed very carefully as comparative data classes. It can be argued that association with road features or soil groups, or with other factors, will vary between the two classes of sites in some way critical to our understanding of the Chacoan system as a whole. Too few of these sites are dated now to resolve matters, but perhaps we could propose that sites which really were constructed in one short episode might be in less productive agricultural soils along major roadways and did, indeed, function as transport centers.

Finally, why the 50 year spread in clusters of dates? What is happening in the San Juan Basin *between* the periods of these clusters? Do we come to discover that the bulk of small outlying (or isolated) P-II occupations have dates which also fall *between* the construction episodes at major sites? Let us propose that they do so cluster (perhaps about A.D. 975, 1025, 1075 and 1125). We might then argue that the history of the Chacoan system was one of episodal aggregation and dispersal — the terminal dispersal following cessation of construction at the large centers.[1] Such a model might conform quite closely to the general view taken by Cordell and Plog (1979), who argue an unstable Anasazi system, prone to fluctuating settlement patterns and displaying only modest population growth after A.D. 900 or 1000.

On the other hand, what if smaller P-II settlements (such as those recorded on the CGP survey) dated narrowly *within* the range of major construction episodes at the *Bonito Phase* sites? We should then have more of a case for population increase as an intensifying force on the system.[1] Since it could be argued that the prelude to abandonment would occasion the creation of many dispersed sites shortly after A.D. 1100 in either case, the A.D. 1060-1080 period would provide the proper perspective. Since the period from A.D. 1060 to 1080 was apparently one of both major construction and population aggregation, it would be unlikely for many isolated clusters of P-II (Hosta Butte Phase, we suppose) sites to date narrowly to this period *unless* there was also an episode of significant population increase prior to it. We

---

[1] Dr. Mark E. Harlan (University of New Mexico) advises us that excavations in the Pittsburgh-Midway project (McKinley County, New Mexico) indicate contemporaneity between small P-II sites and a nearby Chacoan outlier. Is this pattern demonstrable elsewhere?

will come to know which was the case as more investigators spread their interests beyond the largest sites, and more come to grips with the need to establish tight temporal control within major phases, rather than primarily between them.

Finally, the aggregating tendency is again pronounced during the P-IV period, some spectacularly large sites having been constructed. The focus of development shifted eastward, at least temporarily, into the Galisteo Basin. Those sites suggest a well-developed network in ceramic trade, as both Chupadero B/W, White Mountain redwares, and late Zuni area polychromes are also present. Nonetheless, it is primarily the settlements in the major river settings which endured, at least episodally, to the P-V horizon.

Photo 4: An excavated Coalition period site on the Pajarito Plateau near Los Alamos, New Mexico. This site was excavated by the late F.C.V. Worman, then archeologist at Los Alamos Scientific Laboratory. Photograph courtesy of F.C.V. Worman.

Photo 5: From the mouth of Bat Cave, looking north, across the Plains of San Augustin. Bat Cave, excavated by Herb Dick (1965), yielded numerous perishable artifacts dating from pre-ceramic periods to later Mogollon periods. The general area also contains Paleo-Indian material up to the recent historic periods. Photograph by S.L. Peckham, courtesy of the Museum of New Mexico, Santa Fe.

Photo 6: Gigantes Ruin, near El Morro National Monument. This is a late P-III and early P-IV site. An interesting feature at this site is a hole which extends through the cliff at the back of the pueblo. It is assumed that the rooms of the pueblo at one time enclosed the hole. View is to the north. Photograph by S.L. Peckham, courtesy of the Museum of New Mexico, Santa Fe.

Chapter IV
WEST-CENTRAL NEW MEXICO
(Mount Taylor and Socorro Areas)

INTRODUCTION

In some respects, these regions promise the most fascinating field of inquiry in the archeology of New Mexico. It is here that the Anasazi tradition of northwestern New Mexico is said to blend with the Mogollon of southwestern New Mexico.

Two federal overviews of the area have been prepared and published. These are *Cultural Resources Overview, Mt. Taylor Area, New Mexico* (Tainter and Gillio 1980a) and *Cultural Resources Overview, Socorro Area, New Mexico* (Berman 1979). Berman is available from the U.S. Superintendent of Documents, Washington, D.C., and both are very handy additions to the library shelf. Berman's is more documentary in nature, while the other is more theoretical. Since only Tainter's portion of the Tainter and Gillio volume is of interest to archeologists, it is henceforth cited as "(Tainter 1980a)". Tainter, in particular, has a clear written style and straightforward way of explaining his theoretical positions. This chapter is, like others, meant to be read in conjunction with these two documents.

In this region of New Mexico, the Colorado plateau province meets the basin and range province. The area is characterized by remarkable topographic diversity. Altitude ranges from about 4,500 feet to over 10,000 feet. In the upland areas substantial forest zones occur. In the lower forest elevations these are mixed pinyon-juniper with some Ponderosa pine. As elevation increases, the admixture of Ponderosa also increases (Transitional zone). In the upper zones, spruce and fir dominate (Canadian zone), while in the highest regions, Alpine complexes dominate, the higher mountains (such as south Baldy) rising above the timberline. The lower elevations of western and central Socorro County consist primarily of the grassy plains of San Agustin, an internal basin characterized by high erosion and poor drainage. The lowest elevations of western Socorro County include the famous Jornada del Muerto, a hot, water-scarce region of Sonoran vegetative complexes — a semi-arid desert environment.

The cultural development of this region occurred primarily in the upper Sonoran and transitional zones. Early Mogollon development resulted in village life in the lower reaches of the Gila National Forest between 6,000 and 6,500 feet (see Willey 1966:184, 191 for photographs) by A.D. 200-300. On the other hand, the Mt. Taylor area, along the south rim of the San Juan Basin, has yielded little evidence of settled life until sometime after A.D. 500 or 600. Temperature and rainfall vary dramatically with altitude. Major streams include the Puerco of the west, the Puerco of the east, the Salado, the Rio Grande and the uppermost reaches of the Gila and San Francisco drainages in Catron County (see Map IV.1).

The history of investigations in this area is long and distinguished. Nonetheless, these investigations have focused primarily on the Mogollon occupations of Catron County and the Zuni (Cibola) complexes of southern McKinley and parts of Valencia County. Substantial portions of the region have never been surveyed and, as in other areas, excavation has been rather selective. Thus, not all cultural periods are equally well known. A major theme in research has been the transition to agriculture (Bat, Cordova, Tularosa caves and Pine Lawn phase occupations) and, secondly, the nature of Anasazi-Mogollon contacts (the Acoma culture province).

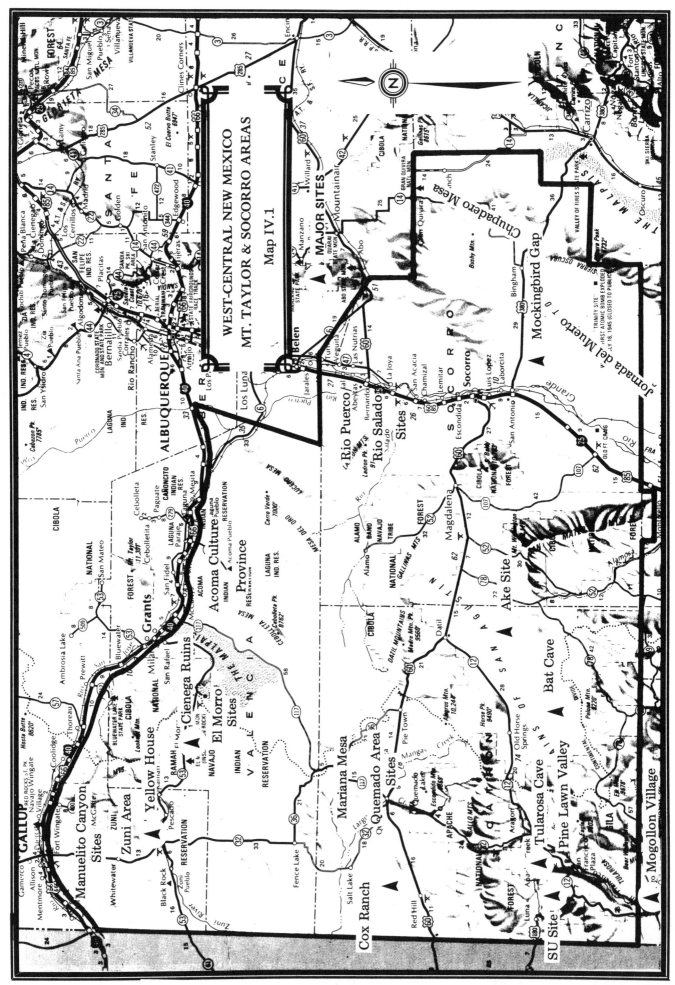

Dr. Tainter has prepared an excellent overview of the Mt. Taylor region. There are two fundamental theses which he pursues throughout: 1) formal similarities and differences in the archeological record cannot be taken as *prima facie* evidence of corresponding ethnic (or socio-cultural) differences in prehistoric populations; 2) the principle of minimum effort (the least cost principle) is broadly applicable in predicting human behavior.

The issues he raises do, indeed, strike very deeply at our understanding of the archeological record. In the first case, at issue is the degree to which one can directly observe cultural (and historical) behavior in archeological remains. The second issue involves the nature of human behavior itself. Since Tainter has provided a summary of culture history in the region that can hardly be improved upon, we will not reoutline the cultural sequence at length here. Rather, we have reproduced the local phase sequences and dates for the region and will provide only a short sketch of important trends (see Tables IV.A-IV.3).

You will notice that very late Puebloan development characterizes both areas (A.D. 650-850). From about A.D. 1000 to 1250, there is a hiatus in occupation in the El Morro district, but not at Zuni. After A.D. 1300, El Morro is again abandoned. Some areas at Zuni are also abandoned but a few continue to be occupied to the Historic period. Now let us turn to the nature of Mogollon-Anasazi features in the archeological record.

It is Tainter's (1980) position that the Mogollon-Anasazi contact zone is more properly understood as an area of economic (and, we presume, political) interaction between *localized populations* that seek to maximize access to ecologically diverse areas and resources. In a paper presented at the 1980 Mogollon Conference, Tainter (1980) presents burial data from the Puerco Valley (New Mexico-Arizona) suggesting local population to have been morphologically (therefore genetically) homogeneous from roughly A.D. 750 to 1250. These data are suggested to indicate that actual population migrations are not an explanation for the mixed archeological characteristics of the Anasazi-Mogollon contact zones during this period. These *mixed* characteristics are prominent in the work of Ruppe (1953) and Dittert (1959) who identified a distinctive *Acoma cultural Province* where square kivas (Mogollon) were mixed with round (Anasazi), and brownwares (Mogollon) were mixed in assemblages with graywares (Anasazi). There is also discussion of kiva orientation (N-S, Anasazi; E-W, Mogollon), etc. (see also, Ruppe and Dittert 1952, 1953).

While one must accept Tainter's point that these differences in archeological traits cannot generally be demonstrated, in an empirical way, to covary with ethnic or linguistic affiliation, it is also the case that neither do morphologic similarities or differences in burial populations demonstrate nor counter the point.

One's language, material habits and ethnic identification are quite independent, in theory, of one's genetic attributes. One need not look beyond the 100 million or so sons and daughters of non-Anglo-Saxon immigrants to this nation for a demonstration. It is also demonstrable, however, that very distinct physical or racial differences between interacting populations can contribute to, or enhance, a tendency to maintain separate linguistic and ethnic identity, as well as in less biologically interactive populations. Thus, we note the tendency among Asian populations with whom we interact economically (abroad) and as co-residents of our own neighborhoods to maintain a high degree of ethnic, linguistic and biological integrity. In short, a clear case against migrating population to account for supposed Anasazi-Mogollon distinctions cannot be made from burial data. That is, it cannot *usually* be demonstrated that the formal attributes of the archeological record in a given locale have either a genetic or ethnic-linguistic explanation.

Table IV.A — AGRICULTURALIST SEQUENCES — MT. TAYLOR DISTRICT
(After Tainter 1980a:96)

	EASTERN SUBAREA (Puerco Drainage)	SOUTH-CENTRAL SUBAREA (Acoma)	NORTH-CENTRAL SUBAREA (San Mateo Valley)	NORTHWESTERN SUBAREA* (Puerco-Manuelito Canyon) (Gallup & West)	SOUTHWESTERN SUBAREA** (Zuni & El Morro)	PECOS CLASSIFICATION (General)
A.D. 1600					Historic	
1500		Cubero				
1400						Pueblo IV
1300	Mesa Verde	Kowina		Kintiel	Late Formative (El Muerto) (Scribe S at El Morro)	
1200	Late Chaco D / Early Chaco D / Late Chaco C		Ceramic 7			Pueblo III
1100	Chaco C / Early Chaco C	Pilares	Ceramic 6	Houck		
1000	B/C Transition	Cebolleta / Red Mesa	Ceramic 5	Wingate / Red Mesa	Middle Formative	Pueblo II
900	Chaco B		Ceramic 4	Kiatuthlanna		
800	Late Chaco A	Kiatuthlanna	Ceramic 3	White Mound		Pueblo I
700	Chaco A	White Mound			Early Formative	
600			Basketmaker ?	Lupton/La Plata		
500	Trujillo/Early Chaco A					Basketmaker III
A.D. 400						

*   Weaver's (1978) sequence is presented here, rather than Gladwin's (1945), because it contains more recent data, and because Gladwin's has generated so much controversy.
** Dates after Marshall and other (1979:257)

122

Table IV.1
ZUNI AND RAMAH—EL MORRO AREAS*

Developmental Sequence		
Local Phases/ Pecos Equivalent	Settlement, Trade, etc.	? Ceramics
Historic/ Late P-IV and P-V (1450—present)	Few sites, large to small. Most along major drainages & lower elevations than during 1200's. Proto-historic Zuni cities of Cibola founded. New ceramic complexes (glazes & polychromes). No further occupation of El Morro. Only spotty occupation in Zuni Reservation area.	M, N, O, P, Q — starts with Pinnawa Poly & ends with Zuni Poly (after 1800).
Late Formative/ Late P-III and P-IV (1150—1450) (Scribe S & El Muerto at El Morro)	Increase in site size; sites move to higher elevations (to east) then later to lower elevations south & west of Nutria/Pescado drainages. At A.D. 1250 El Morro area again populated—dramatic increase in population—sites clustered in *defensive* settings. At 1276 smaller sites abandoned & few large sites (500 rooms) constructed. These sites abandoned at A.D. 1300.	Ceramic groups G, H and I, J, K, L
Middle Formative/ Late P-II to Early P-III (ca. A.D. 1000-1150)	Settlement shifted to bottomlands along major drainages. Multistory masonry pueblos w/rectangular kivas constructed. At El Morro there was a hiatus in occupation during this period.	Ceramic groups E, F
Early Formative/ BM-III — Early P-II (A.D. 650-1000)	Small pithouse villages gradually replaced by above-ground architecture. Sites located in many settings but highest elevations avoided. Anasazi ceramic assemblage. No Mogollon redwares but Forestdale smudged is found. Pop. pressure during P-I forced expansion to marginal areas by Early P-II.	White Mound B/W Lino Gray Kiatuthlanna B/W Kana'a Neck Banded
Basketmaker II	No materials recorded. No pueblo occupation at Zuni prior to A.D. 650. None at El Morro prior to ca. A.D. 850.	Ceramic groups B/C/ D.
Archaic/Paleo Indian	Not adequately documented in either locality. A few isolated points have been found.	None

* Data from Watson, LeBlanc, and Redman (n.d.) and LeBlanc (1978) and others cited in Tainter (1980a:90-92) and Marshall 1978 (in Hunter-Anderson 1978)

? See Marshall's ceramic stratification in Hunter-Anderson (1978:31-41, esp. p. 31)

Table IV.2
THE ACOMA CULTURE PROVINCE*

Acoma/Cebolleta Mesa Phases/Pecos Equivalent	Settlement, Trade, etc.	+ Typical Diagnostic Ceramics (see Table IV.3)
Acoma (1600-present) P-V	Historic Acoma & settlement along Rio San Jose	Hawikah glazes; Ashiwi & Acoma poly's
Cubero (1400-1600) P-IV — P-V	Acoma area & Acoma Pueblo settled. Few sites survived Kowina phase.	Pinnawa & Kwakina glazes
Kowina (1200-1400) Late P-III to P-IV	Pop. aggregated into large sites on high mesas or woodlands. Major change Great Kivas in sites. Pop. intrusion from SW inferred (Mogollon)	(Kowina Ruin = 300 rooms) Tularosa B/W; Kowina B/W; St. John's polychrome
Pilares (1100-1200) Early P-III	Less settlement in higher topographic divisions. At end of period settlement shifts to flat-topped mesas. Sharp decrease in external trade. Northern & southern districts diverge (masonry vs. adobe architecture). Highest population.	Cebolleta B/W, local Tularosa B/W
Cebolleta (950-1100) P-II	Transition to larger sites. Late in period mountain meadows are heavily occupied. Cebolleta B/W indicates disruption of Chacoan influence. Proportion of brownwares increases. Great diversity in ceramic trade.	Cebolleta B/W
Red Mesa (870-950) Late P-I/Early P-II	Sites in higher topographic settings vacated. Early jacal surface units; later L-shaped masonry roomblocks (over 15 rooms). Ceramic trade differs between the two kinds of sites.	Red Mesa B/W Socorro B/W
Kiatuthlanna (800-870) P-I	Sites located on secondary drainages, mesa tops, etc. Pithouses w/surface structures. Increasing use of linear or crescentic jacal surface units. Brownwares increase. (Mogollon influence assumed.)	Kiatuthlanna B/W
White Mound (700-800) BM-III—P-I Transitional	Sites in wide variety of settings. Small pithouse settlements w/some surface rooms & cliffside shelters. Few sites recorded. Few brownwares or absent.	White Mound B/W
Lobo (1800 B.C.-A.D. 700)	Late hunter-gatherer stage. Late Archaic artifacts found w/P-I ceramics at north end of Cebolleta Mesa.	
San Jose (3000 B.C.-1800 B.C.)	As described by Irwin-Williams (1973). In situ development from earlier periods.	

* Data from Dittert (1959)
+ See following table for complete ceramic assemblage.

Table IV.3
CERAMIC CHARACTERISTICS OF TEMPORAL DIVISIONS IN THE ACOMA AREA*

Phase	Ceramics
LOBO 1800 B.C.–A.D. 700	Aceramic.
WHITE MOUND A.D. 700-800	White Mound B/W, Lino Grey. Intrusives: Alma Plain, Alma Neck Banded, redwares.
KIATUTHLANNA A.D. 800-870	Kiatuthlanna B/W, Kana-a Grey. Intrusives: San Juan Redware, Alma Plain, Alma Neck Banded.
RED MESA A.D. 870-950	Red Mesa B/W, Socorro B/W, Kana-a Grey, Exuberant Corrugated. Intrusives: Wingate B/R, Alma Scored, San Francisco Red, Forestdale Smudged, Plain Brown ware. Pilares Brown near end of period.
CEBOLLETA A.D. 950-1100	Cebolleta B/W, Socorro B/W, Kana-a Grey, Exuberant Corrugated, Tohatchi Banded, Northern Grey Corrugated, Pilares Banded. Intrusives: Gallup, Escavada, Puerco varieties of Puerco B/W, Reserve B/W, Kwahe'e B/W, Wingate B/R, Puerco B/R, Forestdale Smudged, Starkweather Smudged Decorated.
PILARES A.D. 1100-1200	Cebolleta B/W, Tularosa B/W (Acoma variety), Tularosa B/W (Tularosa variety), Socorro B/W, St. Johns Polychrome, Pilares Banded, Pilares Fine Banded, Los Lunas Smudged. Intrusives: Puerco B/W, Snowflake B/W, possibly Tularosa B/W (Tularosa variety) and St. Johns Polychrome.
KOWINA A.D. 1200-1400	Acoma & Tularosa varieties of Tularosa B/W, Kowina B/W, Kowina Indented, St. Johns Polychrome, St. Johns Polychrome with glaze paint, North Plains B/R, North Plains Polychrome, Kowina B/R & Polychrome, Pinnawa & Wallace Polychromes, Pilares Fine Banded, Los Lunas Smudged. Intrusives: Early Klageto B/W, Springville Polychrome, Pinedale B/R & Polychrome, Klageto B/Y & Polychrome, Heshotauthla Polychrome, Fourmile Polychrome, Pinnawa R/W, Reserve Plain Corrugated, Houck Polychrome, Querino Polychrome, Mesa Verde B/W, Reserve Indented Corrugated, Tularosa Patterned Corrugated.
CUBERO A.D. 1400-1600	Pinnawa Glaze-on-white, Kwakina Glaze-Polychrome, Pinnawa Glaze-Polychrome, Acoma Glazes, Northern Grey Corrugated, Kowina Indented, Indented Brownwares. Intrusives: Matsaki Polychrome, early Rio Grande Glazes.
ACOMA 1600–Present	Hawikuh Glaze-on-red, Hawikuh Glaze-Polychrome, Ashiwi Polychrome, modern Acoma Polychromes. Intrusives: Ashiwi & Zuni Polychromes, Tewa Polychrome, Laguna types, Dinetah Utility (rare).

* after Dittert (1959), and as appears in Tainter (1980a:59)

In a world in which *in situ* population growth is slow, populations are isolated, and intermarriage and trade are infrequent, one might find the distribution of genetically distinct population to covary with certain attributes of the archeological record. In such a case it would seem reasonable to infer ethnic and/or linguistic differences also. In most cases, however, the distribution of the genetic characteristics of geographic races is clinal, and rather few of these characteristics can actually be demonstrated from skeletal materials. In spite of these difficulties, a broad-scale study of burial data from the Chaco Canyon area south to the Mimbres area and from east-central Arizona to the eastern flanks of the Sangre de Cristo, Manzanos and Sierra Blanca Mountains would be highly informative. It would be important to know if there is evidence for *any* biologically (at least morphologically) distinctive pockets of local population west of the plains after about A.D. 500.

It was, of course, an early and important theme in the study of Southwestern prehistory to determine what distinctive (racial) populations might exist in the area. A great deal was initially made of the cephalic indices of various skeletal populations. Most archeologists will recall that a major diagnostic feature separating the BM-III period from the Pueblo I was the occurrence of round-headed physical types in burial populations. Later, it was realized that cranial deformation (from cradle boards) accounted largely for the differences in cephalic index, and the Pueblo period ceased to be viewed as an influx of distinctive populations displacing the original Basketmaker (Wormington 1947).

Since the attribute of cephalic index cannot be determined from archeological survey, in any case, different diagnostic features for the same BM-III/P-I phases came to be determined somewhat differently from excavation as opposed to survey. In survey, the diagnostic attributes of the P-I period depended on both architecture and ceramics. Slab-lined cists, ephemeral traces of cobble-based jacal surface structures, and few deep pithouses, coupled with the general absence (or scarcity) of painted wares, would be likely to receive an Early P-I designation. The same ceramic assemblage found in association with many distinct pithouse depressions would most likely be noted as a *late BM-III* village. One cannot help but wonder how many sites in the Laboratory of Anthropology survey files remain diagnosed as P-I from excavations of 40 or more years ago on the basis of cranial deformation in skeletal remains. One cannot also help but wonder how many sites have been relegated to one or another category during survey on the presence or absence of 3 or 4 sherds of White Mound or Kiatuthlanna Black-on-white. At any rate, it has been many years since much of the available skeletal material was analyzed (some of it never has been). It would be extremely valuable to do so, for the issue of analyzing recently excavated burials is becoming increasingly sensitive.

A second point to raise about the Mogollon-Anasazi interaction sphere has to do with Tainter's suggestion that interacting populations will style cultural symbols to enhance that interaction. Specifically, he refers to kiva shape in addition to other attributes. While this may be plausible, we suppose that a fundamental change in ceremonial structures would also imply a fundamental change in ceremonial/religious ideology. The general form of Tainter's argument would account, as an example, for the distribution of mosques and the Muslim faith in black Africa where, generally, no great migrations took place. In this historical case, the major interaction involved slavery, and the actual adoption of Islam in smaller black villages (and among nomads) was a rather long, gradual process.

Here we have a case for relative racial stability in the culturally (and archeologically, in the distribution of mosques) transformed population and cultural/archeological stability in the Arab population, while a racially heterogeneous population is brought in (later traded in the European world). While one might make any number of ecological/demographic/economic arguments to explain the Arab slave trade in black Africa, it is the case that *History* provides us a model in which a migrated population (admittedly, the migration was forced) is introduced to an archeologically unchanged context (at least regarding religious architecture) where the racially unchanged population adopts the altered religious architecture. It is also the case that in some parts of sub-Saharan Africa the local adoption of Muslim ways was more pronounced in the upper strata of society. Tainter makes a similar point in a different way.

He cites Wade's (1970) homogeneous (from A.D. 750-1250) burial data from an adjacent portion of Arizona in concluding that formal characteristics of the archeological record vary without evidence for actual population incursion. We modify the point to suggest that until it is demonstrated that the population of west central New Mexico was *not relatively* homogeneous over a wide region after A.D. 750-800, the presence of a homogeneous population in any given area would not inform very greatly on population movement one way or another.

Returning to the Anasazi-Mogollon contact zone, then, it seems essential to know precisely the distribution of kiva morphology and masonry versus adobe architecture, etc. over a wide region. We should then have to know the distribution of ceramic frequencies as well. If square kivas, for instance, were adapted to promote Anasazi interaction with the Mogollon, they should first appear in larger sites where local elites cared to promote the economic interaction. Are square and round kivas contemporaneous within a given archeological site? Indeed, how many sites in the entire region have both? Does the distribution of such features vary not just north-south as Ruppe (1953) and Dittert (1959) suggest, but also by average site size? Tainter (1980a:60) suggests that the distribution of brownwares in the Los Veteados district (southernmost Cebolleta Mesa) could be argued to involve an intrusive population there during the Cebolleta phase (A.D. 950-1100) though he favors the opposite conclusion. That is, a small number of sites in that area are characterized by very high percentages of brownwares, while a larger number of sites display smaller percentages. What are the average sizes of these sites? Do they vary at all by discernible architectural differences (as shown by survey)? Finally, the Cebolleta phase is dated from A.D. 950-1100. This is narrow if one is thinking in terms of 2,000 years of prehistory. It is chronologically gross, however, if one is thinking in terms of changing economic and ideological patterns. How do we even know whether many of these sites are genuinely contemporaneous? How does one account, as well, for the distribution of adobe architecture? Is it not more likely found in the lower, drier, sandier portions of the Acoma culture province, and how contemporaneous is it with masonry materials?

In summary, we have a vast archeological problem presented us in west central New Mexico. The problem is currently more powerful than the precise data we can bring to bear on it over a wide region. Some of these data are available but untabulated, other data can be gotten through additional survey (ceramic, site setting and gross architectural features), while some information can be obtained only through excavation (temporal control and additional burial data). We have included the Mt. Taylor and Socorro districts in the same chapter, partly because we think the Anasazi-Mogollon boundary along the Rio Salado (and southern Cebolleta Mesa) is only half the story.

In Catron and Socorro Counties, the Old Mogollon tradition also begins to undergo substantial change and subregional differentiation about A.D. 800-900. There, it is argued, the introduction of the black-on-white pottery styles (Reserve and Tularosa phases), coupled with increasing differentiation in masonry construction, indicates increasing Anasazi influence. LeBlanc (1979) suggests that the Reserve-Tularosa phases, one-hundred-odd miles south of Cebolleta Mesa, are largely non-Mogollon in character. Nonetheless, he argues that the Mimbres area to the south of the Mogollon Mountains remains culturally intact as a Mogollon entity until abandonment of the Mimbres sites around A.D. 1150. Nonetheless, the Classic B/W pottery and above-ground masonry architecture in the Mimbres area intrude on the clarity of the argument.

Rejoining Tainter's argument (1980:8), we see that the Chacoan interaction sphere extends to maximum ecological diversity in the northern Cebolleta Mesa region. This argument has substantial appeal, for it could indeed account for the currently recorded distribution of Chacoan outliers, though Chacoan ceramics are more widespread. However, in view of the allegedly increasing Anasazi character (let us assume this also to be merely an interaction sphere rather than intrusive population) of the highlands (Reserve Phase) along the southern periphery of the plains of San Agustin, one is required to ask just who is maximizing ecological diversity.

Clearly, one cannot have both Anasazi *intrusion* to the south and Mogollon *intrusion* to the north at roughly A.D. 900 (though some see only Mogollon influence to the north after A.D. 1100) without also assuming that the San Agustin Plains and surrounding highlands were the focus of yet another demographic/economic network from A.D. 800 or 900 until abandonment, a network that would have acted quite similarly to the Chacoan system though on a more modest scale. The plains of San Agustin are neither so vast nor so well watered as either the periphery of the San Juan Basin or the Mimbres area (formed by the Gila, San Francisco and Mimbres valleys). Thus, one could suppose that the lower elevations of the San Agustin Plains were not as attractive for agriculture (few permanent streams) prior to P-II times as other basin regions having more permanent water courses. Population in this portion of the Southwest is not thought to have been increasing dramatically until A.D. 800-900.

On the southern periphery of the San Agustin Plains, Mogollon development in the highlands begins about A.D. 250-300, while in the Cebolleta Mesa region, Laguna, and at Zuni, early Basketmaker remains are not recorded. Basketmaker occupation is thought to begin about A.D. 700 (White Mound phase) throughout most of the southern portion of Tainter's overview area. Though Tainter (1980a:68) indicates that Basketmaker II materials have recently been found on La Jara Mesa (Powell 1978) west of Mt. Taylor, early Basketmaker remains in the Mt. Taylor district must be counted as exceedingly rare. Though future survey and excavation could alter our perceptions of the archeological record in this respect, the case is currently good for continued hunter-gatherer presence in the Zuni highlands until A.D. 500 or 600, perhaps a bit longer in some areas. This brings us to the principle of least effort.

THE LATE HUNTER-GATHERER QUESTION IN THE MT. TAYLOR AREA

The continued existence of hunting-gathering populations, after others had been transformed to the agricultural strategy, is not quite the enigma it might appear at first glance. In Chapter II (Theoretical Perspective) we present a model of the transition to agriculture based on the interaction of the two subsistence strategies.

It seems clear that cultigens arrived in the west-central part of New Mexico by roughly 2000 B.C., or earlier. Yet, the first strong evidence for sedentism and nascent village life is usually taken to be the Basketmaker II and analogous occupations (Pine Lawn phase). Such occupations are found in Catron County, scattered about the central San Juan Basin and in the area of Albuquerque's West Mesa. In the upper Puerco drainage (Irwin-Williams 1973) this period is spanned by the En Medio Phase (800 B.C. — A.D. 400) and the Trujillo Phase (A.D. 400-600). They are, however, not well documented in the Mt. Taylor area.

The ethnographic record is replete with cases of hunters-gatherers who survived, concurrently with neighboring agriculturalists, into the historic eras of one or another part of the world. The several Apachean groups in the Southwest evidenced varying propensities for part-time agricultural pursuits (Basehart 1973) into historic times. It is usually suggested in the literature that they were *opportunistically* agricultural. That is, when environmental conditions were propitious, they practiced some agriculture. A more perceptive suggestion is that casual agriculture is practiced in times of poor hunting. Indeed, historic Mescalero Apache groups occasionally stole seed corn from Puebloan groups or Spanish settlers for planting (Basehart 1973).

The least effort or least cost principle, of course, predicts that there will be resistence to labor-intensive subsistence strategies. In many portions of the semiarid Southwest, agriculture was a very marginal pursuit over any substantial span of years. Any labor invested in crops would have failed to produce a return on labor in several years of each ten. An additional several years might produce only an even return on calories invested in agricultural labor. Under such circumstances, the only type of agriculture that would make sense, given relatively low population density, would be casually tended stands in a few more favored local areas. This is precisely the type of agriculture practiced by the historic Mescalero when it was practiced at all. It may have been the type practiced by late Archaic populations as well.

What is required for much of the Southwest, given the least effort principle, is not an explanation for the continued presence of hunters-gatherers, but, rather, an explanation for the adoption of agriculture to any degree at all.

There are several traditional anthropological arguments about agriculture that ought to be revised. 1) Agriculture is a high return strategy which is fairly secure, and it is either causatively (Boserup 1965) or possibilistically related to major population growth. It can easily be argued that uncertain rainfall cycles, small-cobbed Chapalote corn and only modest technological experience, lead to the conclusion that agriculture can be fragile, not very productive and would not support substantial population growth.

2) The principle of least effort is broadly applicable in modeling or predicting human behavior under several very constraining assumptions. The principle should read: *Given equal outcomes (or returns) under reasonably predictable circumstances and the choice of several alternative modes of achieving the outcome, the least cost solution will generally be selected.* Thus phrased, this principle does indeed predict a broad array of behavioral solutions to short-run problems. That is, decisions are made largely on the basis of short-term self-interest, as Cordell and Plog have recently argued (see Cordell and Plog 1979). It does not, however, predict or account for the facts of cultural evolution (nor of biological evolution, for that matter).

To understand why we make such a sweeping statement, one must consider the nature of the relationship actually expressed by the least cost principle. This principle says that when one holds the return constant, a way will be sought to lower the investment needed to achieve the given return. In other words, it predicts *efficiency* as the primary goal of human behavior (one can also hold the investment constant and increase the return — increased efficiency is still the result, though the available power will increase). Efficiency in the extreme, however, produces no available energy to do work. We are not just being esoteric here; classic hunters-gatherers are literally so efficient that they are nearly homeostatic. Population doesn't grow, technology and social organization are highly conservative – they adhere so tenaciously to the least cost principle that they have avoided major evolutionary change.

The course of cultural evolution, however, is one of succession by larger and more complex cultural systems. Energetically, these are more powerful. It is the case that cultural systems often seek a *great cost* solution to problems. In Chapter II we called this the power drive. For instance, it could be argued that the Federal Bureaucracy of the U.S. generally seeks a *most cost* solution to any given problem. This is not a gratuitous comment — the U.S. has been an enormously power-specialized system, and our bureaucracy has helped to maintain this specialization by inducing vast energy inputs to fuel the system. We are the locusts (see Chapter II) of the contemporary world.

Power-specialized behavior is induced by several conditions — intense competition, highly unpredictable circumstances ("work hard to save for a rainy day") and catastrophe ("I am working twenty-four hours a day and can't manage to stay even"). Or, as Wade (1970) astutely points out, at A.D. 1100 to maintain population levels women had to average six births apiece.

Intense competition does not, so far, appear to have been a feature of the archeological record until the placement of many BM-II sites in suggestively *defensive* situations (Bluff Site, Promontory Site, Hilltop Site -- Early Pithouse or Pine Lawn phase) about A.D. 250-350. We can presume, then, that the adoption of agriculture here was either a response to unpredictable circumstances or to misfortune. In Chapter II, we select minor misfortunes on the part of some in the Archaic population as the precipitating condition. We then combine the least cost principle with the great cost principle (i.e., power with efficiency) to model a series of subtle moves away from the preagricultural space/population balance. We rephrased these principles to reflect their underlying meaning: power versus efficiency.

In short, as early agriculturalists met with modest success, they opened up additional space to hunter-gatherer population expansion. In order to offset the demographic effects of periodic crop failures, agriculturalists increased fertility, though many babies may have starved as their mothers' milk dried up from inadequate diet. At the extreme, very rapid weight loss and/or a body weight to fat ratio of 22% or less in women dramatically increases irregularity of the menstrual cycle and inhibits normal ovulation. We don't think seasonal cycles of weight loss have been adequately pursued as a possible factor inhibiting fertility in hunter-gatherer female populations. The burial data Tainter cites are evidence of this attempt to maintain demographic power nearly a millenium later. With this kind of fertility, reduction in the causes of mortality results in explosive growth.

At any rate, those who pursued seasonal sedentism following an agricultural harvest, increasingly lost access to foraging landscape as nomadic population increased. This induced both increased storage in good years and, in bad years, increased trade with others in different locales who also stored. Is it possible that the development of rabbit fur and turkey feather blankets, etc. among Basketmaker populations of 500-1000 B.C. was partly a response to restricted hunting range? Or had the general population already grown so much as to make larger game generally unavailable for making garments?

We argue that there would have been little investment in labor to create permanent structures until general resource competition substantially prevented mobility, and made the protection of stored surpluses a consideration, and until agricultural population had stabilized, to a point at which labor became a less premium commodity. In order for the agricultural adaptation to stabilize, we argue, agriculturalists would have had to create an economic/-breeding network with others of their own kind.

The rapid spread of ceramics from A.D. 200-400 and the increasing tendency to small settled villages in a few locales argues that a certain degree of ethnic differentiation between hunters and agriculturalists had already begun to take place. What language groups in the area diverged about 1600-2000 years ago (see Hale and Harris 1979)?

GENERAL TRENDS IN THE MT. TAYLOR REGION

The process of increasing agricultural intensification from A.D. 200 to 500 or 600 is manifest in small village archaeological remains only after a substantial period of gradual population deregulation and ethnic and linguistic differentiation. Specifically, we suggest that the period of the terminal Archaic-Early Basketmaker was one of increasing agricultural dependence by a few, while also one of increasing numbers of hunters-gatherers. The general absence of early Basketmaker remains in the Mt. Taylor area is intelligible if agricultural populations were intensifying their sedentary strategy and reducing space needs until A.D. 500-700 in the northern highlands of the Chuskas and San Juan Basin. Meanwhile, one can argue, the same process took place in the Gila Wilderness area. Agricultural populations could have been withdrawing to more circumscribed areas, leaving the Zuni highlands as uncontested hunter-gatherer territory.

This view might be contradicted by Martin and Plog's (1973) suggestion that the period from A.D. 500-700 was one of decreasing dependence (Mogollon area) on agriculture, and of population decline. We suggest the alternative notion (next chapter) that early agricultural populations may have adjusted settlement into lowland areas during this period. Specifically, we should like to see more independent dates for ceramic scatters in the Jornada area.

We characterize the period from A.D. 200-500 as one of major ethnic differentiation coupled with increasingly complex and separate trading patterns. Thereafter, until about A.D. 700, the picture becomes extremely complex. Do we have partial population loss and collapse back to hunting-gathering? Lithic assemblages should generally reflect this, if so (manos and metates becoming scarce, etc.). Have we agricultural experimentation in new geographic locations, not heavily investigated? We need to excavate and date early plainware ceramic scatters in both higher and lower elevations to see what might be uncovered in the way of post molds, shallow pitroom stains, etc. Are portions of the San Mateos and Zuni highlands generally uninhabited (A.D. 1-800) as Schaafsma (1978) suggests? Or are late Archaic lithic assemblages (San Jose points may outlast the alleged dates for the period) fully contemporaneous with BM-II and BM-III in western New Mexico?

From A.D. 700 to roughly A.D. 1150, we see increasingly widespread trade, the disappearance of hunters-gatherers altogether from west central New Mexico (whether by retreat or adaptive conversion) and possible deemphasis of ethnic differentiation (this goes back to Tainter's arguments on the interaction spheres).

After A.D. 1150, however, we see the collapse of a 200 year old Chacoan/Basin economic network in the Pilares phase, followed by restructured settlement and trading patterns— an upland economic network (P-III). This is then interrupted by episodes of abandonment in the late P-III period, and sites again become defensively located. Some sites are abandoned with assemblages nearly intact. Others are burned in a short period of substantial disintegration at the juncture of the P-IV horizon. Following this period, several distinct subsistence adaptations seem to have been achieved, leading into the historic period. Martin and Plog (1973) discuss different adaptive agricultural strategies among the Hopi, Zuni and Rio Grande pueblos. One cannot help but characterize the late 12th and 13th centuries as a calamitous period which both opened and closed with substantial population movements. The first occurred when the Chacoan network disintegrated, the second with abandonments in the higher mesas and woodlands. We offer several additional thoughts on changing economic patterns and abandonment in the conclusion of this chapter.

Now let us turn to Socorro and Catron counties — the more distinctly Mogollon portion of the geographically interwoven cotraditions.

THE SOCORRO AREA

BACKGROUND

This study area includes all of Socorro and three-quarters of Catron County, New Mexico. Driving south on I-25 from Belen, N.M., one would proceed due west to the Arizona state line to describe the northern boundary of the Socorro unit. About 20 miles north of Truth or Consequences, N.M., there is a sign which says Sierra County. Again, look west to the Arizona state line — this is the southern boundary of the study unit. East of the Rio Grande the Socorro area proceeds roughly to Carrizozo, N.M. (actually Valley of Fires lava flow), thence north to Corona, N.M., thence northwest again to the original boundary near Belen.

The overview published by Berman (1979) does not include the eastern portion of the area as drawn here. Nonetheless, the BLM and Forest Service asked us to abide by the map (see Map I.1) reproduced in the introductory chapter, and so we have here*. This area east of the river includes the lowlands of the Rio Grande, the northern Jornada del Muerto, northern Oscura range (the area of the Trinity atomic bomb site) and the higher lands of Chupadero Mesa to the north of Highway 380. These eastern areas contain the northernmost branch of the Jornada-Mogollon (Lehmer 1948). Marshall (1973) has described the Socorro and Corona archeological expressions in this eastern portion. The southern Jornada region is discussed more fully in the next chapter.

The major focus of Berman's overview is upon the westernmost portions of the Socorro district, an area of substantial forest and highlands. The Jornada cultural zone is in the eastern lowlands, the Mogollon-Tularosa area is in the southwestern mountains, and the Anasazi area is primarily to the north of the plains of San Agustin. Each of these alleged cultural systems has been described by different phase sequences, and hence there is substantial confusion for the uninitiated.

Berman has organized her overview sequentially from Paleo-Indian to Archaic and Formative — then to P-II, then to P-III and to P-IV. She has done this to avoid using multiple sequences, and indeed, as Martin and Plog (1973) have complained, we have burdened ourselves with cultural series which tend to bewilder, rather than elucidate. In spite of that, these various archeological phases are not so well cross-dated as one might suppose. For those reasons we will pay some attention to that subsequently.

First, it is essential, in reading Berman's overview, to grasp the locations of different planning units as she describes cultural patterns. She sometimes uses the federal administrative areas as designators and at other times uses names of mountain ranges.

It is important to realize that the Gila Forest (southwestern quarter) is a mass of substantial uplands and mountains which contains the Alpine branch of the Mogollon (Danson 1957) or the Cibola branch (Wheat 1955). This area is characterized as the Pine Lawn branch in later Mogollon development (about A.D. 900-1000) by Wheat (1955).

Though there is no well-defined boundary, the Quemado planning unit (northwest quarter) is generally characterized as the Cibola (or Zuni) branch of the Anasazi. The distinction has much to do with the early distribution of Cibola graywares as opposed to Mogollon brownwares. The area east of the Continental Divide is not well surveyed.

---

* This map has since been revised.

132

Data from the Cibola Forest (three areas) are only modest. Little systematic survey has been conducted in the area. The BLM lands of the Driveway, Stallion and Ladron planning units are not well surveyed either. Recently, Human Systems Research (Wimberly and Eidenbach 1980) has surveyed in the lower Puerco and Salado drainages — between Belen and Socorro, N.M., near the Rio Grande. The data they so carefully present sheds an entirely new light on adaptive process in the region's prehistory and (Eidenbach 1980) on the nature of the Mogollon-Anasazi boundary.

Thus, as one reads the Berman overview, be advised that the data presented are primarily from the western mountains and highlands of the region. For instance, in Chapter 6 (p. 60) she discusses patterns in altitudinal shifts during the later sequence (A.D. 1000-1300), but her data are from an altitude range of 6,200 feet (Pine Lawn Valley) to about 8,500 feet (Gallo Mountain Ranger Station). Altitude varies in the entire Socorro region from 4,500 feet (on the Rio Grande) to 10,700 feet (South Baldy, Magdalena Mountains) and this range of variation is greatest in the *eastern* half of the area — the little-surveyed portions. In short, she has captured less than half the true variance in available data. Let us turn, then, to a short discussion of the cultural sequence.

CHRONOLOGY

Berman (1979:28) follows "Haury/Martin" in providing these sequence dates as follows:

> Pine Lawn: A.D. 1-500
> Georgetown: A.D. 500-700
> San Francisco: A.D. 700-900
> Three Circle: A.D. 900-1000

These phases are followed in the Mimbres area by the Classic Mimbres, generally given as A.D. 1000-1200. We discuss the entire sequence in detail in the following chapter, and will only present a brief discussion here. We have, from tree-ring dates gotten in the Mimbres Foundation excavations, plus our own intuitive judgments, provided our own suggested dates in the following chapter.

Formative Chronology, This Volume

> Pine Lawn: A.D. 250?-550
> Georgetown: A.D. 550-650
> San Francisco: A.D. 650-850
> Three Circle: A.D. 850-1000?
> Mangus: A.D. 925-975 — Boldface B/W
> Mimbres: A.D. 975-1150

Our chronology requires a brief clarification here. It is notable that there are no reliable construction dates for a Classic Mimbres roomblock before about A.D. 1050 (from among 300 dendro dates produced during the Mimbres Foundation's work). There are also no reliable tree-ring dates for Three Circle construction after A.D. 900 in the Mimbres. Thus, we argue (in the next chapter) that the missing construction dates are a function of dispersal during the late Three Circle phase, followed by reaggregation in the Classic Mimbres sites at, or just before, A.D. 1050. We note that Mimbres Boldface (Mangus B/W) appears first in sherd scatters in lowland areas of the Jornada-Mogollon, followed shortly by Classic Mimbres Black-on-white in small quantities (Lehmer 1948). Dr. Whalen (co-author of the overview discussed in the following chapter) uses the Boldface as a horizon marker for the Mesilla phase (A.D. 500-1100) in the area of the southern Tularosa Basin. Since El Paso Polychrome is now known to occur in some Classic Mimbres sites, the beginning dates for the ware have been placed at just after A.D. 1100 (Way 1979). Thus, the Boldface, which appears earlier in Jornada sites nearer to the Mimbres Valley is perforce an earlier horizon marker, for many sites in the Tularosa Basin that have Classic Mimbres Black-on-white have neither the Boldface nor El Paso Polychrome. Thus, there is a peak occurrence for each ware, sequentially, in lowland areas. We would guess these peaks at 950-975 (Boldface); 1050-1075 (Mimbres) and about 1150-75 for early (direct rim) El Paso Polychrome.

Since Graybill (1973) and others argue for slightly different dates in the upper Gila or upper Mimbres areas, we recognize that a temporal gradient for phases probably exists in the Mogollon heartland. We think these gradients may have to do with altitude differences. Finally, we should note that LeBlanc does not agree that there exists a Mangus phase *in the Mimbres Valley*. Since other investigators are mixed on the existence of this phase, it may exist elsewhere. We present the case as best we can. Other research will be required to resolve it.

In terms of the present study area, Berman presents chronology (p. 28 and beginning of each succeeding chapter introductions) which is a bit confusing. The following table places these chronologies side by side for easy comparison.

Table IV.4
COMPARATIVE CHRONOLOGIES
MIMBRES, SOUTHWESTERN SOCORRO and GENERAL PECOS (MT. TAYLOR) DISTRICTS

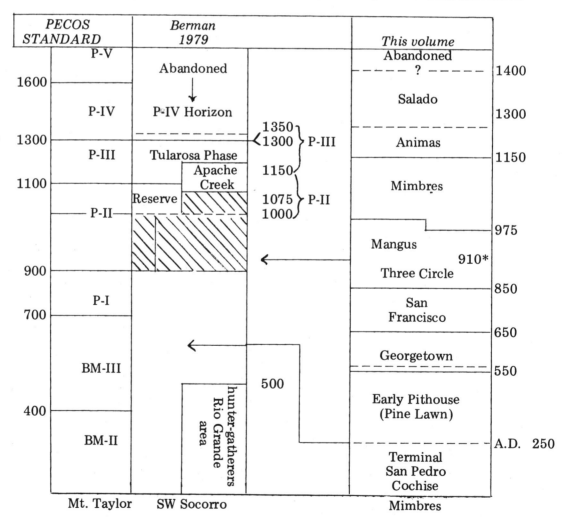

* Prior to A.D. 910, Berman uses the San Pedro—Three Circle sequence.

It should be remembered that the Pecos classification has been recognized as inadequate in some respects for a long time. Most field archeologists readily admit this, but are, at the same time, hopelessly addicted to the classification.

THE FORMATIVE
(Pine Lawn through Three Circle of the Mogollon-Mimbres Sequence)

The early and well known Pine Lawn phase was first excavated and reported in this area (see Martin and Plog 1973). The earliest Pine Lawn phase is only one expression of a region-wide phenomenon constituting the early evidence for small sedentary village life in the Southwest.

Actually, there is substantial variability in these pithouse settlements. Village size varies from only several to fifteen or twenty pithouses. There is substantial variation in such dated remains — a range being from the mid A.D. 200's to about 600. It is during the early part of this period that the first brownware ceramics consistently begin to appear in pithouse structures.

Earlier pithouses are known from the terminal Archaic (primarily to the south and west of this area) but their gradation into early Pine Lawn villages has not been well studied. A-ceramic sites of the period blend with ceramic ones, and relatively few are well dated. Dr. Cordell (1979) mentions Talus village near Durango, Colorado (mid A.D. 200's). Dr. Tainter points out that such sites are often in plateau environments away from major permanent streams. His point is important, for the West Mesa sites he discusses are rather like sites in the Hueco Bolson that are discussed in the overview of Southwestern New Mexico (next chapter). These also date as early as the A.D. 250-400 period. It is not at all certain that these early sedentary or semisedentary villages are, adaptively, the same phenomenon. Little evidence of agriculture was obtained at the Winn Canyon site (Fitting 1973) to the south along the Gila River (elevation 4,100 feet), while substantial (even remarkable) evidence for storage facilities was obtained from the Talus Village site in the upland of the Colorado Plateau (over 6,000 feet).

In Martin and Plog (1973:373-386) such sites in Arizona include the Bluff Site, Broken Flute Cave (transitional to succeeding phase), and Obelisk Cave (Graywares). The SU Site in the Pine Lawn Valley of the southwestern Socorro district is one of the best known of these sites and is described in Martin and Plog (1973) and in Willey (1966). No one will be able to specify the conditions under which sedentism and regular agriculture took place until all such sites are studied as a unit. That is, one must arrange the data from 50 or 100 of these occupations according to altitude, assemblage, storage facilities, exposure and botanical remains. An initial glance at the evidence suggests that these sites are spread over nearly 75,000 square miles, and vary in altitude by roughly 2,500 feet, but cluster around 6,500 feet on the one hand and 4,500 feet on the other.

Because of these difficulties much has been written about village size, kiva development and the nature of economic-social organizational adaptation to account for the presumed adaptive complexity which takes place between the earliest of these villages and those of succeeding phases. Nonetheless, the upsetting fact remains that we do not yet know what is being adapted to. Our evidence of Archaic occupation is so spotty, and these villages so few, that we don't even know if the population density requirements that most scholars (including ourselves) have come to suppose as a precondition for sedentism can be demonstrated.

The succeeding Georgetown phase (A.D. 550-650) is enigmatic. In the Pine Lawn Valley, Georgetown occupation is very modest. After the attainment of substantial village size there is a near hiatus in occupation. Berman reports that Georgetown and San Francisco phase occupations are scarce in many parts of the Cibola Forest. LeBlanc reports them from the Mimbres drainage. Thus, Martin and Plog (1973) suggest a generalized population decline for the A.D. 500-700 period. Indeed, in the Point of Pines region of Arizona, Breternitz (1959) discusses the evidence for and against an occupational hiatus in the A.D. 600-800 or 900 period.

From excavation at Tularosa Cave (Martin and Plog 1973), there is evidence for a reduction in the utilization of corn as an important food resource. Yet in spite of this evidence, many (if not most) excavators see a continued trend towards increasing social-economic and technological complexity in succeeding periods. Pithouse size increases (but declines in Pine Lawn Valley); there is trade in the early San Francisco redwares, and community house (kiva) architecture becomes increasingly differentiated. These developments proceed in spite of an alleged decrease in population and lessened dependence on corn.

Many sites of the period are known only from cursory surveys and consist of plainware scatters (Alma Plain). Since it is equally possible that population dispersed, instead of declined, we need to know the distribution of such scatters. It may be that pithouse villages were only seasonally occupied for many centuries. Many have argued it. At some point, it will be necessary to have a distributional map of such plainware scatters over a wide region. These could then lead to a program of test excavation of a number from various environmental-altitudinal zones, which may prove that there are some ephemeral architectural remains associated with these. Some archeologists have proposed that pithouses without hearths are summer season units, while those with hearths are winter season units. Nonetheless, there is no conceivable pattern of seasonal transhumance that would generate such a phenomenon between pithouses in the same site or in the same general altitude zone.

For instance, one might suppose that Mogollon populations hunted in the highlands during fall and collected in the lowlands during spring or summer. This might produce occupations in lower elevations without hearths in pithouses, but one would have to ask: why construct a pithouse at all unless the collecting activity was recurring and of substantial duration? Perhaps it was agricultural pursuits that shifted seasonally to the lowlands. In that case winter occupation units would generally have hearths and a lithic assemblage geared primarily to hunting — unless the unprocessed corn were carried upland. Under those circumstances, the assemblage would evidence both grinding and hunting implements, but have more volume of storage, since cob corn would have greater volume.

Who, on the other hand, would carry cob corn a substantial distance uphill? Under what circumstances would the cob be useful enough as fuel to be worth transporting? In short, we can easily conceive of an upland hunting and a lowland collecting/agricultural strategy. We can conceive of lowland sites with no hearths and substantial grinding equipment, and upland sites the reverse. Yet we don't have the likely lowland sites to account for such a pattern, unless at least some Jornada-Mogollon lowland sites are contemporaneous, for there is substantial evidence that such activities took place in those. Few are dated, but even if they were dated to the A.D. 500-800 period, how would we know whether these represented a permanent lowland specialized population that traded with the upland, or a seasonally transhumant one? In either case, who would build a small summer pithouse next to, or even a few hundred yards from, a winter one? A large, deep pithouse buffers the temperature extremes of both seasons.

We have gone on at some length about pithouse adaptation for several reasons. First, there are ceramic scatters in the study area about which we know little. Secondly, it is hard to suppose different pithouse forms in similar settings at identical time periods. However, changing climatic circumstances, or changing temporal factors, could produce such a pattern (if, for example, it got warmer in the highlands). Currently, we control neither well enough to produce an adequate explanation. Third, Berman has lumped the Formative with Pueblo I in the northern part of the Socorro district.

In traditional temporal terms, this is appropriate, for P-I is alleged to overlap the Georgetown (late) to Early Three Circle period. Yet the P-I in the north is defined by the presence of the Cibola Grayware series (Lino Gray, Kana'a Neckbanded, etc.) and surficial storage rooms. On page 40 Berman (1979) comments that pottery *did not appear until Basketmaker III times.* This is misleading to the casual reader, for Lino Gray ceramics are generally dated to A.D. 450 from the Four Corners region, yet there are earlier dates (A.D. 32 ± 138 from BR-45 west of Bernalillo — see Reinhart 1968) which are considered controversial. Some of the earliest wares in the Anasazi district are Mogollon (or Mogollon-like) brownwares. Though this has often been taken to argue a later development to the north, one must recall that a small Basketmaker III pithouse site without ceramics automatically gets a Basketmaker II designation. Architecturally, the same site *with* ceramics would be designated BM-III.

Judge (in press) has recently summarized the early (Paleo-Indian—Basketmaker III) sequence for the San Juan Basin and notes 102 BM-II sites and 934 BM-III sites in the San Juan Basin. Most of these range in date from about the time of Christ (a few are early BM-II to 500-900 B.C.) to about A.D. 950. Such sites, collectively, are not rare except by comparison with the enormous number of Pueblo sites. While there is little temporal control, it would be thoughtless to suppose that the trends leading to sedentary village life were not apparent in both regions.

Additionally, Berman suggests that during the P-I period, the northern portions of the study area had already moved to above ground architecture. This may be so, but again there is little temporal control. That is, in the highlands of the Gila Forest we know large pithouse villages endure to about A.D. 900 — these in the Anasazi sequence would generally be classified by survey archeologists either as a very late Basketmaker village or a Multicomponent BM-III—P-I pithouse village. If Red Mesa Black-on-white were on the site (A.D. 950 or a bit earlier: Breternitz 1966) it would probably be considered to contain either an Early P-II or intrusive component as well.

Martin and Plog (1973:194) summarize the situation. After A.D. 700, and markedly by A.D. 1000, the character of the Mogollon area changed to one like that of the Anasazi, with above-ground architecture, great kivas, and the Chaco-like black-on-white pottery. This reference is to the development of the Mimbres B/W and Reserve (overlaps with Gallup B/W) wares. At this juncture the Gila Forest area is believed to be sufficiently different from the Mimbres to the south of the Mogollon rim (right along the southern boundary of the study unit) that the local Reserve-Tularosa sequence may be said to begin.

Both Reserve Black-on-white and Red Mesa Black-on-white are said to appear in this area (Catron County) about A.D. 940-950 (A.D. 850-870 to the north), and surface structures begin to be built. LeBlanc (In LeBlanc and Whalen 1979) states that Boldface Black-on-white was being produced by A.D. 900, and he comments on a transitional style to the Mimbres Black-on-white which developed rapidly to its classic style. LeBlanc rejects the notion of an Anasazi intrusion, and views the Mimbres Whitewares as *in situ* developments from earlier Three Circle Red-on-white. We believe (noted in next chapter) that LeBlanc's position may be stated too firmly. Many authorities would disagree with him. Nonetheless, Tainter (1980) has argued that the Chaco interaction sphere extended only far enough into the Zuni highlands to maximize ecological diversity. In essence, he sees an economic rather than a population intrusion. Again, others (Ruppe and Dittert 1952) would disagree. They view the south side of Cebolleta Mesa to the north of Catron County as the dividing line or mixed zone between the two systems.

In short, by A.D. 900 or 950, the nature of trade, ceramic development, architectural development and settlement pattern becomes enormously complex in an extremely short period of time. Since Berman has not focused on the A.D. 900-1000 period in great detail, we will continue from that point.

THE RESERVE—TULAROSA or P-I/P-II to P-III/P-IV HORIZONS (A.D. 910?? - 1325?)

This period is broadly bracketed by the declining incidence of Mimbres Boldface Black-on-white and the increasing appearance of new styles of utility wares in association with a locally made black-on-white known as Reserve (but stylistically similar to Gallup B/W). The end of this period is marked by abandonment in the western and highland portions of the study area by A.D. 1325 (probably A.D. 1300-1310).

In the uplands this period is introduced by a curious pause or disruption in settlement pattern. The larger Three Circle phase (Boldface Black-on-white) pithouse villages move increasingly to above-ground architecture, but areas that had not been occupied in the Three Circle period are settled throughout the highlands. This period has been given several local phase names, but one of the best known sources is Breternitz's (1959) report on the Nantack phase at Point of Pines, Arizona (just to the west across the State line). The phase name is unimportant. What does matter is that the changing settlement patterns of the A.D. 900-1000 period are bracketed by ceramic seriation and cross-dating.

In Breternitz's study we have a pattern, or model, for small sites characterized by a 10th century pithouse occupation and a slightly later Reserve and/or distinctly later Tularosa masonry component. Remember, that Breternitz's site contains the later St. Johns Polychrome (3 sherds, 2 in pithouse fill, one in later room fill), but only in minute quantities, even though there was a tremendous kiva excavated there. Nonetheless, the general pattern in the region at this time is for many outlying small sites to cluster in upland meadows within a mile or two of such a great kiva. In the Pine Lawn Valley, 60 such small units (the majority are masonry units) are scattered across several square miles, but only one kiva exists. This represents a distinct break from the previous pattern of one, or more, alleged kivas per cluster of pithouses.

In short, there is dispersal to many areas previously unoccupied, lack of aggregation in formal village structure, and a scarcity of kivas. Many such sites are assigned to the Reserve phase. Nonetheless, the evidence suggests that a number of pithouses are first constructed before the later surface roomblocks. The earliest of these surface units are of jacal construction, followed by cobble masonry units. Both Nantack and Pine Lawn Valley are at about 6,000 feet in altitude. As just mentioned, there are sixty such sites in the Pine Lawn Valley. Only three have more than ten rooms, and these can be argued to be just slightly later in time.

Thus, one proceeds through time from Mogollon pithouse villages of 10-20 "rooms" with kiva (about A.D. 900), to ten rooms or fewer, often without kiva (from A.D. 950 or 1000 to A.D. 1050 or 1100), and to increasing size (during the late Reserve phase) in the 1100's, at 10-20 rooms. These changes all take place in the wetter forested zones.

Notably, this changed settlement pattern occurs in the slightly lower mountain meadow regions (Rice 1979:40) first. That is, the change begins in the Pine Lawn Valley (6,000 feet) and similar areas. This adaptation then proceeds to move into the higher elevations. As this pattern proceeds, sites become slightly larger. This marks the period of maximum occupation of the upland areas, sites being very numerous. This period is Berman's P-II (A.D. 1000-1100) *Reserve* phase. Nonetheless, very few sites of these periods have been subjected to absolute dating techniques, and we are concerned that the ceramic cross-dates in the region may be too gross to be very accurate in identifying the precise timing of major changes in settlement patterns.

Site size varies throughout the highlands, from two or three rooms to 30 (Peckham 1958). In the Pine Lawn Valley, these Reserve phase pueblos average 62 m² in size. In the Tularosa and San Francisco valleys — slightly higher in elevation — they are about 30 m². We note also that the early Pine Lawn phase pithouses were larger than the average. There is substantial variability in masonry, orientation, etc. throughout the period. Berman (1979), follows Rice's (1975) interest in pursuing Danson's survey data and discusses the case for the later (mid A.D. 1100's-1300) Tularosa phase sites shifting to slightly lower elevations (generally, below 7,000 feet; the Gallinas Spring site and a few others, being exceptions).

The later Tularosa phase sites vary substantially in altitude. The architectural details are also complex. The tendency is to proceed from small linear to L-shaped roomblock to large sites organized around open plazas. Multistory units on the plaza are reported (see sketch, p. 162, of Mogollon village — Complex 1). Finally, Danson (1957), Bluhm (1960) and others have reported walled, closed-plaza sites, which are thought to be very late, in the forest areas. The large Gallina Springs site does not quite represent this pattern. Excavations there were recently conducted by Dr. Tainter. For good descriptions of similar sites see McGimsey's report of excavations on Marianna Mesa (1980).

One of the more complex settlement events in the Socorro district involves the apparent abandonment of the Gila Forest area at A.D. 1300-1325. At the very end of this period one finds St. Johns Polychromes in association with the early Zuni glazes.

A great deal of speculation surrounds such abandonments, and it is often argued that the subsequent Salado (P-IV) occupation in the lower Rio Salado drainage of Arizona is related to these late P-III occupations in the Gila Forest area. Some scholars therefore propose an actual migration into the Salado drainage. The enclosed plaza sites exhibit certain related ceramic types (Roosevelt Red, Pinto/Gila Polychromes, etc.) and lack kiva features. To the west, the earliest Salado components are argued to be semi-subterranean pitrooms associated with Pinto/Gila Polychromes and either Tularosa or Roosevelt Black-on-white. Later Saladoan sites are substantial roomblock masses enclosing a great yard or walled court. These are described in Martin and Plog (1973).

Whether the Salado in Arizona is related by actual migration (the majority view 20 years ago) or by economic interchange of similar pottery styles, etc., is not quite the issue here. What is important is that the A.D. 900 period and the A.D. 1200-1300 period are times of major shifts in settlement pattern and cultural identity in the western Socorro district. Trade increases, social complexity increases, the size of largest sites increases, but fewer and fewer sites occupy the forested highlands until all are abandoned. So Tainter (1980a) calls for a general theory of abandonment. But how are we to construct one? Most of us sense general climatic/ecological trends at work. In the next chapter we will point out correlations between tree-ring width and broad cultural patterns and will argue in terms of winter or summer dominant rainfall shifts. It is half an argument at most, but others have recently focused on portions of the Colorado Plateau (Euler, et al. 1979) as an upland refugee area in time of drought. We like the approach, but feel certain that it will continue to stimulate as much debate as agreement. Let us turn to the eastern portion of this area for some comparative notes.

EASTERN RIO GRANDE SUBAREA

In the Socorro region we have only an imperfect picture of settlement pattern. Berman mentions the survey work to be performed in the eastern part (Stallion and Ladron planning units) of the region. The report (Wimberly and Eidenbach 1980) should be widely available soon.

We have previewed this report, and it is a real eye-opener. The survey was conducted in the lower Puerco and Salado (see map — this is *not* the Arizona Salt or Salado River) Rivers near their juncture with the Rio Grande. The survey was broken into sample units stratified by environmental zone. Elevation ranged between 4,800 feet and 5,900 feet, elevations not much represented in the data from the western portion of the region. Rainfall here averages between 8.5 and 10 inches (Rio Grande to Magdalena). Specifically, the Rio Puerco drainage in the survey area had elevations ranging from roughly 4,800 to 5,100 feet. Twenty sites were recorded in just under six square miles. These ranged from Early P-I to P-IV (Glaze A). Three Late P-II/Early P-III sites were recorded. One of these is structural (adobe and mixed adobe/-masonry construction). From surface inspection, the authors estimate 32 rooms, including a C-shaped unit surrounding a plaza area.

In the Rio Salado drainage (their Loma Blanca and La Jencia units; see Wimberly and Eidenbach 1980:89), 37 sites were recorded. These include BM-III (including two pithouses), Early P-I, Late P-I, Early and Late P-II sites and three P-IV (one Glaze A, one Glaze D and one Glaze C,D,E) pueblos. The Glaze A pueblo was approximately 75 rooms surrounding a large plaza, with one kiva in the plaza and one outside. While there is obviously not the temporal control one would have from excavation data, the ceramic seriations were done by M. Marshall (in Wimberly and Eidenbach 1980:165-187). We can take that to mean that the identification of ceramic materials is of high quality. There is a smattering of Mimbres Boldface Black-on-white in the Late P-I and Early P-II, there are the Red Mesa Black-on-whites and Wingate Black-on-reds, and *later* there are Rio Grande Glaze A's (also C, D, E). These earlier Black-on-whites and Black-on-reds, Marshall suggests (in Wimberly and Eidenbach 1980:184), "indicate an occupation which extended into the early P-III horizon, ca. A.D. 1050-1100. . .". The presence of Cedar Creek Polychrome at Site P-4 ". . . indicates Late P-III—Early P-IV horizons" (ibid). The Rio Grande Glazes indicate an early P-IV horizon (A.D. 1300-1325).

In summary, there are 57 sites in roughly ten square miles, surveyed foot by foot. Site placement is primarily along the contact zones between diverse ecological/physiographic units. Twenty-four of these are structural (not merely ceramic or lithic scatters). Of these, eleven are P-II components. THERE IS NO P-III (A.D. 1100-1300) PERIOD SITE AS ORDINARILY DEFINED FROM CERAMIC MATERIALS. In the Gila Forest, confusion is created because some consider that sites are P-III only if St. Johns Polychrome is present. Others include all those with Tularosa Black-on-white as the Tularosa (A.D. 1100-1300 period).

Nonetheless, Berman (1979) states that sites in the Pine Lawn Valley do not undergo the full Tularosa phase transition and appear to have been abandoned. These are at 6,000 feet. Some of the highest sites, above 7,000 feet, do not undergo the Tularosa transition, either. The Apache Creek phase sites do not, and some are located as high as 8,000 feet. Nonetheless, it is misleading to accept the idea that abandonment is related only to elevational changes, though nearness to the major drainages does seem to be a more meaningful pattern in later site placement. Altitude by itself means little. Some lands above 6,500 feet are rather sparse on vegetation. Compass exposure and soils are important factors. The San Agustin Plain itself is 6,700-6,800 feet high. That is, substantial portions of the Driveway unit (BLM grasslands) are higher than some areas characterized as mountain meadows. The pinyon-Ponderosa transition zone varies substantially from area to area in altitude. To say that the Gila *Forest* or Cibola *Forest*, etc. is abandoned by 1300 would substantially mislead persons from other portions of the country who do not realize that noticeable portions of a National *forest* in New Mexico contain nothing more notable than an occasional stunted pinyon or juniper.

In the lower Puerco and Salado, Wimberly and Eidenbach (1980:227) conclude:

140

". . . . Until approximately A.D. 1000, population appears to have been sparse and dispersed, albeit clustered near the water sources. During the following two hundred years, traits listed from excavated sites suggest relationships with the populations of the northern and western Plateau margins. After about A.D. 1200, locally (middle Rio Grande) developed material culture appears to attain predominance (i.e., brownware ceramics and adobe architecture). Mera (1940) has recorded a number of site locations of what he terms the Rio Grande Glaze period. Dating from approximately A.D. 1300 to the historic eras, the period in the general region is characterized by the production of mineral glaze painted pottery. Markedly unusual sites are dated to the early years of the Glaze period. These sites are on high isolated mesa positions which suggest a 'defensive' orientation (Mera 1940).

"In the Salado drainage at La Jara Butte, on the Rio Grande near San Acacia just down from the Salado confluence at Indian Hill, and on the Puerco at Hidden Mountain, are three examples directly related to the study area. The sites are sizeable, more than 150 rooms, reasonably well constructed of locally available masonry elements, and appear to contain limited amounts of cultural materials. The ceramic type in association, Rio Grande Glaze A, although poorly dated, is believed to have been short-lived (less than 75 years).

"Following the Glaze A period, sites are generally larger, located in less defensible positions, and longer lived. The reason for the defensive location of the Glaze A sites is, to date, totally unknown. The problem has not been examined. Middle and late Glaze period sites are situated in more conventional drainage associated positions. One such site was recorded in the Salado study area (there are undoubtedly others), and Pottery Mound is the most substantial example on the Puerco. With an estimated 500 rooms and a population of 1,000 people or more, the occupation of Pottery Mound undoubtedly substantially effected environmental conditions on the lower Puerco.

"At about the time of earliest Spanish contact, it appears that populations occupying the Puerco and Salado moved to several major villages in the middle Rio Grande. Continual Athapascan incursions originating from or passing through the two drainages are reported by the Spanish throughout the Colonial period. Spanish livestock was apparently grazed on the two drainages but no attempt was made to establish a settlement until almost one hundred years after the 1680 Revolt which succeeded in ousting the Spanish colony for ten years."

[Wimberly and Eidenbach 1980:227]

What we find striking is the absence of the P-III sites in the lower Puerco or Salado. This is some 100 miles to the east of the Reserve-Pine Lawn area. We could be talking about an altitudinal-vegetational variance, or simply about differentiated cultural/economic systems.

No Chupadero Black-on-white (A.D. 1150-1400+; cited in Marshall 1973) was described from the ceramic samples, particularly for the several glazeware sites. Neither could Marshall identify the San Marcial phase (Mera's type site LA 1151) from ceramic materials. We will return to these points in the overview of this chapter.

In other words, the archeological records of the western and eastern portions of the Socorro study area are remarkably different, but little intervening survey has been conducted, and dated sites are too few to amplify the causes of such differences. For instance, only *one* Apache Creek phase pithouse has ever been absolutely dated (A.D. 1159, Cutting).

CONSIDERATIONS FOR SURVEY

BACKGROUND

The geographic extent of the Socorro-Mt. Taylor area requires some comment. The area north of I-40, with the exception of Acoma and Laguna lands, is not included in this discussion of the survey area. Dr. Tainter's overview discusses acreages that are properly considered the San Juan Basin. We suppose that he extended his discussion northward because of the economic/cultural relationships which may have obtained between many of the Zuni-Cebolleta Mesa area sites and the Chacoan system. Nonetheless, our discussion here, estimates of acreage, areas surveyed, etc. is south of I-40, with the noted exception.

The history of archeological survey in the Mt. Taylor-Socorro districts is long and distinguished. Leslie Spier (1917) and Frank Roberts (1932) surveyed and excavated in the Zuni region. Recently the University of New Mexico conducted a major study of the Yellowhouse area (Hunter-Anderson 1978). To the east, Ruppe and Dittert's (Ruppe and Dittert 1952, 1953, Dittert 1949, 1959, Ruppe 1953) surveys and reports (and theses) identifying the Acoma culture province are classics. Danson's (1957) surveys in west central New Mexico are not much less cited. Research in the Gila National Forest has been conducted by a number of the most respected and most careful scholars in American archeology (among them, Martin, Haury, Rinaldo and others). Knowledgeable professionals like Peckham, Schaafsma and Wiseman of the Museum of New Mexico have worked in the area. New Mexico State University staff have surveyed and/or excavated in the area, Beckett (1973) having prepared his thesis on the distribution of Cochise (Archaic) sites in the region. The Zuni Archaeological Program is active in the northwestern portion of the region. Human Systems Research has conducted recent surveys near the mouth of the Puerco and Salado drainages. Mera (1940) conducted earlier surveys in the eastern area along the Rio Grande and Chupadero Mesa.

In spite of these investigations the area remains only partially understood. This is in part because two cultural cotraditions (Mogollon and Anasazi) appear to blend (whatever the style of argument) as one approaches the central portion of this region from either the north(west) or south. So as one moves east-southeast from Zuni or east-northeast from Alma, N.M., archeological understanding and intensity of survey decline. If two such gradients are joined to form a triangle south of Gran Quivira (easternmost portion of the study area), the figure adequately conveys a gradient of declining certainty in the data base (see Map IV.2).

In a sense this is not surprising, for the region is vast, topographically diverse and not well cut by highway systems in several areas. As computed here, the area includes over 12,200,000 acres (see Table IV.5). While only one-sixth of the State of New Mexico, this region is nonetheless four times the size of Connecticut — that is, between 19 and 20 thousand square miles. As in most other areas of New Mexico, the land is under diverse ownership and stewardship. About 39% of the land is under private ownership. Most of these lands are held by ranching interests, many of these families having pioneered the area at the end of the last century. Access to these lands depends primarily on good will, but as in most other areas of New Mexico, there is a history of active interest in and tolerance towards archeologists. The Albuquerque Archeological Society has been active in the area, as have a number of persons in the Reserve, Socorro and Magdalena areas. Access to private land depends, of course, on the approach and behavior of the archeologist wanting to do research.

ACCESS TO INDIAN LANDS

Indian lands account for about 17% of the total acreage. While the Zuni people are conservative in some respects, they have an active archeological program which regularly conducts survey on Zuni lands. The northern Zuni Reservation, and Manuelito Canyon to

142

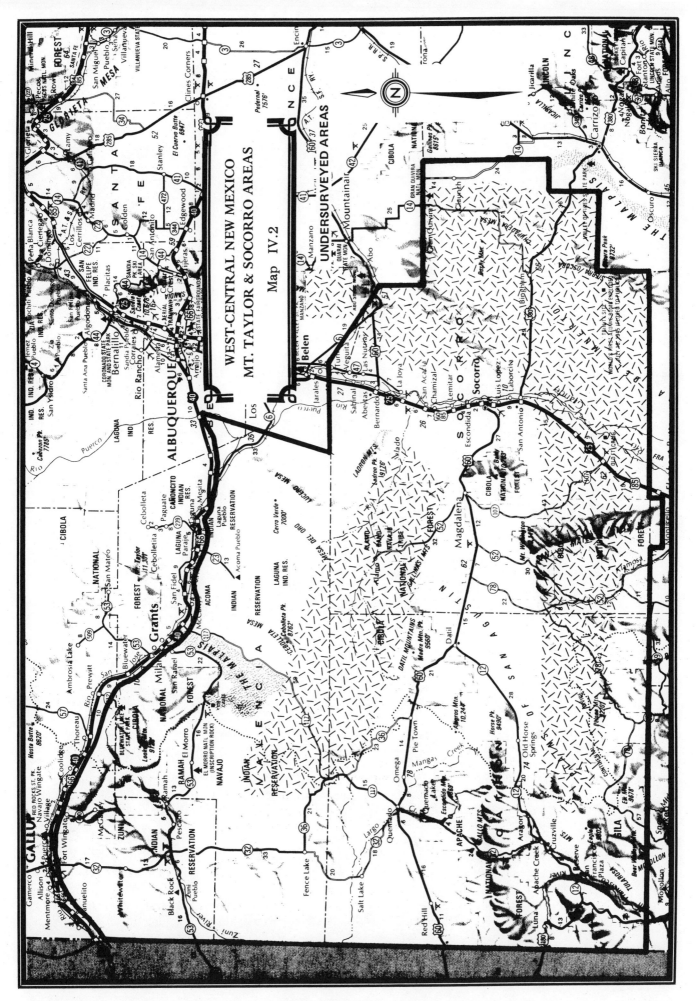

WEST-CENTRAL NEW MEXICO
MT. TAYLOR & SOCORRO AREAS

Map IV.2

Table IV.5

WEST-CENTRAL NEW MEXICO – LAND OWNERSHIP

Land Ownership	MT. TAYLOR		Catron County	SOCORRO, NEW MEXICO		
	Valencia County	Percent		Socorro County	TOTAL ACREAGE	Percent
BLM	404,028	9.71	593,742	947,016	1,540,758	19.34
NPS	1,040	.024	0	371	371	.004
BIA	13,385	.32				
Bureau of Reclamation			0	4,055	4,055	.05
Corps of Engineers			0	39,170	39,170	.49
Fish and Wildlife			0	278,766	278,766	3.49
Forest Service	519,083*	12.47	1,513,546†	651,772†	2,165,318†	27.18
State	251,746	6.05	533,037	609,517	1,142,554	14.34
Indian	1,175,646**	28.25	0	56,680	56,680	.71
Private and Miscellaneous	1,795,566	43.15	1,063,997	1,674,467	2,738,408	34.37
TOTAL ACRES	4,160,494		3,704,302	4,261,760	7,966,080	

* Includes Forest Service lands from McKinley County.
** Includes Zuni and Ramah Navajo lands from McKinley County; Laguna lands from Sandoval County and Bernalillo County.
† Additional Forest Service lands from Sierra County.

the west, have been heavily surveyed. At Laguna, lands in the Mt. Taylor region and in a wide area around Grants, New Mexico have been pretty extensively surveyed. The Ramah Navajo, Laguna and Acoma peoples have all granted access to archeologists.

It should be remembered, however, that grants of access are not pro forma; that the Governor's offices are *always* contacted first to inquire as to how the petition is to be made to the Council or Governor. One must be prepared to make a gracious and thoughtful request, and then allow time for a decision to be conveyed. The taking of collections is generally discouraged or prohibited, and if you are permitted to take any, you must remember that artifacts are the property of the Tribe, not of the archeologist or institution conducting survey. Finally, many areas are considered sacred. These days, one is often asked to avoid certain general areas that have religious significance.

There are, of course, different concepts of land and its meaning in different societies. In Anglo society we think of our homes as a refuge, as a place wherein we have the right of privacy, if we wish it. The law of the land secures these privileges for us. Most Indian peoples view their land precisely as we view our own houses. In short, access to these lands varies from time to time and person to person. The southern portions of Zuni, Acoma and Laguna are not as well surveyed as the northern areas (near I-40). Much less survey has been conducted at Ramah (Navajo) and very little on lands of the Alamo (Puertocito) Navajo on the north slope of the Gallinas Mountains.

FEDERAL AND STATE LANDS

Federal and State lands comprise just over 50% of the total land area of this region. Access is easy, but antiquities permits are required for survey on all these lands. Most of us are quite used to these procedures. For those that are not, the State Archeologist of New Mexico is also (by both statute and tradition) the Director of the Laboratory of Anthropology (a Division of the Museum of New Mexico) in Santa Fe. This office (State Lands) or the State Historic Preservation Officer (also Santa Fe) will help you initiate your requests or advise you.

The two big land holders are the Bureau of Land Management and the U.S.D.A. Forest Service. East of the Rio Grande, the U.S. Army maintains a joint use area associated with its missile tracking facilities. Access south of the highway to Carrizozo requires special arrangements.

Survey coverage on lands administered by the Bureau of Land Management (much of these lands are in Berman's Driveway unit and east of the Rio Grande in Socorro County) has been minimal. The southern units of the Cibola Forest (Datil Mountains, San Mateo Mountains, Gallinas Mountains, Magdalena Mountains) are not well surveyed (again, refer to Map IV.3).

IMPACTS AND PRIORITIES

The major areas of impact run in a band along I-40, both north and south of the highway. These are occasioned by uranium development in the Grants uranium belt (the lower elevations of the Mt. Taylor area in Tainter's overview), and general population expansion around Grants-San Rafael and to the west around Gallup, New Mexico. Fortunately, these lands are among the most heavily surveyed in the state. A substantial part of the State's contract archeology is carried out in this region. Thus, while there is important loss to the archeological record, there is also a financial base for continued survey under federal law. In short, though impacts are intense, so is research. Matching grant surveys that may take place after this volume appears should focus primarily on thematic surveys to make National Register nominations.

Elsewhere in this region, there are few mining activities, though there is some exploration. The primary impacts are from timbering, an unusual degree of erosion along the plains of San Agustin, and pot-hunting or vandalism. Perhaps half the sites in the region are vandalized — more than in the central San Juan Basin but much less than in Mimbres country to the south. The areas north of Route 60 (over the crests—northward) to the southern portions of the Indian lands, are practically unsurveyed and reported as not so heavily vandalized. To the east of the Rio Grande, the western edge of the Chupadero Mesa country and the northern Jornada del Muerto are substantially unsurveyed (Mera was through there in the '40's) or unreported. From the Rio Grande to the west across the San Mateo Mountains the area is little surveyed, though said to be more highly vandalized.

Throughout the area, most surveys have been conducted primarily within several miles of major drainages and along passable roads. While the northernmost tier of the region has seen much contract archeological work, the area south of Cebolleta Mesa has seen little.

It will be essential to conduct additional survey in the areas outlined on the map to resolve the Anasazi-Mogollon issue. Since BLM/Forest Service and State lands are all involved (again, see Table IV.5), it would seem worthwhile to propose a joint venture of some kind, and we shall shortly make a proposal for acreages to be surveyed.

THE DATA

It is almost impossible to reconstruct actual survey coverage and intensity of coverage *accurately* from disparate sources. The following data are only a reasonable approximation of survey coverage and the number of recorded sites.

In the northern unit of this 20,000 square mile area, we calculate a total of 2,119 recorded sites. Some of these data are reported and summarized in Wimberly and Eidenbach (1980), but we exclude portions of the upper Puerco not on the Laguna Reservation, and surveys in the Mt. Taylor area not on Indian lands (i.e., Allan *et al.* 1976; Carroll *et al.*1979, etc.). These figures include the Zuni area. In addition, the Bureau of Indian Affairs, Albuquerque area office, has recently conducted a large sample survey in the higher elevations of Cebolleta Mesa for a proposed timber sale on Acoma Reservation lands. Their data are not included, but should make an interesting addition to Ruppe and Dittert. Pueblo sites recorded (Broster, personal communication) are not so large or varied as those recorded by Ruppe and Dittert, but substantial Paleo-Indian materials were recorded — a fascinating addition to Judge's (1973) Rio Grande survey, which is discussed by Tainter (1980a).

We compute the area of this northern unit at approximately 6,700 square miles. Thus, recorded site density for the region is high compared to the surface area estimated as actually surveyed. In calculating survey coverage, we compute all thematic and reconnaissance surveys at 10% of general surface area. We know that this is not genuinely accurate, but it is the method employed by Wimberly and Eidenbach (1980), so we decided to keep any margins of error consistent throughout the volume. We compute surveyed lands at roughly 210 square miles. We calculate site density at ten sites per square mile surveyed. While site density was rather low in the Lower Puerco/Salado surveys, averaging just under six sites per square mile, it was phenomenally high in the Yellowhouse Reservoir survey, where in ten square miles (25.3 k^2 — Hunter-Anderson 1978:6), 318 sites were recorded. It was also high at El Morro, 200 sites being recorded in 5-10 square miles (Watson, LeBlanc and Redman, n.d.).

In the southern unit, we had great difficulty computing both area surveyed and number of sites. Many (most, actually) surveys were thematic or reconnaissance, and we had trouble placing many sites in the Gila Forest of Catron County either in this or the Mimbres section. We estimate 165 square miles surveyed and 1,420 sites recorded. These data are summarized in Table IV.6.

146

Table IV.6
ESTIMATED SURVEY DATA*
WEST CENTRAL NEW MEXICO (Mt. Taylor-Socorro Districts)

	Mt. Taylor	Socorro	Entire Region
Square Miles covered:	210 sq. mi.	165 sq. mi.	375 sq. mi.
Number of Sites:	2,119	1,420	3,539
Density Square Miles covered:	10.19 sq. mi.	8.6 sq. mi.	9-10 sq. mi.
Total Square Miles in Area:	6,700	12,500	19,200
Percent of Region Surveyed:	3+%	1.4%	2%

Major under-represented areas: Upper Salado drainage, including North Gallina Slope; San Mateo and South Magdalena Mountains; all of area east of Rio Grande.

- -

*Note: These data are rough estimates, only intended for comparative purposes at the decision-making level. They are not intended for the conduct of formal research.

We note that these data cannot be compared well to data from the San Juan Basin or selected surveys from the Mimbres drainage. Relatively fewer ceramic and lithic scatters have been recorded, compared to other regions. The SJBRUS file (the San Juan Data base) shows that it was not common to record many of these until the 1950's, or later. With the advent of contract archeology, the practice of recording everything has become common. Since comparatively few contract surveys have been conducted in some areas of the Socorro district in the last few years, we feel a strong bias is present.

RESEARCH SUGGESTIONS

The eastern portion of this study area overlaps one of the most undersurveyed regions in the Southwest. From west to east there is, allegedly, a cultural gradient in Archaic times between San Pedro Cochise materials and different plains Archaic traditions. To the north, in the upper Puerco drainage, Irwin-Williams argues, the Oshara assemblages are a distinctive *in situ* lithic tradition which was transformed during the En Medio stage to the Basketmaker. Others do not agree. Lang (1977) views the Galisteo Basin material as having elements of San Pedro Cochise.

In the early Basketmaker III period, it is suggested that there is early Mogollon influence on the Anasazi, brownwares being found in early sites to the north (Sambrito Brown). Many have suggested an alleged Anasazi intrusion into the area. Most cite the appearance of Anasazi whitewares and above-ground architecture. Later, Ford, Schroeder and Peckham (1972) argue Mogollon influence into the north, the contact zone being along the Rio Salado. Again, Wimberly and Eidenbach (1980; and also Eidenbach 1980) decline to accept their argument. Ruppe and Dittert's surveys led to the conceptual formation of the Acoma cultural province, which Tainter (1980a) declines to accept as formulated. The styles of argument do change, but the observation that the area is a complex contact zone does not. The Southwestern corner of the region evidences an early Mogollon development; some of the earliest Anasazi decorated wares are found in the northern portion of the area. Many argue that the Salado occupation was formed here before abandonment in 1300 or 1325, and that reoccupation occurred in the Rio Grande Glaze period in the eastern sector. Finally, the area is thought to divide the early historic Tiwa (to the north) from the Piro to the south.

147

As a practical matter, little survey has been conducted in the eastern areas because the archeological remains, with the exception of a few more spectacular sites like Gallina Spring in the Gallinas Mountains unit of Cibola Forest and Pottery Mound (Hibben 1955, 1975), are not spectacular and lie beyond the core areas of highly published archeological systems. Secondly, some of this back country is hard to get into. For a summary of recent work in the northeastern quarter of the region see Wimberly and Eidenbach (1980). None of the theoretical issues mentioned above will be resolved until a substantial survey is conducted to solve the problem.

Specifically, we propose that a long north-south transect be laid out at the southern boundary of Socorro County, along the east slope of the San Mateo Mountains (just west of I-25), to proceed due north (until it meets State Road 107 opposite San Antonio, New Mexico). One could then proceed north along the west slope of the South Baldy Mountains, roughly to Magdalena, New Mexico, thence due north along the east slope of the Gallinas Mountains. From there one could continue down the northeast slope of the Gallinas, thence across the Salado drainage and then north along the western rim of Lucero Mesa to the southern portion of Cebolleta Mesa. That is a north-south transect of roughly 95 miles. A transect should then be run east, just north of Magdalena, crossing I-25 roughly between Chamizal and Lemitar, and on into the lowlands of the Jornada to the crown of Chupadero Mesa, that is, roughly 65 miles. These two total 160 miles of transect.

Any number of sample designs could be employed. Simple square mile blocks centered on major slope features and ecotones would be appropriate. Such a survey would cross every environmental zone in the region, the entire altitude gradient, and every possible slope exposure. One square mile of four would be ample coverage; i.e. 40 square miles. There are those that propose very small sampling fractions, and there is good justification for this, but we offer several thoughts. 1) National Register sites get lost from small sample blocks. 2) Every square mile block can be controlled for ecological microvariation and restratified for research purposes in any number of ways. 3) Most surveyors will not be able to locate small quadrats in many parts of such country accurately. 4) Square mile units would allow the BLM and Forest Service simply to eliminate certain areas of their lands as surveyed.

Such a survey would crosscut all three of those units of the Cibola Forest which lie in Socorro County. Further, it would crosscut the Ladron, Stallion and Driveway planning units of the BLM. A major historic mining district would be crosscut near Magdalena as well. Valuing labor at $15,000/annum and overhead at 25%, such a survey would cost roughly $250,000 dollars in 1980. It might be possible for a cooperative funding effort to be mounted with the SHPO's office. Since the funds would be on a matching basis (this usually means that an institution or individual puts up half the labor *gratis* and collects only half the cost of materials), the total agency cost would be about $125,000.00.

Such a survey would connect the northwesternmost portion of the Mimbres area to the Acoma culture province and the easternmost Tularosa phase sites to Chupadero Mesa, where, allegedly, there are contemporaneous P-III developments. Distributional maps plotting ceramic frequencies north-south and east-west should be prepared, and all other already recorded sites in the eastern region should have ceramic frequencies plotted and summary descriptions appended (see Marshall, n.d.). If this survey doesn't allow one to locate the spatial correlates of the missing P-III horizon in the Salado and Puerco drainages, permit resolution of the existence of the Socorro Expression's increasingly debatable San Marcial phase, and locate the Chupadero wares missing from the lower Puerco-Salado surveys, then nothing will. We would also be surprised if Paleo-Indian and Archaic materials were not recorded, given proximity to the Mockingbird Gap Clovis site, among others.

148

This area is a real key to understanding cultural process in New Mexico. If we were to see these ceramic distributions and the environmental/geographic correlates for the P-III occupations, we might understand enough to say what excavation data we would require for further solutions. Throughout this volume, it has not been our intention to specify precisely what people ought to do, or precisely what research should be undertaken. Nonetheless, we believe that some version of such a survey in eastern Socorro County and southern Valencia County merits very serious consideration.

Let us turn, then, to National and State Register considerations.

STATE AND NATIONAL REGISTER PROPERTIES IN WEST CENTRAL NEW MEXICO

Our records indicate that there are 44 sites and districts in this region nominated to the State Register. These do not include individual sites in the Manuelito Canyon complex and historic Zuni, Acoma and Laguna. Multiple nominations include the Zuni-Cibola complex, the Manuelito Canyon complex and El Morro National Monument. Five sites are on the National Register.

As in other regions of the state, certain kinds of sites tend to be very heavily represented, while others attract less attention. For an approximate listing of these, see Tables IV.7 and IV.8 below. As Judge (in press) has recently pointed out, it is often very difficult to separate these by component from available descriptions, hence we may have summarized imprecisely. Five of these sites, plus a number in the Zuni-Cibola complex, are on the National Register of Historic Places. We will return to a discussion of these after presenting site descriptions and sketches.

Table IV.7
PHASES OF STATE and NATIONAL REGISTER SITES IN WEST CENTRAL NEW MEXICO

NORTHERN UNIT (Mt. Taylor)*:

Paleo-Indian	No sites
Archaic	1 Site (Comanche Springs)
BM-II	No sites
BM-III	2? (possible components at Yellowhouse & Village of Great Kivas)
P-I	1 site component at Dittert No. 444 (possible components in Manuelito Canyon complex)
P-II	1 site component (possible Late P-II at Gallinas Springs)
P-III	10 sites (see Table IV.8)
P-IV	14? Early P-IV components at most nominated sites. Pottery Mound is *pure* P-IV.
P-V	5 components at 5 sites in Zuni area (+ historic Acoma, Laguna and Zuni pueblos — not subject of this volume).
Total Number	34 Components; 20+ Sites

SOUTHERN UNIT (Socorro County)*:

Paleo-Indian	3 sites (Mockingbird Gap + Ake & Bat Cave (late Paleo-Indian)
Archaic	6 sites (Ake, Bat Cave, Tularosa Cave, LA 3998, 4002, 4010)
Pine Lawn	3 (Mogollon village & components at Bat & Tularosa Caves)
Georgetown/San Francisco	3 (same as above)
Three Circle	4 (same as above + component at LA 3993)
Reserve	6 (Cox Ranch, Tularosa Cave, LA 4029, 4026, 4023, 4033)
Tularosa	Apache Creek, Tularosa Cave, Gallinas Springs, Sandoval Cave, LA 3993, LA 4026, 4029, 4030.
Other	Kiatuthlanna-1-(LA 4032-pithouse village); P-IV Glazeware-1-(Pottery Mound); Zuni Salt Lake-1-(Historic)
Total Number	27 Components; 24 Sites

* Note: We do not have data on all the components that may exist in and around these sites, and we do not yet have an inventory of sites/components in the Manuelito Canyon nomination.

Table IV.8
PREHISTORIC STATE and NATIONAL REGISTER SITES*
WEST CENTRAL NEW MEXICO
(National Register Properties are starred)

Reg. No.	Name	LA No.	County	Phase
MT. TAYLOR UNIT:				
No. 095	Cebolleta Ruin	424	Valencia	Late Pilares-Kowina (P-III — P-IV)
No. 096	Cienega Ruins	425, 426	Valencia	Kowina (P-III—P-IV)
No. 059*	El Morro National Mon.	99, 430	Valencia	Kowina (P-III—P-IV)
No. 109	Pueblo de los Muertos	5536	Valencia	P-III — P-IV
No. 444*	Dittert Site	11723	Valencia	P-II—P-IV (Cebolleta Can)
No. 436	Correo Snake Pit	—	Valencia	P-IV
No. 724	Pottery Mound	416, 8683	Valencia	P-IV
No. 102	Gigantes Ruin	1551	Valencia	P-III—P-IV
ZUNI AREA:				
No. 478	Comanche Springs Site	14904	Valencia	Archaic + BM-III (poss) + P-III
No. 010*	Hawikuh Ruin		McKinley	P-II — P-V
No. 285	Kechipbowa Ruin	8758	McKinley	P-IV — P-V
No. 14	TG&E Route	3984 et al.	McKinley	BM-III? P-III, IV & V
No. 374	Zuni Cibola Complex (NHL)	see below	McKinley	BM-III? P-III, IV & V
No. 103	Heshotauthla Ruin	2114	McKinley	
No. 287	Kwa'kin'a Ruin	1053	McKinley	
No. 286	Kyakiima Ruin	492	McKinley	These are P-III—P-V w/an early component (BM-III ---P-I?) at Yellow House & P-II at Great Kivas
No. 288	Mats'a:kya Ruin	— —	McKinley	
No. 121	Jack's Lake Ruin	433	McKinley	
No. 128	Yellow House Ruin	493	McKinley	
No. 239	Manuelito Complex (NHL)	— —	McKinley	BM-III—P-III—early P-IV
SOCORRO UNIT:				
No. 092	Apache Creek Ruin	2949	Catron	Apache Creek (Reserve-Tularosa) or P-I/II—P-III
No. 424	Ake Site	13423	Catron	Paleo-Indian + Archaic (Mogollon trace)
No. 093	Bat Cave	4939	Catron	Late Paleo-Indian — Mogollon (A.D. 1100)
No. 306	Mogollon Village	11568	Catron	Georgetown—Three Circle Mogollon
No. 204	Zuni Salt Lakes	— —	Catron	Zuni—Historic & Prehist.
No. 125	Tularosa Cave	4427	Catron	Archaic—Tularosa Phase
No. 263	TG&E Route Archeological Sites	3984 et al.	Catron	Archaic—P-III—P-IV + Kiatuthlanna (A.D. 800s)
No. 713	Cox Ranch Pueblo	13681	Catron	Reserve
No. 101	Gallinas Springs Ruin	1178 & 4180	Socorro	Late P-II—Early P-IV (1100—1325)
No. 161	Mockingbird Gap Archeological Site	— —	Socorro	Paleo-Indian (Clovis)
No. 116	Sandal Cave	8696	Socorro	P-II—P-III + Late BM

*This list does not include historic pueblos of Acoma, Laguna, Zuni

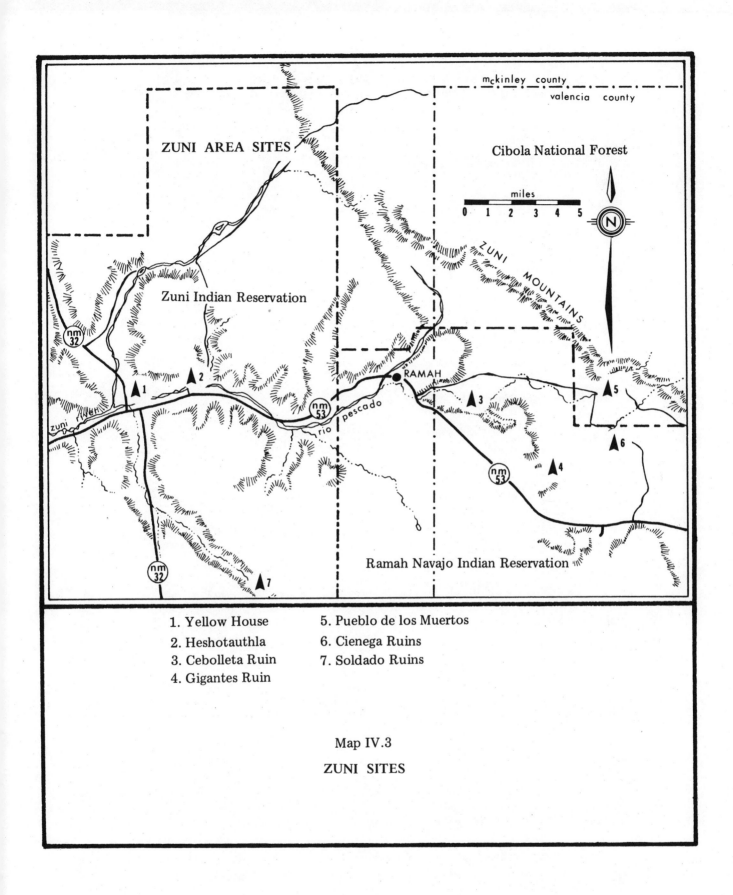

ZUNI AREA SITES

Cibola National Forest

mckinley county
valencia county

miles

0 1 2 3 4 5

N

Zuni Indian Reservation

RAMAH

rio pescado

Ramah Navajo Indian Reservation

1. Yellow House   5. Pueblo de los Muertos
2. Heshotauthla   6. Cienega Ruins
3. Cebolleta Ruin   7. Soldado Ruins
4. Gigantes Ruin

Map IV.3

ZUNI SITES

SHORT DESCRIPTIONS OF STATE AND
NATIONAL REGISTER SITES: WEST CENTRAL NEW MEXICO

CEBOLLETA RUIN (No. 095, LA 424)

This site is situated at 7,000 feet elevation on a low bench along the south side of Togeye Canyon. This site is limited to a single occupation dating roughly to the 13th and 14th centuries.

Two dissimilar architectural units are present at this site, and consist of a square masonry pueblo, 375 feet by 350 feet, and a smaller circular unit, approximately 180 feet in diameter. In addition, there are approximately 20 to 22 kivas and one great kiva. Pottery found includes Tularosa B/W, Klagetoh B/W, St. Johns Polychrome, Wingate B/R, Kwakina Polychrome, Heshotauthla Polychrome, Kowina B/R, and Pinedale Polychrome. This site was reported by Dittert and is discussed briefly by Tainter (1980a) in notes on the *Acoma Culture Province*. This site survived the P-III to early P-IV collapse in the forested areas at least briefly.

CIENEGA RUINS (No. 096, LA 425 and LA 426)

These two sites are situated in a stabilized sand dune area in the El Morro Valley about 3.5 miles north, northeast of El Morro National Monument. The sites are located at 7,220 feet in elevation in a grassland environment.

Both sites consist of oval roomblocks, constructed of roughly shaped basalt. Besides the very unusual layout of these sites, LA 425 exhibits the remains of a masonry-lined water well within the plaza. The self-contained design of these sites does indeed suggest that episodes of site intrusion were occurring. See McGimsey (1980) for descriptions of similar site features from probably contemporaneous sites to the south on Marianna Mesa.

The ceramics found at these sites indicate that LA 425 is slightly earlier than LA 426, but there is a considerable overlap in which both sites were probably occupied at the same time. Ceramics include Tularosa B/W, Klagetoh B/W, Wingate B/R, St. Johns Polychrome, Heshotauthla Polychrome, and Kwakina Polychrome, indicating a date in the 13th and extending into the early 14th centuries.

EL MORRO NATIONAL MONUMENT (No. 059 -- Woodbury's Site)

In addition to the historic inscriptions (dating from 1605-1906) at El Morro, there are the remains of two Indian pueblos, each containing approximately 250 rooms. Eighteen rooms of one pueblo (Atsinna) have been excavated. These pueblos date approximately from A.D. 1250 to 1300+.

PUEBLO de los MUERTOS (No. 109, LA 5536)

This site consists of a large rectangular pueblo constructed of sandstone masonry. There are approximately 200 to 300 rooms with 7 or 8 kivas and a great kiva located in the plaza. The site is situated at 7,280 feet, within the mouth of Muerto Canyon. The primary vegetation is pinyon and juniper, with some ponderosa pine.

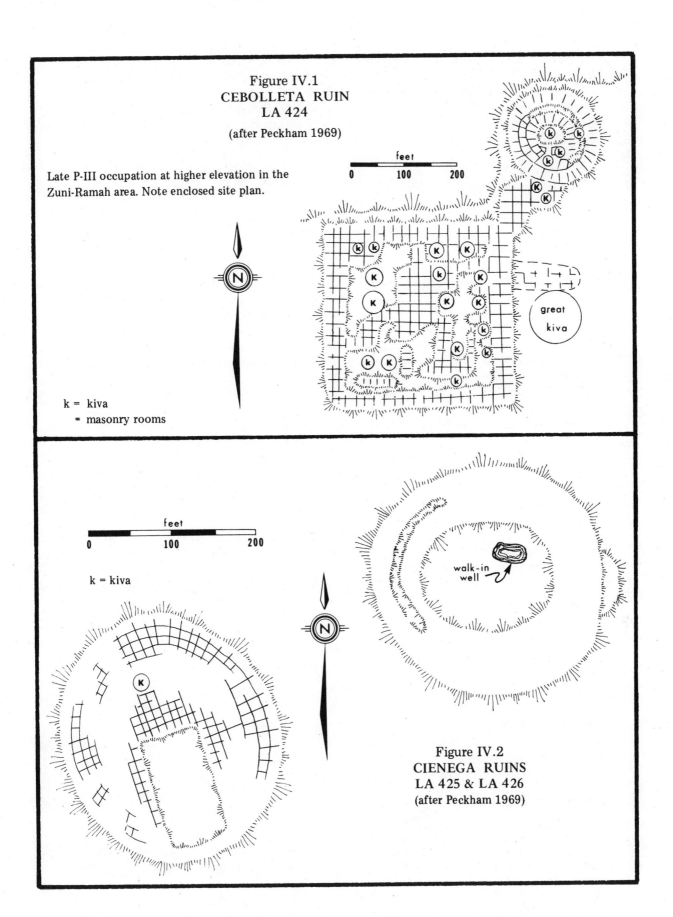

Figure IV.1
CEBOLLETA RUIN
LA 424

(after Peckham 1969)

Late P-III occupation at higher elevation in the Zuni-Ramah area. Note enclosed site plan.

feet
0   100   200

great
kiva

k = kiva
= masonry rooms

feet
0   100   200

k = kiva

walk-in
well

Figure IV.2
CIENEGA RUINS
LA 425 & LA 426
(after Peckham 1969)

153

The ceramics at this site indicate a date within the A.D. 13th and early 14th centuries. The layout of the site is an enclosed plaza, similar in plan to certain of the late compound sites in the Gila Forest (Berman 1980) and some of the smaller Santa Fe B/W plaza sites on the Pajarito Plateau near Los Alamos, New Mexico. Is this site design related to later Salado architectural features, or is it a function of social disintegration and conflict during this period of collapse?

DITTERT SITE (No. 444, LA 11723)

The Dittert site is located near the mouth of Armijo Canyon at the edge of the pinyon-juniper zone, at an elevation of 7300 feet.

The pueblo itself consists of approximately 30 surface rooms and a kiva. Eight rooms and the kiva were excavated by Dittert in 1948. From ceramic evidence, this ruin was found to date between A.D. 950 and 1350, or during the late Cebolleta phase and Pilares phase. According to Dittert (1959), eleven miles north of this site 5-10% of the pottery is brownware sherds. In the area of this site, 15-20% of the pottery is brownwares. At this site in particular, the brownwares total 30%. Further to the south, the percentage is around 50%. Recent survey data (Wimberly and Eidenbach 1980) suggest that this ceramic distribution has both temporal and geographic correlates.

CORREO SNAKE PIT (No. 436)

This site consists of a natural geologic feature, formed by a hot mineral spring. The site resembles a cone with a depression within the center, approximately 16-35 feet in diameter and 29 feet deep. The site most likely symbolized a *sipapu*, and was used in pre-Spanish times by the Acomas, and later by the Lagunas.

Material recovered from the depression includes beads, dart and arrow material, wood objects, projectile points, pot polishers, fetish stones, pottery, textiles, sandals, turquoise pendents, prayer bundles, leather and 908 prayer sticks. The pottery found includes Glaze A Red, Puerco B/W, Zuni Glaze, and Tularosa B/W. Judge (1973) briefly discusses material obtained from this site.

POTTERY MOUND (No. 724, LA 416 and LA 8683)

Pottery Mound is a large Pueblo ruin located in the Puerco Valley at approximately 5,000 feet in elevation. The site itself is constructed of adobe, and covers an area of approximately seven acres. Ceramic remains from this site indicate a date of 1300 to 1450. Hibben (1975) published a volume on kiva art from this site, and the University of New Mexico field school worked there during the summer of 1979. This P-IV site postdates the upland collapse in the Gila Forest and El Morro/Cebolleta Mesa area. There are over 500 rooms at the site, and population has been estimated at more than 1,000.

GIGANTES RUIN (No. 102, LA 1551)

This site is situated at the head of a canyon on a narrow promontory which projects from the southwest side of a cliff. A natural feature at this site consists of a small window which has eroded through the cliff which forms the northern limit of the site.

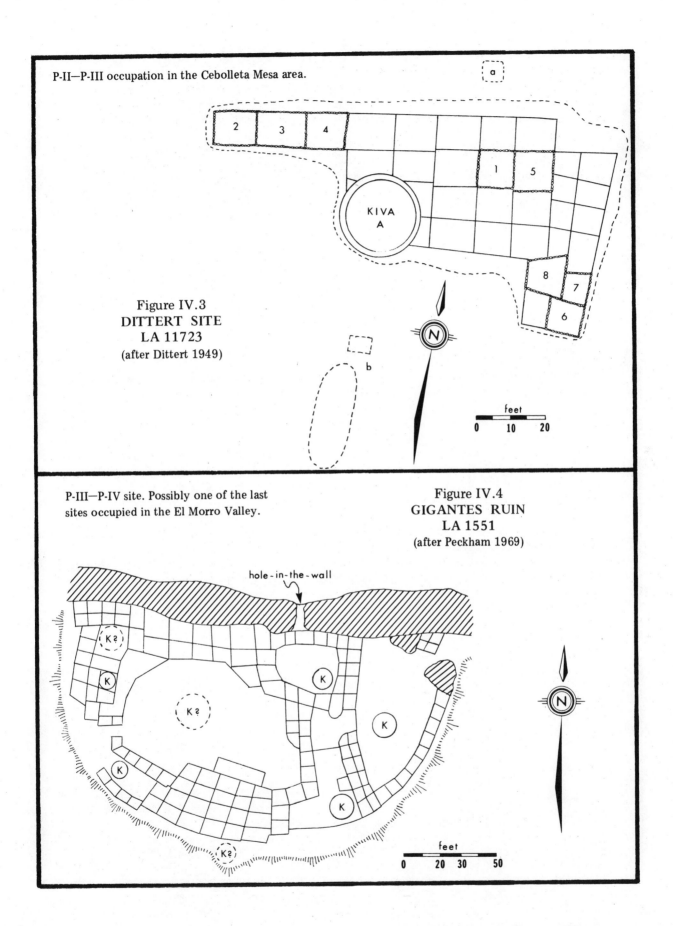

P-II—P-III occupation in the Cebolleta Mesa area.

Figure IV.3
DITTERT SITE
LA 11723
(after Dittert 1949)

KIVA
A

feet
0   10   20

P-III—P-IV site. Possibly one of the last
sites occupied in the El Morro Valley.

Figure IV.4
GIGANTES RUIN
LA 1551
(after Peckham 1969)

hole-in-the-wall

feet
0   20 30   50

155

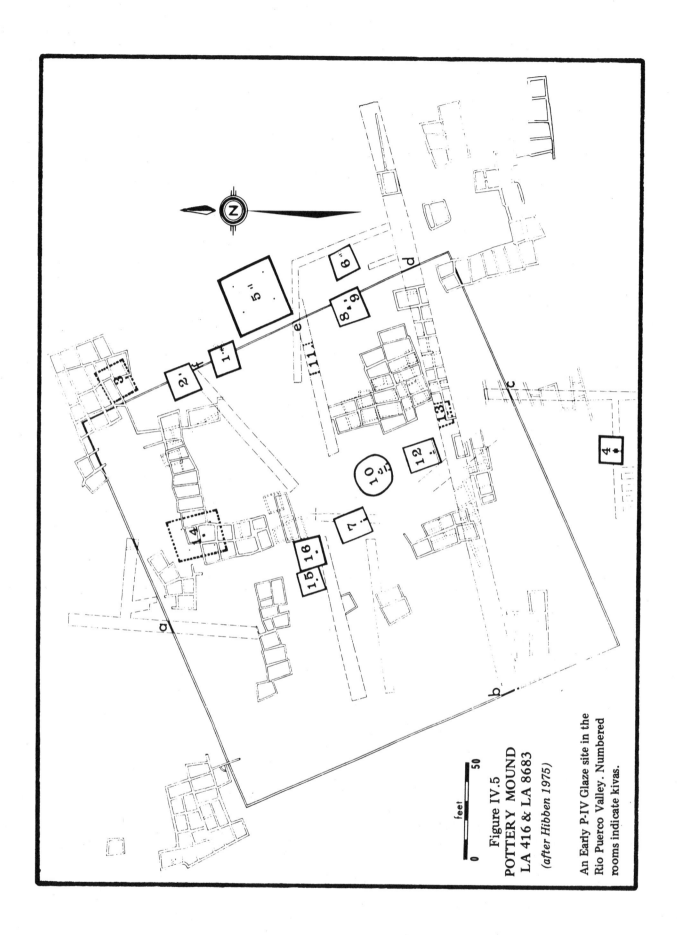

Figure IV.5
POTTERY MOUND
LA 416 & LA 8683
(after Hibben 1975)

An Early P-IV Glaze site in the
Rio Puerco Valley. Numbered
rooms indicate kivas.

feet
0   50

Compared to several other sites in the El Morro Valley, Gigantes ruin is small, with approximately 125 rooms and five to eight kivas. Construction consists of sandstone masonry.

Ceramics found at Gigantes ruin consist of Tularosa B/W, Klagetoh B/W, Wingate B/R, St. Johns Polychrome, Heshotauthla Polychrome and Kwakina Polychrome. Also, unlike other sites in the area, this site exhibits Pinnawa Red-on-white. These types suggest a date from A.D. 1175 to 1450, which is longer and later than most nearby sites. This may be one of the relatively few sites in the area that survived the A.D. 1300-1325 abandonments. Is site setting any different than for those sites that experienced the A.D. 1200-1325 P-III collapse?

COMANCHE SPRINGS SITE (No. 478, LA 14904)

Comanche Springs site is located approximately 4.5 miles west of the foot of the Manzano Mountains, at approximately 5,400 feet. Occupation of this site began during the Archaic period (~3000 B.P.) and includes a possible Basketmaker III pithouse, some Anasazi use at approximately A.D. 1200 and several structures of Hispanic origin used at 1600-1700.

Numerous examples of projectile points, lithic debris and fire-cracked rocks from the Archaic period have been recovered from Comanche Springs. Numerous bison bones have also been recovered.

The later components have yielded glaze decorated pottery and Spanish Majolica sherds. Just when were bison an important resource in the area? Many scholars have proposed that late Puebloan groups moved into the plains to hunt bison and/or partly abandoned agricultural pursuits. Other Archaic bison kill sites should be located, since the availability of bison in late Archaic times in western New Mexico might have forestalled the stimulus for agricultural development in plentiful areas.

ZUNI-CIBOLA COMPLEX (Reg. No. 374, National Historic Landmark)
(Descriptions cited from *Master Plan for Proposed Zuni-Cibola National Cultural Park, New Mexico* 1971)

VILLAGE OF THE GREAT KIVAS (LA 631) -- Located on the north side of the Nutria Valley at the mouth of Red Paint Canyon, about 17 miles northeast of Zuni Pueblo, the Village of the Great Kivas is representative of the prehistoric occupancy of the area from the 11th into the 13th century A.D. This site exhibits, in its architecture and its ceramics, solid evidence that peoples of southern Mogollon tradition lived beside or among peoples of the northern Anasazi tradition. Situated at the base of a high cliff — decorated with many petroglyphs and a few pictographs — the ruins consist of three separate house blocks, associated trash areas, and two great kivas, covering about three and a half acres. The excavated portions of these ruins are in fair condition. This site was excavated and reported by Roberts (1932).

YELLOW HOUSE (LA 493) — This ruin — the Zuni name it Heshotathluptsina — is located at the intersection of New Mexico State Highway 32 and 53, on the north side of the Rio Pescado opposite the mouth of Horsehead Canyon, thus readily accessible to the traveling public. Covering roughly an acre and a half, this late prehistoric site is probably representative of the 14th-century ancestral Zunis. Ceramics found on this site suggest that a 9th or 10th-century habitation may also have existed here. Unexcavated and well-preserved, Yellow House appears as large mounds of rock and debris, with walls that may stand nearly five feet. This site provides a link between the Village of the Great Kivas and the early prehistoric period of the Cities of Cibola.   This site was also recorded during the recent Yellowhouse Dam survey (Hunter-Anderson 1978) and was mapped by Mike Marshall.

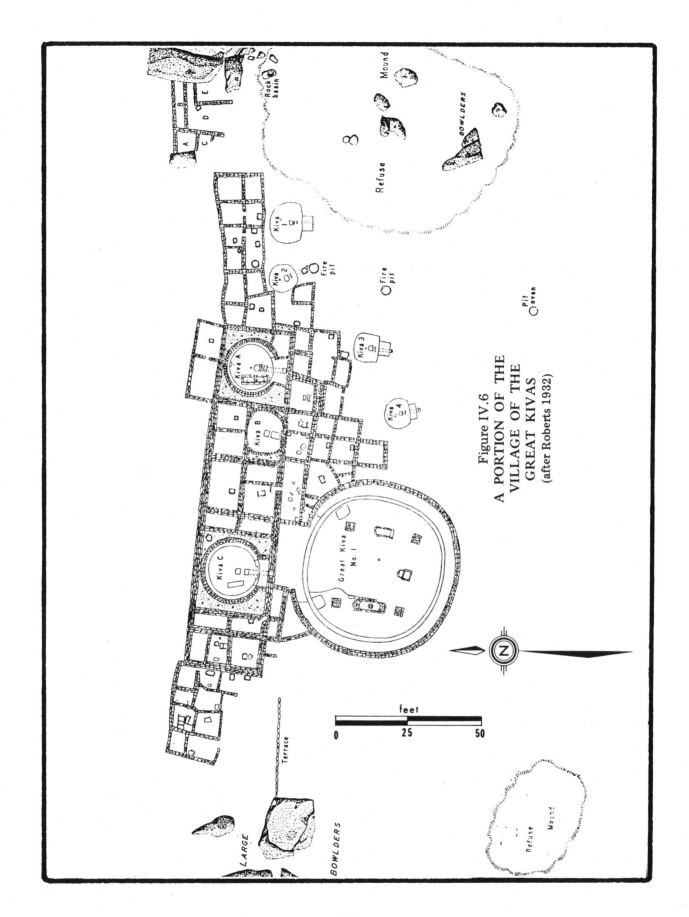

Figure IV.6
A PORTION OF THE
VILLAGE OF THE
GREAT KIVAS
(after Roberts 1932)

158

HAWIKUH (LA 37) — Situated about 16 miles southwest of Zuni Pueblo, this was the first of the Cities encountered by Coronado in 1540. Extensively excavated and backfilled, Hawikuh now appears as a formless mass of rock and pottery strewn over a low hill. Most of the more than 400 rooms excavated were backfilled, and thus are expected to be in an excellent state of preservation. Excavations were carried out during the first two decades of this century by F.W. Hodge. At the base of the hill on which Hawikuh is situated are the remains of the 17th-century mission of La Purisima Concepcion de Hawikuh, consisting of a church, its convent, and outbuildings. These historic ruins are in a poor state, but enough photographs and reports exist to provide guidance for a restoration program.

KECHIPBOWA (LA 8758) — This ruin is located about three miles to the east of Hawikuh on the northern escarpment of the Ojo Caliente Wash. It has a small, continuous-nave, 17th-century stone church. In this century, the robbing of stone has reduced the walls from their original height, but the structure could be accurately restored from accumulated photographic and archeological evidence. Limited parts of the pueblo have been excavated and the exposed walls have been found in fair condition. The remains of an earlier pueblo, similar to those of the prehistoric circular kivas near Hawikuh, underlie the structural remnants. Slab-type houses that may represent 8th or 9th-century prehistoric occupations are found near the pueblo. While this site contains historic remains, its major value lies in demonstrating the development of Zuni culture during the 15th and 16th centuries, prior to the arrival of the Spanish. Kechipbowa should provide the archeological link between Yellow House and the late prehistoric period of the Cities of Cibola.

HALONA — This is one of the Cities of Cibola. It underlies the present-day Pueblo of Zuni. Halona is also the present day pueblo of Zuni. This site is one of the six Zuni pueblos visited by Coronado in 1540. The exact founding date of Halona is uncertain, but sherds dating to the 1300's have been found here.

KWAKINA (LA 1053) — Extensive low-mounded ruins located about six miles west of Zuni Pueblo, on the north bank of the Zuni River, are the only remains of this village. Cultivated fields surround the site. Approach is by an almost impassable, severely rutted road with some cross-country travel also required. The site is significant as one of the unstudied Cities of Cibola.

MATSAKYA — This site, believed to have been the largest of the Cities, lies three miles east of Zuni. At present, it appears as a great mound of debris; no standing walls are visible. There are probably hundreds of rooms, walls intact, beneath the mound. Matsakya possesses religious significance for the Zunis.

KYAKIMA (LA 492) — This site is situated on a knoll under the southwest corner of Towayalane, four miles southeast of Zuni. The site, large and in good condition, is built on four terraces. Kyakima, like Matsakya, possesses religious significance for the Zuni.

[End of Cited Material]

HESHOTAUTHLA RUIN (No. 103, LA 2114)

Heshotauthla Ruin consists of the remains of a large polygonal pueblo, constructed of sandstone masonry. Ceramics at this site have yielded small amounts of pottery dating to the early 11th century, but most of the ceramics date to the 13th and 14th centuries.

JACK'S LAKE RUIN (No. 121, LA 5534)

The Soldado ruin is situated on a low rise along the west bank of Soldado Canyon, at an elevation of 7,100 feet. The ruin is constructed of sandstone masonry, and consists of two major plaza areas surrounded by roomblocks. One portion of the site is rectangular in shape and is connected to a circular roomblock. Three kiva depressions, within the plaza areas, are also present. Ceramics from Soldado Ruin suggest a date within the 12th and 13th centuries. Again, we have a large site which was abandoned during late P-III times.

MANUELITO COMPLEX (NHL – No. 239)

This area contains such sites as Tower Ruins and the Great Ruins. Ruins in the canyon area date from Archaic periods (isolated Paleo-Indian point finds are also reported) to abandonment between 1300 and 1325. The most spectacular ruins are well-built coursed masonry structures. The main plaza area and roomblocks are tremendous. The area abounds with St. Johns Polychrome and Tularosa Black-on-white. It, like most sites in the San Juan Basin and Socorro areas, was abandoned between 1300 and 1325. Nonetheless, occupation in the canyon area was intense and long-lived compared to that in most other localities in New Mexico. See Tainter (1980a:86-88) for a short discussion. Weaver (1978) has written his doctoral dissertation on the area.

APACHE CREEK RUIN (LA 2949)

This site is situated on a low terrace along the west bank of the Tularosa River, near the confluence of the Tularosa River and Apache Creek. The site consists of an estimated 13 pithouses, four masonry roomblocks, and a great kiva. There are about 35 to 40 rooms altogether within the roomblocks. The Apache Creek site was occupied primarily near the end of the Mogollon period, and has components attributed to the Reserve phase, the transitional Apache Creek phase, and/or the Tularosa phase. Recall that Apache Creek phase sites (A.D. 1075-1200) are considered enigmatic because of the pithouse rooms and the frequent failure to reach the full P-III characteristics (including presence of certain ceramics, i.e. St. Johns Polychrome) of other Tularosa phase sites in the Gila Forest area.

AKE SITE (LA 13423)

The Ake site is a multicomponent site, consisting of Paleo-Indian, Archaic and Mogollon occupations. The oldest component is a Folsom occupation which produced a number of Folsom points, tools, and the remains of muskrat and bison.

The next component consists of a Cochise culture occupation. This occupation yielded numerous manos and metates along with cores, waste flakes and tools. The final prehistoric use of this site is indicated by several sherds from a single Alma Plain vessel. The Ake site was excavated by Pat Beckett (1980).

BAT CAVE (LA 4935)
(Dick 1965)

One of the most famous sites in the Southwest, Bat Cave yielded evidence of corn at 3000 B.C. This date was derived early in the use of the C-14 technique and some scholars reckon a 2000 B.C. date. The monograph reporting the excavation is but one of a distinguished

160

series of reports produced over many years by the School of American Research in Santa Fe. This monograph is, we suggest, required reading. Bat Cave is located on the southern margin of the Plains of San Agustin.

MOGOLLON VILLAGE (LA 11568)

This site consists of 19 or more pithouses, situated on a mesa top at 5,140 feet elevation, on the left bank of the San Francisco River. This village was occupied during the Georgetown, San Francisco and Three Circle phases (ca. A.D. 600 or 700 to 900). These phases predate the alleged split between the Mimbres sequence in the south and the Reserve/Tularosa phases in the Socorro district. Note the "bean-shaped house" 5A (refer to Martin and Plog 1973:91 for descriptions).

ZUNI SALT LAKE

An important Zuni sacred place where the Zuni people gathered salt in early historic times. Zuni Salt Lake is mentioned in Bolton's (1949) accounts of the Coronado expedition and is mentioned briefly in the recent Tainter (1980a) overview of the Mt. Taylor area. It is located northwest of Quemado, New Mexico.

TULAROSA CAVE (LA 4427)

This cave, at 6,792 feet in elevation, was occupied as early as 2300 ± 200 B.P. (300 ± 200 B.C.) in the lowest level. It was excavated by Paul S. Martin (Martin and Plog 1973:276) who found numerous examples of corn, squash, beans, nuts, and seeds, with manos and metates, flaked tools, basketry, sandals and a wide array of ceremonial objects were also recovered.

From 150 B.C. to A.D. 1200-1250, the assemblage of artifacts increases in variety and quantity. The Tularosa Valley area experienced population increase between A.D. 900-1200. It is from decreasing evidence for use of corn at this cave and the scarcity of Georgetown-San Francisco phase pithouses in the Pine Lawn area that Martin and Plog (1973) infer a population decline between A.D. 500 and 700 in the region. LeBlanc (Chapter V) declines to accept this proposition, for he sees substantial use of corn during the Georgetown occupations of the Mimbres Valley. Until LeBlanc's excavation data are available to us, we favor Martin and Plog. Nonetheless, the issue is not resolved. We have tentatively suggested a general dispersal of population at this (A.D. 500-700) period.

TG&E LINE

These descriptions are, admittedly, somewhat cryptic. Nonetheless, this is a good type of nomination, for highly variable archeological remains are protected.

LA 3984 — L-shaped pueblo, 25 rooms (1050-1100)
LA 3990 — waffle garden
LA 3993 — nine separate pueblos of 2-20 rooms each, one great kiva, 7 other kivas
       (A.D. 950-1050; 1175-1275)
LA 3998 — Archaic site, 7 hearths, pits, flakes and tools
LA 4000 — fieldhouse, one room (A.D. 1300)
LA 4002 — Archaic, flakes, manos
LA 4010 — Archaic, flakes, burnt rock, one mano

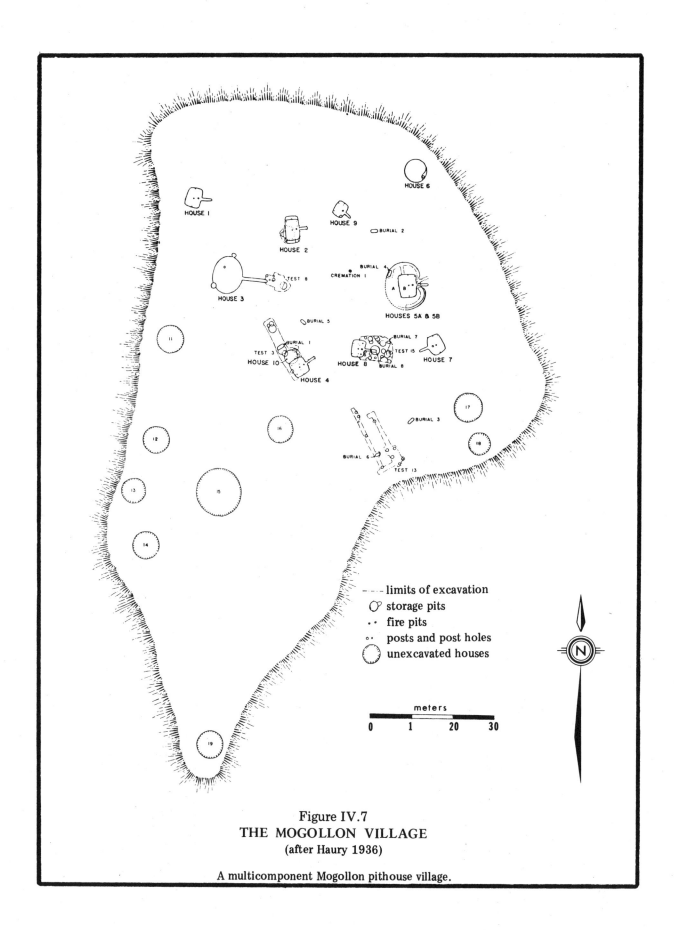

Figure IV.7
THE MOGOLLON VILLAGE
(after Haury 1936)

A multicomponent Mogollon pithouse village.

162

LA 4015 — petroglyphs

LA 4023 — pueblo, block-shaped, 20 rooms and one kiva (A.D. 1000's, major occupation during 1100's)

LA 4026 — series of pueblos, 200 rooms total, great kiva (A.D. 1100-1250)

LA 4029 — L-shaped pueblo, no kiva depression (A.D. 1000's, second component A.D. 1100-1250, Tularosa)

LA 4030 — pueblo of 50 rooms — 2 components (A.D. 1100-1250, Tularosa; earlier A.D. 1000's)

*LA 4032 — pithouse village (Kiatuthlanna phase, A.D. 800's), number hundreds of pithouses and slab rooms

LA 4033 — two small pueblos, 8 rooms total (A.D. 1000's)

*This is an amazing size for a pithouse village. We wish we had the full data available to us at this writing.

COX RANCH PUEBLO (Mogollon Pueblo — LA 13681)

This pueblo consists of the largest Reserve phase (A.D. 950?-1150?) village known, with an estimated 300 rooms. It is located north-northeast of Red Hill, New Mexico and south-southwest of Zuni Salt Lake. The site is situated on the western slope of a wide canyon, near the canyon wall at approximately 6,600 feet. Mike Marshall analyzed a small sample of ceramics from this site and found an equal number of Anasazi Graywares and Mogollon Brownwares.

GALLINAS SPRINGS RUIN (LA 1178, 1180)

This is an extremely large pueblo located in the southern foothills of the Gallinas Mountains at an elevation of 7,400 feet. Surface remains indicate 400-500 multistoried rooms arranged in three to six tiers around a semi-enclosed plaza. There are four kiva depressions in the plaza. Ceramics are alleged (Davis and Winkler 1962) to include degenerate Mesa Verde Black-on-white, and perhaps intimate a post-A.D. 1300 occupation of Mesa Verde immigrants. Others (Wimberly and Eidenbach 1980) question this interpretation. Dr. J. Tainter of the Cibola National Forest conducted excavations there several years ago, and his forthcoming reports may resolve many questions regarding this massive ruin, occupied until about A.D. 1300-1325.

MOCKINGBIRD GAP ARCHEOLOGICAL SITE

This site is located ten miles east of San Antonio, one-quarter mile south of Highway 380. One hundred and fifty Clovis points have been found here. In addition, possible post holes have been discovered, suggesting a structure. The site dates broadly to 9000-6000 B.C. Investigations have been conducted here by R. Weber of the New Mexico Bureau of Mines (Socorro). Judge's (1973) classic study of Paleo-Indian occupation in the Rio Grande Valley makes many references to this site (1973:45,75,160,247,252,255,285-86).

SANDAL CAVE (LA 8696)

This cave is located in Nogal Canyon, south of San Antonio, New Mexico. A large number of pictographs are present, suggesting a shrine. Examples of sandals, cordage, wood, arrow foreshafts, fire sticks and corn cobs have been recovered. Ceramics including Wingate Black-on-red, Mimbres Black-on-white, Chupadero Black-on-white, El Paso Polychrome are found around Sandal Cave, indicating a date of ca. A.D. 1000 to about 1250.

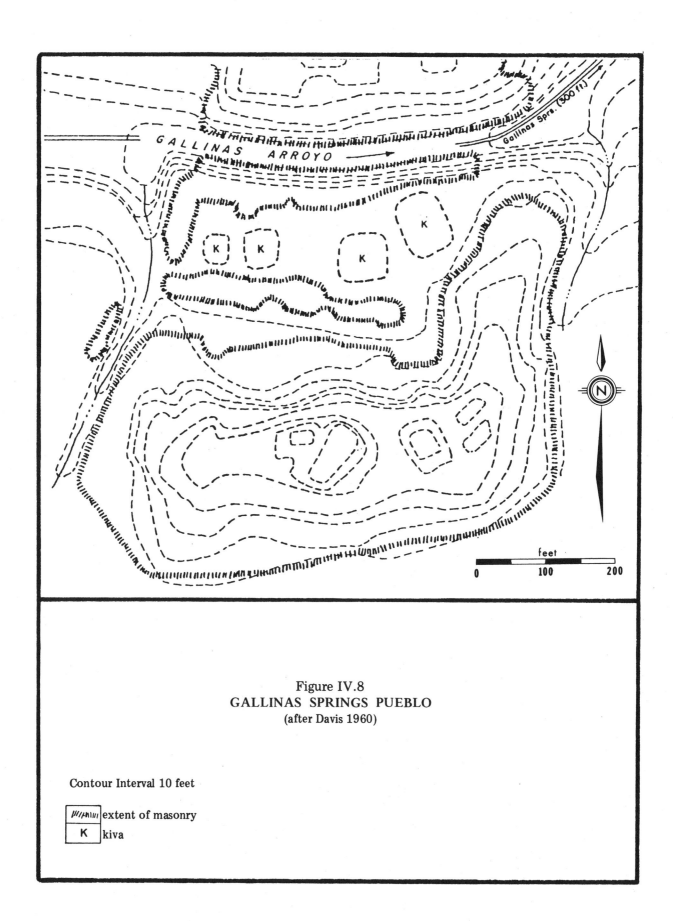

Figure IV.8
GALLINAS SPRINGS PUEBLO
(after Davis 1960)

Contour Interval 10 feet

|〰〰| extent of masonry
| K | kiva

164

DISCUSSION

In the Mt. Taylor unit, no Paleo-Indian sites have been nominated either to the State or to the National Register. Nonetheless, Judge (1973) had recorded over 50 Paleo-Indian sites, from Folsom through Cody. Two notable clusters of these lie near the confluence of the Rio San Jose and the Rio Puerco, and between the Puerco and the Rio Grande just north of Belen, respectively. Thirty of Judge's site assemblages were analyzed intensively, 1,513 artifacts being involved (1973:65). Only one substantial Clovis campsite was recorded (Site 13JB5), campsites of that period being very seldom reported (1973:73, 75). Judge's site data should be reviewed (he should also be consulted) to determine whether a thematic nomination would be appropriate for one of these site clusters, particularly since the Rio Abajo area south of Albuquerque is becoming rapidly urbanized. In addition, the Bureau of Indian Affairs' recent survey on Cebolleta Mesa has recorded a surprising quantity of Paleo-Indian material around one prominent rincon. Broster (1980) has recently presented a paper on these finds, and the data should be reviewed, for they suggest a spectacular intensity of Paleo-Indian utilization in that area.

In Socorro County, three Paleo-Indian sites are on the State Register (Mockingbird Gap; some material from Bat Cave, and the Ake Site). Only the Ake Site is on the National Register. Other Paleo-Indian localities are reported from the plains of San Agustin and from portions of the Jornada del Muerto to the east. The Laboratory of Anthropology files should be searched to locate any campsites that may be recorded, and R. Weber of the New Mexico Bureau of Mines should be consulted on his knowledge of the area's lithic sites, as should P. Beckett of New Mexico State University, Las Cruces. Paleo-Indian occupation of western New Mexico is neither well known nor systematically known. Our judgment is increasingly firm that Paleo-Indian occupation of New Mexico was both far more intense and widespread than was believed a few years ago. In every region of substantial erosion, Paleo-Indian finds have been recorded. The distinctive nature of the early Bat Cave material (Dick 1965) still has not been placed in a conclusive interpretive or chronological context (C-14 was a brand new technique when the Bat Cave samples were analyzed).

Archaic materials are included from Comanche Springs, Ake, Bat and Tularosa caves, and the TG&E survey (LA Nos. 3998, 4002, and 4010, respectively). Many more Archaic remains are known from the region. In Socorro and Catron Counties, much material evidences Chiricahua and San Pedro Cochise characteristics. North of Route 60, lithic materials are said to resemble the Oshara materials of the upper Puerco more closely (Berman 1979:17). Most of the Archaic material in the area that has been subjected to formal analysis comes from cave sites (Tularosa, Cordova, Bat, O Block, Lemitar Shelter, etc.). Of these, only Bat Cave is on the State Register. A number of these caves, together with smaller rockshelters, should be considered for a thematic National Register nomination. Since stratified dry cave deposits represent one of the scarcest and most precious investigative resources on the transition to agriculture, it is most pressing that any deposits yet undisturbed (or only partly disturbed) be protected. Moreover, other sites similar to the Ake campsite must be identified. Irwin-Williams' (1973) Oshara sequence has not been adequately confirmed and dated elsewhere. Our notions about the shift to agriculture in New Mexico rely on too little data.

Early Basketmaker/Early Pithouse occupations have been nominated from the southwestern quarter of the study area. The only architectural (as opposed to cave) site representing the A.D. 500-900 period is Mogollon Village (LA 11568). LA 4032 is a substantial Anasazi pithouse village of the Kiatuthlanna Phase (A.D. 800's). Lino Gray and Kana'a wares appear at Yellowhouse (LA 493) in the Zuni area, but we have no detailed information on the component. Since pithouse village occupations are said to have developed early in the Mogollon, but village life to have been arrested until after A.D. 500 in the north, early Anasazi components

165

simply must be identified. Sites like LA 4032 undoubtedly merit National Register nomination. No small, early pithouse occupations have been nominated, and this should be done. The Gila Forest should seriously consider the merits of a *Mogollon Villages* district nomination in which Pine Lawn, Three Circle and Reserve occupations will be represented. In Valencia County, any pre-P-II pithouse occupations should be sought out and given special attention. Wimberly and Eidenbach (1980) recorded one where datable material was eroding out. Chapter IX suggests a plan for capitalizing on such situations during survey.

P-II/Reserve phase occupations are underrepresented among nominated sites. Cox Ranch Pueblo (LA 13681) is on the National Register. The smaller Reserve phase sites are, in fact, more representative and should be identified and nominated. Several of the Apache Creek phase pithouses (Late P-II/Early P-III) should be identified, as should P-II occupations in the eastern (Rio Grande) portion of the area. One well-preserved and unusually formally aligned site was recorded (Wimberly and Eidenbach 1980:148) as HSR 903/S-27.

As for P-III/Tularosa phase occupations, P-III sites are well represented among nominated sites in the Mt. Taylor area. The Gallinas Springs site in the Cibola National Forest represents a Tularosa period occupation, but smaller ones in the Gila Forest are not well-represented. No P-III occupation in the lower elevations of the Rio Grande/Jornada del Muerto is represented. It is not even certain that a P-III occupation is represented in the area. This needs to be pursued -- surely there are sites near Chupadero Mesa (far eastern end of Socorro County) recorded during Mera's, or later, surveys that should be represented.

P-IV occupation in the Zuni area is well represented. There is apparently no P-IV occupation in the Gila Forest. Nonetheless, several enclosed plaza sites have been noted in that area, and are probably very late P-III or P-IV. Such sites are associated with the Gila Polychrome and thought to represent an early Salado formation. All site files should be reviewed to identify those sites having the enclosed plaza arrangement. Any that might represent early Saladoan components ought to be field-verified and nominated.

In the Rio Grande area, the only nominated Glazeware site is Pottery Mound (LA 416/ LA 8683). The recent Puerco/Salado survey for the Corps of Engineers (Wimberly and Eidenbach 1980) identified two substantial sites representing the P-IV occupation. HSR 903/L-10 (LA 285) is a 75-room pueblo arranged around a central plaza. Two kivas were present, and stratigraphy was generally intact. This is an excellent Glaze A ruin, which may immediately (1325-1350?) postdate abandonment in the western portions of the region. This site is a likely candidate for both the State and National Registers. HSR also recorded a 40 room Glaze D pueblo during this survey. In addition, Pottery Mound should also be on the National Register. Since these Rio Grande Glaze sites are within relatively easy distance of Belen and portions of I-25, now is the time to select a number for nomination. These Glazeware pueblos represent a continuum right to the protohistoric period (late 1500's) in the area. We suggest that a *Rio Abajo Glazeware Pueblos* thematic nomination be considered. It would be optimal to select sites which represented the glazeware sequence as fully as possible. A number of resource persons could be consulted for suggestions (among them, Drs. Hibben, Ellis, Cordell, and Schroeder; Mr's. Peckham, Marshall, Schaafsma, Wimberly, Eidenbach, and A.H. Warren, among others).

P-V Protohistoric/Historic pueblos have been nominated at Zuni, Acoma and Laguna. M. Marshall has been requested by the Historic Preservation Bureau to conduct a survey of the Piro culture area along the Rio Grande. We believe that several nominations will be forthcoming. Persons interested in this period should consult the Schroeder (1979) article on historic pueblos, which appears in the *Handbook of North American Indians*, Volume 9. The amount of data (and we presume, labor) contained in this article is enormous.

GEOGRAPHICAL AND GENERAL CONSIDERATIONS

The State and National Register in west central New Mexico are represented by 44 nominations of prehistoric sites. Compared to that in several other regions of the State (southwestern New Mexico and the plains) this is a good numerical representation. Approximately two (the Zuni and Manuelito complexes contain a number of sites) of each 100 recorded sites is nominated to the State and/or National Registers. We find, however, that these nominations focus primarily on a rather narrow geographic belt from Manuelito Canyon (near Gallup, New Mexico) to Zuni and El Morro and to Cebolleta Mesa in the north. They focus, secondarily, on the Gila National Forest in Catron County. Socorro County is seriously underrepresented, with only two Register sites. That is, the roughly 10,000 square miles of Catron, Valencia, and portions of McKinley County (Zuni-Manuelito area) are represented at roughly four or five sites per 1,000 square miles, whereas Socorro County (7,000 square miles) has about one-fifteenth the representation by land surface.

The nominations over-represent the large Late P-III occupations to the near exclusion of other time periods. We believe these lacunae can be dealt with through a *Chiricahua Caves* thematic nomination; a *Mogollon Villages National Register District* nomination centered on the Gila Forest, and the *Rio Abajo Glazeware Pueblos* thematic nomination along the Rio Grande. Ideally, the *Mogollon Villages* district could be structured to include Pine Lawn-Tularosa and Salado phase occupations, including both large and some small occupation units from each phase.

The Jornada del Muerto and west flanks of Chupadero Mesa will require more survey before lack of information from that area can be overcome. Some individual nominations of Paleo-Indian sites, stratified Archaic sites, early Anasazi Basketmaker materials and P-II occupations in the lower elevations will likely have to be made piecemeal. The three thematic nominations we have suggested here would require only moderate additional fieldwork, but perhaps a bit more extensive in the Rio Grande than elsewhere.

It is our position here that each site reported in a well-known monograph (Bat Cave, Cordova Cave, Tularosa Cave, Wet Leggitt, SU, Pottery Mound, and so on) should, at the least, be nominated to the State Register, even if most of the material has long ago been carried away for analysis.

OVERVIEW – WEST CENTRAL NEW MEXICO

THE ANASAZI-MOGOLLON PROBLEM

This particular region perplexes us more than most. Perhaps this is because the Mogollon and Anasazi cotraditions join here in some way. We say *in some way* because we are not genuinely satisfied that any particular argument thus far proposed has really explained cultural variability in this general region.

Tainter (1980a:54-66) argues against the idea of changes in the Acoma culture province as a consequence of commingled populations. Rather, he argues an economic relationship which varies through time. Elsewhere, he refers to burial data which suggest homogeneous populations in the region (except later at Zuni). In his argument about the nature of the Chacoan interaction sphere (1980a:110, 112-113), he argues (as he does in a later paper also; see 1980) that the Chacoan system expanded until it optimized maximal ecological diversity, but not beyond the maximal. Thus, he argues that the northern portion of the Acoma culture province was mixed in archeological attributes on account of economic interactions with the Chacoan system. His argument is appealing, but inconclusive on two accounts: 1) survey and excavation in areas to the south and east (see Chapter VI), including the lower Puerco/Salado, indicate the presence of Chacoan ceramic wares in P-II sites located in a region which far *exceeds* the maximal diversity that can be obtained by extending economic links to the upland periphery of the San Juan Basin. Indeed, the Red Mesa and Cebolleta (A.D. 950-1100) phases have the highest diversity of trade wares; 2) on page 105 Tainter (1980a) counters Marshall's and Stein's comment that burials are scarce in Chacoan towns and their subsequent suggestion that Bonito phase architecture is public architecture. He states that of the hundreds of pueblo sites in the overview area which have been excavated or tested, only one (LA 4487) contains enough burials to represent most of what was probably the living population (1980a:105). Since we know the Chacoan system began to collapse about A.D. 1125, we may presume that most of the population, not being buried in such sites (large or small, according to Tainter) wandered off elsewhere. How, then, is it unreasonable for Dittert and Ruppe to argue a sharp increase in population (including site intrusions) during the later Pilares (A.D. 1100-1200) phase and early Kowina phase (A.D. 1200 to 1300) with a decline in external trade during the Pilares phase?

As we said earlier, mortality in any long period of time is, inevitably, 100%, while at any given time and place the statistics assume their ordinary meaning to us. Accepting the fact that Chacoan towns were *abandoned* by A.D. 1150, all those born before about A.D. 1075 have to be buried *someplace*. Tainter's use of the *least cost* principle doesn't suggest that they would have been carried very far, though a few high status individuals might have been. We think most of those born before A.D. 1100 are buried in the smaller sites surrounding Chacoan towns and, very few of these have been excavated.

In any case, we should like to see the burial data from these several hundred excavated sites in summary form, for if Tainter *is* able to demonstrate that burials cannot account for Chacoan population since the early inception of the regional system (A.D. 950 or 1000), then there may be a case for continual, or periodic, episodes of dispersal or abandonment throughout the system's history.

We had always conceived of a largely *in situ* population growth for the P-II — "Early P-III" sites associated with the Chacoan network, but it is a deepseated human instinct that one goes home to die. Further, we had assumed home to be the smaller, nearby Hosta Butte phase sites. In view of the data Tainter cites, we must now ask: just where are these home places?

Secondly, do we have a data base from burials large enough to determine gradations in physical type, south to north from Reserve, New Mexico to the San Mateo outliers and the Red Mesa Valley? If we do, we should ask someone to reanalyze these data and bring these to bear on the Anasazi-Mogollon problem.

As Tainter suggests, shifting economic networks merit very serious investigation. Eidenbach (1980) points out that the plainwares in the Salado district show a strong Mogollon influence in surface treatment (including graywares), while decorated (painted) wares are generally classifiable as Anasazi. So the ceramic assemblages as a whole are mixed. Since one major difference between the brownwares and graywares (Shepard 1965) is the use of carbonaceous versus non-carbonaceous paste, one would need to determine source clays throughout the region to discover whether localized sources of material accounted in part for the grayware-brownware distribution. Secondly, only by conducting refiring experiments can one determine whether some of the graywares were actually produced in a reducing atmosphere. Third, what is the distribution of Anasazi versus Mogollon surface treatments in utility wares from one part of west central New Mexico to another; that is, north to south and east to west?

Suppose, for instance, some area is found where Anasazi surface treatments occur on brownwares. We should then need to know the source of clays utilized. If Dittert and Ruppe are correct in saying that external trade collapsed during the Pilares (A.D. 1100-1200) phase, then could we not propose to test the proposition that local clay deposits account for some changes in the graywares and brownwares? Additionally, we note that the hue or surface color of ceramics depends partly on the type and quantity of fuel used to accomplish the firing. Wimberly and Rogers (1977) demonstrated that variation in the hue of redwares in the Three Rivers drainage correlated with altitude, hence immediate availability of firewood for fuel. Brownwares are characteristic of the plains, lowland basins and desertic settings throughout the Southwest. Let us also, then, propose to test the proposition that the proportion of brownwares increases with declining altitude and/or linear distance from fuel sources in west central New Mexico.

In BM-III sites within the Anasazi region, brownwares are recorded (Sambrito brown is one variant). As both Tainter (1980a) and Cordell (1979) have noted in their overviews, a number of these sites are in environments like that of the west mesa — distant from heavily wooded areas. Finally, most of the ceramics in Chaco Canyon were imported, including utility wares. These imports came from more heavily wooded areas such as the Chuska slope, the Red Mesa Valley, and to a more modest extent, from Mesa Verde (Windes 1977). Is it possible that Chacoan sites in the central basin, including small satellite communities, could not generally have produced their own graywares on account of fuel scarcity? If so, the percentage of locally made wares even in the smaller communities should decrease through the 11th and 12th centuries. Would the percentage of brownwares increase with presumed episodes of drought throughout the Anasazi-Mogollon contact zones?

We do not, of course, know the answers to these questions, but feel they should be asked. There is enormous information content in ceramic assemblages. Many attempts have been made to correlate language group with ceramic styles. The cases have occasionally proven definitive, but far more often are inconclusive. Yet it is by no means time to accept the impasses that have arisen between the schools of thought that stand for the economic/adaptive argument as opposed to the cultural/historical one. What if it is discovered that in one or another time period the incidence of brownwares does indeed covary with the geographical correlates suggesting firewood scarcity? What if it is discovered, on the other hand, that Mogollon versus Anasazi surface treatments of plainwares vary independently of color variation? In such a hypothetical, but pleasant, outcome those on both sides of the argument could share a victory in research.

That is, we believe that the Mogollon-Anasazi contact zone has both an historical and and ecological meaning in the general sense, and an economic versus idiosyncratic one in the particular. A regional ceramic analysis could be proposed, in the context of a survey such as was suggested earlier. Such a survey, of course, would have to be set up to take collections for analysis. In any case, we believe that the no collections survey has been pushed too far. It denies verification of field identifications and limits necessary laboratory analysis in cases where specific research problems would otherwise be proposed. The ceramic research we propose here would have to be well planned and well-funded. In justifying the cost of such a program, we point out that nearly all the State-National Register sites in the region have been nominated on account of size or architectural features. Few have been nominated because they inform broadly on the major unanswered questions about cultural development in the Southwest (Mogollon Village, Bat Cave, Tularosa Cave are exceptions). How will we know which sites are significant to the resolution of Anasazi-Mogollon contact over time unless we identify them also by specific assemblage attributes?

HUNTERS-GATHERERS-AGRICULTURISTS

A second theme requiring thought involves the interaction of agriculturalists and hunter-gatherers. This has been suggested by Tainter (1980a) as an important research topic for this region. Chapter II (Theoretical Perspective) introduces the idea of differently regulated population/space regimes between hunters-gatherers and agriculturalists. In west central New Mexico, most sources agree on the possibility that hunters-gatherers continued their way of life until roughly A.D. 500. We are not convinced that hunters-gatherers would have disappeared even then, for population densities may not have pressured them out of this region, or forced them to intensify until roughly A.D. 800-900.

The essential points are these. In regimes where there are favored areas of productivity dramatically exceeding that of surrounding regions, hunting-gathering populations are drawn inward. Density pressure is then created at the core of such regions, even though areawide population may not have saturated. Those who practice storage during a season of maximal dispersal confer an adaptive advantage on those that do not. Thus, hunter-gatherer population expands into the dispersal season space vacated by those who store.

Over time, those who practice part-time agriculture are the population at risk. Fertility and infanticide cease to be space dependent, and become storage dependent. Each failure on the part of early agriculturalists creates episodes of competition for collecting lands, particularly acute in a winter-scarcity regime. Each early success only permits the hunter-gatherer population to increase, since additional space is being vacated.

In good years, agriculturalists have vegetable produce to trade with hunters-gatherers. Generally, maize would have been traded for meat and/or hides. The trade of agricultural products to hunters-gatherers destresses their population-regulating mechanism, and further eliminates risk to them. Since agricultural produce represents substantial caloric return per acre compared to production in the hunter-gatherer system, any agricultural foodstuffs they obtain represent a great space subsidy in their own system. Since the agricultural produce obtained requires more energy investment per calorie to produce than does the collection of large game, there is also an initial direct labor subsidy to the hunter-gatherer by the agriculturalist.

Having lost access to space, at least seasonally, the agriculturalist obtains meat and other wild resources in trade. In good years this balances the diet; but in bad years hunters-gatherers have little to trade. So even if the caloric value of wild meat traded for corn is high, the trade is unequal, for the agriculturalist can obtain little during crisis, and that obtained is not (either in quantity or kind) generally storable through to the next crop season. *Nor does it provide seed corn following a crisis.*

Finally, when agriculturalists learned to minimize the effect of crop failures by trading widely among their own kind, and exchanged women primarily among themselves, they were able to protect their fertility ratio and stabilize their population as compared to the hunters-gatherers. This implies increasing ethnic differentiation.

In New Mexico, very early defensively located agricultural villages suggest a few agriculturalists in a sea of hunters-gatherers. In good years there would be little conflict, but in periods of notable oscillation in temperature or rainfall, competition could have been intense.

Small pithouses, dating to the San Pedro Cochise (terminal Archaic) in southwestern New Mexico, suggest that Archaic populations were already seasonally sedentary, storage facilities being present.

170

Later (A.D. 250), sites such as Talus Village near Durango, Colorado, suggest an extremely high proportion of storage to habitation facilities, even in the absence of ceramics. Such storage clearly suggests that population had grown to such a point that access to collecting areas during poor times was insufficient to sustain existing population.

During the early Pine Lawn phase, sites such as the SU occupation in Pine Lawn Valley do not really seem to have been defensive in location. Was this a period when the major transformation to agriculture had taken place regionwide? Or was this a climatic optimum in which agricultural production was stable? We do not yet know.

During the A.D. 250-550 period, ceramic production became widespread, and trade intensified. This suggests a period when pockets of agriculturalists established broad networks amongst themselves. The northern network we consider to be Anasazi, the southern, Mogollon.

After A.D. 800 or 900, population expanded rapidly and major shifts in settlement pattern took place, P-II occupations having expanded *widely* into basin environments. In episodes of particularly variable rainfall (A.D. 950-1000; Cordell 1979:7), population pressure would have been too great for agriculturalists and hunters-gatherers to co-exist in poor years. Does this period represent the conversion of remaining hunters-gatherers to an agricultural strategy, or were they forced into isolated mountain regions, or even outward to the plains? Again, we do not know.

It appears that sometime after 1300 bison hunting on the plains permitted hunters-gatherers and agriculturalists to co-exist along the plains contact zones, bison hunting being productive enough to subsidize the agricultural populations to the east of the Sangre de Cristo, occasionally. Nonetheless, a pattern of "raid and trade" prevailed between the Plains and Pueblos even into historic times, suggesting a very fragile co-existence. We discuss these relationships more fully in later chapters (see Chapters VI and VII).

From Archaic times (perhaps Paleo-Indian, i.e., the Bat Cave sequence) onward, there is at least some evidence for cultural differentiation between major population systems which crosscut west central New Mexico. These relationships and boundaries (all disputed) need to be investigated in detail. We have presented a model here of the development of sedentism and agriculture which accords broadly with the archeological record of the region. In order to write a more detailed account, we would need to have far more information on shifting quantity and seasonality of rainfall from about 500 B.C. onward. Many climatic reconstructions have been proposed, but none has been accepted as definitive. Our position here is that shifting season of rainfall is generally more critical to deregulating a hunter-gatherer system than is the quantity of rainfall.

ABANDONMENTS

The whole subject of abandonments cannot be subsumed under one explanatory variable, because there are multiple events of abandonment in west central New Mexico. Only about one of each one hundred recorded sites in the region (about 35 of 3,519) survived into the P-V period, and nearly all of these appear to be reoccupations. The majority of these, then, are not thought to represent continuous occupation preceeding the early P-IV period (about 1350). In the Pine Lawn area there is no transformation to the Tularosa phase, as defined by the presence of St. Johns Polychrome. In the Apache Creek area, few sites seem to have been occupied after A.D. 1250. Elsewhere, in Manuelito Canyon, Cebolleta Mesa, the Gila Forest, and the El Morro Valley, sites were abandoned sometime between A.D. 1250 and 1325. In the lower Puerco and Salado districts, sites were not occupied past the P-II—Early P-III horizons (about A.D. 1100 or 1150), and reoccupation did not occur until after the appearance of Rio Grande Glaze A (A.D. 1300-1325).

Clearly, the identification of equivalent phases and chronologies from one archeological district to another is critical. One cannot do a gross ceramic seriation (i.e., P-III, A.D. 1100-1300) or rely on a dozen dendro dates to resolve the issue of simultaneous episodes of abandonment. Such episodes of abandonment need to be separated chronologically and by environmental zone.

Further, the identification of certain phases by the presence or absence of such items as St. Johns Polychrome introduces another and entirely distinct problem. Is a separate chronological phase being identified, or is it that St. Johns Polychrome identifies a specialized trade network in which only a few sites are included? What, for instance, is the mean size and variation in size and/or architectural features between sites in a given region which have St. Johns Polychrome, as opposed to those which do not?

St. Johns Polychrome is "one of the most widely traded ceramic types in the Southwest" (Martin and Plog 1973). Nonetheless, an initial investigation into its distribution suggests a pattern which is indeed unexpected. For the moment, we have reviewed data only from the CGP and Seboyeta surveys in the San Juan Basin (Windes 1977; Carroll, et al. 1979); from survey in the lower Puerco-Salado (Wimberly and Eidenbach 1980); from survey in the Three Rivers drainage (Wimberly and Rogers 1977); from survey in the White Sands National Monument (Wimberly and Eidenbach 1980a); from data compiled by Smiley (1979) for the southern Tularosa Basin, by Jelinek (1967) for the middle Pecos, and by Leslie (1979) for the plains of the eastern Jornada (Trans-Pecos). So the pattern suggested is clearly just tentative.

From more than 1,250 ceramic sites in widely scattered basin areas, a sample of over 200 thousand sherds indicates 49 sherds of St. Johns Polychrome! Forty-four of these came from

Table IV.9
ST. JOHNS POLYCHROME* — BASIN FLOOR DISTRIBUTIONS

Area	Author	No. Sites	No. Sherds in Sample	No. Sherds St. Johns
Eastern Jornada	Leslie (1979)	300	175,000	None
Southern Tularosa Basin	Smiley (1979)	Not given	4,782	43
Seboyeta Mesa	Carroll, et al. (1979)	13 Pueblo	136	None
Central Tularosa Basin	Wimberly & Rogers (1977)	66 ceramic	5,612	1
West central Tularosa Basin	Wimberly & Eidenbach (1980a)	13	2,000+	None
[the Bradfield Site (Lehmer 1948) near White Sands Missile Range HQ. had traces]				
Northwest San Juan Basin	Windes (1977)	750+	15,400	4 (B/R)
Puerco-Salado	Wimberly & Eidenbach (1980)	57	4,756	None
Middle Pecos	Jelinek (1967)	64	30,000 +	1
TOTALS		1,263+	237,000 +	49

* These surveys all describe early, mid or late P-III or chronologically overlapping occupations. We are not able to judge the consistency with which St. Johns B/R; Wingate B/R and St. Johns Polychrome have been identified.

the west slope of the Sierra Blanca-Sacramento chain. St. Johns Polychrome is often reported from sites at higher elevation in the Sierra Blanca region, from elevated portions of the Gila and Cibola National Forests, the Cebolleta Mesa region, the Zuni area, from the Chuska Mountains, from sites on the Pajarito Plateau near Los Alamos, N.M., and from sites in the elevated portions of the Taos district (see Cordell 1979). It is reported from the Montoya site (LeBlanc and Whalen 1979) in the upper Mimbres district, and a few of the Chacoan outliers (Marshall, Stein, Loose and Novotny 1979). These latter are in the more elevated (about 6,500 feet) portions of the San Juan Basin (though these sherds are generally said to occur in later Mesa Verdean occupation). It is reported in the Cimarron district and at Mesa Verde, as well as from the east face of the Chuska Mountains. These are all higher elevations and generally well-forested regions.

While these data are too modest to be conclusive (particularly since St. Johns may post-date most Chacoan occupation) they clearly suggest that St. Johns Polychrome is widely traded in an *upland* network. Further, they raise questions about the absence of a P-III occupation (defined for the moment on the ceramic "dates" of St. Johns as A.D. 1175-1300) in low-lying areas other than the Puerco-Salado drainages. On the other hand, it may merely be that St. Johns is traded into a few large sites in these regions, but more research is required. We will report our continuing investigations of this tradeware when our data are more complete.

For the moment, then, we turn again to the Berman overview (1979) and to her assertion that Tularosa phase sites are generally at lower elevation than are Reserve phase sites. [We have reviewed Rice's (1975) data and also a more recent treatment in Stafford and Rice (1979).] This may be so in certain portions of the Gila Forest, but Danson (1957) indicates many smaller (Reserve) sites along the base of Mariana Mesa, and Dittert (1949) indicates many contemporaneous Red Mesa phase and early Cebolleta phase occupations in lower elevations. It would appear that the P-II (900 to 1100) occupation of west central New Mexico was involved in an extensive trade network. Recall Dittert's claim for great diversity in ceramics during the late Red Mesa and early Cebolleta phases. This network was interrupted (Pilares phase), then replaced by a restructured upland trade network.

Rather than characterize Reserve and other local P-II occupations as higher in elevation, we may conclude that they occupied the greatest range of elevations in the study area. Tularosa phase occupations, including equivalent P-III occupations such as those of the Kowina phase, did not move to lowland elevations. Instead, they appear to have narrowed or tightened their range of settings. Thus, abandonment of a given altitude zone must not be taken as abandonment of a region. In addition, Rice (1979) suggests that late 12th century Tularosa phase sites will *always* be larger than earlier Reserve phase sites in the adjacent Apache National Forest. Nonetheless, Cox Ranch Pueblo (see State Register site descriptions) comprises 300 rooms — vastly larger than any sites Rice (1979) discusses as demonstrating the pattern. Clearly, if we are to unravel the causes of abandonment, we must identify episodes of reaggregation and shifting site location. These patterns, then, must be taken separately from actual abandonment of a region. We must also determine the extent to which the presence or absence of certain tradewares may have caused sites to be assigned to the wrong period. We require a great deal more chronological control, both from excavation and from micro-seriation of ceramic assemblages, to isolate each of these complex events.

At this juncture we may tentatively conclude that trends during the several centuries which preceded collapse were toward: 1) a narrowing range of site setting; 2) a major restructuring (or several) of a more generalized trading network to a specialized one; and 3) aggregation into larger communities.

SOME SUGGESTED RESEARCH TOPICS

1. How does one account for the continued existence of hunters-gatherers north of Highway 60 until A.D. 500 or so? Can no BM-II—early BM-III occupation be found in this area?

2. The late Paleo-Indian/Archaic differentiation in lithic assemblages — north to south and east to west (Chiricahua and San Pedro Cochise versus Oshara traditions).

3. Why is Georgetown-San Francisco phase occupation so scarce in the Pine Lawn Valley?

4. The Pine Lawn area has early Pine Lawn (A.D. 300-500) occupation and Three Circle-Reserve occupation, but Georgetown-San Francisco and Tularosa phase are scarce/absent. In what way is the Pine Lawn like the Reserve phase occupation? Are, then, Georgetown-San Francisco and the Tularosa phase also somehow like each other, but different from the first two?

5. What is the regional nature of split phase occupations? How common are they? Do different phases belong together systematically as pairs in many locales? Do these patterns vary by altitude zone?

6. LeBlanc (next chapter) claims that Georgetown-San Francisco components in the Mimbres are not so scarce as to indicate population decline following the Pine Lawn phase. Is he correct? Is it because the sites he has excavated there are 1,000 feet lower in elevation than the Pine Lawn Valley?

7. Why is there no apparent P-III occupation in the lower Puerco-Salado drainages? Where else is P-III missing? Or is this a function of limited chronological control?

8. Is the Anasazi-Mogollon boundary economic or ecological? Is it a real ethnic barrier? How do you demonstrate any given case? Burial populations from the "mixed" zone? Are they also mixed?

9. Abandonment? How many episodes? Shifting trade patterns? Shifting altitude zones? Climatic catastrophism? Population aggregation?

10. How many terminal dates do we have? Which are dendro? C-14? Archeomagnetic? How do they pattern? Do they pattern differently in different altitude zones?

11. Apache Creek phase. Why the late pithouse occupation? Why several places in the Southwest at roughly this time period? Who are these people? Have burial populations been adequately compared to other Mogollon burial populations? Are they homogeneous?

12. Formative Salado. Is this area the crucible of formation? How good are our dates? How do we demonstrate migration?

13. The San Marcial phase. Does it occur ceramically only at Mera's site, LA 1151? What other local black-on-whites are contemporaneous? Why the tendency for highly localized ceramic wares at certain time periods and not others?

14. Shifting economic patterns over time. We need overlay maps showing clinal distributions of ceramic types by time period.

Chapter V
SOUTHWESTERN NEW MEXICO
(Mimbres and Jornada-Mogollon Areas)

BACKGROUND

The Mogollon tradition has dominated the attention of archeologists in southwestern New Mexico for nearly 100 years. Though the various branches of Mogollon culture extend over a vast area of New Mexico and adjacent Arizona, with ill-defined boundaries trailing off in northern Chihuahua and southwest Texas, the focus of this first section is on the Mogollon-Mimbres proper, as opposed to the Jornada-Mogollon, which follows (Lehmer 1948).

MOGOLLON-MIMBRES AREA

BACKGROUND

Geographically, we are speaking of an area which is loosely defined by the southern boundary of Socorro County (extended westward to the Arizona state line) on the north, the Arizona boundary on the west, the Mexican border on the south, and the Rio Grande on the east, excluding that portion of Dona Ana County lying west of the river. This area of roughly 15,000 square miles is the geographic heartland of the Classic Mimbres tradition.

The northern portions of this area are characterized by extensive upland valleys and mountain ranges rising to 10,000 feet in altitude. From west to east these form a series of basin and ranges defined by the Upper San Francisco, the Upper Gila, and the Upper Mimbres river drainages. These are cool, well-watered uplands where vegetation zones, growing season and temperatures vary markedly with altitude and exposure. As one moves south these rugged, well-timbered uplands open up into a classic semi-desertic basin and range province. Mountains are less lofty, moderately to only poorly timbered, and upland meadows are replaced by desert floor, quite sandy in places and characterized by the Sonoran vegetative zone. Rivers such as the Mimbres gradually disappear into the sandy plains of the desert floor. From the standpoint of human adaptation, there is remarkable geographic, climatic and vegetational diversity to manipulate, either through changes in altitude or by north-south movement.

The Classic Mimbres tradition (roughly A.D. 1000 to 1150) is famous among archeologists for its spectacular ceramics. The boldness of naturalistic figures in black-on-white, the splendid symmetry, the excellence of craftsmanship — such features stimulate fascination and desire in art-loving humans. It must be that these ceramics draw the focus of the mind, for the archeology of southwestern New Mexico has been dominated by a single-mindedness that would be remarkable elsewhere. This mood seems to have influenced much of the literature — forgiveable in one sense, but frustrating in another.

Dr. LeBlanc (LeBlanc and Whalen 1979) and his collaborators carefully unfold the Classic Mimbres as the center of a highly restricted *universe* in the overview of southwestern New Mexico. While important and previously unpublished data are presented, the archeology of the Mimbres Valley is the primary focus of the overview. Cultural development there is presented as more geographically isolated than appears warranted. Relationships (spatial and temporal) between developments in the Pine Lawn, Redrock Canyon, Gila Cliff, San Simon and Little Colorado are obscured. For these reasons it is essential that we present here a brief sketch of Mogollon prehistory with some discussion of the many unresolved problems that continue to beg for solution.

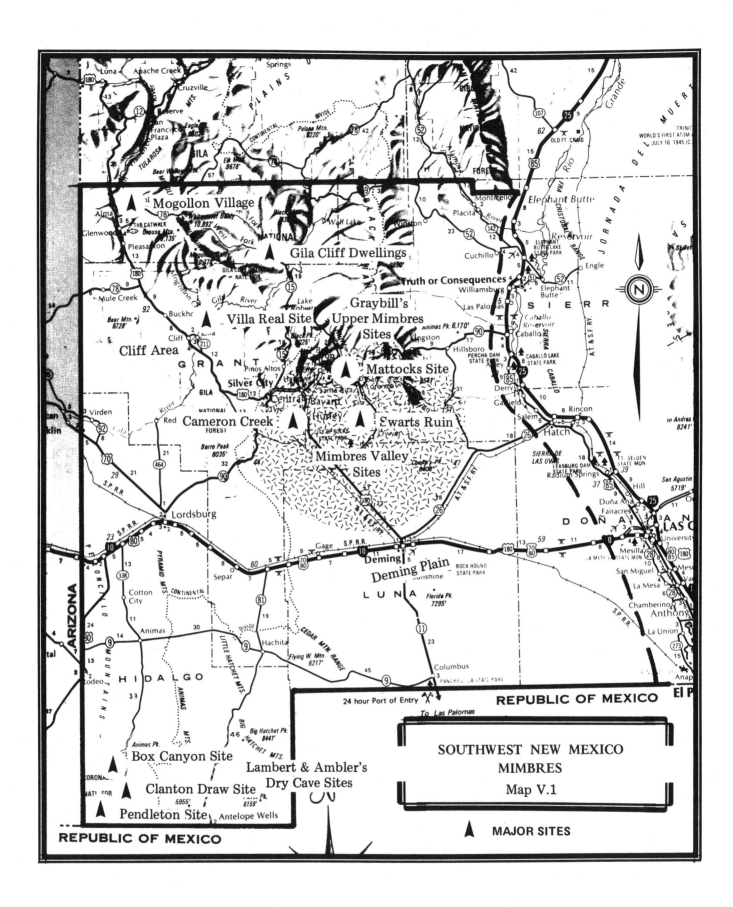

SOUTHWEST NEW MEXICO
MIMBRES
Map V.1

▲ MAJOR SITES

176

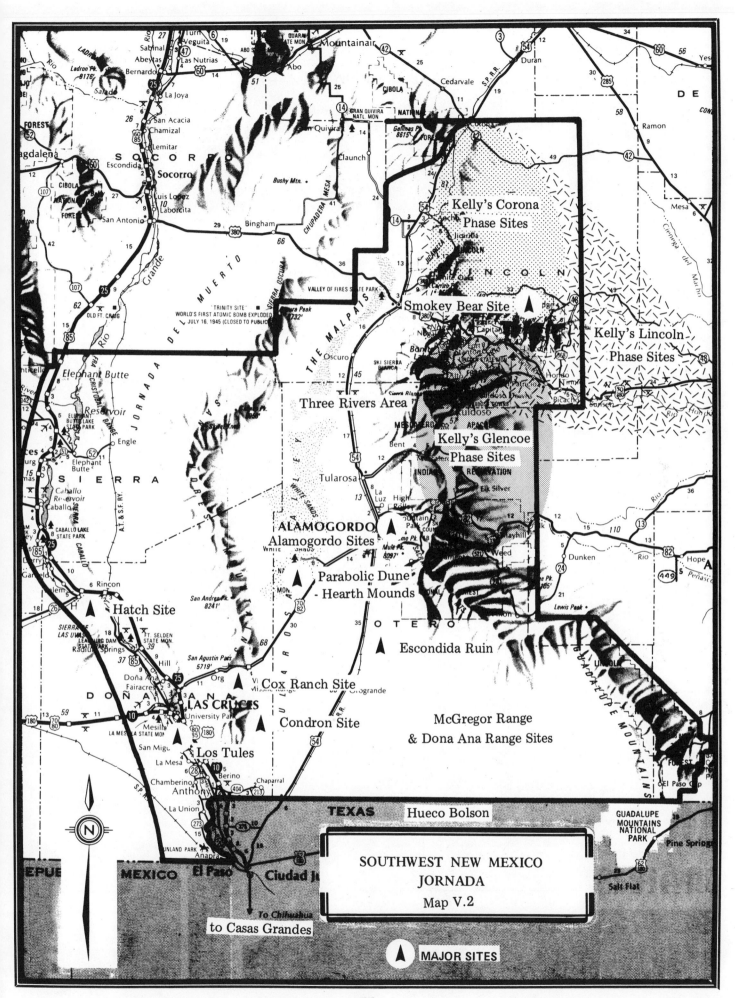

Kelly's Corona Phase Sites

Kelly's Lincoln Phase Sites

Smokey Bear Site

Three Rivers Area

Kelly's Glencoe Phase Sites

Alamogordo Sites

Parabolic Dune - Hearth Mounds

Escondida Ruin

Hatch Site

Cox Ranch Site

Condron Site

McGregor Range & Dona Ana Range Sites

Los Tules

TEXAS Hueco Bolson

to Casas Grandes

SOUTHWEST NEW MEXICO
JORNADA
Map V.2

▲ MAJOR SITES

THE CULTURAL SEQUENCE

THE EARLY MOGOLLON
(A.D. 250-550? Early Pithouse = Pine Lawn = Mogollon I = Al Cabo = Hilltop)

CHRONOLOGY

The early Mogollon is variously dated at 200 B.C. (Wheat 1955:185); A.D. 200 (Anyon, Gilman and LeBlanc 1980:i); 100 B.C. (Willey 1966:188); or 600 B.C. (Martin and Plog 1973); if one accepts the alleged first appearance of Alma Plain pottery at one cave site.

Chart V:1
A COMPARISON OF MOGOLLON CHRONOLOGIES

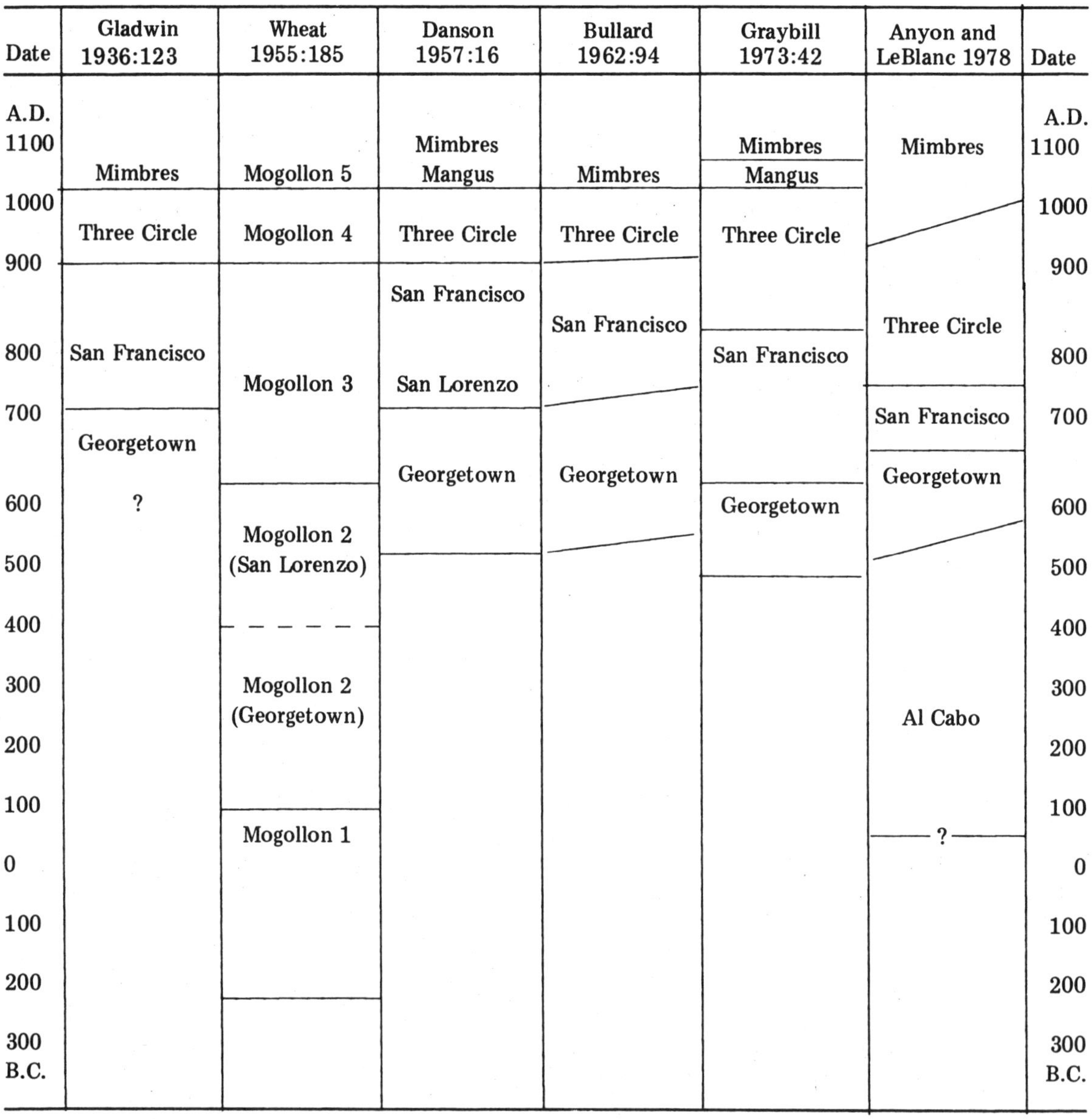

Date	Gladwin 1936:123	Wheat 1955:185	Danson 1957:16	Bullard 1962:94	Graybill 1973:42	Anyon and LeBlanc 1978	Date
A.D. 1100	Mimbres	Mogollon 5	Mimbres / Mangus	Mimbres	Mimbres / Mangus	Mimbres	A.D. 1100
1000	Three Circle	Mogollon 4	Three Circle	Three Circle	Three Circle		1000
900			San Francisco			Three Circle	900
800	San Francisco	Mogollon 3	San Lorenzo	San Francisco	San Francisco		800
700						San Francisco	700
	Georgetown		Georgetown	Georgetown		Georgetown	
600	?	Mogollon 2 (San Lorenzo)			Georgetown		600
500							500
400		– – – –					400
300		Mogollon 2 (Georgetown)				Al Cabo	300
200							200
100							100
0		Mogollon 1				—?—	0
100							100
200							200
300 B.C.							300 B.C.

178

This first Mogollon phase is variously termed the Early Pithouse (LeBlanc and Whalen 1979); the Al Cabo (also LeBlanc and Whalen 1979); Mogollon I (Wheat 1955), the Pine Lawn (Willey 1966); the Pine Lawn-Georgetown (Bullard 1962), or The Hilltop Phase.

In fact, the diagnosis of transition from the San Pedro Cochise (final Archaic period) rests on the first appearance of Alma Plainware pottery. The conflicts arise, in some cases, over the validity of stratigraphy in cave deposits (Martin, et al. 1952 and Bullard 1962 re: Tularosa and Cordova Caves) and, in others, from a lack of datable material. The earlier appearance of ceramics seems to have occurred to the west and south.

Preceramic, or aceramic, pithouse sites also are known from several areas and, of course, cultigens have been dated to roughly 3000 B.C. (some sources suggest 2000 B.C. for the Bat Cave cultigens) in the now classic report of excavations at Bat Cave (Dick 1965). Why the addition of ceramics is viewed as so important, while the settlement and subsistence characteristics of the later San Pedro Cochise are given lesser attention, is not immediately comprehensible. At any rate, the other dates for the appearance of ceramics in the Pine Lawn and Forestdale (north and west of the Mimbres Valley, about 100 miles) areas appear to be about A.D. 250-300 at the Bluff Site (Douglass 1942), at Bat Cave (Dick 1965:18) and at the SU Site (Martin and Plog 1973). It is well to recall that preceramic pithouse habitations also occur to the north in the Albuquerque area. Reinhart (1967, 1968) has described such an occupation, termed the Rio Rancho Phase, dated (C-14, two dates) at between 1000 B.C. and A.D. 1. Martin and Plog (1973), following Breternitz (1966), give the dates of A.D. 300-950 as best dates for Alma Plainwares.

The Lino graywares of northern New Mexico appear at about A.D. 400 and have been used to distinguish the Anasazi from the Mogollon. Nonetheless, there is substantial evidence that brownwares predate the graywares in the Anasazi area, extending into the Albuquerque, Navajo Reservoir, Taos and Cimarron areas, although extremely rare in these last (see discussion in Cordell 1979:43).

SETTLEMENT

The early Mogollon pithouse sites in the Mimbres and Pine Lawn (see also Chapter IV) areas are generally characterized by placement on high knolls, or mesas (the SU Site is an exception) which appear to offer defensive advantage. Such pithouse communities were only modest in size, but they are, nonetheless, of surprising scale if one argues that they represent the *first* move to sedentism. Martin and Plog (1973) suggest an average of 17 pithouses per village. Stafford and Rice (1979, Vol. I: Chapters 4 and 5) have summarized Mogollon settlement data which include portions of Arizona. They indicate that while six of the ten sites that have been excavated from this period are *large* (over ten pithouses), the majority of sites which have been surveyed (and not excavated) are very small and are far more numerous than the larger sites. Such sites are recognized from surface survey by pithouse depressions (often easy to overlook) and ceramic scatters consisting mainly of Alma Plainware, occasionally with a low frequency of San Francisco Redware. LeBlanc limits this to 1% or 2% of the ceramic assemblage in defining this phase (LeBlanc and Whalen 1979:Chapter 3).

These early sites are in generally elevated locales, most being in areas which range between 6,500 to 7,500 feet or more in elevation. Most overlook substantial drainages, that is, overlook upland and mountain valleys. Stafford and Rice (1979) report numerous sherd and lithic scatters on the valley floors in an adjacent area of Arizona, apparently without evidence of structures, that they believe date to this period. Lekson (1978), who surveyed the Redrock Canyon drainage (well to the west of the Mimbres Valley, near the Arizona border) in 1978, for his Master's thesis, also reported many sherd scatters in the drainage, but without the painted wares as diagnostics, no chronology was assigned. Minnis (1979) reports that many sherd scatters were recorded during the extensive Mimbres Foundation surveys, but no particulars are reported in the overview other than that many of these are plainware scatters located in desert areas.

ARCHITECTURAL FEATURES

Pithouses during this period display notable variation in size, shape, depth and orientation, and are not standardized with regard to internal features.

Martin and Plog (1973:92) give the average size of Pine Lawn Phase pithouses as 30 m² for the very early occupation. Excluding Room 2 (very large) at the Winn Canyon Site (Fitting 1973), those pithouses excavated averaged 26 m². Martin and Plog (1973:92) state that the size of Pine Lawn pithouses decreases through time until roughly A.D. 500 when they average 17 m². We are not certain of this figure, since it is the same that Bullard (1962) offers for the average size of all Mogollon pithouses. LeBlanc (LeBlanc and Whalen 1979:Chapter 2, pg. 126) does not provide figures regarding pithouse size in the Mimbres valley prior to the later Georgetown Phase. He does note, however, that superpositions of pithouses and episodes of remodeling, unlike later periods, are absent during this period. This suggests single, short term occupations to him.

The variation in internal features between pithouses of this period has led to substantial commentary and speculation in the published literature. The absence of hearth features in some pithouses seems to have troubled archeologists the most. Rice (1979:79) comments that approximately 50% of the early pithouses lack hearth features. Because of the high elevation setting, they argue that pithouses without hearths must represent summer occupation. Stafford (1979) goes on to create a model of settlement-subsistence based on seasonal sedentism. While it certainly appears likely that the inhabitants of these early pithouse villages were less sedentary than the residents of later occupations, two observations should be made.

In the first place, Fitting's (1973) Winn Canyon Site (he suggests occupation from A.D. 300-500) which is situated at just over 4,000 feet in elevation, has hearth features in four of the six rooms excavated (1973:24). Altitude and the need for hearths would seem to have a correlation opposite to that suggested by Stafford (1979:115-117). This points out an important problem with the Early Pithouse period — too few sites have been excavated to make compelling comparisons. For instance, the SU Site has more variability in structures than have the Winn, Mogollon, and Harris sites; it has produced more sherds per room and far more manos than other similar sites. If there was better temporal control over particular rooms in excavated sites, one might learn whether the frequency of hearths had implications for climatic shifts over time.

Stafford (1979:117) then notes that as room size increases, the probability of having associated hearth features also increases. This may not be so surprising, for a small room or pithouse is more easily warmed by body heat from a given number of individuals than is a large room. On the other hand, the largest room at the Winn Canyon Site (Room No. 2, about 50 m²) had no hearth; the other room (No. 3) lacking a hearth was the smallest room excavated (diameter of smallest to largest is ratio of 1:1.92). It is simply going to take more than ten excavated sites spread from the Black River drainage of Arizona to the Mimbres Valley to permit a solution to seasonality of occupation and population patterns. Nonetheless, we doubt the strength of the no hearth/summer occupation versus hearth/winter occupation concept. After all, why would anyone make the labor investment in a summer season pithouse at all — surely not to escape the heat at 7,000 feet in altitude, and surely not to store as yet unharvested grains? If different ecological associations for each could be demon-

180

strated or botanical samples indicated differing subsistence bases, then the model would be more plausible (we will return to another possibility shortly).

POPULATION

Population estimates and demographic trends are important themes in archeology. Martin and Plog (1973:81) view the early pithouse period as one of gradual population increase until roughly A.D. 500. They argue for population decline between A.D. 500 and 700. Their argument is based on evidence for declining rainfall during this period (Hevly's rainfall chart in Martin and Plog 1973:52) and on the dramatic (80%) drop in the incidence of corn cobs from these levels of Tularosa Cave. LeBlanc (1979:125-128) takes pointed issue with this interpretation, citing methodological difficulties at Tularosa Cave. While it is true that Martin and Plog's evidence bears most directly on the Pine Lawn area and the adjacent portions of Arizona (Hay Hollow Valley, Black River, etc.), and there is always the potential for stratigraphic mixing in cave sites, LeBlanc offers no evidence to the contrary.

He has not based his contention on specific data extracted from the Mimbres Valley itself. He has not marshalled data from pollen profiles, flotations, or local tree-ring studies to support a claim that corn utilization and rainfall remain at pre-A.D. 500 levels in his study area. In addition, LeBlanc (1979:128) suggests that succeeding Georgetown Phase sites are rare in the Mimbres Valley, sites which, he argues, represent the transition from earlier to later settlement patterns. For the time being, we decline to accept LeBlanc's position. Until disproven, the period should be considered one of accelerating population increase at the time of Christ, peaking about A.D. 500 and likely declining thereafter. We present another possibility below. LeBlanc (1979:127) suggests a population of 350-500 persons for the entire Mimbres Valley, with one or two villages early in this period, culminating in four to eight villages.

There are probably as many reconstructions of population/room counts as there are archeologists. Demographic reconstructions based on architectural features are a risky business in the best of circumstances. For this time period, the circumstances are *very* tenuous. Too few sites are carefully dated from excavations and few are diagnosed to this period from survey.

Martin and Plog equate the large size of early (A.D. 200-500) Mogollon pithouses (when compared to the later phases) with large family size. The large family size is argued to be adaptive for hunting-gathering activities. If by *family* they mean an extended family which is largely a lineage group, perhaps so. If they mean a large nuclear family, we think not, for it is the agriculturalist who faces the heavy labor demands which enhance the value of many offspring, not the hunter-gatherer or casual horticulturalist.

SOCIAL ORGANIZATION

Every recent monograph on the Mimbres-Mogollon goes on at length about social organization (LeBlanc and Whalen 1979; Stafford and Rice 1979). The various reconstructions take too wide a variety of forms to allow reasonable discussion here. Suffice it to say that most are highly speculative and can be separated into two broad schools of thought. The first state that the large rooms represent communal structures which are redistributive centers, somehow related to lineage or clan organization — an organization which binds together related nuclear families who occupy surrounding pithouses. The second school of thought views pithouses as the abode of some form of extended family (usually a lineal descent group) for whom the communal structure represents a community level of redistribution or ceremonial activity that transcends lineage ties.

One has the feeling that the patrilineal band, transforming eventually into a clan, is on

181

many minds. There must be some rule in archeology that unless one has pottery styles, or some such, for evidence one never actually names the kin group that has been discussed for many pages. We, like the lady who tells her age, will say *Patrilineages*. Yes, this is actually a possibility. The patrilineal band hunts large game occurring in non-migratory herds (Steward 1955) and is thought to operate to resolve local population/resource imbalances (Birdsell 1968). In a long-inhabited and population-saturated area, geographical population pressure would induce self-regulatory population behavior (see earlier chapters). Under such circumstances, tropical forest groups of South America such as the Akwe-Shavante (Maybury-Lewis 1967) who are patrilineal (though uxorilocal in residence) and horticulturalists six months of the year are notable with respect to two characteristic features. They have very strong institutions of the men's house (sometimes called bachelor's house) and they are extremely bellicose. The men's house is hostile to and absolutely excludes women. Such features are merely a continuum of the population regulating behavior (including men's hut and hostility toward women) of the Ona of Tierra del Fuego in a K-selected population regime[1] (Stuart 1980). Such systems are thought to derive their structure and unusual proclivity for warfare from the stresses of shifting to seasonal agriculture and the subsequent increase in the productive value of female labor.

If the Mogollon represent a shift from an older patrilineal hunting society and if the early communal structures are, in fact, men's societies linked to patrilines, one should not find female burials in them. Burials might well be bimodally distributed between young adult to subadult males (ages 10-18, perhaps) and elder males (widowers). In spite of published accounts of female burials in *early* kivas, the problems of temporal control over contemporaneous structures in early sites leave the question open. The matter of burials brings us to the next discussion.

BURIALS

The burial data from this area of the Mogollon merit a complete review and recompilation. It is a sad fact that the vast majority of sites in this area have been pothunted and the burials destroyed. Old collections of skeletal remains require seeking out and reanalysis. For the moment we shall have to present a picture which is unsatisfactory in its sketchiness.

---

[1] Actually, we are not certain that the Akwe-Shavante are classically patrilineal. The point is that their system maintains highly uniform size among villages over a wide region, precluding a marked heirarchy in *site* size. This operates at the village level like Ona population at the band level; i.e. forces villages to spread out and stress the boundaries of the territory. Local demographic conservatism is balanced against the need to assert density control over potential *encroachers*. This is essential since encroachment during the trek (collection) season cannot be met defensively, for there are no protective population aggregates at that time. Actually, such a system would have to fluctuate between repeated episodes of demographic conservatism and local population increase. One would expect some kin mechanism capable of alternating between endogamous and exogamous behavior. The logical solution to such a problem would be to have some mechanism whereby the definition of *kin* and, therefore, marriageable females, could change. The consequence of such behavior would be for a regional population system alternately to expand and contract, even without similar environmental flux as a conditioning factor. For any population that was seasonally agricultural and seasonally mobile, the structure would tend to be very complex. The demographic needs and consequences of the agricultural enterprise are very much at odds with the labor, space and demographic requirements of *most* hunting and collecting regimes. Such systems would tend to have a structure within a structure, that is, some dual or moiety system within a descent system. This might have bearing on both the complexity and elusiveness of eastern Pueblo social organization.

Table V:1
SELECTED DATA – BURIALS OF THE EARLY PITHOUSE PERIOD

Site	No. Rooms Excavated	Extramural Stripping	No. Burials	Average per Room
SU	25	some	54	2.2 (rounded)
Harris	34	some	50	1.5
Bear	17	some	40	2.4
Winn	6	no	7	1.2

Bez (1979:667-686) discusses burial practices and mortuary offerings for the early pithouse period. Several patterns in the available data emerge. Early pithouse villages, though, are often thought to be lacking highly structured managerial components which result in ranking and well defined status positions (Plog 1974). It is expected, therefore, that there will be a notable difference in the structure of the mortuary remains between the late sites and early sites. Such differences should manifest themselves in ill-formed interment areas. Few status markers which cannot be correlated with age and sex dimensions and status symbols in a technical and personal mode which denotes achievement (Stickel 1968) should be expected.

Bez notes that burials at the SU Site do not seem to be spatially localized, while at the Harris Site bodies buried in the trash areas cluster around three nearby houses. At Bear Ruin ten burials of forty are spread randomly through the trash areas, while the remaining thirty fall into two tight clusters. At the SU and Harris sites mortuary goods suggest little complexity in status differentiation. The Bear Ruin, on the other hand, displays a marked variability in grave goods which crosscut age and sex differences. Bez concludes that the complexity of organization at this time period merits reevaluation.

We conclude that several important problems currently prevent proper comparisons of burial data. First, lack of tight chronological control (particularly Winn Canyon and late, Georgetown, phases of the Harris Site) makes comparisons of levels of complexity, for a given time period, problematic. Second, the inattention to extramural excavation prevents accurate comparisons between site size and burial populations. Third, since primarily larger sites of this time period have been excavated, we are uncertain that burial studies based on them would accurately reflect conditions in the more numerous smaller sites. For instance, LeBlanc has noted that in the Mimbres Valley during the Classic period (A.D. 1000-1100), large Mimbres sites average five burials per room, while as one moves outward from the Mimbres Valley to sites like Saige-McFarland, the average is one-half to one and one-half per room.

In spite of these difficulties, several tentative observations can be made. The average burial *per room* is 1.8, not unlike smaller, outlying Classic Mimbres sites over half a millenium later. Since the Harris and Bear Ruin sites likely are a bit later in date (Georgetown transition) than the other two, the contrast in average number of burials between them cannot be attributed to temporal differences. Harris (Mimbres Valley) and Winn Canyon (Gila) have the lowest frequency of burials, while the SU Site (Pine Lawn) and Bear Ruin (Salt River) to the west have a higher frequency. Perhaps a review of other data would suggest a geographical cline in burial frequency showing more intense population pressure to the north and west at this time period. It is also notable that the SU and Bear Ruin sites display a notably higher frequency of manos and metates per room than the Harris or Winn Canyon sites. This leads us into a short discussion of subsistence.

SUBSISTENCE

Most sources note a substantial reliance on hunting and gathering, coupled with maize agriculture, during this time period. Chapalote corn, squash, beans and cotton (it becomes common between A.D. 100-300) are present in sites of this period. The archeological record is heavily influenced by reports from dry cave sites such as Tularosa and Bat caves (again, to the north and west). Collected resources include pinyon (underemphasized in the literature), acorns (in lower elevations), deer, jackrabbit, cottontails, rodents and various bird species. The incidence of deer remains is quite high in many sites, and assemblages (chipped stone and points) associated with hunting vary markedly from site to site (remarkably high at Winn Canyon, remarkably low at the Harris Site). Either there are notable local variations in subsistence dependence during this time period or excavation techniques have introduced nonexistent variability.

Rice (1979) views subsistence as seasonal, with winter/summer habitation a possibility in neighboring portions of Arizona. LeBlanc (1979:128) argues against the applicability of Rice's model to the Mimbres Valley. He states, "It seems that the EP [early pithouse] pattern was essentially the same as the LP [late pithouse] pattern. Fairly large villages were occupied almost continuously or completely continuously throughout the year with major dependence on agriculture" (1979:128129). He goes on to say:

> "Rice seems correct in arguing that if most occupation occurred in pithouses, but sites were seasonally occupied, then there would be substantial differences among pithouses. This might include the presence or absence of hearths, storage, facilities or artifact classes. TO DATE THERE IS NO INFORMATION THAT SUCH DIFFERENCES REALLY EXIST" (1979:129) [emphasis ours].

In view of the published descriptions indicating great variability in pithouses and artifact assemblages for sites of this period, LeBlanc's would appear to be a controversial statement. LeBlanc also dismisses the likelihood of seasonal use of pithouses coupled with seasonal use of nonarchitectural sites. Pottery would be expected in such sites, according to LeBlanc, but "few, if any, sherd and lithic scatters seem to contain pottery that relate to the EP period, although such pottery is not particularly diagnostic [i.e., Plainware scatters] .... these are the only data presently available" (1979:129-130). He concludes that the shift to sedentary agriculture had occurred by the Early Pithouse period in the Mimbres Valley. Given Breternitz's (in Martin and Plog 1973) best dates of A.D. 300 to 900 for Alma Plainwares, *any* sherd scatter in the Mimbres Valley not containing a high proportion of painted wares *could* belong to this early period. Moreover, Anyon (1979) and LeBlanc (1979) both argue the primary use of the boldface (elsewhere Mangas) and Classic Mimbres Black-on-white bowls as mortuary items. If they are correct, why are these diagnostics often found in sherd scatters at all?

In short, substantially different patterns of subsistence are argued for the Mimbres area and adjacent portions of Arizona. The case is currently unclear. Intensive survey to locate isolated plainware sites and provide spatial and ecological data for the isolated lithic and sherd scatters would be most welcome.

SUMMARY

This early phase is generally agreed to end about A.D. 550-600 (see Chart V:1). If one accepts the fact that over a space of 300 miles (NW-SE) nothing happens according to a stationmaster's schedule (under conditions of low population density), then there is nothing problematic in such a terminal date. What is problematic is the portrayal of an important time period in the shift to agriculture and sedentism from too few excavation data and a remarkable absence of published (intensive) survey data. In the study area, survey data are further biased by over-representation of the major river valleys to the exclusion of other areas.

We simply do not have an adequate picture of settlement size, number of settlements or resource exploitation from sites in the Mogollon area. Substantial variation in excavated assemblages, architectural features, burial practices and subsistence behavior can be inferred from published reports. These, coupled with problematic, and scarce, dates have led to many differing characterizations in the literature, which are generalized to the whole Mogollon from the data in one or another locale. The degree of actual variability is obscured by inconsistent surveys and excavation practices. It is impossible at this moment to say in what degree such variation is due to time, spatial distance, varying ecological circumstances, or capricious methodology.

Theoretically, new ideas must also be raised. For instance, LeBlanc has suggested a population of 250-500 in the entire Mimbres Valley during this period. The Mimbres surveys (by the Mimbres Foundation) have sampled the approximately 1,200 square miles of the Mimbres Valley. That is, LeBlanc is suggesting a population density which ranges between 1 person per 5 and 1 person per 2½ square miles. This is well within the pure hunter-gatherer range of population density (Lee and DeVore 1968) and would not seem to meet the density conditions for village aggregation and stress leading to full sedentism under normal climatic circumstances (we return to this in the Mimbres Summary).

Secondly, Rice has proposed distinct winter/summer season pithouses. This might make more sense if one supposed that the period in general was characterized by erratic shifts between winter and summer dominant rainfall patterns. Under such circumstances, one would expect different agricultural strategies to be essential. In the winter rainfall regime, crops would have to be planted early to maximize the benefits of soil moisture. Under such circumstances, corn would often have to be harvested in an immature state. Human selection would be for fast maturing corn. Since higher elevations would present late frosts, such sites would have to maximize plantings on southern or southwest facing slopes and above low-lying pockets of cold air. If Rice is correct, such sites should have a high proportion of hearths.

In the summer rainfall regime, soil moisture would have to be maximized by planting in a variety of locales (as do the Hopi), with some plantings in stream beds. Human selection would favor slow maturing corn which would survive to late summer rains. Such sites would likely face east or north to avoid intense late afternoon sun and would likely have fewer hearths. Because many sites are located along major river drainages and these generally flow northeast to southwest in this country, there might be distinct clusters of sites on one bank, then another, as one moved up or down river. In short, we might argue the possibility of two distinct patterns: *a winter rainfall pattern* with south or southwesterly facing slopes below the site, small (small varieties of cultigens usually mature more quickly), fast maturing varieties of corn, often harvested in an immature state, and a higher incidence of hearths; *a summer rainfall pattern* would be characterized by east (or north) facing slopes away from the site, (larger varieties of corn over time?), corn picked mature, and fewer hearths. Corn would be planted in low-lying areas. The implications of the Chapalote/Harinoso de Ocho shift, somewhere between A.D. 700 and 900, might be significant in this respect. At any rate, cob and kernel development should be quite different for the same variety under the two contrasting conditions. The *summer pattern* sites might also have a lower mean elevation, even if by only 50 or 100 feet.

Such a model would be quite useful in organizing the data we do have and structuring designs for future survey. Some elements of it may even prove supportable. It will be discussed more fully in the conclusion of the chapter.

THE GEORGETOWN PHASE (A.D. 550-650?)

CHRONOLOGY

In the recently published *Handbook of North American Indians*, Woodbury and Zubrow (1979, V.9) follow Wheat (1955) in assigning the Georgetown Phase to the time period between A.D. 100 and 400. Nonetheless, Danson (1957), Bullard (1962), Graybill (1973), Anyon (1979) and Anyon, Gilman and LeBlanc (1980) argue a time frame between A.D. 500 and 700. In LeBlanc's overview he favors A.D. 500 (or slightly later) to A.D. 650. These variations are not so problematic as one might suppose, if it is borne in mind that this phase is used to describe several distinctive patterns in the archeological record.

First, there is a notable shift in site placement, from high, inaccessible promontories to the lower first terraces above major streams. Second, the proportion of San Francisco Red ceramics increases noticeably (10-20%) and, third, round to D-shaped pithouses are common. Wheat's earlier dates are less difficult to absorb if it is understood that he placed less emphasis on the shift in site locations. We prefer to keep that emphasis for reasons that will be obvious.

In the Mimbres area, dendrochronological dates from the Harris Site of this period range from A.D. 582 to about A.D. 624 (Anyon 1979). We judge these dates to suggest a reasonable time frame of A.D. 550-650.

SETTLEMENT

Actual sites of this phase are quite few in number, and most of them are small, smaller in fact than many of the sites (last section) thought to be earlier. There are five pithouses of this period at the Harris Site, according to Woodbury and Zubrow (1979:59) and four at the Starkweather Site. It is very difficult to determine just which pithouses at the Harris Site, for example, belong in this or an earlier phase. We judge it possible that the Winn Canyon Site overlaps with this time period, even though Fitting felt it to be earlier. The percent of San Francisco Red at the Winn Canyon Site was 6% (Fitting 1973:26) and Room 2 (the large ceremonial room) contained 19% San Francisco Red. These frequencies are much higher than most scholars allow as diagnostic of the earlier phase. Either the percentage of San Francisco Red is a good time marker or is evidence of increasing economic differentiation. The case is quite unclear. Future surveys should record every ceramic scatter possible to provide actual percentages of plain, red and painted wares.

In spite of the scanty evidence, we can suppose 5 to at most 15 pithouses per site as an average, with the caveat that these sites are suspiciously scarce (see Population) and few sherd scatters have been analyzed. There is clearly a shift between inaccessible bluff and accessible riverine settings. LeBlanc is in the minority for arguing full sedentism at this period.

ARCHITECTURAL FEATURES

According to Anyon (1979, citing Wheat, it would appear), the average pithouse size during this period is 14.3 m^2. Stafford and Rice (1979) indicate that the occurrence of hearth features increases somewhat from earlier periods. Construction timbers (like some of the latest sites in the early pithouse phase) tend to be of riverine species (cottonwood, etc.). This is one primary reason that dendrochronological dates are scarce for this period.

Communal architecture increases slowly in distinctiveness. Grooved floor features occur in later components of the SU, Bluff and Crooked Ridge sites (Martin 1979:67). Anyon (1979) points out that such *kivas* began to have distinctive ovoid wings or bulges. Most Georgetown

Phase sites also have later pithouse components superimposed on them. LeBlanc's (1977) Diablo Site is an exception.

POPULATION

In view of the scarcity of these sites in the Mimbres area, Martin and Plog's (1973) argument for population decrease in the period from A.D. 500-700 cannot be ignored. Assuming a starting date of A.D. 600 as one of gradual population increase (based on the Harris Site date of A.D. 582vv), if LeBlanc's argument is to be accepted, the Mimbres area would have to have had a very modest population base from which to develop the population necessary to account for the Three Circle Phase which he argues begins about A.D. 750. From the known room counts in the Mimbres Valley attributed to this phase, we could suppose a base population of 50 persons. This seems impossibly small, even allowing Martin and Plog's argument.

Projecting this population forward at a doubling rate of every 40 years we would arrive at a figure of only 800 by the year A.D. 760. Assuming sedentary agriculture, as does LeBlanc, the early Three Circle Phase (if LeBlanc's date of A.D. 750 is used — we don't) would only have had a population density of one person to 1.5 square miles in the Mimbres Valley. By the eve of the Classic Mimbres at A.D. 960, if population had continued to double at the same rate, there would have been a population of 25,600. At an average size of 25 pithouses per late Three Circle Phase site (Minnis 1979) the entire inventory of sites could be figured at 200. Though this might be a plausible figure, demographers (Cowgill 1975) would find nearly 400 years of such sustained growth to be remarkable. The twenty modern pueblos required the 80 years between 1860 and 1940 to double in population, but only 30 years to double again by 1970 (Simmons 1979a:221). The next doubling will likely be about an 18 year span, yielding a population in 1988 of 65,000 to 67,000. This (1980) census should show a population of about 42,000 to 44,000.

Since the period between A.D. 450 to 500 and A.D. 650-700 suggests population loss (Martin and Plog 1973) and rearrangement of settlement-subsistence (changes in site location) we can presume disintegrating influences similar to that suffered by modern pueblos between 1860 and 1900. Thus, a terminal Early Pithouse/Georgetown population of 50 at A.D. 600 might double by A.D. 680 and again by A.D. 710, and again by A.D. 730 and again by A.D. 750, and still equal only 800 persons. Eight Three Circle sites of twenty pithouses each would account for the entire population. If one accepts LeBlanc's suggestion of 500 persons at the end of the Early Pithouse period and no population loss, then the archeological record is short by about 90 pithouses at the beginning Georgetown if one allows 4-6 m² space per individual (Casselberry 1974). By the end of the Georgetown Phase, this flaw in the archeological record would be remarkable.

We have already argued (see previous section) that the population figure of 500 is too low to have created the density requirements for sedentism. At 15,000 square miles for the entire region in question, we can suppose a density of not more than 2-3 square miles per person as the *absolute minimum* to meet our requirements, that is, provide enough *background* population to maintain tension on high density pockets such as the Mimbres Valley. At A.D. 500 a population of 5,000 to 10,000 at minimum would be required regionally to have sustained villages characteristic of the Early Pithouse Phase. At an average size of 7-10 pithouses (LeBlanc 1979) and five individuals per pithouse, we require 100-200 such sites in southwestern New Mexico as a minimum at *any given time*. Assuming a use span of 60 years each, from A.D. 250 to 550, we are looking for 500-1,000 pithouse sites of this size (ten pits), and an additional 200-400 such sites for the Georgetown Phase even if it only lasted 120 years.

There are only several conclusions possible: 1) the lack of systematic survey which crosscuts major drainages has flawed the archaeological record to a remarkable degree; 2) there was enormous population loss during the A.D. 500-700 period; 3) the majority of the population during the first half millenium after Christ never lived in identifiable pithouse villages at all; or 4) some combination of these three factors is responsible. We favor the latter idea.

SOCIAL ORGANIZATION AND BURIALS

No particular conclusions can be drawn from data presented in LeBlanc's overview. The data from Bear Ruin in Arizona (which overlaps this time period) suggest some increasing social complexity evidenced by increased clustering of burials, and notes grave goods which crosscut age and sex differences. LeBlanc, conversely, suggests that Georgetown Phase burials have few grave goods, no particular orientation, and tend to be scattered about. The later Mogollon characteristic of subfloor inhumations and ceramic bowls *killed* as grave goods seems not yet to have become a firm pattern in the Mimbres.

SUBSISTENCE

LeBlanc argues for uninterrupted reliance on corn agriculture, coupled with hunting and gathering. Stafford and Rice (1979) emphasize the seasonal aspects of subsistence and the wide variety of wild plants and animals taken. Martin and Plog (1973) argue from the Tularosa Cave data that the period is one of relapse to the hunting-gathering way of life. While that may not hold for the study area, the lack of settled villages suggests a retrogression. Again, deer, rabbits, rodents, wild grasses, acorns, pinyon, wild succulents, bird species and some domesticates (corn, beans, squash, cotton) are characteristic of the period.

SUMMARY

The Georgetown Phase is difficult to interpret, the evidence being scanty. It seems to be characterized by a few small to medium sized villages, population loss or dispersal and increased dependence on foraging. Again, the archeological data may be weakened by a century of focusing on river basin survey and the importance of painted ware sites.

THE SAN FRANCISCO PHASE (A.D. 650-850?)

CHRONOLOGY

Different scholars place the San Francisco Phase at slightly differing time periods. Gladwin (1936) suggests roughly A.D. 700 to 900, Bullard (1962) A.D. 700-750 to roughly A.D. 900, Graybill (1973) about A.D. 650-850, and Anyon, Gilman and LeBlanc (1980) A.D. 650-750. Haury (1936) placed the terminal date at A.D. 900.

The dendrochronological samples that Anyon (1979) has compiled for this phase range from A.D. 625 to 755. However, the cutting dates all cluster between A.D. 736-748. Again, these come from only a few sites and the tight clustering cannot be expected to hold everywhere. Nonetheless, we favor Graybill on the matter.

These sites are characterized by more rectangular pithouses, Mogollon Red-on-brown and San Lorenzo Red-on-brown. At this juncture a problem arises. Anyon (1979:173-176) has difficulty in deciding the temporal interpretation of the Three Circle Red-on-white ceramics. In his first proposal on phase sequences (p. 173), he suggests dates of A.D. 700-800 for the San Francisco Phase. Several pages later, he suggests dates of A.D. 650-750 and accepts that scheme because he feels the later terminal date for the San Francisco would not allow enough time for ceramic development (in 200 years) from the Three Circle Red-on-white,

Boldface Black-on-white, the Transitional Black-on-white, and then the beginning of Classic Mimbres. *The Transitional* Black-on-white was being produced in developed form by A.D. 900 (Anyon 1979:175). The problem of rapid ceramic development, coupled with the dramatic rise in the number of Three Circle Phase pithouses, goes against Anyon's notions of gradualism in cultural evolution, so the terminal date for the San Francisco Phase is adjusted backwards. The cutting dates cited above, however, really preclude termination of this phase at A.D. 750 if the ceramics in pithouse floor contexts suggest that the Mogollon Red-on-browns are diagnostic. Anyon suggests, without making a point of it, that the Three Circle Red-on-whites are actually found in modest quantity during this phase. The whole case is confused by the conflict between underlying assumptions about ceramic development on the one hand, and the evidence of substantial increases in site size on the other. The issue is further confused by the fact that Mogollon Red-on-brown and Three Circle Red-on-white both have best dates of A.D. 775-950 (Martin and Plog 1973). We feel most comfortable with dates of A.D. 650 to about A.D. 852, assuming some overlap with the earlier Georgetown Phase.

SETTLEMENT

During this period the number of pithouses in the Mimbres area increases markedly. The average size of sites increases to perhaps 15-20 pithouses per site, with some sites having considerably more. Site placement is firmly fixed on first terraces over rivers and *in situ* development on sites of the previous Georgetown Phase seems to be the rule. Most settlements include one or two clusters of pithouses with associated kivas (one or two per site). Again, house units seem to have no highly patterned arrangement. Most of the sites are in higher elevation settings (above 6,000 feet) though some may be at lower elevations (the Winn Canyon Site is at an elevation of 4620 feet, Fitting 1973) and simply not recorded on surveys. This could be especially so if such sites tended to be smaller, were less likely to have the fancier wares, and, being lower, were on the banks of smaller drainages where they became buried by silting from upstream areas.

ARCHITECTURAL FEATURES

Anyon (1979) cites the average pithouse size as 15.3 m^2. We have computed variation in the diameter of structures as 1:1.72, comparing the small to the large. Anyon views the development of *lobed* communal houses as becoming gradually more distinctive from residential units. There is still a substantial percentage of pithouses without hearths, though pithouses become much more rectangular and less variable in size and internal features. Pithouses show more careful interior finish and rampways become common. The entrances, or rampways, have no single compass orientation, though the larger structures seem to have a northeast orientation (Anyon 1979:199-200).

POPULATION

It is difficult to obtain exact room counts for this period, since interpretations of dates from excavated pithouses often hinge on the percentage of San Francisco Red to Mogollon Red-on-brown, and for some investigators the presence of the red-on-whites is diagnostic of the Three Circle Phase. The evidence suggests definite population increase that falls short of dramatic. Martin and Plog (1973:320) cite the reconstructions of population trends developed by S. Plog in the late 1960's. These suggest that population (Little Colorado R.) in an adjacent area did not begin to increase dramatically until about A.D. 850, that is, until the succeeding Three Circle Phase.

SOCIAL ORGANIZATION

No shifts in basic organizational features seem to be suggested by the data as discussed by Anyon (1979). Nonetheless, in the neighboring Forestdale region, Stafford and Rice (1979) have lumped the Pine Lawn and Georgetown phases together because of the later shift to the Reserve phases in that district. They view the shift there as representing a move toward smaller communities (though the exact temporal relationships between the two areas is not well studied, this would appear to be slightly later — about A.D. 900) in more upland settings with a decrease in the larger sites at slightly lower elevations. In that area they view the relatively few kivas, when compared to the substantial number of small settlements, as suggesting a social order based on economic redistribution (small scale) over a fairly generous locale. Unlike Willey (1966) and some other scholars, LeBlanc and Anyon point out that the Mogollon Red-on-brown wares diagnostic of the phase are common in the Pine Lawn and Jornada regions (north and east), but are scarce in the San Francisco and Gila drainages to the south and west. This, of course, raises questions about the Mogollon-Ootam relationships and the southwestern shift of the Mogollon which McGregor (1974:226) discusses during the A.D. 700-900 *Adjustment Period*. Whatever the social arrangements might have been, they appear not to have been moving toward a similar shift in the Mimbres area itself during the San Francisco Phase.

BURIALS

During the San Francisco Phase there is a very modest increase in grave goods, especially ceramics. It is during this period that the *killing* of mortuary ceramics becomes established as a pattern. *Killing* was more often accomplished by simply smashing the bowls, though some did have holes punched through the bottom, as was characteristic of later periods. Because of the varying interpretations of just which pithouses at which sites represent a San Francisco Phase occupation, we have not been able accurately to summarize burial data. For instance, Wheat (1955:63) suggests that the majority of the burials at Mogollon Village and at the Harris Site are of the San Francisco Phase. Anyon's (1979:214) reading of Haury (1936) suggests to him that the case for the temporal placement of these burials is quite unclear.

The situation can be summed up with this statement: "Very little can be said about the Mimbres branch of the San Francisco burials except that they are liberally scattered throughout the villages, often in old storage pits and abandoned pithouse depressions" (Anyon 1979: 214). With one exception, the subfloor burials characteristic of later periods appear not to have been a significant feature of this period.

SUBSISTENCE

Here again, few specific trends are discernible from data suggested in the LeBlanc/Whalen overview. This period, however, is one in which new varieties of corn are known to have been introduced to the southwest. Specifically, Martin and Plog (1973) note the introduction of 8 rowed corn (Harinoso de Ocho), of larger cob and less flinty character. New varieties of beans and squash replaced previously favored varieties and cotton assumed greater importance. At the same time, basic changes in manos and metates took place, larger trough metates with more grinding surface replacing the smaller.

A wide variety of animal remains is still found in sites, though a detailed study comparing frequencies of remains from site to site and between regional varieties of the Mogollon has yet to be attempted. Martin and Plog (1973) suggested increased sedentism, generally, during this period, coupled of course with substantially increased dependence on cultigens. LeBlanc and Anyon (1979) view the period as one of continued sedentism based primarily on cultigens, while Stafford and Rice (1979) focus on the continued tendency toward seasonal shifts in the subsistence base (though not nearly so marked as in the Pine Lawn-Georgetown Phase).

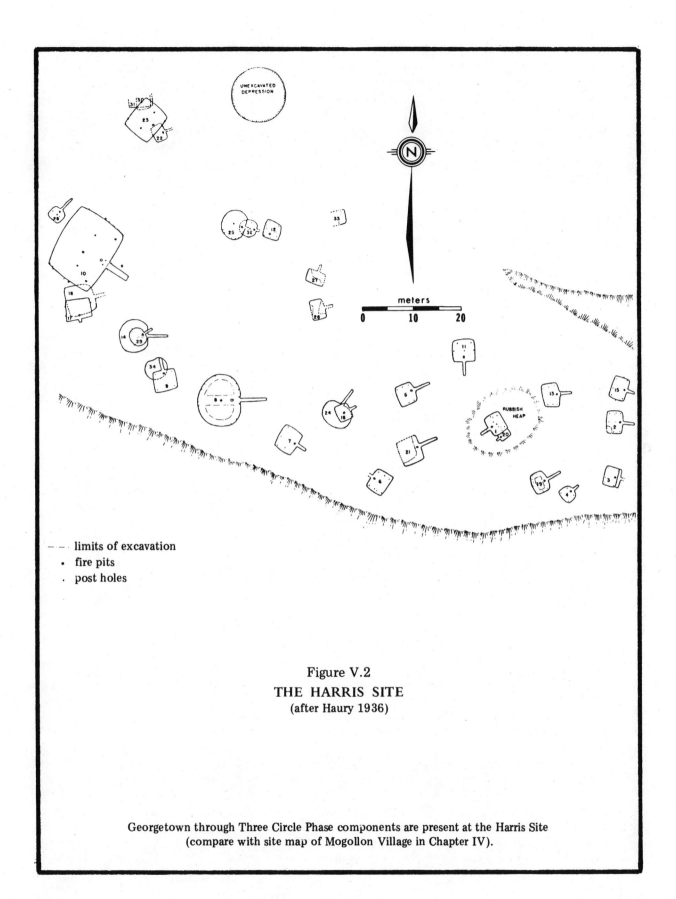

limits of excavation
fire pits
post holes

Figure V.2
THE HARRIS SITE
(after Haury 1936)

Georgetown through Three Circle Phase components are present at the Harris Site
(compare with site map of Mogollon Village in Chapter IV).

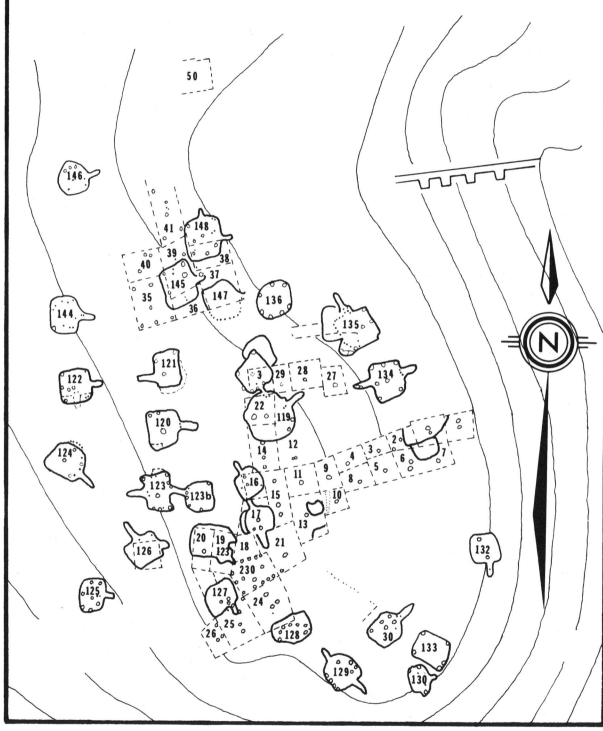

Figure V.3
CAMERON CREEK SITE
(after Bradfield 1929)

Classic Mimbres roomblocks superimposed over earlier pithouses. This is typical in the Mimbres District.

The return to the use of pine species (as opposed to *riverine*, mainly cottonwood) for both construction and fuel is suggestive. This is like the pattern of the earliest pithouse period and unlike the transitional period between it and the Georgetown Phase (ca. A.D. 500-600).

SUMMARY

During this period there are substantial changes in agriculture, generally, in the Southwest, though the details of these changes need to be clarified for the Mimbres itself. Site size increases, though not dramatically and population increases, again not dramatically. Large game and a wide variety of smaller game and wild vegetal foodstuffs supplement an increasing dependence on maize, beans and squash. The Harinoso de Ocho type of corn makes its appearance. There is little evidence for increasing social stratification from burial goods, but the size of pithouse units does increase to a degree. Though sites of this period are, comparatively, well-dated to the north in the Pine Lawn-Reserve area, they are less well-dated here (the temporal placement of rooms at the Harris Site being a point of contention). Anyon (1979; Anyon, Gilman and LeBlanc 1980) seems more than vaguely uneasy about in-the-ground identification of this phase due to superposition of later Three Circle Phase pithouses over the earlier.

THE THREE CIRCLE PHASE (A.D. 850-975 or 1000?)

CHRONOLOGY

Almost all sources agree on the period from A.D. 900-1000 as the best general time frame for the Three Circle Phase. LeBlanc and Whalen (1979) and Anyon (1979), however, suggest that the phase extends from A.D. 750 to 1000. Graybill (1973) also suggests a broader time span in the upper Mimbres drainage.

As we stated earlier, both LeBlanc and Anyon feel a longer temporal span is necessary to account for the development of several distinctive ceramic types in rapid succession: Three Circle Red-on-white, Boldface Black-on-white (also known as Mangus Black-on-white), and the Transitional style of Black-on-white leading to the Classic Mimbres. Again, the question of just what is being described arises. If we assume (as do Anyon and LeBlanc) that ceramic development is gradual because cultural evolution is itself gradual, then the shorter time span of A.D. 800-1000 is troublesome. It is especially troublesome since LeBlanc has emphasized the existence of a series of transitional pottery styles between the Boldface (Mangus) and the Classic Mimbres. Separating Boldface B/W and Transitional B/W allows him to emphasize his point that the succeeding Mimbres was an *in situ* development lacking evidence for Anasazi intrusion as a causative agent, black-on-white ceramics notwithstanding. In order to maintain this view of Mimbres development, he is forced to deny any cultural penetration. This seems to confuse rather than clarify the issue.

The tree-ring dates cited for this period range from A.D. 801 to 964 (Anyon 1979: 157-165, Chart 6, 167-168). The single early (A.D. 801) date is a *vv* sample from House No. 4 at Harris Village. The post A.D. 900 dates are from one pithouse (each) at the Wheaton-Smith and the Mattocks Site (LA 676) and, being from roof fall, are problematic. Most of the other dates (and all of the cutting dates) cluster between A.D. 858 and 898. In view of this, Graybill's suggested chronology seems quite reasonable.

SETTLEMENT

During the Three Circle Phase there is a remarkable *in situ* expansion of village size, at least in the larger sites. The number of pithouses increases, and most are superimposed over earlier pithouse settlements. Martin and Plog (1973) suggest an average of 50 pithouses per village during this period. Minnis (1979) suggests 24.5. Obviously there is local variation.

193

At the same time, new settlements increase along secondary drainages. In this case LeBlanc and Anyon's judgment is in agreement with that of Stafford and Rice (1979) and of Zubrow (1971), who have noted a similar pattern in adjacent areas of Arizona. Though Minnis (1979: 617) suggests that the average size of Three Circle pithouse settlements is 24, with variation of from 1-100 pithouses, he also notes that a number of these sites have 60-70 pithouses. It is not possible at the moment to determine precisely how many of these units were occupied at a given time, on the average. Nonetheless, site size is at least double that of the preceeding San Francisco Phase.

During this period the appearance of the Three Circle Red-on-white in quantity and the Boldface Black-on-white (Mangus) ceramics is a dramatic change from the earlier Mogollon Red-on-browns. These ceramic developments have led to assumptions that they represent influences from the Anasazi area (the black-on-white color scheme) and from the Hohokam (the appearance of naturalistic anthropomorphic designs). As noted earlier, the Whalen and LeBlanc overview rejects the notion of Anasazi influence, but does not seem to have taken a strong position on the Hohokam. What is important is that the Three Circle and Boldface ceramics have a much wider distribution than the Mogollon Red-on-brown. LeBlanc views this as evidence of trade, during this period, to all the cardinal directions. It would be relatively simple to separate *trade* from *influence* if ceramic clays were compared to source clays for the entire region by spectrographic analysis.

ARCHITECTURAL FEATURES

As a generality, architectural features don't change dramatically during the earlier part of this phase. There are, however, several trends that merit comment.

In the first place, the average size of pithouses decreases to 13 m² and average *depth* declines. The size of *communal* structures increases in relation to the size of habitation units. By our computations (and we believe our data to be imperfect) the ratio of smallest diameters to largest diameters of these pit structures is 1:2.92. That is, size decreases and variation between the smallest and largest increases in comparison to the Georgetown Phase. Pithouses become true straight-sided rectangles.

Pithouses are often superimposed, one upon the other, and these rectangular pithouses often have cobble masonry *half* walls supporting the interior of excavated portions. There are generally one or two communal houses or kivas per site. Pithouse ramp orientations tend increasingly to favor southeastern exposure.

POPULATION

The Three Circle Phase is quite clearly one of rapid population increase. In Martin and Plog (1973:320), population trends for the regions nearest the Mimbres, the White Mountain and Little Colorado show the beginning of rapid population increase at A.D. 1050 and 850 respectively. Given the number of Three Circle cutting dates which cluster around A.D. 850-860, we are able to argue that population in this area began a notable surge between A.D. 850 and 900, as it did also in the Mesa Verde and Chaco areas to the north. Further, we may argue that construction dates clustering as closely as one or two years apart in the same site represent either aggregation from outlying areas or the establishment of new families based on *in situ* population growth. If we accept Martin and Plog's (1973) argument that A.D. 500-700 was a period of population decline and apply the growth pattern of the contemporary Pueblos as exemplifying population dynamics following catastrophe, we are able to create a speculative but useful population model.

If we accept LeBlanc's upper estimate of 500 as the *pre-catastrophe* population in the

Mimbres Valley and assume no loss during Martin and Plog's hiatus, thereby suggesting homeostasis, we can project the first post A.D. 700 doubling at A.D. 780 as 1,000 people. The second doubling would be at A.D. 810 with 2,000 people, the third at A.D. 830 with 4,000, and the fourth at A.D. 850-860 with 8,000 people. Considering the influence of modern medicine in the pueblos, we are giving maximum credit to these Mimbres folk. Nonetheless, at A.D. 850 the entire hypothetical population (still assuming the old hunter-gatherer ratio of one *head of household* to five dependents) could have been accomodated in about 1,300 to 1,400 pithouses. Population would have been about five persons per square mile in the Mimbres Valley but only one pithouse per square mile would have been necessary to accomodate the population, or 55 average Three Circle sites of 25 pithouses each.

Significantly, we note that pithouse size increased to a maximum during the San Francisco Phase (15.8 m²). The first two hypothetical population doublings clearly fall within this previous phase, and it is reasonable to argue that expansion was partially absorbed by larger pithouses containing more children. The next hypothetical doubling at A.D. 830 appears more problematic, since there is no associated cluster of cutting dates to demonstrate the construction inevitably needed to accomodate such growth. The short doubling time would logically have required the establishment of new families. Either the dendrochronological record is flawed by its modest sample size or there was an expansion into new site settings. The cluster of construction dates at A.D. 850-860 suggests that a generation of children were coming of age in rapid succession, a generation whose mothers may still have been reproductively active. This appears to usher in the Three Circle Phase with its smaller, more numerous pithouses.

LeBlanc and Anyon have noted the absence, generally, of tree-ring dates between phases which are otherwise recognizable from ceramics and architecture. We think it likely that population expansion was outward (budding) in some instances and should not be surprised to find that some *missing* dates will yet be retrieved from modest outlying sites — sites having fewer diagnostic ceramics.

SOCIAL ORGANIZATION

Many scholars argue for increasingly complex social-organizational features during this period. This is inferred from increasing differentiation in burial goods, increasing village size, and increasing size of communal structures. Since pithouse size declines, one can also suppose a decrease in family size. Yet a decrease from 15.8 m² (San Francisco Phase) to 13 m² (Three Circle Phase) is clearly not sufficient proof of a shift to nuclear family organization. Beyond invoking the generality that a growing system tends to stratify and become organizationally more complex, we think it overly speculative to fill in particular details.

BURIALS

In the Three Circle Phase, the pattern of intramural subfloor burials takes hold. In Three Circle sites where this is a strong pattern, Anyon (1979:219) suggests there is a transformation to later Classic Mimbres population centers. This is a really fascinating observation. As evidence, Anyon points out that neither the Harris Site (Mimbres Valley) nor the Lee Site (Gila Valley) is overlain with a Classic Mimbres component. Only two intramural subfloor burials were found in each from among roughly the same number of excavated pithouses (30-35).

If this pattern were to be further documented, it might provide the basis for valuable insights. For instance, let us suppose the co-occurrence of Classic Mimbres Black-on-white, above ground cobble/masonry pueblos and a high proportion of intramural subfloor burials to be indicators of a Classic Mimbres site. If we further suppose that these indicators are related, processually, in some way, then sites lacking one or more of these features can be presumed to have been developed through a different succession of adaptive responses.

As Anyon points out, sites with such burials are rare in the Gila drainage (two burials thus far discovered) and absent (thus far) in the San Francisco drainages, but not in the Mimbres (83, thus far). Significantly, the LeBlanc/Whalen overview (Survey chapter) indicates that as one moves away from the Mimbres Valley proper, the average number of burials and burial bowls per room decreases fivefold (also, the average site size decreases).

Might we suggest that sites where subfloor burials are few or absent tend to produce, or trade in, the Three Circle or Boldface style ceramics and continue to be characterized by rectangular pithouses in later periods? Might we also suggest that some smaller outlying sites, classified as Three Circle or Mangus Phase, may be contemporaneous with early Classic Mimbres sites in the Mimbres Valley where the Mimbres Black-on-white does lie above the Boldface, stratigraphically?

In other words, we may resolve LeBlanc's and Anyon's unwillingness to accept the Mangus Phase *in the Mimbres Valley* (LeBlanc and Whalen 1979; Anyon, Gilman and LeBlanc 1980) with the Gladwin's (1934) description of it from survey in the Mangus Valley, by proposing that these represent different kinds of sites, partially contemporaneous, and if we suppose also that ceramic development was more rapid in one (the large) than the other.

Anyon, Gilman and LeBlanc (1980:12-15) make a very nice case for precisely this interpretation and recognize the potential contemporaneity of such sites, but come to an opposite conclusion because "LARGE Three Circle Phase pithouse villages were replaced in a very short period of time by LARGE surface pueblo sites generally in the same location . . . . This is demonstrated by the lack of structures that might be characterized as transitional between pithouses and above-ground masonry pueblos on THESE sites . . . . and the close design similarity between ceramics from the two kinds of structure" (Anyon, Gilman and LeBlanc 1980:13). In other words, we think Mangus and Mimbres phases may have much the same relationship in southwestern New Mexico as have Hosta Butte and Bonito Phase in the San Juan Basin. That is the difference between *bigs* and *littles* and the inevitable differences in rates of demographic, economic and technological change between them. Since the crucial prior condition appears to be the number and style of burials, we will return to that and applaud Anyon for his impressive observation, leaving our own explanation until a bit later, lest we get out of phase here ourselves.

Other characteristics of Three Circle burials are also of interest. Flexed burials increase in numbers. Boldface Black-on-white bowls are often *killed* by smashing, though no (later) Transitional (to Classic Mimbres) Black-on-white bowls were smashed. The Transitional bowls are increasingly killed by hole-punching in the bottom and increasingly placed over the face or head, as opposed to covering the knees or at the side, as is more common with Boldface Black-on-white. No Boldface bowl placed over the skull is known. Plainwares and undecorated ollas were not generally used as grave goods and Three Cirlce Phase handled pitchers were used almost exclusively as grave goods.

Of 85 Three Circle Phase subfloor burials which Anyon discusses (1979:215-220), 65% (55) were children under the age of ten. Twenty-eight of these (50%) had *no* grave goods. There are 41 bodies in the entire sample without grave goods, which is about 48%. Forty-three percent of the adults (n30) are without grave goods. Thus, children are slighted as regards grave goods to only a modest extent.

There is notable variability in the quantity of grave goods, from modest to substantial, and Anyon notes that burial goods for different burials occurring in the same pithouse may be rich to none. Since we have not seen data summarized by age, sex, quantity of goods, etc. within pithouses, we do not know whether age/sex differences lead to such disparity in grave goods within the same living unit. Also, we should like to see summarized the number of burials per pithouse and the size of those pithouses as well as the range of ceramics found in each. Finally, few extramural burials are reported and this is undoubtedly a function of excavation technique (though a number of extramural burials are reported for the Three Circle Site).

Finally, during this period turquoise is added to the inventory of burial goods and occurs in some quantity, along with shell and other small items. Macaw feathers may first appear. There is the suggestion of increasing status differentiation, but its specific form (hereditary vs. ascribed, etc.) is uncertain. Again, burial data from southwestern New Mexico needs to be carefully reevaluated, particularly in view of the massive recent destruction of burials from pothunting.

SUBSISTENCE

The LeBlanc/Whalen overview (1979) argues for heavy dependence on floodplain agriculture without irrigation techniques during this period. Some sites are in secondary drainages and employ a similar strategy. Pollen counts for corn are common. The relative scarcity of beans and squash is generally agreed to be a function of less certain preservation.

Curiously, the inhabitants of Three Circle villages return to ponderosa pine for construction timbers, though pollen profiles and hearth ash remains suggest cottonwoods to be still common in the floodplains. The remains of deer and cottontails are the most common faunal materials in those sites in the Mimbres area.

In the Black River district in an adjoining portion of Arizona, and the Reserve area of New Mexico, Stafford and Rice (1979) emphasize the shift to smaller sites in more upland settings (A.D. 900-1000), representing the transition to the Reserve Phase, which represents a break from the larger settlements in lower elevations. They suspect a broadening of foraging activities. Curiously, no one makes much of pinyon nuts as a potential food item which can be, intermittently, gathered in great quantities. Clearly, more subsistence data are needed.

SUMMARY

The Three Circle Phase is one of substantial population increase, of continued *in situ* village growth for many, but not all, sites, and of increasing dependence on agriculture. Pithouse size decreases, communal structures increase in size, and pithouses become straight-sided and half-walled. Burial goods increase, variations between grave offerings are noticeable, infant mortality is suspiciously high and new grave goods occur; i.e., turquoise and macaw feathers. There is a rapid transition from Three Circle Black-on-white to Boldface (Mangus) Black-on-white to Transitional Black-on-white. LeBlanc views trade as farflung, outward, from the Mimbres Valley. Specifically, Mimbres Boldface and Classic Black-on-white, which appear in the Jornada Mogollon to the east, are presumed to have been traded to that region. Since clay and temper analysis have not located source materials, this interpretation must be considered tentative. Suffice it to say that either population movement or economics were more expansive during this period than previously.

There is still notable dependence on wild game, deer and rabbit, but construction timbers revert to upland (rather than cottonwood and other riverine) species.

THE CLASSIC MIMBRES (A.D. 975-1150?)

CHRONOLOGY

Almost all sources agree that the Classic Mimbres begins about A.D. 1000, and most assign terminal dates between A.D. 1200 and 1250. The Cosgroves (1932) suggested a beginning date of A.D. 950, and on the basis of ceramic styles, this is tempting to Anyon, Gilman and LeBlanc (1980:17). Nonetheless, they opt for the A.D. 1000 date. They give a terminal date of A.D. 1150, based on the fact that no cutting date that postdates A.D. 1117 has been determined from among 300+ tree-ring samples. In fact, they favor A.D. 1130 as a likely terminal date. Curiously, they argue pointedly that the sequence leading to *abandonment* of the Mimbres district is unlike other abandonment phenomena in the Southwest.

Recall that in Chapter III we made a point of the Chaco phenomenon losing its magnet effect about A.D. 1130, after the last construction dates for the phenomenon, dates which are widely published. We are not so creative in pointing this out, for Chaco Canyon is listed in Martin and Plog (1973:320) as *abandoned* in A.D. 1150, this based on an earlier manuscript by S. Plog (1969). Why, then, have Anyon, Gilman and LeBlanc (1980:33) elected to conclude: "Thus the abandonment of the Mimbres region does not appear to be linked to the abandonment seen in other regions of the Southwest which occur during the A.D. 1200's"? It is, of course, the case that *neither* Chacoan nor Mimbres abandonment is related to abandonments of the later P-III period (see concluding chapter of this volume).

Several additional points should be made about chronology. No reliable (cutting) tree-ring dates exist for a Three Circle Phase pithouse after A.D. 900, and not a single construction (cutting) date has yet been recovered for a Classic Mimbres building which predates A.D. 1050 (Anyon, Gilman and LeBlanc 1980:17). There is thus a remarkable paradox. There is an unbroken stylistic sequence of transitional pottery forms, but a full 150 year gap in evidence for construction of sites which are conventionally thought to be the result of rapid transitional events. At the end of this phase, however, there is said to be a complete break to the *non-Mogollon* Animas tradition by A.D. 1175. We are thus presented with cultural continuity in the context of a 150 year *gap* in chronology on the one hand and dramatic cultural succession on the other, with only a 25-45 year discontinuity.

Mind you, we are not sneering at Anyon, Gilman and LeBlanc's (1980) observations. We have in most cases accepted their data and observations, but have been led, at times, to different conclusions. It could be that the vagaries of selecting sites for excavation could produce such a picture. That is, there is a gap in dates between Three Circle and Mimbres construction in *large* sites. One could conclude that the intervening dates will be found eventually in very *small* sites scattered about, as we have suggested for the Mangus. This line of thinking again points towards the Mangus Phase as a small site phenomenon, that is, a period of relative dispersal such as Stafford and Rice (1979) have described for the Three Circle-Reserve Phase transition which occurred to the north and west (the Nantack phase in Point of Pines, Arizona; see Breternitz 1966).

Anyon (1979) characterizes the later Classic Mimbres as a period of population pressure outward to more marginal areas, but lesser dependence on agriculture in large Classic Mimbres sites (lower pollen profiles). We could revise this scheme to suggest *two* such episodes of dispersal and relative decline in occupation at larger sites, followed by subsequent collapse inward to aggregated conditions, one at A.D. 950-1050 and again from A.D. 1125-1175 (the final aggregation being Animas in character). We could then view each episode as symptomatic of adaptive stresses leading to major reorganizations of society. The symmetry of this approach is pleasing, and accords better with developments elsewhere. And, important to the purpose of this volume, additional survey could shed substantial light on the problem by identifying likely sites from size (smaller) and transitional ceramic assemblages, sites which might later offer the missing dates upon excavation.

On the other hand, we wish to point out that the observations of the Mimbres Foundation staff call to mind certain features of the Classic Maya collapse (Culbert 1973). In that volume evidence for increasing mortality at the end of the Early Classic Mayan period is discussed. That mortality is followed by a curious pause or dislocation (lack of dated stelae for 110 years) and then rapid onset of the Mayan Classic development. We see a pattern here: mortality, ill-defined reorganization or pause and the onset of the power drive we discussed in Chapters II and III. It is also the pattern in late Medieval Europe between the first plagues and the Renaissance (roughly A.D. 1300-1500). We will return to this line of thinking later in summarizing this chapter.

SETTLEMENT AND ARCHITECTURE

In the period, from roughly A.D. 950 to 1100, archeological sites in the higher elevations of the Forestdale region of Arizona are said to be uniformly small (Stafford and Rice 1979). These average ten rooms or less in size, the point being that such sites are almost always smaller than later ones in the same area dating to the 12th century. Still there is substantial increase in the number of sites. The number of these sites increases particularly in the higher elevations, and there is a shift to surface architecture, including jacal construction. There are relatively few kivas at this time. For instance, in one portion of Danson's (1957) survey (Pine Lawn, Tularosa and Apache Creek Valleys) there were 60 Reserve Phase sites to a single kiva. In those regions to the north and west there is substantially more evidence for Anasazi (or at least non-Mimbres) influences. Whether these involve actual population movements or changing economic networks, as Tainter (1980) has argued, is not known.

In the Mimbres area itself there is a huge number and variety of sites. These range in size from 4-5 room sites to a maximum of about 200 rooms. The smaller sites (under 20 rooms) are the most numerous. The mean size for all sites is given as 19.6 rooms (LeBlanc and Whalen 1979). In the survey data summarized in Chapter 9 (LeBlanc and Whalen 1979), the author has provided histograms of Mimbres site size for a population of 500 sites. It seems fairly clear that Classic Mimbres sites in the Mimbres Valley fall into four basic size clusters. These are 2-5 rooms, 10-20 rooms, 30-50 rooms, and 120-200 rooms. These are in the proportion of 10:5:1:1, respectively (our calculations). Given these proportions, there may be little structural difference between 30-50 room and 120-200 room sites. On the other hand, there are no Classic Mimbres sites recorded which are 70-100 rooms in size. This absence of smooth gradation in size argues for a heirarchical difference between these two size clusters that is not suggested by simple proportions. Moreover, the absence of sites with 70-100 rooms is in marked contrast to the previous Three Circle Phase, where 70-80 pithouses were regularly the largest such sites. In the Classic Mimbres the largest sites seem to have attained a scale unknown in previous periods, and the largest were two to three times the size of the next smallest. In view of Eudoxus' Theory of Proportions, the ratio of 1:1 for 30-50 and 120-200 room sites should not be equal if these sites do fill different structural roles in the Mimbres system (see Euclid's *Elements*, Book V). There would, of course, be no paradox if smaller Mimbres sites were substantially under-reported from survey, or if field estimation of site size was too erratic to be meaningful.

In contrast, Graybill's (1973) survey of the upper Mimbres drainage (far north of the study area) yields a mean site size of 9.4 rooms (N = 168). These cluster at 2-5 rooms, 10-20 rooms, and 30-50 rooms. Twenty to 30 room sites are very scarce and large sites (over 100 rooms) are not reported. Thus, we have a heirarchy of three clusters by size, and in contrast to the Mimbres, the largest site category is missing altogether. This is more like the late pithouse phase (Three Circle) and the structural break appears to be in the 20-30 room range.

Lekson's (1978) survey of the Redrock Canyon area (N = 77) suggests strong similarity to Graybill's data, mean site size being 9 rooms.

The comparison of these three surveys is, in fact, difficult since each author uses different phase designations. The most serious problem is that their data have been restructured to eliminate Mangus Phase sites. If, as we have suggested, these overlap temporally with the end of the Three Circle Phase and the beginning of the Classic Mimbres, particularly in outlying districts characterized by smaller sites, then comparisons will be distorted. Nonetheless, it is reasonable to state that the Classic Mimbres, in terms of settlement heirarchy, is only *classic* in the Mimbres Valley itself. This, of course, proceeds only from known survey data. Future survey could substantially alter the picture.

During the Classic Mimbres, there is an expansion into secondary drainages (which partially overlaps similar expansion during the Three Circle Phase) and also into lower elevational desert settings, allegedly unlike the previous pithouse periods. This is likely a generally accurate characterization over a wide area, for it is thought to be shortly before A.D. 900 that pithouse occupation of the Tularosa Basin to the east increases in the higher elevations, and shortly after A.D. 1000 occupations containing Mimbres Black-on-white increase in the lower settings. Recall, however, that the early ceramic scatters in the adjacent lowlands of the Jornada are primarily Boldface Black-on-white (Lehmer 1948). In the Mimbres area, many sites in the lower, drier elevations are thought to be non-architectural and are characterized as large ceramic scatters. This may not be so if such sites were of puddled adobe construction, a non-Mimbres trait usually associated with later Animas (Black Mountain) and Salado phases. We shall return to this possibility in the forthcoming section on the Jornada-Mogollon.

Architecturally, Mimbres sites are usually portrayed as representing a distinct break from prior periods, for great emphasis has been placed on the appearance of surface masonry pueblos at about A.D. 1000. Such sites are characterized by square to rectangular rooms arranged in linear roomblocks and constructed of cobble masonry, adobe mortared. These roomblocks typically have one kiva each; a common configuration being two roomblocks, 10-12 rooms each and each with its kiva.

While there is little doubt that the Classic Mimbres represents a restructuring of earlier society in several important ways, these changes may be overly dramatized in the literature. During the previous Three Circle Phase, pithouses assume the fully rectangular shape characteristic of later periods and are often half-walled with cobble masonry. We are guessing that the tendency of pithouse walls to collapse under close spacing, compounded by increasing drainage problems under the same circumstances, led first to half-walled masonry, then to above ground architecture. Pithouse flooding, even if occasional and not severe, would have had a nasty effect, for water has its way to the lowest spots — to subfloor storage pits, and ruined food supplies could have been disastrous. This would have been partially so under conditions of winter dominant rainfall patterns, with early spring rains that rotted remaining seed corn before planting time. If this is so, we would expect an inverse relationship between spacing of pithouses and the speed of transition to Classic Mimbres architecture. Since site size is obviously a correlate, we may propose a pattern of small site size, relatively great spacing between pithouses, and slower (or ceramically, more confused) transition to classic architecture. Arguing the extreme, some sites likely did not make the transition at all, and this may have depended on general setting characteristics as well.

Finally, the earlier existence of above ground architectural features has not been adequately considered, though known in the literature. For instance, above ground structures are known (from the Blue River Valley) which date to the Early Pithouse period and are associated with the Alma Plain and Rough wares (Rice 1975:61). In the Pine Lawn Valley surface structures are known from very early (either preceramic or aceramic) Mogollon sites (Arnold 1943:252, 267). It is probable that the traditional emphasis on intramural excavation and only secondary interest in extramural stripping in the Mogollon has contributed substantially to impressions of dramatic architectural shifts during the Classic period. It is not, perhaps, that the archeological record *per se* is so flawed; rather, peripheral vision may have been neglected. Hence, with the inward focus upon rooms and their subfloor burials, the immediate architecture is inevitably noticeable, while the more distant surroundings are blurred.

During the Classic Mimbres there is a substantial drop in the average size of rooms. It is confusing that pithouses are compared to surface rooms quite inconsistently. In Martin and Plog (1973) two surface rooms are said to count as one pithouse unit. Early reports and more recent ones are also very different in approach. In reports such as Kidder's *Pecos* (1958, but reporting work done 30-40 years prior) great care is exercised to give both total room counts and by phase. In recent reports there is often so much homage paid to "science" that the investigator forgets his subject and obscures important data. We calculate room size as about 10 m^2, but since Martin and Plog give 12 m^2 at A.D. 1000 (1973:90), we will say here 12 m^2, or less, a sharp drop from the Three Circle Phase.

POPULATION

All sources agree that the Classic Mimbres was a period of substantial population increase. Our own argument is that population may have peaked between A.D. 1050-1100 and then held fairly steady prior to the final building episodes in the Mimbres (ca. A.D. 1117). The data are not currently available to support this contention strongly. The cluster of Mimbres construction dates from A.D. 1060-1080 and the expansion of Mimbres economic influence (from ceramic data) allow the argument to be made tentatively. That is, we argue a population curve chronologically similar (the pattern of tree-ring dates is also amazingly similar) to that proposed by Martin and Plog (1973: 320) for the Chaco Canyon area.

SOCIAL ORGANIZATION

Most researchers have attempted in one way or another to reconstruct certain aspects of Mimbres-Mogollon social organization from studies of ceramic styles, burial goods, village layout and the like. As we have said previously, such studies usually produce very tentative results.

In the Mimbres area, the smaller size of habitation rooms and decreasing numbers of manos and metates per room is generally taken as indicating an increasing shift to nuclear family organization (Martin and Plog 1973). The increasing distinction between habitation rooms and ceremonial or kiva rooms is taken as an additional indicator of change in social organization, as is the tendency to incorporate kivas in each of several roomblocks. The major discussion regarding these changes is whether, taken all together, they *in toto* represent a shift away from kin-based, or kin-integrated, society. In certain portions of adjacent Arizona, the evidence (one kiva to 60 sites in Reserve area — see above) suggests that social organizational features were distinct from those of the Mimbres (where kivas become incorporated in roomblocks) during this period. These architectural differences do really seem suggestive, but it is impossible to draw specific conclusions, particularly since temporal control is modest for small Reserve Phase sites.

LeBlanc (LeBlanc and Whalen 1979) reports research conducted by Dr. Catherine LeBlanc (we have not reviewed the original paper) on styles of Mimbres naturalistic designs to determine whether certain common animal designs (such as antelope, lizard, etc.) were clan designators. It was discovered on analysis that such design variations were likely attributable to manufacture in five or six primary locations throughout the Mimbres, rather than as clan designators used as such. This may be the case. Nonetheless, it would be important to have maps of all the Classic Mimbres burials with design elements for each burial, the burials being designated by age and sex where possible.

Gilman (1979), the author of Chapter V (The Classic Mimbres) in the LeBlanc/Whalen volume, has done a nice job of summarizing possibilities for future research. The author points out that naturalistic bowl designs and geometric ones seem to be associated with infant and adult burials, respectively. Again, this is not conclusive, for the range of societies having different modes of identifying children from adult members is wide and no specific inferences can be drawn. Moreover, there is no rule that says the principle of identification will be the same for both children and adults. It could prove to be the case that children's bowls are personal name markers of some kind, while adult bowls are corporate designators with quite different symbolic and organizational overtones. If the time or season of a child's birth gave rise to names, as was common in MesoAmerica (and elsewhere), it should be possible to determine so. The frequency of births throughout the year is asymmetrical. One would have merely to plot birth frequencies by month (data from the Pueblos would do) and see if the frequencies of the major naturalistic design followed the same curve. If it did, the frequency curves could be fitted together. Since some of the creatures depicted have seasonal connotations, one might be fortunate enough to reconstruct elements of seasonal patterns in birth and naming practices that were associated. It might also be that the patterned distribution suggested an underlying moiety system or a system of related, ranked lineages.

In summary, we argue that social organization may have undergone substantial changes during this period. The incorporation of kivas into roomblocks argues against anything like classic patrilineal systems with men's houses, since these are always spatially separate. Besides, such a system does not generally produce population at high rates. It seems likely that religious and economic factors were increasingly strong integrative forces, as many have argued. Though the specifics are obscure, and may always remain so, the possibilities for additional insights, based on available data, are rich.

BURIALS

Late Mogollon sites in Arizona, such as the Grasshopper, Carter Ranch and Jewett sites, all have indications of status burials which crosscut age and sex differences (see Stafford and Rice 1979:672-687, for summaries). In the Great Kiva at Grasshopper it was determined that subadults were better endowed physically than those buried in surrounding areas (Clark 1967). Whittlesey's (1978) dimensional model of burial data for Grasshopper also tends to confirm two social classes based on ascribed status.

In the Mimbres area itself, these kinds of analyses have not been completed, or at least not published. Nonetheless, there are marked differences in grave offerings, both in quantity and kind. Such differences can be attributed in part to age and sex, but the confirmation of inherited vs. achieved status will require further investigation.

The Classic Mimbres burials tend to be subfloor and intramural, and most often have Classic Mimbres bowls inverted over the face/head. Some cremations are known (more characteristic of the later Animas and Salado phases). Extramural burials are also known, but the limited extramural excavation that has characterized so much research in this area precludes an accurate assessment of proportions (Gilman 1979).

Grave goods suggest trade over a fairly wide area. These include shell from the Pacific and/or Sea of Cortez. Shell items are thought to represent finished items only, as no waste from manufacture is found. Other grave goods include turquoise and macaw feathers (though some are thought to appear in the Three Circle Phase). Interestingly, LeBlanc (1979) suggests that there are few outside ceramic wares represented in the Mimbres at this time. Those that are more common are primarily the Reserve Phase Black-on-White wares (north and west) which are viewed as continuations of the Red Mesa Black-on-White and Kiatuthlanna, thus of the Cibola Whiteware series. We are thus presented with a picture of trade which suggests little influx of ceramics *late in the Mimbres Sequence* (A.D. 1100+?), but substantial import of non-ceramic status goods, particularly from the Hohokam area. Since Classic Mimbres ceramics have a broader distribution to the east, these classes of material culture cannot be said to account for economic patterns. One has to suspect, therefore, that a great deal of food was beginning to move about. It seems likely that clay source and temper analyses of the more ubiquitous Mimbres-Jornada-El Paso Brownware series would shed more light on trade patterns than have the classic decorated wares. There are those scholars who feel that this brownware series represents the *tin cans* of the southern Southwest. They, along with El Paso Polychrome, begin to appear in enormous quantities at Casas Grandes in the late 11th and 12th centuries. This argument merits serious consideration.

The available burial data is interesting in quite another way as well. The greatest number of burials per room is found in the large sites of the Mimbres Valley itself (Galaz, Mattocks, etc.) and the average per room is something over five burials (Gilman 1979). As one moves outward to distant sites like Saige-McFarland, burials per room are one-quarter to one-fifth as numerous. The quantities of grave goods follow precisely the same patterns. As we mentioned earlier, this appears to be a continuation of a trend beginning in the late Three Circle Phase (ca. A.D. 900-950). Again, because of excavation procedures, we do not know whether this is attributable to differential proclivity for intramural burials in the largest sites, or can be accounted for by variance in length of occupation among sites. Our working assumption is that there are real differences in short-term mortality, though this may later be disproved. The point is that these numbers of burials are rather like Kidder's (1958) *Pecos* and unlike those for Classic Chacoan sites (Tainter 1980).

SUBSISTENCE

The patterns of subsistence appear to have undergone several notable changes in Classic Mimbres sites. In the first place, there is evidence for decreased dependence on corn, for pollen counts drop sharply as the phase proceeds. Most large sites still rely on floodplain agriculture, but the use of riparian species for firewood and construction declines markedly; yellow pine, pinyon and juniper replace these.

Jackrabbit bones increase markedly (replacing cottontails) and Gilman (1979) suggests that these represent an invasion of jackrabbits into agricultural facilities. The incidence of deer remains also drops markedly, becoming quite scarce in the later Mimbres. The incidence of bird bones increases dramatically; these include teal, prairie chicken and quail — species *not* found in late pithouse phases.

To the west in the Gila Valley (at LA 5356), the incidence of faunal remains is similar, but not identical. Fish, cottontail, jackrabbit, turtle, gopher, various bird species and deer appear, in that order. There is, in short, a clear shift to smaller species and wide variety. These may indicate a scouring strategy occasioned by failing agriculture, as Anyon, Gilman and LeBlanc (1980) suggest. It also is evidence of a shift we discussed in Chapters II and III (see also Stuart, in press) to a subsistence spectrum we have characterized as the *power niche*. Unlike several other parts of the Southwest, this period of classic development is not associated with irrigation systems of increasing scale.

SUMMARY

The Classic Mimbres appears only to have been *classic* in the Mimbres Valley and adjacent areas. As one moves outward from this center, the scale of development becomes more modest. The average size of recorded sites diminishes by a factor of 3 and the sites of largest scale (120-200 rooms) are not found at all. The number of burials per room, unlike that at Classic Chacoan sites, is remarkable. The frequency of burials and the quantity of mortuary offerings declines as one moves outward from the Mimbres Valley. The decline appears to exceed the proportional diminution in site size, though this may be an artifact of methodology, it suggests different adaptive process from one area to the next. This further suggests (following Myrdal's model of economic attraction rather than the Flannery/Binford version) that outlying sites were donors of population from time to time.

Population increase at the beginning of the phase appears to have been substantial and to have leveled off quickly. The major architectural change is to above ground cobble masonry roomblocks incorporating kivas. We have proposed that the shift to above ground architecture is functionally related to pithouse wall weakness and flooding caused by reduced surface (to carry away runoff) as the spacing between structures is reduced. Some smaller sites (10 rooms and less) are thought to be only seasonally occupied, for assemblages are sometimes very modest. This suggests to us an economic heirarchy more than a seasonal dichotomy. Most primary classic sites overlie late pithouse sites, and the classic seems also to have expanded outward into agriculturally more marginal environments; some of these latter sites arose from earlier pithouse occupations.

Trade in certain exotic items (shell, macaw) seems to have been farflung, primarily to the south and west. Ceramic trade was primarily to the east (the Jornada). Late in the period, external ceramic trade is truncated. Whether these Mimbres ceramics to the east represent trade or population expansion is not known. We suspect both, because of the increase in occupation in the El Paso and Tularosa Basin areas about A.D. 900. Geographical distribution of ceramics vs. other exotics is asymmetrical.

Social organization seems to have shifted towards smaller family units, and changes in the placement of kivas suggest changes in basic integrative mechanisms, but the specifics are not known and may never be. There is evidence from burial data for increasing social (economic) stratification, but again the underlying principle is not yet apparent.

Dependence on corn agriculture appears to have declined late in the phase. Reliance on smaller and more diverse faunal species increased while large game hunting decreased markedly. Upland species dominated in fuel wood and construction, and there seems to have been movement into secondary settings.

The precise beginning of the phase and the placement/existence of the Mangus Phase is problematic, as is the interpretation of large vs. small sites. The Mimbres period is now thought to end by A.D. 1130-1150 and a sharp break to the non-Mogollon Animas tradition is proposed. Since the hiatus in construction dates between the previous Three Circle and the Mimbres Phases is much longer than the post Mimbres hiatus leading to the Animas, there is a substantial paradox from the evolutionary perspective (Note: Our treatment of the Classic Mimbres is brief, for we find Gilman's chapter of the Whalen/LeBlanc overview to have raised many issues for future investigation. We note also that on p. 343, Gilman does put the decline of the Chaco system at A.D. 1130 — neglected elsewhere in the volume).

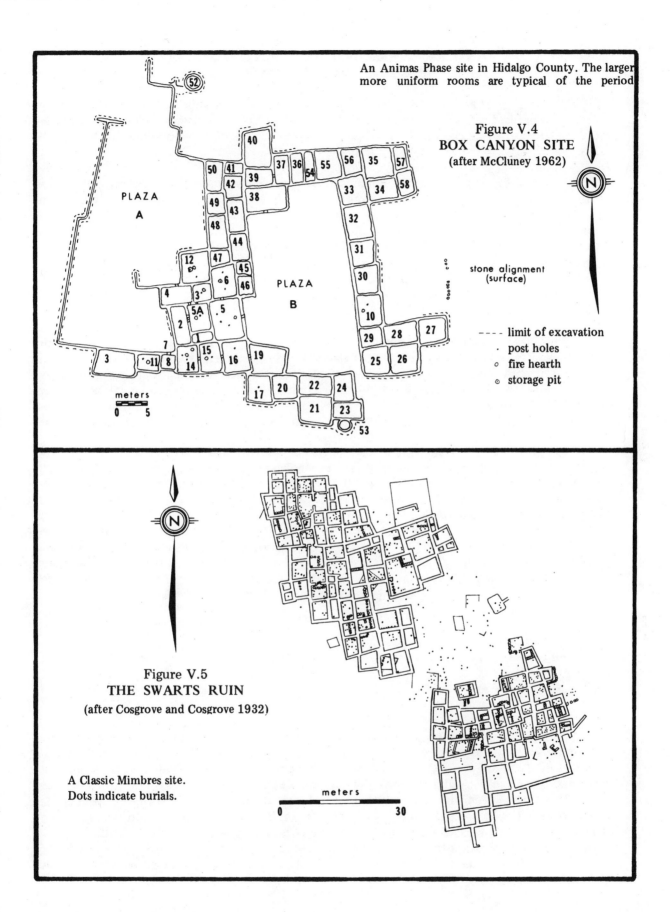

An Animas Phase site in Hidalgo County. The larger more uniform rooms are typical of the period

Figure V.4
BOX CANYON SITE
(after McCluney 1962)

PLAZA A

PLAZA B

stone alignment
(surface)

---- limit of excavation
· post holes
○ fire hearth
⊙ storage pit

meters
0   5

Figure V.5
THE SWARTS RUIN
(after Cosgrove and Cosgrove 1932)

A Classic Mimbres site.
Dots indicate burials.

meters
0   30

205

THE ANIMAS PHASE (A.D. 1150 or 1175 to 1375 or 1400?)
(Elsewhere: Black Mountain Phase and El Paso Phase)

The Animas Phase will only be treated briefly here. Animas Phase sites were first recognized from excavation at Pendleton Ruin (Kidder, Cosgrove and Cosgrove 1949). Later, other sites were identified in Hidalgo County (McCluney 1962). Here, too, the chronology is problematic and few firm dates (if any) are available.

Most scholars agree that the Animas sites represent a sharp departure from Mimbres cultural patterns. The precise nature of this departure is, however, the subject of substantial argument. This phase is considered by LeBlanc and Rugge (1979) to be basically a Casas Grandes culture having contemporaneous (or nearly so) regional variants, the Animas, the Black Mountain and the El Paso. The Animas focuses on Hidalgo County, the Black Mountain area is to the north in the Mimbres Valley, while the El Paso Phase is found to the east in a broad area to the north of El Paso (see Map V:2). Schaafsma (1979) is in essential agreement. He views these archeological phenomena as comprising one geographically heterogeneous interacting group either heavily influenced by or centered in Casas Grandes.

The either/or is the real crux of the matter. One may side with DiPeso (1974), and view these sites as population outposts of Casas Grandes, or one may emphasize the economic influence of Casas Grandes upon remnants of Mimbres populations. This latter is in the style of Tainter's (1980) arguments regarding the Acoma cultural province and its relationship to the Chacoan economic sphere. One can also hedge bets and go with the either/or — most authors have taken this course (Lambert and Ambler 1961; McCluney 1962; Schaafsma 1979).

LeBlanc (1976) has suggested that the rise of Casas Grandes forced the earlier Mimbres population to migrate, thus accounting for the Mimbres depopulation. This would have occurred during DiPeso's Buena Fe (A.D. 1060-1205) Phase, when the city of Casas Grandes was just beginning to emerge. This inference strikes us as overly simplistic. It would seem to us improbable that an emerging system like Casas Grandes could exert such pressure on the Classic Mimbres (a system at its height) *unless* other (and major) factors were already intervening. LeBlanc and Rugge (1979:379) point out that there is evidence for different physical populations in the Animas and Black Mountain (Mimbres) areas at this time. They view continuity in burial practices (killed bowls over faces) between Classic Mimbres and the Black Mountain Phase (their phase is designated from one site) sites as suggestive of some population continuity in that region:

> There is reasonable evidence (e.g. burial practices) that part of the Animas
> population were descendants of the Mimbres population, but other groups seem
> to have been included. There is also reason to believe that the mix of population
> was not the same in the Hidalgo area as it was in the Mimbres—Deming area.
> (LeBlanc and Rugge 1979:379-380)

We are non-plussed on two accounts. If Black Mountain populations were, in part, descended from actual Mimbres folk, why have LeBlanc and his collaborators (LeBlanc 1979; Anyon 1979; Anyon, Gilman and LeBlanc 1980) characterized the Animas/Black Mountain as *non-Mogollon in character* (Anyon, Gilman and LeBlanc 1980:18)? Second, what data do support the contention that there was a physical *mix* of population? Are these references to Lambert and Ambler's (1961) samples of hair from U-Bar Cave (Hidalgo County) analyzed by Duggins (1961:99-101)? If so, we point out that the hair was thought to be unlike (in one variable) that of other Southwestern groups such as Zuni, Hopi, Mesa Verde, Basketmaker — no reference was made to comparisons of samples from Classic Mimbres sites *per se*. Or, perhaps the reference is to Reed's (in McCluney, n.d.) analysis of burial remains in the Joyce

Wells Site (1963 season's material)? Substantially more data than we have been able to discover would be required to arrive at firm conclusions about the physical mix of populations during the Animas Phase.

LeBlanc and Rugge's (1979) notion that some population moved on and some stayed on has a certain appeal. Without evidence for remarkable catastrophe in the Mimbres at A.D. 1125-1150, it would be hard to imagine that everyone moved on at once. It is equally hard, as we have said, to imagine that an emerging Casas Grandes could provide so prodigious a push — a century later, perhaps, it could have happened, but at this juncture, it is unlikely. In spite of the fact that LeBlanc (1976) and LeBlanc and Rugge (1979) have not made a good case for their model, we think the idea that remnant populations were encroached upon both demographically and economically makes some sense.

The sharp break between Mimbres and Animas (may we subsume the one Black Mountain Phase site?), we suspect, is more apparent than real. The rapid disappearance of Mimbres Classic pottery, like the currently rapid disappearance of the Lincoln Continental argues for a failed economic structure but not necessarily the evaporation of an entire system. Mortality was high during the Classic Mimbres in its core area, but in outlying districts may have been lower. It is reasonable to argue that the Mimbres Valley area became the most unstable about A.D. 1130, along with the largest of outlying sites. Increased mortality and scrounging for diverse foodstuffs argue for substantial dislocation in economics and the investment of labor. Arguing that the largest Mimbres sites were Classic bowl producers argues that the production centers were vulnerable economically at this time. In short, one could say that business went bad; labor was needed to scrounge and (what with mortality and all) the good life in the large sites lost its appeal and many people drifted away. This would account for the cessation of a ceramic style.

With reduced population in the larger sites, the need to continue construction would also have been eliminated, hence the end of construction dates from dendro samples. Do not forget that post-Classic burials and a wide variety of tradewares from all directions, including the Ramos and Chihuahua polychromes, occur on a number of large Classic Mimbres sites (Gilman 1979:279; how this squares, temporally, with the characterization of truncated ceramic trade at the end of the Classic Mimbres, we are not certain), but these are scarce or absent at the smaller and outlying Mimbres sites. Since many of these tradewares come also from the north (St. John's, northwest; Chupadero, northeast) and there is little evidence of non-Mimbres construction, no one invokes the Casas Grandes colonization idea. These are merely ephemeral post-Classic occupations. Nonetheless (see last chapter and Chapter III), they are *crucial* to understanding regional events. The point is that these tradewares place Casas Grandes and non-Casas Grandes goods in the same area at the same time (A.D. 1200's). Disruption in the prior pattern of few external tradewares occurred primarily in the large sites, not the small (*precisely* like Chacoan outliers in the San Juan Basin). Other sources maintain that the Mimbres lasted until A.D. 1200-1250. It probably did in spots, but not primarily in the locale of the Classic Mimbres. Mimbres occupation would have continued in the *highlands* of the upper Mimbres drainage and such sites would be smaller (9-10 rooms).

More to the point, the Animas Phase, as currently known, is characterized by large villages, averaging 125 rooms, which are located in lower elevations and more desertic settings. These areas, however, are in generally good agricultural soil and represent substantial alluvial catchments. The style of architecture is a sharp break from the Mimbres; typically U-shaped pueblos of puddled adobe (rather than cobble masonry), enclosing plazas and lacking kivas. Rooms averaged 16-17 m² — like the earlier San Francisco Phase, but in sharp contrast to the previous Mimbres (and Three Circle). In short, population was aggregated, substantial areas were uninhabited and there were abrupt changes in architecture. We don't know how abrupt, actually, for larger Mimbres sherd scatters in similar environments seem not to have been tested archeologically to determine (by coring, perhaps) whether there were also Mimbres villages of puddled adobe. We suspect there were.

The Animas Phase (from ceramic dates) probably peaks about A.D. 1250-1275 and is said to continue in one region or another until after the collapse of Casas Grandes. In subsistence, we again note the use of riparian trees for construction and firewood (unlike Classic Mimbres) as in the later pithouse phases. The reliance on bird species disappears, and the use of deer again assumes the subsistence role it played during the early Three Circle Phase. The range of faunal remains narrows considerably, and corn and corn remains are again very prominent in botanical material. In the Box Canyon and Clanton Draw sites (Cutler and Eickmeier 1962: 48-52), there is a substantial increase in the percent of 12-rowed corn (Pima-Papago and Oñaveno — soft and hard, respectively) of medium to small cobs. That is, the predominance of Hariñoso de Ocho (medium to large cobbed and soft) which is notable from A.D. 700-1100 was reversed (peak percentage—A.D. 700-900).

Organizationally, the loss of the kivas suggests that yet other modes of social/economic integration emerged. Village size, though large, did not exceed the size (nor match the largest) of Mimbres sites, and the economic network was drawn together over vast space in relatively open environments. This is conceptually quite like the Chaco model we discussed in Chapter III. Casas Grandes and its related economic sphere seems to have picked up where Chaco left off. There seems little doubt that the fall of Casas Grandes (A.D. 1340) was related to the Great Drought of 1276-1299. Curiously, as in the aftermath of the Chaco system, when the Classic Mimbres sites begin to lose their magnet effect, we again see some evidence of decapitated bodies, burned structures, etc., both in the Mimbres and Animas Valleys.

Unlike the Mimbres Classic sites, there are relatively few burials in the Animas sites. The pattern is rather more like that of the smaller outlying Mimbres sites (.5-1.5 burials per room) or the earlier San Francisco Phase sites. In short, the Animas is, in some respects, rather like one part of the Chaco system; in other respects it is similar to the partly contemporaneous Tularosa Phase in east central Arizona. There also, one sees an increase in the size of settlements, with certain areas (Pine Lawn Valley, New Mexico) depopulated during the Reserve-Tularosa transition and a shift to lower elevations (Rice 1975), particularly areas of level plateau. Is it possible that the Hidalgo County Animas sites are of the late A.D. 1200's to early 1300's, while the Black Mountain Site is a century earlier?

Sites of this phase merit far more attention in southwestern New Mexico than they have been given. Hidalgo County is not well-represented in the Museum of New Mexico site files or in publications. Though Dr. Frank Findlow of Columbia University has conducted substantial survey in the area, his data are just now becoming available to us here in New Mexico and we have not had time to review them for this volume. Much more remains to be done.

THE SALADO PHASE (Est. 1300?-1450?)
(The Cliff Phase)

The Salado is a phase wrapped in controversy. Chronologically, it is quite problematic. It is, of course, best known in the Gila and Salt drainages of Arizona. Some scholars include both Tularosa Black-on-white and later Gila Polychrome (also Tonto and Pinto) and the associated sites in this phase (McGregor 1974). Others consider it to include only the polychrome period. The phase is known from Casa Grande and Los Muertos in Arizona. It is found in both upland and desert settings, but is *classic* in the areas surrounding major riverine systems.

Characteristically, Salado sites are said generally to take the form of compounds enclosing pueblo-type rooms. Construction is massive, in lower elevation settings consisting of poured adobe and in upland settings of cobble and adobe construction. In the Cliff area of New Mexico, 18 sites are recorded, while 3 are described in the Mimbres Valley. Room size averages 21 m², and there is very little variation in room size. Burial practices are variable, some being cremations (with killed pots) and others being inhumations with whole vessels. This has led to no end of speculation about different populations living side-by-side. Martin and Plog (1973:312-317) offer as reasonable a general overview as can be found.

LeBlanc (1979) views the Salado in New Mexico as a continuation of the Animas (suggesting Casas Grandes population?), others (see McGregor 1974) view the Salado as occasioned by migrations from the Flagstaff area of Arizona, first to the Gila-Salt drainages of Arizona and later to southwestern New Mexico. Writings on the Salado are characterized by conflicting speculations, and in view of scarce data we find these quite unproductive. For the moment, we side with Martin and Plog merely because their interpretations of *in situ* development and local growth of status heirarchies are simple and straightforward. The real point, however, is that much more survey work must be done in extreme southwestern New Mexico before final pronouncements are made.

Recall that there is thought to be a Salado component also at the Pendelton Ruin (Kidder, Cosgrove and Cosgrove 1949), and that a moderate quantity of the Gila Polychrome ceramics was found at the Box Canyon Site (both sites are in Hidalgo County) during Mc-Cluney's (1962) excavation. The temporal relationship between the Animas and Salado phases is a very open question, and we should not be surprised to discover substantial overlap. The termination of the phase is equally problematic. This is compounded by variable data (some unpublished, some hearsay, some apparently not worked up) from excavations.

More to the point, the period seems to be characterized in New Mexico by 30-100 room sites (LeBlanc 1979:388). LeBlanc elsewhere (p. 394) suggests a range of 12-250 rooms, but some of these data are based on hearsay. There is argued to be a strong dependence on corn agriculture. All of the sites described are near substantial watercourses, though no irrigation systems are described for New Mexico. The reliance on deer as a faunal resource was pronounced and perhaps as elsewhere, the production of cotton blankets was characteristic (note that cotton is a commercial crop today in the Animas Valley). Based on subsistence data, it seems safe to assert that the Salado follows the Great Drought (1276-99).

LeBlanc (1979:393) views the abandonment of most of the Cliff area sites as quite rapid, citing rich *in situ* assemblages which include semi-cooked food. Not all sites show this pattern, but it seems common. Curiously, the Villareal Site (Lekson 1978), a very small 5 room pueblo overlying two earlier pithouses, contains a most problematic ceramic assemblage: Boldface Black-on-white (Mangus), Classic Mimbres, Tularosa Black-on-white, Chupadero Black-on-white, Playas Red, El Paso Polychrome and Gila Polychrome. These "are all present in relatively similar frequencies in all units INCLUDING THE PITHOUSES [emphasis ours]. Contrary to Lekson's assessment, this cannot represent a contemporary assemblage" (LeBlanc 1979:398).

This site genuinely upsets LeBlanc, for a 400 year (or longer) span of ceramics is represented in a context which raises questions about the neat stages of cultural development that are supposed to be reflected in successive ceramic styles. LeBlanc (1979:348) explains it thus: "The best interpretation of this site is that it was first a late pithouse village. It was next used intermittently during the Classic and Animas periods. Finally, it was used as a Salado field house".

Several questions merit consideration. How are two pithouses considered a village, and later, five rooms considered a fieldhouse? Where is the Classic Mimbres architecture that is missing between the pithouses and the Salado? Now, it may be as LeBlanc (1979:398) says, "that the preponderance of the pottery found represents accidentally associated sherds and a high degree of mixing". On the other hand it may be, as we have suggested throughout this chapter, that small sites in this region do not follow the same pattern as the large. What does a five room Salado site look like anyway? Maybe Salado architectural techniques predate the Salado ceramic phase in southwestern New Mexico. Maybe Classic Mimbres architecture and modest *Salado* architecture are contemporaneous — the occurrence of each being dependent on size of site, local materials, and general aridity of setting. Alternatively, maybe some small pithouse sites never underwent the transition to Classic Mimbres architecture (in microcosm) at all and were continuously occupied until a later Salado period. Pithouses, after all, were occupied *very* late to the east in the area we are about to discuss, so late, in fact, that the last occupants of the last pithouses between the Gila and the Pecos may have looked out that little entry ramp one day, into Apachean faces. We want to know the answers to these speculations. Until substantial survey in southwestern New Mexico has been conducted to record many hundreds more smaller sites, and has targeted perhaps a hundred of these for eventual excavation, we shall have none.

The Villareal Site is, to our mind, the most interesting one discussed in the entire LeBlanc/Whalen overview of 30,000 square miles. It is interesting because it does not fit the pattern it is supposed to fit. It is, of course, dismissed as a mistake -- an impossibility. What if a second or third is found? Will they all be flukes? Now, some of the more established researchers will question our theme in this section; many have already set their ideas. Nonetheless, we assert that there has been far too much attention lavished on the large Mimbres sites and the excavation of the most attractive ceramics. The appropriate question is not, *who is right?* but *who will shift their focus to the small and mundane and eventually provide more refined answers?*

THE JORNADA AREA

The eastern portion of this study area is herein termed the Jornada unit. While the Jornada branch of the Mogollon (Lehmer 1948) is focused in this area, it is certainly not bounded by it. The Eastern Branch of the Jornada is east of the Pecos River and extends eastward into Texas. Jornada sites, characterized by the ubiquitous brownwares, extend south into the Big Bend country of Texas, west of the Rio Grande River and far south into Chihuahua.

The formal administrative boundaries of this study area are outlined on the map (V:1) at the beginning of this chapter. Physiographically, the lower areas include the Lower Rio Grande Valley, the Tularosa Basin and the Jornada del Muerto. Upland areas include the San Andres-Chupadero Mesa chain, the Capitan Mountains and the Sierra Blanca-Lower Sacramento chain. Unlike the western portions of southwestern New Mexico, these upland areas are much less extensive, opening either into extensive internal basins or into the plains to the east. The major watercourses are the Rio Grande to the west and the Rios Bonito, Tularosa and Sacramento in the Sierra Blanca-Sacramento system. This latter highland system is well-watered and densely forested, but the lowlands of the Tularosa Basin and Jornada del Muerto are hot and dry. Just where the western boundary of the Jornada belongs is a subject of differing opinion — the lower elevations west of the Rio Grande will do, as a generality.

Unlike the Mimbres area, the focus of archeological research has not been so narrowly on the sites (or rooms) where one or another remarkable ceramic types is found. There is, therefore, a much better balance to recent research interests in the area, though excavation data are very limited when compared to those for survey. Archeological research in the area has a long history, but most attention has been focused on the Jornada Mogollon since the late 1930's and 1940's (Mera 1938; Lehmer 1948).

Excavation in the Jornada has been much more modest than in the Mimbres, the San Juan Basin or the upper Rio Grande. Thus, the preponderance of archeological information has been gathered from survey. Temporal control is very problematic. The vast majority of square mileage covered in archaeological survey lies south of U.S. 82-70 (which runs from Las Cruces to Alamogordo, then east through the Lincoln National Forest). The major lowland surveys in the south have been conducted on the Dona Ana and McGregor Missile Ranges (Beckes 1977) and in Fort Bliss (Whalen 1977, 1978).

To the north, in the Three Rivers portion of the Tularosa Basin, several smaller, but well-reported surveys have been conducted by Human Systems Research (1973; Wimberly and Rogers 1977). The plains north of the Capitan Mountains (extreme northeastern corner of the study area), most of the Tularosa Basin north of U.S. 82-70, and the Jornada del Muerto are nearly unstudied.

In the mountain areas (and the Hondo Valley to the east), the Sierra Blanca and Capitans have been partially surveyed and reported by Kelley (1966). The San Andres Mountains, the Oscuras and the Sacramentos are essentially unsurveyed. A great deal of the unsurveyed acreage lies on the White Sands Missile Range and in the so-called *cooperative use area* and the Lincoln National Forest. In the past year, the Bureau of Indian Affairs has conducted extensive survey on the Mescalero Reservation. Their report is currently in preparation, and together with Dr. Kelley's thesis and several surveys and excavations by Wiseman, Peckham and Farwell (various reports, see Wiseman 1979) of the Museum of New Mexico, we can consider the area of Sierra Blanca fairly well reported by comparison. All other areas north of U.S. 72-80 (excluding the Three Rivers drainage) and the Sacramentos (the Lincoln Forest) are high on any critical list of archeological priorities. This area and the adjacent easternmost portion of the Socorro Planning Unit (V-NM, see preceding chapter) may represent the largest contiguous block of nearly unsurveyed, unexcavated and unpublished acreage in the American Southwest. The center of this area can be spotted on any road map — follow New Mexico Highway 380 east from San Antonio to Carrizozo, then NM 54 south to Alamogordo, then U.S. 82-70 west to Las Cruces; turn north on Interstate 25 and return to San Antonio.

RESEARCH PROBLEMS AND CHRONOLOGY

Fortunately, this section of the overview can be brief, for the object of this volume has been to summarize survey priorities and identify investigative themes that broadly encompass those research interests, which, by consensus, are especially important to the archeologists working in a given region. In this case, the task is easy, for Beckett and Wiseman (1979) have provided us an edited volume containing papers from the First Jornada-Mogollon Conference. It is essential reading and contains a number of really excellent papers. Since we have no improvements to suggest, their summary is reproduced here verbatim:

> *The full sequence of prehistoric occupation from the Llano Complex (ca. 13,500 B.P.) to abandonment about A.D. 1400 is known to exist in part, if not all, of the Jornada Branch (Marshall in Human Systems Research 1973). In spite of this, very little is known about Paleo-Indian and Archaic sites, and most of what is known is in the form of limited survey data and a few excavations (Smith, Smith and Runyan 1966; Human Systems Research 1973:Section V). In fact, at least two basic Archaic affiliations underlie the Jornada Mogollon sequence, but there is apparent disagreement as to the boundaries of both (Beckett this volume and Leslie this volume). The prehistoric ceramic periods are better known in that, overall, several sites and house structures have been partially or totally excavated. However, aside from the El Paso Phase pueblos in the southern Tularosa Basin, when compared to the size of the region, few sites have been dug of any time*

period. *Practically every new excavation project produces new variability for the architectural record, and certain kinds of structures or rooms (such as for socio-ceremonial purposes) are only suspected or are poorly known. The study of different ceramic-period site types and functions is in a rudimentary stage at best, and much-needed excavations outside of structures are relatively new (Brook this volume and Whalen this volume).*

The question of abandonment (about A.D. 1400), usually on a subregional basis, has been addressed to some extent (Jelinek 1967; J.H. Kelley 1966; Leslie this volume; Mera in Scholes and Mera 1940). Wimberly and Rogers (1977) have even suggested that some peoples remained behind. It seems reasonable to assume that the immigrants from the Jornada Branch sites went in a number of directions and that their descendants combined with several different historically known groups. The reasons for the abandonment are mostly obscure, and the directions the people took (beyond what is primarily speculation at this time) remain to be demonstrated.

Historic groups known to have inhabited the Jornada Branch include the Lipan and Mescalero Apaches, the Mansos, and the Sumas, to name a few. There is a break or hiatus in the archaeological and historical record in the occupation of the area between approximately A.D. 1450 and October, 1590 when the Castaño de Sosa expedition encountered a group of Indians probably just north of the present New Mexico/Texas border (cf. Hill 1916:314). These Indians, whose dogs carried goods loaded on their backs, might have been the forerunners of the Apache Indians who for the next few centuries were to play havoc with the settled eastern Pueblos, Spanish and later Anglo-American penetrations into the area. While several sites are known to exist, many remain to be discovered, others undoubtedly need to be correctly identified (was Honea's [1965] Caballo Site really a preceramic site?), and many must be investigated. Hispanic and Anglo history have fared only a little better in that a few studies have included some sites; we are awaiting final reports on the Brantley Reservoir Project by Southern Methodist University and the Human Systems Research project at Dog Canyon.

Paramount to the success of any fine-grained analysis of archaeological data is the construction of an accurate chronology. Thus far, such a chronology does not exist for the Jornada Branch, and most dates which have been derived from individual projects are based on ceramic data. Limited use has been made of tree-rings, archaeomagnetic sampling, and radiocarbon determinations, but much remains to be done before a reliable chronology adequate for intra-regional and regional comparisons will be a reality.

The Jornada Mogollon has traditionally been viewed as a cultural backwater to the rest of the American Southwest. Although Schaafsma (this volume) has given some reason to doubt that this was true for the latest known prehistoric phase (El Paso Phase), the Jornada provides an excellent 'laboratory' for the study of cultural conservatism. Not only does the branch appear to be marginal to the rest of the Southwest, but several areas within the branch (such as the Guadalupe Mountains, Kelley's [1966] Glencoe Phase, and the Eastern Extension) were apparently marginal to the more 'progressive' portions (such as the El Paso and Lincoln [Kelley 1966] Phases). Tainter (this volume) has suggested one direction of inquiry into this phenomenon, but others must be formulated and all should be investigated in depth before the problem can be resolved.

212

Several aspects of the cultural system(s) of the Jornada are now or should soon become the objects of inquiry. Since many of them are highly complex and the data for their solution are disparate and time-consuming to gather, it is anticipated that these studies will require lengthy investigation. For instance, given the high physiographic, floral, faunal, and climatic diversity of the Jornada, it is logical that human adaptation at different times and under different technological conditions varied. Some evidence as to subsistence patterns has been collected, but not nearly enough is now in hand to allow much more than the recitation of some of the foods consumed. To what extent did the various species contribute to the diet? Did some species form economic mainstays or provide 'prime mover' impetus to the use of certain areas (such as various authors have suggested for acorns and prehistoric settlement in the Eastern Extension)? Why is it that at least one site near Roswell has an abundance of bison bone while others nearby and of the same approximate age have little. How does this all fit in relative to the newly investigated Garnsey Bison Kill (Speth this volume)? Or what about the Guadalupe Mountains? Did they have a year round population or are the cultural remains those of seasonal agricultural and/or other peoples who lived in the surrounding 'flatlands' as Applegarth (1976) has suggested to an extent and others have postulated more generally. Were the large El Paso Phase villages of the southern Tularosa Basin, with their dozens of rooms and very scant trash, really year round habitations as one might deduce from their imposing size? Did true ditch irrigation exist in connection with El Paso Phase existence as implied by numerous writers or did some less intensive technology prevail? What is the meaning of what may have been the dominant variety of corn in the Sierra Blanca-Capitan highlands; this corn has been characterized as fairly homogeneous and relatively 'primitive' compared to that which was available at contemporary villages in the Rio Grande, for instance (report by R.T. Ford on corn from the Bent Project [Otero County] — on file with Wiseman). It seems, on the strength of present evidence, that beans were also grown in the Sierra Blanca-Capitan highlands but that not all villages had them. Did some wild resources take the place of beans and fill the complementary role (nutrition-wise) with corn or did the Indians lack the innate sense of nutritional balance so frequently attributed to them and as now doubted by Callen (1973)? The overall impression being gained by a number of researchers is that there was a greater mobility in even the sedentary groups of the Jornada than is normally attributed to village-dwelling groups. Perhaps this is one reason why the major ceramics of the region are so similar and widespread. (It should be noted that the above ideas were in part or in whole arrived at independently by at least three people with whom Beckett and Wiseman have talked to over the past two years. They are S. Applegarth, J.H. Kelley, and M. Wimberly).

The prospect of widespread human movement brings up the aspect of trade. One fact that has been evident from nearly the beginning of organized inquiry into Jornada prehistory is the occurrence of a large number of trade ceramics representing Casas Grandes, the Salado, the Mimbres, the Western Pueblo, and the Middle Rio Grande. Others have suggested that commodities contained in the pottery may have resulted in the importation of these wares. But how often does one use a bowl as a container for transport? This is not to say that some commodities were not 'packaged' in ceramic vessels, but one should keep in mind that functional and/or aesthetic considerations probably prevailed in many if not most instances. As examples, 'everyone knows' that (today) the best water vessels are obtained from Acoma (ceramic fabric very much like Chupadero Black-on-white), Picuris makes the best bean pots, and Santo Domingo produces excellent dough bowls. And what about all the porcelain shipped to the New World from China, and the widespread trade of Spanish majolica in New Spain? Then there are the shell ornaments from both Gulf of Mexico and Pacific Coast species. What were the commodities used in the exchanges? J.H. Kelley (1966) has suggested that the Lincoln Phase site of Bloom Mound near Roswell was a Southwest-Plains trade center similar to the later, more powerful Pecos Pueblo. The presence of turquoise sources (Orogrande and in the vicinity of Nogal Peak southwest of Capitan, New Mexico) and archaeological finds of copper bells, Alibates chert implements (including diamond-shaped, alternately bevelled knives), and differential distributions of shell ornaments are indicators of inter-regional trade. Intra-regional trade has been indicated in an initial study by J.H. Kelley (this volume), and Whalen (this volume) suggests approaches to the basic nature of trade relationships. The beginnings have been made, but more thorough treatments of the subject must await the future. To this end, Bronitsky (1977) offers several trantalizing ideas with regard to trade as an ecologically instigated socio-economic phenomenon.

Another aspect having important bearing on the reconstruction of the culture history and the elucidation of cultural process of the Jornada Mogollon is that of demography. Mobility in connection with subsistence requirements is suggested above, and abandonment of the region appears to have taken several directions. Hints of the first intra-regional abandonments, undoubtedly preludes to the more general abandonments about A.D. 1400, have been noted by J.H. Kelley (1966) for the upper Rio Penasco and by Leslie (this volume) for southeastern New Mexico. These two areas might serve as the initial focal points for more intensive studies, particularly since, if the inference is correct, they may have constituted some of the more marginal areas inhabited by the Jornadans. The growing evidence for multiple violent deaths (at the Salt Cedar Site [Collins 1968], Bloom Mound [J.H. Kelley 1966:Appendix 8], and the Block Lookout or Smokey Bear Site [Wiseman 1976]) is probably highly significant even though it is not known at this time whether internecine warfare, marauding nomads, or some other problem(s) were the cause.

The most recent studies applied to the Jornada Mogollon are those of rock art and archaeoastronomy. The former has already produced some very provacative ideas (Schaafsma and Schaafsma 1974) which need to be assessed against both new rock art data and any other types of archaeological and ethnographical data which can be brought to bear. As recently discussed with V.R. Brook (personal communication with Wiseman), are terraces on the rims of some El Paso Polychrome bowls (cf. Moore 1947) part of the Katchina Cult Complex which Schaafsma and Schaafsma postulate passed through the Jornada Mogollon on the way to the Rio Grande Pueblos? Are distributions of rock art styles as potentially effective in determining socio-cultural boundaries as Mobley (this volume) suggests? And what does the content of rock art tell us about the artists and their societies (cf. Brody 1977)?

Archaeoastronomy has been a 'rage' lately, but even some of the hardest skeptics have to listen to the studies produced by Wimberly and Eidenbach (1977b), Eidenbach (this volume), and Brook (this volume). These works represent the first concentrated inquiries in the Jornada area into what students of Pueblo ethnography have known for decades to be a major facet in subsistence and ceremonialism. Such studies, carefully executed, should be encouraged.

Lehmer's 1948 work was a synthesis of the data then available on the Jornada Branch. Since that time, much new information has been gained, and

214

it has become apparent that many of Lehmer's ideas and constructs have been or are in need of replacement. The area encompassed by the Jornada Branch has been greatly enlarged, and the cultural complexity is obviously greater than be envisaged [sic]. With every substantive (and even some not so substantive) project comes vital, sometimes startling data. It is this aspect, perhaps more than any other, which has engendered such a strong interest in the region. Even with this renewed interest, archaeological studies in the Jornada Mogollon lag far behind those of many areas in the Southwest. The field is wide open. It is hoped that this conference will have served as a catalyst in which shared knowledge and ideas will continue to emerge from the new and renewed friendships that were formed from this common bond 'the Jornada Mogollon' research area.

And finally, the response of the conference participants as revealed by their attendance, remarks, subsequent actions and desire for a second conference has been most gratifying — perhaps the most gratifying part of the entire effort.
(Wiseman and Beckett 1979:397-401)

We have only several comments to add. First, the authors refer to questions regarding the nature of lithic traditions in the Jornada. This reference focuses on Beckett's (1979:224) investigations, which suggest that the San Pedro Cochise (Archaic) lithic tradition terminates on the west side of the San Andres Mountains, while the east side has lithic affinities in an unnamed Archaic tradition from west Texas . The implication, of course, is that the San Andres range divided two different population systems during the later preceramic periods.

The idea of how Jornada population systems behaved is one of the fundamental themes underlying Jornada archeology. In the same volume, Tainter (1979) has presented a paper on Jornada demography and cultural evolution. He concludes:

. . . . given population growth, any adaptation a population may make becomes obsolete and cultural change becomes necessary. With higher rates of population growth, adaptations become obsolete more frequently and rate of cultural change will thus increase. The topographic diversity of the western Jornada area would have conditioned such population growth, while in the topographically homogeneous plains growth would have been much less rapid. With the influence of population growth on cultural change, the prehistory of the western Jornada would have been characterized by a succession of adaptations which were comparatively short-lived, while in the prehistory of the eastern Jornada extension the stability of cultural adaptations should be noticeably higher (Tainter 1979:382).

Tainter's argument is good, but we differ on two counts. In Chapter III (San Juan Basin-Paleo-Indian Adaptation), we argued that, over time, the density restrictions on preceramic populations in intermontane areas would create population conservatism, whereas the expansive plains environment would not. Thus, until San Pedro Cochise times at least, we would argue for more cultural conservatism in the western Jornada than to the east. Later, with the shift to agriculture (at least part-time) in the western areas, one can argue a *fast-breeder* population relative to eastern plainsmen (Tainter would agree). Episodes of population growth in the western Jornada would have generated instances of dispersal east to the plains, particularly in the A.D. 900-1150 period and right after A.D. 1250. Because of the drought conditions of A.D. 1276-1299, any population movement at that time would have been short-lived indeed if based at all on agriculture. Pueblo-like adaptations on the periphery of the plains should have been the shortest-lived of these Jornada adaptations if adjacent plainsmen could continue to disperse under stress. That is, those trapped in an unstable agricultural strategy could make extensive use of the landscape; i.e., episodally *escape the trap*. In that case, their rate of cultural change would be lower, and certainly the archeological evidence of it, would

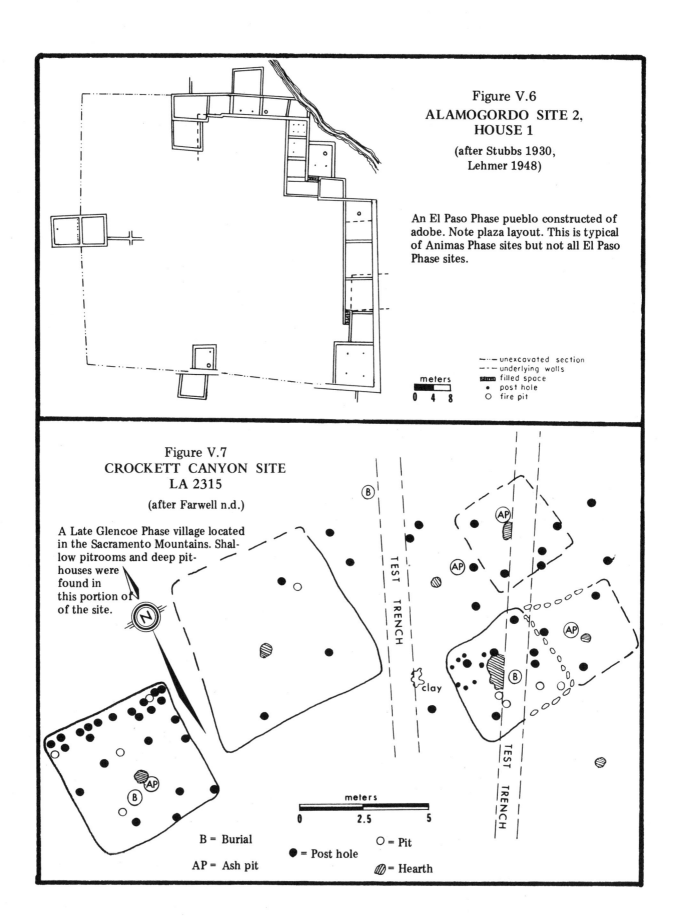

Figure V.6
**ALAMOGORDO SITE 2,
HOUSE 1**

(after Stubbs 1930,
Lehmer 1948)

An El Paso Phase pueblo constructed of
adobe. Note plaza layout. This is typical
of Animas Phase sites but not all El Paso
Phase sites.

-·--·- unexcavated section
-·-·- underlying walls
▨▨▨ filled space
• post hole
○ fire pit

meters
0   4   8

Figure V.7
**CROCKETT CANYON SITE
LA 2315**

(after Farwell n.d.)

A Late Glencoe Phase village located
in the Sacramento Mountains. Shallow pitrooms and deep pithouses were
found in
this portion
of the site.

TEST TRENCH

clay

TEST TRENCH

meters
0   2.5   5

B = Burial

AP = Ash pit

● = Post hole

○ = Pit

▨ = Hearth

216

be less visible. In Chapter II we noted that it is an establishing agricultural population which suffers most in episodes of drought, relative to hunters and gatherers. That is, the late A.D. 1200's should have eliminated Jornadan's occasional ability to maintain a toehold on the plains (end of the Maljamar Phase?). See the following chapter for data which lend tentative support to this possibility.

Actually, we do not yet know the answers. Dr. Tainter could be correct. Until better dates and climatic data are obtained for the Jornada it is sporting to consider all reasonable arguments, for diverse views stimulate the detective process as does nothing else.

As a second point, we should like to address Beckett and Wiseman's comment about primitive corn in the Capitan-Sierra Blanca area (Wiseman 1979:61; Kelley 1966). This, of course, pleases us no end. Some readers will have noted that in the Mimbres section it was suggested that one particular agricultural strategy focused on small cobbed, fast-maturing corn — a strategy designed around bimodal rainfall distribution, with the winter season dominant. We characterized this as a higher elevation strategy which depended heavily on hunting-gathering as an alternative in periods of fluctuating rainfall. Since it was proposed that this strategy depends heavily on winter soil moisture recharge, it may be *less* dependent on stream-bed placement in periods of very high rainfall (with winter dominant). Its optimum period as an adaptation (based on tree-ring width — see conclusion of chapter) should have come at about A.D. 825-850 and again about A.D. 1200-1250. At less than optimum conditions, snow melt will preserve the spring germination for a time as rainfall declines and summer rainfall becomes predominant.

Under a summer dominant rainfall regime, larger and more productive varieties of corn can be grown, but they require a longer growing period and optimum soil moisture retention — at lower elevation.

In this part of the Jornada the Early Glencoe Phase (A.D. 900-1100?) sites were located on streams, and this was a period of declining and dramatically varying rainfall becoming more summer dominant. The Late Glencoe and Corona phases (ca. A.D. 1100-1200) had site place-ment on larger streams as well — had they become more water dependent?

If these speculations are correct, then these higher elevation archeological manifesta-tions would have partially lost population downward as summer dominant, less abundant rainfall conditions peaked at about A.D. 1100. In short, the decline in rainfall which started about A.D. 870 (Martin and Plog 1973:51; Cordell 1979:7) should have led precisely to the temporal pattern of site placement Wimberly and Rogers (1977) suggest for the Tularosa Basin — a slight downhill shift in site placement starting about A.D. 900. About A.D. 1000, as the trend continued, populations would have shifted noticeably downhill to lower its expo-sure to the higher standard deviation in rainfall which occurs in the highest elevations. They would also have maximized crop size through optimizing the growing season for existing corn varieties, and by growing an increasing mixture of larger, slower maturing varieties. Spring soil moisture would have been maximized by locating increasingly near streams or alluvial fans below slopes with an exposure that created a relatively late snow melt above (an east slope?). Such soils should be among those with the highest moisture retention properties. By A.D. 1100, with the summer dominant pattern established, the move to basin floors in areas of major streams would have been predominant.

As rainfall again increased slightly after A.D. 1125 and became temporarily more bimodal in distribution, the trend would have been to shift agriculture upwards again. Thus, when absolute dates are someday obtained, the lowest sites in the major basins surrounding the Sierra Blanca district should cluster in dates from A.D. 1075-1125, the quality of soil being most important, since nearness to water will have been maximized. The majority of sites in the higher alluvial fans should show a bimodal distribution of dates, clustering around A.D. 950-1000 and A.D. 1150-1175. The majority of highest sites will have dates clustering more closely to the *winter-dominant* rainfall optimums we propose — that is, near A.D. 850-900 on the one hand and A.D. 1200-1250 on the other.

The remains of corn should be slightly different in these classes of sites — the lowest elevations (A.D. 1100 cluster) having a greater tendency toward larger varieties (even if slightly larger, but still likely flinty). Corn varieties should, on the average, be most "primitive" or "chapalote-like" in the higher elevation sites and most homogeneous. Where they are not, the dates for such a site should tend to be more off center from the clusters that we have proposed. After A.D. 1125 some population again moved upwards — this is the earliest *Lincoln Phase*, which we speculate peaked at about A.D. 1250 in the higher elevations and involved some actual population movement upward. It seems to us that the first dates on the Lincoln Phase should occur in the lower valleys (Penasco-Hondo) and in the highest elevations last (Ruidoso) (see Kelley 1966). Dates in these different Lincoln Phase sites should also be staggered with elevation — perhaps by 20-40 years from the lowest to the highest valleys. The adaptation would have again shifted downward as the *Great Drought* conditions approached after A.D. 1250. That is, Lincoln Phase sites in the lower elevations should show an early and late building component, say A.D. 1175 and 1300, while in higher elevations single or continuous occupation is, we speculate, more likely.

Thus, we think Lincoln Phase sites will cluster uphill-downhill as follows: the earliest and generally lowest A.D. 1150-1170; higher A.D. 1190-1210; highest A.D. 1230-1250; lower again at A.D. 1270-1290. Thus, dates at some sites (particularly in similar settings) should have a bimodal clustering about 80-100 years apart.

During these shifting conditions we think active trade between the various altitude zones would have been heavily stimulated by the need to integrate upland and lowland adaptations economically. Such integration would have mixed the different agricultural outcomes which occurred in the highlands and lowlands under fluctuating conditions. Particularly during the A.D. 950-1050 period and again between A.D. 1150-1200, fluctuating winter-summer patterns would have alternately favored sites in different agricultural settings. The relative scarcity of kivas or ceremonial rooms and richness of local ceramics (and their changing patterns of trade) suggest a strong local economic network at these times.

This is, of course, speculative. But, we think it worth pursuing and in line with existing evidence. We have not said that population *ceased* in the different altitude zones, only that the focus shifted. Thus, there should be sites in each zone with more continuous occupation — we are talking about proportions of sites occupied in a certain zone. Finally, the general population increase supposed for the area between A.D. 1150-1300 may be testimony to the effectiveness of a summer rainfall agricultural strategy combined with an economic network to integrate the upland winter strategy. In short, any uphill movement after A.D. 1150 was probably into a zone already containing increased population. Though Kelley (1966) notes only one allegedly defensive site, we suspect the move involved some conflict here and there.

Abandonment? We've done enough speculating here. Let's leave that for the conclusion of the volume, when the strength of statewide patterns can be applied. It is fair to emphasize that the backwardness of the Late Glencoe and Corona (and at least in corn, the Lincoln) phases is in timing and, in its upland pithouse setting, quite like the Largo-Gallina and Apache Creek phases of the same time period. The Gallina is alike in another respect as well — there are also Puebloan roomblocks on or near a number of late Gallina sites — roomblocks which are thought to postdate slightly, or barely overlap in time with, the Gallina components (A.D. 1250-1300, or thereabouts). The Analogy to the P-III of the Upper Rio Grande (Chapter III) is also apt.

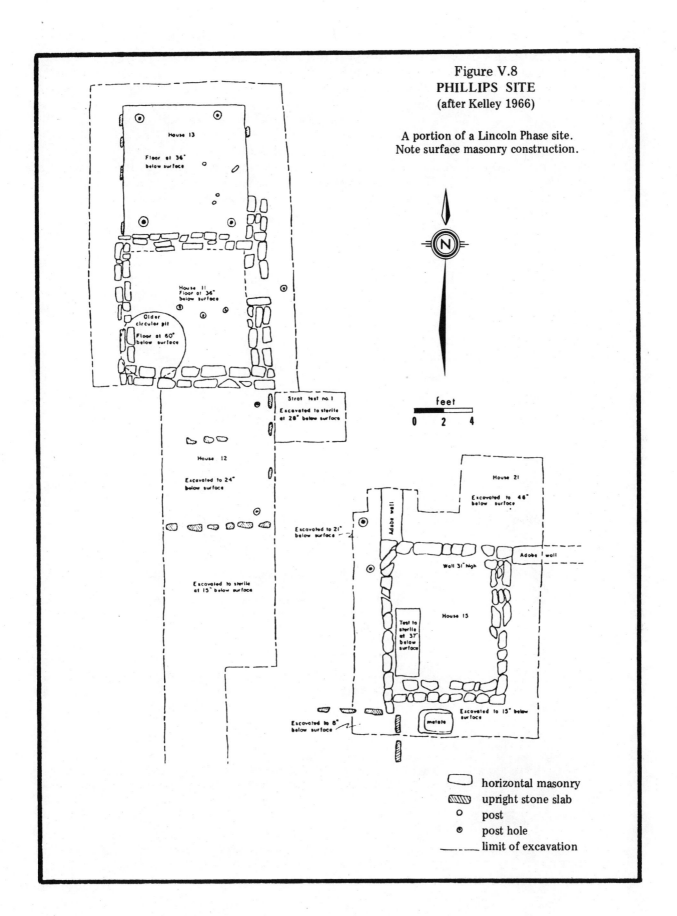

Figure V.8
PHILLIPS SITE
(after Kelley 1966)

A portion of a Lincoln Phase site.
Note surface masonry construction.

N

House 13

Floor at 36"
below surface

House 11
Floor at 36"
below surface

Older
circular pit
Floor at 60"
below surface

Strat test no. 1
Excavated to sterile
at 28" below surface

House 12

Excavated to 24"
below surface

Excavated to sterile
at 15" below surface

Excavated to 21"
below surface

House 21

Excavated to 46"
below surface

Adobe wall

Adobe wall

Wall 31" high

House 15

Test to
sterile
at 37"
below
surface

metate

Excavated to 15" below
surface

Excavated to 8"
below surface

feet
0   2   4

horizontal masonry
upright stone slab
post
post hole
limit of excavation

219

Following this discussion we have presented some outlined notes taken by Mr. Gauthier from Dr. Kelley's (1966) doctoral thesis. These are included as a short reference for the general reader. Whalen's full discussion of the Jornada should be read in the LeBlanc/Whalen (1979) overview. We have not outlined his work here since, unlike the Mimbres portion, we felt his presentation was not at such odds with the majority of the existing Jornada literature. Since he did not discuss the upland adaptations at length, we included them here.

We mention, though, that Dr. Whalen discusses a very early (A.D. 250) and extensive pithouse occupation in the Hueco Bolson. If accepted and confirmed in other areas of the Jornada, it will have substantial impact on ideas about when and where the shift to sedentism took place in New Mexico. Regarding the western Jornada's relationship to the Mogollon population of the Mimbres district, we argue a dominant economic network between the two until the disruptive shifts in the seasonality and predictability of rainfall between A.D. 850-1050 required a strong localized economic network to integrate the different agricultural settings. Frankly, we think some Mimbres population migrated into areas like the Tularosa Basin early in that dislocation. As the local network saturated its ability to solve problems at about A.D. 1200, sometimes having too little and in good years, too much, the Casas Grandes economic sphere seems to have offered trade with regions farflung enough that local conditions could be offset. This seems to have been particularly true in the southernmost lower elevations of New Mexico, but we are very uncertain about the precise timing of these developments.

NOTES ON SIERRA BLANCA

(Derived from J.H. Kelley [1966]: *The Archeology of the Sierra Blanca Region, Southeastern New Mexico.* Unpublished Ph.D. Dissertation. Department of Anthropology, Harvard University, Cambridge)

A. GLENCOE PHASE (early 900-1100; late 1100-1200)
   1. Early Glencoe Phase — 90% Jornada Brownware with Chupadero B/W, Mimbres Boldface, Three Rivers R/T.
       a. Hondo Valley first to change to Lincoln Phase, Ruidoso Valley the last.
   2. Late Glencoe Phase — Chupadero B/W, El Paso Polychrome, Lincoln B/R, Three Rivers R/T, small amounts of Gila Polychrome, Ramos Polychrome, St. John's Polychrome, Heshotauthla Polychrome, Rio Grande Glaze I.

   — Early Glencoe was mostly subsistence gathering (including mesquite beans) with marginal agriculture of maize.
   — Hunting became more important in *Late Glencoe* as evidenced by large number of projectile points and scrap bones.
   — Early Glencoe metates — open-ended trough.
     Late Glencoe metates — closed trough with mano rests.
   — Corner-notched points more popular in the the south with side-notched points in the north.

Glencoe Phase, in general: sedentary population late to develop and thinly spread. Village sites tend to be located in narrow limits of pinyon-juniper belt of the Upper Sonoran Zone, close to the Transitional Zone, where there is water and alluvium for farming — 5400' to 6200'. Estimated 5-10 pithouses in villages.

B. CORONA PHASE (Early P-III, 1100-1200)
   1. Pottery: major types Jornada Brown and Chupadero B/W.
   2. Sites located near water, in upper Sonoran pinyon-juniper belt.
   3. Site layout -- open and scattered arrangement of small house units, few to up to 50 units can be scattered over ten acres. Paucity of trash, no extended occupations. House units of 1-9 rooms outlined by upright slabs. Shallow pithouses with jacal superstructures. Rooms with no hearths or with flagstone floors, probably for storage.

   — Corona Phase has some major cultural traits which were *out-of-date* elsewhere in the Southwest.

220

C. LINCOLN PHASE (mid P-III - early P-IV, 1200-1300+)
  1. Includes all of Corona Phase area plus some to the south.
  2. Abandoned in Glaze I times, *but a few Glaze II and III sherds indicate sparse population afterwards.*
  3. Site locations — Upper Sonoran, pinyon-juniper belt.
      a. Linear roomblocks fronting east with plaza and kiva.
      b. Enclosed square built around small plaza.
      c. 10-20 rooms to 120 rooms. Linear pueblos much smaller than those built around plaza.
      d. Ceremonial structures; square and deep.
      e. Several pueblos built on deep cultural fill (in situ growth?).
  5. Pottery — corrugated replaced Jornada Brown as main utility ware. Also present: Chupadero B/W and Capitan variant, Lincoln B/R, Three Rivers R/T, El Paso Polychrome imported from Tularosa Basin.
  6. Considerable temporal and some geographical overlap with Late Glencoe Phase.
  7. Maize is a retention of small-eared corn type when the larger type was available — due to drought-resistant adaptation?
  8. Slab Metates; trough with one end closed; mealing bins beginning to appear.

ECOLOGICAL VARIABLES

  1. Village sites influenced by requirements of crops.
      a. Glencoe Phase — located immediately adjacent to streams.
      b. Corona Phase — sites on tributaries of large streams.
      c. Lincoln Phase — sites clustered in main valleys or ridges further from water than Corona Phase.
  2. Defense not a factor — only one site, Block Lookout Site (Lincoln Phase) defensive site.
  3. Population believed to be highest during Lincoln Phase.

Lincoln and Glencoe sites usually have a high percentage of projectile points to vegetable food processing tools. Hunting played a major role. In addition, an abundance of animal bones supports this interpretation.

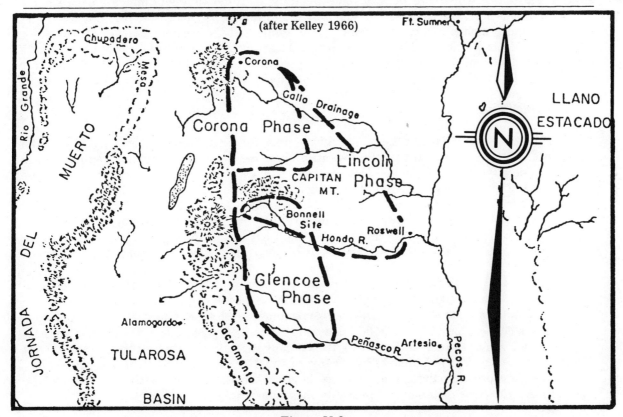

Figure V.9
GEOGRAPHIC DISTRIBUTION OF LINCOLN-CORONA-GLENCOE PHASES

CONSIDERATIONS FOR SURVEY

BACKGROUND AND PRIORITIES

Our primary objective in this volume is to set the stage for future survey work in the various districts of the state and to outline priorities. The geographic extent of southwestern New Mexico as overviewed here is quite staggering (see Table V:2) — nearly *20 million* acres, or roughly 30 thousand square miles.

These acreages are under diverse ownership or stewardship. Private lands are most extensive (28%), followed by Bureau of Land Management (26%), Forest Service (15%), and Corps of Engineers and State lands in nearly equal proportions (13% each). Unlike the Northern Rio Grande and San Juan Basin, where 40% of all lands are Indian owned, there is only 2% Indian land in this study unit. Private lands occur in about equal proportions in both areas (roughly one-quarter). The lands most difficult of access would include the White Sands Missile Range and the Mescalero Indian Reservation.

Fortunately, a major survey of Mescalero lands was conducted during the summer of 1979 under the direction of Mr. Bruce Harrill of the Bureau of Indian Affairs, Albuquerque Area Office. This was a sample survey of ¼ section quadrants in high altitude settings, and the report is in preparation as of this writing (May 1980); it may be available by the time this document is published. This is fortunate, for an extensive survey of Mescalero lands may never again be possible. Considering the conventional wisdom that *there is nothing up there anyway*, the results of this survey are most interesting. Mr. Broster of the BIA (personal communication) suggests that when site density data are fully analyzed they will indicate between 1-2 sites per square mile, on average. The majority of these will be small; the kind not always recorded on more thematic surveys — which have dominated the western portion of this study area. In fact, our reading of Forest Service reports from the Gila Forest to the west suggests that reported sites may be substantially under-represented there. This may be due to the fact that the majority of Forest Service surveys have been small and scattered — primarily occasioned by small land trades, road placement, etc., or it may be due to less interest in recording the very small sites.

The White Sands Missile Range should be more fully surveyed. For security reasons the area is not generally open, but the administration there has had a good cooperative relationship with archeologists in the Tularosa, New Mexico area. If it is borne in mind that the range cannot just stop business to accomodate archeologists, then a well-planned survey should be possible. There are some extensive sites in the area that date to the A.D. 1000-1200 period and historic ranching remains (1870 on to mid 1950's) are rich and important. The historical events in this area that are associated with Anglo expansion during the late 19th century figure prominently in the political geography of New Mexico and its quest for statehood.

The area between Las Cruces and El Paso has been subjected to rather more survey than other areas in southwestern New Mexico. Most of these, however, have been amateur weekend excursions or small surveys occasioned by expanding development in the Las Cruces area. Again, these surveys have tended to be small and scattered. The records of the El Paso Archeological Society need to be gone through systematically. Specific mention of their work did not figure prominently in the LeBlanc/Whalen overview. They are a most distinguished society with a long history of publication, and any large systematic survey in that area should be coordinated with their material, and probably their personnel.

The other federal and state lands in this portion of the state should present no particular difficulties of access. Private lands can be difficult or easy, depending on the landowner and

Table V:2

SOUTHWEST NEW MEXICO
LAND OWNERSHIP (in Acres)

	Hildago County	Lunas County	Dona Ana County	Otero County	Grant County	Sierra County	Lincoln County	TOTAL ACREAGE	Percen
BLM	740,771	747,067	1,143,793	929,578	292,472	824,687	518,924	5,197,292	26.08
NPS	0	0	50,393	84,706	0	0	0	135,632	.68
Water and Power Resources Service	0	0	418	0	0	19,650	0	20,068	.10
Corps of Engineers	0	0	486,267	1,459,752	0	517,754	172,160	2,635,933	13.22
NASA	0	0	4,198	0	0	0	0	4,198	.021
NMSU Agriculture Research Svc.	0	0	105,713	0	0	0	0	105,713	.53
International Boundary Comm.	0	0	8,173	0	0	632	0	8,805	.044
Forest Service*	76,589	0	0	563,472	884,193	363,154	398,783	3,102,244	15.56
State	354,431	534,951	286,910	449,908	367,685	361,195	300,841	2,655,921	13.32
Indian	0	0	0	460,402	0	0	0	460,402	2.31
Private or Miscellaneous	1,034,298	610,462	348,695	300,502	996,450	613,088	1,719,052	5,601,463	28.10
TOTAL ACRES	2,206,080	1,892,480	2,434,560	4,248,320	2,540,800	2,700,160	3,109,760	19,927,671	

*Includes Forest Service land from Eddy and Chavez Counties; portion of Forest Service lands in Lincoln County transferred to central New Mexico; portion of Forest Service lands in Sierra County transferred to Socorro, New Mexico.

223

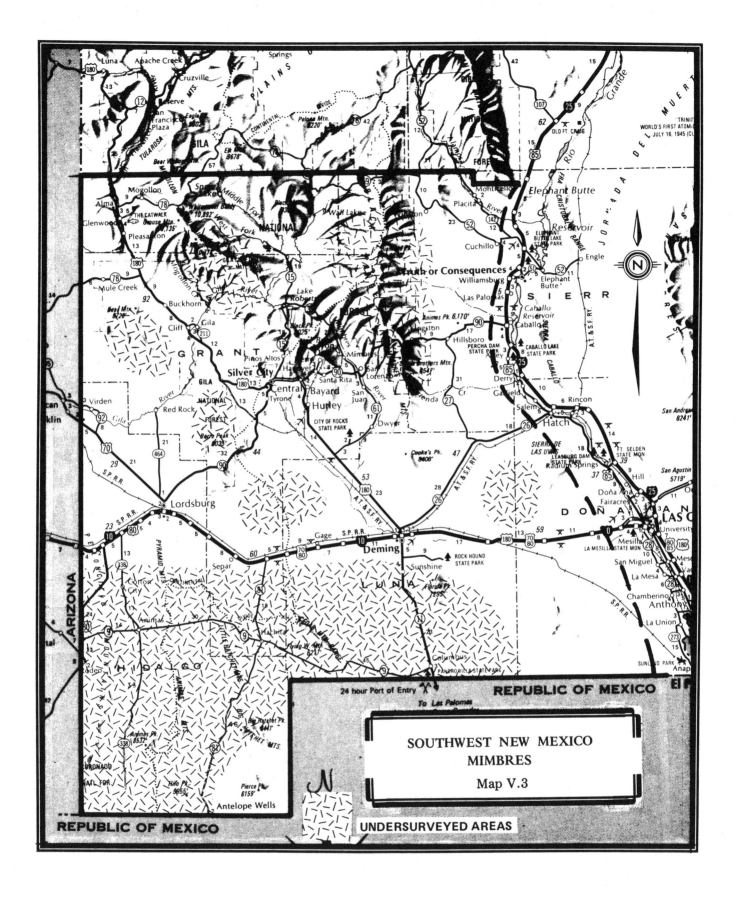

SOUTHWEST NEW MEXICO
MIMBRES

Map V.3

UNDERSURVEYED AREAS

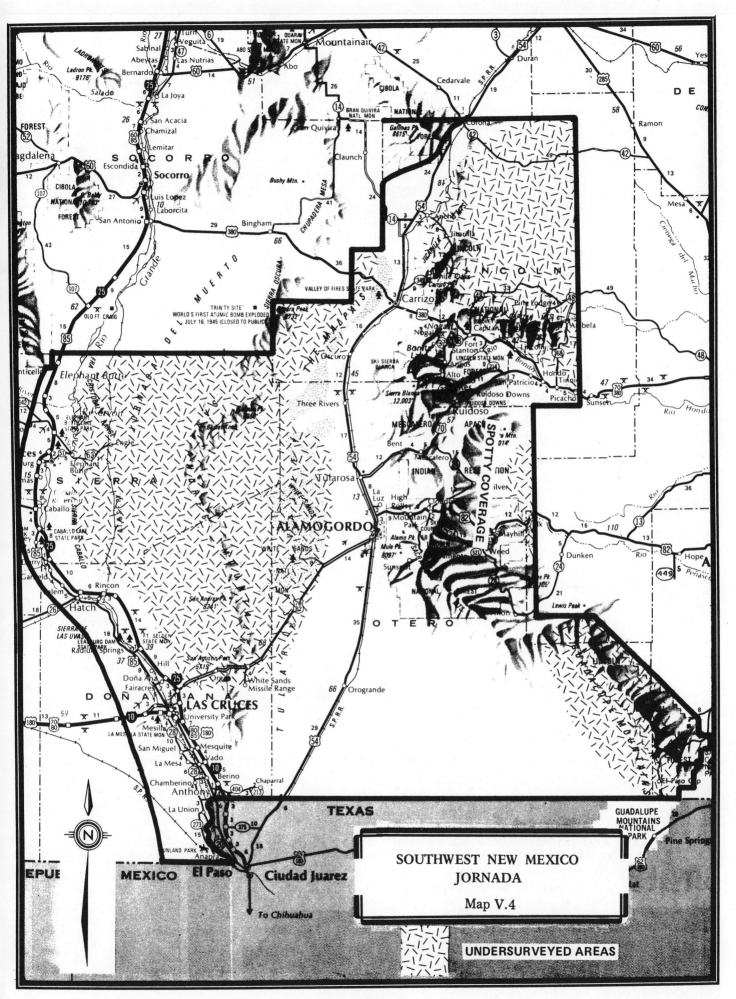

SOUTHWEST NEW MEXICO
JORNADA

Map V.4

UNDERSURVEYED AREAS

225

the approach. Most of the ranching families in the region are both hospitable and, historically, have been very good to archeologists, and not a few of them are highly knowledgeable.

Larger, systematic survey has been conducted in the Tularosa Basin (Wimberly and Rogers 1977) and the data are detailed. Survey has also been conducted in the Mimbres Valley by the Mimbres Foundation (no full monograph has yet appeared), and in the Gila and San Francisco drainages. Minnis (in LeBlanc and Whalen 1979) has summarized certain of these data, but no overall picture of survey in southwestern New Mexico is available. Dr. Findlow of Columbia University has surveyed extensively in Hidalgo County, but again, we have seen no report. In the early 1960's, the School of American Research surveyed and excavated in Hidalgo County (Lambert and Ambler 1961; McCluney 1962), else we should know little at all of that region from published literature. In the 1930's, Kidder and the Cosgroves did some survey in the southernmost tip of Hidalgo County (Cosgrove and Cosgrove 1932; Cosgrove 1947; Kidder, Cosgrove and Cosgrove 1949). The University of New Mexico surveyed in the Alamo Hueco Mountains in 1952, but again, no report has been published.

Our judgment is that, in the entire region, only the general areas of the Gila and Mimbres drainages — a triangle formed by El Paso-Las Cruces and Columbus, the east central portion of the Tularosa Basin, Sierra Blanca (Kelley 1966 and BIA, in preparation), and the McGregor and Dona Ana Missile Ranges south of the Las Cruces to Alamogordo highway, can be said to be well known archeologically and to have been treated in a systematic way. All other areas we view as of high priority for archeological survey.

Impacts on archeological resources in the area fall into three major categories: pothunting, timbering and population expansion/casual access. The Classic Mimbres sites in the Mimbres-Gila and major side drainages (Cameron Creek) are estimated to be 95% destroyed by pothunting, hence the urgency of the Mimbres Foundation's work in the 1975-1980 period. Apparently, the smallest Mimbres sites and sites of other time periods are not nearly so vandalized. This is particularly fortunate because the smaller sites represent the most crucial lacunae in data from the region. Timbering activities are primarily in the Gila and Lincoln Forests and the Mescalero Reservation. We view extensive survey in the Gila and Lincoln Forests as very important. The corridor between El Paso and Las Cruces is the major focus of population expansion and related development.

Since most surveys in the region have followed river drainages, we view surveys planned to crosscut major upland regions as essential. Survey data from the major river projects need to be collected and written up (James Fitting is also rumored to have yet unpublished survey data which were not included in his 1972 report on the Cliff area). Before any major new surveys are commissioned for the SHPO's program, a contract should be let to draw all these data together and coordinate these with the Museum of New Mexico's computer project for site files, and publish them, for the singular focus of a centuries' publication in southwestern New Mexico has been upon excavation results. The recent Jornada-Mogollon conference (Beckett and Wiseman 1979) is a good general overview of research interests in the eastern section of the study area, but again, survey results are scattered throughout the various papers in the volume.

THE DATA

As best we can estimate from disparate sources, the following summary is a reasonable approximation of current survey data. Of 15,000 square miles in the western portion of the study area (again, see Map V:1), we estimate that 150-160 square miles have been surveyed systematically, though the object of many surveys was to record the larger architectural sites. This is just over 1% of the total land surface. In contrast, we estimate the survey coverage of the San Juan Basin (as of 1980) at approximately 4%, or roughly 600 square miles. The

LeBlanc/Whalen overview lists a total of 1,871 recorded sites from files at the Museum of New Mexico, northern Arizona University, the Arizona State Museum and Gila National Forest (Silver Nity, New Mexico) and known survey accounts by individual investigators. This is an average of 12.5 sites per square mile surveyed. However, in view of the thematic nature of many of the surveys and their river-valley orientations, the figure should be taken cautiously.

The most extensive of these surveys in the Mimbres Valley, conducted by the Mimbres Foundation, covered fairly diverse topography adjacent to the river, and also in desert areas around Deming. Site density was 5.5 per square mile. We are surprised at the modest density, since this is almost identical to the densities obtained by Graybill (1973) in the upper Mimbres drainage. Since sites in outlying areas are much smaller, it is interesting that site density in the Gila drainage is substantially higher. These range from 8 sites per square mile (Lekson 1978) to 25 sites per square mile (Morris 1968). Fitting's survey in the Cliff area appears much like Lekson's. We estimate at least *37,500* recordable (excluding pot drops and the like) sites in the western region; that is two and one-half per square mile as an average. In other words, a century of surveying the greatest apparent concentrations of sites in the most productive riparian zones has yielded not higher than a 6% sample, numerically, of visible archeological remains, and perhaps only half that.

Initially, we thought this sample to be highly biased in comparison to other areas, for about 43% of all recorded sites are Classic Mimbres (about 800). That is, a 150 year period accounts for something under one-half the recorded remains. There are two recorded Paleo-Indian sites in the area and sixteen Archaic sites (there are also the ubiquitous unidentified lithic scatters). These account for an additional 2% of recorded sites. Thus, 55% of the recorded sites account for 1100 years of deposition (A.D. 200-Early Pithouse to A.D. 1450-Salado, less 150 years of Classic Mimbres). That is slightly more than 0.9 sites per depositional year (exclusive of the Mimbres) as opposed to 5.5 sites per depositional year during the Classic Mimbres; the average for the entire 1250 years being 1.5 sites per depositional year.

At first we doubted that the Classic Mimbres had anything like five or six times the visible site output of all other architectural phases and suspected this to be largely a distortion based on the thematic nature of archeological work in the region. Thus, we created a comparison with data derived from Dr. Waite's SJBRUS files for the San Juan Basin. Using the BM-II through P-III—P-IV transitional sites, we argue a similar (for comparative purposes) time span of A.D. 200-1450 and a total of 7,521 sites. This gives us a depositional output of roughly 6 sites per year for the full sequence, as opposed to 1.5 for the Mimbres-Mogollon. Excluding the P-II and P-III transitional sites in the SJBRUS file, the site average per year is 4. Using the P-II and P-II—P-III transitional sites as roughly A.D. 900-1050, we get 3,200 sites for the 150 year period or an output of roughly 22 sites per year; a ratio of exactly 5.5 to 1! As in the Classic Mimbres, the P-II and P-II—P-III sites were precisely 43% of the total known sites; a striking similarity!

We were not able to arrive at the figures we preferred, for we believe the correct comparison would be derived by lumping the Late P-II and P-II—P-III and Early P-III (to A.D. 1150). Alden Hayes (1975) has long argued that distinctions between Early-Late P-II and P-III should be made. We agree, and think the Pecos classification is mistaken in separating Late P-II and Early P-III in the San Juan Basin. In any case, since these transitional sites are believed to be more numerous, we could be looking at an output of sites of something like 6 to 1 for the period A.D. 975-1125. Temporally and developmentally, we think this might be the correct comparison to the Classic Mimbres.

Several other points should be made. Since we earlier suggested the sample known from the San Juan Basin to be roughly four times the acreage of that for the Mimbres, we adjusted our site numbers from the San Juan data by dividing by 4 to see if there was rough comparability. These data are summarized in the table below:

Table V.3
COMPARISON OF SURVEY DATA*
SAN JUAN BASIN AND MOGOLLON--MIMBRES

	San Juan	Mimbres	Adjusted to Equal Acreages (÷4)
Sq. Mi. covered	600	150	150/150
Total sites (Ceramic)	7,521	1,871	1,880/1,871
Site Density/Sq. Mi.	12.5	12.5	12.5/12.5
Sites/yr. A.D. 200-1450	4	.9	1/.9>
Sites/yr. at peak	22 (A.D. 900-1050)	5.5 (A.D. 1000-1150)	5.5/5.5
% Sites in Classic to Total Ceramic	43%	43%	43%/43%
No. Sites in Classic	3,200	804	800/804
No. Sites Aceramic or preceramic	733 (SJBRUS)	217 5 survey sample = (see Minnis 1979)	% = 11/<12
No. Sites post Classic	201 (P-III/P-IV thru P-V)	85 (Animas-Salado	% of N = 2.5/4.5

*Note: These data are *best estimates only*, drawn from quite disparate sources — we do not intend them for research purposes! There is *no* control over site size and other critical variables.

Several tentative conclusions can be drawn. The parallels in these data are very striking and were completely unexpected. We offer *no* explicit explanation for the similarity of these rough data. Initially, we thought that comparisons between overview areas would be impossible and meaningless, in view of vastly different archeological coverage and incompleteness of site files. First we tried to compare sites by type and also by temporal periods — this process led to complete disarray. Then we decided that bias in recording sites and in deciding which remains were *sites* and which were not might be roughly equal in both areas over the course of a century. Therefore, output (production) of sites per year was thought useful in the same sense that we currently fuss over the number of *housing starts per year* — a measure of the productive capacity of a cultural system.

The striking similarities in these data suggest that computerization of the site data from other areas of New Mexico should be conducted *before* massive surveys are funded. Since we have (currently) no real control for site size in the Mimbres area and little control by chronological period in any area, full research into adaptive process cannot yet be conducted on an interregional basis. Nonetheless, it would appear that it is not primarily the *size* of the data base (or acreage surveyed) in a given area that is critical — it is the quality of the data in its detail. The quality of data in a given region and its weaknesses need to be evaluated before really worthwhile survey can be conducted.

Further survey could demonstrate that site density (or any other factor) in the San Juan and Mimbres varied more widely as survey coverage increased, for it is reasonable to argue that as survey coverage in the Mimbres increases, relative site frequency will go down, the most concentrated areas of deposition already having attracted attention. But, frankly, we don't really know. What we do know is that smaller sites everywhere, but particularly in higher altitudes, minor drainages and desert areas, are substantially undersurveyed in the Mimbres. Hidalgo County is likewise substantially undersurveyed. On the other hand, these striking similarities tell us that we will never understand Southwestern prehistory by research compartmentalized region to region, for here we have some tentative evidence that Mogollon and Anasazi are somehow parts of one greater pattern. Future surveys need to be designed specifically to increase the *comparability* of available data region-to-region.

Finally, though the site density per square mile is, tentatively, 12.5 in surveyed areas of both the San Juan Basin and southwestern New Mexico (west of Rio Grande), it does not seem possible that each area (15,000 square miles each) could contain 186,500 visible or recordable sites! We know that site density varies wildly from one microregion to the next, and substantial areas are not apparently occupied at all — particularly those between major population systems. It seems safe to assert that archeologists over the last century have been very efficient at recording disproportionate concentrations of sites.

A summary of survey data east of the river must await more survey and the BIA report of the Mescalero survey. Nonetheless, our calculation is that ca. 1500 km² or roughly 600 square miles of the eastern (Jornada) unit has been surveyed (Whalen 1979:Tables 34 and 36). About 2,000 sites in all are recorded. While this seems quite similar to the western unit's survey data, the surface base is roughly four times larger, being 4%, as in the San Juan Basin. Roughly 4 sites per square mile would be the average. We are not able to compute site output for this region. Optimally, we would lump the Transitional Pueblo and Early Pueblo (A.D. 1100-1250 or 1300), but the lack of temporal control makes this currently impossible. Site output per year per square mile surveyed would appear to be roughly .4 (perhaps as low as .35) for the entire period of A.D. 200 to 1400, that is, one quarter of the output of the western unit. There is a definite A.D. 1100-1300 peak, but we don't know its true magnitude — it also appears to be roughly between 4 and 6 to 1 (1,000, or 50% of these sites are definite Pueblo; i.e. half in 300 of 1200 years = 4 to 1 plus undetermined ceramic scatters).

Finally, we wish to reemphasize the points we have made so that there is no misunderstanding. The similarity of the Mimbres and San Juan survey data suggest a remarkably similar *rate* of site creation over substantial runs of time and vast acreage. These do not compare, in any real way, the relative size or complexity of the Mogollon-Mimbres or Eastern Anasazi cultural systems. Rather, we state that site creation (output) per year per square mile is identical as an average. We also state that site creation (output) per square mile per year increased by something on the order of five-fold during easily recognizable Classic phases (which are also better dated than most others). Thus, the same *rate* of overall development seems remarkably similar and in each case the period from A.D. 900-1150 is marked by increased site creation (depositional output) per unit time and space. We argue that this is further evidence, though totally unexpected, for the power drive phenomenon discussed in earlier chapters. We will return to this in the summary of this chapter. For the moment, however, let us turn to the more practical matter of National and State Register properties in the region.

STATE AND NATIONAL REGISTER PROPERTIES IN SOUTHWESTERN NEW MEXICO

Our records indicate that there are 15 sites in southwestern New Mexico on the State Register, four of which are also on the National Register of Historic Places. Several of these have been added recently due to the vigorous work of the Mimbres Foundation. These sites are listed below in Tables V:4 and V:5 (dates and phases approximate).

The pattern of nominated sites is quite interesting. By temporal phases these are arranged as follows:

Table V:4
**ARCHEOLOGICAL PHASES OF STATE AND NATIONAL REGISTER SITES
IN SOUTHWEST NEW MEXICO**

WESTERN UNIT: (Mimbres Area)

Paleo-Indian	No sites
Archaic	No sites
Early Pithouse/Pine Lawn	No sites
Late Pithouse, Georgetown	2 sites (Burrow Springs, Woodrow)
San Francisco	4 sites (Mattocks, Upton, Woodrow, Wheaton)
Three Circle	4 sites (Mattocks, Upton, Woodrow, Wheaton)
Mangus (real or not)	No sites
Classic Mimbres	5 sites (Woodrow, Treasure Hill, Mattocks, Upton, Wheaton)
Animas/Black Mountain	1 site (Montoya)
Tularosa	1 site (Gila Cliff)
Salado	2 sites (Kwilleylekia, Janss)
Apachean	No sites

Total Number 10

EASTERN UNIT: (Jornada Area)

Paleo-Indian	No sites
Archaic	2 sites (Alamogordo and components of Parabolic Dunes)
El Paso	2 sites (Three Rivers, Escondida)
Lincoln	1 site (Feather Cave)
Apachean	1 site (components of Parabolic Dunes)

Total Number 5

Table V:5
**STATE AND NATIONAL REGISTER OF CULTURAL PROPERTIES
SOUTHWEST NEW MEXICO**
(National Register Properties are starred)

Reg. No.	Name	LA No.	County	Time Period (Approx.)	Phase
No. 52	Three Rivers Petroglyph and Pueblo Site	4921	Otero	A.D. 900-1300 (peak at 1150-1250)	El Paso
No. 99	Escondida Ruin	458	Otero	A.D. 1150-1350	El Paso
No. 126*	Woodrow Ruin	2454	Grant	A.D. 500/700?-1200	Georgetown—Classic Mimbres
No. 152	Alamogordo Site	456	Otero	2000 B.C.	Archaic
No. 156*	Feather Cave	— —	Lincoln	A.D. 1200	Lincoln
No. 221	Kwilleylekia Ruins	4935	Grant	ca. A.D. 1450	Salado
No. 314*	Burro Springs Site No. 2	11609	Grant	A.D. 700	Georgetown—San Francisco
No. 353	Treasure Hill	16241	Grant	A.D. 1000-1150	Classic Mimbres
No. 434	Parabolic Dune Hearth Mounds	— —	Otero	2000 B.C. + later occ.	Archaic + Pueblo & Apache
No. 500	Janss Site	12077	Grant	A.D. 1425	Salado
No. 501	Mattocks Site	676	Grant	A.D. 700-1150	San Francisco—Classic Mimbres
No. 502	Montoya Site	15075	Grant	A.D. 1175-1300	Animas (Black Mountain)
No. 504	Upton Site	15030	Luna	A.D. 700-1150	San Francisco—Classic Mimbres
No. 505	Wheaton Smith Site	— —	Grant	A.D. 800-1150	San Francisco—Classic Mimbres
No. 63*	Gila Cliff Dwellings National Monument	13658	Catron	A.D. 1200	Tularosa

Table compiled to August 1979

SHORT DESCRIPTIONS OF STATE AND NATIONAL REGISTER SITES
(National Register Properties are Starred)

THREE RIVERS PETROGLYPH AND PUEBLO SITE (LA 4921)

This site consists of a ridge formation where many examples of petroglyphs are located, along with the remains of prehistoric pithouses and surface pueblos. The structures are located south of the petroglyph area on the first bench above the highest river terrace, approximately 200 meters north of Three Rivers Creek, at an elevation of 5,000 feet.

The Three Rivers Pueblo site was recently surveyed by Human Systems Research and reported by Wimberly and Rogers (1977). Previously, portions were excavated by New Mexico State University and the Bureau of Land Management (Bussey, et al. 1976). The ceramic remains from this site indicate an occupation range from A.D. 900 to 1300, with the major occupation dating from A.D. 1150 to 1250. As such, its earlier components reflect the substantial expansion noted for both the P-II period in the San Juan Basin and general processes leading to expansion during the Three Circle and Early Mimbres Classic. The A.D. 1150-1250 occupation should reflect the general nature of early post Mimbres occupation, variously termed Animas, Black Mountain, El Paso, etc., depending on geographic locus. The setting is substantially like those in the Animas Valley of Hidalgo County.

ESCONDIDA RUIN (LA 458)

The Escondida Ruin is situated on an alluvial fan and sand dune area about five miles west of the base of the Sacramento Mountains, near the east edge of the Tularosa Basin at an elevation of 4,100 feet. The site consists of an El Paso Phase pueblo covering an area of approximately 0.2 miles x 0.3 miles. There are the remains of three parallel, discontinuous adobe roomblocks containing 60 to 80 rooms, and possibly more are present, but are obscured by drifting sand. Again, adaptive similarities and contrasts with other post Mimbres sites are indicated.

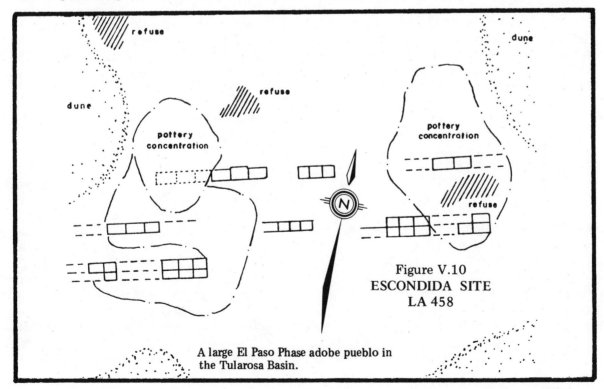

Figure V.10
ESCONDIDA SITE
LA 458

A large El Paso Phase adobe pueblo in the Tularosa Basin.

KWILLEYLEKIA RUINS (LA 8674)

Kwilleylekia Ruins consist of a large Salado Phase pueblo located on the banks of the Gila River near the town of Cliff, New Mexico. The site includes a compact adobe pueblo, a plaza type pueblo and a linear roomblock. The Salado Phase is the last pueblo occupation in the Mimbres area. This pueblo was believed to have been occupied from A.D. 1325 to the A.D. 1500's. Cremated burials have been excavated at Kwilleylekia, a trait which is not common in earlier sites of the area. There is also evidence that a plaza type ball court may exist in the south mound. This site is partially excavated and is open to the public.

BURRO SPRINGS SITE NO. 2 (LA 11609)*

This site consists of perhaps the largest pitroom village in the Southwest with an estimated 200 pitrooms which extend over 15 acres. Burro Springs Site No. 2 is an early Mogollon settlement. One pitroom has been excavated which revealed a rectangular structure, 12 feet x 16 feet, with a sloping, south-facing entryway. Ceramic material recovered from this pitroom consisted primarily of plain brownwares, with a trace of Three Circle Red-on-White, Mogollon Red-on-Brown and Mimbres Boldface Black-on-White. This site is located on a high terrace on the west side of the Burro Springs Valley, at an elevation of 5,780 feet.

TREASURE HILL (LA 16241)

Treasure Hill is a classic Mimbres ruin with an estimated thirty rooms, an undetermined number of pitrooms and two possible kivas. More rooms are probably present, but are under, and adjacent to, a county road. The Cosgroves excavated and reported on two rectangular kivas at Treasure Hill (Cosgrove 1923). This site is located in the Arenas Drainage, about three miles northwest of the Cameron Creek Ruin.

WOODROW RUIN (LA 2454)*

This site is situated on a high bench above the west bank of the Gila River at approximately 4,600 feet in elevation. The site dimensions are 900 feet x 500 feet. Thirty-three pithouses are confirmed and more probably exist, but are covered by later occupations. In addition, 16 roomblocks and two great kivas are present, along with numerous plaza areas. One plaza area, located at the north end of the site, may in fact be a ball court.

The ceramic remains at the Woodrow Ruin indicate an occupation from A.D. 700 to A.D. 1200. This site represents a presumed Georgetown-Classic Mimbres Phase development in the Gila River drainage. As noted in previous sections, the contrasts between larger sites in the Mimbres and outlying drainages (in ceramics, grave offerings, room size, burials per room, etc.) are at least as instructive as the more commonly emphasized similarities. Since the elevation of this site (and others in the Gila drainage) averages 1,000-1,500 feet lower than large, Late Pithouse-Classic sites in the Mimbres basin, there should be adaptive contrasts from the outset of occupation. Why, for example, has Fitting's (1973) Winn Canyon site (at 4,200 feet) no later occupation while the Woodrow Site has later components? How do early assemblages from the two kinds of sites compare?

ALAMOGORDO SITE (LA 456)

This site consists of a rock shelter that was occupied primarily during the Archaic period. Large quantities of perishable materials, dating 4,000 B.P., have been recovered by excavations conducted by New Mexico State University (Bussey, Kelly and Southward 1976).

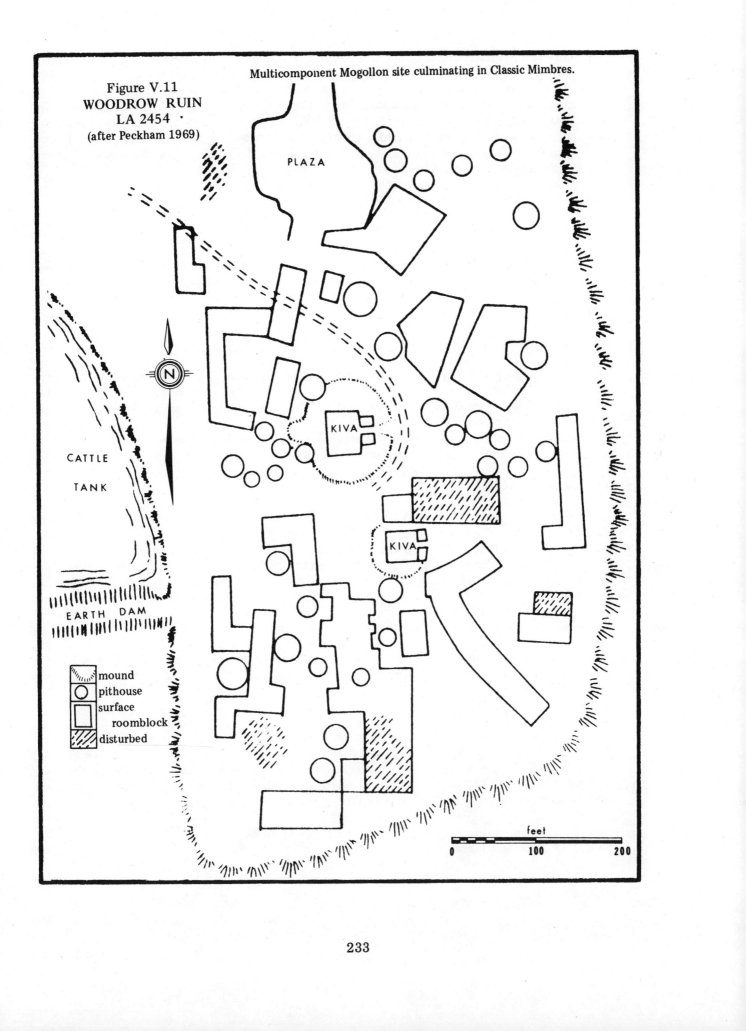

Figure V.11
WOODROW RUIN
LA 2454 ·
(after Peckham 1969)

Multicomponent Mogollon site culminating in Classic Mimbres.

PLAZA

CATTLE
TANK

EARTH DAM

KIVA

KIVA

mound
pithouse
surface
roomblock
disturbed

feet

0   100   200

233

The site is located on the edge of a canyon, ten miles east of Alamogordo. The data from cave sites in the Alamogordo area, including Fresnal Shelter (excavated also), need to be compared with those from cave excavations to the northwest (Tularosa and Bat caves) and those from caves excavated to the southwest (Hidalgo County; Lambert and Ambler 1961). Since the Archaic occupations of southwestern New Mexico are so little known from detailed excavation at open sites, continued attention to identifying and protecting dry cave sites is imperative. Such deposits will continue to provide the major data on the shift to agriculture in this portion of New Mexico for some time to come.

FEATHER CAVE*

Feather Cave is considered to have been an important shrine to the prehistoric Pueblo people in the Fort Stanton-Lincoln areas. A large number of perishable items have been recovered from this cave site, along with a stone altar containing numerous arrows. The site is located on the south side of Mt. Capitan at an elevation of 6,200 feet. Ceramic remains indicate occupation around A.D. 1200. Ellis and Hammack (1968) have reported on the possible religious aspects of this site.

PARABOLIC DUNE HEARTH MOUNDS

This site is located near the eastern and southern borders of White Sands National Monument at an elevation of 4,000 feet. The major features of this site are the preserved hearths that date from Archaic (4000 B.C.), Pueblo and Apache periods. The heat from the hearths had changed the gypsum sand into an impure plaster of paris and, when moisture was later added, a hardened cast of the hearths was created. There is little difference between the hearths of different periods, indicating similar subsistence strategies over a lengthy period of time.

JANSS SITE (LA 12077)

The Janss Site is located on the first terrace above the Mimbres River at the upper end of the Mimbres Valley. The elevation is 6,200 feet. The site consists of a 30-room adobe pueblo of the Salado culture. A date of approximately A.D. 1425 has been assigned on the basis of C-14. Of five known Salado period components in the Mimbres Valley, two have been destroyed by bulldozers. Since the focus of the Salado is to the west (ca. 150 miles), the Salado sites in the Mimbres area should offer regional contrasts to those in Arizona. LeBlanc (1979) suggests these to be smaller and not typical in every respect. Is there a continuum of Salado, or puddled adobe, sites extending to the east even further? Do the local differences become great enough that puddled adobe sites extending along the southern tier of New Mexico and Texas are thought unrelated? Better dating of similar puebloid constructions in southeastern New Mexico and adjacent Texas is clearly required to resolve the issue (see following chapter).

MATTOCKS SITE (LA 676)

This site consists of a 200+ room pueblo and several pithouses. The site is located on the first terrace above the Mimbres River at an elevation of 5,880 feet. The pueblo is constructed of cobbles, with the rooms arranged in four roomblocks, each with plaza areas, several pithouses and a possible kiva. The Mattocks Site dates to A.D. 700-1150. Again, this is a Classic Mimbres site evidencing the *in situ* development from the Late Pithouse period to termination about A.D. 1130-1150.

MONTOYA SITE (LA 15075)

The Montoya Site is an adobe pueblo of 50 rooms. This post-Mimbres site contains larger

A Salado Phase site in the Mimbres Valley. Note adobe construction and large rooms.

Figure V.12
JANSS SITE
LA 12077
(after LeBlanc 1976)

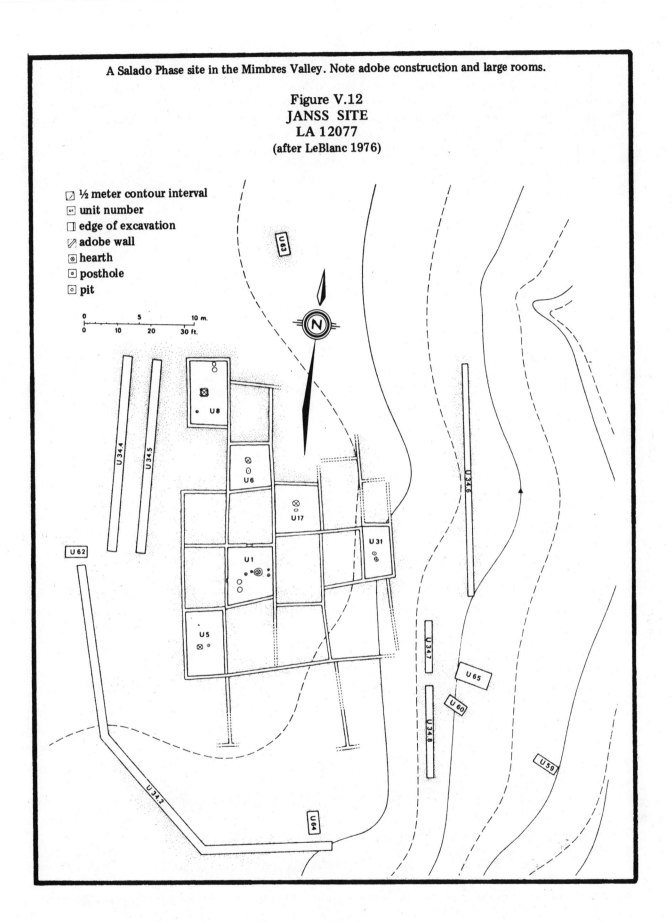

rooms than earlier sites. The rooms are up to 30 feet long, and have as much as 30 m² of floor space. In addition, burials consist of both cremations and regular interments; there are also decapitated burials. The site is at 5,200 feet in elevation. The occupation is roughly A.D. 1175-1300, a local Animas (Black Mountain) manifestation. Evidence for similar conflict associated with the demise of post-Classic occupations occurs in the Gallina highlands (albeit in stockaded pithouse settlements) at the same time roughly 300 miles to the north (see summary, this chapter).

UPTON SITE (LA 15030)

The Upton Site consists of two superimposed villages located on the first terrace above the Mimbres River (in the lower valley) at an elevation of approximately 5,000 feet. At least six pithouses are known, but it is likely that 30 to 36 are present. The pithouses date from A.D. 700 to A.D. 1000. The latest occupation consists of about 150 surface rooms arranged in three roomblocks. This portion of the site is Classic Mimbres and dates to A.D. 1000-1150. A possible ball court is also present at this site and is indicated by a large, long double lobed mound. The site is both lower in elevation and more southerly than the largest concentration of Classic sites.

WHEATON SITE

This site contains the remains of a pithouse village, a superimposed surface pueblo and a historic homestead. A total of six pithouses are known, although another six are estimated. The pithouses date between A.D. 800 and A.D. 1000. The surface pueblo consists of 25 continuous cobble rooms and dates to A.D. 1000-1150. The rooms at this pueblo are somewhat smaller than those at other Mimbres sites.

The Wheaton Site is located on the first terrace above Gallinas Creek (a major tributary of the Mimbres River) at an elevation of 5,700 feet. This site is significant, since it is located outside the Mimbres Valley proper. Rather little attention in the literature has been lavished on the larger sites in secondary drainages.

GILA CLIFF DWELLINGS (LA 13658)*

These are well preserved cliff ruins occupied between A.D. 1175 or 1200 to 1300. They represent the major evidence for Tularosa Phase occupation in southwestern New Mexico. There is only one other (much smaller) Tularosa Phase site in the area, and a possible component at a third site. The relationships between Tularosa occupation and Animas (Black Mountain) or Early Salado are not well known. The major Tularosa occupation is to the north of the southern boundary of Socorro County, New Mexico. These cliff dwellings are contemporaneous with similar Mesa Verdean and Gallina Phase *cliff dwellings* in the Upper Rio Grande and Four Corners region. Though these cliff sites are widespread at this time, and are quite notable in the public mind, they are a numerically rather rare type of site when compared to other P-III occupations.

DISCUSSION

In the Western Unit, two Paleo-Indian localities have been recorded and a number of Archaic sites (San Pedro Cochise) recorded, but none are nominated. These site records should be reviewed to see if any register eligible sites are included. Any site of these periods which suggested from survey records that even a portion was intact would qualify. Additional sites of the Archaic/Cochise periods could be expected in surveys of eroded pockets and at little-surveyed higher elevations. The lack of substantial erosion in this region (compared to the San Juan Basin, Estancia Basin and the southeastern Llano Estacado) undoubtedly accounts in part for under-representation of sites in these early time periods, but those known are often also ig-nored.

No Early Pithouse period sites in the Mogollon sequence appear on either the State or National Register. Nonetheless, LeBlanc has documented their presence in the Mimbres Foundation surveys and Fitting (1973) excavated a portion of the Winn Canyon Site. Winn Canyon is either Early Pithouse (Al Cabo or Pine Lawn, as you prefer) or Early Georgetown (we have not seen published dates, but we think this is our oversight, for Fitting is said to have published them after the cited 1973 report.). In either case, Winn Canyon would be a likely Register candidate in view of its unusual assemblage (see earlier sections) if the rest of the site is still reasonably intact.

Later Pithouse Occupations. Site files should be gone through to see if additional George-town components (especially scarce) are in condition to be preserved. Additionally, the major surveys in the region should be reviewed to identify very small pithouse sites (in secondary drainages, etc.) for nomination. Most of these may have only a very small admixture of dec-orated wares. If this were done correctly, the object would be to stratify sites according to altitude zones and by major drainage. That is, in each of the Gila-San Francisco-Mimbres drain-ages, several intact sites of 3-5 pithouses should be nominated. In three major drainages one might nominate three higher and lower sites in each (this implies northern to southern distribu-tion as well). If a secondary drainage or two are included for contrast, 12-15 sites might be involved in a thematic nomination.

Mangus Phase. We still think this phase represents a *major* unresolved issue in regional prehistory. It is not at all satisfactory that no sites thought to be Mangus are on either registry. These sites will also be smaller, from all indications, and contain assemblages of Mimbres Bold-face and, perhaps, Transitional Black-on-white. Since we have speculated that the Mangus is a small site phenomenon which represents a dispersal about A.D. 900 (due to a winter to summer rainfall shift, coupled with decreased moisture — see Overview, this chapter), it is essential to have sites of this period represented and preserved. Our notion is that some of these will be rectangular pithouses and some may also have modest surface structures. The same selec-tion strategy suggested in the preceding paragraph would be appropriate.

Classic Mimbres. Since these sites are generally (95% pothunted) partially destroyed, any remaining ones that are intact (probably very small) should be nominated. No field house types are represented. The outlying sites (like Saige-McFarland) merit more representation. None of the extensive (LeBlanc 1979) sherd scatters in desert areas is included; some of these are *huge* and should be nominated. These large sherd scatters could prove very productive for test excavations.

Animas/Black Mountain. Since sites of this period are considered Black Mountain in the Mimbres and Animas in Hidalgo County, it is essential that Hidalgo County sites (*true Animas*, we suppose) be reviewed for nomination. This can be done immediately since Dr. Findlow's (Columbia University) survey forms are now available; the McCluney (1962) sites can also be reviewed.

Salado. Because of the unusual questions raised by Lekson's Villareal Site, additional Gila Polychrome sites should be identified, even if very small, and several likely candidates should be nominated.

The lack of recorded Apachean remains in the area suggests more a problem for future surveys than review of existing site files.

In the Eastern Unit, several Paleo-Indian finds are mentioned in Wimberly and Rogers

(1977:2). Broilo (1973:225) mentions Folsom and Cody from campsites in the southern Tularosa Basin, and Hester (1962) mentions a Paleo-Indian site near Alamogordo in his discussion of the Elida site material from Roosevelt County, New Mexico. These occur in elevations of 4,000 to 5,000 feet. The files of the El Paso Archeological Society should be reviewed and this period be represented.

Archaic sites in the Eastern Unit should be reviewed as well. Both Paleo-Indian and Archaic remains are present, the famous Naco and Lehmer sites are to the south and west and lie across a political boundary which puts them outside the scope of our inquiry. Such sites are favorites of collectors. Anything thought to be only partially collected or intact should be protected, if possible.

Pre-A.D. 900 Jornada-Mogollon [Lehmer's (1948) Mesilla Phase]. Though occupation of this region by agricultural populations clearly builds up in the A.D. 900-1300 period, earlier sites are mentioned. Dates are extremely scarce in the region (north of the Hueco Bolson) and this certainly generates a problem; surface assemblages are often scant. Nonetheless, a few sites that might date to this period should be targeted for a modest testing program. Any that emerge with datable material should be considered for nomination.

El Paso Phase. A broader range of these sites should be included in the Registers. There is substantial subregional variation in the architecture, ceramic assemblages and locations of El Paso Phase sites. Again, as with the Mimbres, this phase should be represented by 12-15 well chosen sites adequately covering local and temporal variability. Again, small sites are not represented.

Other Later Phases (Geographical variants) — Corona (southern), Late Glencoe, Lincoln. Type sites for these phases should be identified from Kelley's (1966) survey data. It is especially important that several of the very late pithouse occupations in the upland areas be preserved. Stewart Peckham and others at the Museum of New Mexico have excavated/recorded a number of these in the Lincoln-Angus, New Mexico area (Wiseman 1979; Farwell and Oakes, n.d.). They should be consulted, for these are most important sites. It has been our view throughout that pithouse occupations are as much (or more) a kind of adaptation, associated with higher elevation and *winter rainfall* agricultural strategies (see final chapter for full exposition), than they are a temporal stage of cultural development. Since our control over the climatological data improves as we approach the present, pithouse occupations of the A.D. 1100-1400 period (A.D. 1100-1275 in the Gallina) offer an outstanding opportunity for major research into the mechanics underlying all of Southwestern prehistory.

GEOGRAPHICAL AND GENERAL CONSIDERATIONS

The State and National Registers currently consist of 15 sites in a 30,000 square mile area. That is, one site for each 2,000 square miles. This is one-fourth or less (depending on the number of Chacoan outliers ultimately accepted for inclusion, but formally nominated; see Marshall, Stein, Loose and Novotny 1979 for a listing of these) the representation by unit of space than for the San Juan Basin-Upper Rio Grande areas.

Hidalgo County, inexplicably, is not represented at all, in spite of unusual preservation in many cave sites (Lambert and Ambler 1961) and its being the alleged focus of the Animas (Casas Grandes related) occupation. Even though Hidalgo County may be one of the least surveyed and certainly unpublished counties in New Mexico, archeologically speaking, enough sites are known to justify review there for potential nomination prior to additional survey.

Luna County has only the Upton Site (Mogollon-Mimbres Classic). The area is generally desertic, bisected by low-dry basin-range topography in the south. Sites in desertic environments are under-represented in the published literature, and undersurveyed during formal projects. Luna County overlaps the presumed gray area between Mimbres and Jornada branches of the Mogollon. It is not reasonable to suppose that there would be no nominatable sites which represent the temporal or geographic transition between Mimbres Classic-Animas and/or Animas-El Paso geographic foci.

Dona Ana County. The trans Rio Grande is not represented; that is, there is not a single Register site in the lower Rio Grande (of New Mexico) drainage itself. These comments should suffice: this area is the focus of the El Paso Phase expression (Schaafsma 1979; Whalen 1979), the heavily inhabited modern corridor between El Paso, Texas and Las Cruces, New Mexico, and represents the east of river vs. west of river population systems argued by some. Site survey records for Dona Ana and Luna counties need to be reviewed urgently for potential nominations (again, the El Paso Archeological Society records plus the Museum of New Mexico records need to be consulted).

As a general statement, the higher elevations and the desert areas in southwestern New Mexico are under-represented on the Registers, in survey and in publication. As a practical matter, this means that federally controlled land in the area (primarily Forest Service-high elevation, and BLM-low elevation) is more noticeably under-represented than is private land along the major river drainages. While we don't applaud the situation, it is easy to resolve; both in access for additional survey where needed, and in cooperation with ongoing federal programs.

FINAL COMMENT

It might appear from this section that we advocate a massive series of additions to the State and National Registers. In one sense this is true, for this area of New Mexico is quite under-represented and also quite prone to selective site destruction without the attendant contract archeology to offset the loss (as in the San Juan Basin and the Carlsbad gas fields). We suppose that something on the order of 70-80 sites should be nominated, from known sites, to the State and National Registers in this area. This does not need to be the bureaucratic nightmare it might first appear, for if we break these into clusters of thematic nominations, such as Mimbres-small sites, Mangus Phase sites, El Paso Phase sites, dry cave sites (Hidalgo County might merit a *National Dry Caves Archeological District* nomination) then the paperwork should be manageable. Probably not more than 15-20 individual nominations would be merited. We advocate a relationship between our State Register and National Register wherein they are used as coordinated tools.

Numerically, the registers are currently very modest. Representationally they are biased to the larger sites in a 700 year time span (A.D. 700-1400). The registers certainly consist of less than one site of two hundred already recorded, and most probably one site in three hundred (assuming a current total site population of 4,000 in all of southwestern New Mexico with 15 Register sites); that is one-half of one percent or less. If one accepts our estimate that there are an average of 2.5, or more, sites per square mile in the region, then 60-70,000 recordable sites might approximate the actual archeological remains in the area. That is, currently recorded sites represent about 2-3% of land surface (both units), but possibly 6-8% of the site population ($1/15$th — $4,000 \div 60,000$). Now, these are only estimates, but conservative ones: 2.5 sites per square mile is 1/5 the site density of already surveyed areas (12.5 square miles) in the western unit and in the San Juan Basin. It can reasonably be argued, therefore, that each current Register site stands for or represents 4,000 sites actually recordable and on the ground; that is *one fortieth of one percent*, and it assumes that archeologists have already been expert enough to locate site concentrations three to five times denser than the average. There is no danger that adding several score nominations will over-represent the actual archeological record in this region!

239

Finally, notions of significance should take into account our analysis (see last section — Survey Considerations) suggesting site output during the Classic Mimbres at 5.5 times the annual rate for other periods. The San Juan data suggest the period just prior to the later Chacoan Classic to be one of high output also. Early P-II might be quite like the Three Circle Phase and anecdotal evidence suggests Three Circle Phase sites to be common compared to all periods but Classic Mimbres. That is, the five sites which represent the Classic Mimbres are a sample from sites that are *five or six times more common* than sites of all other periods — 50% of the registers *do* represent roughly 50% of the site population (43% Classic), a good symmetry. These sites are not significant, however, on account of scarcity. They are important because they are multicomponent and because so many Mimbres sites have been vandalized. The point is that an equal representation on account of scarcity for sites in other periods would require them to be nominated at a rate of five to six times that of the Classic sites for every one found. One might continue to nominate one of 100 Classic Mimbres sites as they are surveyed in the future. However, on the basis of scarcity, five or six of each hundred (if a hundred each of all other periods could ever be found) from other periods would be an equal accounting.

Small sites of ephemeral materials or small building units (small cobbles) will be destroyed by random process much more quickly than large sites constructed of larger masonry units. Thus, an architecturally *well-preserved* small site of such materials is, proportional to its numbers, much rarer than the large. These factors should play far more heavily in considerations of scarcity and states of preservation, when determining significance, than they have in the past.

OVERVIEW — SOUTHWESTERN NEW MEXICO

Obviously, any overview of the archeology of a region as vast and unsystematically surveyed as this quarter of New Mexico can only be speculative at present. The western portion of the study area is known primarily from excavation, the eastern portion primarily from survey. While chronology has nowhere proceeded beyond the problematic, it is virtually uncontrolled in any precise terms in the eastern, Jornada, area. Cultural development in the two areas is similar at the most general level. Whalen (1979) has characterized the Jornada development as later and more modest in scale than in the Mimbres. This seems accurate enough, but it does not tell us a great deal.

In this overview there are several lines of thought that merit pursuit, while others do not. First, the Mimbres area is generally viewed as slightly earlier in intensive development than elsewhere in New Mexico. This appears true if comparison is made to more easterly regions, while it is less so if one looks north and west. We have generally presumed the shift to agriculture earliest in the southwestern New Mexico area. In truth, the evidence rests on data from Bat and Tularosa caves, slightly to the north, and unpublished evidence from Fresnal rock shelter in the far eastern highlands of this study area. This is doubly confusing, for the Pine Lawn area of New Mexico moves into the expected developments early, while there is little evidence for similar events in the Tularosa Basin, the lower Rio Grande and desertic areas. On the other hand, the Hueco Bolson to the south (in Texas) has yielded a number of A.D. 200-300 dates for small pithouse sites. Nonetheless, there is less evidence for agriculture both in more modest ground stone assemblages and in lesser quantities of carbonized corn.

Clearly, this shift to agriculture is a complex phenomenon — perhaps not associated with one environmental zone; not associated perfectly with the length of time cultigens are known in a given region, and only imperfectly correlated with architectural features (pithouses). In short, it makes no sense to pursue the agricultural development question based on current data in this portion of New Mexico, for we are not even able to separate early architectural sites which are agricultural from those that are not. Thus, we leave the focus of the preceding chapter and concentrate here on comparing sequences of development and the general characteristics of those sequences.

There are three specific kinds of arguments we wish to advance here. First, the trajectory, or pattern, of development in the Mimbres area is, in its characteristics and in its timing, strikingly like that of the Chaco-Anasazi in the San Juan Basin and its highland periphery. Second, the nature of these developments is directly related to major shifts in the quantity and timing of rainfall. Third, the developments to the east (Jornada) are rather unlike the first two, in timing, but like other areas of the Southwest (such as the Little Colorado and Hopi areas). That is, there are two basic developmental and population schedules in New Mexico and adjacent Arizona, here referred to as *schedule one* and *schedule two* systems. All of these arguments will be phrased in terms of cycles of power and efficiency. In Chapter III (San Juan Basin) a general picture of such phases was suggested. In Chapter IV (Socorro-Mt. Taylor) demographic power was discussed briefly in the context of sedentism and infant mortality. Here we hope to convince the reader that power drives at the cultural level exist and can be demonstrated from ordinary archeological data.

DEVELOPMENTAL TRAJECTORIES IN SOUTHWESTERN NEW MEXICO: THE EVIDENCE

There are six general categories of evidence which indicate the most basic and general mechanics of Mogollon and post-Mogollon development. The focus here is upon the Mimbres data because of the more detailed information from excavation, but generalized data from the literature of Southwestern archeology are also used where appropriate.

RAINFALL AND TREE-RING WIDTH

Hevly's general chart reconstructing mean tree-ring widths is reproduced in simplified form in Martin and Plog (1973:52). This chart (reproduced below) is for the Little Colorado area — not in, but adjacent to the western portion of this study area.

(after Hevly, in Martin and Plog 1973)

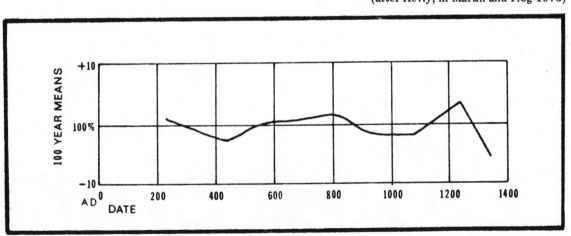

TREE-RING INDEX

The point of this chart is that relative quantity and seasonality of rainfall can be inferred from it. Many scholars have felt that the general character of such a reconstruction offers only limited utility in climatic and subsistence reconstruction. In spite of the risks, we have come to put great stock in the general patterns indicated (we started this project opposed), with this proviso: highs (above the mean but bottom of chart) represent *both* increased moisture and winter dominant moisture, while lows show decreased moisture and summer rainfall relative to the previous 100 year mean (Martin and Plog 1973:51:Table 5).

You will notice that the tree-ring mean width is crossed at roughly A.D. 300, again at A.D. 550-570, again at approximately A.D. 875, at A.D. 1125 and about A.D. 1280. There is confusion in Martin and Plog between Hevly's table on page 51 and the chart on page 52. On page 51 the A.D. 200-400 period is characterized by declining moisture as the tree-ring width falls below the mean (*left* in Martin and Plog's terms) while in the A.D. 1100-1300 period moisture is also said to decrease while the mean tree-ring width is going the opposite direction. Confusion aside, focus on these observations. The mean is crossed at the above dates. The peaks in one direction (below the mean as drawn and indicated in Martin and Plog's text, p. 52, but labeled +10 on chart) come at roughly A.D. 450 in the A.D. 300-550 period and A.D. 1000-1100 in the A.D. 875-1125 period. In the other direction, the peaks come at roughly A.D. 850 in the A.D. 550-845 period and about A.D. 1240 in the A.D. 1125-1280 period. For the moment all we are required to consider is the developmental similarities and difference between each of the two time periods above and below the mean. One also needs to bear in mind that the mountain areas will have considerably more moisture at a given time period and that rainfall fluctuations peaked between A.D. 950-1000 (Cordell 1979:70).

PHASES. The best dates for the various Mimbres phases will be reviewed here to show their fit to the tree-ring width chart. Anasazi temporal phases will be noted for contrast. Ceramic sequence is also noted. The cross-datings are, of course, approximations.

A. Early Pithouse A.D. 250 to 550, Alma Plainwares, high site setting. Anasazi-Very Late Basketmaker (II) and Early Basketmaker III.

Tree-ring width — this phase falls precisely between the first two points where the mean is crossed. The intervening period is characterized by a low in rainfall about A.D. 400 and allegedly biseasonal rainfall patterning.

B. Georgetown A.D. 550 to 650 (perhaps A.D. 700), San Francisco Redwares; site setting lower on river benches. Anasazi-Basketmaker III (roughly A.D. 500-700 -- too close to differentiate overlaps with local phases in the San Juan Basin).

This period falls in the first upswing (gradual) in tree-ring width. We view this as a period of slightly increasing rainfall and an increasing shift to winter season rainfall (Hevly argues biseasonal moisture).

C. San Francisco Phase A.D. 650-850; Mogollon R/B; San Lorenzo R/B; Three Circle R/W (Early); *in situ* site development.
*Anasazi—P-I (roughly A.D. 700-900; too close to differentiate)

*Here the major difference is the shift to surface (jacal) rooms in the Anasazi area *in lower elevational settings*. Cordell (1979:10) and Hayes (1975) both suggest that the high density of P-I sites was near perennial streams on the northern periphery of the San Juan Basin; quite like San Francisco and Three Circle Phase settings in the Mimbres area.

This period terminates with a peak in tree-ring width above the mean, just as it begins its sharp downturn to cross the mean again at about A.D. 870. We see a peak in rainfall and dominance in the winter season of a bimodal rainfall distribution.

D. Three Circle A.D. 850-975 (ignores Mangus or Transitional — the last actual tree-ring date of A.D. 964 is problematic); Three Circle R/W; Boldface B/W (Mangus); Transitional B/W; sites extend into secondary drainages.

If you accept Mangus as small outlying sites and note the farflung distribution of Three Circle and Boldface ceramics, then a certain dispersal phenomenon is arguable. In addition, roughly A.D. 900 is the period when pithouse occupation rapidly increases to the east in the Jornada area in lower elevations than the Mogollon heartland, but above the basin floors.

Anasazi—P-II Early (Hayes 1975) A.D. 850 (Red Mesa B/W) or 900 — ca. A.D. 975. Late: A.D. 975-1050 or A.D. 1100. This is interesting. The Early P-II is characterized by maximum geographic dispersal (Lipe 1978); a variety of pottery types, etc. The Late P-II, however, is viewed by Rohn (1977) as poorly understood at Mesa Verde (high-wetter setting), and possibly associated with population loss in some areas (Hayes 1975). There are shifts in settlement pattern toward the end of this period and summer rainfall is thought to have been good (Schoenwetter and Eddy 1964). We are safe in assuming some parallel between the poorly understood *Late P-II* at Mesa Verde and the controversial earlier *Mangus* phase and (contemporaneous?) Animas phase in southwestern New Mexico.

E. Mimbres: A.D. 975-1125 or 1150 (first tree-ring dates about A.D. 1050). Mimbres B/W; *in situ* development plus more extensive movement into secondary locations. Large villages are numerous.

Anasazi—Late P-II (A.D. 975-1050) plus Early P-III (A.D. 1050-1150 or 1175)[1]. The last Chacoan construction dates are about A.D. 1125, as in the Mimbres. The Late P-II is the large town phenomenon, culminating in the Chacoan outlier network.

One problem, as we have suggested earlier, lies in the existence of a gap in tree-ring dates between Three Circle and Mimbres Classic (A.D. 900-1050), and in the fact that early to late P-II in the San Juan Basin occupies just this period. We suspect a scarcity of tree-ring and/or C-14 dates from excavation in the San Juan Basin at about A.D. 1000 as well. Someone may care to review the San Juan excavation data in detail to compare this. Just as most now realize that there has been temporal and classificatory confusion between Hosta Butte (small) and Bonito Phase sites in the Anasazi area, we now suspect confusion in the Mimbres between Mangus and Mimbres phase sites. The difference, of course, with Mangus sites is that the *scale* of development was more modest, hence the small sites have not attracted much attention and some question the very existence of the phase.

F. Animas A.D. 1175-1375 (perhaps A.D. 1400); Casas Grandes Polychromes. Sites are fairly large, on good agricultural soil; population aggregation in relatively few sites in lower desertic settings is presumed. The economic network (and, some argue, population) of the preceding cultural continuum is replaced.

Anasazi—Late P-III; about A.D. 1175-1325. This period is characterized by McElmo and Mesa Verde B/W ceramics and intense upland development in the Rio Grande (Chapter III). There is at least a partial disruption of previous economic and architectural patterns. The major site clusters are in the Chuska Mountains, Mesa Verde, and Pajarito Plateau. The generally dry settings of the Animas sites confuse us no end on a comparative basis.

Importantly, in both areas, population declines; some site settings become defensive; some die in unfortunate fashion and the locus of population shifts. In the San Juan Basin, the

---

[1] It is here that one of the great flaws in application of the Pecos Classification is nearly insurmountable. Some investigators use it as a temporal horizon, others as architectural/ceramic. Hence, many Chacoan sites are classified Late P-II in the SJBRUS file, while others are P-II/P-III transitional, and yet others are Early P-III.

first shift is to the north and east (Mesa Verde, the Gallina and the Upper Rio Grande). In the Mimbres, population centers shift south (Hidalgo County, Animas and Casas Grandes) and east (Jornada transition to pueblo -- i.e. above ground architecture -- period is allegedly about A.D. 1100, and the dense settlement is in El Paso Phase sites).

This period is one of generally increasing rainfall, which peaks around A.D. 1250, then declines noticeably during the Great Drought of A.D. 1276-1299, and finally turns upward about A.D. 1300-1350. Again, there is a bimodal rainfall pattern; and, we argue, winter dominance about A.D. 1200-1250.

POPULATION

Population is a much more speculative venture. Nonetheless, the following general patterns can be argued.

Mimbres -- A.D. 200-550, increasing; A.D. 500 or 550-700, decreasing (Martin and Plog 1973) or static, or dispersed (this volume); A.D. 700-900, increasing, A.D. 900-1100, increasing dramatically; A.D. 1100-1300, decreasing. Construction peaks for the Three Circle and Mimbres phase sites come at A.D. 850 and 1050, respectively.

Anasazi--Chaco (Martin and Plog 1973:320). Other published data indicate that population began growing rapidly at A.D. 900, peaked at A.D. 1000, began declining immediately, and that abandonment followed at A.D. 1150.

In comparative terms, we would argue that dramatic Mimbres population increase begins about A.D. 875, peaks about A.D. 1050, and declines at A.D. 1080, and that Mimbres Valley abandonment comes at A.D. 1150 or before. This is like the presumed Chaco population curves, and, at most, is but 25 years off center. In contrast, we argue that Sierra Blanca/Jornada population increase started at least a century later and peaked about A.D. 1250, Animas/El Paso abandonment coming about A.D. 1350. Population-wise there seem to be two basic schedules. An early peak, early abandonment phenomenon includes the Chaco, Houck and Mimbres areas as well as portions of the Little Colorado.

There is also a late peak, late abandonment phenomenon, which includes Mesa Verde, Tsegi, Canyon de Chelly, White Mountain, the Pajarito Plateau, Sierra Blanca, the Gila Forest, Cebolleta Mesa, the Gallina, and portions of the upper Little Colorado. These all peak at A.D. 1200-1250, and are abandoned about A.D. 1325. The Jornada's (*not* Eastern Jornada, discussed in next chapter) El Paso phases and the Animas belong here. Again, regarding the tree-ring chart, the first population peak comes in the middle of the decreased, summer dominant moisture regime at roughly A.D. 1000 to 1050 (Cordell 1979:7) which follows a period at A.D. 950-1000 of dramatically oscillating rainfall levels. We argued in earlier chapters (especially Chapter II) that such instability triggered or accentuated the demographic power drive. Here you have it, right on schedule, with the early peak (P-II equivalent) population systems. The next period of increased standard deviation in rainfall comes in *some* areas (mostly uplands) at A.D. 1150-1199 (Cordell 1979:7), followed by the A.D. 1200-1250 population peaks. The less demographically powerful *schedule two* (P-III) systems, being geographically distinct from the first, may have involved population movements as well.

Clearly some areas, such as the Hopi and Rio Grande, represent migrations as well as natural population increase. We believe this to be the case as well in the Sierra Blanca region and in many other areas. Some of these represented final adaptations and achieved survivor status (into the historic), as Martin and Plog (1973) have correctly pointed out. The influence of migrations cannot be discounted for some *schedule two* (generally P-III to *early* P-IV) systems, but these are at best *half* an explanation. On the other hand, we do largely discount migration for *schedule one* population peaks (P-II systems, temporally) and argue early *in situ* natural population increase to be the norm for these.

Population declines are, in some sense, even more problematic, for we don't really know how people reacted to a failed subsistence system. We generally assume them to have died or migrated, with perhaps the sorriest of the lot lingering on in the shadows of their former grandeur. On the other hand, we rarely suppose that they might have behaved in such a way that we could not identify what happened even if we excavated every square inch of New Mexico. In the case of the alleged A.D. 500-700 population decline in the Pine Lawn area, we suspect that all is not as it appears, for many plainware ceramic scatters are found in desert settings. Clearly in the Mimbres, there are very few Georgetown Phase sites of this period, but population is definitely increasing in early Basketmaker III times to the north. What there is, rather, is some evidence for declining agricultural dependence and some scarcity in sites — particularly in the A.D. 550-600 period. Let us turn momentarily to burials, which add an important dimension.

BURIALS

The most general of trends will be mentioned here. We fervently hope someone will, one day, be encouraged to draw all the burial data together for each developmental period in New Mexico. We think such a sample would exceed 5,000 burials in all and be quite worthwhile.

In the Mimbres region, the frequency of burials changes substantially over time. There is poor control over the dating of many burials, but the trend is clear. Early pithouse burials average 1.8 per room, with variation between sites of the period at a ratio of 1:2 (sites having the *most* burials per room average almost exactly double the least — see Early Pithouse section). Georgetown burial data is scarce, but may be partially included in that for the Early Pithouse period (the dating problem). San Francisco Phase burials have been described as liberally scattered in sites. We don't have a figure, but presume it to be slightly higher than Early Pithouse to earn the description. Three Circle Phase burials are more numerous yet, averaging above two per room (we would guess perhaps 2.5 to 3 in the larger sites, but cannot arrive at a firm figure of the number of rooms from which Anyon's (1979) sample of burials (N85) was derived.

In the Classic Mimbres, the large sites average about 5.5 burials per room, while the smallest in outlying districts average just under one per room. We note that the ratio of human remains in the small classic sites to the large is in roughly the same proportion — 1 to 5.5 as the figures we calculated for the site output per year per total square miles surveyed for the Classic period.

Comparing the Early Pithouse and Classic Mimbres periods, we note that the variance in human remains has increased from 1:2 to 1:5.5, whereas, comparing the overall average of the two time periods, the Mimbres Classic has only doubled the average number of corpses per room. Comparing site size (rooms) to burials is also interesting. Early Pithouse sites average 7-10 rooms, while large Classic (N500) Mimbres sites average 19.6 (LeBlanc 1979). That is, between the Early Pithouse and Classic periods, when one doubles mean site size, one also doubles the burials in direct proportion. During the Classic Mimbres, however, sites in the Mimbres district average 19.6 rooms while, in the uppermost Mimbres and Gila River drainages, mean site size is 9.2 rooms. That is, when one doubles mean site size from one subregion to the next in that time period, the number of burials increases not by a factor of 2, but by a factor of 5.5.

Thus our tentative argument is that, site size being equal, mortality during the Classic Mimbres increases by several fold in large sites while in small sites it remains like that of the Early Pithouse period. Until someone is able to argue from age/sex data of skeletal remains or obtain dates from excavation that indicate twice the generational depth (length of occupation) is the norm for Classic rooms on large Mimbres sites, we will stick with the argument of proportionally higher mortality in the larger Mimbres sites.

During the Animas Phase, burials per room decline markedly to between one-half and (nearly) two per room, depending on the site. The sample of excavated Animas sites and the partial excavations preclude a meaningful average, but it appears to have dropped to the same, or less, than the Early Pithouse period.

The situation is quite different in the Chaco Anasazi region, for burials become quite scarce between A.D. 900 and 1300 (Cordell 1979). They are certainly not scarce later at Kidder's (1958) excavation of Pecos. That is, they are scarce from Early P-II to P-III, during the Anasazi florescence and shift into the Upper Rio Grande. Unless smaller Hosta Butte Phase sites are excavated and begin turning up remarkable numbers of burials, there is an argument for an immense distinction between the two systems. Mimbres burials go up during the Classic period, while Chaco Anasazi go down.

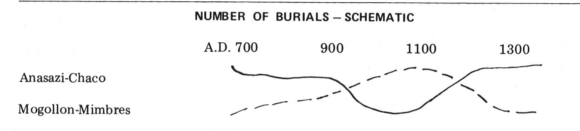

NUMBER OF BURIALS — SCHEMATIC

A.D. 700   900   1100   1300

Anasazi-Chaco

Mogollon-Mimbres

Even if many burials are eventually excavated at Hosta Butte sites, we would still have an important distinction between the two systems. Mimbres burials would *decrease* in number per site as sites got smaller, while Anasazi burials would *increase* as sites got smaller.

One can either argue that the more complex system was generally better able to protect its population or that large sites were a demographically/economically successful adaptation for the Anasazi, but not the Mimbres (What might this have to do with irrigation?). If the latter is true, Mimbres burial data should yield skeletal evidence for increasingly good nutrition and robustness as site size *decreases*. The reverse would be true for the Anasazi, if future excavation indicated that biological advantage was not generalized in both large and small sites. *Status* burials in the *largest* Mimbres sites would then be osteologically more like the *ordinary* burials from the *smallest* Mimbres sites than like the remains of nonstatus burials from the same large sites. A partial solution to these questions undoubtedly already lies unsifted (or perhaps merely untouted) in the general literature. We will return to this paradox in the conclusion which follows shortly.

ARCHITECTURE

Architectural data and pithouse/room size has often been compiled in published literature to aid in interpreting archeological phases. Few generalized statements have been made, for only one clear pattern has emerged to most eyes. That is, as Mogollon development progressed through time, pithouse (finally, room size) decreased through time. This has generally been suggested as indicating an increased tendency for nuclear family formation — fine. We hope to convince the reader, however, that the data hint at much more. We have taken the following data from a variety of sources and added some from recent excavations. For these reasons do not expect it to match Bullard's (1962) or anyone else's precisely. Again, it is the general pattern that matters. In addition, gross calculations of variance in large to small rooms are offered. Again, these are not formal coefficients of variation (that should be done, and has been in several cases, yet we leave that task to others); they are just a ratio of small to large room size.

Table V:6

MOGOLLON PITHOUSE AND ROOM SIZE AND RATIOS OF VARIATION

Comparative Anasazi Diversity Index from Martin and Plog (1973)

	Mogollon Phase	Dates	Size (m^2)	Variation as a Ratio
	1. San Pedro Cochise (Hay Hollow)	prior to A.D. 250	7-8	Substantial (data sketchy)
	2. Pine Lawn (Early Pithouse) (Late Pine Lawn 18 m^2)	A.D. 250-550	25	Less substantial (data sketchy)
ANASAZI INDEX	3. Georgetown	A.D. 550-650	14.3	1:2
A.D. 650-850,14.5	4. San Francisco	A.D. 650-850	15.8	1:1.72
A.D. 850-1050,22.3	5. Three Circle	A.D. 850-1000	13	1:2.92
A.D. 1050-1200,17.6	6. Mimbres Classic	A.D. 1000-1150	12	1:4<
A.D. 1200-1250,18.6	7. Animas	A.D. 1175-1375	17	1:2 (data sketchy)
	8. Salado	A.D. 1375-1450?	21	1:1.25

You will notice from the table that room size and variation are consistently patterned. As room size increases, variation in size decreases. There are several episodes of increasing and decreasing room size. Room size increases from terminal Archaic (San Pedro Cochise) to Pine Lawn, then decreases again before alleged episodes of abandonment or population loss in that area. Room size increases through the Georgetown and San Francisco phases and then decreases again in the Three Circle and Mimbres. It reaches a low before alleged abandonment by Mimbres populations. Thereafter, room size increases to the terminal Salado.

Below is Hevly's tree-ring chart and 100 year mean. Below it are plotted the preceding data from Table V.6.

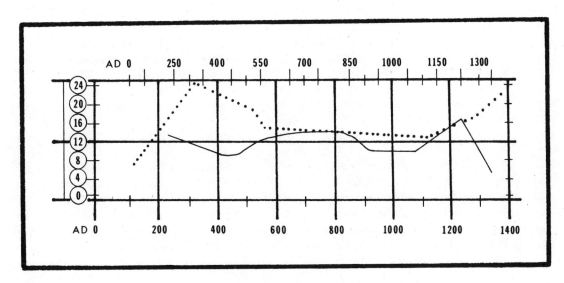

247

The directions of change are strikingly like the trends noted in Hevly's chart. Now, our argument is not that tree-ring width and room size vary directly, or that the relationship is causal, but that the general patterns of change are similar. There is apparently lag time between the disrupted climatic period from A.D. 300 and 550 and response in room size. Also, room size appears to increase through the alleged 1276-1299 *Great Drought* decline. However, we don't yet know much about the Animas-Salado transition; they may not represent the cultural continuum LeBlanc tentatively supposes. The points are these. The high points of room size (about A.D. 250-300; about A.D. 800-850, about A.D. 1250; and A.D. 1400-1450) all fall in the high peaks on Hevly's chart. The lows in room size (just prior to BC/A.D.; A.D. 550 and A.D. 900-1100) come in periods of decreased tree-ring width and, arguably, moisture, which is summer dominant (Martin and Plog 1973:51).

If we look at the trends of rising and falling room size in light of other general archeological data, yet additional patterns emerge.

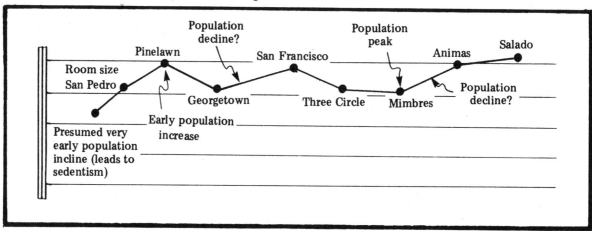

Though there are many chronological problems with the placement of early phases, and demographic data are largely impressionistic, it is possible to argue that population increases (and size variance with it) as room size decreases. Population is either static or in decline as room size swings upward and room size variance decreases. In each complete cycle of room size downswing, followed by increasing room size, basic cultural adaptations are restructured. That is, the fundamental cultural *phase* changes take place between the peaks of large room size.

Thus, we find altered site placement, changes in degree of agricultural dependence and change in ceramic styles as one moves from the Pine Lawn to the San Francisco phases. Sites are scarce in the Georgetown Phase, and difficult to identify and characterize. The same type of phenomenon recurs as one swings from San Francisco to Three Circle to Mimbres and Animas. In each case, the downswing in room size is entered with recognizable cultural continuity, but ceramic sequences change notably (and speed up). There are changes in site size and placement (Three Circle sites average 24 pithouses in the Mimbres while Classic Mimbres sites average only 19.6 rooms — a *decrease* in site size). Finally, cultural continuity is said to be disrupted with the advent of the Animas, when room size again increases. Recall that though Classic Mimbres site size may decrease, the number of sites is remarkable when compared to all but the Three Circle period in the Mimbres.

The cultural diversity index summarized by Martin and Plog (1973:210-212) and explained therein is presented in Table V.6 for contrast. For the Anasazi, maximum experimentation, complexity, and adaptability came between A.D. 850 and 1050, the terminal period (about A.D. 1200) becoming quite homogeneous (1973:213). The Anasazi index is at its peak while room size is smallest and variance in size is greatest in the Classic Mimbres period. Between A.D. 650-850, Anasazi experimentation, etc. (environmental) was quite low. This comes during the peak room size during sequential Mogollon *in situ* development, one pithouse site being invariably superimposed upon the other. In short, we argue that the dynamic curves of the two systems (Chaco and Mogollon-Mimbres) are nearly identical. This only adds to the impression of similarity in development we suggested in the previous comparison between Mimbres and Anasazi archeological phases. We argue that decreasing room size and increasing variance in size do indirectly reflect population dynamics and rates of cultural change. That is, the large room-low variance pattern is related to the efficiency phase and the small room-high variance pattern is related to the power phase of a cultural system (the data from the Upper Rio Grande presented in Chapter III do not refute this interpretation for the P-III—P-IV shift in that region, either).

The gross nature of architectural change follows a pattern like that outlined for Paleo-Indian and Early Archaic projectile points in Chapter III. That is, size increases over time, divergence between the large and small becomes pronounced, and there is then rapid replacement by the small. In other words, the functional differences between the large and small become great; that is, specialization takes hold. The rhythm, or pattern, then repeats itself through time, though succession or replacement by other systems may be involved.

In the Mimbres sequence, room size first increases (San Francisco). There is then increasing specialization between small rooms (residential) and large rooms (ceremonial) in the Three Circle Phase. The large rooms (ceremonial) become rarer still compared to small in the Classic Mimbres. The sequence terminates with the Animas/Salado, and though rooms are again somewhat larger, the specialized, overly-large rooms are gone entirely. This type of pattern appears over and over again in technological change. For instance, in our society, automobiles show increasing size, peaking in the late 1960's. Small, specialized European cars begin to take hold at that time. Until several years ago American manufacturers domestically produced cars of greatly different size/weight characteristics. We are now going through a period when small cars are quickly replacing the large and the largest that remain have been trimmed in size from their predecessors.

At a recent symposium, we commented on this pattern in architecture and Mr. Albert Schroeder of Santa Fe posed an interesting question in response. He pointed out that as Navajo family size grew, a family merely built successively larger hogans to accommodate the growing number of children. We are grateful to Mr. Schroeder for the observation, for it allows us to illustrate this pattern.

In the tables and schematic which follow, section 2 shows the hypothetical construction of hogans through an 88 year period starting with year 0 — the founding family's initial hogan. The assumptions are these: the woman's reproductive span is 20 years. An average of 8 children are produced per couple at the rate of 2.5 years between births. Part 6 shows the order of appearance of the three sizes of hogans. The first cohort of children establishes hogans after 22 years of elapsed time, and so on. The ages at producing the first child are shown for the first two cohorts (1-4 and 4-8). In reality, such events will not all happen at the same time. This is not a demographic model, however. It is merely intended to illustrate hypothetical construction events.

You will notice that construction events start off slowly (10 year spacing), followed by a two-year burst in construction at elapsed years 20-22. Then follow 8 years of no construction, then the *2-8* pattern again repeats itself. At years 40-42-44, the pattern of elapsed time between construction episodes is 2-2, followed by a 6 year elapsed period. Then there are 2 years, 2 years and *again 8* (year 54-62 elapse). The point is this: the cycles of construction *speed* up and *slow* down. They are like power peaks. Average hogan size for each generation (denoted by ↓) is summarized in Table V:7.

The point here is that the short construction generations (6 years) produced hogans of smaller average size than the longer (12 years) construction generations. In the schematic (No. 5) it will be seen that hogan size increased to maximum (here size key 3) until an episode of constructing small hogans occurs. Size increased again at year 32, but does not change in year 40, then peaks in year 42 and is again succeeded by more numerous small hogans in year 44. In section 5 it will be seen that large hogans (size 3's) *are always followed* in time by small hogans (size 1's). In reality, nothing in the actual world, and certainly not in the archeological record, follows such a rigid schedule. Nonetheless, this illustrates the tendency for small size to succeed large and for average hogan size to decrease, not merely as a function of the number of hogans created by each generation, but also in the shorter generational spans.

In other words, the short generational pattern, spanning 6 years, produces only large and small hogans. That is, the coefficient of variation in size would be greater than in the longer generational spans, as we have argued. Again, the general pattern is small to large, followed again by the small hogans. Long *generations* are followed by shorter episodes characterized by higher coefficient of variation in size and lower average hogan size. The short construction generation, high variation and low room size form a constellation of characteristics that constitute a power phase.

If one looks at the Mimbres tree-ring dates, it will be seen that construction dates appear to cluster a few years apart. These clusters should be identified formally (the r, v and vv, etc. being treated as separate series to see how they correlate). The dates from rooms of larger.than average size (assumes increasing family size is being accomodated) from those of smaller average size (assumes episodes of new family foundings) should be separated to create two series. Where the dates of *smaller* rooms cluster, they should show a lower coefficient of variation in size than for the entire series of small rooms. These would belong to a power peak, the specialized subset of small rooms having been analyzed separately.

By such a method, comparing the spacing of clusters and separating series into large and small rooms, we think the actual episodes of age cohort room construction (at founding of nuclear family) could be reconstructed by a good mathematician/programmer for the Classic Mimbres sites.

The hogan model, though completely hypothetical, suggests that the tightest date clusters for all Mimbres rooms (large not separated from small) might have the greatest overall coefficient of variation in room size. These clusters of dates might vary in length of time between them -- the length of time oscillating between longer-shorter, longer, etc. Using only the 11r dates from different rooms LeBlanc has published for one site, these can be broken into five separate temporal series: 5-11-10.5 and 10 years apart. Is this accidental or somehow like the 6 year-12 year alternating generational spans of the hypothetical hogan model? We need to know.

Figure V.13
SCHEMATIC
A MODEL OF HOGAN REPLACEMENT

1. Hogan output per generation:
   39 hogans for 44 years = roughly 1.13 hogans per year.
   174 hogans for 66 years = roughly 2.5 hogans per year.
   448 hogans for 88 years = roughly 5 hogans per year.

2. Construction Patterns:

```
                          5                 8                      24
Years                                                          42
Elapsed 0       10        20↓       22      30      32      40      ↓      44
  N1    —10— N1  —10— N1   —2—  N4  —8— N4  —2— N4  —8— N4  —2— N4  —2— N16
 Size 1      Size 2   Size 3  1-4      4-8     1-4     5-8     1-4      1-4
                        x    Size 1  Size 1  Size 2  Size 2  Size 3   and
                                                              x       2-6
                                                                    Size 1

        50↓       52        54        62        64 ↓    66      72↓     74        76
  —6—  N4  —2— N16  —2— N16  —8— N16  —2— N16  —2— N64 —6— N16 —2— N64 —2— N64
        5-8     5-8 2nd G 1-4 2nd G 5-8 2nd G 1-4  2nd G 1-4 3rd G 5-8 2nd G 5-8 3rd G 1-4
       Size 3  Size 1   Size 2   Size 2   Size 3   Size 1   Size 3   Size 1   (3rd G)
         x                                   x                  x             Size 2

        84        86 ↓      88
  —8—  N64  —2— N64  —2— N25  —6—
        5-8     3rd G 1-4 3rd G 1-4 4th G
       Size 2  Size 3   Size 1
         x
```

Key: Years elapsed in series: 30 - top data line
       Years elapsed to next construction event: —2—
       No. hogans constructed: N4
       Denotes generation: (G)
       Size of hogan: Size 1, small; Size 2, medium; Size 3, large.
       ↓ denotes end of a generation's construction activities.
       x denotes end of childbearing for a given generation's females and terminal occupation in a large hogan.

3. Size 1 = 1 - family founded
   Size 2 = 2 - family grows to 4
   Size 3 = 3 - family grows to 8 — Elapsed time = 20 years or 1 child per 2.5 years

4. Schematic of first few years:

```
Elapsed Year   0        10       20      22       30       32       40      42   44
Hogans        ①        ②        ③      ④16     ⑧16      ④       ⑧      ④  0000
                                         ③18     ⑦18      ③       ⑦      ③  0000
                                         ②20     ⑥20      ②       ⑥      ②  0000
                                         ①22     ⑤22      ①       ⑤      ①  0000
                              Age of children     11    (Size 2) (Size 2) (Size 3) x⁵
                              founding families                            x children
                              1 - designated child 1-8                      2nd Gener.
```

5. Order of appearance: Hogan Size by Generation.

```
                                                      not shown above
   1 2 3↓1 1 2 2 3↓1 3↓1 2 2 3↓1 3↓1 2 2 3↓1  [3↓ 1223 ↓ 13 ↓]

      x       x   x     x   x     x
   20   20 yrs. 6 yrs 12 yrs 6 yrs  12 yrs  6 yrs 12 yrs 6 yrs.
          ⌞ length of construction generation ⌟
```

Table V:7
AVERAGE HOGAN SIZE AND GENERATION SPAN

*Size Factor/N Hogans	Span	Average Size	Elapsed Years
6/3 hogans]	20 yrs.	2.0	20
39/21 hogans]	20 yrs.	1.9	42
28/20 hogans]	6 yrs.	1.4	50
128/64 hogans]	12 yrs.	2.0	64
112/80 hogans]	6 yrs.	1.4	72
512/256 hogans]	12 yrs.	2.0	— year 86
448/320 hogans]	6 yrs.	1.4	— year 94
2048/1024 hogans]	12 yrs.	2.0	— year 110-116
1792/1280 hogans]	6 yrs.	1.4	

*Sum of all hogan size factors (1, 2 or 3) for N hogans constructed

SUBSISTENCE

It is important to note (*vis a vis* Hevly's tree-ring widths) that there are at least two episodes in which scholars suspect reduced dependence on agriculture. These are between the Pine Lawn and Georgetown Phases and during the late Classic Mimbres Phase. During the Mimbres there is a definite shift to broader spectrum foodstuffs and smaller species. In an earlier chapter we characterized this as a power niche. At the end of *both* the Pine Lawn and Mimbres periods there is evidence for decreasing dependence on corn. These episodes both occur during declining rainfall (somewhat summer dominant the first time and heavily summer dominant the second). Also, in both the Georgetown and Animas phases (which dated to the tree-ring width upswings on Hevly's chart) riparian tree species are used in construction. Shifts in dependence on different varieties of corn will not be discussed here, but in the conclusion of the chapter.

Throughout this section, we have been emphasizing patterns in the data and comparisons between Mimbres phases and major cultural traditions. These several lines of comparative evidence are drawn together to create the sketch which follows.

THE MIMBRES: A CONCLUDING SKETCH

Clearly, the Mogollon developmental sequence in the Mimbres areas closely follows that of the San Juan, or Chaco, Anasazi.

From well-dated initial pithouse sites (ceramic) in both areas to the stunning similarity of terminal construction dates for the Classic sites in the Chaco and the Mimbres areas, we are offered a picture of symmetrical timing in archeological developments. While the Anasazi sequence shifted to predominantly above ground architecture (in basin settings) before the Mimbres, we have suggested that such a shift may have been associated with village density and the need for above ground storage facilities. This architectural factor and the later (how much later is uncertain) appearance of black-on-white series pottery in the Mimbres are really the only evidence for supposing Anasazi (or some other) influence in the ultimate organizational complexity of the Mimbres. Since earlier surface architecture (thought to be storage rooms) has been largely ignored in the Mimbres, more field investigation may resolve the problem.

POWER PHASE

The Mimbres Classic (and secondarily the Three Circle phase) are the power phases of the Mogollon-Mimbres sequence. Several lines of evidence suggest that this was so. First, these are the periods of greatest construction, Classic Mimbres sites having an averaged output of 5.5 sites per year in surveyed acreages and accounting for 43% of all recorded sites (identical to Chaco Classic site data). Room size is at its smallest, variance in size between the largest and smallest sites and between large and small rooms is greatest during the Classic period. Ceramic development is very rapid just prior to the Classic Mimbres. There is expansion of Mimbres sites into secondary settings and wide distribution of Mimbres ceramics. Once the Classic Mimbres was well-developed, however, there was little continued transition in ceramics and architecture.

Changes in subsistence, increased burials and rapidly changing burial practices in the Three Circle Phase all indicate rapid development from A.D. 900 to about 1050. It is in the larger, mortality-prone late Three Circle phase sites with subfloor burials that massive Classic Mimbres construction later takes place (see discussion of Anyon's observation). Again, the pattern of mortality (stress) actuates the power drive! Exotic trade goods become common and status differentiation increases. The picture is one of rapid change and rapid exhaustion of resources (food and fuel). The system peaks in complexity, and expands outward almost simultaneously.

THE EFFICIENCY PHASES

Development during the Georgetown and San Francisco phases is primarily *in situ*. The size of pithouses peaks, ceramic development is relatively slow, burials are more modest in numbers and burial practices change slowly. Large game is hunted, and subsistence is similar throughout each phase. Kivas do increasingly differentiate from other structures, but not nearly so notably as in the Three Circle Phase. Population growth is slow. The picture is one of slow or slight development and substantial conservatism. There are few exotic goods and little evidence in burials for notable status differentiation. The late Animas phase may also be efficiency dominated, but too few data are available.

ENVIRONMENTAL FACTORS: ADAPTIVE MECHANICS

Hevly's tree-ring chart is interesting because the general trends of development can be plotted so easily against it. We know it is only an indirect indicator of rainfall and its seasonality, and we know that too much attention to simple relationships is risky. Nonetheless, one object of this volume is to outline speculations that will stimulate interest and generate topics for future research.

We view development from the Georgetown to earliest Three Circle (A.D. 550 or 600-850) as a response to fairly consistent environmental conditions — gradually increasing rainfall and biseasonal patterning, increasingly winter dominant to about A.D. 800 or so. At about A.D. 870, rainfall began decreasing and the seasonal distribution shifted somewhat. By A.D. 950-999 average rainfall began oscillating wildly. We argue (Chapter II) that increasing stress set off the need to compensate adaptively and that it was enhanced, if not induced, by this fluctuating rainfall. This, we argue, induced increased childbearing to offset infant mortality. Coupled with increasing environmental and technological experimentation, the old adaptive structure of Mogollon-Mimbres society began to repattern.

At about A.D. 950, fluctuating rainfall was sometimes summer dominant and sometimes winter dominant. We argue that this also induced dispersal as a response, but dispersal we think was of two kinds. Unable to determine which agricultural conditions would prevail, some dispersed into lowland, more desertic environments. while others moved upland into the upper reaches of secondary drainages. We speculate that the vast majority of these sites were small. Many in desertic areas would likely have been constructed of ephemeral materials and/or easily eroded puddled adobe. Due to disruption from the more central economic network, painted wares would be relatively scarce, often absent. We think it possible that many of the extensive sherd scatters in the desert survive from this pattern — many architectural features having eroded or gone unnoticed.

Simultaneously, those moving into the uplands were trying to maintain the older adaptation, perhaps increasing elevation to maximize the available rainfall. We argue this to be the basic nature of the Mangus Phase, Boldface Black-on-white sites.

Ultimately, however, the summer dominant drought-prone rainfall pattern prevailed. This fact, and tentative ceramic data, permit us our conclusions. We expect that the first response under such circumstances would be for most (not all) to disperse upward and outward to maintain the old adaptive pattern. The majority of these sites should contain the earlier ceramics — Three Circle, Boldface and Transitional Black-on-white. The incidence of Mimbres Black-on-white on such sites should be disproportionately low, often absent. The desert ceramic scatters mentioned in the literature tend to support this pattern, for Boldface Black-on-white appears nearer to the Mimbres heartland. The majority of the most distant desert ceramic scatters, however, should be slightly later in time. Therefore, Mimbres Classic Black-on-white should be disproportionately high compared to other Mimbres painted wares on the majority of these. In some cases the Boldface will be absent altogether, as it often is in the northern Tularosa Basin.

Thus, in some old Mogollon population nodes, this pattern of oscillating dispersal started about A.D. 870 and alternated between the forest and desert settings during the mid to late 900's, terminating with preponderant desert and lower drainage dispersal by 1050-1100. On the ground, this means some small sites in high, forested settings will terminate the ceramic sequence, for instance, with Three Circle Red-on-white. Others will contain no (or little) Three Circle, but contain substantial Mangus (Boldface), though little Classic Mimbres (or none). In some situations, previous pithouse occupations may give the appearnce of continuous ceramic development (Georgetown-Mimbres) while many outlying small sites, not far distant, will show discontinuous ceramics — some leaning to the early sequence, some to the later. Most of these occupations will be very short (20-40 years?).

As a generality, phase dates in the northwesternmost portion of the Mimbres study unit may average a bit earlier than in the southeastern portions. Since the variance in rainfall also increases with altitude, the need for economic restructuring would be greatest and most immediate in the higher elevations. During the peak of this upland dispersal phenomenon, about A.D. 925-975, there may be a 20-40 year lag or gradient in ceramic development which is clinal northwest to southeast. These gradients are both altitudinal in nature. Precisely the *reverse* seems to have occurred with changing styles and depths of pithouse construction, shallower pithouses having occurred first in the Mimbres Valley and later in the Reserve district. Thus, without absolute dates, phase transformations are contested by different investigators, who place different emphasis on the diagnostics of architecture as opposed to ceramics.

In view of the alleged more general 100-200 year time lag in some developments between the Mimbres Valley and the Tularosa Basin, it also seems reasonable to propose a similar gradient, from the New Mexico-Arizona state line to the Mimbres Valley, of perhaps 50-100 years (more similar geography) throughout the entire cultural sequence from the Pine Lawn phase onward. Again, phase transformations, in essence, do not occur simultaneously in different altitudinal/ecological zones. This is an important feature of Mogollon, if not Southwestern, archeological development.

In short, we suggest that the dispersion started about A.D. 870-900, the greater tendency being to seek secondary upland settings, while a few upper desert locations were settled. Many of these latter were still shallow, rectangular pithouses. By A.D. 950-999 the oscillations in rainfall had created an intense need for greater economic integration over a wider region. Increased exotic goods and desirable (and valuable) ceramics resulted. Social organization likely came to be based more on economic alliances than on kinship. By A.D. 1000-1050, rainfall and its seasonality settled down (oscillations dampened). Dispersal into the lower riverine and desert settings predominated. By A.D. 1050-1100, older sites along major drainages expanded rapidly, as did newer sites along the primary watercourses in desert areas.

This, we suppose, was partly from *in situ* population increase and partly from reaggregation of those who had previously dispersed upward and outward, their adaptive response failing more often during the summer dominant regime. By A.D. 1050-1100 the agricultural adaptation to summer-dominant rainfall was well established.

In the central Mimbres and other major drainages, this adaptation was fragile. Population substantially overtaxed resources in the larger, older sites. Mortality was higher than in the small outlying sites. Though some undoubtedly moved in to replace those who died (as happened in plague-torn Europe during the A.D. 1340-80's), this again enhanced the aggregating tendency, and a few very modest irrigation systems appeared. The Mimbres, however, was never able to integrate the pockets of agricultural production over so broad an area as was the Chaco Anasazi. Organizationally, it was less able to prevent want in bad years in the larger sites — hence, under episodes of stress it was prone to dispersal. The Chaco Anasazi, for a time at least, was able to offer greater benefit by integration with its largest sites. Hence, at least for a time, it was more aggregation-prone under short-term episodes of stress. In other words, when subsistence crises occurred for a year or so in the San Juan Basin at A.D. 1050, one generally tried to get *into* a Chacoan town, while when crops failed in a Mimbres town, one generally *got out*. This we argue from the burial data in both areas. It implies, of course, the much higher organizational level for the Chaco Anasazi, which is also documentable in other ways.

If a MesoAmerican hand *was* involved in the peak organizational levels in both areas, it by comparison, failed its task in the Mimbres, for subsistence shifted back partly to scouring for small game and gathering during the terminal Classic. This does not prove or disprove such influence. Rather, it may be that the geography to the south and east of the San Juan Basin was not so advantageous to a vast interconnected system. Regional ecological diversity could be lower in the Mimbres district than in the San Juan Basin, when perimeters are included. Dr. Tainter's (1980) argument about the Chacoan economic sphere extending only far enough to include maximal ecological diversity is discussed in the previous chapter. His argument merits attention. Though not in final form, it is very pleasing in several respects. It may also be that the Mimbres population base was simply too small to generate the labor needed to run a Chacoan-type system. We do not yet know. We are not quite able to accept the MesoAmerican hand in the form in which it is often portrayed in the literature. Nor are we ready, in view of trade items, introduced varieties of corn and presumed ball court features, to close the door on it. If that hand was there, its greatest utility would have been in dealing (since Georgetown times) with the unprecedented situation of summer dominant, drought prone rainfall. We point out though, that the MesoAmerican planting calendar would have been useless unless changing patterns of seasonality in rainfall could be accomodated.

Finally, the episodes and nature of Mimbres dispersal into the several altitude zones is almost identical to the timing and sequence of occupation increase and development in the Tularosa Basin and adjacent areas. This implies actual population expansion into portions, at least, of the Jornada.

THE POSTSCRIPT

What happened to the Mimbres populations? They might finally have got the summer dominant adaptation going fairly well, but conditions again changed. The bimodal distribution of rainfall again returned, more winter dominant, along with slightly increased moisture.

Again, there was some shift to highland areas — pithouse adaptations returning to the Sierra Blanca system and the Gallina highlands far to the north. In both areas this was a time of some turmoil (A.D. 1150-1250).

Therefore, we will argue that some Mimbres populations again dispersed into the upper river drainages between roughly A.D. 1125 and A.D. 1200. Don't look primarily for Classic Mimbres architecture at this period. Rather, look for small unobtrusive settlements of pithouses in secondary and/or upper creek drainages (6,000 feet and up) having primarily Mimbres Black-on-white as painted wares and, perhaps, no fancy wares at all. Why? This is one strong pattern for the early P-III period elsewhere in New Mexico at this time (Apache Creek Phase, Late Glencoe Phase, Early Gallina Phase), and it is possible that it was a feature of post-Classic Mimbres decline here as well.

In southwestern New Mexico as the Mimbres Classic broke up, the Casas Grandes system seems to have played a strong role in reestablishing economic networks south and east of the Classic Mimbres area. The Animas-El Paso Phases likely peaked with the increasing rainfall and decreasing standard deviation in rainfall that has been noted in other areas of New Mexico (Cordell 1979:7). The highland adaptations did not work so well as they once had, for they were benefitted by higher rainfall, but also much higher deviations in rainfall from year to year. That is, such systems worked best as mixed agricultural/hunting-gathering systems under relatively low population density. The Mimbres population had grown too large for this option to resolve all its problem.

It is in this that we may have a clue to the Pine Lawn-Georgetown Phase shift. The previous rainfall dislocation resulted, perhaps, in population decline. More accurately, we think it resulted primarily in simple dispersal and a substantial retrogression by agriculturalists into the hunting-gathering niche. Hence, there would be some defensive site locations and, we argue, still many existing hunters and gatherers to put pressure on the landscape. We think Martin and Plog's (1973) argument for decreased agricultural dependence has merit, but think site scarcity may be due to creation of more *Archaic-like* sites for a time than *Mogollon-like* sites. We also think that an early decline in rainfall (A.D. 350-550) and/or increasing summer rainfall dominance, would have generated pressure to adopt new varieties of corn. Perhaps the 8 rowed dent corns and the similar Oñaveno might have appeared first about A.D. 400-500 and those classed as Hariñoso de Ocho (and some related varieties) shortly thereafter, perhaps A.D. 500-600. This is a bit earlier than Martin and Plog (1973) have argued. If general climatic conditions increasingly favored some of the earlier *Chapalote-like* corn varieties again from A.D. 600 to 850 (the winter rainfall agricultural strategy), it seems reasonable to argue that any new varieties introduced in the first summer dominant rainfall episode (A.D. 350-550) would not become very common or predominant until the second similar episode, starting about A.D. 900. What studies have compared corn varieties where temporal control was precise enough to demonstrate such a case?

In each of these two great episodal decreases in tree-ring width (A.D. 300-550 and A.D.

870-1125), population dispersal, decreasing dependence on agriculture, reaggregation and finally a new adaptive structure is an arguable sequence. As we have said, following the Mimbres Classic, a complete retrogression into the hunter-gatherer niche was not possible due to general population pressure. As far as ethnically distinct hunters and gatherers are concerned, there is only one time period in which we are able to conceive of sedentary population as dense enough in southwestern New Mexico to preclude full-time hunters and gatherers in substantial numbers. That is the period from A.D. 900-1150 in the western unit (but perhaps not along the southern periphery) and perhaps not at all in the eastern (Sierra Blanca-Tularosa Basin-Jornada) portion.

We are very uneasy about the origins of the Apache in this area. Wouldn't you think that those who allegedly followed the buffalo so recently onto the eastern plains would have at least had the recurved bow? The Navajo did, but many groups of early historic Apache used a simple reflex bow. That is more the stuff for deer hunters, don't you suppose? In view of the very close relationship between the two (Navajo and Apache), how does one account for this difference? We are not going to state that the Apache were much longer *in situ* than historical accounts suggest. Yet, we openly speculate on the matter in the next chapter, and sense that others may begin to propose it ere long. While we don't know that we could be won to such an argument on the basis of the current data, we do feel that the issue merits a very careful reconsideration.

Photo 7: A general view of the Woodrow Ruin. This site is perhaps one of the last, large Classic Mimbres sites that has not been completely destroyed by vandals. The woman standing in one of the great kiva depressions, at the center of the photograph, is Barbara Peckham. Photograph by S.L. Peckham, courtesy of the Museum of New Mexico, Santa Fe.

Photo 8: A cluster of Chupadero B/W ollas. These vessels were excavated at a site near Angus, New Mexico, in the Sierra Blanca region. Chupadero B/W is widely distributed throughout the southeast quarter of New Mexico. Photograph by R.E. Farwell, courtesy of the Museum of New Mexico, Santa Fe.

Photo 9: A deep pithouse near Angus, New Mexico, in the Sierra Blanca region. Note the extreme depth and the typical four-post roof support system of this P-III pithouse. Photograph by R.E. Farwell, courtesy of the Museum of New Mexico, Santa Fe.

Chapter VI
SOUTHEASTERN NEW MEXICO

BACKGROUND

From the archeological standpoint, southeastern New Mexico encompasses the eastern extension of the Jornada-Mogollon culture area. Compared to most other regions of New Mexico, little archeological attention has been focused on the southeast plains. Perhaps this is so because the region is vast, the visible archeological remains are not so remarkable as in the Anasazi and Mogollon heartlands, and the archeological record is poorly substantiated from independent chronology.

Geographically, we are speaking of an area which is bounded on the west by the eastern flanks of the Sacramento and Guadalupe Mountains. The region is bounded on the south and on the east by the borders of the state of Texas, and on the north is bounded roughly by a line drawn from the junctures of Torrance, Guadalupe and Lincoln counties, northeastward to Quay County at the Texas border. The area thus encompassed includes slightly more than 26,000 square miles. As with the other major regions of New Mexico, our point of departure for discussion is a recently prepared overview entitled *A Cultural Resource Overview for the Bureau of Land Management, Roswell District* (Camilli and Allen 1979). This overview, prepared by staff of the University of New Mexico, is still in draft form, and we may presume that some future revisions might be in store. Nonetheless, it is an excellent introduction to the archeology of southeastern New Mexico. Unlike several of the other overviews for New Mexico, the Camilli and Allen overview is focused on survey data, which is, of course, to our advantage here.

The eastern portion of this region is characterized by extensive uplands which adjoin the Guadalupe and Sacramento ranges. Maximum elevations range to about 6,500 feet. As one moves to the east, these upland areas open into the Sacramento plain, which is characterized by mixed grassland zones and some woodlands, depending on specific topography and elevation. As one moves further to the east, the Diamond A plain slopes down gradually toward the Pecos Valley and is characterized by mixed grassland zones. The Diamond A plain ranges from roughly 3,500 to 4,500 feet in elevation. Next, one enters the valley of the Pecos, which bisects southeastern New Mexico from north to south. The valley of the Pecos itself ranges from 3,400 feet in elevation in the north to roughly 2,800 feet in elevation near the Texas border.

As one proceeds to the east of the Pecos River, elevations again increase, but not notably. The eastern margins of the Pecos drainage are known as the Mescalero plain, and are characterized by desert grassland complexes. The easternmost section of southeast New Mexico is known as the Llano Estacado. The Llano Estacado is characterized by extremely low relief, internal drainage, and elevations ranging roughly from 3,800 to 5,000 feet. The Llano Estacado is also characterized by mixed grassland communities. It is separated from the Mescalero plain by a topographic feature which varies in height from 400 or 500 feet to low, dune-covered ridges. This landform is called the Mescalero pediment. Portions of the Mescalero pediment are substantially eroded, and it is not surprising that many Paleo-Indian remains have been recorded along this topographic feature (see Map VI.1).

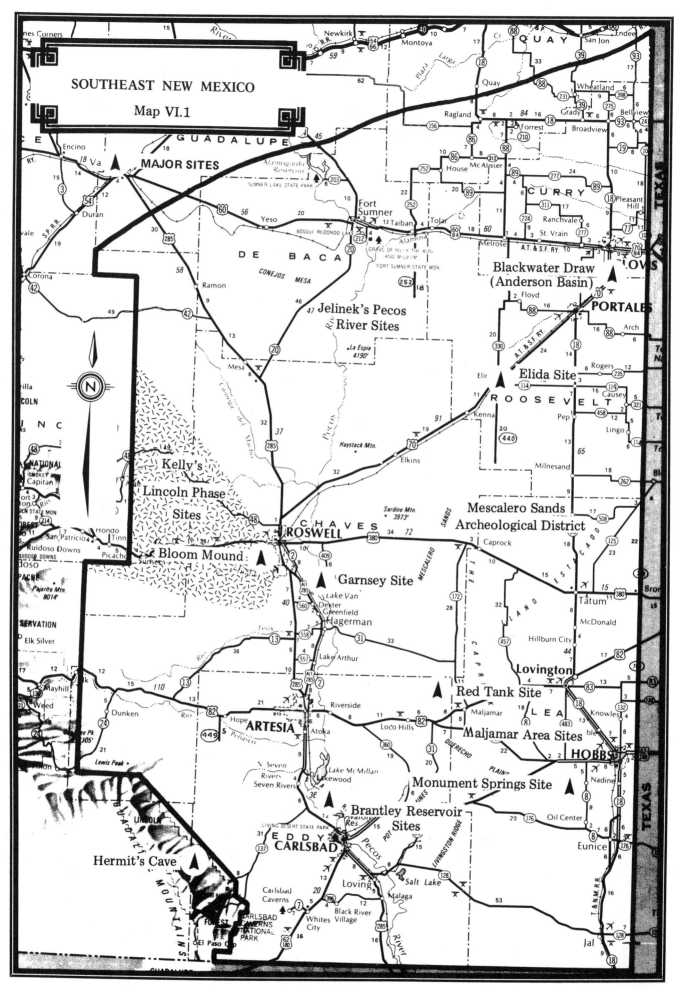

SOUTHEAST NEW MEXICO
Map VI.1

MAJOR SITES

Blackwater Draw
(Anderson Basin)

Jelinek's Pecos
River Sites

Elida Site

Mescalero Sands
Archeological District

Kelly's
Lincoln Phase
Sites

Bloom Mound

Garnsey Site

Red Tank Site

Maljamar Area Sites

Monument Springs Site

Brantley Reservoir
Sites

Hermit's Cave

Except for the eastern flanks of the Sacramento-Guadalupe Mountain chain, there is little elevational variance to manipulate in adjusting to changing conditions of subsistence. Nonetheless, the area receives greater rainfall than does the San Juan Basin or portions of southwestern New Mexico. Rainfall, in general, varies between 14 and 15 inches annually throughout the region. In order to achieve an equivalent annual rainfall, one must generally move into the higher elevations, above 6,500 feet, in western New Mexico. Climatic reconstructions for southeastern New Mexico may not accurately apply to the western, more heavily populated portions of the state, for here weather patterns are conditioned by the Gulf of Mexico air masses. To the west of the central highland spine of New Mexico, however, climate is dominated by air masses from the Pacific Coast area.

In historic times, substantial buffalo populations are known to have inhabited at least the more northern areas of southeastern New Mexico. Pronghorn, deer, and other smaller species were also common. Woodlands, however, were rather uncommon east of the Sacramento-Guadalupe chain, and in many areas wood was scarce as a resource. Camilli (Camilli and Allen 1979) discusses a wide variety of plant and animal resources which were available to inhabitants of southeastern New Mexico. In general, the climate is remarkably similar throughout the region and is characterized as a continental, semi-arid type. That is, dry winters and rainfall maximum in late summer are characteristic. A number of permanent streams, such as the Hondo, crosscut southeastern New Mexico from east to west. Arising from the Guadalupe and Sacramento Mountains, such streams flow into the Pecos River. As one moves to the east, however, onto the Llano Estacado, water, and certainly permanent water, becomes an increasingly scarce resource. Let us turn then, to a short sketch of the archeological record.

THE CULTURAL SEQUENCE

THE PALEO-INDIAN PERIOD
(10,000 B.C. to 5,000 B.C.?)

Paleo-Indian research has enjoyed a very special focus in southeastern New Mexico. The Camilli and Allen (1979) overview presents the Paleo-Indian period in some detail, as do both the Cordell (1979) and the Tainter (1980a) overviews. In this volume, our discussions of the Paleo-Indian period appear primarily in Chapter III (San Juan Basin) and Chapter VII (Northeast Plains). In this chapter we will only discuss the Paleo-Indian period in a brief and general way, for our object in this volume has been to direct research to areas and to issues that have not been completely treated in the literature. Thus, while the Paleo-Indian remains in southeastern New Mexico are important in the history of archeology, there is also little fear that Paleo-Indian studies will be overlooked in future archeological research.

Major Paleo-Indian sites in southeastern New Mexico include Blackwater Draw (two localities), Milnesand, Burnet Cave, the Elida Site, and Hermit's Cave. Eleven radiocarbon dates have been derived from three of these sites (Hermit's Cave, Burnet Cave, Blackwater Draw locality 1). These dates range from 12,900 B.P. to 7432 B.P. -- that is, roughly 10,000 B.C. to 5500 B.C. There is thus a possible pre-Clovis occupation at Hermit's Cave. This stratum at Hermit's Cave, plus the controversial occupation at Sandia Cave, and a few scattered Sandia points in the Estancia Basin, represent several of the few arguable pre-Clovis occupations thus far known in New Mexico. In no case is the evidence incontrovertible. Clearly, however, Paleo-Indian occupation becomes regular and fairly well known by Clovis times, that is, roughly 9,000 B.C.

Interestingly, in Roosevelt County, Clovis, Folsom and Midland materials occurred in about equal proportions (Broilo 1973). This does not appear to be the case, however, in northwestern Mexico (Chapter III), where later materials classifiable as Belen and Cody appear, in fact, to be more common than in southeastern New Mexico. This observation is nonetheless tentative.

We point out that the majority of known Paleo-Indian materials in southeastern New Mexico occur either along the eastern escarpment of the Guadalupe chain in the west of the study area, or along the Mescalero pediment and adjacent portions of the Llano Estacado in the eastern portions of the area. There are few Paleo-Indian localities in the approximately one-half of southeastern New Mexico which is in the Pecos drainage. As we will see in Chapter VII (this volume), there seems to be a similar situation for northeastern New Mexico, and indeed this same pattern is strikingly clear for the San Juan Basin. That is, while a number of Paleo-Indian localities are known from the periphery of the San Juan Basin, few are documented in the central basin area.

Of more interest to us here is the common characterization among survey archeologists of southeastern New Mexico as *Paleo-Indian country*. Just how accurate is this characterization? Below you will see summarized those data which we have been able to derive from the literature (Table VI.1). We wish to point out that we have no notion of how many Paleo-Indian localities may be known in each area to collectors or amateurs unless they have been mentioned in the published literature. Thus, the figures we provide do not *certify* the number of actual Paleo-Indian localities; they give only those known formally or reported anecdotally in the literature. These figures do not include many isolated point finds.

Table VI.1
COMPARISON OF KNOWN PALEO-INDIAN SITES AND LOCALITIES

	Northwestern N.M.	Southeastern N.M.	Northeastern N.M.
Formally Recorded:	59 (Judge 1973) 13 (San Juan Data Base) 16 (Broster, p.c.) 5 (Elyea, *et al*. 1979)	26 (Camilli & Allen 1979)	25 (this volume)
Colloquially Reported:	N? finds in Mt. Taylor area (Judge, p.c.) N? finds in Gallup-Manuelito area (Tainter 1980a:86)	80 (Wendorf & Hester 1975)	
Formally Reported: TOTAL	94	26	25 (No *hearsay* sites incl.)
Coloquially Reported: TOTAL	?	80 (includes some in Texas)	0
TOTAL N.M.	94+	106<	25
Major Excavated Sites	**3 (Sandia Cave, Rio Rancho, Dunas Altas*)	5 (Blackwater Draw-2 localities, Milnesand, Burnet Cave, and Hermit's Cave)***	3 (San Jon, Sapello-R-6, Folsom)
Dated Paleo Sites	1 (Sandia Cave-disputed)	3	2

* (Dunas Altas had a Folsom component — not published)

** (Test excavations have been conducted at Ojito Springs, Comanche Springs and Alamo Muerto; see Judge 1973:45)

*** (Analysis of Warnica's Elida site material was published by Hester in 1962, but these were surface collected)

If one includes the peripheries of the San Juan Basin rather than the central basin itself, a striking situation can be argued for the quantity of known Paleo-Indian remains when compared to those known for southeastern New Mexico. Judge (1973) recorded 59 Paleo-Indian sites and localities along the central Rio Grande drainage, which forms the southeastern border of the San Juan Basin. In addition, the San Juan Data Base included components for 13 Paleo-Indian sites. Moreover, the NIIP Survey (Elyea *et al.* 1979) recorded five additional Paleo-Indian localities in the Gallegos Wash area which borders the northwestern periphery of the San Juan Basin. Finally, the recent BIA Timber Survey has reported 16 Paleo-Indian sites and localities in the Cebolleta Mesa area and near Stone Lake on the Jicarilla Indian Reservation (Broster, personal communication).

Broster points out that the survey is by no means complete, and more Paleo-Indian localities are expected in the Jicarilla Reservation. Thus, there are 94 formally recorded Paleo-Indian sites and localities in the San Juan Basin and its environs — an area which we colloquially refer to as *not having Paleo-Indian occupation*. In "Paleo-Indian country", however, that is, southeastern New Mexico, we note that 26 (Camilli and Allen 1979) Paleo-Indian localities have been formally recorded and an additional 80 (Wendorf and Hester 1975) have been summarized in the literature after informant interviews with amateur collectors. We did not trouble to discover how many of these later 80 sites were in Texas, though we know it to be a number. In short, there are fewer than 106 Paleo-Indian sites and localities formally reported in southeastern New Mexico, that is *Paleo-Indian country*, whereas there are more than 94 known in northwestern New Mexico. We point out that in both cases we have not included most known isolated point finds in the category of Paleo-Indian locality.

In northeastern New Mexico 25 formally reported Paleo-Indian sites and localities are known (Chapter VII). In this region there has been no summary of sites known only to collectors. Several striking implications emerge. First, there are more *formally* recorded Paleo-Indian sites and localities in the San Juan Basin and adjoining areas than in all of the plains provinces of eastern New Mexico combined. Secondly, there are nearly as many, if not fully as many, Paleo-Indian sites and localities known in the San Juan Basin and environs as are known in the Paleo-Indian country of southeastern New Mexico.

In view of the fact that members of many survey crews in the San Juan Basin maintain that they have never observed (and in some cases have never seen anywhere) Paleo-Indian materials in the field, we suggest that the average survey crew in the San Juan Basin does not expect to find, nor is particularly *tuned* to finding, Paleo-Indian materials. On the other hand, surveyors in southeastern New Mexico both expect to find and are often especially skilled at finding Paleo-Indian materials. Thus, we may argue that San Juan Basin surveys underrepresent actual Paleo-Indian materials. This is particularly so where many of these finds involve only fragments of projectile points which, in any case, are quite difficult to identify even for experts highly skilled in such identification. In short, southeastern New Mexico, claimed to be Paleo-Indian country, will be shortly eclipsed in published sites and localities by the San Juan Basin as the BIA Surveys continue. More to the point, survey crews operating in the San Juan Basin must come to expect the possibility of Paleo-Indian materials and learn to identify these, particularly assemblages which contain distinctive drills and scrapers, but where no diagnostic points themselves occur.

The general scarcity of Paleo-Indian materials in the central San Juan Basin, the central portions of the northeast Plains, and from the Pecos drainage itself, forces us to face another problem which will be controversial in some quarters. As we have said, Paleo-Indian materials are suspiciously scarce in the central San Juan Basin and in the valleys of the Canadian and Pecos rivers, respectively. While we do not know the reason for this, we must face the fact that there are only several logical alternative explanations. Dr. Cordell (1979) has suggested that Paleo-Indian materials are primarily known from those areas which are substantially eroded.

We point out that the majority of Paleo-Indian materials have been recovered either from eroded landforms such as mesas and pediments, or highly eroded areas such as portions of the Estancia Basin, the Rio Grande Valley and the Llano Estacado. Thus, one must face the possibility that the paucity of Paleo-Indian materials in other basin and river drainage areas is due to their being buried by erosional process.

Secondly, one can propose that the basic Paleo-Indian subsistence strategy involved systematic entrapment of game along notable landforms. These have relief which may have permitted game entrapment. In this case we might propose that the Paleo-Indian strategy involved fall and, perhaps, spring transhumance from the broken peripheries of major basin areas to and from intervening lower elevations. The diagnostic materials thus found along the peripheries of the San Juan Basin, the northeast plains and the Pecos drainage might represent such a hunting strategy. If erosion is not the cause of relatively scarce remains in the intervening lower areas, then we must argue that Paleo-Indian assemblages in those areas are simply not recognizable to most field archeologists. In this case, more field archeologists certainly need to learn what Paleo-Indian assemblages look like when they do not contain diagnostic projectile points. In many cases, however, if such remains do occur in basin floors, they might contain scrapers and drills. Thus, it should not be impossible eventually to identify such assemblages *if they exist*.

To summarize, the general Paleo-Indian settlement strategy as we see it now in New Mexico may be a function of: 1) post-depositional erosional process; 2) the actual hunting strategy of Paleo-Indian populations; 3) the inability to recognize intervening assemblages not associated with hunting strategies. Archeologists must face this issue and determine which of these three variables, or which combination of these three variables, accounts for the pattern of Paleo-Indian remains that has been identified. Finally, field archeologists must disabuse themselves of the idea that western New Mexico, and northwestern New Mexico in particular, is not Paleo-Indian country in the same sense as the southeast plains.

HOW MANY PALEO-INDIAN POINTS ARE THERE IN NEW MEXICO, ANYWAY?

All manner of demographic reconstructions for Paleo-Indian populations have been proposed in the literature. As Camilli points out (Camilli and Allen 1979), Hester (1975:255) has suggested a ratio of hunters to dependents of between 1:1 and 1:2. This is altogether too conservative, for not less than three dependents (that is, a wife and two children) would be required per hunter for a biologically viable population. Stuart (1977) has suggested that the average number of dependents per big game hunter is four or five, including the aged. Population density estimates range from a high of one person per square mile to a low of about 14 square miles per person (Wilmsen 1973, cited in Camilli and Allen 1979:52). Though Camilli dismisses Wilmsen's assumption on population density as violating the ethnographic record, she never cites just which ethnographic data make such a reconstruction implausible. Stuart (1977, 1980) has demonstrated that the Ona populations of Tierra del Fuego were induced to internal competition and dramatic population regulation at a density somewhere between 7 and 9 square miles per person. The Ona hunted under circumstances which can be argued to have been at least as profitable as in major portions of New Mexico and, moreover, had the bow and arrow, which would have given them substantial technological advantage over Paleo-Indian populations. Thus, we may suggest the logically densest population that can reasonably be argued for Paleo-Indian populations in New Mexico to be one person per six square miles.

If we construct hypothetical populations based on a high, a medium and a low population density for New Mexico, and also construct a ratio of hunters to dependents that varies from a low of 1:3 to a high of 1:5, we may compute possible numbers of hunters for the entire state of New Mexico. If we further make some assumptions about the number of Paleo-Indian points which were used, broken or lost per week, therefore requiring replacement in manufacture, we may then create expectations for the total number of Paleo-Indian points that would have been manufactured and deposited in New Mexico over roughly a 4,000 year period of Paleo-Indian occupation. These hypothetical data are summarized in Table VI.2.

Table VI.2
PALEO-INDIAN POINTS: HOW MANY?

	High	Medium	Low
Assumed Population Density:	1/6 mi^2	1/14 mi^2 (Wilmsen)	1/60 mi^2
Total Population, N.M.	20,000	8,000	2,000
Number Hunters:Dependents	1:3	1:4	1:5
Total Number of Hunters	5,000	1,600	330
Points used/broken, lost per year*	[100/year]	[75/year]	[50/year]
Points Manufactured per Year	500,000/year	120,000/year	16,500/year
Total Points for 4,000 year Occupation	2 Billion	480 Million	66 Million
Total Points Deposited per Square Mile	16,640/mi^2	4,000/mi^2	550/mi^2
As above, per Acre	26/acre	6.25/acre	.85/acre
Predicted Recovery of Points @ 2% Survey of New Mexico	40 Million	9.6 Million	1.32 Million

* Predicted number of points at 10% of above usage rate.

	[10/year]	[7.5/year]	[5/year]
Total Paleo Points	200 Million	48 Million	6.6 Million
Predicted Number Known from 2% Survey	4 Million	960 Thousand	132 Thousand

You will notice from the above table that, assuming a high population density of one person per six square miles and a ratio of three dependents for each hunter and a use of 100 points per year, that is two per week, the total number of points manufactured and deposited during 4,000 years of Paleo-Indian occupation would have been *2 Billion*. This is impossibly high as a figure, for in this case there would be no less than 26 Paleo-Indian points per acre if distributed evenly throughout New Mexico. At the suggested 2 percent of intensive survey in New Mexico which has been conducted thus far in the history of archeological research, there should then be *40 million* Paleo-Indian points known to collectors and museums and in recorded site forms. At the low end of our scale, we may suppose a density of one person per 60 square miles, and a ratio of hunters to dependents of 1:5. In this case there would only be 330 hunters in the entire state of New Mexico at a given time. Nonetheless, if each required the manufacture of 50 points per year, there would be a total of 66 million Paleo-Indian points for the period of occupation, and the predicted recovery of points at 2% survey, state-wide, would be *1.32 million*. The only case that we can reconstruct which might even approximate the number of known Paleo-Indian points is one based on these low population figures and a point manufacture rate of 5 points per year per hunter. In this case the total number of Paleo-Indian points would be 6.6 million, 132 thousand being known from surveys in New Mexico during the last century.

In Judge's (1973) Paleo-Indian survey of the Rio Grande Valley, 480 square miles were *surveyed*. In all, 201 Paleo-Indian points were recovered from 59 sites and localities, that is one Paleo point was recovered for each 2.4 square miles. Our lowest case figure predicts that there would be 132 Paleo-Indian points for each of these 2.4 square mile units. So Judge's recovery rate is approximately three-quarters of one percent of our lowest predicted value. We may conclude then, that: 1) Paleo-Indian occupation of New Mexico was impossibly small; 2) that Paleo-Indian hunters seldom hunted; or 3) our recovery rates for Paleo-Indian points from surface survey are well below 1% of the actual remains.

Those who might wish to argue that Paleo-Indian occupation was as small as our lowest case, or smaller, should bear in mind that substantial Apachean occupations in historic and protohistoric times have produced *fewer recorded Apachean sites than we have known Paleo-Indian sites.* Thus, it may be argued that at impossibly small population levels Paleo-Indian remains would not generally be visible at all. The most important thing that we could ever know from ethnoarcheological investigation, or from ethnographic data, would be the average number of points that similar hunters expended in a year's time. With these data, and a range of plausible population densities, we could refine predictions regarding the number of Paleo-Indian points which may be expected in New Mexico. Further, we could, as is proposed in a forthcoming chapter, experiment with laying out projectile points (real or facsimiles) in one acre plots, for instance, to see at what point artifact density would create visibility for an ordinary survey crew. It occurs to us that there must be some critical artifact density threshold for survey crews to record such point finds at all. If we knew the range of threshold densities that obtained for several different survey crews, we could then retrodict from known Paleo-Indian surveys the total number of points which, in all probability, had been missed during survey. Let us turn, then, to the Archaic period in southeastern New Mexico.

THE ARCHAIC
(5,000 B.C.? to A.D. 1000?)

The Archaic period in southeastern New Mexico is, as elsewhere, not well known. Nonetheless, several generalities can be offered. Unlike western New Mexico where roughly 11% of recorded sites are lithic scatters or aceramic, but like the Northeast Plains, over one-half of the recorded sites in southeastern New Mexico are aceramic. Nonetheless, relatively few of these contain diagnostic lithic materials, and may date anywhere from perhaps 5,000 B.C. to at least A.D. 1000 (the Yeso Creek site). Others, of course, may even represent later occupations not associated with ceramic production, but this is currently speculative. If one includes the Yeso Creek site, then, four *Archaic* sites have yielded radiocarbon dates in southeastern New Mexico. These are Blackwater Draw, Locality No. 1, the Howell Site, GS-3, and Yeso Creek. These dates range from roughly 4000 B.C. to A.D. 1000.

Most *Archaic* remains in southeastern New Mexico have been seriated chronologically on projectile point types. Nonetheless, as we discuss in the chapter on the Northeast Plains, this is indeed a risky proposition. We may presume that chronological control over such Archaic remains as contain diagnostic points is probably half a millenium at best, and ordinarily no greater than 1,000 years. In other ways, characterization of Archaic sites from recovered projectile points in southeastern New Mexico is perplexing to us. For instance, Henderson (1976: 45) includes Jay points with Paleo-Indian components. No explanation is offered for this. We had thought ourselves somewhat daring when in Chapter III we proposed that Jay assemblages might be partly contemporaneous with Cody materials. In at least one other case an investigator has included Milnesand components as early Archaic, again without special explanation. Thus, it is almost impossible to determine just how many Paleo-Indian, as opposed to Archaic, assemblages have been properly diagnosed in southeastern New Mexico. For instance, Henderson (1976) lists six Paleo-Indian components, but as we have said, these include Jay points and we are not told how many of the six components contained Jay points.

What is notable with regard to Archaic assemblages in southeastern New Mexico is that no remains which suggest an early agricultural subsistence base have ever been recovered. This is in direct contrast to a number of Archaic sites west of the central highlands in New Mexico. Secondly, those few Archaic assemblages which have been excavated or tested indicate that large mammal procurement was not a feature of Archaic adaptations. Again, this is unlike western New Mexico, where more Archaic assemblages are known to have produced remains of deer, antelope and, occasionally, bison. Most of the faunal remains recovered from Archaic sites in southeastern New Mexico include turtle, rabbit, and rodents. In other respects, however, recovered sandals, basketry, etc., very much resemble Archaic/Proto Basketmaker assemblages in western New Mexico. Thus, we may presume that the general technological and subsistence patterns were similar in many ways, but that agricultural strategies were either little known or unproductive in southeastern New Mexico. Big game hunting also appears to have been a limited subsistence strategy.

To our knowledge, no one has ever computed the number of Archaic projectile points (primarily *dart* points) recovered per site or locality, as Judge (1973) did for Paleo-Indian materials in the central Rio Grande. Obviously, no one would currently be able to say what the intensity of Archaic occupation or Archaic hunting strategies might have been when compared with other portions of the Southwest. Clearly, such a study is merited.

With approximately 900 aceramic sites recorded in southeastern New Mexico, it is still not possible to argue for a very intense Archaic occupation. The San Juan Data Base indicates that 2,200 Archaic and aceramic sites have been recorded in that region. Considering that approximately one-fourth the survey coverage of southeastern New Mexico has been completed when compared with the San Juan Basin, the Archaic *or aceramic* remains there would be proportionately equal to 2,160 sites in the San Juan Basin (four times survey coverage less 40% difference between 15,000 mi^2 and 26,000 mi^2). We point out that, with fewer ceramic occupations in southeastern New Mexico, there has been a longer-term tendency to record such sites, while it was uncommon to do so until perhaps 15 years ago in the San Juan Basin. Thus, the true proportions of these kinds of sites may not be reflected in site files. Secondly, we are faced with the possibility that Archaic-like adaptations in southeastern New Mexico have a substantially longer temporal span than in the northwest, where the agricultural strategy was clearly being induced by Basketmaker II times. It is also quite possible, though little discussed, that many of the scatters of fire-cracked rock and non-diagnostic lithic debris in southeastern New Mexico may date to the early historic and protohistoric plains occupations of the area. It seems essential for datable hearth features to be investigated in more detail and brought under chronometric control, whether through archeomagnetic technique or the recovery of C-14 datable material. Nonetheless, as in other instances, the striking similarity in certain comparative survey data is surprising. Have we a situation in which the intensity of Archaic occupation in eastern and western New Mexico was essentially equal until BM-II times? Or is a more modest occupation made to seem larger by the site accretions of an additional millenium in the east? Since agriculture is currently thought to be a density-related phenomenon, we have a profound need to produce an answer.

Finally, we suggest that point typologies be more carefully refined in determining relative chronological sequence. This is, of course, not a simple proposition in practice and would require further excavations. We know that Johnson (1967) has derived point types as a series of period markers for Archaic assemblages. Johnson's period III extends from 4580 B.C. to A.D. 110, and is based on fourteen C-14 dates. His period IV extends from 350 B.C. to A.D. 1245, and is based on seventeen C-14 dates. Though Camilli (1979:63) concludes that "this interpretation invalidates reliance and relative dating in reference to point forms", it is important to point out one apparent pattern. These later Archaic periods all overlap temporally between 350 B.C. and A.D. 110. This is not so surprising, for in fact it well brackets the traditional Basketmaker II period. This further strengthens the argument presented in Chapter II for divergence in major subsistence strategy and technology rather than the discrete evolutionary succession of changing technological forms. In short, we expected this, and have provided for it theoretically. Now we must ask how we may refine these patterns chronologically. Again, we suggest that the kinds of technological analysis in point forms that Judge (1973) has conducted would be productive when applied to our concepts of increasing and decreasing size and variance in size as indicators of the power and efficiency phases in systems.

In this context, perhaps the most productive research that could be conducted would be to continue Judge's specific analyses of Paleo-Indian assemblages into the Archaic assemblages commonly referred to as Jay, Bajada and San Jose. It is our conception that the Jay points and the Bajada points will fall far more closely into the Paleo-Indian technological range than the San Jose. Such an analysis would, of course, contribute substantially to any interpretation regarding major episodes of technological discontinuity and, perhaps, demographic discontinuity in the archeological record.

Secondly, we point out that a major unknown is whether Paleo-Indian points recovered in the context of Archaic materials represent primary or secondary, that is curated, deposition. Since in southeastern New Mexico many Archaic localities also produce Paleo-Indian materials (the case is similar elsewhere), this is not a point to be overlooked. Again, following Judge's (1973) line of thinking, if Paleo-Indian points were curated and reused by later populations there would almost certainly be noticeable differences in hafting technique. Thus, we may propose that Paleo-Indian points found in purely Paleo-Indian localities be studied as a comparative assemblage with Paleo-Indian points recovered from Archaic localities. Because foreshaft materials and the details of hafting techniques would be different, it is our conception that patterns of point breakage should also be different between the two kinds of projectile assemblages. It is also not unlikely that substantial modifications would be required in the basal areas of Paleo-Indian points hafted by later Archaic populations. While these are only speculations at the moment, they are relatively easily solvable problems, and would make a substantial contribution to interpretive methodology.

In concluding this section, we point out that we intuitively doubt high densities of Archaic populations in southeastern New Mexico prior to A.D. 700-800. We further suppose that if more *unknown* lithic occupations can be dated in southeastern New Mexico, it will be seen that a number of these overlap temporally with later ceramic period occupations. That is, we specifically propose that, for a time at least, relatively sedentary ceramic occupations occurred in the same general regions with people who continued to follow a more mobile and less technologically weighty adaptive strategy. Nonetheless, faunal assemblages recovered from those few Archaic remains which have been excavated indicate that life was hard on the plains until the first millenium of the Christian era. Thus, it would appear that the temptation to adopt an agricultural strategy would have eventually been strong when it became possible to pursue such a strategy. In short, we suspect that while the need was there (and perhaps the temptation) for a long time, the conditions were not right to pursue agriculture until roughly A.D. 900. Let us turn, then, to an appraisal of later period occupations in southeastern New Mexico.

CERAMIC PERIOD OCCUPATIONS
(A.D. 900? to A.D. 1450 or 1550?)

Something less than a thousand ceramic period sites have been recorded in southeastern New Mexico. Of these, approximately two-thirds are mixed ceramic and lithic scatters. The number of structural sites, therefore, is only a few hundred, unlike portions of western New

Table VI.3
STANDARD CHRONOLOGICAL SEQUENCES FOR THE SOUTHERN HIGH PLAINS,
CANADIAN RIVER VALLEY and SOUTHEASTERN NEW MEXICO

	Northeastern New Mexico (Wendorf 1960)	Plains-Panhandle Area (Suhm et al. 1954)	Southwestern Llano Estacado Eastern Variety of the Jornada Branch of the Mogollon (Corley 1965)	Middle Pecos Valley (Jelinek 1967)
A.D. 1700	Historic Nomads	Historic Stage		
1600				
1500				Historic
1400	Panhandle Aspect— Antelope Creek Focus	Neo-American Stage Antelope Creek Focus	Ochoa Phase	Post McKenzie
1300				Late McKenzie
1200			Maljamar Phase	Early McKenzie
1000	Pueblo Aspect		Querecho Phase	Late Mesita Negra / Early Mesita Negra
900				Late 18 Mile
800				Early 18 Mile
700	Archaic?	Archaic?	Archaic?	
600				
500				Archaic?
400				
300				
200				
100				
A.D. 0				
B.C.				

269

Mexico. One of the larger Pueblo period or Mogollon sites in southeastern New Mexico is Bloom Mound (Kelley 1966), which is somewhere between 10 and 12 rooms in size and lies a few miles up the Hondo River west of Roswell, New Mexico. Most structural sites in this part of the state have from two to three to perhaps twenty or thirty structures. The majority of these were small shallow pithouse depressions, often badly eroded. A few sites having surface roomblocks are known, the majority constructed of adobe.

Even in these sites, direct evidence for maize agriculture is scanty, though Jelinek (1967) did recover cobs of maize in his excavations near Fort Sumner in the northern portion of the study area. There are two basic phase sequences for the region; one in the north (Jelinek 1967) and one in the south (Corley 1965; Leslie 1979). There are only eleven independently dated ceramic period sites in all of southeastern New Mexico. These have produced a total of twenty C-14 dates which range from A.D. 700 ± 95 (Laguna Plata) to A.D. 1845 ± 100 (Garnsey site — contaminated sample). These dates, though few, seem to fall naturally into three spans: about A.D. 800 to 1000, approximately A.D. 1100 to 1360, and roughly A.D. 1450 to 1560. There is reasonable evidence for agricultural pursuits in the northern portion of the study area from roughly A.D. 900 to perhaps A.D. 1250. In the southern portions of southeastern New Mexico an agricultural strategy is assumed, but has little evidence to demonstrate it. Sometime after A.D. 1250, most sources agree, there was a return to buffalo hunting as a major subsistence focus. Let us first look at Jelinek's sequence for the middle Pecos Valley.

Jelinek has divided occupation in the middle Pecos Valley into seven phases which are post Archaic. These are outlined in Table VI.4.

For analytical purposes we have lumped these into four phases which are equivalent to the Pecos classification. It will become apparent shortly why we have done this. First, bear in mind our discussion in the last portion of the chapter on southwestern New Mexico, where we discuss major altitude shifts in the Sierra Blanca-Capitan area. Secondly, the reader will also wish to refer to the final chapter of this volume where we present settlement patterns statewide. Those discussions will make the characteristics of these phases as we have grouped them here more intelligible in terms of general, regionwide, systematic settlement shifts.

The Early 18 Mile phase (A.D. 800-900) yields evidence of the first few sites which may be permanent settlements and occur in areas of agricultural potential. Associated ceramics include Lino Gray and brownwares. Later in this phase a number of well established, fairly small, sedentary communities are noted. These have shallow pithouses and occasionally small contiguous surface rooms. This later period has been termed the Late 18 Mile phase. Jelinek suggests a date of A.D. 900-1000. Interestingly, Red Mesa B/W appears at this time in association with Jornada Brown.

We have herein separated the Early and Late 18 Mile phases. It is our judgment that the Early 18 Mile phase represents the early lowland development which occurs nearly statewide with P-I sites and is contemporaneous with the Late BM-III development in the highlands. Though such a trend has not been well documented for the Mimbres region in particular, many ceramic scatters are known in that area which date prior to the Classic Mimbres occupation, and we have proposed an early occupation there in lower elevations, which requires further investigation. This Early 18 Mile phase we judge to be contemporaneous with early highland development in the Sierra Blanca region (Capitan Phase) and elsewhere (Late San Francisco and Three Circle Phases; the Rosa Phase, etc.). In every other region of New Mexico where the data are available, this period of highland development peaks between A.D. 700-900. Thus, we judge the Early 18 Mile phase to be dated somewhere between A.D. 750 and 850, for it is the case elsewhere in New Mexico that *P-I sites* in lower elevations generally date to just before or just after A.D. 800.

Figure VI.1
BLOOM MOUND
(after Kenyon Kobean, in Kelley 1966)

A Lincoln Phase site near Roswell. There are few large known structural sites in southeast New Mexico.

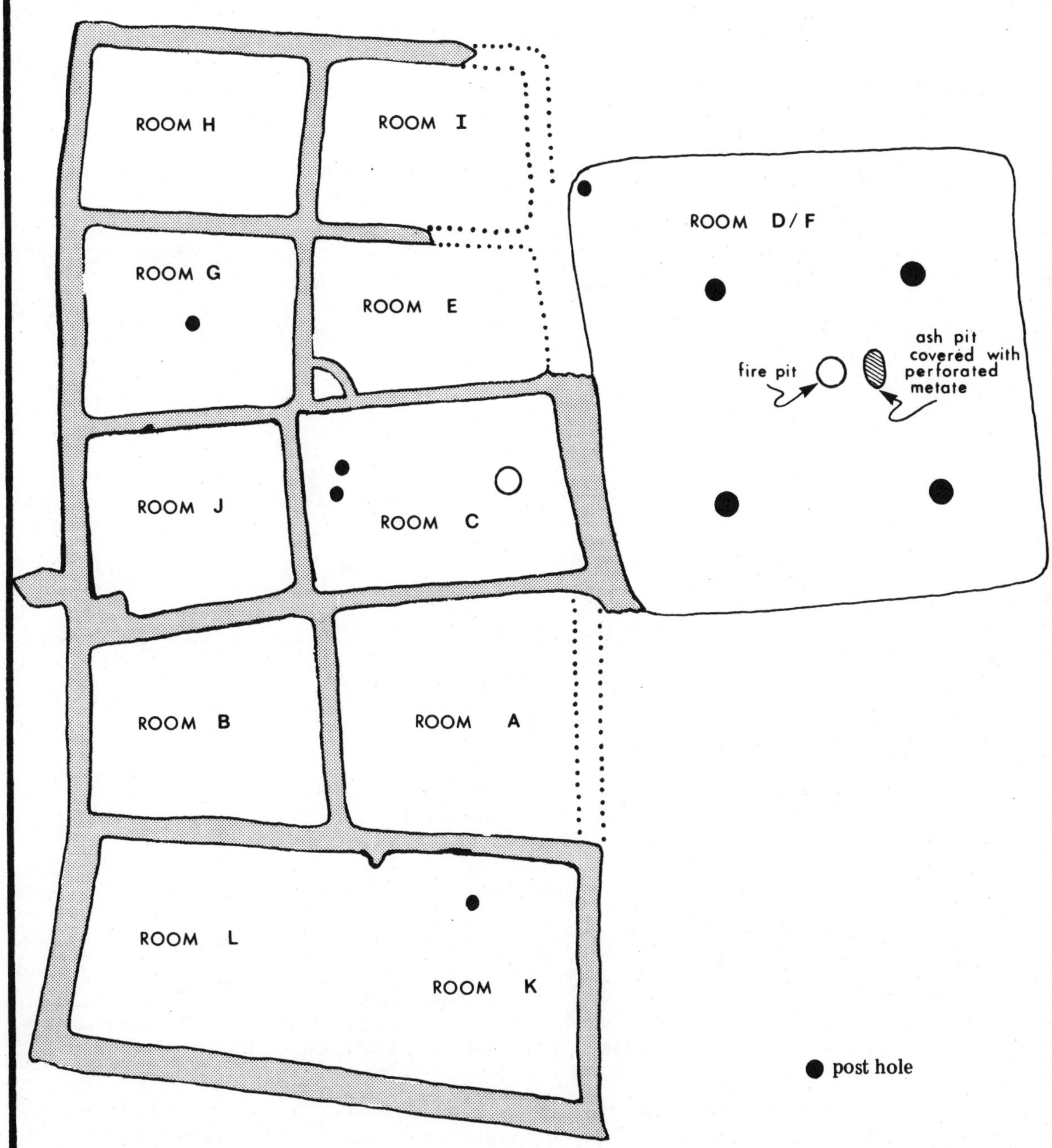

271

Table VI.4
A SUMMARY OF PHASE CHARACTERISTICS
IN THE MIDDLE PECOS VALLEY*
(Northern Portion of Southeast Plains)

Pecos Equivalent/Phase Dates		Settlement/Trade	Diagnostics
P-IV	Post McKenzie (A.D. 1350—?)	Temporary camps (lithic and ceramic scatters) in locations not favored by earlier occupations.	Few sherds Rio Grande Glaze 1. App. of basally-notched points.
MAJOR SHIFT TO BUFFALO PROPOSED — — — — — — —			— — — — — —
P-III	Late McKenzie (A.D. 1250—1350)	One very large site & few small surrounding scatters. Appearance of bison bones in numbers. Drop in *Zea* pollen.	Middle Pecos B/W Brownwares re-reduced. Traces of St. Johns Poly., Santa Fe B/W, Three Rivers R/T.
	Early McKenzie (A.D. 1200—1250?)	Only three sites but rather large. Less than a dozen intrusive sherds.	McKenzie Brown Middle Pecos B/W Traces S.Fe B/W Triangular side-notched points
— — — — — — — — — — — — — — — APPEARANCE OF SANTA FE B/W — — — — —			
P-II	Late Mesita Negra (A.D. 100—1200)		Graywares increase & Brownwares decline as phase ends. Brownwares and first appearance of Chupadero B/W late in phase.
	Early Mesita Negra (A.D. 1000—1100)	Larger sites & more intense occupation than at any other time. Fairly wide variety of tradewares from both north and southwest. Notable scarcity of large mammal subsistence remains.	+ Red Mesa B/W Socorro B/W Mimbres B/W Cebolleta B/W Reserve B/W
Early P-II	Late 18 Mile (A.D. 900—1000)	Well established, small sedentary communities. Shallow pithouses & small contiguous surface rooms (arch. features scarce). No similar highland sites. Trade with eastern Anasazi and Jornada Brown.	Red Mesa B/W; Jornada Brown, Middle Pecos Micaceous
Late BM-III/ P-I	Early 18 Mile (A.D. 800—900)	Few sites; first possible permanent settlements in potential agricultural areas. Lino Gray (Anasazi influence). Equivalent to early Capitan Phase in Lincoln area.	Lino Gray & points similar to Shabik'-eschee Village.
	Archaic (5000 B.C.?— A.D. 1000?)	A few scattered lithic localities, many w/no diagnostics & therefore uncertain temporal horizon.	Jay points to San Jose (scarce)
	Paleo Indian	5 Paleo point bases recovered during survey; 4 of the 5 were found on later sites having no other Paleo materials. 5th was isolated point find. Bases are not typed, but several look to be *Midland* points.	5 Paleo bases, Plate 7, following p.175

* Abstracted from Jelinek (1967)

The Late 18 Mile phase, which Jelinek dates A.D. 900-1000, is the period in which the first well-established communities can be documented. The appearance of Red Mesa B/W, and Jelinek's judgment that there are no similar highland sites in the Sierra Blanca region, leads us to conclude that this phase is equivalent temporally and adaptively to the later downhill shift that we proposed during Mangus phase development in the Mimbres area. Importantly, Jelinek notes that trade is with the eastern Anasazi rather than with nearby highland areas. This point cannot be overly emphasized. Since Red Mesa B/W is now known to date a bit earlier than Jelinek had supposed, we place the dates of this phase at approximately A.D. 850 or 875 to A.D. 950 or 975.

Following the Late 18 Mile phase is the early Mesita Negra phase, which Jelinek dates A.D. 1000-1100, and the late Mesita Negra phase, dated A.D. 1100-1200. It is in this period that the most intense occupation and larger, though not notably large, sites occur. In the Middle Pecos there are more sites of the early and late Mesita Negra phases than in all other periods combined. Notably, an extensive trade network in ceramics develops, for associated ceramics include Reserve B/W, Cebolleta B/W, Mimbres B/W, Socorro B/W, and the continued presence of some Red Mesa B/W. At the very end of this phase there is the first appearance of Chupadero B/W, and graywares again increase as brownwares decline. This is evidence of interaction with the extensive basin trade networks which we have discussed in the last several chapters. In fact, these data are so like those for west central New Mexico (see Chapter IV) that one forgets that 150 linear miles intervene.

In this region, there is evidence of trade with the Mimbres interaction system, the west central New Mexico interaction system, and the Chacoan system. Recall, however, that Red Mesa B/W is not demonstrated to have been generally manufactured in Chaco Canyon. Rather, it was produced in a number of localities along the southern highland tier of the San Juan Basin, directly west of the Middle Pecos area. The appearance of Chupadero B/W between the early and late Mesita Negra phases marks the faltering of basin florescence and gradual re-establishment of a trade network with adjacent highland areas. Thus, though modest in proportions, the Late 18 Mile and the Mesita Negra phases, collectively, are parallel to and reflect the mechanics of classic P-II development elsewhere in New Mexico. Therefore, we date these three phases, collectively, at roughly A.D. 875 to 1140 or 1150.

Notably, Mimbres B/W occurs in the middle of the Mesita Negra sequence, but is not found in later phases. So the Classic Mimbres system is as we have argued — contemporaneous with basin expansions elsewhere. Investigators should reconsider the tendency to date occupations to the late A.D. 1100's and 1200's on the basis of Mimbres B/W in lowland ceramic assemblages. We point out that Jelinek is one of the few investigators to have correctly placed the Mesita Negra phases in accordance with the Mimbres B/W (LeBlanc's dendro dates were not known in 1967). The only adjustment we make then in Jelinek's dates is to begin these phases slightly earlier and to terminate them at A.D. 1150 instead of A.D. 1200. Though these adjustments are speculative, no absolute dates being available for these phases, the weight of nearly 700 reports and publications leads us to suggest that our speculation is not idle.

The early and late McKenzie phases are represented only by several large structural sites, with a few surrounding ceramic and lithic scatters in evidence. These two phases are represented in too few sites, in our estimation, to merit separate nomenclature. Nonetheless, Jelinek's judgment on their relative temporal placement appears to have been very astute. The early McKenzie phase is characterized by a dramatic decline in intrusive ceramics, there being only a few sherds of Red Mesa B/W (thought to be reused from earlier occupations) and traces of Santa Fe B/W. It is at this time that the general shift in settlement patterns throughout New Mexico is again to the highlands.

Elsewhere, we note that at Cebolleta Mesa the period is also characterized by dramatic disruption in ceramic trade and a rapid aggregation into highland settings. LeBlanc (1979) has also noted the relative modesty of external trade into the Mimbres area for later P-II and early P-III ceramics. The large site representing the late McKenzie phase evidently represents the aggregation and downhill shift that we have noted between Late P-III and Early P-IV times elsewhere. Jelinek has dated the late McKenzie phase as A.D. 1250-1350. Our own judgment is that the McKenzie occupation represented at this site is most probably an A.D. 1280 or 1290 to 1300 construction episode, for no Rio Grande Glaze 1 wares appear. In short, the McKenzie phases, though aggregated in site size, are modest numerically because they fall in the earlier and later portions of the P-III period of highland development.

The post McKenzie occupation Jelinek dates to A.D. 1350+, and notes that these are primarily temporary camps, that is, lithic and ceramic scatters in locations which were not favored by earlier occupations. This, of course, indicates either some shift in subsistence or in environmental factors. On these sites a few sherds of Rio Grande Glaze 1, both Red and Yellow, are notable. Our own opinion is that the post-McKenzie occupation is better dated to just after A.D. 1300. We note that in the late McKenzie occupation evidence for maize pollen decreases dramatically and the appearance of bison bones in some sites is notable. It is at this time that there appears to be a major shift in subsistence focus. Jelinek has supposed that at roughly this time, that is somewhere around A.D. 1300, there was a return to bison hunting and once sedentary populations abandoned the agricultural strategy to take up a more no-madic life in the plains.

We accept Jelinek's judgment with several minor modifications. It is the case that the appearance of bison bones and increased grassland production seem to fall somewhere in the A.D. 1250-1300 period. This is not surprising, for Reher (1977) has noted that buffalo populations peak not generally during *but following an episodal climatic optimum* for grass production. We judge that climatic optimum to have been in the form of both increased and winter dominant rainfall, which was discussed in the last chapter. Such a pattern would logic-ally lead to colder, slightly wetter, and more moisture retention conditions for grassland production in the southeast plains. Jelinek has suggested that the increased moisture came in the summer months, but we decline to accept this position. Thus, we suggest that the tempor-ary optimum in buffalo population came perhaps just about A.D. 1250-1275, maybe a little later.

Following this period there is little evidence from dated bison remains for substantial bison remains in sites until A.D. 1450-1550. So bison hunting appears to us, tentatively, to involve *two* major episodes — the first around A.D. 1250-1300 and the second A.D. 1450, and later on to historic times. This second optimum in buffalo population would coincide with what Reher has termed the Little Ice Age, which he notes lasted from roughly A.D. 1500 to 1800, a widely known and well documented climatological episode, worldwide.

In the southern portion of the study area, occupation has been generally divided into three major phases. These are the Querecho phase, generally dated from A.D. 950-1100 to 1150; the Maljamar phase, generally dated A.D. 1100 or 1150 to 1300; and the Ochoa phase, generally dated from A.D. 1350 to 1450. We note that many investigators include an interlude phase between the Maljamar and the Ochoa.

Though a purely agricultural strategy is not so well documented for this region at any time, we view the Querecho phase and the Maljamar phase, collectively, to be the equivalent, temporally and ceramically (Mimbres B/W, Cebolleta B/W followed by Chupadero B/W), to P-II/Early P-III development. We note that the Maljamar phase sites are larger pithouse villages than those found at any other time of occupation in this region, and they occur in the same locations as the earlier Querecho phase sites. Though the dates for these two phases are given as A.D. 950-1300, collectively, we should like to revise this judgment to suggest that the

Ochoa and Maljamar phases are also dated roughly from A.D. 950 to 1150 or perhaps 1200.

Leslie (1979) notes the abandonment of other areas of the southeastern plains at the end of the Maljamar phase. Specifically, we are proposing here that at the end of the Maljamar phase those populations which actually had pursued either an agricultural (conjectural) or an intensive collecting (more likely) strategy that depended on summer dominant rainfall to produce the harvest during P-II times, would have moved into other areas, specifically into adjacent highlands. Much has been made of the shin oak available along the Mescalero pediment of the southeast plains, and while we don't know the answer, we should like to discover if harvestable quantities of acorns from the miniature oak are dramatically affected, not solely by the quantity of rainfall but by shifts in seasonality of rainfall.

We place the post Maljamar-pre-Ochoa interlude at roughly A.D. 1250-1350, both on the basis of ceramics (appearance of Lincoln B/R, Glaze A Red and Yellow, Ramos and Gila Polychromes) and on the notion that this was again a time when populations were beginning to move out of highland areas. We suspect a 50-60 year hiatus between the Maljamar and post Maljamar materials, but this is currently speculative. In the southern region, bison were never as plentiful as to the north. But few bison remains have been recovered from sites in the eastern extension of the Jornada-Mogollon until Ochoa phase times. We suppose that the earliest Ochoa phase developed may have involved some bison hunting, perhaps at about A.D. 1350 as proposed. Nonetheless, we believe that the Ochoa phase is in fact comprised of two episodes — the early at the very beginning of this period and, later, a semisedentary period also made possible by a later optimum in buffalo population which began perhaps as early as A.D. 1450 but continued into the earliest historic period, perhaps A.D. 1550. We suppose that such semisedentary or recurring settlements would also have had to have been in areas where collectable resources were substantial.

In any case, cultural development in the eastern Jornada-Mogollon requires *much* further investigation. The general complexity, coupled with the lack of dated sites, and trade networks which, in later times, extended into Texas, all combine to leave us far from satisfied with our characterization of the southern portion of this study area. Many important details are missing from the published literature. For instance, we know (Leslie 1979) that the post-Maljamar/pre-Ochoa period saw a substantial rise in El Paso Polychrome. What we do not know is whether those polychromes are direct rim style (pre A.D. 1260 — see Whalen 1979) or the post A.D. 1260 rim treatments. We suspect that the post A.D. 1260 material evidences the dramatic increase in these assemblages, but hard data is needed to be certain.

In summary, we propose that culture development in southeastern New Mexico loosely parallels developments in both the Anasazi and Mogollon areas to the west between roughly A.D. 800 and A.D. 1300, though on a far more modest scale. We know that the evidence for dependence on agriculture in this region is generally modest, the more so as one moves to the south and east. Nonetheless, Jelinek's observations for declining maize production and remarkable dependence on small animals, such as rodents and turtles, during the Mesita Negra phase, is quite like LeBlanc's observations for the trend in Classic Mimbres subsistence.

P-III development seems to have taken place almost everywhere in the highlands. We propose that, at least from the Pecos drainage to the west, the episodes of abandonments which Jelinek and other investigators have seen, occurred at this time and are related to archeological phenomena such as the Lincoln expression. In the Shinnery Oak belt to the east and along the Mescalero pediment, we are not so certain that populations would have been influenced by the same kinds of climatic change. Nonetheless, we note that everywhere in the Southwest, beginning somewhere around A.D. 1200, there is more evidence for large game hunting from then on than there is during P-II periods. Thus, we may presume that the first period of dependence on agriculture or on relatively stable collectable wild resources

Table VI.5

PROPOSED SOUTHEASTERN NEW MEXICO CHRONOLOGY AND PHASE CORRELATIONS

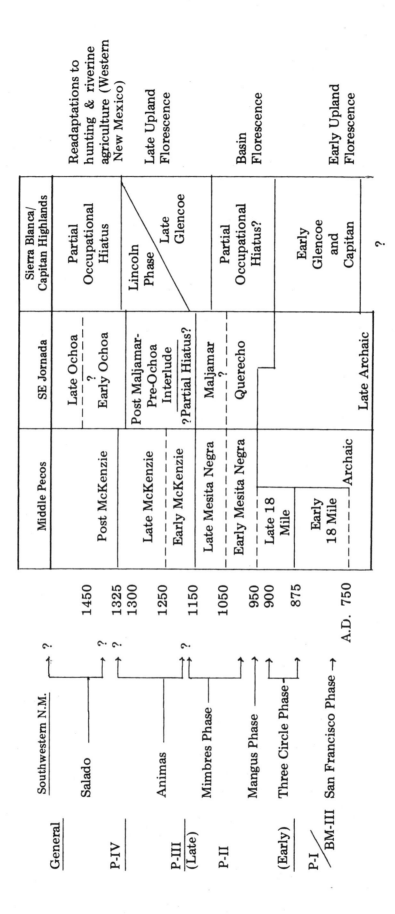

General	Southwestern N.M.	A.D.	Middle Pecos	SE Jornada	Sierra Blanca/Capitan Highlands	
	Salado	1450 ?	Post McKenzie	Late Ochoa ?	Partial Occupational Hiatus	Readaptations to hunting & riverine agriculture (Western New Mexico)
P-IV		1325 ?		Early Ochoa		
	Animas	1300 ?	Late McKenzie	Post Maljamar-Pre-Ochoa Interlude	Lincoln Phase	Late Upland Florescence
P-III (Late)		1250 ?	Early McKenzie	?Partial Hiatus?	Late Glencoe	
P-II	Mimbres Phase	1150	Late Mesita Negra	Maljamar ?	Partial Occupational Hiatus?	Basin Florescence
	Mangus Phase	1050	Early Mesita Negra	Querecho		
(Early)	Three Circle Phase	950 900	Late 18 Mile		Early Glencoe and Capitan	Early Upland Florescence
P-I / BM-III	San Francisco Phase →	875	Early 18 Mile	Late Archaic		
		A.D. 750	Archaic		?	

terminated by roughly A.D. 1150 and was followed by a return to agricultural dependence after A.D. 1300 in some areas and to bison hunting in others. In the general sense, developments in the southeastern plains are not so unlike development elsewhere in New Mexico. The proposed abandonment of agricultural strategies for buffalo hunting makes great sense to us. After all, one has only to invoke the principle of minimum effort to suppose that a less labor-intensive strategy with higher yields would have been attractive to those who were able to pursue it (see also Tainter 1979).

Devolution is a common fact in both the archeological and ethnographic records, but anthropologists have been slow to accept this. In the terms that we have presented in this volume, devolution, in this case, would simply be tantamount to a return to the efficiency niche described in Chapter II. In this case we should then expect that the structural complexity of the system would be eroded by return to an incompatible less labor-intensive strategy. With the abandonment of the irrigation strategy in agriculture among the western pueblos at roughly the same time that buffalo hunting became episodal in the east, structural complexity in the west never again equalled the Chacoan system. With less to lose, structurally, the shift appears more dramatic in southeastern New Mexico, but the comparative magnitudes of simplification may be little different, in reality.

One question, of course, is just who were these people in the middle Pecos and in the eastern extension of the Jornada-Mogollon? We believe that extensive burial studies would have to be made and compared with excavated sites in the Sierra Blanca-Capitan region to determine the facts of the case. Our strong suspicion is that at times the majority of population involved in Chupadero Mesa-Sierra Blanca developments was neither Anasazi nor Mogollon physical types. We believe it most likely that many sites on the eastern periphery of Mogollon-Anasazi development were first founded by western New Mexico physical types, following the final expansion of the basin interaction spheres in the early A.D. 1100's. Then we would suppose that with a shift to highland areas, followed by collapse of the highland systems, any remaining sites in these regions, that is, in the lower elevations (Chupadero Mesa, the east flank of Sierra Blanca, and perhaps even in the Galisteo Basin), would show a pattern in which founding populations were either Anasazi or Mogollon population types. Very rapidly there would be an admixture of plains physical types.

In short, we are not at all convinced that populations participating in the pre A.D. 1000 highland developments (*very* modest) in the Sierra Blanca-Chupadero Mesa region, for instance, were of the same physical type as populations in the Mogollon heartland. We think it more likely that the P-II expansion was by western physical types followed by complex admixtures. We would like to know, and far more excavation will have to be conducted to determine the case. Our proposed chronology of southeastern New Mexico is shown in Table VI.6. Let us turn, then, to survey and National Register considerations.

CONSIDERATIONS FOR SURVEY

BACKGROUND AND PRIORITIES

Archeological survey in southeastern New Mexico has generally been sporadic and thematic. There have been many surveys to locate Paleo-Indian remains, but many of these have never been published. Nor is there much contract archeological work in this area when compared to northern and western New Mexico, an exception being the Carlsbad area and other regions where substantial gas fields are in operation in far southern New Mexico. By far the finest general monograph on the region is Jelinek's (1967) survey of the middle Pecos Valley, roughly from Fort Sumner to Roswell, New Mexico, but even his data base is small, fewer than 60 sites having been summarized (the CGP survey in northwestern New Mexico was 750+; see Reher 1977).

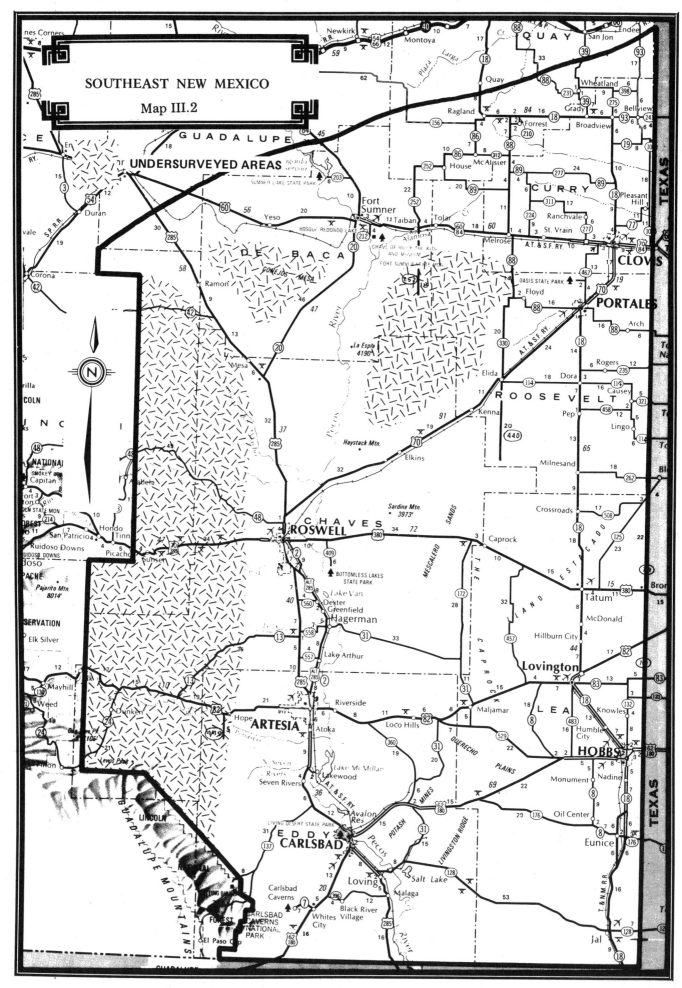

SOUTHEAST NEW MEXICO

Map III.2

Geographically, this is a huge region, comprising nearly 17 million acres. Camilli and Allen (1979) suggest a figure of slightly over 18 million acres, but portions of their study area are discussed with the northeast plains in a succeeding chapter. Thus, southeastern New Mexico as defined here consists of 26,000-odd square miles. Unlike other portions of western New Mexico, 63% of the acreage in this region is privately owned. Most of the rest of the acreage is rather evenly divided between the Bureau of Land Mangement and the state of New Mexico, there being no Forest Service and small military holdings in the region (except Cannon Air Force Base near Clovis). There are *no* Indian lands involved, and unlike most other parts of New Mexico, federal holdings are a minor portion of acreages.

Private lands in southeastern New Mexico, and perhaps lands pertaining to Cannon Air Force Base near Clovis, would be the areas that would involve potential difficulty of access. In most portions of southeastern New Mexico, land owners have been relatively generous with archeologists in permitting them to conduct survey. Occasionally however, the publication of site locations and the name of property owners creates problems. Few land owners want amateur collectors traipsing across their land without permission, so archeologists must be attentive to the formalities and the protection of privacy.

Unlike other parts of New Mexico, with the possible exception of northeastern New Mexico, there have been no really large surveys conducted in southeastern New Mexico. The most extensive surveys are those reported by Jelinek (1967) and the Brantley Reservoir study (Henderson 1976). The data contained in the Jelinek report appear to be very complete and useable. The Brantley Reservoir report is more interesting theoretically than it is with respect to data. Leslie (1979) has summarized survey data from the southeastern area of the region. His summary is interesting, but again the data are not complete. The Lea County Archeological Society has conducted extensive surveys from time to time, along the southern portions of the Llano Estacado and the Mescalero pediment in particular, focusing much of their work in the Maljamar area.

Leslie (1978) has also summarized a great deal of data on projectile points from collections in southeastern New Mexico and southwest Texas. Hester (1962, etc.) did the same some years earlier. Eastern New Mexico University in Portales is also active in the area, having its own contract archeological program. In spite of these activities, it is still very hard to summarize survey data from the area accurately, for again, many surveys which have been conducted are small, scattered and/or thematic. Others are simply not widely known in the literature and the genuine extent of archeological survey in southeastern New Mexico is very hard to appreciate. The Camilli and Allen (1979) overview summarizes most of the site form data available in university museum and agency files. Nonetheless, a great deal more information could be obtained, we believe, from the active amateur societies in the region, who, in any case, publish regularly.

In general, the Fort Sumner area has been surveyed (Jelinek 1967). The area from north of Roswell in an arc to Hobbs, New Mexico, along the Mescalero pediment, has been rather extensively, though often thematically, surveyed. In addition, the general area around Carlsbad, New Mexico has been fairly well surveyed compared to other portions of southeastern New Mexico, as have some of the gas fields in the area of Jal. Kelley (1966) surveyed portions of the Hondo drainage from a few miles west of Roswell to the Lincoln-Capitan area. Twelve square miles of the lower Pecos south of Artesia, New Mexico was surveyed for the Brantley Reservoir study.

Other portions of the area are simply not well known to the formal archeological literature. In particular, the region west of the Pecos to the highlands of the Sacramentos, Guadalupes and Capitans is literally unknown (except for Kelley's sites). Recall that Kelley's

Table VI.6

SOUTHEASTERN NEW MEXICO: LAND OWNERSHIP (In Acres)

	Quay	Guadalupe	Curry	De Baca	Roosevelt	Chavez	Lea	Eddy	TOTAL ACREAGE	Percent
BLM	819	49,584	0	35,377	7,706	1,175,977	430,054	1,411,180	3,110,697	18.33
NPS	0	0	0	0	0	0	0	44,195	44,195	.26
Bureau of Reclamation	1,026	240	0	4,565	0	0	0	27,211	33,042	.19
Corps of Engineers	50	0	0	0	0	0	0	0	50	.00029
Fish and Wildlife	0	0	0	0	3,231	23,310	0	0	26,541	.15
NMSU Agriculture Research Service	0	34	0	0	0	0	0	0	34	.0002
State	237,714	177,810	60,667	243,570	211,140	703,706	873,748	477,730	2,986,085	17.60
Private and Miscellaneous	1,605,511	1,691,692	837,898	1,230,728	1,350,403	1,957,475	1,508,358	579,865	10,761,925	63.44
TOTAL ACRES	1,845,120	1,919,360	898,560	1,514,240	1,572,480	3,860,468*	2,812,160	2,540,181*	16,962,569	

*Forest Service lands in Chavez and Eddy counties transferred to Southwest New Mexico

study, like Jelinek's, only recorded between 50 and 60 archeological sites. The upper Penasco drainage between Hope and Elk, New Mexico, needs to be surveyed. Also, the lands bordering the eastern boundary of the Mescalero Apache Reservation are not well known archeologically. To the north of the Capitan Mountains the area between Ancho, White Oaks, Pine Lodge, and to the east as far as the Pecos River has not been systematically surveyed. These areas are primarily considered the Sacramento and Diamond A plains. While there is some flatland in these areas, there is also substantial relief, and major arroyos crosscut the region west to east.

To our knowledge, Conejos Mesa and surrounding regions in DeBaca County are not surveyed. Thus, though the Corona expression (Marshall 1973) has been defined in the northwest portion of this area and the Lincoln and Capitan expressions in the west central portions of the area, none of the intervening lands have been surveyed systematically. The specific nature, extent and chronological placement of any intervening archeological remains is not known, for instance, with reference to Jelinek's chronology. It is our expectation that the westernmost portions of this area will contain a substantial Late P-III to Early P-IV occupation. In addition, pithouse occupations of unknown temporal affinity (the majority, but not all, are thought to be P-III) are colloquially known in the area, but as is pointed out in Chapter VII, only a few of these have been excavated (see Table VI.7 for land ownership in southeastern New Mexico).

Impacts on archeological resources in the area fall into three major categories: 1) surface collecting and pothunting, 2) gas and some oil field development; and 3) erosion, probably in that order. There are no major centers of population that are rapidly increasing within the region. Since the majority of archeological sites in the region are under private ownership, the state and the Bureau of Land Management should definitely intensify their efforts to create substantial districts of protected archeological remains.

THE DATA

Camilli and Allen (1979) list something over 1200 archeological sites in the region. We point out that they have included only those sites for which they were able to obtain reasonably precise locational data. Here we have also included all those sites which have been recorded, but for which data are inadequate. In addition, we also include many sites which are recorded by institutions and agencies outside of New Mexico, or for which site forms have not been forwarded to the Laboratory of Anthropology in Santa Fe. Our total, as best as we can retrieve it from the literature, is 1,816 sites in 26,000 square miles. We estimate (though with great difficulty) that the equivalent of 280 square miles has been surveyed, more or less systematically.

We point out, however, that it is difficult to compute an acreage-covered figure for sites that were individually and occasionally recorded. For instance, just how much intensive survey did Mera (1938) conduct in all? Also, however excellent in other respects, Jelinek (1967) does not tell us specifically how much area was surveyed. His survey (1967:42) was primarily between Fort Sumner and La Aspia along the Pecos, a distance of perhaps thirty miles. It is almost impossible to compute the actual ground coverage, but we have judged it at 16 square miles. We leave it to others (perhaps Jelinek himself would care to comment) to determine whether this is reasonable in computing his survey coverage.

We had similar problems throughout and can offer no good resolution at this moment. We can suggest, however, that one of the most important bits of data which may be contained in the introduction to an article or a report of survey is the actual person hours spent in intensive survey. Judge (1973) put this information in his study of the Rio Grande Valley. In the case of Judge's Paleo-Indian survey, we compute his 930 hours of field time at 7 square miles of coverage, based on an average of 40 acres per person per day. While this may not genuinely reflect Judge's field time, since others also aided in the project, it is nonetheless a tangible way to make different survey reports comparable when computing coverage.

At any rate, we compute survey of southeastern New Mexico at just over 1% of ground coverage. At 280 square miles surveyed for 1,816 sites, we have an average site density of 6.5 sites per square mile surveyed. This compares with 12.5 sites per square mile as surveyed in the Mimbres. This compares also to the 12.5 sites per square mile density for the San Juan Basin area in New Mexico. This is a slightly higher site density than we have determined for northeastern New Mexico, where the figure is 5 sites per square mile. We point out that in each of the undersurveyed areas of New Mexico — that is, the Mimbres, the Jornada, southeastern New Mexico and northeastern New Mexico — survey has tended to focus along the major river drainages, except for the lower Rio Grande, and we do not know that these figures accurately reflect site density over a broad region.

Tentatively then, site density in the eastern 40% of New Mexico is approximately half that of western New Mexico from the data as we now know them. Whether this reflects any real differences in population densities or merely substantially different archeological visibility, due to the continuing nonceramic adaptations in many portions of eastern New Mexico, is not known. It would be foolish at this point to generate demographic reconstructions of any sort from these data, though some day, with more accurate figures and control over site size as well, it might be done. In any case, site density on a given survey seems to range from a low of about 2 or 2.5 sites per square mile to a high of about 10 to 12 sites per square mile. Again, this is a magnitude of difference when compared with the range of densities for larger surveys in western New Mexico.

Since there is such poor chronological control over recorded sites in southeastern New Mexico, we are not able to do a comparative *site output analysis* as we did between the Mimbres and San Juan Basin regions. This is unfortunate, for we feel that such a study would be highly instructive. Nonetheless, many surveys, even recent contract surveys, only list sites as ceramic or aceramic, or perhaps identify sites as black-on-white ceramic as opposed to brownware ceramic. The Brantley Reservoir survey (Henderson 1976), for instance, describes painted ceramic wares as *Black-on-white Period*. This could be anything from Mimbres Black-on-white (A.D. 900+) to Chupadero Black-on-white (ca. A.D. 1100 to 1400+). This tells us next to nothing about precise chronological placement, since black-on-white sites, even in southeastern New Mexico, may span roughly A.D. 800 or 900 to 1400 or 1500 (some Tabira Black-on-white is even later).

Table VI.7
ESTIMATED SURVEY DATA: SOUTHEASTERN NEW MEXICO*

Square miles covered: 280 mi²
Number of sites: 1,816
Density of square miles covered: 6.5 sites/mi²
Total square miles in area: 26,000
Percent of region surveyed: 1+%

Major underrepresented areas: Pecos River between La Espia and Roswell, the Sacramento and Diamond A Plains north of Carlsbad to Corona, New Mexico (minor exception is Kelley's survey in the Hondo Valley area west of Roswell); portions of the Llano Estacado between Portales and Hobbs.

*Note: These data are rough estimates only. They are not intended for the conduct of formal research.

In summary, we applaud Camilli and Allen's (1979) attention to site data, for no other overview attempted to do this in any detail. While we feel that their results were excellent when compared to the problems encountered, we nonetheless maintain that the job is not yet done. For instance, we note that there are (by our count) fifteen dated archeological sites in southeastern New Mexico. Ironically, it is the only area in the state where Paleo-Indian remains are better dated proportionally than are later period occupations. Fifteen independently dated sites represent just about one dated site for each 1,800 square miles. If we were writing an overview of the archeology in the state of Delaware, for instance, we would, on this basis, have only *one* independently dated site for interpretive purposes. So the archeological profession places an impossible burden upon itself in correctly interpreting cultural development in southeastern New Mexico. That is, only one site of 115 formally recorded is dated independently, while in the San Juan Basin something on the order of one site in fifty has been dated. Chronological control, additional intensive survey, and bringing the substantial work of amateur investigators into the formal literature, must be rated the top priorities for archeological research throughout southeastern New Mexico.

STATE AND NATIONAL REGISTER PROPERTIES IN SOUTHEASTERN NEW MEXICO

Our records indicate that there are ten nominated sites and archeological districts in southeastern New Mexico which appear on the State Register. Three of these (Painted Grotto, Mescalero Sands and Blackwater Draw) are also on the National Register of Historic Places (see Table VI.8). Since the Mescalero Sands archeological district includes 33 sites, there are 41 sites in all nominated. Even with this district nomination to raise the total number of sites, there is approximately one site nominated for each 600+ square miles. Without this one district nomination, the number of sites drops to 9, and there would then be approximately one site per 2,700 square miles which had been nominated to either the State or National Register.

As we have said elsewhere, our minimum estimate of the number of recordable sites in any major region of New Mexico is 2.5 sites per square mile. Thus, we estimate that there are not less than 65,000 recordable sites in southeastern New Mexico. In these terms, State and National Register nominations each stand for approximately 1,500 sites or more which actually occur in the archeological record. The geographic representation of these sites is unusual in another respect. In southeastern New Mexico there are no nominated sites in Curry County, in DeBaca County, or in the eastern one-quarter of Lincoln County which is included in this study area. Roosevelt County has only one nominated site (Blackwater Draw), while Lea and Eddy counties have three each. Chaves County has two nominations which (because of Mescalero Sands) total 34 sites. Let us turn, then, to brief descriptions of these nominated archeological properties.

SHORT DESCRIPTIONS OF STATE AND NATIONAL REGISTER SITES
SOUTHEASTERN NEW MEXICO
(National Register Properties are Starred*)

No. 498   PAINTED GROTTO*

The Painted Grotto consists of a rock shelter located within Carlsbad Caverns National Park. Nearly the entire back wall of the rock shelter is covered with well-preserved pictographs. In addition, a large rock in the rock shelter has several grinding surfaces present, indicating use as a metate. The rock shelter is located within a canyon, about 100 feet above the canyon floor. It is not known which culture group is responsible for the pictographs.

Table VI.8
STATE AND NATIONAL REGISTER OF CULTURAL PROPERTIES
IN SOUTHEASTERN NEW MEXICO
(National Register Properties are starred)

Reg. No.	Name / LA No.	County	Time Period (Approximate)	Phase (if known)
No. 498*	Painted Grotto/—	Eddy	?	?
No. 159	Lusk Ranch Site/—	Eddy	(9000-6500 B.C.?)	Folsom, Midland Plainview
No. 168	Red Tank Site	Eddy	(A.D. 1500)	(Late Ochoa?)
No. 433*	Mescalero Sands/— Archeological District (33 sites)	Chaves	(A.D. 950-1100)	Querecho and poss. Archaic and/or Apache
No. 160	Mescalero Sands Site (included in above)			
No. 155	Burro Tanks Site/—	Chaves	500 B.C.-A.D. 1500	Multicomp.
No. 171	Taylor Peak Site	Lea	(9000-4000 B.C.?)	Paleo-Indian & Archaic:Clovis, Folsom, Plainview & Archaic.
No. 167	Rattlesnake Draw	Lea	(9000-10,000 B.C., + later components)	Paleo-Indian & Archaic
No. 162	Monument Springs Site	Lea	Multicomponent	Paleo-Indian through Maljamar
No. 002*	Anderson Basin (Blackwater Draw)	Roosevelt	(9500-5000 B.C., + other preceramic components)	Paleo-Indian & Archaic

Table VI.9
NOMINATED PROPERTIES BY TEMPORAL PERIOD:
SOUTHEASTERN NEW MEXICO

Period	No. Nominations (by components)
Paleo-Indian	5
Archaic	5 (components at other sites)
BM-II or III equiv.	1 (Monument Springs)?
P-I equiv.	0? (alleged Hueco Phase)
P-II equiv.	35 (components and Mescalero Sands)
P-III equiv.	2 (Burro Tanks & Monument Springs components)
P-IV equiv.	2 (as above)

No. 433   MESCALERO SANDS ARCHEOLOGICAL DISTRICT*

The 33 archeological sites within the district consist of seasonal campsites utilized for hunting and gathering activities. The major utilization of this area occurred during the Querecho phase (A.D. 950-1100) of the Jornada Mogollon (Corley 1965:36). In addition, it is believed that the Mescalero Apaches also utilized this area for gathering foods.

Several areas within this district also exhibit large quantities of bone fragments and little or no pottery. This may suggest an Archaic period occupation, or possibly Apachean hunting camps. This confusion shows that more detailed chronologies are needed for this area. The Mescalero Sands site is located approximately 35 miles east of Roswell.

No. 171   TAYLOR PEAK SITE

The Taylor Peak site consists of a possible *stratified* Paleo-Indian and Archaic site. The site is exposed along a recent arroyo exposing bison bones and lithic artifacts. Clovis, Folsom, Plainview, Midland and early Archaic points were found on the surface. The site is located about four miles northwest of Maljamar, New Mexico.

No. 168   RED TANK (BOOT HILL) ARCHEOLOGICAL SITE

This is a large midden site which has produced vast amounts of material for private collectors. Numerous burials have been found here, along with many shell items and trade items. The site dates to the late prehistoric period at about A.D. 1500. The site is located about nine miles northwest of Maljamar, New Mexico (Corley and Leslie 1960).

No. 167   RATTLESNAKE DRAW

This site consists of a stratified Paleo-Indian site and later occupations. Artifacts recovered from this site include Clovis points and Archaic milling stones. In addition, there is a shallow well dating to the Archaic period (Agogino, Smith and Runyan 1966). The site is located about twelve miles west of Buckeye, New Mexico.

No. 162   MONUMENT SPRINGS SITE

This site dates primarily from A.D. 100 to A.D. 400, with earlier and later occupations also evident. The major part of the site consists of a pithouse village and a very large midden area. Midland and Plainview material and late prehistoric material have also been found at this site. Monument Springs is located about four miles west of Monument, New Mexico.

No. 159   LUSK RANCH SITE

The Lusk Ranch site is located in a sandy draw, exposed in several areas by wind erosion. Mammoth and bison bones have been found here, along with Folsom, Midland and Plainview projectile points. The site is located about 25 miles northeast of Carlsbad, New Mexico.

No. 155   BURRO TANK SITE

This site was occupied from approximately 500 B.C. to A.D. 1500 (though probably not continuously). The ceramics from this site indicate a long sequence of recurring occupations, which is somewhat unusual in this area.

There is an extensive midden at this site with surface rooms and possible pit-rooms. The site is approximately 15 miles northwest of Maljamar, New Mexico.

No. 002   ANDERSON BASIN (BLACKWATER DRAW SITE)*

This area has produced much information on Early Man. Archeological investigations began at this site in the 1930's and have continued up to the present. Evidence from the Anderson Basin indicates that numerous Paleo-Indian groups killed extinct megafauna and camped in the area. Projectile points identified as Clovis, Folsom, Milnesand, Scottsbluff, Eden, Angostura, and Plainview have been found here. In addition to the Paleo-Indian material, Archaic and possibly Jornada Mogollon artifacts are found at Blackwater Draw (see the works of Agogino and others cited in Camilli and Allen 1979). Blackwater Draw is one of the most famous Paleo-Indian sites.

DISCUSSION

Unlike other portions of New Mexico, half of the nominations for this area include Paleo-Indian components. Here it is the later period sites which are substantially underrepresented — something of an irony when compared to all of western New Mexico. Nonetheless, additional Paleo-Indian remains merit nomination to both State and National Register, for stratified deposits in particular are exceedingly rare and any known should be reviewed and nominated before the depredations of collectors take their inevitable toll. For instance, neither the State or National Register include such well known sites as the Elida (though the materials *are* all in private hands, sites such as this should be nominated as soon as they become known), the Milnesand, nor Hermit's Cave. The Taylor Peak site, for instance, probably belongs on the National Register as well as the State Register. No Paleo-Indian materials west of the Pecos have been nominated. This situation should be rectified.

Apparently no Archaic remains in southeastern New Mexico have been nominated for their own sake. Rather, Archaic components often co-occur with Paleo-Indian deposits, and for this reason there are several components on the registers. Nonetheless, a number of *pure* Archaic deposits are known. Site forms should be reviewed, and those eligible for nomination should be nominated, for the Archaic sequences are not well known nor well dated in southeastern New Mexico. Ironically, there are more dated Paleo-Indian sites in southeastern New Mexico than there are Archaic. Since most known Archaic remains are highly deflated and sites have been substantially disturbed by erosion, any known stratified Archaic deposits merit nomination and would provide immensely valuable archeological information.

Later period occupations, unlike other portions of New Mexico, are seriously underrepresented in State and National Register properties here. All of the late period sites which have been nominated occur in and around Maljamar, New Mexico, and represent the Querecho-Maljamar-Ochoa phase sequence of the southeastern Jornada-Mogollon. We point out with great dismay that no site which represents Jelinek's Middle Pecos Sequence appears on either register. We point out that no site which represents the eastern extension of the supposed Corona expression has been nominated. We point out that no sites which might represent Kelley's (1966) Lincoln and Capitan phases have been nominated.

Thus, it is the case that only one of the local phase sequences which postdates the Archaic period is represented at all, on either the State or National Register. Certainly, if it is at all possible to do so, a National Register archeological district should be created along the Pecos from just south of Fort Sumner to just south of 18 Mile bend. Such a district would include sites of all of the phases which Jelinek identified. It might appropriately be called either the *Middle Pecos National Archeological District* or perhaps the *Bosque-Redondo National Archeological District*.

Second, it is essential that Kelley's (1966) site data be gone through and a representative nomination of Lincoln and Capitan expression sites be made. This also merits nothing less than either a thematic or National Register district nomination, perhaps entitled the *Lincoln National Archeological District*. In the northwestern portion of the area, the Corona focus has been defined, as said earlier. This area, and portions of the eastern flanks of the central highland spine where the Lincoln and Capitan expressions have been defined, will require both a careful review of existing site forms and additional survey. In each of these three cases a National Register district nomination is *paramount*, in our view.

Finally, the area around Maljamar, New Mexico contains such a rich array of sites, some of which are already nominated to the National and State Registers, that it would appear appropriate to consider a *Maljamar National Archeological District* which incorporated additional sites not now nominated in a thematic nomination of broader scale. We are certain that the Lea County Archeological Society and others in the area would consider cooperating in such a proposed venture.

We point out also that early pithouse occupations, that is, perhaps A.D. 400-900, are variously suspected or known from the east slopes of the Sacramento Mountains and highly probable in the east slopes of Chupadero Mesa. Where these higher elevations intrude into southeastern New Mexico, such sites should be sought out and nominated. This would require additional survey, but in the overview of this volume we suggested that deep pithouse villages occur in the higher elevations at roughly A.D. 500-900 and again in the A.D. 1100-1300 period. We believe that such pithouse occupations along the eastern flanks of the highlands of New Mexico would be an important element in understanding cultural process and cultural affiliations in Anasazi and Mogollon prehistory. In short, we believe that the information contained in such sites would be priceless in unraveling questions with regard to both economic and physiological relationships between early Anasazi-Mogollon and Plains populations. We accord these sites our very highest priority for additional survey and protection.

GEOGRAPHICAL AND GENERAL CONSIDERATIONS

As we mentioned previously, the State and National Registers in southeastern New Mexico comprise ten nominations consisting of 41 archeological sites. Also, we mentioned that there are no nominated archeological sites in Curry County, in DeBaca County, in the eastern one-quarter of Lincoln County which falls into this study area, and only one nominated site in Roosevelt County.

In fact, if one circumscribes a circle around Maljamar, New Mexico having a radius of roughly 30 miles, seven of the ten nominations to the State and National Registers fall in it. Obviously, the rest of southeastern New Mexico is substantially underrepresented (70% of the nominations fall within 10% of the area), both from a geographical standpoint and from the standpoint of the number of eligible sites, of those recorded, which merit action and preservation.

One must consider that there are no nominated prehistoric sites in Quay County, only one in Guadalupe, and none in Torrance County east of Estancia, New Mexico. In other words, it is possible to describe an area bounded roughly on the west by sites such as Abo and Quarai, and on the north by the pictograph site at Santa Rosa, on the east by Blackwater Draw, between Clovis and Portales, and on the south by the Caprock district near the juncture of State 380 and 172, thence west to Hondo, New Mexico and northwest again to Estancia. The area thus described takes in nearly 10,000 square miles and contains not one site nominated to the State or National Register. In comparative terms, then, an area the size of the state of Maryland contains no National or State Register nominations. This is clearly not a tenable situation, and when it is considered that northeastern New Mexico is also substantially underrepresented in the National and State Registers, it must be concluded that the eastern portion of New Mexico, in general, has been neglected from the Register standpoint. We believe that the rectification of this situation should be a high priority.

As mentioned earlier, erosion is an important factor in the destruction of archeological sites in eastern New Mexico. For this reason, stratified deposits, even those which are not intact, would merit very serious consideration for nomination. It would probably be advisable, in fact, to overnominate sites in eroded areas in southeastern New Mexico. It is certainly the case that however many sites might be nominated, eventually, time and erosional process alone will reduce both the integrity and the number of such sites with or without the protective intent of any legislation. It is clearly a case where the site base will diminish in many areas, and any which are still intact and not severely pothunted should be protected as best they can be.

This philosophy, if applied, would appeal most to the generally reducing nature of the archeological data base in southeastern New Mexico, and also to the relative rarity of stratified deposits. Both these factors contribute substantially to any logical determination of significance. In short, while we could argue that the most common type of site in the universe of northwestern New Mexico might be a ten-room, stratified and undisturbed P-II village, in southeastern New Mexico we would be forced to argue just the reverse. This transferal, or inversion, of priorities may be difficult for some, but it is the case that one standard of conventional wisdom based on site type and scarcity cannot be adequately transferred from one major region of New Mexico to another.

We conclude this section, then, with the strong suggestion that the National and State Registers be substantially expanded in southeastern New Mexico. Specifically, we have proposed that a Bosque-Redondo National Archeological District would be appropriate as a nomination to include Jelinek's type sites. Secondly, we have proposed that the Corona and Lincoln expressions be considered for additional survey and either thematic or district nominations, as the case warrants. Finally, we have suggested that a district or thematic nomination be prepared for the area around Maljamar, New Mexico. Such nominations would rectify the most obvious current lacunae, though other nominations of either a district or thematic nature will undoubtedly arise in the course of time and seem logical. Unfortunately, we do not know enough about the archeological record of southeastern New Mexico in its entirety to propose an exhaustive and adequate series of the types of nominations which would be necessary. Perhaps future survey and investigation will permit others to make such proposals.

OVERVIEW — SOUTHEASTERN NEW MEXICO

The archeology of southeastern New Mexico is exceedingly complex and presents formidable difficulties of field methodology which are not encountered in the same degree in western New Mexico. Too few dated sites have been used to construct local archeological sequences, and no broad regional chronology appears to prevail. It is of course possible that no such regional chronology is appropriate, and this in fact is one of the major questions which future archeological research must face.

Cultural development in southeastern New Mexico is in some ways quite similar to the more widely familiar archeological record of western New Mexico. In other, and perhaps critical ways, differences are also dramatic. In view of important similarities with the Puebloan regions and equally important similarities with the plains provinces, just what is the appropriate theoretical, classificatory and interpretive balance when applying investigative technique in southeastern New Mexico? We don't know.

Our knowledge of Paleo-Indian development is perhaps too sketchy to make complete comparisons. Nonetheless, we accept Judge's (1973) interpretation that the intensity of Paleo-Indian occupation in northwestern New Mexico was more modest than that in the eastern plains areas. Nonetheless, we have pointed out that formally recorded Paleo-Indian localities in the San Juan Basin and its environs at least equal localities recorded in southeastern New Mexico. We do not suggest that this contradicts Judge's interpretation; rather we think it reflects on a tendency to assume basic differences where in some cases the formally reviewable data do not support such an interpretation.

We note also that the *majority* of Paleo-Indian remains in southeastern New Mexico are in fact found along areas such as the Mescalero pediment. Thus, any characterization of Paleo-Indian occupation must take this into account, along with the pattern determined in the San Juan Basin, and the pattern which will be outlined in the forthcoming chapter for northeastern New Mexico. These all suggest a very strong association with peripheral topographic features rather than with open plains/playa environments. We wish to know whether this apparent pattern is a function of erosional process on the one hand, or Paleo-Indian hunting strategies on the other. We certainly do not yet know.

Archaic occupation in southeastern New Mexico appears to have been protracted and fairly intense, but data to make adequate comparisons is not available. What is apparent from excavation to date is the general absence of any evidence for agricultural strategies during the Archaic period. Tentatively, we will argue that geographic compression east of New Mexico's highland spine was not sufficient to induce the dependence on such a strategy. That is, as we argued in Chapter II, when presented with the possibility, hunters and gatherers simply walked away from stressful situations and stressful locations.

It is pretty clear that the Archiac strategies lasted until quite late in southeastern New Mexico. Perhaps it is appropriate to state that Archaic-like hunting and gathering strategies were always a feature in parts of southeastern New Mexico. Nonetheless, we consider it likely that agricultural strategies and hunting and gathering strategies co-existed in relative proximity in portions of southeastern New Mexico from perhaps A.D. 850 to perhaps A.D. 1100. We have explained in Chapter II why this should not be so difficult to accept, for the space requirements of agriculturalists are reduced to the advantage of surrounding hunters and gatherers under most circumstances.

In addition, we view it as possible that an agricultural strategy and a hunting and gathering adaptation coexisted, at least in the eastern portions of the Sierra Blanca-Guadalupe highlands, even earlier. And we ask if earlier sedentary adaptations, perhaps pithouse villages, might not someday be found where an agricultural adaptation might be demonstrated as early as, say, A.D. 400-500. Recently such agricultural settlements have been demonstrated from the southern portions of the Tularosa Basin, and it is not impossible that we should have it here as well. If such early occupations were found on the eastern periphery of southeastern New Mexico, we would then either have to revise our notions about geographic compression as a function of highland topography or, alternatively, conclude that there was an earlier and more dramatic population expansion in the Southwest than has previously been supposed.

Later occupations in the middle Pecos and in the eastern Sacramento Mountain areas along the Sacramento and Diamond A plain appear to parallel both Mogollon and Anasazi developmental trends closely. That is, there was a rather notable expansion of sedentary farming communities during the P-II period, followed by increasing moves into the highland areas and, late in the P-III period, by substantial aggregation of population into few but larger communities. Some time, then, during the late A.D. 1200's to early 1300's, there appears to have been an episode of notable dependence on bison hunting. This, of course, is unlike development in most areas of western New Mexico with regard to the specific fauna exploited.

Nonetheless, we tend to view this an an episode rather than a singular trend which endured into the historic period. There is rather more evidence for bison hunting at roughly A.D. 1300, and again around A.D. 1500 and onwards, than there is evidence for continued dependence on bison in the Pecos area throughout the period. So while populations in western New Mexico generally abandoned areas in the A.D. 1300's where there were no riverine environments, and resettled into agricultural settings along permanent streams, we agree with Jelinek that the agricultural strategy was largely eliminated from the adaptive repertoire in southeastern New Mexico.

The case, however, for those Jornada-Mogollon sites east of the Pecos is not at all so clear, and we can only surmise that, for a time at least prior to A.D. 1300-1350, developments in the middle Pecos and in the southeastern Jornada were similar, though not identical. Specifically, we suspect that the subsistence base west of the Pecos and south of Roswell may never have been agricultural in nature. Perhaps it is most appropriate in considering the balance of plains and pueblo developmental trajectories to suggest that the Pecos itself may have formed some sort of demarcation. Again, this is only a tentative suggestion and we are open on the matter.

In short, a great deal of additional archeological research will be essential in southeastern New Mexico before our picture of the archeological record can be substantially refined. We have no doubt that additional investigations will give us some interesting surprises, both about kinds and intensities of occupation, one subregion to another. For the moment then, let us turn to the northeast plains.

Photo 10: San Jon Site. The arrow indicates the primary excavation area at this Paleo-Indian site. Note the site placement with its relationship to the surrounding topography. Photograph by S.L. Peckham, courtesy of the Museum of New Mexico, Santa Fe.

Chapter VII
NORTHEASTERN NEW MEXICO AND CENTRAL NEW MEXICO

NORTHEAST NEW MEXICO

Few efforts have been made by New Mexico archaeologists to define any cultural complexes within this region (northeast New Mexico)... [Campbell 1976:8]

... more systemic archaeological investigations are necessary before reliable conclusions concerning the overall archaeology of northeastern New Mexico can be made. [Thoms 1976:32]

Northeastern New Mexico has received very little attention from archaeologists in recent years, although rich and varied remains are known to exist there ... [Wendorf 1960:55]

... archaeologists have avoided this region almost entirely. [Wiseman 1978:1]

The Dry Cimmaron river valley and the entire northeast portion of the state of New Mexico exist in a virtual archaeological vacuum. It is not that archaeological sites do not exist in the region, but that research in the area has been alarmingly minimal and incomplete. [Oakes 1979:79]

INTRODUCTION

The quotes given above serve to illustrate the numerous problems that confront archeologists working in northeast New Mexico. Part of this problem stems from the fact that the archeological remains in this area are not as visually spectacular as in other areas of New Mexico, and so they have not attracted many archeologists. This former lack of interest plagues contemporary investigators with such problems as an inadequate working chronology and inaccurate cultural identifications.

The problem of chronology is rooted in the lack of absolute dates (radiocarbon, dendrochronology, archeomagnetic, etc.) retrieved from sites in northeast New Mexico. In the past, most sites have been cross-dated by pottery and projectile points, which has resulted in a loose chronology. For example, there are several projectile point forms which are dated from 4000 B.C. to A.D. 1000, or a period spanning 5,000 years! It is difficult for the archeologist to define cultural sequences or to speak of changing cultural adaptations based on such a gross time span.

The problem of cultural identity has been hampered by the assignment of different names to the same cultural phenomena. This seems to be caused by the different orientations of the various investigators. Those investigators from the east side of the Texas-New Mexico border view many of the archeological remains in northeast New Mexico as of plains, or an eastern origin, and those with experience from the west side of the border attribute similar archeological remains to a marginal Basketmaker/Pueblo culture.

Table VII.1

COMPARATIVE ARCHEOLOGICAL SEQUENCES -- NORTHEAST NEW MEXICO

A.D./B.C.	Wendorf (1960) Northeast NM	Thoms (1976) Northeast NM	Levine & Mobley (1976) Los Esteros	Mobley (1978) Los Esteros	Hammack (1965) Ute Dam	Lang (1978) Conchas Res.	Glassow (1980) Cimarron Area
A.D. 1800	Historic Nomads	Apaches	Plains Period	Plains Period	Plains Nomads	Plains Nomads	Jicarilla 1750-1900
1700							COJO 1550-1750
1600							
1500	Hiatus?				Panhandle	Plains Village	Hiatus?
1400	Panhandle	Panhandle					
1300	Pueblo	Pueblo / Apishipa	Pueblo	Pueblo	Pueblo		Cimarron 1200-1300
							Ponil 1100-1250
		Neo-Indian (Plains-Woodlands)				Plains Woodland	Escritores 900-1100
							Pedregoso 700-900
							Vermejo 400-700
1000	Archaic	Archaic	? Archaic	Archaic	Archaic	Archaic	Archaic
A.D. 200							
1000							
2000							
3000							
5000	Plano / Paleo-Folsom Indian	Paleo-Indian	Paleo-Indian	Paleo-Indian	? Paleo-Indian	Plano / Folsom / Clovis Paleo-Indian	? Folsom ?
7000							
10,000	Clovis						
11,000 B.C.							

292

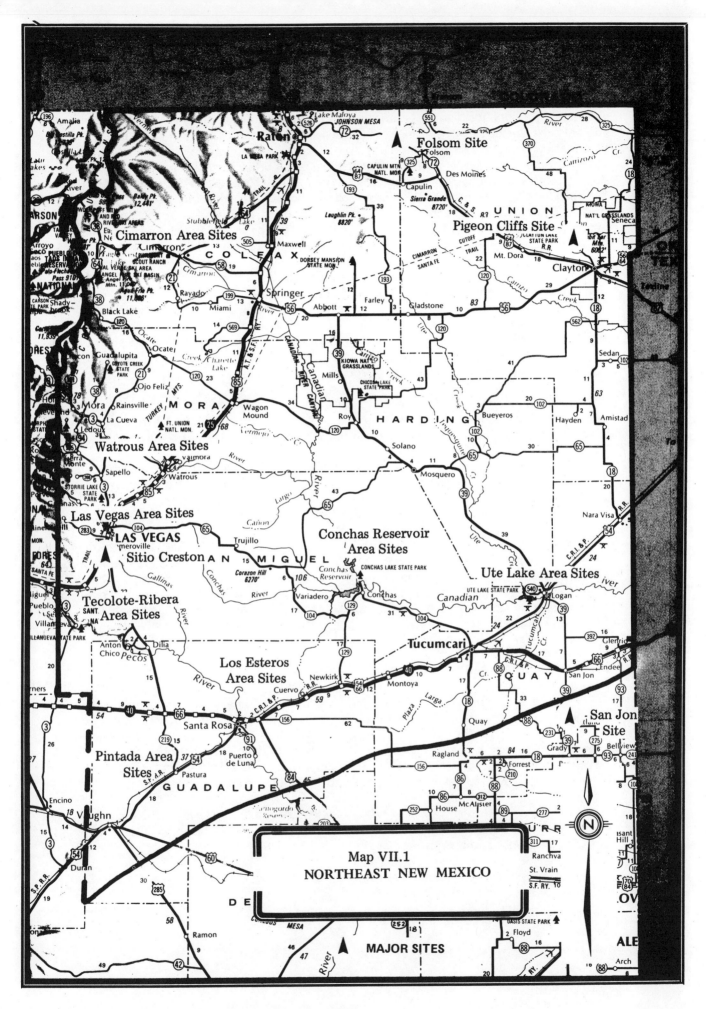

Map VII.1
NORTHEAST NEW MEXICO

MAJOR SITES

293

As yet, no Forest Service-Bureau of Land Management Cultural Resource Overview is available for the area of northeast New Mexico. This document has been commissioned but is only in the beginning stages. J. Gunnerson will be the author of this volume, which will cover not only the northeast portion of New Mexico, but portions of Texas, and Oklahoma as well. Fortunately, there are several good reviews available for the area (Wendorf 1960; Campbell 1976; Thoms 1976) and a number of archeological reports which also contain regional discussions (Hammack 1965; Kirkpatrick 1976; Levine and Mobley 1976; Lang 1978; Glassow 1980). The site files at the Laboratory of Anthropology, Museum of New Mexico, were consulted for additional archeological data that are not represented in the literature. These summaries and the site data from the Museum are the basis for this chapter. In Table VII.1 general culture chronologies based upon these sources are presented .

Geographically, northeast New Mexico includes all of Union, Colfax and Harding counties and portions of Mora and San Miguel counties (see Figure VII.1). The northern portions of Guadalupe and Quay counties are also included in this area, even though the Forest Service-Bureau of Land Management joint cultural overview units place these two counties in southeast New Mexico. Their inclusion in northeast New Mexico was based on the desire to achieve a better understanding of the range of brownware ceramic complexes in northeast New Mexico, as well as for general comparative purposes.

The boundaries of this area are the Colorado-New Mexico border on the north, the Oklahoma, Texas-New Mexico border on the east, roughly Interstate 40 on the south, and the eastern boundary of the Carson and Santa Fe National Forests on the west.

The western portion of this area is characterized by a high mountain range — the Sangre de Cristos — where elevations range up to 13,000 feet. From the mountains numerous streams emerge, most of which flow east for twenty or thirty miles and then turn to the south. The major drainages in this region include the Pecos, Canadian, Ute and Dry Cimarron rivers.

West of the mountains are the Las Vegas and Raton Plateaus. These features are mostly flat or rolling plains with several areas of canyons and mesas. The plateaus are bounded to the southeast by the Canadian Escarpment, which is a major topographic feature consisting of lava-capped mesas and sharply entrenched streams. Nearly the entire area contains Upper Sonoran vegetation, with transition zone flora encroaching on the lower slopes of the Sangre de Cristos. The higher zones of the mountains are characterized by Canadian zone vegetation; the area near Logan, New Mexico contains a small pocket of Lower Sonoran vegetation.

THE PALEO-INDIAN PERIOD IN NORTHEAST NEW MEXICO

The first conclusive evidence of early man in North America was uncovered at the now-famous Folsom type site in the late 1920's. This site produced 19 distinctive Folsom projectile points associated with 23 bison of an extinct subspecies (Wormington 1957:25). Despite this important discovery of early man in northeast New Mexico, the Folsom type site, the San Jon Site (located immediately south of the study area), and an unreported site near Sapello, New Mexico, are the only excavated Paleo-Indian sites in this area.

Paleo-Indian sites in northeast New Mexico are much better known from surveys and from evidence found in private collections. The following sites are listed in the site survey files of the Laboratory of Anthropology:

LA 3647	Clovis, Folsom, Plainview	LA 8121	Folsom type site
LA 4558	Eden	LA 8135	Folsom
LA 6232	Folsom	LA 6819	Unknown Paleo-Indian
LA 6776	Unknown Paleo-Indian	LA 8129	Unknown Paleo-Indian
		LA 12586	Folsom

Other Paleo-Indian sites located in northeast New Mexico, but not listed in the Laboratory of Anthropology site files, include those reported by Baker and Campbell (1960). They list eight sites in which Clovis, Folsom, San Jon, Plainview, Milnesand and Meserve projectile points were encountered (see Figures VII.2 and 3 for locations of these sites and others listed below).

In the Clayton area, at Pigeon Cliffs, Steen (1955) found a projectile point described as a reworked, fluted Clovis point similar in shape to a Meserve projectile point. This projectile point was found beneath a stratum radiocarbon-dated at approximately 6,000 B.C. (Steen 1955, 1976). Within this same stratum, but laterally removed, were a basin metate and mano.

Campbell (1969, 1976), reporting on sites in Las Animas County, Colorado, north of the study area, lists one example of a Clovis point and Folsom material from two other sites. He also states that Folsom points have been found on the eastern periphery of Raton Mesa as well. Plano material (parallel-flaked projectile points) was reported from eight sites located in canyon areas. Campbell (1976:48-9) sees a shift in site placement from the open steppe areas (Clovis and Folsom) to canyon areas (Plano horizon) over a period of time. He feels that this shift may be due to a climatic episode that brought about the extinction of megafauna and caused more hunting activities to be located in canyon areas where species such as deer were found (1976:49).

In the Cimarron area, Folsom points have been found by local collectors. Additional evidence of Folsom occupation in northeast New Mexico is reported from Ute Dam (Hammack 1965), and finds near Newkirk, New Mexico indicate Folsom and Plainview as well (Lang 1978). Anderson's (1975) survey near the Folsom type site reported one isolated Plainview projectile point, and noted that Scottsbluff and Alberta projectile points have been found in the Mesa de Mayo area near the New Mexico-Colorado border. In addition, two projectile point fragments, with transverse parallel flaking, possibly belonging to the Firstview Complex, were found at two multicomponent sites in her study area (Anderson 1975).

The distribution of these Paleo-Indian sites and projectile point finds is illustrated in Figures VII.2 and 3. Two trends are apparent from these figures. First, nearly all sites and reported finds are located in two north-south oriented *bands*. It appears that the geography, and possibly the elevation, in this portion of the state are strong contributing factors to Paleo-Indian site placement. The easternmost band generally parallels the Canadian Escarpment; the western band is placed against the foothills of the Sangre de Cristo Mountains and, at the northern locations, against the Trinidad Escarpment. Elevation of these features is at approximately 7,000 feet on the Sangre de Cristo foothills-Trinidad Escarpment, and at 5,000 feet on the Canadian Escarpment.

The second point to be made has to do with the location of the various site types. The higher elevation site *band* consists of Clovis, Folsom, Plainview and Cody artifacts. The lower elevation band, near the 5,000 foot level, consists of Clovis, Folsom, Plainview, Cody, San Jon, Milnesand and Meserve materials. The Clovis, Folsom, Plainview and Cody projectile points are present in both areas, but the San Jon, Milnesand and Meserve projectile points are limited to the areas of lower elevation.

In a previous section, we (see Chapter III) discussed the possible distribution of generalized and specialized projectile points as defined by Judge (n.d.) and discussed by Cordell (1978:15). Briefly, the fluted and laterally thinned projectile points (Clovis, Folsom, Midland, Plainview, Meserve, Milnesand and Frederick) are referred to as generalized points. The constricted or indented base projectile points (San Jon, Firstview, Alberta, Eden and Scottsbluff) are specialized points. Generalized points are suspected to represent a wide range of animals

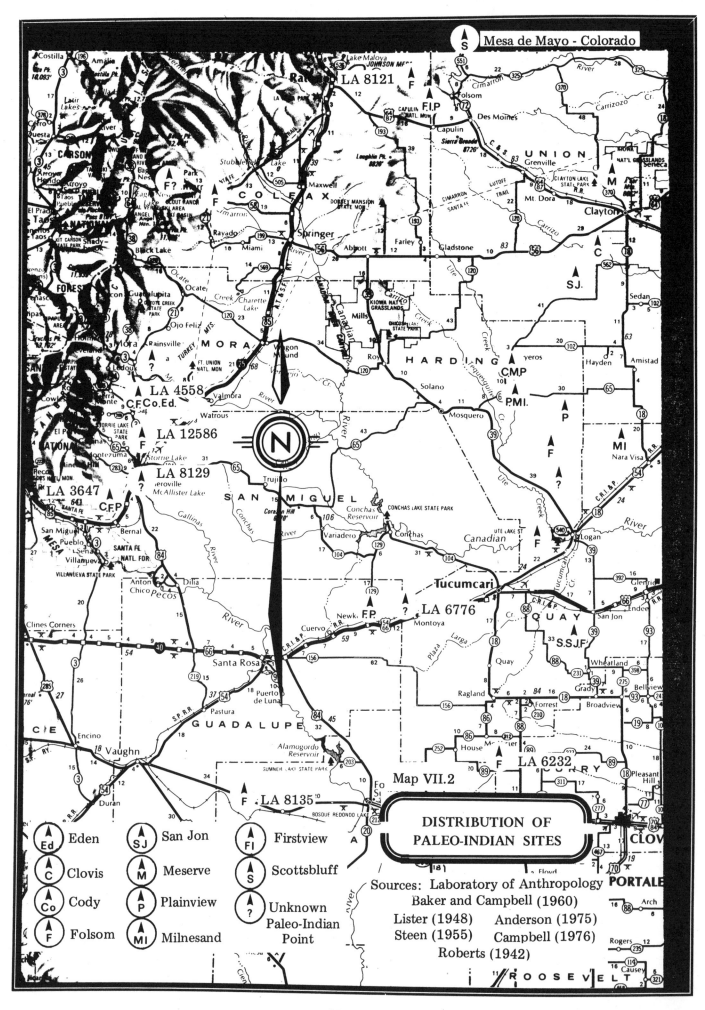

Mesa de Mayo - Colorado

LA 8121

LA 4558
C.F.Co.Ed.

LA 12586

LA 8129

LA 3647
C.F.P.

LA 6776

S.S.J.F.

LA 6232

LA 8135

Map VII.2

**DISTRIBUTION OF
PALEO-INDIAN SITES**

Sources: Laboratory of Anthropology
Baker and Campbell (1960)
Lister (1948)   Anderson (1975)
Steen (1955)   Campbell (1976)
Roberts (1942)

Ed	Eden
C	Clovis
Co	Cody
F	Folsom
SJ	San Jon
M	Meserve
P	Plainview
MI	Milnesand
FI	Firstview
S	Scottsbluff
?	Unknown Paleo-Indian Point

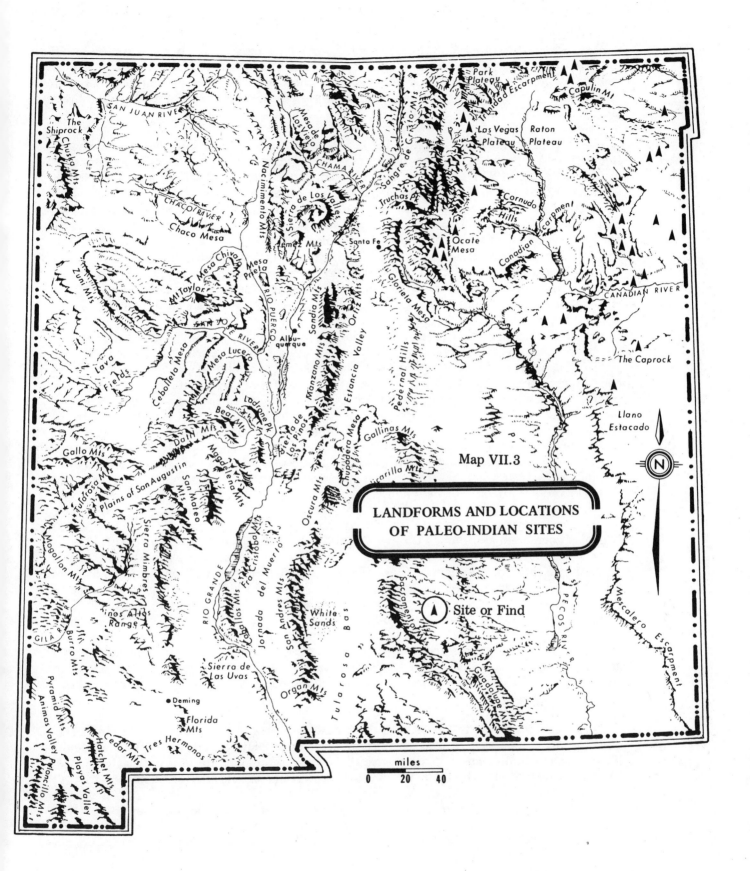

Map VII.3

LANDFORMS AND LOCATIONS
OF PALEO-INDIAN SITES

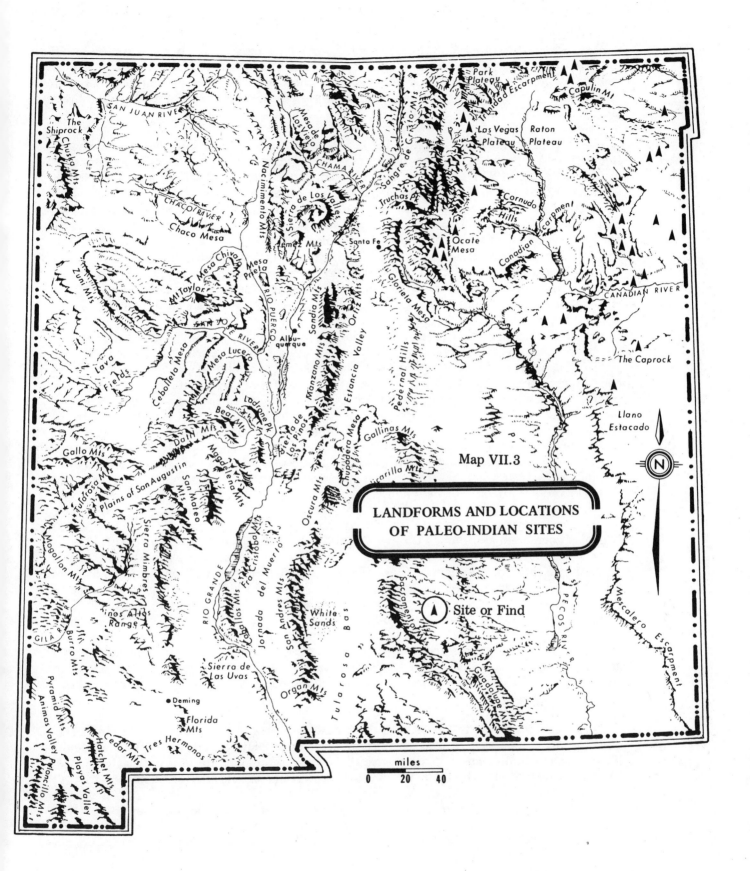 Site or Find

297

hunted, while specialized points are designed for killing bison only. If these two types of projectile points do indeed represent different hunting or subsistence strategies, then the generalized projectile point should be found over a wide area and in several different environmental zones. In contrast, the specialized projectile points should be found where the bison are — on the plains (see Chapter III).

Refering to the distribution of Paleo-Indian projectile points in northeast New Mexico (see Figures VII.2 and 3), the generalized points are widely distributed (the predominant type in both site *bands*). The specialized projectile points (in this case San Jon, Firstview, Scottsbluff and Eden) appear to be limited largely to the lower elevations of the plains, with some exceptions. The first exception includes a Scottsbluff site (LA 4558) located north of Sapello, New Mexico, which is believed to be a quarry site (Cordell 1978:16) and therefore not indicative of subsistence pursuits. Although the site (also referred to as R-6) is labeled a Scottsbluff site, Mr. John Broster, who worked on this site, informs us that only one Scottsbluff projectile point was recovered from excavations, while thirty or more Eden projectile points were found. The second exception includes a Firstview and a possible Alberta projectile point which have been reported immediately north of the New Mexico-Colorado border in the Mesa de Mayo area (Anderson 1975:131). This area is around 7,000 feet in elevation, and can be considered a part of the Trinidad Escarpment, or the high elevation band. Generally, this northern area (along the New Mexico-Colorado border) contains quite a mixed assemblage, which also suggests a long period of occupation or use. From this area the following projectile point types have been reported: Clovis, Folsom, Plainview, Plano (types not specified), Alberta, Scottsbluff and Firstview. This broad assemblage of Paleo-Indian projectile points may represent the terminus of northern and southern nodes following migratory game (again, see our discussion in Chapter III), and the mixing of assemblages would be expected to occur here. Most important, however, is the reported Alberta projectile point (Anderson 1975:131) found in this area. Alberta points are generally considered to represent northern plains manifestations (Cordell 1978:15-16), and this occurrence may indicate the southern extent of this style, and therefore probably of the northern hunters themselves.

Another distinction between these two clusterings of Paleo-Indian sites (the two *bands*) is one of temporality. Although Cordell (1978:15) has pointed out several inconsistencies in dated Paleo-Indian points, it is possible to make several general statements concerning trends over a period of time. Evidence of Clovis, Folsom and Plainview occupation (ca. 9500 to 7500 B.C.) is present in both areas. The later periods (ca. 7500 to 5500 B.C.) are generally limited to the lower elevation areas, along the Canadian Escarpment. To the north, in southern Colorado, Campbell (1976) noted a shift in Paleo-Indian site placement through time from open steppe areas to canyon areas. Broilo (1971) noted a similar shift at Blackwater Draw away from playas to other areas of permanent water (streams, etc.). Broilo felt this trend coincided with a general drying period, which forced herds of megafauna away from playa water sources to other sources of water. Such a trend would also force big game hunters to shift their hunting areas and campsites.

No site placement trends such as those described by Campbell (1976) or Broilo (1971) are apparent in northeast New Mexico. The reported sites plotted in Figures VII.2 and 3 most likely represent kill or attempted kill sites. The distribution along the major topographic features perhaps indicates the truth of our statement (Chapter III) that the tendency to hunt migrating game was to *press them against the eastern spine of the Rockies*. To this we can only add that the hunters were pressing game against the Canadian Escarpment as well.

This phenomenon of Paleo-Indian site location near these topographic features needs further investigation. The existing site data generally do not note the locations of immediate features such as cliffs, drainages, etc. in relation to site placement. Assuming that most of these sites represent kill sites, a survey centered on these features could give several insights into

298

the hunting methods utilized by these big game hunters. Such a survey could employ the type of site pattern/prediction methods used by Judge (1973) in his Paleo-Indian study in the Rio Grande. The hunting methods utilized by these big game hunters most likely include bison jumps, drives and ambush. A survey along these topographic features could identify such hunting strategies. Information could also be collected to determine if these hunting strategies change over time. Since the average number of bison per kill site increases through the Paleo-Indian period, changes to more efficient or cooperative hunting techniques should also become apparent.

The mechanics of bison migrations are not well known — especially for the extinct species hunted by Paleo-Indian groups. It is generally accepted that large numbers moved north and south annually, manipulating latitude for suitable grazing areas. This is probably best illustrated by the distribution of Paleo-Indian sites in northeast New Mexico. The two north-south oriented site *bands* perhaps reflect kill sites during migration. However, it should also be kept in mind that the same type of manipulation could also be accomplished by east-west movements (manipulating altitude instead of latitude). An east-west migration would conceivably use the foothills of the Sangre de Cristo as summer pasture and the open, southern plains as winter pasture. If some bison moved in an east-west migration pattern, the herd size would probably be smaller (less grazing room in the foothill areas) and more localized. Possibly, skeletal differences, indicating different populations, could be delineated by studying a number of individuals from different latitudes. The science of migrating animals is extremely complex. There are several species not all of whose members migrate at the same time or speed or even at all. What is sorely needed is a study of *bison ecology* or *megafauna ecology* to see just how these animals behaved. Such a study should include details concerning herd aggregation, dispersion, migration, speed of migration, population dynamics, etc. We believe that the behavior of big game (elephants, bison, horse, camel, etc.) is an extremely important key for understanding Paleo-Indian archeology.

Megafaunal statistics are not the only ones lacking, however. Both Cordell (1979:20) and Martin and Plog (1973:159-160) have pointed out that these big game hunters probably did not rely entirely on large mammals for food. Both suggest that big game most likely consisted of only 50 percent of the diet. If this is true, we know only one-half of Paleo-Indian subsistence behavior. If we examine the documented tools used for subsistence activities of ethnographically known big game hunters (e.g. Cheyenne), two patterns emerge. First, the tools are indicative of a division of labor by sex, and second, most tools not associated with big game hunting would not preserve in an archeological context:

Tools Associated with Male Subsistence Activities	Tools Associated with Female Subsistence Activities
Lance points	Digging stick* (tubers and roots)
Arrow points	Twig broom & deerskin thimbles* (prickly pear fruit)
Butchering tools (knives, scrapers, etc.)	Stone maul (breaking bones for marrow and breaking
Stone mauls	firewood)
Lance and Arrow shafts*	Small handstone (crushing berries and seeds and pulverizing dried meat)
	Tanning kit (scraper, flesher, draw blade* and softening rope*)

* probably would not preserve in an archeological context.
After Hoebel (1960)

Assuming that our analogy of big game hunters of the 1800's and Paleo-Indian big game hunters is close, then not only have archaeologists concentrated on half of Paleo-Indian subsistence, but on only half of the basic social organization as well. It should be pointed out, however, that a small grinding stone was uncovered at Blackwater Draw and, in the Paleo-Indian levels at Pigeon Cliffs, a mano and metate were found. Since those tools associated with big game hunting (male activities) are most likely to be preserved, our knowledge of Paleo-Indian is quite limited, and hypotheses on demographic trends or group size are based on incomplete data .

THE ARCHAIC PERIOD
(6000-5000 B.C. to A.D. 1000+)

Unlike other areas of New Mexico, the Archaic occupation in northeast New Mexico began early and persisted until late. There appears to be considerable overlap of the beginning and ending of the Archaic period with earlier and later horizons. Most investigators date the Archaic period from 6000-5000 B.C. to A.D. 1000, or for a period lasting nearly 6,000 or 7,000 years. Although this occupation is nearly one-half of the total time that man has been known to have occupied the northeast portion of New Mexico, very few details are known about the period.

The distribution of sites attributed to the Archaic and of those sites which contain culturally unidentified lithic scatters is plotted in Figure VII.4. Most of these sites were recorded in the late 1950's and early 1960's as part of the Museum of New Mexico highway salvage archeology program, and therefore cluster along highways. Documentation of these sites generally consists of location only, although a few site forms describe the artifacts.

The early Archaic period in northeast New Mexico is virtually unknown. As Wendorf so aptly stated (1960:57), "At this point [the early Archaic period] our view of the prehistoric developments in northeastern New Mexico become [sic] clouded due to the absence of systematic research".

Steen's (1955, 1976) excavations at the stratified Pigeon Cliffs site near Clayton revealed an early Archaic occupation. Materials recovered from this site included a large stemmed and tanged projectile point, a graver of Alibates flint and numerous bones of extinct bison. This site was dated at approximately 6000 B.C. and is contemporaneous with or even earlier than late Paleo-Indian materials (Frederick Complex) located to the south on the Llano Estacado (Campbell 1976:86). Steen's Pigeon Cliffs site is important because of the early C-14 date indicated for the Archaic period in this area.

Campbell (1976:86) believes that the contemporaneous occurrence of these two different complexes (Archaic and Paleo-Indian) may be due to environmental differences. The Llano Estacado area, which is a large grassy plain, may have continued to support large herds of animals longer than the area around the Pigeon Cliffs site, which is basically a canyon area. Possibly this canyon area would be more favorable for hunting small game and collecting wild plants (Campbell 1976).

Other possible early Archaic sites have been reported from Ute Dam (Hammack 1965) and at Los Esteros (Mobley 1978). An excavated early Archaic site is located near the town of Folsom (Honea 1964). This site was a highway salvage excavation, which fortunately yielded a radiocarbon date of 2650 ± 130 B.P., or around 700 B.C. (Anderson 1975). Artifacts from this site (LA 8120) included a one-hand mano, flakes, scrapers and projectile points. The projectile points from this site are corner-notched points between three and four centimeters long.

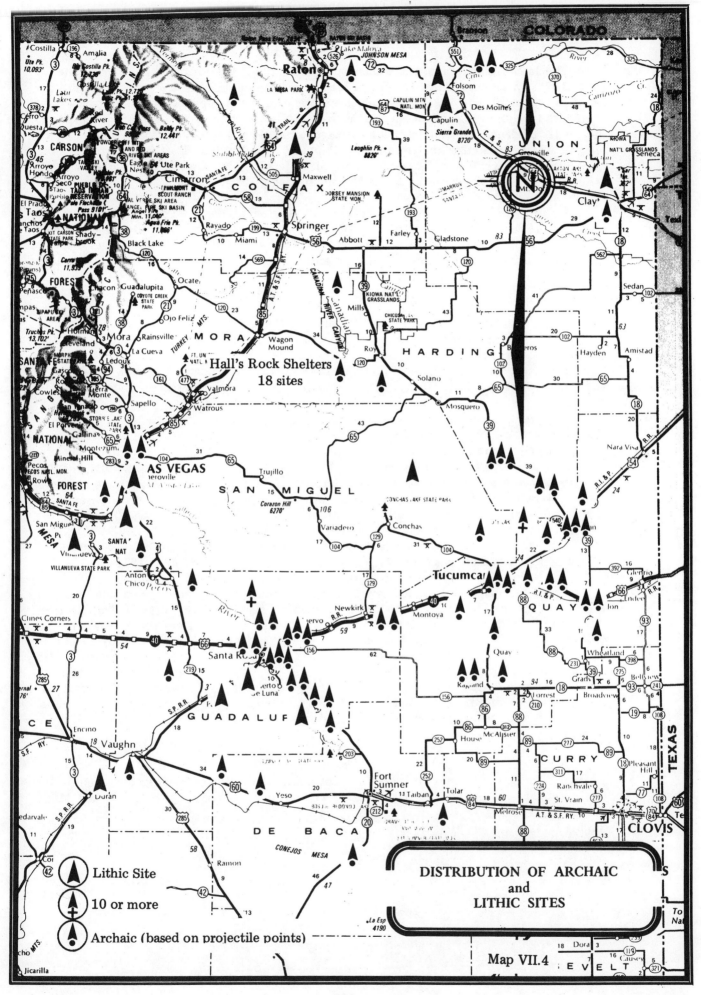

Hall's Rock Shelters
18 sites

DISTRIBUTION OF ARCHAIC
and
LITHIC SITES

▲ Lithic Site

▲ 10 or more

⊕ Archaic (based on projectile points)

Map VII.4

The later Archaic period is somewhat better known from surveys and excavations by Lang (1978), Wiseman (1978), Mobley (1978) and Campbell (1976). Lang (1978), using survey data and artifacts from private collections, believes that there was an actual intrusion of people into the upper Canadian River area from the Rio Grande area at around the first century A.D. Evidence for this intrusion is based upon projectile point style (corner-notched points), which are similar to Basketmaker II points found in late Rio Grande Archaic sites. In addition, nearly 50 percent of this style of projectile point is made of obsidian which is believed to have originated in the Jemez Mountains (Lang 1978:26-27).

Unfortunately, these results were not duplicated at nearby Los Esteros Reservoir. Mobley's (1979) excavations included a site, radiocarbon dated at A.D. 60 ± 40, in which obsidian and other exotic lithic material made up less than two percent of the lithic assemblage. In addition, Alibates flint was also present, but again, in very small quantities (Mobley 1979:218). Most of the lithic material utilized by late Archaic populations was from local sources.

Other known Archaic sites include some of Hall's (1938) rock shelters located near the Canadian River, which probably date to the late Archaic period (Campbell 1976:86). Late Archaic sites are also known from the Dry Cimarron drainage (Renaud 1930), Ute Reservoir (Hammack 1965), Los Esteros (Mobley 1978, 1979), near Logan, New Mexico (Wiseman 1978), the Cimarron area (Glassow 1980) and near Folsom, New Mexico (Anderson 1975).

A major problem for survey archeologists working in northeast New Mexico is that of assigning a culture label and date to lithic sites which lack diagnostic artifacts. Generally, sites without ceramics are considered pre-ceramic, and therefore, designated as Archaic. As previously pointed out by Wiseman (1978), in two large surveys where a large number of lithic sites were recorded (Los Esteros and Ute Reservoir), the cultural and temporal designations applied were quite different for these similar types of sites. At Ute Reservoir, Hammack (1965) believed that most of his lithic scatters probably post-date A.D. 1000 and are the remains of protohistoric Apache groups. At Los Esteros (Levine and Mobley 1976), lithic sites without diagnostic artifacts are believed to date prior to A.D. 900 and are affiliated with the Archaic period (this belief was later modified, however; see Mobley 1979).

From the discussion given above, we can see that quite a bit of confusion exists as where to place the lithic sites in a cultural or temporal framework. In northeast New Mexico, the dating of lithic sites or Archaic sites should be a high priority, since these lithic sites *are probably the most common site type* in this area. Witness Glassow's study (1980), in an area of high pueblo site density, where a total of 164 sites or 54 percent of the recorded sites found were unidentified lithic scatters, or Lutz and Hunt (1979), who recorded 212 sites in an area just across the border in Colorado in which 154 sites, or 72 percent of the total, did not have any diagnostic artifacts and could not be placed within a cultural-temporal framework. It appears that many archeologists in this area are unable to use about one-half or more of their data.

At around A.D. 200 the appearance of corn, pottery and the bow and arrow in certain areas of northeast New Mexico marks the beginning of the Plains Woodland or Neo-Indian or Basketmaker or Late Archaic period, depending upon the investigator (Campbell 1976; Thoms 1976; Lang 1978; Glassow 1980). Basically, this period is an adaptation which is similar to the former Archaic subsistence strategy (hunting and gathering), but with the addition of agriculture and a few technological innovations. It should be kept in mind, however, that agriculture was not adopted in all areas.

Two different subsistence trends become apparent during this period. In the northern area (Cimarron area) there is a trend to increased sedentism and the beginnings of a strong reliance on agriculture (Glassow 1980). To the south (Los Esteros area), hunting and gathering subsistence strategy continued at this time, and continued through the entire pueblo period.

Glassow's study (1980) of agricultural development in the Cimarron area revealed an occupation by semi-sedentary agriculturalists that began around A.D. 400. The earliest period, the Vermejo Phase, A.D. 400-700 (one radiocarbon date at A.D. 510), is similar to Basket-maker II cultures recorded in other areas of the Southwest. This phase is characterized by circular, masonry-walled houses, corner-notched projectile points, evidence of domesticated corn, and the absence of pottery.

Mobley's study at Los Esteros focused upon subsistence practices, exploitive ranges, technological behavior, tool assemblages, lithic material types, and stylistic variability in tools and rock art between Archaic sites and sites that dated to the Pueblo period (1979:212). The results of these studies indicate that there is a great deal of continuity between sites of the Archaic period and the Pueblo period (radiocarbon dates range from A.D. 60 ± 44 (one date) to A.D. 1100-1200's (five dates). Mobley concludes that an Archaic adaptation (without any evidence of agriculture) continued in the Los Esteros area until at least A.D. 1300 and possibly up to A.D. 1400, based upon ceramic tradewares (Mobley 1979).

Elsewhere in northeast New Mexico at this time the appearance of cord-marked pottery indicates the beginning of the Plains Woodland period. This period is not at all well known in this area; most information about Plains Woodland sites comes from Colorado and other states. It is believed that Plains Woodland groups were semi-sedentary agriculturists (corn was recovered from several cave sites, which are believed to date to this period, along the Canadian River) and occasionally constructed circular masonry dwellings. The artifact assemblage consists of small corner-notched projectile points, one-hand manos, a variety of lithic tools and, rarely, cord-marked pottery (Campbell 1976). Sites listed in the Laboratory of Anthropology site files which may be Plains Woodland sites are: LA 803, LA 1499, LA 1762, and LA 15867 (Oakes, 1979). In addition, Gunnerson (1959) noted cord-marked sherds on sites near Clayton, and a cave site excavated by Mera (1944) may also date to this period (Figure VII.6).

THE ANASAZI PERIOD

Anasazi occupation in northeast New Mexico is generally believed to have begun around A.D. 1000. This date is based upon ceramic cross-dating, but, as mentioned above, there is evidence of earlier Anasazi remains in the Cimarron area (Glassow 1980).

A number of pueblo sites in this area have been excavated or tested, but these usually consist of only a brief report, or contain unusable data. Two sites, located near Watrous and Tecolote, have yielded tree-ring dates which cluster in the first half of the thirteenth century.

The site files at the Laboratory of Anthropology indicate that there are four major clusterings of Pueblo sites (Figure VII.5):

1. Pintada Canyon area (elevation around 5,500 feet)
2. Ribera-Tecolote area (elevation around 6,500 feet)
3. Watrous Valley area (elevation around 6,500 feet)
4. Cimarron area (elevation around 6,400 to 7,500 feet)

DISTRIBUTION OF PUEBLO SITES

Map VII.5

Brownwares

* 1200—1300+
✕ 1100—1200
+ 1000—1100
Ⓑ Brownwares Only

Graywares

● 1200—1300
⊟ 1100—1200
▲ 1000—1100

The Pintada area contains a number of Pueblo sites located along Pintada Arroyo. These sites are characterized by the presence of Chupadero Black-on-White and brown Utility wares, and most likely date from the Pueblo III (A.D. 1200 to 1300) to the early Pueblo IV period (A.D. 1400's). No systematic survey is known from this area, nor are any sites known to have been excavated. There are also extensive outcrops of petrified wood, suitable for lithic tools, found in the Pintada area (Mobley 1979).

The pueblo sites in the Pintada area range from large adobe pueblos, measuring up to 175 meters by 75 meters (Laboratory of Anthropology Site Survey Records — LA 1286, field map by R. Wiseman), to small, single or two-room structures, outlined by upright slabs. There are also reported sherd scatters and rock shelters. For the most part, however, the sites in this area (with the exception of those sites recently recorded) suffer from a lack of adequate documentation.

The Tecolote-Ribera area is another area of apparent high site density. Most of the sites listed in the Laboratory of Anthropology site files are located along the Pecos River, between Ribera and Villanueva; another group is located near Tecolote. Most sites date to the Pueblo III period, but a few also contain sherds belonging to earlier and later periods. As in the Pintada area, there is a definite lack of systematic survey in this area, and only one excavated site has been reported.

The excavated Tecolote site, LA 296 (Holden 1931; Fergusson 1933) consists of ten house mounds and a long ceramic sequence which includes Red Mesa Black-on-White, Kwahe'e Black-on-White, Santa Fe Black-on-White, Galisteo Black-on-White with small amounts of Socorro Black-on-White, Chupadero Black-on-White, Tularosa Black-on-White, Wingate Black-on-Red, Puerco Black-on-Red and St. Johns Polychrome. Five tree-ring dates retrieved from Tecolote range from 1171r to 1259vv (Robinson, Harrill and Warren 1973).

The Watrous Valley area also suffers from a lack of archeological documentation. However, the Laboratory of Anthropology site files indicate several pueblo sites within the general area. Portions of one site, the Lynam site, have been excavated (Lister 1948). Ceramic materials from this site include Santa Fe Black-on-White, Wiyo Black-on-White, Chupadero Black-on-White, Kwahe'e Black-on-White and Chaco II, which suggests an occupation from A.D. 1100 to 1300+. Another excavated site near Mora, New Mexico consists of a circular room constructed with horizontally placed slabs (Moorehead 1931). Campbell (1976) suggests that this site may be affiliated with Plains Woodland or Apishapa cultures. Just how this site fits in is currently unclear. Tree-ring dates have also been recovered from a site in the Watrous Valley, although which site is not known. The published dates range from 1179vv to 1214v (five dates total) with one date at 1212r (Robinson, Harrill and Warren 1973).

Most of the recorded pueblo sites in the Watrous Valley contain house mounds; LA 311 consists of five house mounds. The Lynam site is described as a large L-shaped pueblo, 120 feet long and 100 feet wide (Lister 1948).

Based upon ceramic evidence, the sites in the Watrous Valley area appear to have been settled and abandoned earlier, but with some overlap, than those in the Tecolote-Ribera area. Santa Fe Black-on-White is present at two sites, along with Puerco Black-on-Red and Wingate Black-on-Red. St. Johns Polychrome is not listed in the area, although it is present in the Tecolote-Ribera area. In addition, there appears to be a strong showing of Red Mesa Black-on-White at two sites (LA 726 and LA 727). Red Mesa is rare in the Tecolote-Ribera area.

The Cimarron area contains the largest quantity of recorded archeological data in northeast New Mexico, largely due to the efforts of the Archeological Program at the Philmont Boy Scout Ranch. Both systematic surveys and excavations have been conducted by this group (Lutes 1959; Kirkpatrick 1976; Glassow 1980) and the quick output and content of the published results would shame many other institutions.

A cultural sequence beginning at approximately A.D. 400 and lasting until A.D. 1300 has been defined in the Cimarron area (Glassow 1980). The earliest phase, the Vermejo, A.D. 400 to 700 (radiocarbon dates), has been mentioned earlier in this chapter. Briefly, this occupation is similar to Basketmaker II occupations found in other parts of the Southwest, but dates slightly later. No pottery has been found at sites of this period, but evidence of corn is present. Structures at Vermejo Phase sites are simple, above ground, circular houses with horizontally coursed masonry walls about one meter high. The superstructure and roof construction at these sites is not known, but postholes are present in the floor of one structure (Glassow 1980:71).

The succeeding phase, the Pedregoso Phase (A.D. 700 to 900, radiocarbon dates) is known from only one definite site in the Cimarron area. This phase is characterized as being similar to the Sambrito Phase in the Navajo Reservoir district, although no undisturbed house structures have been found. Ceramics appear for the first time in this phase in the form of crude, thick and oxidized sherds (Glassow 1980). Both beans and corn have been recorded for the period (Kirkpatrick and Ford 1977).

Following the Pedregoso Phase is the Escritores Phase, believed to date from A.D. 900 to 1100 (ceramic cross-dates). Pithouse architecture is reminiscent of the Dennison (Vivian and Clendenen 1965) and Sedillo sites (Skinner 1965) located near Albuquerque. Kiatuthlanna Black-on-White, Red Mesa Black-on-White and Kana'a Neck-banded pottery are typical at sites of this period (Glassow 1980:73).

The Ponil Phase (A.D. 1100 to 1250, ceramic cross dates) is, geographically, the most extensive phase in the Cimarron area. Above-ground domiciles reappear during this period, usually as multiroom structures, along with numerous rock shelters (Lutes 1959; Glassow 1980). The pottery associated with sites belonging to the Ponil Phase includes Taos Gray (punctate and incised), Taos Black-on-White or Kwahe'e Black-on-White.

The final Pueblo period in the Cimarron area is designated the Cimarron Phase (A.D. 1200-1300, ceramic cross dates). Larger multiroom pueblos constructed of adobe or masonry accompanied by ceramic assemblages of Cimarron Plain and Santa Fe Black-on-White are indicative of the phase.

Some interesting observations were made by Glassow in his recent publication on the Cimarron area (1980). First, he recognizes a shift in settlement from the upper canyon areas (higher elevation — around 7,200 feet) during the Vermejo Phase (A.D. 400-700) to the lower canyons and plains margins (around 6,500 feet) during the later periods (1980:103). He also charts the variation in site frequency by phase from his survey area (Table VII.2) which seems to indicate an extremely low population density during the Pedregoso Phase (A.D. 700-900). Several comments are warranted by these observations.

In Chapter III, we delineated certain periods when most site locations were in upland settings or lowland settings. Briefly, the Basketmaker III and Pueblo III periods are characterized by site locations in high upland settings. The Pueblo I, II and IV periods are characterized by a general shift in site locations to lower elevations.

It is interesting to note that in Glassow's study area most of the sites are above 6,500 feet (high elevation) and Vermejo phase sites (dates to the Basketmaker III period) are quite common. The following Pedregoso phase (dates to the Pueblo I period, A.D. 700-900) is nearly absent in the area. This extremely low site frequency during the Pedregoso phase may

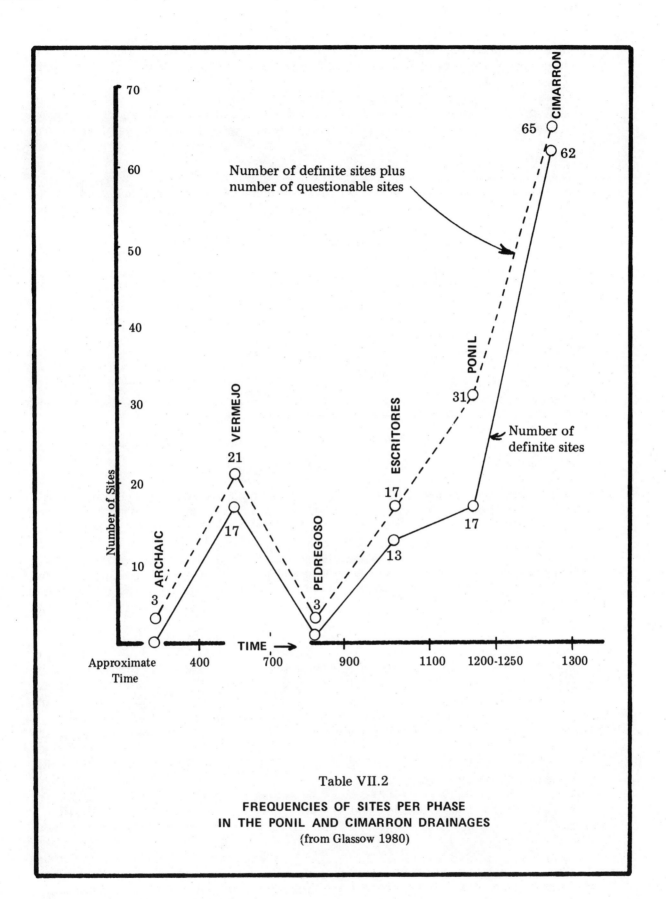

Table VII.2

FREQUENCIES OF SITES PER PHASE
IN THE PONIL AND CIMARRON DRAINAGES
(from Glassow 1980)

307

indicate a shift from the high elevations to lower elevations — possibly outside Glassow's survey area. Where the sites of this period are located is unknown, but locations below 6,500 feet are a good possibility.

Elsewhere in northeast New Mexico, the situation is not as clear. The following table was drafted to illustrate altitude locations for a sample of 47 pueblo sites (Table VII.3).

Table VII.3
ELEVATION TABLE FOR NORTHEAST NEW MEXICO PUEBLO SITES
(Excluding Cimarron Area)

	Period	P-II	P-II/III	P-III	P-III/IV	P-IV	P-V*
	No. in Sample	7	3	18	13	2	4
Elevation	7000	1	0	0	0	0	0
	6500	0	1	1	0	0	0
	6000	2	2	7	3	0	2
	5500	3	0	5	5	2	1
	5000	1	0	5	5	0	1

*probably Apache Sites

This table reveals that during the Pueblo II period (approximately A.D. 900-1100) sites are distributed fairly evenly throughout various altitudes, with a slight concentration between 5,500 and 6,000 feet. Transitional Pueblo II-III sites are located between 6,000 and 7,000 feet, indicating a shift to higher elevations. The following Pueblo III period sites are found from 5,000 feet to 6,500 feet. This distribution is fairly even, with a slight concentration at 6,000 to 6,500 feet. The later Pueblo II-IV period sites show a slight movement down in elevation, concentrating between 5,000 and 6,000 feet. The few data available for the Pueblo IV period indicate occupation between 5,500 feet and 6,000 feet, or a continuation of lower elevation occupation.

The trends outlined in Chapter III may apply to northeast New Mexico, but are not clear-cut. One problem with attempting this analysis is that the individual site data for this area are not very reliable. In most cases the frequency of ceramic types is not given, making period placement rather tenuous. Also, the locational accuracy of these sites (and therefore the sites' elevation) is sometimes questioned. And finally, another variable which needs more examination is the fact that on the east side of the Sangre de Cristo Mountains the average temperature is lower than on the west side (Cordell 1978:68). This would probably affect the altitude placement of a site in this area, making direct comparison with other areas difficult, unless this variable can be adjusted.

The distribution of Pueblo sites and sites with Pueblo pottery is given in Figure VII.5. Two comments need to be made concerning this distribution. First, prehistoric pueblo pottery found on the plains is usually attributed to the presence of Pueblo farmers or Pueblo buffalo hunters (c.f. Krieger 1946; Collins 1971:89). However, when historic pueblo pottery is found on the plains, it is automatically assumed to be a tradeware on an Apache site. It is curious that, with one exception, prehistoric sherds are not considered tradewares as well. The exception is Mobley's work at Los Esteros (1979) in which Pueblo pottery, located in areas away from Pueblo sites, is viewed as tradeware rather than as evidence of Puebloan occupation.

Our second comment concerns the distribution of Mogollon and Jornada brownwares and Anasazi graywares. The brownwares have quite a wide distribution and are found as far north as Clayton, New Mexico. The dominance of brownwares suggests that the plains dwellers at this time had contacts primarily with Puebloan groups to the southwest, rather than with the Anasazi groups to the west.

In contrast, the Anasazi graywares are, for the most part, limited to the eastern foothills of the Sangre de Cristos. The graywares do occur on the plains, but in very small amounts. However, in the Cimarron area the earliest pottery is described as a thick, oxidized pottery (a brownware). Succeeding pottery is typical Anasazi grayware. Again, as in the Navajo Reservoir, Rio Rancho area and certain areas of the San Juan Basin, we see that the earliest pottery in Anasazi areas is a brownware and is later followed by graywares.

The age of the brownware sites on the plains is not known. The brownwares are not a well dated or defined pottery type and, on the plains, are usually not found associated with decorated pottery types, making precise chronological placement impossible. More of these sites should be dated by methods independent of artifact types.

THE PANHANDLE ASPECT
(The Antelope Creek Focus, Apishapa Focus and Plains Woodland)

The post-Anasazi developments in northeast New Mexico are commonly referred to as the Antelope Creek Focus of the Panhandle Aspect. Archeological sites belonging to this phase are generally characterized by contiguous-room pueblos, defined by rows of upright slabs. It is believed that Antelope Creek populations relied both on agriculture and bison hunting for subsistence (Krieger 1946; Wendorf 1960). Occupation of this area is generally considered to have occurred from A.D. 1300 to 1450, based upon dated Pueblo tradewares. This culture is better known in the Texas and Oklahoma Panhandle areas, where it was first defined and where most work has been applied to these sites (Campbell 1976:6).

The origin of the Antelope Creek Focus is believed to lie in a general Plains Woodland tradition. As mentioned earlier in this chapter, the Plains Woodland period (ca. A.D. 200 to 1000 in northeast New Mexico) is nearly identical to Basketmaker II or early Basketmaker III cultures defined elsewhere in the Southwest (Lang 1978:29). Small corner-notched projectile points, dart points, cord-marked pottery, grinding stones, and circular houses constructed of horizontally placed slabs characterize this period in the northern areas. One possible Plains Woodland site, the Cross L Ranch Site, LA 15867, has been excavated (Oakes 1979). However, the site layout and artifact inventory suggest that this site may actually date to the Apache period.

By A.D. 1000, the Plains Woodland period was replaced by the Apishapa Focus (Campbell 1976). Apishapa sites are characterized by upright slabs, usually defining a single room. Most rooms are circular or oval, with square rooms occurring rarely. Campbell (1976:88) reports the presence of at least 20 Apishapa sites in northeast New Mexico. One possible Apishapa site, Sitio Creston (LA 4939), located near Las Vegas, New Mexico, has been excavated (Wiseman 1974).

Apishapa Focus sites differ from the earlier Plains Woodland sites in house type and material culture (Campbell 1969:389-402). Dart points are still present along with corner-notched points, but the dominant projectile point form is now side-notched. Ceramic types consist of cord-marked ware, which is not as deeply marked as the earlier wares, and is very close to Borger Cord-marked. Houses are characterized by a wall base of upright slabs and, presumably, a cribbed-log superstructure. There is an increasing number of rooms per site, along with a trend to occupy more defensive positions (Campbell 1969).

The succeeding Antelope Creek Focus sites are generally larger and contain from six to eighty rooms. Rooms are rectangular, although several other shapes are also present. The method of wall construction also differs from earlier types. Antelope Creek walls are characterized by two parallel rows of upright slabs, with the interior space filled with adobe and rubble. Succeeding rows of upright slabs were placed on top of, and inset slightly over, the lower courses. This was continued until the desired wall height was achieved. In cross-section, such a wall would look like a very steep-sided pyramid. Pottery from these sites consists of cord-marked ware and Pueblo tradewares from the Rio Grande Valley. The most common form of projectile point is a side-notched point, usually referred to as a Harrell point.

The distribution of Panhandle sites in northeast New Mexico is given in Figure VII.6. Because of the low number of sites, this figure emphasizes our lack of knowledge of this culture. What we do know of Panhandle sites in northeast New Mexico has been summarized by R. Campbell (1976, 1969) from data collected primarily in Colorado and from sites reported in the literature from surrounding states. Here, from Campbell's (1969) evidence, in southeast Colorado at least, there is evidence of population increases and apparent altitudinal shifts through various periods. The period from roughly A.D. 1000 to A.D. 1300, the Apishapa Focus in southeast Colorado and northeast New Mexico, is generally an upland occupation. From Campbell's (1980) site distribution maps it appears that the primary trend is for site locations between 5,000 and 6,000 feet. Population is rapidly increasing at this time in southeast Colorado. No data on population dynamics are available for New Mexico.

Sometime after A.D. 1300, there is a shift to lower elevations and to areas along permanent water courses. The upland areas of Colorado and New Mexico are thought to be virtually unoccupied by these groups. This period, the Antelope Creek Focus, is also characterized by population aggregation into larger villages. Again, we see that agriculturalists shift site locations after A.D. 1300 from upland areas to lowland areas, and also aggregate into larger villages.

In New Mexico, sites affiliated with the Panhandle culture are not well known. Basic knowledge, such as chronology, total artifact assemblage and house type, is not completely understood. Despite Campbell's (1969, 1976) seriation of house forms (from circular with horizontal masonry to circular or oval with upright slabs to rectangular with upright slabs) questions have recently arisen concerning their correct temporal placement (Lintz 1978). Artifacts associated with Panhandle sites are not well dated. The projectile point forms (corner-notched, side-notched or triangular without notches) have very long time spans, making exact phase or cultural placement next to impossible. This will be discussed in a later section.

In the area south of Las Vegas, New Mexico a number of sites which may be Panhandle sites have been recorded. These sites (LA 12078 through LA 12099) are currently under study by New Mexico Highlands University, directed by Robert Mishler. Vertical slab foundations are present at most of these sites, but as yet none has been dated. Underlying one of these structures is a pithouse, but it too has not been dated or reported. Wiseman (1975) excavated a site in this area believed to date to the early 1100's. This site, Sitio Creston, LA 4939, consisted of eight circular stone rooms similar to Apishapa sites described by Campbell (1969, 1976). The pottery from Sitio Creston, which occurred in a very low frequency, is described as being similar to Taos Gray (Wiseman 1975).

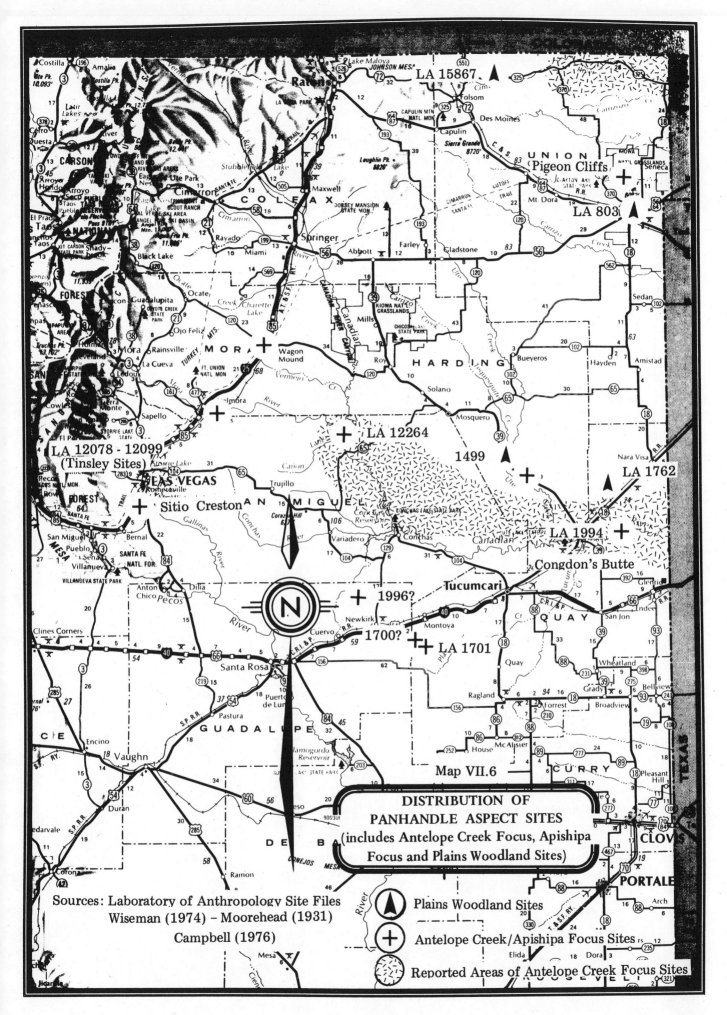

Map VII.6

DISTRIBUTION OF PANHANDLE ASPECT SITES
(includes Antelope Creek Focus, Apishipa
Focus and Plains Woodland Sites)

Sources: Laboratory of Anthropology Site Files
Wiseman (1974) – Moorehead (1931)
Campbell (1976)

▲ Plains Woodland Sites

✛ Antelope Creek/Apishipa Focus Sites

⬤ Reported Areas of Antelope Creek Focus Sites

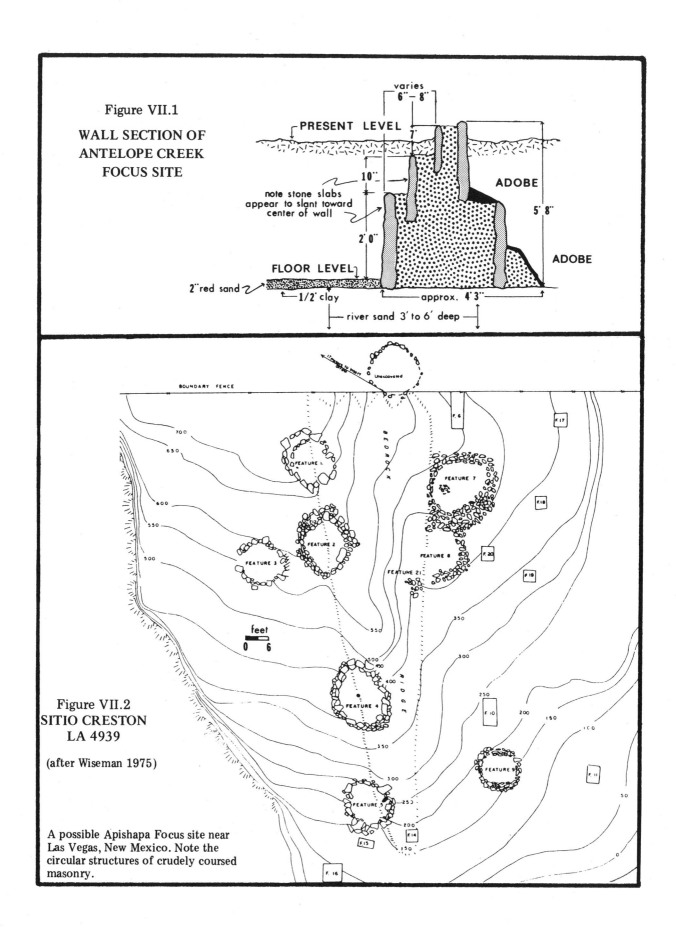

Figure VII.1

WALL SECTION OF ANTELOPE CREEK FOCUS SITE

varies 6'' – 8''

PRESENT LEVEL

7'

10''

note stone slabs appear to slant toward center of wall

ADOBE

5' 8''

2' 0''

ADOBE

FLOOR LEVEL

2'' red sand

1/2' clay

approx. 4' 3''

river sand 3' to 6' deep

Figure VII.2
**SITIO CRESTON
LA 4939**

(after Wiseman 1975)

A possible Apishapa Focus site near Las Vegas, New Mexico. Note the circular structures of crudely coursed masonry.

BOUNDARY FENCE

BEDROCK

RIDGE

Unexcovered

FEATURE 1

FEATURE 7

FEATURE 2

FEATURE 8

FEATURE 3

FEATURE 21

FEATURE 4

FEATURE 9

FEATURE 5

feet
0   6

The chronological ordering of these sites is unclear. Neither is it understood how these sites relate to nearby pueblo sites. Are there overlaps between occupations, or are these Panhandle sites later than the Puebloan occupation? Wendorf's (1960) statement that the Panhandle culture arrived from the east after A.D. 1300 needs to be revised. From Campbell's (1976) work we see that there is probably considerable time depth of Panhandle culture in this area, long before A.D. 1300, and that population movement, through time, is to the east.

Abandonment of the area by Panhandle groups is generally believed to have occurred around A.D. 1450 (Wendorf 1960). Campbell (1976), on the other hand, notes that several sites along the Canadian River in New Mexico may have been occupied well into the 1500's. This late occupation is viewed as a conservative group living in "small villages of circular slab-foundation houses with a poorly developed ceramic industry" (Campbell 1976:90).

ATHAPASKAN ARCHEOLOGY IN NORTHEAST NEW MEXICO

Nearly all of our knowledge of Athapaskan archeology in New Mexico is based upon the work of J. Gunnerson and D. Gunnerson. Their studies are the primary sources for Athapaskan archeology. These studies have recently been summarized in J. Gunnerson's article in the *Handbook of North American Indians*, Volume 9 (1979).

Most of the known Athapaskan sites in northeast New Mexico are believed to be Jicarilla Apache sites. Several of these sites have been excavated and reported. This has resulted in quite a wide variety of defined house forms. Excavations and surveys by Gunnerson (1959, 1969) in northeast New Mexico (particularly along the foothills of the Sangre de Cristos) have dealt with these sites, most of which post-date A.D. 1600.

House types defined by excavation include multiroom pueblos, pithouses and stone circles commonly referred to as tipi rings. The Glasscock site, located near Ocate, is an excavated Apache pueblo which contains seven contiguous, adobe-walled rooms, arranged in a L-shape. Artifacts recovered at Glasscock included Ocate Micaceous sherds, Pueblo and Mexican tradewares, lithic tools, manos and metates and projectile points. The projectile points are described as small triangular forms, either side-notched or unnotched. However, Gunnerson (1979:165) illustrates one example of a corner-notched point. Other sites reported by Gunnerson include the Sammis site near Cimarron, where a pithouse, surrounded by a low wall or a ring of cobbles, was excavated. Again, the dominant artifacts at the Sammis site were Ocate Micaceous sherds, Plains-type stone tools and Mexican tradewares (1979).

The final house or site type discussed by Gunnerson (1969, 1979) is the tipi ring. These ubiquitous stone rings are widely distributed throughout the plains and are notorious for their general lack of artifacts. Gunnerson (1979) describes similar sites located near Cimarron and Las Vegas, New Mexico. Artifacts at these sites, when they are present, consist of ceramics (Ocate Micaceous, Perdido Plain, and Pueblo tradewares) and occasionally stone and metal artifacts. Tipi ring sites may date anywhere from the 1400's up to the late 1800's.

Most scholars generally agree that the Athapaskans (both Apache and Navajo groups) were late arrivals in the Southwest, appearing shortly before Coronado's arrival in 1540. Gunnerson (1979) believes they enter at sometime early in the 1500's. In northeast New Mexico these early Apache groups are seen as nomadic hunters who shortly adopted agriculture and began building small pueblos. Early Spanish documents describe Apache pueblos east of the Taos mountains, with ditches and canals to irrigate their fields.

The distribution of Gunnerson's (1979) Apache sites, and Apache sites from other sources, are plotted in Figure VII.8. The overall distribution of Apache sites is strikingly similar to the distribution of Paleo-Indian sites. This distribution, particularly that of tipi ring sites, reflects, in our opinion, a similar subsistence strategy — big game hunting. We emphasize the tipi ring sites, since these sites are thought to be the remains of highly mobile bison-hunting groups. The distribution of tipi ring sites is generally along two major land forms

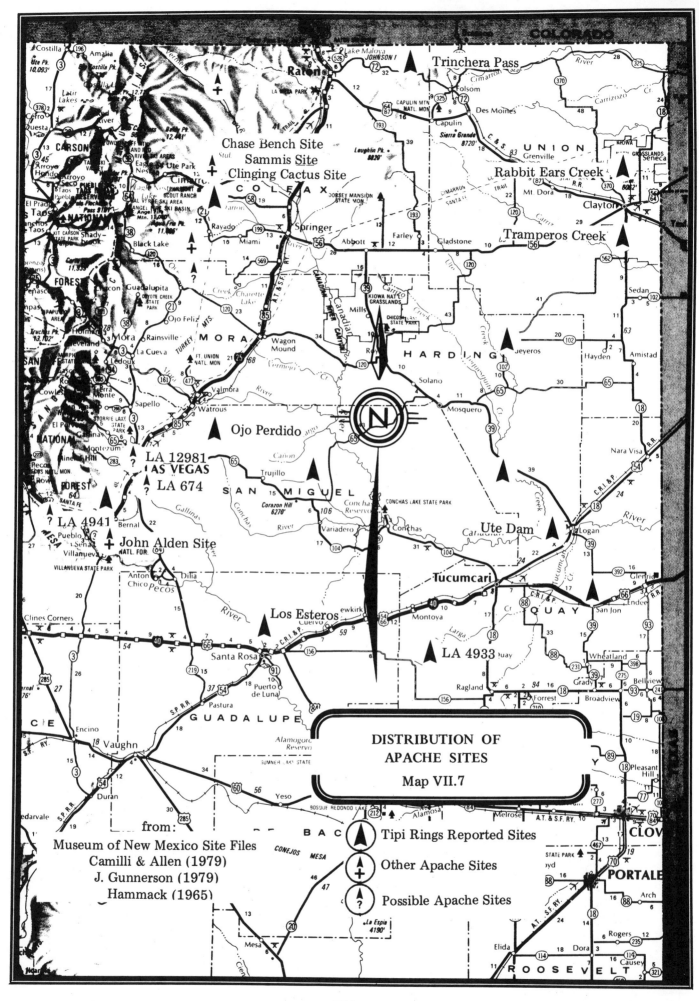

DISTRIBUTION OF
APACHE SITES

Map VII.7

from:
Museum of New Mexico Site Files
Camilli & Allen (1979)
J. Gunnerson (1979)
Hammack (1965)

Tipi Rings Reported Sites

Other Apache Sites

Possible Apache Sites

— the Sangre de Cristo foothills and the Canadian Escarpment. Again, two altitude zones are represented, one at approximately 5,000 feet and the other between 6,500 feet and 7,000 feet. However, as with the Paleo-Indian sites, more research is necessary. There are probably hundreds more of these sites, but they have not been properly recorded. Campbell's (1969:440) distribution map of historic sites in New Mexico reveals several more possible Apache sites for which we have no records. Other types of Apache sites, such as pueblos and pithouses, discussed above, are limited to the Sangre de Cristo foothill area. Most of these probably reflect a semi-sedentary or even a sedentary farming population (Gunnerson 1979).

The age of Athapaskan groups in New Mexico has long been a source of debate among archeologists. Various Athapaskan groups are generally believed to have arrived in the Southwest at around A.D. 1500 or slightly later. This date is based primarily upon negative evidence, since no known Athapaskan site has been reliably dated earlier than A.D. 1500.

Linguistic evidence for the age of Athapaskan groups in the Southwest is also ambiguous. Some (Hoijer 1956) believe the original split between Athapaskan speakers in Canada and those that migrated to the Southwest took place approximately 1,000 to 600 years ago. There is evidence that the Kiowa language is very close to the Tanoan languages (Hale and Harris 1979), and Gunnerson (1979:162) remarks that the Jicarilla and Kiowa Apache languages are very similar. It has also been offered that the various Tanoan languages (Towa, Tewa, Tiwa) and Kiowa split at about the same time (Ford, Schroeder and Peckham 1972:34). This idea, along with dental morphology evidence from the Trinidad Lake area in southeast Colorado, where skeletal remains dated from A.D. 1075 to 1190 are believed to be Athapaskan (Turner 1977, cited from Cordell 1978:106), perhaps indicates an in-place separation of certain Apache groups (Kiowa and Jicarilla?) and Tanoan language groups. The so-called Puebloan groups that lived along the foothills of the Sangre de Cristos in northeast New Mexico may actually be the source of the later Kiowa Apache groups and Jicarilla Apache, providing that the Kiowa and Jicarilla languages are indeed closely related (Ford, Schroeder and Peckham 1972:34). Currently the case is unclear. However, we should keep in mind that elsewhere in New Mexico, various farming groups on the eastern margin of Pueblo territory later became bison hunters at around A.D. 1200 (Jelinek 1967).

The earliest recorded date of Apaches in New Mexico is 1525, recorded by the Coronado Expedition of 1540. Information gained by Coronado from Pueblo Indians indicates that in 1525 the Teya (possibly Plains Apache?) attacked several pueblos in the Galisteo Basin and also attacked Pecos but were driven off (Hammond and Rey 1940; Lambert 1954; Kidder 1958; Gunnerson 1979). This group of raiders then began trading with the pueblos. The Coronado expedition also noted that in 1540 the Teyas and Querechos (both assumed to be Apaches, although the Teyas may have spoken Caddoan; Schroeder n.d.) were trading meat and hides to the Pueblo Indians for corn. This information indicates that by the first half of the sixteenth century, Apachean groups had already established a trading pattern with Pueblo groups that would last until the eighteenth century. We wonder how long it would take for such a pattern to emerge. We would suggest that the beginnings may have been before 1500.

In northeast New Mexico, nearly all Apache sites have been dated by the presence of Ocate Micaceous pottery, which is believed to have been made from A.D. 1550 to 1750 (Gunnerson 1979). This ware is very similar to pottery produced at Taos and Picuris Pueblos. It has been suggested that Ocate Micaceous was actually produced at these pueblos (Schaafsma 1976). Excavations at Taos Pueblo indicate that micaceous pottery becomes the dominant type around A.D. 1550 (Ellis and Brody 1964) or at the same time that it appears on Apache sites to the east of Taos. Clearly, petrographic analysis is needed to determine the source of this pottery. *If* it is shown that this pottery was actually made at Taos Pueblo or Picuris Pueblo at around A.D. 1550, and traded to Apaches, we need to find out what a pre-Ocate Micaceous Apache site would look like. Are they the numerous, undated stone rings found throughout the Plains? Or, are the numerous, undated lithic scatters found throughout northeast New Mexico representative of early Apache sites? We feel that this discussion serves to indicate that more research is needed to clarify the time depth of Athapaskan groups in New Mexico.

Despite questions of when the Athapaskan groups arrived in New Mexico, interactions between Plains Indians and Pueblo Indians began around A.D. 1300, usually indicated by Plains-type artifacts present at Pueblo sites and Pueblo pottery at Plains sites (Krieger 1946; Wendorf 1953; Lange 1979). This interaction is often viewed as a symbiotic relationship in which during favorable climatic episodes, Pueblo groups would trade surplus corn, beans and squash to the nomadic Plains Indians for meat and hides. During droughts, when crops were scarce and hunting was poor, raids by Plains Indians became common (Kelley 1952).

We perceive that certain pueblos were trade centers or economic centers in much the same way that, in the contemporary world, there are centers of commerce. Pecos Pueblo was a dominant trade center during Glaze V times or during the A.D. 1500's and 1600's (Kidder 1958). This is indicated in the archeological record by the appearance of Plains artifacts in levels dated to this period, and by numerous historical accounts. After A.D. 1700, when Pecos was declining as a trade center, the trade emphasis had shifted to Taos, where well documented trade fairs were held. Bloom Mound, located near Roswell, New Mexico, may have been a trade center during the A.D. 1300's (Kelley 1966). There are probably many other Pueblos located on the eastern periphery of Pueblo territory that functioned at one time or another as trading centers. It is important to note, however, that these centers shifted through time.

During the historic period the relationship between Pueblo Indians and Plains Indians was characterized by lively periods of trade and devastating periods of raids. This pattern of trade and raid is examined in Table VII.4. Here we have plotted the relative annual precipitation from A.D. 1500 to A.D. 1820 (based upon tree-ring data from the northern Rio Grande) and the incidence of skirmishes or raids between Plains Indians (Apache and Comanche), Pueblo Indians and Spanish colonists, derived from information in Kenner (1969).

Although the evidence is not conclusive, several trends are apparent from this chart. First, most Apache raids correlate with periods of drought, although there are several exceptions. These exceptions are usually a disagreement between the historical documents and the climatic conditions indicated by the tree-ring data. Such a disagreement in the period around A.D. 1670, where the tree-ring data reveals a short period of above-average precipitation, but the historical references indicate this to be a period of great drought, during which many Pueblo Indians and Spaniards starved. The period from A.D. 1663 to 1670 is documented as a time of epidemics and severe Apache raids as well as drought. The severity of these calamities led to the abandonment of the Jumano and Tompiro Pueblos in the Salinas District (Vivian 1964). The years from A.D. 1770 to 1780 are historically documented as a period of drought and of severe Comanche depredations, but the tree-ring evidence suggests that relatively moist conditions prevailed. Another favorable climatic episode occurred from approximately A.D. 1705 to 1725, indicated by tree-ring data. This was also the time of many Comanche raids, and therefore does not fit the pattern of raiding during drought periods.

The occurrence of Spanish slave-raiding expeditions and retaliatory raids appears to coincide with favorable climatic conditions, with one major exception. In 1779, Governor Juan Bautista de Anza defeated the Comanches in a major engagement which virtually ended Comanche depredations against New Mexico (Kenner 1969). Climatic data indicate that this action took place during a severe drought.

Pueblo uprisings against the Spanish appear to coincide with drought periods. The

Table VII.4

CLIMATE INDICATED BY TREE-RINGS AND APACHE RAIDS

rebellions of 1650, 1680, 1692 and 1694 all occurred during periods of drought. Of course, drought was not the sole factor behind the revolts — most likely drought was only a minor factor. The major causes of rebellion were the encomienda, repartimiento and the suppression of native beliefs. However, since the Spanish were collecting tribute in the form of food and labor, any drought or decrease in food production would have had serious effects upon the Pueblo Indian food supply.

Although the evidence is far from conclusive, several points merit further comment. Raids by Plains groups usually occurred during dry periods when game and wild plants were in short supply. This would also be a period when the Pueblos would not have any crop surpluses to trade. We can assume that drought conditions would not be as severe for Plains nomads (no massive population loss or loss of large tracts of territory) as it would be for the Pueblo Indians (see Chapter II). The ability of Pueblo Indians to survive the effects of a drought would be limited by their capacity to store food. The option to disperse or return to a hunting and gathering strategy is already closed by existing hunters and gatherers -- the Plains Indians — who are undergoing food shortages themselves. During such periods of drought, the Plains Indians could either simply disperse or raid the Pueblos.

The option of raiding would, in effect, permit population increase of hunter-gatherer groups, much the same way as trading for food would (again, see our discussion in Chapter II). By 1650, such a population increase may have closed the option to disperse among certain Plains groups. The settling of the Jicarilla Apache in semi-sedentary or even sedentary agricultural villages along the eastern foothills of the Sangre de Cristos suggests that population pressure was forcing more intense food production methods. The Jicarilla Apache in turn became the target of later Comanche raids.

The Pueblos lost more during dry climatic episodes. They not only had to cope with starvation; they also suffered from raids. Their losses were great -- territory (i.e. the Salinas Pueblos) and lives (from starvation and raids), and their options consisted mainly of looking into an empty storeroom or finding another Pueblo group who would take them in. However, during favorable climatic episodes, a lively trade ensued, benefitting both sides. In addition, the Pueblo Indians and Spanish colonists could muster enough men for retaliatory raids and slave raids against the Plains Indians during these favorable periods.

Although this discussion is simplistic, it points out, in a general way, trends between Plains and Pueblo populations. Of course, the situation is much more complex, and better climatic, population and historical records are needed. A close examination of the Pueblo-Plains relations would be an excellent test of the theory of roles played by agriculturalists and hunters and gatherers presented by us in Chapter II.

CENTRAL NEW MEXICO

INTRODUCTION

Central New Mexico encompasses what is generally referred to as the Salinas District. This area brings to mind many famous Southwestern archeologists such as Hewett, Mera, Hibben, Vivian and Hayes, who have all worked in the region. The ruins of the massive Spanish missions and the large Indian pueblos have inspired articles, many of which border on the romantic (c.f. Walter 1916; Lummis 1925). It is these large mission structures which have been the subject of most archeological investigations for the last seventy years in central New Mexico.

Like northeast New Mexico, no Bureau of Land Management-Forest Service Cultural Resources Overview is yet available for central New Mexico. Archeological surveys in this area have been almost non-existent, so there is really no consensus as to what is actually out there, and in what frequency. The Laboratory of Anthropology site files were consulted for additional archeological data that is not reported in the literature. The files were found to be highly biased to pueblo sites. A total of 106 sites are listed in the Laboratory of Anthropology site files as located in central New Mexico (see Table VII.10). The individual site data is limited, with the site location and a listing of ceramic types usually the only information given.

Central New Mexico is located at the approximate geographic center of the state. Its boundaries are the same as those of Torrance County, with the addition of the Cibola National Forest Service lands in the Manzano and Gallina Mountains. The major land forms within this part of New Mexico include the east slope of the Manzano Mountains, the Estancia Basin, Chupadero Mesa and the northern end of the Gallina Mountains (see Figure VII.9).

Elevation variability (and therefore, vegetation variability) is greatest on the west side of central New Mexico, due to the Manzano Mountains. The highest peaks in the Manzano Mountains are about 10,000 feet high. From the crest of the Manzanos, the terrain slopes to the east, occasionally cut by several eastward-flowing, entrenched drainages. Vegetation along the east slope of the Manzanos consists of Canadian and Transition life zones.

Thirty miles east of the crest of the Manzano Mountains lies the Estancia Valley or Basin. Within this basin are the famous Salt Lakes (also referred to as the Laguna del Perro or Salina Lake). Around the margins of these old lakebeds are salt deposits which were used by the Indian populations (both Pueblo and Apache) and later by the Spanish colonists. Historic references to these salt deposits indicate that contracts were issued to various Pueblos to mine and transport the salt. Salt was also an important export commodity from the early historic New Mexico colony. Most of this salt found its way to Chihuahua, where it was used in the silver smelting process. In much earlier times, these lakes also attracted herds of large mammals which were hunted by Paleo-Indian groups. A number of Paleo-Indian sites are found around the ancient shoreline.

The southern area of central New Mexico is dominated by Chupadero Mesa and the northern end of the Gallina Mountains. Chupadero Mesa is an elevated area (around 6,500 feet to 7,000 feet) forested with pinyon and juniper. This is the area in which Mera (1931) defined Chupadero Black-on-White. Many pueblo sites have been recorded here and many more are known, but not recorded.

East and north of the Estancia Basin are large expanses of plains, occasionally interrupted by mesas. For the most part, however, this is an area of low topographic relief, supporting an Upper Sonoran vegetative community. Drainages in this area are mostly eastward-flowing. The most important drainage is the Pintado, where a high density of Pueblo sites are located. This clustering of Pueblo sites is discussed in the Northeast New Mexico section.

PALEO-INDIAN AND ARCHAIC PERIODS

Two well-known Paleo-Indian sites have been excavated in central New Mexico. These are the Lucy Site (LA 4974) and Manzano Cave (LA 4932). The Lucy Site lies in a series of blowouts, situated above the old shoreline of prehistoric Lake Estancia. A mixed assemblage of Paleo-Indian projectile points (Sandia, Clovis, Folsom and Midland projectile points) and Archaic material (Pinto Basin-like projectile points and manos and metates) have been recovered at Lucy (Roosa 1956). Manzano Cave is another multicomponent site with Paleo-Indian and Archaic artifacts. One Sandia point, and several points similar to Gypsum Cave points, have been reported from Manzano Cave (Hibben 1941; Wormington 1957). In addition, four grooved stone balls, thought to be bolas, were also reported.

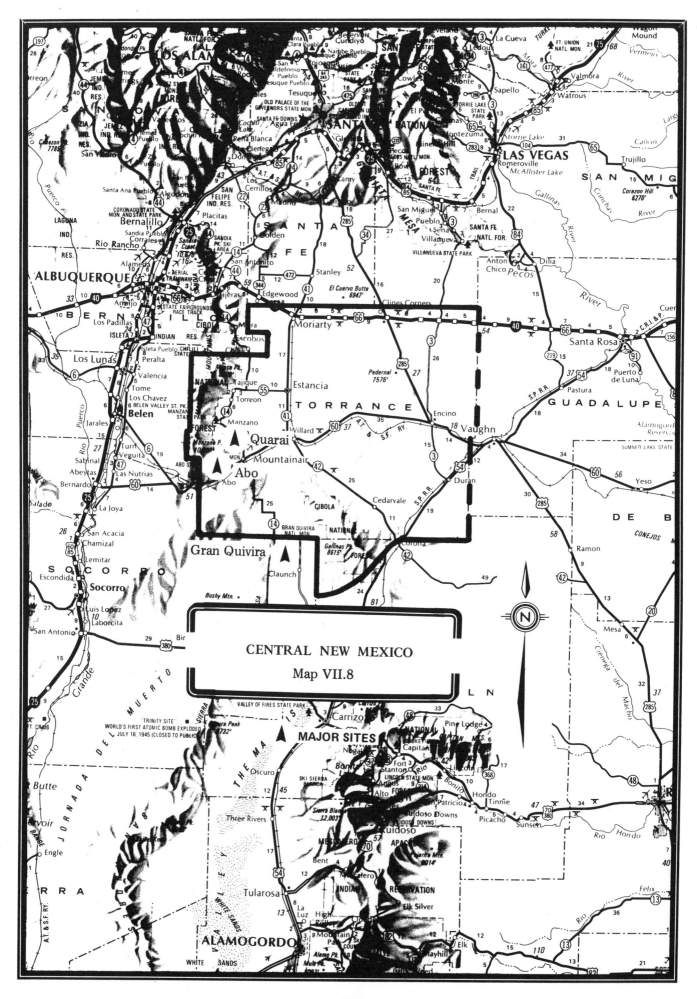

CENTRAL NEW MEXICO

Map VII.8

MAJOR SITES

Other Paleo-Indian sites and finds have been reported by Haynes (1955). Nearly the entire range and sequence of Paleo-Indian point types has been reported from central New Mexico; most of the points were found by private collectors. The distribution of Paleo-Indian sites in this area is not as clear as is the distribution in northeast New Mexico. There are two major clusters of Paleo-Indian sites located at the north and south ends of prehistoric Lake Estancia. These are primarily Folsom sites (Lyons 1969) but Clovis, Sandia, Milnesand and Agate Basin projectile points are also found here (Haynes 1955).

Another region where Paleo-Indian sites are found is east of prehistoric Lake Estancia, generally in elevated areas. Data concerning site location and associated topographic features are generally lacking, although most appear to be located against mountains or mesas, and some are located on mesa tops. Clovis, Sandia, Folsom, Eden, Milnesand and Midland projectile points are reported from these areas.

Paleo-Indian site placement in central New Mexico appears to be where most archeologists think these sites should be located — near playas (Lake Estancia) and on areas of high ground which could be interpreted as lookout sites. Earlier in this chapter we discussed Paleo-Indian site placement in northeast New Mexico, where it appeared that site location was largely controlled by topographic features. The same type of situation is present in the San Juan Basin, where we (see Chapter III) have indicated that most sites are located on the fringes of the basin, or where topographic variability is highest. We need to determine if the trends in Paleo-Indian site placement in northeast New Mexico and in the San Juan Basin are as they appear, or if it is a lack of systematic survey or soil deposition that creates these apparent site placement trends. In central New Mexico, where soil erosion is severe, this pattern is not so evident. This may indicate that Cordell (1978) is correct when she states that "... we might be looking at areas in which surfaces of the appropriate antiquity are exposed, rather than at geographic features which were selected as activity loci by Paleo-Indian groups" (1978:133).

THE PUEBLO PERIOD

The Indian pueblos and Spanish missions in central New Mexico are well known. There are two state monuments and one national monument established to honor and preserve these mission and pueblo sites. The missions at Quarai and Abo State Monuments have been excavated, but the associated Indian pueblos are virtually untouched (Ely 1935; Toulouse 1949). At Gran Quivira, two mission structures have been excavated. Portions of two separate pueblo roomblocks have also been excavated (Vivian 1964).

The earliest known Puebloan occupation in central New Mexico consists of a pithouse village located near Gran Quivira. There are at least nine pithouses at this village, two of which have been excavated (Green 1955; Fenega 1956). The majority of the pottery recovered from these pithouses was Jornada Brown (70 percent or more). Lino Gray or Kana'a Gray was present in low frequencies; San Marcial Black-on-White was reported from one pithouse. The excavators bracket the occupation from A.D. 600 or 700 to A.D. 900, based upon these ceramic types.

The succeeding periods (from approximately A.D. 900 to 1300) are difficult to deal with due to a gap in the literature and in the site records. Vivian (1964) and Mera (1940) view Pueblo development in this area as very similar to developments occurring in the Rio Grande Valley, but with strong influences or ties to the Jornada Mogollon region, based upon the high incidence of Jornada Brownwares. Following the abandonment of the Jornada area at around A.D. 1400, these groups moved north into the central New Mexico area. It was this immigration that was partially responsible for the large pueblo population centers at such sites as Gran Quivira, Pueblo Colorado and Tabira, and also involved the elements of the

Pueblo population referred to as the *Jumano* or the *rrayados* or the tatooed or body-painted groups (Vivian 1964:146). The later Pueblo developments in the Gran Quivira are then viewed as a very conservative population, out of the mainstream of Puebloan development. This conservatism is primarily indicated by a lag in certain architectural traits (kivas) and the persistence of mineral paint-decorated pottery (Chupadero Black-on-White) and Jornada Brownwares, which continued in use up to and during the historic period. The continued use of a mineral paint black-on-white pottery is seen as conservatism, but it should be realized that, after A.D. 1300, whatever the paint type in use in any area, that paint type remained in use until Spanish colonization. Such areas as the Pajarito Plateau, Chama area, Jemez area, Picuris and the Gran Quivira area decorated their pottery with the same type of paint in use in the A.D. 1200's, and only the Rio Grande Valley area south of Santa Fe, where glaze decorated pottery became the dominant type, changed paint types after A.D. 1300.

Toulouse and Stephenson (1960) have defined a cultural sequence in this area, based upon the results of a limited reconnaissance near Gran Quivira. This sequence is given below (1960:40):

Table VII.5
PHASE SEQUENCE — GRAN QUIVIRA REGION*

Claunch Focus (Pueblo III, ca. A.D. 1200-1300):

Jornada Brown	Chupadero B/W
Los Lunas Smudged	Indented Corrugated Utility
San Francisco Red	

Arroyo Seco Focus (Pueblo III, ca. A.D. 1200-1300; contemporaneous with Claunch Focus):

Chupadero B/W	Corrugated Utility
St. Johns Polychrome	

Gran Quivira Focus (Early Pueblo IV, ca. A.D. 1300-1425):

Chupadero B/W	Cieneguilla Glaze-on-Yellow
Agua Fria Glaze-on-Red	Jornada Brown
San Clemente G-P	Indented Blind Corrugated

Pueblo Colorado Focus (mid Pueblo IV, ca. A.D. 1400-1500):

Chupadero B/W	Largo G-P
Tabira B/W	Little Colorado Polychrome
Agua Fria G/R	Jornada Brown
Cieneguilla G/Y	Indented Blind Corrugated

Pueblo Pardo Focus (Late Pueblo IV, Early Pueblo V, ca. A.D. 1500-1600 or 1650):

Tabira B/W	Kotyiti G-P
Tabira Plain	San Lazaro G-P
Chupadero B/W	Jornada Brown
Plain Smooth Utility Ware	

Salinas Focus (Pueblo V, ca. A.D. 1600-1675):

Tabira B/W	Salinas Redware
Tabira Polychrome	Mexican Majolica
Kotyiti G-P	Plain Smooth Utility Ware

---

*(Note: The dates and period designations are our additions)

322

The two earliest foci defined by Toulouse and Stephenson (1960) are the Claunch Focus and Arroyo Seco Focus, both of which probably date from A.D. 1200 to A.D. 1300. Claunch Focus sites are small, one to three room surface structures, irregularly arranged, with no definite plaza areas. In contrast, the contemporaneous Arroyo Seco Focus sites are well planned pueblos, usually arranged around a central plaza area. It needs to be emphasized that St. Johns Polychrome is present at Arroyo Seco Focus sites and is absent from Claunch Focus sites. We feel that this may indicate a slight temporal difference. If the altitude shifts described in other areas of New Mexico are also present in the Gran Quivira area, the Arroyo Seco Focus sites should represent the higher altitude settings and later sites (see our discussion in Chapters III and IV).

The succeeding Gran Quivira Focus is viewed as a period when influences from the south (Jornada Mogollon area) are accepted into a Puebloan context (i.e., Jornada Brownwares in an Anasazi Pueblo). This trend began in the previous Arroyo Seco Focus and Claunch Focus, where both Mogollon and Anasazi traits are present but separate, but are joined together in the Gran Quivira Focus. During this period there is also an increase of intrusive ceramics, primarily in the form of Rio Grande Glaze A types. Sites are situated in easily defensible positions, such as mesa tops or ridge crests.

During the Pueblo Colorado Focus, most sites continue to be located in defensible positions. Sites generally consist of several roomblocks, from five to thirty or more rooms, irregularly arranged around one or more plaza areas. Jornada Brownwares continue to dominate the ceramic assemblage, but Chupadero B/W, Tabira B/W, Rio Grande Glazeware and Little Colorado Polychromes are also present.

Following the Pueblo Colorado Focus is the Pueblo Pardo Focus. This period is also characterized by sites which contain numerous roomblocks irregularly arranged around several plaza areas. Again, Jornada Brownwares are the dominant ceramic type. Also occurring are Tabira B/W, Chupadero B/W and numerous Rio Grande Glazewares. This period lasts until the beginning of the early historic period.

The final Pueblo period in this area is referred to by Toulouse and Stephenson (1960) as the Salinas Focus. Sites such as Gran Quivira, Abo, and Quarai are representative of sites of this period. Large pueblos with regular building patterns, arranged around numerous plazas, are characteristic of the Salinas Focus. In addition, several pueblos also contain large Spanish mission structures. The ceramic assemblage still consists of Jornada Brownwares, along with Tabira B/W, Tabira Polychrome, Rio Grande Glazewares and Spanish influenced types. Schroeder (1979) has recently discussed the historic period in this area. The interested reader is referred to his article for more information.

Although the cultural sequence developed by Toulouse and Stephenson (1960) is based upon a small amount of data, several trends merit further comment. The earliest periods, the Claunch Focus and the Arroyo Seco Focus, are believed to be contemporaneous occupations, but with one focus displaying Jornada Mogollon affinities, the other Anasazi. Here, as in west central New Mexico, there is the same problem of the Anasazi-Mogollon boundary (see Chapter IV). These different traditions merge in later periods, but exactly what joins and how it joins is still a problem.

Defensive sites appear during the Gran Quivira Focus, or during Glaze A times — A.D. 1300-1425. Other defensive Glaze A sites have been reported from the Puerco-Salado area (Wimberly and Eidenbach 1980), but elsewhere (in the Rio Grande Valley) most sites are not in defensive positions. This may indicate that sites dating to the Glaze A period in this area (near the southern boundary of the Pueblo area) are frontier settlements with occasional periods of strained relations with other groups which necessitated the establishment of defensive communities.

During the following period, the Pueblo Colorado Focus, site locations continue to be in defensive positions. This is in contrast to most other sites dating to this period (ca. A.D. 1400-1500) where site location is not in defensive positions. One exception includes Pecos Pueblo, where a wall was constructed around the pueblo perimeter, at about this same time (Kidder 1958). Again, we see that pueblos located on the frontiers occupy defensive locations or, at Pecos, construct defensive works. There also appears to be a shift from the south to the east frontiers for the locations of defensive Pueblo sites.

The site files at the Laboratory of Anthropology contain data on 106 archeological sites located in central New Mexico. Of these 106 sites, 90 are pueblo sites. Among the 90 pueblo sites, only 45 sites are well enough documented to enable us to place them in temporal categories based upon ceramic type. These are listed below (also see Table VII.10):

Period	No. of Sites
P-II	4
P-II — P-III	1
P-III	7
P-III — P-IV	3
P-IV	16
P-IV — P-V	8
P-V	6

(Source: Laboratory of Anthropology Site Files)

This small amount of information emphasizes the lack of systematic research in central New Mexico. The data available are biased to the large sites with surface structures, and generally ignore the smaller sites. Very few pithouse sites are recorded in this area, but one pithouse site has been excavated, and nine pithouse sites were recorded during a reconnaissance near Gran Quivira (Caperton n.d.). Dating of these sites has been accomplished by ceramic cross-dating, although the dominant type is usually a plain brownware which can date from A.D. 300 to 1650+. Succeeding periods indicate a rapid increase in the number of sites until the Pueblo IV period. During the transitional Pueblo IV-V period there is a decline in the number of sites (by one-half), and another slight decrease during the Pueblo V period. Transitional sites (i.e., P-II—P-III or P-III—P-IV) occur less frequently than sites that belong to one single phase. This indicates that sites were usually abandoned, and that new houses were established in different areas. Unfortunately, where these shifts to new site locations occurred is not known. In other areas of New Mexico, during certain times, occupation would tend to cluster at certain elevations (see our discussion in Chapter III). We assume that such altitudinal shifts are also present in central New Mexico but, given the quality of the data from this area, we must await the results of future surveys and the collection of more reliable data before any definite statements can be made.

The postulated influx of Jornada Mogollon groups at around A.D. 1400, following the end of the San Andreas Phase (Vivian 1964:145), appears to fit the overall rise in the number of sites during the Pueblo IV period. But again, there have been no systematic surveys that estimate the number of rooms per site, or even a systematic survey that documents only the number of sites per phase. More research is needed to determine if there is an actual increase of sites or rooms per site during this period. The question of Mogollon-Anasazi interactions in central New Mexico is as much of a problem as it is in west central New Mexico (see Chapter IV). Here, in central New Mexico, the dates are slightly different, but the postulated intrusions of various groups is a dominant theme. The early Spanish documents suggest two distinct groups living at Gran Quivira; one group practiced tatooing or body painting and the other group did not. Vivian (1964) believes the decorated portion of the population (referred to as the Jumanos or rrayados) is the remnant of the Jornada Mogollon who migrated north to the Gran Quivira area at around A.D. 1400.

Burial data from a number of sites in central New Mexico and in the Jornada Mogollon should be reviewed. First, it is important to determine if two distinct human groups can be segregated from central New Mexico burial populations. Burial data from the Jornada Mogollon area should be compared with data from central New Mexico to determine if these were, indeed, Jornada Mogollon groups in this area. Comparisons with Plains Indians should also be undertaken, since other groups also called Jumano or rrayado by the Spanish were known to inhabit the plains east of Gran Quivira in early historic times. Quite possibly this faction of the population could be from the plains instead of the Jornada area.

Obviously, considerable additional data are necessary for central New Mexico. Most studies have been confined to the area around Gran Quivira and Chupadero Mesa, and virtually nothing is known from the areas to the north around Tajique or Chilili.

CONSIDERATIONS FOR SURVEY

BACKGROUND AND PRIORITIES

Northeast New Mexico and central New Mexico together comprise an area of 12,276,653 acres or nearly 19,182 square miles. Unlike other parts of New Mexico, federally controlled lands are at a minimum here. The most extensive group consists of private holdings (85 percent in northeast New Mexico and 73.8 percent in central New Mexico), many of which are large ranches. State-owned lands comprise the second largest holdings, making up approximately 13 percent in both areas, followed by Forest Service lands (10.6 percent in central New Mexico and 1.2 percent in northeast New Mexico). The remaining small percentages of lands are controlled by the Bureau of Land Management, National Park Service and Fish and Wildlife Service (see Tables VII.6 and VII.7).

As previously stated, archeological research in this portion of New Mexico has been spotty at best. Early research in northeast New Mexico was conducted by E.B. Renaud, who excavated several sites in the Dry Cimarron area (1929, 1930) and reported on a number of petroglyph sites (1936) and stone enclosure sites (1942a). His studies were followed by Mera's excavation in the Jaritas Rock Shelter (1944) and E.T. Hall's excavation of a series of rock shelters along the Canadian River (1938). Other research at about this same period was performed by several individuals interested in tracing the extent of Panhandle Aspect sites from Texas and Oklahoma into New Mexico (Mason 1929; Holden 1930; Moorehead 1931). By far the single most important study during this period was at the Folsom site, where the first conclusive evidence of early man in North America was found (Wormington 1957).

Highway salvage surveys and excavations were conducted by the Museum of New Mexico beginning in the late 1950's (Honea 1964; Laboratory of Anthropology Site Files) and these operations continue today at a rapid pace (Wiseman 1975, 1978; Farwell 1979; Hannaford 1979; Oakes 1979; Koczan, n.d.; Seaman, n.d.). Both prehistoric and historic period sites are covered in these reports.

More recent studies have consisted of reservoir surveys and excavations (Steen 1955; Hammack 1965; Levine and Mobley 1976; Lang 1978; Mobley 1978) and Indian Land Claims (Schroeder, n.d.). Other types of research, which include Ph.D. dissertations (Anderson 1975; R. Campbell 1976; Glassow 1980) and other funded projects, have also been completed or are still in progress (Gunnerson 1959, 1979; Kirkpatrick 1976; J. Campbell, personal communication).

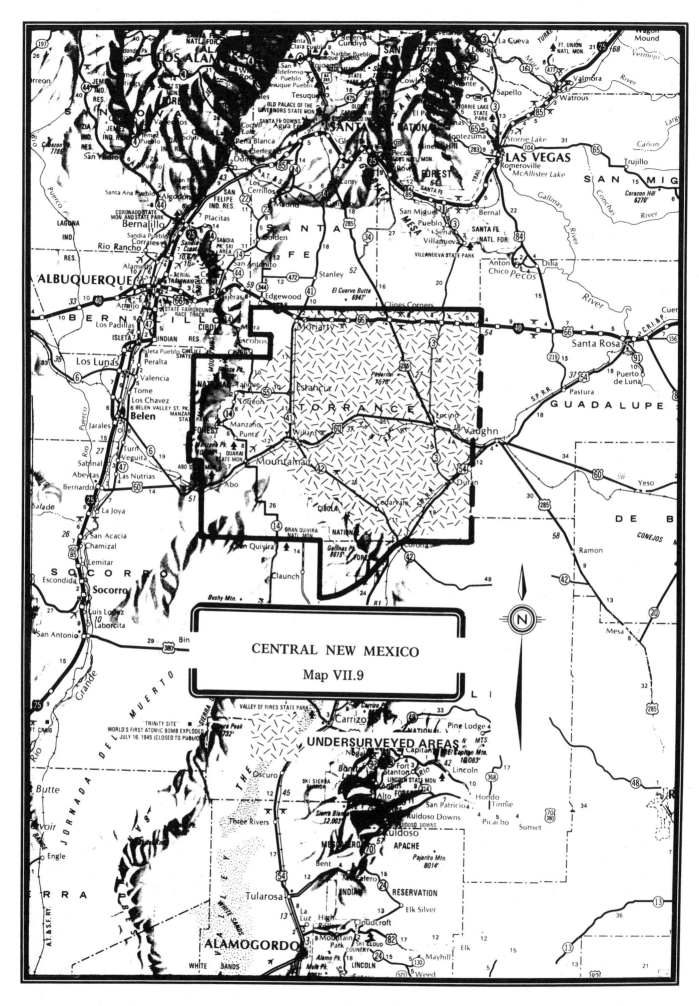

CENTRAL NEW MEXICO

Map VII.9

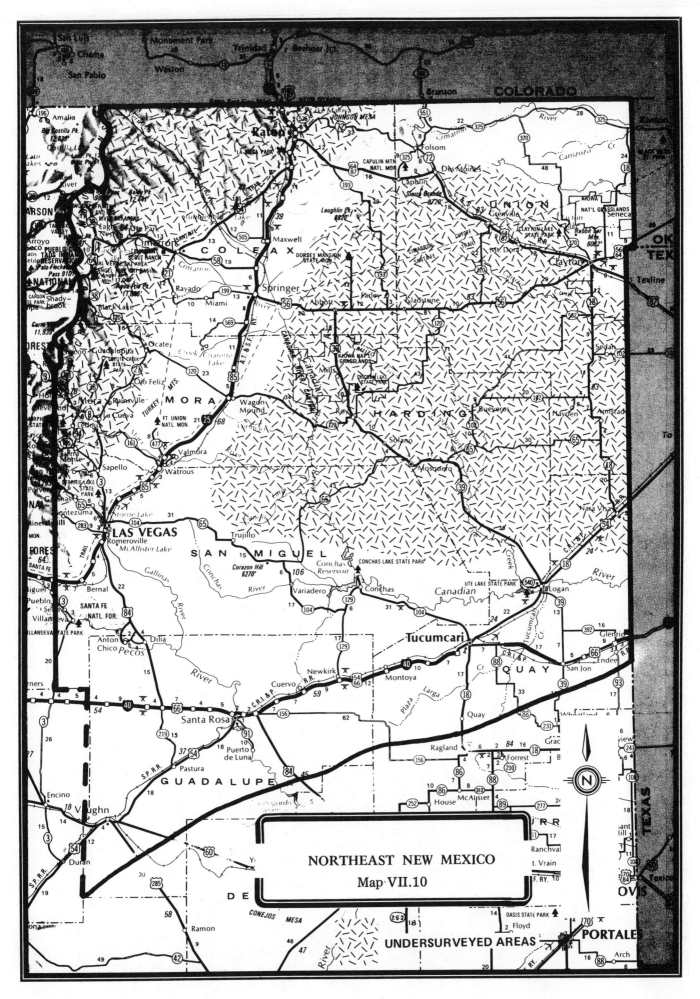

NORTHEAST NEW MEXICO

Map VII.10

UNDERSURVEYED AREAS

Table VII.6
LAND OWNERSHIP – NORTHEAST NEW MEXICO (PLAINS NEW MEXICO)

Land Ownership	San Miguel	Mora	Colfax	Union	Harding	TOTAL ACREAGE	Percent
BLM	35,756	7,561	261	503	5	44,086	.43%
NPS	341	721	0	680	0	1,742	.017%
Fish and Wildlife	7,614	0	2,663	0	0	10,277	.102%
Forest Service*	0	0	0	57,534	70,545	128,079	1.27%
State	173,808	81,638	278,189	441,946	344,981	1,320,562	13.12%
Private and Misc.	2,494,424	1,050,168	2,120,769	1,942,217	952,789	8,560,367	85.04%
TOTAL ACRES	2,711,943	1,140,088	2,401,882	2,442,880	1,368,320	10,065,113 or 15,727 mi^2	

*Forest Service lands in San Miguel, Mora and Colfax Counties transferred to Upper Rio Grande.

Table VII.7
LAND OWNERSHIP – CENTRAL NEW MEXICO

Land Ownership	Torrance County	Percent
BLM	44,373	2.0%
NPS	240	.0108%
BIA	0	0
Forest Service*	234,657	10.61%
State	299,805	13.55%
Private and Misc.	1,632,465	73.81%
TOTAL ACRES	2,211,540 or 3,456 mi^2	

*Includes Forest Service land from Lincoln and Valencia Counties.

Archeological research in central New Mexico has concentrated primarily on excavation. In the early 1920's, Edgar L. Hewett, then of the School of American Research, directed excavations at Gran Quivira. Most effort was concentrated on the large mission church (San Buenaventura) but portions of the Indian pueblo were excavated as well. In addition to this work at Gran Quivira, the missions at nearby Abo and Quarai were also excavated and stabilized in the 1930's (Ely 1935; Toulouse 1949). The pueblo ruins at Abo and Quarai have largely been ignored, except for a few test excavations during the excavation and stabilization of the missions.

One pueblo dating to the Pueblo IV period, Pueblo Pardo, has been reported (Toulouse and Stephenson 1960). Vivian (1964) excavated an early mission structure at Gran Quivira and one roomblock, also dating to the early historic period. Al Hayes also conducted excavations at Gran Quivira in the mid 1960's, but no report is yet available. Only one pithouse site has been reported (Green 1955; Fenega 1956). These early sites are believed to be fairly numerous, but are sorely underrepresented in the Laboratory of Anthropology site files and in the literature.

Paleo-Indian research in this area has documented two well-known sites -- the Lucy Site, LA 4974 and Manzano Cave, LA 4932 (Hibben 1941; Roosa 1956). Manzano Cave also contains material from Archaic and Pueblo periods. Additional Paleo-Indian studies include Lyons (1969; Lyons and Switzer 1975) who prepared his doctoral dissertation on Paleo-Indian and Archaic materials in this area, and Haynes (1955), who published on finds from private collections.

Surveys have been conducted in the area around Gran Quivira (Mera 1931, 1940, 1943; Caperton, n.d.). These were not systematic surveys, but are better referred to as a reconnaissance or thematic survey (see Figure VII.9). In central New Mexico the most outstanding problem is a lack of systematic survey. Many sites are known, but the actual numbers by period and the distribution are not known. Spectacularly large pueblo sites are present in this area, along with massive Spanish missions — and it is to the historic mission structures that 99 percent of the archeology has been directed. Very little is actually known of earlier periods beyond the fact of their presence.

The archeology of northeast New Mexico is only partially understood. This is in part due to a lack of attention during a period of time when sites in other parts of the state were being dated by dendrochronology and temporal/cultural sequences were being developed for these areas. This portion of New Mexico was seemingly ignored by these investigators when cultural chronologies were developed. Another problem was the lack of datable material (tree-rings) and the unspectacular nature of most sites in the area. These factors have contributed to a general lack of knowledge of northeast New Mexico.

Most recorded archeological sites in northeast New Mexico are located near the east side of the Sangre de Cristo Mountains and, to a lesser extent, along major drainages and along Interstate 40. This leaves nearly the entire central portion of northeast New Mexico with virtually no archeological surveys or excavations. This gap in the data base is quite significant. As discussed earlier in this chapter, the Paleo-Indian sites and the later tipi ring sites were found to cluster on each side of this gap in the data (along the Sangre de Cristos and Canadian Escarpment). It is possible that this observation may be totally incorrect, since little work has been conducted in this large area separating the two clusterings of sites. Only more systematic survey will be able to determine this.

IMPACTS AND PRIORITIES

The northeast portion of New Mexico is very poor in mineral resources. Unlike the San

Juan Basin and Mount Taylor areas, which are currently suffering severe impacts from mineral extraction (coal and uranium) and related activities, northeast New Mexico and central New Mexico are virtually untouched by this type of impact. One exception is in the Raton Coal field, located in western Colfax County, which will probably see an increase in coal mining in the near future. Fortunately, these impacts will be somewhat mitigated by Dr. J. Campbell, University of New Mexico, who is currently conducting systematic surveys and excavations in this area. Dr. J. Campbell also informs us of a stratified cave site, which is planned for excavation, that may solve some of the problems relating to chronology in this area.

The extraction of helium gas and carbon dioxide may also cause land modification in the near future. Drilling for helium is, or has been, undertaken near Estancia (central New Mexico) and near Des Moines and Bueyeros (northeast New Mexico). Drilling for carbon dioxide gas will most likely increase rapidly, since this gas is used to recover more oil from nearly depleted fields. Since most of this area is privately owned, archeological surveys for drill pads and pipelines are not usually conducted.

Other sources of adverse impacts upon the archeological record include road construction, reservoirs, vandalism and erosion. It is fortunate that the Museum of New Mexico, Laboratory of Anthropology has a good working relationship with the State Highway Department which results in investigations of many sites which would otherwise be lost. Several projects (survey and excavation) have been completed or are near completion. We are unaware of any reservoirs being planned for this area. Previous reservoir studies (Ute Reservoir and Los Esteros Reservoir) have produced several good monographs. Conchas Lake was not surveyed prior to inundation, since archeological salvage programs in the Southwest were generally not conducted during this time (late 1930's). However, Lang (1978) has recently surveyed a large tract of land adjacent to Conchas Reservoir. In the event that more reservoirs are constructed in this area, we can only hope that the projects will measure up to or surpass the quality of the previous reports.

Vandalism is not as serious in northeast New Mexico as it is in other parts of the state. However, some very important cave sites have been looted (such as LA 18798). In an area where the chronology is not very well known, we should look upon stratified cave sites as veritable archeological gold mines. More cave sites should be sought out and be preserved or carefully excavated, if vandalism is a threat.

Increasing population and urban spread is not a problem in northeast New Mexico. In fact, the most recent census indicates population loss or no change in this area. Population in central New Mexico may begin to increase due to its proximity to the Albuquerque area. An increase in population would also mean more construction (possibly impacting sites) and more site vandalism. This is a remote possibility at this time. Sites in this area, however, have already been vandalized. One site (Pueblo Blanco) has been particularly hard hit. The unfortunate thing is that most of the vandalism at Pueblo Blanco was conducted by a misguided amateur archeology group from the southern part of the state. Evidently the historic trash mounds were looted in an attempt to train members in excavation techniques. The result of this activity is a two-page report. Such things cannot be allowed in the future.

Erosion is presently not much of a threat in northeast New Mexico, according to erosion maps. But in central New Mexico, large portions have been severely wind-eroded. This has been both a boon and a serious loss for archeologists. Many buried Paleo-Indian sites have been exposed which otherwise would have gone unnoticed. Unfortunately, many arrowhead collectors frequent these sites and remove the diagnostic artifacts. Judging by the literature on this area, most collectors are more than happy to show their collections to interested persons, so all is not lost.

330

THE DATA

Given the fact that fewer archeological studies have been conducted in northeast New Mexico and central New Mexico than in other areas of the state (with the possible exception of the Southeast Plains), we feel that our estimates of land surveys in northeast New Mexico are probably the most accurate. The small amount of existing data made it possible to collect information on nearly all recorded sites and surveys in this portion of New Mexico. This information is qiven in Tables VII.9, VII.10 and VII.11.

Table VII.8
SITE DENSITY: NORTHEAST NEW MEXICO

Survey	No. of Sites	Area Surveyed in Square Mile	Sites per Square Mile
Los Esteros (Mobley 1979)	246	28	8.7
Conchas Reservoir (Lang 1978)	13	2.75	4.7
Folsom area (Anderson 1975)	74	20*	3.7
York Canyon area (J. Campbell, n.d.)	28	12	2.3
Las Vegas area (N.M.H.U., Mishler)	22	4*	5.5
Total		66.75	Avg. 4.98
			(5 sites per square mile)

Area Surveyed:

66.75 sq. mi.	(from projects listed above)
20 * sq. mi.	Ute Dam (Hammack 1965) — high estimate
20 * sq. mi.	Cimarron area (Glassow 1980) — low estimate
10 * sq. mi.	Museum of New Mexico Highway Surveys — high estimate
10 * sq. mi.	Other surveys — high estimate

126.75 sq. mi. TOTAL SURVEYED
or 125 sq. mi. (rounded-off figure)

Surveys in Adjacent Southeast Colorado (for comparison):

Las Animas County area (R. Campbell 1976)	1187	221	5.37
Las Animas County area (Lutz and Hunt 1979)	212	15.75	13.4

*Estimate

We estimate that approximately 125 square miles have been surveyed in northeast New Mexico, or 0.8 percent of the total land area. This figure was arrived at by adding known acreage counts and estimated counts. From the larger surveys we computed site densities by averaging these projects (see Table VII.1). Site density average is about five sites per square mile, but there is quite a bit of diversity between surveys. Levine and Mobley's (1979; and Mobley 1978, 1979) survey of Los Esteros Reservoir indicates a site density at almost nine sites per square mile in contrast to Lang's survey (1978) of Conchas Reservoir (Lang's survey was outside of the actual reservoir, and no areas adjacent to the river were surveyed) where site density was found to average 4.7 sites per square mile. This perhaps indicates that site density is higher in areas adjacent to river areas, and that site frequency decreases away from such areas.

Table VII.9

SITE TYPES AND NUMBERS — NORTHEAST NEW MEXICO
(From Site Files at the Laboratory of Anthropology and Sources Cited Below)

No. of Sites	
77	Lithic Unknown and Archaic Sites
46	Pueblo Sites
55	Historic Anglo or Spanish
10	Panhandle Aspect Sites (includes sites designated as Antelope Creek Focus, Apishipa Focus and Plains Woodland Sites)
8	Paleo-Indian
4	Unknown, with pottery
6	Tipi rings and possible Apache Sites
9	Petroglyph Sites
11	Sites with Pueblo pottery and lithic scatters, located away from Pueblo settlements.
9	Unknown, no data or unidentifiable features.

235	Sites listed in the Laboratory of Anthropology Site Files

+

57	Ute Dam (Hammack 1965), 46 lithic sites, 6 tipi ring sites, 5 historic sites LA 5540—LA 5592
18	Hall's rock shelters (Hall 1938), probably Archaic and Plains Woodland (?) LA 5332—LA 5349
22	Tinsley Sites, most are probably Panhandle Sites (Apishipa ?) LA 12055—LA 12099
246	Los Esteros (Levine and Mobley 1976; Mobley 1978), 133 prehistoric, 69 historic, 44 multicomponent. LA 18454—LA 18698
304*	Cimarron area (Glassow 1980), 3 Archaic, 21 Vermejo Phase, 3 Pedregoso Phase, 17 Escritores Phase, 31 Ponil Phase, 65 Cimarron Phase, 164 Unknown (mostly lithic scatters without diagnostic artifacts).
74*	Folsom area (Anderson 1975), 55 lithic sites (mostly Archaic?), 3 cave sites, 2 buried sites, 14 sites with structures.
28*	York Canyon area (J. Campbell, personal communication), 12 historic, 4 Apache, 12 Archaic or lithic sites.
13*	Conchas Reservoir area (Lang 1978), 5 lithic sites, 1 lithic and ceramic site, 2 Petroglyph sites, 2 Historic sites, 2 Unknown with structures, 1 with slab cists.

997	TOTAL Archeological Sites
	(1,000; rounded-off figure)

*Sites not listed in the Laboratory of Anthropology Site Files

Table VII.10

LIST OF RECORDED SITES IN NORTHEAST NEW MEXICO
(From Site Files at the Laboratory of Anthropology)

Lithic Unknown and Archaic:

(77) LA 1759, LA 1760, LA 2756, LA 3644, LA 3900, LA 3901, LA 3902, LA 3903, LA 3904, LA 3905, LA 3946*, LA 5876, LA 6555, LA 6586, LA 6763*, LA 6768, LA 6769, LA 6771, LA 6772, LA 6773, LA 6774, LA 6777, LA 6779, LA 6780, LA 6781, LA 6782, LA 6801, LA 6802, LA 6803, LA 6805, LA 6806, LA 6807, LA 6816, LA 6819, LA 6901, LA 6909, LA 6910, LA 6911, LA 6912, LA 8000, LA 8008, LA 8009, LA 8010, LA 8012, LA 8013, LA 8014, LA 8015, LA 8016, LA 8017, LA 8027, LA 8120, LA 8122, LA 8123, LA 8124, LA 8126, LA 8127, LA 8128, LA 8131, LA 8133, LA 12295, LA 12296, LA 12982, LA 13278, LA 13459, LA 13478, LA 15281, LA 15282, LA 16318, LA 16710, LA 16711, LA 16712, LA 16713, LA 18297, LA 18700, LA 18703, LA 18798, LA 18119

Pueblo Sites:

(46) LA 237, LA 296, LA 310, LA 311, LA 313, LA 339, LA 508, LA 509, LA 567, LA 671, LA 674, LA 726, LA 727, LA 929, LA 1245, LA 1246, LA 1247, LA 1286, LA 1287, LA 1288, LA 1289, LA 1290, LA 1480, LA 1561, LA 1562, LA 1563, LA 1564, LA 1697, LA 1761, LA 1763, LA 1843, LA 2052, LA 2053, LA 2103, LA 2105, LA 2106, LA 2107, LA 2108, LA 2200, LA 3307, LA 3308, LA 3906, LA 12268, LA 12269, LA 12270, LA 21975

Historic Anglo or Spanish:

(55) LA 2734, LA 2735, LA 3543, LA 4940, LA 4970, LA 4971, LA 4973, LA 5050, LA 5152, LA 5159, LA 6762, LA 6764, LA 6765, LA 6766, LA 6778, LA 6808, LA 8011, LA 8865, LA 8878, LA 8880, LA 9074, LA 12744, LA 12983, LA 13116, LA 13117, LA 13418, LA 13419, LA 13420, LA 13421, LA 15209, LA 15280, LA 15283, LA 15284, LA 15285, LA 15399, LA 15848, LA 15928, LA 15929, LA 15932, LA 15933, LA 15934, LA 15953, LA 15954, LA 15955, LA 15956, LA 15957, LA 15958, LA 16316, LA 16317, LA 16698, LA 18298, LA 18701, LA 18702, LA 18716, LA 20197

Panhandle Aspect Sites (includes Antelope Creek Focus, Apishipa Focus and Plains Woodland):

(10) LA 803, LA 1499, LA 1700, LA 1701, LA 1762, LA 1994, LA 1996, LA 4939, LA 12264, LA 15867

Paleo-Indian Sites:

(9) LA 3647, LA 4558, LA 6232, LA 6776, LA 8121, LA 8129(?), LA 8135, LA 12586, LA 6819

Unknown, with Pottery:

(4) LA 2233, LA 2234, LA 2754, LA 2755

Tipi Rings and Possible Apache Sites:

(6) LA 4933, LA 4941, LA 8130, LA 8134(?), LA 12981, LA 13467

Petroglyph Sites:

(9) LA 10944-LA 10951 (8 sites), LA 16955

Sites with Pueblo Pottery and Lithic Scatters, Located Away from Pueblo Settlements:

(11) LA 1498, LA 1699, LA 1764, LA 1879, LA 6767, LA 6775, LA 6804, LA 8001, LA 13477, LA 18120, LA 18121

Unknown, No Data or Unidentifiable Features:

(9) LA 3941, LA 4930, LA 5438, LA 5592, LA 5877, LA 6008, LA 6770, LA 13280, LA 13281

*ceramics were also found

Table VII.11
LIST OF RECORDED SITES IN CENTRAL NEW MEXICO
(From Laboratory of Anthropology Site Files)

No.   *Percent*

Paleo-Indian Sites:
2   (1.8%)   LA 4932 (Manzano Cave), LA 4974 (Lucy Site)

Lithic? Sites:
7   (6.6%)   LA 2539, LA 6778, LA 6809, LA 6912, LA 6913, LA 6914, LA 6915

Rock Art Sites:
1   (0.9%)   LA 8989 (rock art near Abo)

Pithouse Sites:
1   (0.9%)   LA 2579

Pueblo II Sites:
4   (3.7%)   LA 304, LA 305, LA 472, LA 1567

Pueblo II-III Sites:
1   (0.9%)   LA 503

Pueblo III Sites:
7   (6.6%)   LA 323, LA 1568, LA 1793, LA 1846, LA 2023, LA 2333, LA 2334

Pueblo III-IV Sites:
3   (2.8%)   LA 198, LA 200 (Tenabo), LA 2548

Pueblo IV Sites:
16   (15%)   LA 83 (Pueblo Pardo), LA 197 (Montezuma Pueblo), LA 199, LA 324, LA 1185, LA 1187, LA 1190, LA 1268, LA 1349, LA 1566, LA 1847, LA 2091 (fortified pueblo near Pueblo Colorado), LA 2538, LA 1540, LA 2541, LA 2543

Pueblo IV-V Sites:
8   (7.5%)   LA 51 (Pueblo Blanco), LA 95 (Quarai), LA 97 (Abo), LA 120 (Gran Quivira), LA 381 (Tajique), LA 474, LA 476 (Pueblo Colorado), LA 847 (Chili)

Pueblo V Sites:
6   (5.6%)   LA 371, LA 372, LA 383, LA 473, LA 3544, LA 5195

Unknown (No Data) Sites:
3   (2.8%)   LA 475, LA 2545, LA 2546 (pot drop)

Pueblo (?) Sites:
45   (42.4%)   LA 9001—9045 (45 sites described as pithouses, pueblos, rock circles)

Historic Anglo or Spanish Sites:
2   (1.8%)   LA 17117, LA 20190

106   Sites Total Recorded in Laboratory of Anthropology Site Files

The situation in central New Mexico is not as clear. Most of the sites recorded in this area have low LA numbers, indicating that they were most likely recorded by early surveys where interest centered on large masonry ruins, and smaller sites were ignored. Mera's interest (1931, 1940) centered upon the distribution of certain ceramic types and the distribution of Pueblo sites during specific time periods. A later survey (late 1960's) focused upon locating sites roughly contemporaneous with Gran Quivira (Caperton, n.d.). This reconnaissance, carried out over a two month period, centered on Chupadero Mesa and covered approximately 480 square miles. A total of forty-five sites was recorded. Clearly, this reconnaissance does not reflect the actual site density in this area.

In addition to the investigations listed above, a gas pipeline survey (Fenega 1956) and various highway surveys have been conducted (Laboratory of Anthropology site files).

From this information, we estimate that only 20 square miles have been surveyed (and this is probably a very high estimate). This would be one-half of one percent of the total land area. The site files at the Laboratory of Anthropology indicate a total of 106 sites located in this area (see Table VII.11), which computes to 5.3 sites per square mile. Of course, this is only guesswork and should be taken with a grain of salt. Actually, we believe that site density in central New Mexico is much higher — erosion has exposed many Paleo-Indian and Archaic sites. It is common knowledge that Pueblo occupation here was quite dense.

STATE AND NATIONAL REGISTER PROPERTIES
IN NORTHEAST NEW MEXICO and CENTRAL NEW MEXICO

There are nine sites in central New Mexico and northeast New Mexico listed on the State Register of Cultural Properties. As in other areas of the state, certain types of sites are underrepresented, or missing entirely from the Register, and some types of sites are very well represented. Five sites are also listed on the National Register, and two more have been nominated, but as yet no action has been taken to list these. These sites are listed below:

		LA No.	County	Phase or Period
Northeast New Mexico:				
No. 426	Hidden Lake Pictograph Panel	—	Guadalupe	Apache
No. 497[1]	Indian Writings	—	San Miguel	Archaic
No. 009*	Folsom Site	LA 8121	Colfax	Paleo-Indian
No. 145	San Jon Site	LA 6437	Quay	Paleo-Indian, Archaic, Pueblo(?)
Central New Mexico:				
No. 238*	Quarai State Monument	LA 95	Torrance	P-IV, P-V[2]
No. 122[1]	Tabira (Pueblo Blanco)	LA 51	Torrance	P-IV, P-V[2]
No. 108[1]	Pueblo Colorado	LA 476	Torrance	P-IV, P-V[2]
No. 064*	Gran Quivira National Monument	LA 120	Torrance/ Socorro	P-IV, P-V
No. 001*	Abo State Monument	LA 97	Torrance	P-IV, P-V

* National Register properties
[1] nominated to National Register
[2] a possible P-III component is present

No. 238*   QUARAI STATE MONUMENT (LA 95)

Quarai consists of the ruins of several pueblos and a Franciscan mission and church. The earliest occupation at Quarai is a small pueblo constructed of masonry and adobe. Ceramics from this portion of the site indicate an occupation from A.D. 1250 to the end of the fourteenth century. The area was probably abandoned then, or only sporadically reoccupied.

The major pueblo ruin at Quarai consists of a large masonry pueblo, containing up to 1,000 rooms, arranged around five small plaza areas. The founding date of this pueblo is controversial. Some scholars believe that it was founded in 1609, following an order by the Viceroy of New Spain to consolidate the Indians into fewer settlements. Others believe that the settlement of Quarai predates the Spanish period, and that there was a continuous occupation until the 1670's. The major feature at Quarai is a massive Spanish mission, constructed in the early 1600's.

Quarai was abandoned prior to the Pueblo Revolt of 1680. This period, immediately before the revolt, was characterized by a severe drought and increasing inroads by Apache raiders. Quarai, along with all the other Salinas pueblos, was abandoned during this period (see Schroeder 1979 for a discussion concerning the abandonment of Quarai and other pueblos in the area).

No. 122   TABIRA (PUEBLO BLANCO) (LA 151)

Tabira contains a large masonry pueblo and the remains of a Spanish mission. Ceramic remains from the pueblo ruin indicate an occupation that began around A.D. 1200 and lasted until the 1670's. However, a major population increase occurred during the fifteenth and sixteenth centuries.

The Spanish mission of Tabira was probably constructed around 1630. This mission was excavated and reported by Stanley Stubbs (1959). Depradations by Apaches and a severe drought probably caused the abandonment of Tabira in 1672.

No. 108*   PUEBLO COLORADO (LA 476)

This is a large masonry pueblo containing up to 800-1,000 rooms in twenty-one roomblocks and four or more kivas. Ceramics from Pueblo Colorado indicate that the pueblo may have been first settled as early as A.D. 1200, although the major occupation and building activities took place between A.D. 1325 and 1625.

Unlike other pueblos in the immediate vicinity, Pueblo Colorado saw a decline in population and eventual abandonment, during a period when other villages were increasing in size. It is possible that Apache depredations may have been responsible for the early abandonment of Pueblo Colorado. This site is nominated to the National Register.

No. 064   GRAN QUIVIRA NATIONAL MONUMENT (LA 120)

Gran Quivira is another large masonry pueblo with a Franciscan mission and church. There are approximately 17 roomblocks, numerous kivas and plaza areas within the pueblo.

Excavations at Gran Quivira began in the 1920's under the direction of E.L. Hewett. Later excavations have been conducted by Vivian (1964) and Al Hayes. Gran Quivira was abandoned in the early 1670's due to persistent droughts and Apache depredations.

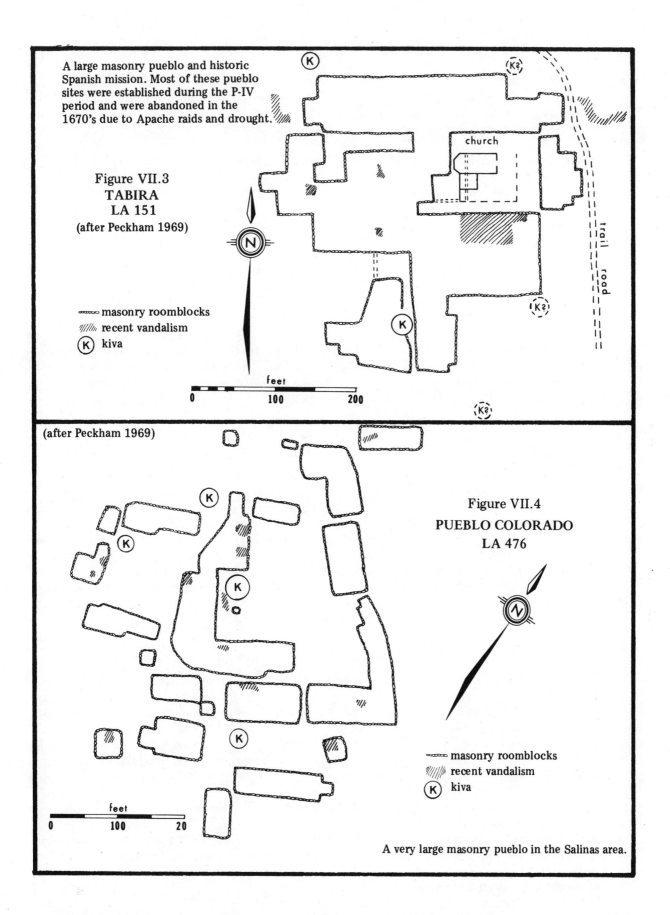

A large masonry pueblo and historic Spanish mission. Most of these pueblo sites were established during the P-IV period and were abandoned in the 1670's due to Apache raids and drought.

Figure VII.3
TABIRA
LA 151
(after Peckham 1969)

church

trail road

------ masonry roomblocks
///// recent vandalism
(K) kiva

feet
0   100   200

(after Peckham 1969)

Figure VII.4
PUEBLO COLORADO
LA 476

------ masonry roomblocks
///// recent vandalism
(K) kiva

feet
0   100   20

A very large masonry pueblo in the Salinas area.

No. 001   ABO STATE MONUMENT (LA 97)

The masonry ruins at Abo were first occupied in the early A.D. 1300's; occupation continued until the late 1600's. A Spanish mission was constructed at Abo in 1629. This mission has been excavated (Toulouse 1949) but the pueblo is virtually untouched. Like the other late pueblos in the immediate vicinity, it was abandoned in the early 1670's.

No. 009*   THE FOLSOM SITE (LA 8121)

The Folsom site in northeast New Mexico provided the first conclusive evidence of Early Man in the New World. Excavations began in 1926, conducted by the Denver Museum of Natural History. The museum was informed of the existence of the site by a local cowboy named George McJunkin. The site proved to be a kill site, from which the remains of twenty-three extinct bison were recovered. Ninteen distinctive projectile points were also found. These points, which were fluted, were named Folsom points, after the nearby town of Folsom (Figgins 1927; Wormington 1957).

No. 426   HIDDEN LAKE PICTOGRAPH PANEL

This pictograph is a single panel in which three dominant anthropomorph figures are framed by a horned serpent and rows of stepped lines. The pictographs, located near Santa Rosa, are believed to be the only recorded works of early historic Apaches in eastern New Mexico. This particular example of rock art has been studied by Gebhard (1958) and more recently by Schaafsma (1972:124-128).

No. 145   SAN JON SITE (LA 6437)

The San Jon site is known principally as a Paleo-Indian site, but an Archaic component and a possible Puebloan component (indicated by Jornada brownware sherds) are also present. San Jon projectile points (named after the site) were found here, associated with extinct bison. Folsom and Scottsbluff projectile points have also been found here. Frank Roberts excavated and reported this site (1942). Although this site is outside our boundaries for northeast New Mexico, we included it in this section because of its situation relative to topographic features. Like most of the other Paleo-Indian sites in northeast New Mexico, the San Jon site is situated adjacent to a major topographic feature, in this case the northern edge of the Llano Estacado, or the *Caprock*, as it is locally known. The persistent occurrence of Paleo-Indian sites in such topographic situations in northeast New Mexico requires more study.

No. 497   INDIAN WRITINGS

This archeological site is commonly referred to as the *Indian Writings*. It is believed, on the basis of comparison with other plains styles studied by Schaafsma (1972), that these abstract figures date between 1500 or 1400 B.C. and A.D. 900. These particular petroglyphs, located at Conchas Lake, consist of a group of five panels which cover an area of approximately 70 meters along the face of a sandstone cliff. Rakes are the most common motif at this site. Also present are concentric circles, wavy lines, dot rows, sunbursts, bird tracks, and other patterns.

DISCUSSION

In northeast New Mexico two Paleo-Indian sites are listed on the State Register (the Folsom Site and the San Jon Site). The Folsom site is also listed on the National Register. These sites are significant both in the history of the discipline of archeology and for the information retrieved from these sites.

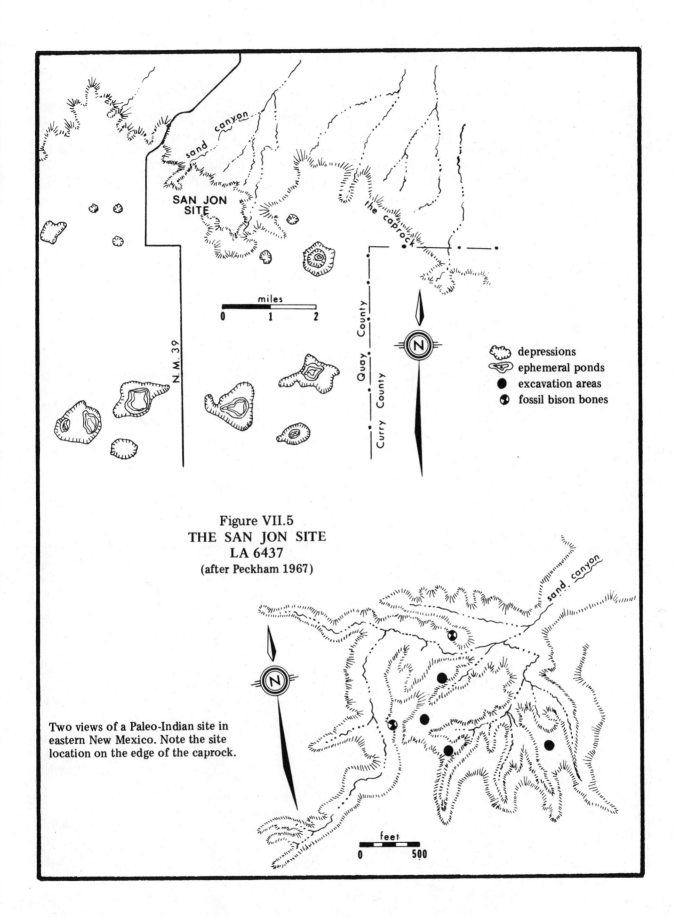

Figure VII.5
THE SAN JON SITE
LA 6437
(after Peckham 1967)

Two views of a Paleo-Indian site in
eastern New Mexico. Note the site
location on the edge of the caprock.

339

Both sites follow a pattern found at nearly all Paleo-Indian sites in northeast New Mexico; they are situated against a major topographic feature. The Folsom site is located in a small draw, backed up against Johnson Mesa, and the San Jon site is located at the edge of the Caprock. The consistent placement of Paleo-Indian sites adjacent to these features suggests to us that they represent kill sites in which these features played an important role — possibly as jumps, or drives, or simply hiding (ambush) places. We suggest that surveys be centered upon these features (the Canadian Escarpment and the east foothills of the Sangre de Cristo range) to determine what kind of sites these are. Possibly a thematic survey (*Paleo-Indian Kill Sites?*) could be performed to record a number of these for the State and National Registers.

In central New Mexico no Paleo-Indian sites are listed on either the State or National Register. This is an unfortunate oversight, since many Paleo-Indian sites (such as the Lucy Site) are known from the area. Again, many sites are located with topographic features, and many others are found along the shoreline of ancient Lake Estancia. A survey in this area is needed to document these sites, since many have been surface collected for years. Such a survey, and resulting nominations, would serve both to protect the sites and to add to our information on Paleo-Indian sites. Local collectors would need to be consulted for such a project. This would not be a problem, since many collectors seem to be truly interested in archeology and are willing to share their information.

The Archaic period is grossly underrepresented on the State Register and is nonexistent on the National Register. An Archaic component at the San Jon site and a petroglyph, the Indian Writings, located at Conchas Lake, are the only Archaic sites listed on the State Register. The Archaic adaptation on the plains was the longest, lasting up to historic times in some areas, but is the least understood. What is sorely needed is a series of sites with datable hearths, or obsidian for obsidian hydration analysis, or perhaps a series of cave sites or cliff shelters with intact deposits which would help our understanding of Archaic occupation on the plains.

An Archaic petroglyph site, the Indian Writings, is currently listed on the State Register and has been nominated to the National Register. This site serves to point up the fact that very few petroglyph or pictograph sites are listed on either register for any area of the state. We feel that more should be listed, possibly arranged along the lines of Polly Schaafsma's (1972) unsurpassed study of rock art. Several thematic surveys could be done.

The later periods, from the Basketmaker up to the Pueblo III, are not represented on either register. Possibly some components at Quarai, Tabira and Pueblo Colorado may date to the Pueblo III period, but this information is based upon low frequencies of P-III ceramics. There are *pure* Pueblo III sites in the area, but none is represented.

The largest block of sites on the State and National Registers in this area consists of the large Pueblo IV and V sites. Most of these sites also contain the remains of spectacular Spanish mission churches. Our knowledge of these sites is generally limited to the mission structures, since very little study has been conducted on the pueblo sites themselves.

GENERAL CONSIDERATIONS

Nine sites in northeast New Mexico and central New Mexico are listed on either the State or National Register. This number is quite low when compared with that in other areas of the state. Large tracts of land and certain cultural groups have been totally ignored. In general terms, all periods in northeast New Mexico and central New Mexico (with the exception of the Pueblo IV-V sites in central New Mexico) can be considered underrepresented.

The Paleo-Indian and Archaic periods have already been discussed, and recommenda-

340

tions for surveys and nominations have been made. Several large clusters of Anasazi sites are located in northeast New Mexico (notably in the Pintada area, Ribera-Tecolote area, Watrous Valley area and Cimarron area) which would probably meet criteria for State and National Register listing. These settlements are not well known, and more investigations are recommended. Perhaps a thematic study, such as *Frontier Pueblo Settlements*, could be one line of study.

The Antelope Creek Focus/Apishipa Focus sites are in dire need of further investigations. Our understanding of these sites is very limited. Two possible Antelope Creek Focus sites, Congdon's Butte (LA 1994) and Sabinoso (LA 12264; both sites recorded by S. Peckham, Laboratory of Anthropology site files; Congdon's Butte was first described in Moorehead 1931) are fairly substantial masonry sites and should be nominated to the State and National Registers. This occupation in New Mexico needs basic questions answered about chronology, material culture, range, etc.

Finally, Apache occupation in this portion of New Mexico is represented on the State Register by one site, Hidden Lake Pictograph Panel, located near Santa Rosa. We feel that Apache sites need more representation, to give these sites the same exposure as the large pueblo and mission sites in central New Mexico. After all, Apache inroads were primarily responsible for the abandonment of the pueblo sites. A thematic nomination of Apache sites should include those discussed by Gunnerson (1979) and others located out on the plains. The distribution of tipi rings in northeast New Mexico is nearly identical to that of Paleo-Indian sites, suggesting similar subsistence patterns. With more research we could determine whether these different groups were practicing the same subsistence strategy 6,000 years apart. A possible thematic study subject could be *Apache Bison Kill Sites and Campsites*.

OVERVIEW – NORTHEAST NEW MEXICO and CENTRAL NEW MEXICO

THE PALEO-INDIAN PERIOD

A regional examination of Paleo-Indian sites in northeast New Mexico has revealed a fascinating distribution of sites. The available data indicate that most Paleo-Indian sites are located against two major topographic features — the Sangre de Cristo foothills and the Trinidad Escarpment. This is a trend we have noted over most of New Mexico — a trend that is virtually unreported in the literature.

In central New Mexico the case is not clear. Many Paleo-Indian sites are situated in those areas where most of us think Paleo-Indian sites should be located, that is, near playas or on elevated areas overlooking playas. However, several Paleo-Indian sites in central New Mexico are also located against topographic features. We assume that most of these sites represent kill sites where the local topography is an important variable for determining site location. A survey centered upon such a topographic feature could provide a large body of data on hunting strategies and their evolution.

THE ARCHAIC PERIOD

Our knowledge of the Archaic period in northeast New Mexico and central New Mexico is severely limited. Although this lack of knowledge is present in other areas of New Mexico, the problem is particularly severe in northeast New Mexico because of the great length of time over which hunters and gatherers occupied this area (6000 B.C. to A.D. 1000+). No regional cultural chronologies have been defined in these areas. This complicates the matter of assigning sites to the Archaic period.

Survey data from northeast New Mexico indicate that perhaps the most common site type is an unidentified lithic scatter. On several large surveys, over fifty percent of all recorded sites were of this type. Clearly, more effort needs to be applied to these sites. Possibly the methods utilized by Judge (1973) to distinguish Paleo-Indian sites from Archaic sites without diagnostic artifacts could be applied. His methods include analysis of material type selection, reduction techniques and undiagnostic tools, such as scrapers, in period classifications (Judge 1973).

Near the end of the terminal Archaic period (ca. A.D. 200), two subsistence trends become apparent — agriculture and a continuation of hunting and gathering. The early agricultural sites are located in upland areas, a situation seen elsewhere in New Mexico. Hunting and gathering continues to be a dominant subsistence strategy in some areas up to A.D. 1300 or A.D. 1400. Quite possibly this type of adaptation continued in use even through the historic Apache period. In Chapter II we discussed different cultural trajectories (so often ignored by archeologists) and their relationship to each other. Here, in northeast New Mexico, there are clear examples of different cultural (adaptive) trajectories.

THE AGRICULTURAL PERIOD

Puebloan occupation is generally considered to begin at around A.D. 1000 in northeast New Mexico and as early as A.D. 600 in central New Mexico. However, Glassow's (1980) studies in the Cimarron area have demonstrated the existence of earlier occupations, and pithouse sites are present near Las Vegas, New Mexico which may also pre-date A.D. 1000.

The Panhandle Aspect (Antelope Creek Focus, Apishapa Focus) is generally characterized as agricultural, but with a higher reliance upon hunting than among Puebloan groups. This culture is thought to have occurred after the Puebloan occupation in northeast New Mexico. A recent study by Campbell (1976), however, suggests that there may be considerable time depth in this occupation. No Panhandle sites in New Mexico have been dated other than by means of Pueblo tradewares or projectile point forms (which are not accurate). We know virtually nothing of this period in New Mexico.

It is common knowledge that in central New Mexico there is a high density of Pueblo sites. Unfortunately, very little is known of chronology or numbers, due to a lack of systematic survey and excavation.

THE PROBLEM OF CHONOLOGY

From our review of the literature and site files, we find that there have been thirteen radiocarbon dates retrieved from eight sites. Tree-ring dates have been recorded from three sites. These sites include:

		Site Type (Apprx. Dates)
Radiocarbon Dates:		
1.	Pigeon Cliffs (Steen 1955, 1976)	Archaic (6000 B.C.)
2.	LA 8120 (Honea 1964; Anderson 1975)	Archaic (700 B.C.)
3.	29CX3 (Anderson 1975)	Archaic (A.D. 800)
4.	Helter Shelter (Mobley 1979)	Archaic (A.D. 1100-1200)
5.	Spillway Site (Mobley 1979)	Archaic (A.D. 1100-1200)
6.	Old Coyote Rock Shelter (Mobley 1979)	Archaic (A.D. 60)
7.	Vermejo Phase Sites (Glassow 1980)	Pueblo (A.D. 400-700)
8.	Pedregoso Phase Sites (Glassow 1980)	Pueblo (A.D. 700-900)
Tree-ring Dates:		
9.	Tecolote - LA 296	Pueblo (A.D. 1171-1259)
10.	Site near Watrous	Pueblo (A.D. 1179-1214)
11.	Gran Quivira - LA 120	Pueblo (A.D. 1400's-1500's)

Table VII.12

CHRONOLOGICAL CONTROL: NORTHEAST NEW MEXICO

A.D.

1800	
1700	
1600	
1500	*Gran Quivira
	*
1400	?
1300	*Tecolote
	*
1200	* Los * Site near Watrous
	* Esteros
1100	*
1000	* 29CX3 * Cimarron-Pedregoso Phase
500	* Cimarron-Vermejo Phase

Time

0	*Los Esteros
1000	* LA 8120
2000	
3000	
4000	
5000	
6000	* Pigeon Cliffs
7000	

Plains Bison Hunters

Paleo-Indian

B.C. 9500

Adaptation—

Big Game Hunting (Paleo & Apache)

Hunting & Gathering (Archaic, Apache)

Agriculture (Pueblo)

Agriculture (Panhandle Sites)

Apache

*Absolute dates (tree-ring, radiocarbon)

We estimate that site density in northeast New Mexico and central New Mexico would average around five sites per square mile, or a total of around 96,000 sites. Since only eleven sites have been dated by absolute methods, we calculate that only 0.01 percent of the total site population in northeast New Mexico and central New Mexico has been dated by means other than artifact types! To us this represents a real problem (see Table VII.12).

Most surveys utilize artifact types to place a site in a temporal-cultural framework. However, in northeast New Mexico several projectile point types have a span lasting approximately 5,000 years. Obviously, sites with these types of artifacts need alternative dating methods where possible (see Table VII.13).

Virtually all cultural periods in northeast New Mexico and central New Mexico need to be reappraised. Absolute dates need to be gathered wherever possible, and artifact types need to be redefined into tighter chronologies. A movement back to the basics is sorely needed. This would include refined chronologies, site distributions, site densities, etc. Then we can proceed with research questions.

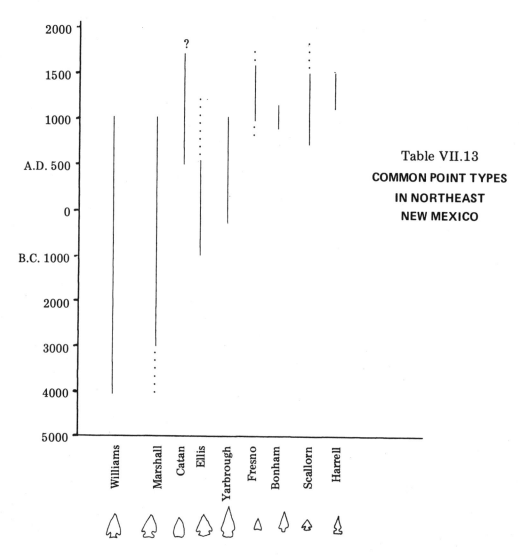

Table VII.13

COMMON POINT TYPES

IN NORTHEAST

NEW MEXICO

Chapter VIII
THE NATIONAL REGISTER AND SIGNIFICANCE

This study is a definition in detail of significance in archeological properties in New Mexico. We have been basing our discussion on the idea that significance consists, among other things, in possibilities for research, and in the selection of sites from different periods or episodes for research purposes. We have implied that such selection will identify and protect those sites which may be investigated to test our ideas about cultural evolution and behavior. Now we should look more closely at the method and theory of site selection. This will lead us to the discussion of survey method in the next chapter.

The nation's list of significant sites is the National Register of Historic Places. We can begin by looking at the legislative history of the Register.

The National Register was created by the Historic Preservation Act of 1966 (Public Law 89-665), which states that "the Secretary of the Interior is authorized to expand and maintain a national register of districts, sites, buildings, structures and objects significant in American history, architecture, archeology and culture, hereinafter referred to as the National Register . . ."

This section (101) of the Act says further that the Secretary of the Interior may grant funds to States for the purpose of preparing comprehensive statewide surveys and plans. The present study, as we have pointed out, is a plan for survey and a definition of significance which will facilitate such survey.

The preamble to the 1966 Act is a declaration by Congress that "the spirit and direction of the Nation are founded upon and reflected in the historic past and that the historical and cultural foundations of the Nation should be preserved as a living part of our community life and development in order to give a sense of orientation to the American people". This is a plain statement of the pervasiveness and breadth of the quality of significance in history and culture, a fact which we will come back to later.

Public Law 89-665, then, describes a national self-examination and evaluation. Thirty-one years earlier, the Congress had enacted the Historic Sites, Buildings and Antiquities Act of 1935. This Act had likewise provided for a "survey of historic and archaeologic sites, buildings and objects" but it had also stated that this was for the "purpose of determining which possess exceptional value" and had placed particular emphasis on the preservation of properties of *national* significance. The 1935 Act had created the system by which National Historic Landmarks were and are designated. It was implicit in the 1966 Act that the National Register of Historic Places was to be a more comprehensive inventory.

The National Register is not described in P.L. 89-665, except as quoted above. For a better understanding of what was meant we need to look briefly at the history of the law's development and passage.

On November 18, 1964 President Johnson received the report of the Task Force on the Preservation of Natural Beauty. It called, among other things, for the preparation of a "comprehensive inventory of the Nation's historic sites and areas . . ." It also said that this should be completed within five years. Here and hereafter the size of the job, and perhaps also its nature, was wrongly estimated. We will come back to this.

It was assumed in the National Park Service and the National Trust for Historic Preservation, created in 1949, would do the work.

President Johnson called a White House Conference on Natural Beauty in May, 1965. In so doing, he added something to the original report when he said that State and local governments should be encouraged in historic preservation. He also referred to a nationwide effort to save "landmarks of beauty and history" and commended the Registry of National Historic landmarks.

At the White House Conference on Natural Beauty, convened May 24, 1965, Gordon Gray, Chairman of the National Trust for Historic Preservation, called for a "national survey to inventory landmarks of all types and grades, of historic, architectural and unique community value".

Earlier in the year, the National Park Service, the Bureau of Outdoor Recreation, and the National Trust had drafted legislation to extend the life of the National Trust and to provide funds to preserve and administer sites, buildings and objects significant in American history and culture. A revised bill drafted in July, 1965 spoke of grants to the Trust on a matching basis to do these things.

As of September, 1965, the Department of the Interior was thinking in terms of grants to the National Trust. In September and October, 1965, a Special Committee on Historic Preservation uder the auspices of the U.S. Conference of Mayors received a Ford Foundation grant and an anonymous donation for the purpose of assembling a report on historic preservation and for writing guidelines on actions to be taken. The report of the Special Committee was entitled *With Heritage So Rich*. Its recommendations included a recommendation for the authorization of grants to States and "a national register, in accordance with carefully prepared standards and criteria, of structures and sites . . . of national importance because of historic, architectural and other cultural values . . . " The report then spoke of "prime national monuments, structures of lesser rank . . . [and] structures of local concern".

In his February 23, 1966 message to Congress President Johnson said that he would recommend "a program of matching grants to States and to the National Trust for Historic Preservation . . . to help preserve buildings and sites of historic significance". S. 3035 was introduced in the Senate on March 2, 1966 by Senator Henry Jackson. It provided for "maintenance by the Secretary of the Interior of a National Register of sites, buildings and objects significant in American history and culture". The transmittal letter from the Secretary stated that "the statewide survey will include sites already determined to be of national significance by the Secretary of the Interior, but it will be aimed primarily at identifying and evaluating other properties that are significant in American history and culture". The letter also referred to the inclusion in statewide plans of "properties of national, regional, State or local historical significance. . ." The letter emphasized preservation of historic sites in rapidly developing urban areas.

On March 4, 1966 the Department of Interior's Office of Legislative Council sent another draft of proposed legislation to the Director of the Special Committee on Historic Preservation. This draft identified national, State, regional and local levels of significance.

A modified version of this bill was introduced in the Senate as S. 3098 on March 17, 1966. It was also introduced in the House as H.R. 13792.

Senate bill 3097 and H.R. 13790 were introduced simultaneously on March 17. Their application was to the Department of Housing and Urban Development rather than to Interior, and they emphasized preservation needs in the cities and local historic or architectural significance.

Committee discussions of the various bills emphasized urban and local preservation, the creation of historic districts by States and communities, levels of significance, and coordination among HUD and other agencies.

In an opening statement on his bill, Senator Jackson referred to "all significant historic properties, not just those that meet the 1935 definition of national significance" and to "a historic preservation program of much broader scope" resulting from aid to States. George Hartzog, then Director of the National Park Service, testifying before a Senate committee, referred to statewide surveys and to national, State and local levels of significance.

Discussion in Senate committee led to the inclusion of references to archeology and architecture in Section 101 of the bill finally presented to the President for signature (this is enough to show what vague and general notions many in Congress had about the nature of historic significance).

The Senate report on the legislation points out that archeology as well as "more obvious aspects of history and culture" should be considered. In House debate, Representative Springer of Illinois mentioned that present criteria for national historic landmarks ruled out graves and birthplaces except in the case of historical figures of transcendent importance. He said he hoped for "less restrictive criteria in the future". Springer was interested in landmark designation for the graves of Thomas and Sarah Bush Lincoln in Coles County, Illinois.

President Johnson signed seven conservation bills, including the historic preservation bill (S. 3035) on October 15, 1966. He referred to the Endangered Species Preservation Act and the Historic Preservation Act together as heritage preservation acts in his statement regarding this approval.

This little review indicates several things. The sites of primary concern at all times were historic sites in urban areas; archeology was an afterthought. No consideration of the choice of a representative sample appears to have been taken; it was assumed that all significant sites would be identified in four or five years. Levels of significance were referred to numerous times. Local, regional and State significance may have been brought up because local and State administrative involvement was considered expedient. No attempt was made to arrive at a basic definition of significance. The inventory was intended to be comprehensive; local, regional and State significance were of greater concern than national, which was already taken care of in existing legislation. Criteria of significance were left to the administering agency to develop. It was understood and explicitly stated by the President that the program contemplated was a conservation program essentially similar to programs of natural conservation.

By the authority created by the law, the Department of the Interior produced criteria for evaluation, which now stand as follows:

The quality of significance in American history, architecture, archeology, and culture is present in districts, sites, buildings, structures, and objects that possess integrity of location, design, setting, material, workmanship, feeling, and association, and:

347

A. that are associated with events that have made a significant contribution to the broad patterns of our history; or

B. that are associated with the lives of persons significant in our past; or

C. that embody the distinctive characteristics of a type, period, or method of construction, or that represent a significant and distinguishable entity whose components may lack individual distinction; or

D. that have yielded or may be likely to yield information important in prehistory or history.

Ordinarily cemeteries, birthplaces, or graves of historical figures, properties owned by religious institutions or used for religious purposes, structures that have been moved from their original locations, reconstructed historic buildings, properties primarily commemorative in nature, and properties that have achieved significance within the last 50 years shall not be considered for the National Register. Such properties will qualify if they are integral parts of districts that meet the criteria or if they fall within the following categories:

A. a religious property deriving primary significance from architectural or artistic distinction or historical importance; or

B. a building or structure removed from its original location but which is significant primarily for architectural value, or which is the surviving structure most importantly associated with a historic person or event; or

C. a birthplace or grave of a historical figure of outstanding importance if there is no other appropriate site or building directly associated with his productive life; or

D. a cemetery that derives its primary significance from graves of persons of transcendent importance, from age, from distinctive design features, or from association with historic events; or

E. a reconstructed building when accurately executed in a suitable environment and presented in a dignified manner as part of a restoration master plan, and when no other building or structure with the same association has survived; or

F. a property primarily commemorative in intent if design, age, tradition, or symbolic value has invested it with its own historical significance; or

G. a properly achieving significance within the past 50 years if it is of exceptional importance.

The criteria for the State Register of Cultural Properties, maintained under State legislation specifically designed to further and to expand on the purposes of the federal law, are substantially similar:

I. The criteria for eligibility for inclusion in the State Register of Cultural Properties and the National Register of Historic Places are the same, with the exceptions identified below.

II. Nominations of historic districts are encouraged.

III. Nominations which promote neighborhood conservation are encouraged.

IV. Nominations which promote urban conservation are encouraged.

V. With a historic district nomination, every structure should be identified as being *Significant*, *Contributing*, *Neutral*, or *Intrusive* to the district. All those structures which are listed as being *Significant* are eligible for listing on the State Register and such listings should be made immediately. Structures listed *Neutral* or *Intrusive* are not eligible for listing on the State Register. Structures listed as *Contributing* may be eligible for the State Register and will be considered on a case-by-case basis.

VI. Criteria for individual significant structures:

    A. A textbook example of a style or method of construction.

    B. An example of a building type which was once characteristic of a particular community or region, but of which few examples now survive.

    C. Be of undisputed quality.

    D. Be the work of a designer or craftsman whose importance in the given community is accepted.

    E. Have historical significance due to important occupants of the structure or to events which occurred there.

    F. As a general rule, the criteria will be more stringent in judging individual structures, than districts.

VII. Additional criteria for evaluation of individual structures and historic districts significant at the national, state, regional or local levels.

    A. Historic districts, structures, buildings, neighborhoods, networks, and cultural landscapes are eligible for listing in the State and National Registers if it can be demonstrated that:

        1. They have been associated with and now illustrate or recall historic patterns or phenomena important to the historic development or identity of New Mexico or one of its regions or communities.

        2. They are visually distinctive or distinctively illustrate styles, methods of construction, vernacular building design, landscape architecture, engineering, or urban planning.

        3. They are essential to the visual or historic character of a particular place or town.

        4. They contain information about or evidence of historic events or processes important to understanding the State.

B. EXCLUSIONS

1. Properties significant *only* for religious or commemorative reasons are not eligible.

2. Structures which have been moved are not eligible, unless no other means of preservation is available.

3. Reconstructed properties are not eligible for the State or National Registers, unless no other example exists and unless the documentation is thorough.

4. Properties that have achieved significance in the last 50 years are not eligible for the National Register unless the nomination indicates that sufficient time has passed to allow professional judgement of significance. Significant structures from all periods are eligible for the State Register.

We may note in passing that the State criteria were written in 1979, and that this explains why they categorize structures (*contributing, neutral*) in a manner recently established by Interior, and use some designations (*networks, cultural landscapes*) which had been suggested not long before by the Heritage Conservation and Recreation Service (the successor agency in historic preservation of the National Park Service), but which had not been adopted, at the time of this writing, by the federal government.

We should also note that from 1969 to 1979 the State professional committee considered the National Register a register for properties of national significance. This is why the number of properties, including archeological properties, on the State Register is so much greater than that on the National Register. This view of the nature of the National Register, as we have seen from our review of the legislative history, was contrary to the Congressional intent, and has since been corrected by the criteria quoted above.

Representative John Seiberling of Ohio proposed extensive amendments and additions to the Historic Preservation Act of 1966 in the Ninety-sixth Congress. His proposals received strong bipartisan support. Detailed recommendations from the National Conference of State Historic Preservation Officers were embodied in the bill (H.R. 5496), which was signed into law by President Carter on December 12, 1980.

The amended law did not change the definition of the National Register of Historic Places, except to include "engineering" among the areas of Register significance. The amended law specified that the Secretary of the Interior was to "establish or revise criteria for properties to be included on the National Register in consultation with national historical and archeological associations".

The amended law also stated that no property could be listed on the National Register if the owner objected. This provision was the result of tax incentives and disincentives created by Section 2124 of the Tax Reform Act of 1976, and some consequent objections to National Register listing by commercial and industrial interests. The provision was introduced into H.R. 5496 in the last stages of consideration by the House of Representatives. It was widely objected to by historic preservation groups as inconsistent with the purpose and philosophy of the National Register, but Seiberling himself advised its acceptance as the price of passage of the bill, and in recognition of the increasingly conservative mood of the Congress. This section of the law explained that in case of an owner objection the Secretary would determine the *eligibility* of the property for purposes of Advisory Council and federal agency information and review.

Let us assume — and we are convinced of this — that the original Congressional intent is well and truly expressed in the national and State criteria. This still does not bring us anywhere near a definition of significance in archeological properties in New Mexico. The federal criterion applicable to most signficant archeological sites in New Mexico, obviously, is the one which says: *that have yielded or may be likely to yield information important in prehistory*. This again begs the whole question; it says that a significant site is important. We need to make a real, a self-sustaining definition of the quality of significance in archeology in all classes of prehistoric sites, structures and objects. Very well then.

The site population of any of the major physiographic areas we have discussed in the last five chapters is probably much larger than that now identified. The sites we know about have certain salient characteristics. Some of them are architectural. In some, the architecture is evidently the product of a long process of technical specialization. Some sites have no architectural features at all. These are sets of artifacts evidently arranged with some conscious purpose or by some particular method of performance of work.

These sites, then, have architectural interest and value in some cases; in some cases they may be able to tell us something about the lives and habits of the people who made them. Our interest in a particular site may vary with the discovery and examination of other sites of similar type or of the same period. It must also be borne in mind that these sites are points or configurations on a map, and at the same time are lines in a perspective; they represent an immense depth in time. Now we are being asked to state which of these sites is significant or important, and which is not. There is a fairly widespread conviction in America that the answer to this question should be simple. It is not simple, but it may in fact be reducible to a formula.

For the purposes of argument, let us consider the possibility that every archeological and historical site is important or significant. That is simply to say that any site may contribute, given the right circumstances, to an inquiry into the lives or means of subsistence of historic or prehistoric people. This may be true, but is evidently not very useful in an administrative point of view. We have to limit, we have to define significance for administrative reasons.

There is something else, also pretty obvious, that we should keep in mind. That is, that significance is relative. Some of the first sites to be put on the National Register of Historic Places, including a number of National Historic Landmarks, were registered because their significance was obvious and unquestionable. Mount Vernon is an example; so is the Palace of the Governors in Santa Fe. Everyone knows what these sites stand for, or to put it another way, the significance of these sites is relative to certain knowledge possessed by many people. There are other sites whose significance is relative to certain knowledge possessed by few people, and there are also sites about which no one knows anything much. Site significance is relative not only to knowledge, but to physical features of other sites. Mount Vernon is a house with some architectural features which were unusual at the time of building but have been widely imitated since.

Before we go to the trouble of establishing some method, probably arbitrary, of calling certain sites important and others not important, we should see if there are already certain forces at work to do this job for us.

There is the fact of change in the physical universe, in this case any major physiographic area which we have defined. Sites are destroyed purposely and by accident by a variety of means, perhaps imparting changed values to those that are left. Sites are also created, even if very slowly, and by processes and for reasons which may resemble the reasons and processes behind the old site population. There are changes, too, in the theoretical universe. The value

351

of certain knowledge and the predictable value of certain questions rise and fall as the state of knowledge changes. Redundancy in our knowledge of sites and of the processes they represent becomes apparent on the one hand; at the same time new questions come up.

The number and nature of sites, then, is limited by these facts. We might say that it is modeled by them, and call them models of significance. The first limiting element can be called a resource model of significance; the second might be called a research model.

The resource model is a map of the resource areas we have defined, e.g. Mimbres-Mogollon. It is a much simplified map; in order to draw it we have to beg certain questions. We have to assume that all the sites fit into a definite number of classes, such as Paleo, Archaic, Pueblo and so on. It might be more appropriate simply to establish arbitrary levels or periods in time, and to group the sites in these. This is analogous to the way in which archeologists lay out a grid or establish levels in a site; the areas thus defined are arbitrary, but consistent; they are units of reference which are used because the physical relationships of artifacts are assumed to be significant and can be measured according to the system thus established. There may be other things on the map, for example, ecological zones or soil types — that is, classifications of the land.

If we take a set of such arbitrary classifications — periods, site types, zones of land and so on, we can use them to make a grid. We can organize the sites that are there according to the way they fall in any one of a number of universe or land areas. We know that our units of reference are arbitrary, but we are also reasonably sure that they are consistently applied to physical phenomena, because they are derived from or based on consistent groups of attributes or are purely arbitrary, as in the case of actual dates.

We could divide up our universe in another way, by interpreting certain groups of attributes as indicating that a site was used in a certain way, and grouping sites according to use across time, rather than by period. You will note that all these possible methods of classification have been used in the course of this study.

No matter what set of classifications we use, we come up with various groups of sites which may be bounded by arbitrary frontiers, for example, the boundaries of an undertaking like a large strip mine. It is then possible to evaluate the sites according to their frequency or rarity, and to require their preservation, or permit them to be destroyed with or without investigation, consistent with that frequency or rarity. Of course, it may be objected that a site which is very rare within the arbitrary boundary of a project may be extremely common elsewhere, perhaps close by. On the other hand, the universe we are using is and will be subject to known conditions (e.g. a mining plan). This makes it possible to manage the sites in that universe, but not elsewhere.

We can apply the same general procedure in a universe that is not fully known, that is, only partly surveyed. For the purposes of our argument, we can accept the theory that, on the basis of probabilistic sampling, the part may be taken for the whole, or that our actual knowledge of the universe may be extended through sampling to a full knowledge of all the units of reference of concern to us.

This resource model has the virtue of relative simplicity, although, as has already been said, it begs the real questions. It has another advantage too. In a model in which the significance of sites changes with the changes in the land itself, the man running the bulldozer determines significance. The destruction of a part of our universe by stripmining causes a corresponding increase in the value of the sites that are left. So when the miner asks which sites are important and which are not, we can tell him to show us his mining plan. To the extent that the plan shows what is going to happen to the land, we can determine significance

352

now and in the future covered by that plan. This may be useful in dealing with the people who think that determining significance should be simple -- much simpler, for example, than running a strip mine.

There are some necessary qualifications of the above. The extent of the investigation of sites before they are destroyed may serve to qualify the extent of change in the significance of other sites in the universe. But this point really belongs to the discussion of research models, as we will show.

A resource model of significance is physical; a research model is theoretical. In a research model the unit of reference is a research question. Here, values rise and fall as questions are answered and asked, rather than according to the number of sites of any given type. If the question, for example, is whether the inhabitants of certain sites made a sort of projectile point, the discovery of that type of point in the sites — with the debitage, presumably, to show that the points were made, not traded — answers the question and makes the sites insignificant.

Notice that effects on the universe define significance in a resource model, while in a research model, the unit of reference, the research question, defines the nature of effects. If the question has to do with the arrangement of sites — their relationship in space — the total destruction of these sites is not an adverse effect if the locations of the sites have been mapped. If the question has to do with the spatial relations of artifacts on a living floor in a single site, merely walking across that floor may adversely affect the site.

A research model is just as arbitrary in its way as a resource model. Who asks the research questions, for example? How many investigators does it take to ask a valid question? Suppose investigators disagree over what questions ought to be asked? There is only one way to deal with these problems. The valid research questions are the ones decided on by the investigator doing the work. Of course he will never ask all the questions nor get all the answers, and some information will be lost. A research model is bounded not only by arbitrary decisions about who gets to do the job and what line of inquiry he will pursue, but by the nature of knowledge and perception.

In contemporary public archeology there are two kinds of sites: those that contain information and those that are susceptible of being preserved and interpreted in place. We have talked about the first kind; we don't seem to have talked about the second, except for suggesting that architectural sites and sites which might interest the general public seem to be more self-explanatory than other sites. They give pleasure; they are good to look at and they tell us, speaking not through an intermediary but for themselves, what their builders were like. Is this a third model? Probably not. These are just cases in which the visitor does his own research, his own looking and understanding, or at any rate some of it, with signs and placards to help him. The difference between a site which contains information and a site which has public value is an imprecise boundary. When the interpretive signs attract more attention and take more time than the site itself, or when the time needed to interpret the site is longer than the time needed to stabilize it, we might suppose that the point of difference is reached.

Our two models of significance do not exclude each other. The resource model shifts with changes in the surface of the area of study, while the research model shifts when questions are asked and answered. The research model replenishes itself by constant reapplication to the resource, and at the same time constantly defines and redefines the nature of effects on the resource. In short, the quality of significance in archeology is a relationship between the physical characteristics of sites and the state of knowledge about sites. This study is an examination of these relationships.

This brings us back to our point of departure. Significance is a formula, but a formula with a practically unlimited number of terms. The formula is not fixed. No inventory and assessment of significance will ever be completed, except by the destruction of all the sites in the inventory area. We, of course, are not too upset about learning that the quality of significance is pervasive and not to be isolated, and that there appears to be no end to the work we are doing. We suspected as much.

Before we end this chapter, we should look at the National Register again. The Register is structured to permit certain kinds of entries. These are as follows:

A district is a geographically definable area, urban or rural, possessing a significant concentration, linkage, or continuity of sites, buildings, structures, or objects united by past events or aesthetically by plan or physical development. A district may also comprise individual elements separated geographically but linked by association or history.

A site is the location of a significant event, a prehistoric or historic occupation or activity, or a building or structure, whether standing, ruined, or vanished, where the location itself maintains historical or archeological value regardless of the value of any existing structures.

A building is a structure created to shelter any form of human activity, such as a house, barn, church, hotel, or similar structure. Buildings may refer to a historically related complex such as a courthouse and jail or a house and barn.

A structure is a work made up of interdependent and interrelated parts in a definite pattern of organization. Constructed by man, it is often an engineering project large in scale.

An object is a material thing of functional, aesthetic, cultural, historical, or scientific value that may be, by nature or design, movable yet related to a specific setting or environment.

[*How to Complete National Register Forms* 1977]

Two additional classifications came into use in 1977.

A THEMATIC GROUP NOMINATION is one which includes a finite group of resources related to one another in a clearly distinguishable way. They may be related to a single historical person, event, or development force; of one building type or use, or designed by a single architect; of a single archeological site form, or related to a particular set of archeological research problems. They can be located within a single geographical area such as a county, or they can be spread throughout a State or even, in the case of a federal agency nomination, throughout the country. Whatever the organizing principle or thematic relationship of the group of resources may be, the nomination should include all known properties within the group that are eligible for listing in the National Register. This means that if properties related to a historical event are to be nominated, every eligible property related to the event should be included; if all eligible courthouses within a State are to be nominated, a nomination should not be submitted for only half of the eligible number; if archeological properties from a specified prehistoric or historic period are to be nominated, the nomination should be based on a survey that can be demonstrated on the basis of an established regional overview such as the State Preservation Plan to be complete enough to identify all eligible sites within a given geographical area.

Thematic Group nominations differ from Multiple Resource nominations in the primary way in which the component properties are related, i.e. thematically vs. geographically. In general, the properties of a Thematic Group will be scattered over a much wider geographical area than those of a Multiple Resource Area where the intention is to identify through a comprehensive interdisciplinary survey all resources of architectural, historical, and archeological significance within the area that are eligible for listing in the National Register. A property included in a Thematic Group nomination, however, may be included in a Multiple Resource Area as well. For example, if a nomination is submitted for buildings in California designed by Frank Lloyd Wright, one of the buildings may be included in a Multiple Resource Area already listed in the National Register.

Thematic Group nominations will generally consist of individual properties related by theme but may in some cases include one or more historic districts as well as individual properties, or even be comprised entirely of historic districts (i.e. a group of districts in a city composed of scattered neighborhoods which developed during the same period because of growth pressures endangered by the development of a single industry). The information necessary for submission consists of:

> *1) a completed nomination form giving a description of the theme chosen and an explanation of how the component properties relate to the theme,*

> *2) attached inventory forms which include brief descriptions, statements of significance, and geographical data for all individual properties.*

> *3) a brief description, statement of significance, and geographical data for each historic district to be included in the Thematic Group, and*

> *4) accompanying visual documentation including maps and photographs. The nomination forms to be used for Thematic Group nominations are the same as those used for individual and district nominations. Inventory forms used may be State, local, or Federal.*

A Thematic Group is by definition a finite group of resources. However, if a property which should have been included in a group is identified through additional research after the group is listed in the Register, or excluded from the original nomination because of an oversight, this property may be added to the group by writing an explanatory letter to the National Register and submitting a continuation sheet or inventory form for the property which provides the data required for any individual property or district included in a Thematic Group.

A MULTIPLE RESOURCE NOMINATION is one which includes all or a defined portion of the historic resources identified in a specified geographical area which may be a rural area, a county, a small town, a large town or city, or a section of a town or city. The size of the area chosen should be determined by historic and/or geographic factors and by the practical factor of its manageability in the nominating process. The nomination should, if possible, be based upon the results of a comprehensive interdisciplinary survey undertaken to identify all of the resources of historic, architectural, and archeological significance within a defined geographical area. The survey data should be carefully analyzed to determine which properties are eligible for listing in the National Register.

Multiple Resource nominations differ from Thematic Group nominations in the primary way in which the component properties are related, i.e. geographically vs. thematically. In general, in the Thematic Group nomination which is by definition a finite group of resources related to one another in a clearly distinguishable way, the component resources of the group will be scattered over a much wider geographical area than those of a Multiple Resource Area. A property included in a Multiple Resource nomination for a particular locality may be included in a Thematic Group already listed in the National Register consisting of all county courthouses in a State.

The information necessary for submission of a Multiple Resource nomination consists of:

1) a completed nomination form giving a general description and statement of significance for the entire defined area, including a description of the scope of the survey on which the nomination is based;

2) attached inventory forms for all individual properties which include brief descriptions, statements of significance, and geographical data;

3) a brief description, statement of significance, and geographical data for any proposed historic district(s) within the area; and

4) accompanying visual documentation including maps and photographs. The nomination forms to be used for Multiple Resource nominations are the same as those used for individual and district nominations. Inventory forms used may be State, local, or Federal.

Surveys used as the basis for Multiple Resource nominations should be as complete as possible. Because of oversights, additional research, new judgements, and/or the increasing age of more recent structures as time passes, however, it may be necessary to nominate additional properties located within the geographical limits of a Multiple Resource Area which is already listed in the National Register. This may be done by writing an explanatory letter to the National Register and submitting a continuation sheet or inventory form for each property to be added which provides the data required for any individual property or district located within a Multiple Resource Area. In addition, if a State office or Federal agency defines a Multiple Resource Area intending eventually to nominate all properties within this area which are eligible for listing in the National Register and has survey data on one or more types of historic properties properties but not on all eligible properties within the area, a Multiple Resource nomination may be submitted with the notation 'partial inventory' and an indication of the type(s) of resources included following the general nomination title. Future nominations may be submitted for other types of historic resources within the Multiple Resource Area after more extensive surveys have been completed, but the geographical limits for each component nomination of the Multiple Resource Area must be identical.

Our emphasis in this study has been and will be on the last two classifications.

Chapter IX
NATIONAL REGISTER SURVEYS FOR NEW MEXICO:
PROBLEMS, METHODS, AND SOLUTIONS

In this chapter we discuss general problems in the methodology of archeological survey.

In order to gain an understanding of survey problems for this study, we reviewed several hundred reports of contracted archeological surveys. From this reading, very general problem areas were abstracted and discussed. Our discussion is not exhaustive, nor is it intended to specify just how archeological surveys should be conducted. It is intended to focus attention on problems that must be addressed by the archeological profession, in general, and prior to the initiation of any large-scale program of National Register surveys, in particular.

Secondly, we suggest project specific priorities for National Register surveys; that is, what kinds of projects are most urgent, where they are most urgent, and how they might be structured to offer us enduring research value. Our primary concern is in the consistency of the site-specific data base, since it, rather than some specific statistical or analytical technique, will be our primary research tool for perhaps a century to come.

Finally, a general plan for National Register surveys is presented.

METHODOLOGY AND A REVIEW OF
CONTRACTED ARCHEOLOGICAL SURVEYS

An important part of this project has focused on a review of contracted archeological surveys in New Mexico. This is so for two reasons. First, it is necessary, in making recommendations, to consider the data and research interests contained in these reports. Second, by identifying points of weakness or inconsistency, it is possible to suggest just which areas of professional practice require substantial attention. For these reasons, a number of institutions were invited to submit reports for review.

Those invited included the contract or research divisions of the following:

	Responded	Provided Reports	
1.*	Yes	1 and bibliog.	The Museum of New Mexico, Santa Fe
2.*	Yes	15	The San Juan County Museum, Bloomfield, NM
3.*	Yes	15	The San Juan Branch of New Mexico State University
4.*	Yes	15	New Mexico State University, Las Cruces
5.	Yes	5 (small surveys)	Eastern New Mexico University, Portales
6.	Yes	(none conducted)	Highlands University, Las Vegas
7.*	Yes	15	The Zuni Archaeological Program, Zuni, New Mexico
8.	NO	—	The Cultural Resource Division, Navajo Tribe
9.*	Yes	5 (several extensive)	The School of American Research, Santa Fe
10.	Yes	(none conducted)	Condie and Associates, Albuquerque
11.	NO	—	Esca-Tech Corporation, Farmington, New Mexico
12.	NO	—	Institute for Anthropological Research, Albuquerque
13.*	Yes	10 (several extensive)	University of New Mexico (OCA), Albuquerque
14.*	Yes	6 (several extensive)	Human Systems Research, Inc., Tularosa, New Mexico
15.	NO	—	Western New Mexico University, Silver City

*Adequately represented.

Of these, only 5 institutions responded fully. Two more were moderately well represented. These are: The San Juan County Museum, The San Juan Branch of NMSU, New Mexico State University in Las Cruces, The Zuni Archeological Program, the University of New Mexico (OCA), the School of American Research, and Human Systems Research. We are very grateful to these individuals, for it is troublesome to pay for, box up, and mail stacks of contract reports upon request. In addition, we should state that several institutions (Human Systems Research and the School of American Research) sent fewer reports simply because they conduct fewer projects. Human Systems Research, Inc. of Tularosa, also xeroxed great piles of climatic data, papers on Chacoan research, and material on southeastern New Mexico, etc. It is unfortunate that other institutions known to be working in the state were not so well represented for formal review purposes.

A number of federal and state agencies were also invited to submit survey reports, planning documents or supporting materials. Federal agencies responding with supporting materials were NPS (Santa Fe — Messrs. Ice and Anderson and Drs. Wait and Birkedal), BLM (Santa Fe — Mr. Flynn) and the U.S. Forest Service (Albuquerque — Dr. Green). However, no federal agency submitted an in-house survey report for review.

It had originally been stated to these institutions that they would have priority in selecting the 12-15 contract reports which best represented their work. In view of the disappointing response from some institutions, the senior author obtained many more contract reports informally and without the specific consent of those institutions to make public any review commentary. For these reasons, we have elected to generalize comments among the many and make few comments specific. These comments are not based, then, on only those reports formally submitted for review.

GENERAL COMMENTS

From the more than 200 contracted archeological reports reviewed from all portions of New Mexico, a number of generalities can be stated. These generalities are based on reports received prior to Christmas 1979. Most are dated between 1975 and 1978.

Contracted archeological reports fall rather neatly into several distinct size-type categories: 1) small-scattered well site and linear surveys; 2) small block surveys, roughly 1-4 or 5 sections, and larger linear surveys (10-50 or 60 miles); 3) moderate size block surveys (10-20 sq. miles), and large linear surveys (ca. 100 linear miles); and 4) large block surveys (well over 20 sq. miles). There are few excavation reports, compared to reports of surveys, and the reconnaissance survey (partial ground coverage and literature search) appears to be currently far less common than five or six years ago (1973-1975).

The research problems involved with the conduct of small, scattered projects in New Mexico has led to a situation in which it appears that at least some institutions have quit trying. In general, these propose no research, appear to use canned statements of research interest, often fail even to mention the specific methods of data recovery, and far too seldom specify whether collections were, or were not, taken. Few contain actual site data forms, and many site summaries or inventories are inadequate in terms of data. The more detailed and explicit of these reports appear to be related to the characteristics of individual field workers who prepare them. Some of the small project reports these individuals have produced are now four or five years old, and several have gone on to conduct other types of projects. In short, there seems to be surprisingly little institutional control over the quality of these reports, and most of the institutions represented had small project reports which varied widely in quality. In general, these small project reports have become more conventionalized over time, the research statements appear in many, serially, in unaltered form, and the bibliographies (in those reports that contain references) are generally highly stylized.

We have commented on the very small projects separately because most institutions maintain that the time/cost constraints of contract archeology create a situation in which these projects defy more elaborate preparation and therefore, do not reflect their research/methodology. We will accept this assertion to a degree, but counter with several observations: 1) certain individuals have produced a series of better than average reports for this class of project, so the possibility for general improvement is already demonstrated; 2) even if no new research is proposed, one can at least be consistent and explicit about methods used for field coverage, data recording, diagnosing the cultural affinity of the site, and samples collected; and 3) since several institutions produce small project reports primarily, one, in effect, is asked to excuse certain institutions from adhering to the conventions of research and methodology alleged to prevail elsewhere. While the conduct of these small surveys has little bearing on the subject of this volume (larger surveys based on matching federal funds), we make one *caveat*. Institutions will not be able to transfer the methods, and reporting standards of most small surveys to larger scale in order to conduct the regionally oriented surveys considered in this volume.

The larger project reports tell a different story. There is, generally, the appearance of more institutional control over quality, but two trends are clear: 1) the general quality of these reports has, in our opinion, been *declining* over the last several years; and 2) there is even greater variance in quality than among the small project reports. Some of the larger survey reports are very competently done, while some are truly abysmal. For instance, one recent, very late (1970's) survey, reporting the results of a 4-5 square mile investigation, recorded more than 125 structural sites. One of these sites was nothing less than a very famous and large Bonito Phase Chacoan town. There are less than 20 pages of text in addition to site forms and site descriptions. No specific research is proposed, the description of field methodology is very vague, and the archeological summary or discussion of the resources is given only 3½ double-spaced pages. The significance of the resources takes up less than a page. Finally, in this report, there is no specific discussion of proposed impacts, and no recommendations about the future committment of resources are offered. We cannot see how such surveys will produce for us either useful planning tools or useful research tools.

Other projects have, of course, proposed explicit research, some of which is quite innovative. But here we insert another caution. An hypothesis by itself is not research. It is merely a question which has been transformed into a statement of relationships thought to be observable, and therefore capable of being tested. If one wishes to conduct research, that is, answer questions, one must also devise a method for observing the phenomena thought to be related. Since it is the weight of many repeated observations which allows one to elevate observations to generalities or to systems of classification, then reason dictates that the method of observation be replicable. It is in this area that the reports reviewed are weakest. A discussion of several major areas of difficulty follows.

PRE-SURVEY PREPARATION

Little pre-survey preparation seems to be a feature of the majority of contracted survey reports. Few reports contain summaries of data and comments about findings from earlier published surveys in the same general geographic area (one exception is the four volume Cochiti Survey; Biella and Chapman 1977-79). Even fewer compare the findings of excavation reports with earlier surveys to determine, for instance, the relationship among characteristics of surface assemblages, presumed cultural affiliation and chronological data established through excavation of similar subsurface components. One study did compare conclusions drawn from surface survey with the results of later excavation at those same sites. This work suggested that surface assemblages are not very good reflectors of subsurface remains. Many archeologists choose to phrase their judgments about the significance of a site in terms of information presumed to be contained in it and therefore recoverable. In contract archeology, most sites are selected for excavation on the basis of surface survey data. Since published literature raises questions about the assumptions which underly such practices, they should not be ignored.

Secondly, without reference to previous literature, already established research questions go ignored, and for those whose preparation time is constrained, a very rich array of ready-made research questions (not research designs) is made available for a long weekend's reading. For instance, a review of Irwin-Williams' (1973) publication on the Oshara Tradition, Kenneth Honea's (1969) study of *Jay* materials, Judge's monograph (1973) on Paleo-Indian occupations, and Reher and Witter's (1977) analysis of Archaic components in the CGP lease, with the survey report of the Navajo Indian Irrigation project (Elyea, Abbink and Eschman 1979), helps one identify several important issues. Stratified Archaic sites are known, but scarce, while stratified Paleo-Indian sites are remarkably rare. Paleo-Indian occupation is highly associated with old playa features and settings where overlooks are available (Judge), and Archaic settlement has been related to areas of high vegetative diversity (Reher and Witter 1977). *Jay* is argued, on the one hand (Irwin-Williams 1973), as an *in situ* development after a break from the Paleo-Indian Period and, on the other, as a possible development evolving from Hell Gap (Honea 1969).

Elyea, Abbink and Eschman (1979) have compared their data to most of these other studies and have proposed a series of necessary research questions which require further implementation. The sites they recorded are, in some cases, *buried*, and so may contain stratified deposits. Moreover, their data raise questions about Judge's assessment of Paleo-Indian site setting; playas and overlooks may not figure strongly. They also question the apparent correlation of Archaic site placement with areas of high vegetative diversity as demonstrated by Reher and Witter (1977). Chapman's (1979) research in Cochiti Reservoir raises even more questions about the "Vegetative Diversity Model" of Archaic site placement. If even several of these buried sites (NIIP) do prove to be intact and to contain stratified deposits, the potential for research could be nothing short of spectacular. What is the stratigraphic context of the late Paleo-Indian and early Archaic? Is the lack of correlation between Archaic sites and vegetative diversity a function of different subsistence strategies in the CGP, the Gallegos Wash and the Cochiti Reservoir areas? Is it a function of alteration to plant communities correlated with degree of erosion, or grazing, etc? Or is it, as Elyea, Abbink and Eschman suggest, a function of distance to water? These questions and others might be answered through excavation, but however important the potential results, excavation is not quite the point we wish to make here.

All of the issues raised above depend in some way upon methodology, and the above authors have all employed different techniques in collecting and analyzing their data. Judge used "site pattern recognition" in his Paleo-Indian studies; that is, he was looking specifically for Paleo-Indian sites in certain settings, but not, as Cordell (1979) points out, in others. The CGP survey was 100% foot surveyed at fairly close intervals organized by control transects. The precise method of Irwin-Williams' (1973) surveys in Arroyo Cuervo is not clear to us from her publication, and the survey by Elyea, Abbink and Eschman (1979) was composed of some block survey plus spot checking because they were resurveying previously surveyed acreage to resolve problems with earlier data. In short, the degree of comparability among the results of surficial survey by these several investigators is not a known quantity.

In a sense, each of these surveys represents ecological/physiographic stratification of some kind. Elyea, Abbink and Eschman relied on Fanale and Drager's (in press) stratification of their survey area into vegetative communities. This stratification is based on remote sensing techniques, and a few on-the-ground problems were noted, but the possibility for replication is undoubtedly high. In the CGP survey, Reher and Witter (1977) relied on a combination of general physiographic features and soil type, coupled with an emphasis on plant communities. The analysis of plant communities and computations of diversity indices were adaptations of techniques used by field ecologists and depended upon Witter's particular ability to distinguish among plant species. These distinctions often depended upon discriminating between stems and root systems, since the area was badly overgrazed in spots. Reher and Witter's vegetative diversity hypothesis was tested independently (Allan, et al. 1975) and confirmed in the NIIP Block II, very near the Blocks IV and V survey area of Eleyea, Abbink and Eschman. Thus, Reher's results might prove to be generally replicable in that portion of the San Juan Basin, but data requirements that not every survey crew can meet are imposed in the field. Finally, Irwin-Williams (1973) and Judge (1973) have described site setting in terms of physiographic features, such as canyon heads, playas, etc. We require a great deal more data about these settings. How many canyon heads in a general region contain the predicted type of site as opposed to those that do not (Judge did attempt a generalization for *playas*)? What range of elevation is intended? What are average temperatures in occupied and unoccupied canyon heads and how could we efficiently obtain those data? What is the vegetative diversity? Does soil type vary, etc? When we say a certain type of site is found in *canyon-head settings*, we should be prepared to say a canyon-head setting ranging between x and y in elevation, that has x degrees arc of exposure to y compass orientation, has x (or several) soil types, x kinds of plant species, and x range of plant diversity and certain average temperature. If the methods for obtaining these data don't exist, then we should be prepared to experiment. We need to know how many of all specific settings were filled, say, during the late Archaic. Why? Is the development of early pithouse architecture (BM-II) a function of increased sedentism, high population density and increased agricultural pursuits? Or were protected cold season settings (caves, rock shelters) simply used up, requiring experimentation with alternative structures? Who currently knows?

In order to prepare for subsequent survey in areas that might yield substantial Paleo-Indian and Archaic assemblages, one should go back to each of these surveys and standardize the methods used insofar as is possible to put the diversely presented data into tabular form. That is, on-the-ground diversity indices should be computed in Blocks IV and V of the NIIP. The Fanale-Drager method should be applied to the CGP study; it might show the same lack of association with site placement as in the NIIP. In that case, one might still need field analysis of vegetative strata in a survey area, whether or not remote sensing techniques are employed. We also have no doubt that Fanale and Drager would like to see the results of field application so that they can refine their method, if problems of practical utility should arise. One would also need to compute average distance from sites to water in each of the survey areas, and exercise substantial control over pedological characteristics. Finally, since Honea has focused on the morphology of Jay points, while Irwin-Williams has focused on the lithic assemblage associated with it, in making their differing suggestions about Paleo-Indian to Archaic lithic transitions, one simply cannot resolve the issue without analysis of both diagnostic materials and remaining lithic assemblages. That, after a short summary, brings us to the subject of field methodology.

Our major points are these: research designs need to be written before one goes into the field. A review of previous literature quickly raises many usable research questions and allows one to identify gaps in the data base and flaws in previous methodology which have obscured the answers sought. The problems of comparability of data and replication of method are so substantial between surveys that pre-survey preparation is of very pressing importance. If one were to pursue the variant results and apply the various methods to increase comparability of the surveys mentioned above, it would be a substantial contribution to Southwestern anthropology. If one then designed several shorter resurveys to fill in data gaps and a series of new surveys using a standardized methodology, one might discover relationships between degree of niche packing and technological change over time. Specifying a factor which conditions technological change is a very major theme in anthropology.

Many contract reports do have research design chapters, and often enough the data collected during survey are said to confirm the hypotheses stated. On the other hand, it is rarer that the methodology of data collection, environmental control and analysis varies with the questions posed. It may be that many general research questions can be addressed through generalized and loosely conventionalized methodology, but in some cases we have read about reputedly good fit between data and very specialized questions without resort to specific methods constructed for the purpose. These instances force us to conclude that such investigators are, at times, either very lucky or write their "proposed research" chapters last. In short, surprisingly few contract surveys yield strong evidence of any specific research planning prior to fieldwork. The Laboratory of Anthropology survey files are rarely used to summarize site data from several hundred (or more) previously recorded sites that are in the general region of the planned survey.

FIELD SURVEY METHODOLOGY AND DATA COLLECTION

Field methodology varies widely from archeologist to archeologist and institution to institution. From contracted archeological reports it is difficult to assess the actual state of the art of field survey, for relatively few reports are explicit about field procedure. There are four major problems we wish to address here: 1) consistent recording of baseline data; 2) sampling sites; 3) diagnosing classification/chronology; and 4) experiment or refinement in methodology.

RECORDING OF BASELINE DATA

The subject of standardizing those data which should be recorded at each site has been a recurring theme at meetings of the New Mexico Archeological Council over the last five years. The issue has not been resolved because the major impediment to resolution has not been adequately addressed. It is necessary to distinguish between data required for purposes of research planning and administrative planning on the one hand, and data required for particular conduct of research on the other. Investigators need to back away from the tendency to propose baseline data based on the specific needs of conducting their own research and focus ONLY on the fewest data which they would require to *sort* archeological sites into categories of greater or lesser research utility to these. Meanwhile, Federal and State agency planners should focus on the minimal data they would require in implementing their administrative mandate.

We view it as counter-productive to devise or construct a central data bank which is so cumbersome in its detail that everyone presumes it will in some way meet their specific research requirements. It is likely that in so doing, there is risk of merely centralizing vast quantities of data which are not comparable. Rather, it is important to have a few basic facts about archeological sites in some central and quickly accessible vehicle. These basic facts should be an abstract of site data recovery forms, rather than the full information from the forms themselves. The forms, of course, should also continue to be centralized at the Museum of New Mexico as they are now, and the archeological profession needs to be altogether more conscientious in seeing that the Museum of New Mexico does, in fact, receive forms for all sites recorded by both amateurs and professionals. Several federal agencies do not currently have their survey work completely represented in the Laboratory site files.

The San Juan Basin Data Base, developed by the National Park Service's Santa Fe branch, is the kind of computerized data file which provides us a concrete basis from which to extend our discussions. We believe a data file containing somewhat (but not much) more information would be optimal. In addition to cultural period, we might require data about elevation, soil type, site size and size of structural units broken into several gross categories, vegetation and more specific information about methodology. The vegetation could be handled by some standard adaptation of the Fanale/Drager remote sensing method or by some adaptation of Camilli's (Camilli and Allen 1979) procedures with remote sensing. We would then need to know if a particular site had also been subjected to a field ecological study which was generally replicable. Elevation would seem to be a simple matter, and most institutions record it, but some still do not, and one must go through remarkable numbers of site files, survey reports and formal excavation reports to retrieve elevation/general exposure data for a sample of, say, 500 sites in a given region. In addition, we need to know not only cultural period, but also whether the diagnostic procedure can be replicated or verified by consulting material contained in the site forms (and, perhaps, samples of material) or archeological reports describing the site.

The current data base does contain information about the method of sampling a site. It startled us to discover that less than 6% of the sites in the San Juan Basin had been subjected to systematic sampling, that 34% had been grab sampled and that fully 59% were unsampled, or sampled by unknown method, or that it was unknown (13%) whether they had been sampled or not. Clearly, we need to attend to this state of affairs. In a general data base, then, we need to know the method of sampling, its degree of replicability, whether information exists to verify the diagnosis of site type independently, and where such information can be found. We also need information on chronology and how it was obtained. Many archeologists use slightly different time periods in adapting everyday application of the Pecos Classification, and similar cultural developments occur at slightly different time periods in different local areas. Thus, we need to know what dates the archeologist has in mind and whether classification and chronology were independently determined and by what means. That is, whether a P-II site, for instance, was so classified on the basis of general architecture, ceramics, lithic attributes, or some independent dating technique, whether obsidian hydration, C-14, archeomagnetic analysis, etc., or all of these.

In short, then, we require some standardized information that is of practical utility and gives a clue as to what research might be conducted with a sample of similarly recorded sites. In addition, we need to know the strength of the data, replicability of method, and where to find the full data. The object, and only object, of such a data base should be to allow us to pose a research question and then sort out a preliminary sample of sites we wish to review for possible inclusion in the actual conduct of our research.

For instance, as we pointed out in an earlier section of this volume, there are important thermodynamic relationships among site size, the size of internal structural units, and energy investments. These involve important implications for the state of the archeological record itself. A small structure requires greater energy investment to create it relative to its mass than does a larger structure. A small structure (size of elements being constant — as in bricks in a building) loses its structure or shape more quickly due to random processes than does a large structure, and the loss of structure decreases as the size of the building units goes up relative to the mass.

Small, simple detached structures (organisms) in nature are more usually subject to repair than replacement, whereas vast, complex interconnected structures are more usually replaced. That is, an amoeba may be divided in two and two whole amoebas will result; an hydra thus separated will grow new proximal and distal portions. While some small lizards will grow a new tail if the old is cut off, an elephant, once having lost its trunk, has rather permanently lost its trunk and shall not survive long in the bargain. These relationships rather dramatically influence what we see during archeological survey and have substantial practical and explanatory utility, as was suggested in discussions of the Chacoan and Mimbres systems. The first of these can be verified, not directly in the archeological record, but either by experiment or by analogy. We have a computer printout from an Albuquerque real estate firm, which indicates that previously occupied houses of roughly 1200 sq. feet were selling at an average of $46.50 per sq. foot (in January 1979), whereas houses averaging 2500 sq. feet in the same neighborhood were selling at $35.00 per sq. foot.

In the archeological record, the second relationship means that archeological sites containing few, small room units will, as a rule, be less well preserved than those containing larger rooms. This is certainly a factor in making judgments of significance when one encounters a well preserved site of this type.

The third means that smaller building units will more often be repaired than replaced or permanently abandoned, whereas large complex structures will more often be abandoned. When one compares the average episodes of modification and reoccupation in a 10-20 room P-II masonry pueblo to those for sites such as Pueblo Pintado, the reality of these relationships in the archeological record becomes apparent.

In order to verify these last two, one only requires size of rooms, number of rooms per site, and the relative size of building units (stone is practical to measure). But consistency and explicitness of method become very important. Thus, one would need to know whether room size was measured from remaining corner to remaining corner, down the apparent centerline of a vague alignment, or from the inside or from the outside of wall fall. One would also need to know whether common statements in archeological reports that "the average size of sandstone clasts were x cm by x cm by x cm" were actual measurements of one, or three, or five, etc. stones, or were judged by eye. In addition, the average thickness of walls would need to be stated. The number of rooms should be distinguished between certainly definable and possible rooms, which many reports do. Total square footage of a roomblock area with measurements of definable rooms within would be most helpful.

What one would need to know in approaching such a data file would be general site size, number of rooms, size of rooms, and some method code that told us whether recording procedures were explicitly stated elsewhere and generally considered replicable. Of the more than 6,000 sites in the San Juan Basin containing visible structures, one could quickly eliminate two-thirds on the basis of inadequate data/method and search out the site files for the remainder to implement the research program. One could sort even further if there were simply *yes* or *no* codes for "features measured"/"artifacts measured"/"methods stated".

One should be able to stratify archeological sites from few rooms to many interconnected rooms and verify that rebuilding and repair was most common in the former and least in evidence in the latter. The same relationship should hold as one arranges sites with small rooms to very large. Thus, it is not surprising that the small P-II sites in OCA's Pittsburgh-Midway excavation program (Harlan, personal communication) yielded much evidence of repair, remodeling and renovation, while Pueblo Alto and Pueblo Bonito at Chaco Canyon show evidence of somewhat less, perhaps, indicating senescence and abandonment.

In addition, one should be able to verify that the smaller the rooms at a given site, the higher the likelihood that they will have lost their apparent structure due to random processes. In other words, small rooms and reports of possible or indeterminate rooms will correlate in archeological reports. This phenomenon has important implications in Southwestern archeology, since so many demographic reconstructions have been based on room counts and small rooms are likely to be vastly underrepresented when compared to large. If this underrepresentation could be verified, and then resolved by computing potential wall mass of indeterminate rooms from the volume and number of boulders in appropriate sample plots (or computing a *loss of structure* factor statistically from the curve of room size, building block size and number of indeterminate rooms), one could compute a *standing mass* for masonry sites of different time periods in the Eastern Anasazi region. Total mass divided by number of units would give a power to efficiency coefficient for sites of different time periods and by different types of sites in a cultural period. One would then be able to order sites temporally in the same phase sequence where other methods failed, or to gain additional control over ceramic seriations which were compromised by subregional lag times in changing patterns of tradeware imports.

Expanding on this theme, one might discover a sucessional break in room size or wall thickness, while traded ceramics remained relatively stable. One could then propose that the sites in the surveyed area were undergoing phase transformation while the pottery producing locale remained stable. If it was also determined that infant mortality (see Chapter III) really did covary with room size, then one might be viewing the onset of a local adaptive failure. By comparing the site setting of the local area and botanical evidence for subsistence (if you later excavate) with similar data from the pottery producing sites, one might see either dramatically different or quite similar adaptive strategies at work in both areas. If the adaptive (or agricultural strategies) were similar, one might then know which kinds of settings were differentially favored at a given time. One might then be able (through comparative soil studies, etc.) to determine whether specific setting degradation or broad-scale climatic/hydrological processes were at work. Why, for instance, do drier basin areas (San Juan, Tularosa, margins of San Agustin Plain, lower Mimbres valleys) floresce on one schedule (A.D. 1000-1100) and uplands (Zuni highlands, Pajarito Plateau, Mogollon Mountains, Sierra Blanca, Mesa Verde) on another (all A.D. 1100+ to 1300)? We have suggested (Chapter V) a shift from summer to winter dominant rainfall as the reason, but how would one prove it?

Alternatively, site settings might be quite similar, but agricultural strategies quite different (irrigation versus dry farming, for instance). One might then be seeing the selective forces leading to differentiated subsistence patterns. The third case would be the one in which both setting and subsistence strategy varied. This might strengthen research into specialization in ceramic manufacture and site placement on poor soils, etc. In any case, one would know where to look, and when, for the appropriate comparative data to highlight adaptive process in the study area.

In order to carry out such a program of research, one would need to have a sample of sites with good temporal control, UTM coordinates (this has become more consistent lately), and a plot of such sites by elevation, vegetative zone and soil type. Computing rainfall and growing season from location, altitude and exposure, one could then compare a rough indicator of agricultural potential with *standing mass* (or energy stored in non-living structure) and a power/efficiency coefficient. Want to bet that the size of Bonito phase rooms increases as the size of Hosta Butte phase rooms decreases at the end of the Chacoan phenomenon? Want to bet that, in a sample of say 500 sites, as the *standing mass* of sites, collectively, goes up the length of occupation for that subset of sites goes down? Did you ever wonder what was the thermal mass or solar coefficient (mass + exposure + rough calculation of wall surface and openings would do) of sites in one time period compared to another, and how that related to pollen profiles suggesting scarcity of firewood? If in addition one controlled the sample by elevation (cold) and by distance to forested areas (access to firewood) how much architectural variation that has been generally attributed to phase differentiation would be explainable on account of site setting factors? Certainly some, but perhaps even enough to change our notion about the architectural diagnostics of some phases. Finally, which sites are thermally designed for year-round occupation and which for specific seasons? Some of these questions *are* raised in research reports, but where would you get the data to conduct a definitive program of research?

We hope someone will accept the challenge to conduct these kinds of studies. We have the technology (computer file programs, plotting capability and LANDSAT imagery for ecological stratification). What we do not yet have is agreement about recording baseline data, consistent field recording procedures and a data file which allows us to separate sites where the data are strong from those that are not. If we can fulfill the need for a consensus on such matters, establish a mechanism to coordinate the effort and encourage field workers to be explicit, someone could accept this challenge and publish a remarkable paper on *Prehistoric Southwestern Architecture: Evidence for Thermodynamic Principle in Cultural Evolution*. Within three to five years, such research could be done in a summer's time without additional fieldwork. To do it now would require the efforts of several substantial field surveys, close coordination between them, and revamping hundreds to thousands of site forms. Finally, the kinds of analysis we propose here (*standing mass* of architecture; thermal storage coefficients, room size/infant mortality) each need to be conducted only several times before such analytical tools became broadly applicable to survey in the Southwest.

SITE SAMPLING

We have two fundamental problems with regard to the subject of site sampling. These can be summed in two questions: what is a site, and what is a sample? Since these questions have nearly as many answers as the profession has archeologists, there is, understandably, substantial methodological disarray and it is a very serious problem.

It is often argued that archeological sites are the remains of past human behavior and that they therefore define themselves. But this is only a theoretical anecdote, or approximation. In practical terms, it is not true either, or we should not be forever arguing about definition on-the-ground. One often hears comments that *"x wouldn't know a site if he fell in it"* or that *"y wouldn't know an artifact sample from a site if his life depended on it"*. We simply cannot afford such sneering, and we think such stylized misbehavior on the part of a few professionals may be contributing directly to a certain vagueness in many of the field reports prepared by young, aspiring field surveyors.

Again, we should let practical concerns dominate our thinking. In the first place, there is substantial inconsistency in the recording and assignment of archeological remains to the categories of *archeological site* and *isolated occurrence*. This ambiguity has invited certain problems. A few contract reports accord only the briefest descriptions to isolated occurrences, which, by most standards, are archeological sites, and do not, thereafter, mention them in recommendations about protective management from direct/indirect impacts. This is professionally unacceptable. We need to create a conventional measure to avoid it. Others distinguish isolated occurrences as sites, but those where the potentially retrievable data are too few to merit the time/cost investment of intensive recording and analysis. This approach has both a strong logical and practical basis. Yet it must be realized that retrievable data depends on both methodology and proposed research. We need to strike a balance between these views and see to it that isolated occurrences are described well enough so that another investigator would know whether the potential information would be valuable to a different research program and where they could be located again on-the-ground.

Most of the problems, however, have to do with scale, or numbers of artifacts and features. Thus, there is a practical need to distinguish between large and small sets of archeological remains without undoing the best efforts of federal and state planners by basing judgments of significance simply upon size. We can all agree that a single artifact or feature is an isolated occurrence, but our semantic usage creates legal and management problems for others. We might wish to refer to a single artifact or feature as either a *single artifact SITE* or *single feature SITE*.

The matter of isolated occurrence vs. site could be resolved many ways. One way would be to take the San Juan Data Base and compute average surface size (sq. meters, for instance) for all sites in the data base or all sites of a particular kind and use this average size as the standard surface unit of measure, or control, for a site. Using such a standard surface measure would tell us how far apart artifacts would have to be before they were considered isolated. If we knew the number or density/sq. meter of artifacts in isolated occurrences vs. sites, we could specify the density factor for determining when, as a practical matter, an artifact scatter became a site. We don't know this because isolated occurrences aren't generally given surface areas and sampled as are some sites. In other words, we have deprived ourselves of the data needed to create a supportable generalization that provides a solution to one of the biggest day-to-day problems in archeological survey.

One suggestion is that we decide on sampling surface units of standard measure until we have such data. Elsewhere we have suggested a circle of 20 meters across (Stuart 1978). By this method, a single artifact is the only artifact in the circle. Two to ten artifacts or features become a scattered artifact *site* (isolated occurrence) and ten or more an archeological *site*. When more than a hundred artifacts are within the circle, in practical terms, it's time to quit counting artifacts and sample (if not 50 artifacts, depending on the survey).

In sampling, it was decided to circumscribe the larger circle around the highest artifact density, then to circumscribe a one meter circle at the center and record everything in it, and then do the same at each point where the long axis of the site crossed the edge of the circle. Three such one-meter sample circles per 20 meter circle equaled a 1% sample of the surface of the control unit. This method was selected because it is easy to circumscribe such circles with standard tapes hung from a spike driven in the ground, because the center of the circle was a logical place to drive the site stake, because the sample circles were a known percentage of the surface of the control unit, and because others could return to the site stake and therefore the exact sample plot. If spikes are driven where the other circles are sampled, then they can also be located again.

Now, we want to be understood clearly here. We have not said that everyone must conduct survey identically. We have not said we know how it should be done. We have not said a sample plot must be a circle. We do not advocate that some (or any) august body shall self-appoint itself archeology's Bureau of Standards. Thus, we repeat: since we do not currently possess *any* broadly supportable body of data that demonstrates what natural size/ density clusters characterize the archeological record in each of the different time periods and various environmental settings, then we must begin to discover how we can best contribute to each other's research and the *a priori* need for some level of control over artifact samples by agreeing in practical terms to do the following.

1) Sample from some consistently definable surface unit. As long as it can be computed in square meters, or in square feet, and your selection method is consistent and definable, someone else has a reasonable chance to use the data. Let us at least decide on either m^2 or ft^2, but not both. Let us not be forever converting one square yard to the equivalent in square meters.

2) State definitively the method employed. Once you leave the site, could someone else return and duplicate your results? If so, good show!

3) Make it simple for yourself. Don't be intimidated by types who squabble endlessly over sampling procedure as an artform. If you can't decide between random and systematic sampling and have proposed no particular research requiring one or the other, cut your sample plots smaller and do one (or more) of each.

4) What if you take a one meter circle as a sample plot, center it on the highest concentration of ceramics (by eye) and get no rim sherds or good sized painted ware sherds? Why not finish your sample plot and also examine and count nearby painted wares?

Tabulate these separately and put the tallies separately in table form with your site description. Label the *controlled sample* table and the *grab sample* tables clearly. We have seen reports where this was done, and it's just fine.

Several additional comments should be made here. If a no collections strategy is employed, the artifacts, once recorded, should be put back in the sample circle where they were gotten — that is, a color coded pin or flag should be driven where each came from and they should be replaced exactly as found. Anyone not willing to follow such *point-plot* procedures is abusing the rationale for the no-collection survey. The no-collection survey has led to other difficulties as well. We have seen reports where ceramics are described in the San Juan Basin as only "black-on-white series pottery". This suggests that some people are having real difficulty making field identification of materials. When such instances occur, and some ideological convention dictates that it is bad form to take collections, we place ourselves in a position where we may never know what such and such a site was, particularly if it is later under a coal mine. And if a site is certain to be part of a strip mine or under 50 feet of water, just what *is* the justification for preserving the sanctity of artifactual context in the first place?

We also must be cautious that we do not deny to the field worker the opportunity to step forward without ridicule and say *I don't know*. We should not espouse any procedure so tenaciously that on-site professional judgment has no role and, further, we deny the tradition and meaning of our profession if we place individuals in such an uncomfortable position that they cannot step forward and ask to be taught new things. Most of us don't know much about a great deal we feel we ought, but we have got ourselves increasingly into an ambience in which we often dare not admit it publicly.

At any rate, if we sample controlled space, then the population sampled is units of space within which artifacts are found. This is not so controversial, for David Hurst Thomas (1975) has completed a number of successful research programs based on it. The demands do not need to be overwhelming, and a site can be sampled in any number of other ways to serve particular research questions. In some manner like that suggested, whether it be squares or circles or what have you, we would come to have the data about site size and artifact densities needed for more refined judgments later on.

The question, of course, will arise as to whether such samples are representative. They are certainly representative of known quantities of space, and if every artifact up to 100 were inspected and the data recorded, we would certainly have representative artifact *samples* of single artifact sites and scattered artifact sites and most small archeological sites, since we would have recorded the entire artifact population. If we also imposed the one meter sample on a number of these, we would soon come to have useful data about representativeness, since we would have recorded both the entire artifact population and the sample. In sites with smaller sample plots we would have a reasonably representative sample of artifact density and control over surface space sampled. At the very least, we can establish by convention a means for generating data from controlled (if not representative) samples that are reasonably replicable from site to site. By convention we can dramatically increase the number of sites with systematic sampling above the current 6% in some portions of New Mexico. That is, if you are going to *grab* (we personally hate the term because it implies sticking the goodies in your pocket), then do so from the same sized unit of space, from a known proportion of space (control unit to total site area), placed according to the same rationale time after time, then simply go on and record everything else you do normally.

From the management perspective we can restructure our wording to make a necessary accommodation about semantic pre-judging of significance, and by demanding that single artifacts and locations and scattered artifacts and locations be recorded with more care (even if few data about each are sought), we can improve our control over a vastly underrepresented portion of the archeological record. Eventually, this would lead us into new areas of research, and could be used to address questions about the actual utilization of apparent population voids and the co-existence of agriculturalists with foragers that were raised earlier in portions of Chapters II and III. By imposing an arbitrary distinction between 2-10 scattered artifacts (or 6 and 12, or whatever) within a given 20 meter (or any other unit) circle and 10 or more (an archeological site), we can prevent large assemblages from being described as more modest packages than they are, whether by research institutions, agencies or individuals. Let us spend our time seeking solutions rather than penetrating motives.

If we do not insist that everything we do have a profound and universally applicable basis in theory, then we can afford the luxury of any solution that is simple, consistent, replicable and usable, without taking opposing theoretical positions. Our other option is to accept the *Six-Percent Solution* we have got now.

DIAGNOSING CLASSIFICATION AND/OR CHRONOLOGY

It is rather hard to understand why the majority of Southwestern archeologists have clung so tenaciously to the Pecos Classification. It is altogether too obvious that there exists substantial conflict between chronological sequences of development and morphological/stylistic change. Since it appears, nonetheless, that the Pecos Classification will be in use at least to the end of the world as we know it, it is necessary that, where possible, the attributes which allow one to classify a site not also be used as the sole method to date it. It is the idea in archeology that periods and phases reflect sequential but largely static characterizations of cultural development. Current usage does not even achieve this goal, and the goal itself is awkward, since archeology has come to be increasingly focused on the dynamics of adaptive or evolutionary change.

The single greatest weakness in the archeological data from the San Juan Basin and Rio Grande is the lack of precise temporal control. Elsewhere in New Mexico there is even less temporal control on a regional basis. There are currently about 10,000 archeological sites in the San Juan Data Base, and fewer than 200 of these have been excavated. Even with current contract projects in progress, it is unlikely that there exists independent verification of chronology for even 2% of the archeological sites in this portion of New Mexico. It is absolutely imperative that archeological survey systematically identify those sites which, a) yield evidence of datable material; b) or by virtue of stratigraphic preservation, might yield datable material, from c) those sites very unlikely to be datable. Recent advances in C-14 dating techniques have been reported which indicate that very small quantities of charcoal and carbonized material are datable, and many sites contain datable obsidian or samples appropriate for dendrochronological or archeomagnetic analysis. It should increasingly become the case that a major object of archeological survey be to collect appropriately recorded and handled samples of such material for analysis.

Diagnosing the classification or cultural affinity of a site is all too often an uneven procedure. It is patently objectionable that lithic sites containing diagnostic artifacts be assigned a cultural period on the basis of one or two artifacts without analysis of associated lithic material, as was pointed out in a separate section. Every time diagnostics are collected, there is created a currently unclassifiable class of sites. Such sites then cannot be registered nor protected under law. It is not rational, either, to assign a cultural period to an assemblage on the basis of recognizing one of 500 or 1,000 pieces of material. If one Paleo-Indian projectile point is found in a scatter of fine grained basalt flakes, it is seen to be out of place, or *curated*, and the scatter is not assigned to the Paleo-Indian period — but when the materials are not so distinctive, few questions are raised. These practices need to be rethought.

Diagnosing ceramic and lithic scatters is also problematic. *Unknown* lithic scatters and *unknown* ceramic scatters are reported in many contracted surveys. Though these two categories superficially look to be symmetrical, they are not. An unknown (Archaic) lithic scatter can span the period from 5000 B.C. (8000 B.C. if dates for the Cimarron material are confirmed elsewhere) to nearly A.D. 1900 (Historic Ute, Apache, Navajo); that is, such sites can be anything from terminal Paleo-Indian onward, a span of at least 7,000 years.

An unknown ceramic scatter, however, has only one-fifth the time range and carries substantially more information, for, in northern New Mexico (unlike the predominantly brownware complexes to the south and southeast), most sites contain identifiable painted ceramics. Therefore, a site described as *unknown ceramic* indicates that, a) the field worker was unable to make an identification; b) the ceramic assemblage consisted solely of plainwares, which were not assignable a classificatory designation (that is, could not be identified as Lino Gray, etc., i.e. BM-III); c) very unusual local or unstudied ceramics were encountered; or d) the sherd sizes are too fragmentary to be identified.

The case of (a) can be eliminated if a systematic sample of the ceramics is obtained for analysis by a ceramicist. The case of (b) can only be eliminated through more detailed technological study of "non-diagnostic" plainwares and attempts to establish chronology; (c) can be eliminated as (a). The fragmentary sherd problem (d) may ultimately be solvable in laboratory analysis, rather than in the field. In short, unknown ceramic scatters either monitor field worker recognition patterns or unusual ceramic attributes, since in some areas of western New Mexico sites with only plainwares are far less common than sites that also contain decorated wares. If (a) is eliminated by collecting a systematic sample and (d) is eliminated by observation, it will be seen that such sites are otherwise unusual and there is little reason that contract reports should so uniformly suggest little significance for them. *Unknown ceramic sites*, as a classification, inherently carries more information than *unknown lithic sites*, and should not be treated identically from the management perspective.

When ceramics and lithics are combined in some proportion on a nonstructural site, anything can happen. If 500 pieces of non-diagnostic lithic material include a half-dozen pieces of decorated ware (let's say Red Mesa B/W), the site may be called *unknown lithic with P-II component* or *P-II ceramic and lithic scatter*. If there are 500 pieces of lithic and ceramic material in equal numbers, the site will likely be classified simply as a *P-II ceramic and lithic scatter*, unless an Archaic point is found. Then it may become a multicomponent Archaic lithic and P-II ceramic scatter. In other words, how many sherds does one drop on a lithic scatter to make it a ceramic period site and *vice versa*? Conventional intuition about proportions of material doesn't yield an adequate answer, so one must study the lithic and ceramic assemblages in more detail than has been customary. Such studies need to be balanced by excavation. Survey alone will not accomplish every goal we have set for ourselves.

On the other hand, one does not change the classification of a ten-room Hosta Butte phase site on the basis of discovering one Archaic point. Of course not, for archeologists know what a Hosta Butte phase site *looks like*. The moral, of course, is that most archeologists know what an Archaic *point* looks like, but fewer know what an Archaic *site* looks like. Apparently, the same holds true for Ute and Apachean lithic sites, since only one of either is recorded in the San Juan Data Base!

This leads us to make a series of suggestions. First, contract reports should state explicitly the specific attributes of particular classes of artifacts and archicture (or other features) that they recognized in assigning a classificatory designation. Controlled samples should be recorded (see last section) which also state the general attributes and proportions of materials in the sample plot not considered diagnostic. Either an actual sample of materials could be collected, or measurements, data and photographs could be taken in the field for ceramic and lithic material, both diagnostic and non-diagnostic. In other words, if a site containing 50,000 pieces of material is diagnosed on the basis of attributes a given field worker recognizes in 20, then the report should say so, and provide some means for analysis of material representative of the rest.

It was suggested earlier that many lithic scatters containing some ceramics were suspiciously close to large Puebloan settlements (Chapman and Biella 1979) and could represent the remains of more nomadic populations that traded with agriculturalists. Many will not care for the theoretical position taken, and will not agree that Archaic adaptations lived on side-by-side with agriculturalists for some period of time. However indelicate to so state, this position is currently quite safe from rejection on any basis other than opinion. A great deal of investigation on the chronology and assemblage attributes of Archaic sites, unknown lithic and/or ceramic a-structural sites will be required before it can be disproved on the basis of data. We should not mind at all being eventually disproven, for some of our more serious chronological and classificatory problems will have been resolved in the effort.

EXPERIMENTAL METHODOLOGY

It should be clear that experimentation and refinement in field and analytical methodology is important to the very future of the archeological survey. Some of these problems are really rather simple. For instance, the whole array of questions regarding recording accuracy as a function of walking patterns, vegetation, speed, etc., can be dealt with straightforwardly. A series of specific suggestions is made in an upcoming section.

The problems of specifying the attributes of site settings in some empirical way is more difficult, but since there is practically no convention on the matter, there is little risk of ridicule even if one goes about it in some very unorthodox way and is, at first, unsuccessful.

Fine-grained analysis of assemblage attributes will also require the creation of methodological avenues to accuracy and efficiency, as will the development of comparable and useful sampling procedures. In short, it is necessary that every survey which purports to conduct research invest a part of the allotted time and budget in creating and refining methodology. It is currently our weakest link, and since none claim it hereabouts as their special domain, it offers a very attractive opportunity to those who would like to create and to publish, yet wish to remain at the fringe of the more hotly contested theoretical imbroglios. We need methodological advancement most urgently, and substantial careers can be made in its pursuit.

GENERAL COMMENTS

The object of this section has been to focus on several difficulties which regularly arise in conducting archeological survey. From the perspective of National Register surveys, there are really only two major goals for such projects: 1) discover and determine which archeological sites, localities or districts merit nomination to the National Register of Historic Places, and 2) obtain data which will permit/enhance regional solutions to understanding the nature of the archeological record. In an administrative/legal sense this involves the quality of significance which we have discussed in the previous chapter. In the research sense, however, *significance* has a more fundamental meaning when the practical aspects of knowing or understanding the archeological record are considered.

It is unlikely that detailed research will ever be conducted at enough individual archeological sites in New Mexico to fundamentally change our collective notions about the broad details for each phase during 12 millenia of prehistory.

Perhaps 700 archeological sites have been extensively excavated in 100 years of research throughout New Mexico. It is likely that as many as one-half of these have been dated by independent means, though not all components of each have been so dated. In short, our chronological hold on the archeological record rests on, at *most*, 1.5% of currently recorded sites (ca. 350 of ca. 23,500 sites). Our knowledge of architectural features, both from surface observation and excavation, is vast by comparison, as is the general nature of the ceramic record. Our command over the specific nature of subsistence strategies, their material remains, and the specific attributes of skeletal populations, is far more modest. These facts are not really surprising, given the time, expense and chance that affect the recovery of desired data from excavation. Nonetheless, the observations must be made that: 1) with a projection of not less than 300,000 recordable sites in the state (2.5 per square mile at minimum) our actual chronological control is *0.15%* of sites (not components) or less; 2) since the preponderance of archeological sites which have been excavated date to the A.D. 1000-1400 period, our chronological control over the other 11½+ millenia of prehistory is infinitessimal, even when statistical techniques are applied to enhance the power of the data. For instance, in the eastern 40% of New Mexico we were able to find only 26 dated sites! Conclusion: it must necessarily be the object of National Register surveys to identify sites which are likely to contain, or are observed to contain, datable material of any kind.

Some method(s) must be constructed to obtain datable material more quickly and efficiently than by extensive excavation procedures, so that surveys can be conducted which actually retrieve and analyze such materials. That is, National Register surveys should provide for limited testing where the probability of obtaining datable material is high and where only modest test excavation is needed to retrieve it, so that a site is not destroyed without planned research. Partly visible hearth features, eroding charcoal and visible material for tree-ring dating (perhaps obsidian) should permit such decisions to be made in the field.

Perhaps we could even learn somehow to core a pithouse depression, much as geologists take samples. Could we produce a device and a method for doing this where there was, say, a 30% probability of obtaining charcoal from burned roof beams and/or hitting a hearth feature on the floor? Could such a core column practically be made large enough (say the cross-section of an ordinary drinking glass) to bring up a stratigraphically intact and analyzable sherd sample? Could a thin, capped plastic casing or sleeve be left in place to prevent *mixing* of the remaining assemblage down the core hole? If you were lucky 30% of the time, you would have pithouse depth, a sherd sample, perhaps a date or two, and, for an hours worth of stripping and cleaning up, the actual pithouse diameter, and a surface sherd sample (post BM-II). We might even learn to handle micro-flotations and pollen samples systematically. Certainly the first few samples should come from pithouses where more excavation is conducted to compare data.

But to the point. Optimally, such a method could be carried out with equipment hand-carried in the field. On the other hand, nothing in life is predictably optimal. Could we go to the New Mexico Bureau of Mines, or a major drilling company, to consult with us and produce such a device? Suppose we could have a device mounted on an ordinary pickup, like a miniature drilling rig (we'll never have to go beyond 3 meters depth and rarely that), compressor operated, perhaps. Could we, for $20,000, create two such units — one for northern and one for southern New Mexico? Let us say that it cost a thousand dollars to have each sample analyzed and datable material processed. What would $100,000 to $200,000 a year of this kind of archeology buy in research data? In just one year it would likely double our knowledge about the BM-II—early BM-III period. Such a device could, of course, be used on buried surface masonry rooms as well.

What kind of research could be conducted? One could certainly continue the long tradition of studying pithouse depth and floor area. Certainly some ceramic studies and botanical studies could be conducted. Perhaps the likelihood of dating wouldn't be percent-wise much lower than for all such units already excavated. For a thousand dollars each and an hour or two of field time, you might know just about as much about most pithouses as if you had excavated, and if you sent out pollen, botanical and C-14 specimens from the core everytime it seemed worthwhile, you would probably know more. More importantly, you would certainly know which pithouses contained materials rich enough to merit complete excavation. From the National Register standpoint, the statements of *potentially retrievable data* would quickly become tangible, supportable and often research-specific.

Now, we don't know that something like this can be done, but we should think on it and every other imaginative possibility. We don't *have* another hundred years to double our data base in the mineral belts of the San Juan Basin or before Albuquerque's planned West Mesa Airport buries most of the remaining unnoticed BM-II/BM-III pithouses under a sea of asphalt.

What, then, do we have? We have an enormous, but inconsistent, data base of survey forms for about 23,000 archeological sites scattered throughout New Mexico (Spring 1980). For all this, who currently uses these files to conduct basic research? Until we learn to use other's survey data regularly to conduct genuine regionally-based investigations, we shall never know just which data are most critical to record in future surveys.

There are approximately (we estimate) 200 BM-II *sites* recorded in the Laboratory of Anthropology series. When you see generalizations in texts about BM-II occupations, do you not wonder about the actual altitude characteristics, associated vegetational communities, general and specific compass exposure, distance to permanent streams and the soils characteristic of site location? Was this a period in which there was no normative behavior in choosing site settings? That is, was this a period of experimentation with sedentism? Or, perhaps, site setting attributes are very uniform. This might suggest that substantial agricultural technique had been worked out long before the advent of visible sedentism. Since this would inform on whether agricultural strategy led to sedentism or whether the population density requirements leading to sedentism also required labor intensive agricultural strategies, the question is not a modest one.

Let us suppose, alternatively, that site setting attributes fell into two or more easily distinguishable categories on differing exposure and soil type. One might then want to excavate several sites from each group to determine whether there was also a temporal difference between the two. One would then want to ask whether such a shift in setting indicated that BM-II populations were changing agricultural strategy or, on the other hand, adapting to changing climatic circumstances over time. Certainly an entire new series of propositions and a new methodology would then be derived to direct future excavation.

Now we are not proposing anything very original, for this is basic SARG research strategy, but we make several complicating observations. In each case of the above, someone would currently have to go back into the field to relocate certain BM-II sites and retrieve previously unobtained data. Some sites are now recorded in detail with regard to specific ecological setting, while others are located only *by ¼ section x, pinyon juniper and east slope Chuskas* (for instance) or merely by section. When one turns to the actual archeological survey reports that recorded these sites (for those where surveys are reported) the disparity between reports is as great as the disparity in the site files. Thus, some sites are described as in a *mesa top* setting, others are in a *gramma grassland setting, open exposure*, yet others are described as located on *soil group IIB, Vegetative Stratification 22Z1, in landform sample stratum F*. In reading the above reports (let us say any 6) you will not, as a practical matter, be able to resolve the different descriptive data, for in some cases additional data do not exist, while in others one simply cannot figure out what was done, methodologically. In yet other cases you would need $50,000 or more to apply one complex ecological approach to the other data sets and still have to go into the field. In several of any six reports you will *never* unravel even how many sites, as opposed to components, were located. You will come to realize that phase was diagnosed differently in several cases (that is, maybe it wasn't BM-II after all) and discover that elevation and/or exposure were not recorded and the sites were not located on either large scale air photos or quad sheets.

The point, and the *entire* point, is that we stand on the frontier of a new kind of research that we could conduct if certain data were consistently available. We have not struck any sort of balance between quality and consistency of generalized data and enormously detailed setting-specific data. It seems obvious to the point of embarrasment to state it, but our basic, unresolved problem in contract archeology is discovering what level of detail we require to conduct research with samples of 500-5,000 sites and how to obtain it consistently, without destroying legitimate diversity of research interests.

Those who advocate *recording everything, in detail* have two considerations to address. Is it economically and logistically practical to do so? Is it even necessary to do so for research purposes? The proposition that prehistoric populations had remarkable accuracy in achieving a detailed ecological *shopping list* of setting attributes in site placement is risky on several grounds. It assumes a degree of technoadaptive sophistication in prehistoric knowledge of the environment that is unequally likely for separate time periods where there is experimentation with different subsistence strategies. It also assumes general conformity to optimizing principles. If these two conditions were regularly met by prehistoric populations we should generally be practicing ethnology, rather than archeology, in portions of the world where substantial climatic catastrophe had not contravened. The archeological record is, itself, the sad evidence of a social entity's failed dream of achieving homeostasis and immortality.

It is, therefore, logically more likely that prehistoric populations typically got the general attributes of site setting right and later fell victim to unforeseen details. Is that not the way our own lives (or perhaps our research?) actually work? And is it not the case that when competition is keenest one can afford the fewest mistakes? That is, remarkably tight fit to a half-dozen or more coinciding variables in site placement is probably symptomatic of unusual regionwide stress, and should be episodal, rather than continual.

In asking ourselves how we might arrange survey reports and site forms to serve these developing research possibilities, we need ask only several questions. If there were striking and systematic variations in general setting attributes from one phase to another, would the data in my report and site forms show it up? Are my data arranged so that anyone reading my report would be able to see any particular patterns that I might have overlooked (my data set being smallish)?

Get this material out front in maps and tables. Get the sites well placed on air photos or quad sheets. After your master survey map, make up separate maps for site placement during each phase and *ceramic group*. Make a map of clinal distributions in one or more lithic and ceramic attributes that you or your laboratory specialist monitored. See Warren (1979) for an excellent example done with Rio Grande Glazewares. If you want to keep it very *broadscale*, prepare distribution maps by percent of two or three *well-known* tradewares. Do bigger sites have more tradewares?

Summarize your data by both sites and components. Put elevation tables by phase under the site map for that period. Put soil charts on a light table, put your quad sheet over it — give us gross soil designations, even if your survey area is small and it's all the same (cite the soil map). Do the same for gross vegetative community. When your survey is added to another hundred surveys, soil association won't be the same and neither will site distribution. Is there anything special in elevation, soil, exposure, vegetation, etc. for sites that are multicomponent? What components *belong* together, which do not?

374

In short, identify patterns in your data even if there appears to be no current explanation for them. If you don't think there is enough variation in your survey area, compare your data to other survey reports, or hunt out 200 site forms from the LA file in your area. Plot them on a map and get them up on the light table. Having read the others, you begin to understand what needs to be recorded during survey. For ideas on variables that can be commonly overlaid from maps (rainfall, frost free days, etc.) see a copy of the recently published *New Mexico in Maps* (Williams and McAllister 1979).

To senior researchers this essayist's role may seem gratuitous, but after reading several hundred contract survey reports with some care, we believe most of the problems with the presentations in these reports have to do with too much attention to the rhetoric of research and not enough to the data actually collected and the potential patterns in it. Our guess is that so much talk has been made of complex hypotheses the last few years that many younger field surveyors (who actually prepare the bulk of survey reports) no longer realize that most research actually begins with basic recognition of patterns in data sets. Further, most initial hypotheses are simply questions about the relationship between two characteristics (attributes, factors, things) that pattern.

For instance, in Chapter III (Upper Rio Grande) we noted that P-I/P-II multicomponent sites *belonged* together in low elevation (below 5500 feet) settings, while P-II/P-III multi-component sets *belonged* together in mid-elevation settings (6000-6500 feet). This is basic pattern recognition, nothing fancy. We then construct a statement. If P-I, which is earlier, temporally, belongs with *lowland* P-II, and P-III, which is later, temporally, belongs with *upland* P-II, then it will logically be the case that *lowland* P-II is earlier while *upland* P-II is later. This is a simple straightforward proposition, or hypothesis, as you like. Next, one selects a method to demonstrate the case. In archeology, several standard methods are available: tree-ring dating, C-14, and archeomagnetic dating of materials that can be obtained through test excavations. Since wisdom dictates that one prepare for failure to locate the datable material on the first few attempts, one also constructs a backup method, perhaps a ceramic seriation constructed from independently dated strata in P-II sites elsewhere. While this might not inform so highly or precisely on your proposition, it could very well tell you whether to continue your research program or reformulate. These are the basic elements of straight-forward research, and is a research design. Recognize a pattern, phrase a question, translate the question into a statement of relationships, select or create a method to observe the related phenomenon (e.g., excavate samples) and analyze the materials. Answer the question.

Since the conduct of research is, in fact, for most of us, systematic capitalization on error, one also constructs an alternate proposition, say about multiple subsistence strategies as a feature of P-II adaptation, in the event that the split elevation occupations are found to be contemporaneous. This requires one to state what faunal or botanical remains would be sought in excavation, how such remains might covary seasonally and how one would retrieve and analyze them.

We genuinely hope that each preparer of a contract survey will become interested in obtaining data and preparing its presentation to highlight the basic patterns. Some will say that it is too expensive or time-consuming to do these things. We suggest that, for most reports, *the length of the ordinary text should be cut, and the number of maps, tables and data summaries should be tripled.* When you write your summary, focus acutely on all the patterns that you are able to identify in your site data, then raise questions. For those that conduct mostly *well site* or *drill hole* surveys, summarize and circulate your findings for all those sites you have located in a given region over a year's time.

It is not that we wish to be unkind or broadly critical of contract survey reports in this section, for as we said earlier, many are excellently done in the field. Far fewer are excellently presented with regard to data and to methodology. The data contained in these reports and resultant site forms will either carry us to new horizons or frustrate us eternally. It is that fundamental, so we had best ponder the alternatives.

Let us turn our attention, then, to establishing priorities for conducting upcoming surveys, which, since they could be implemented without some of the ordinary contract restraints, make some of the suggestions offered here more potentially realizable.

PROJECT SPECIFIC PRIORITIES FOR ARCHEOLOGICAL SURVEY

Obviously, the establishment of priorities for funding archeological survey in New Mexico involves a number of complex issues. There are, of course, as many differing opinions as there are archeologists and federal planners. Most archeologists with whom we have discussed this project are very concerned that their particular research interests not be treated in some exclusionary way. This is a very natural concern and one with which we are in great sympathy. It serves no one to endorse one or another kind of research interest as satisfactory and all others as derelict. It is the lot of the serious scholar to seek such craftsmanship of methodology and excellence of result that others are moved to consider adopting his/her methods and conclusions. More often than not, this pursuit is frustrating and, in order to secure the flattery of imitation, the scholar often has to reformulate ideas and methods many times. In contrast, it is the sycophant who seeks to command imitation. As in every walk of life, there may be some few among us who prefer to prevail by command rather than by craftsmanship. Those few will not be pleased with the suggestions we are about to offer.

On the other hand, federal and state agency personnel often have more of a commitment to longer range planning than have the rest of us who live from archeological project to project. In many cases, federal programs for overviews and planning surveys are already being implemented. In this case, overviews are complete, or nearly so, which summarize a vastly more substantial body of information than any of us will be able to absorb in preparing a single proposal to conduct archeological survey. It is necessary that conventions be established regarding communication so that duplication of effort does not arise.

COMMUNICATION

Each year the State Historic Preservation Officer should prepare a solicitation for proposals to conduct archeological survey well in advance of his/her deadline for funding (3 to 6 months). This solicitation should summarize projects in progress in the various (5) overview units of New Mexico that have been funded by the SHPO's office. The SHPO should also invite representatives of the major agencies who administer land in these units to provide a brief summary of their surveys or overviews/planning documents, completed or in progress. At the same time, the principal investigators of the various institutions that conduct survey under contract, should be invited to do likewise. Each should be provided a sketch map of the several survey planning units and should be asked to shade in the locations of current surveys of 4 sq. miles (2560a) or more, or any linear survey of 20 miles or more. The SHPO's office can act as compiler and issue the shaded sketch map and project briefs to potential proposors. In this manner, the SHPO will have the advice of federal and state agency planners at his disposal in considering potential projects. At the same time, information about contracted surveys will provide a gauge of the degree to which other sources of contract funds are subsidizing priorities in a given area. The risk of preparing a proposal for research which duplicates other efforts will be small. The SHPO should also provide the President of the New Mexico Archeological Council (NMAC) with copies of the solicitation to be distributed to scholars not permanently employed by a given academic or contracting institution.

PROJECT SPECIFIC PRIORITIES

We have given much thought to a simple and straightforward but even-handed method for establishing priorities for matching funds archeological surveys. No method will likely be found which suits every purpose and, since the nature of land-altering activities and our state of knowledge is in constant flux, no set of priorities can become a permanent fixture. It will be surprising, indeed, if this document is even remotely usable five years hence, and no plan or document can replace the exercise of good professional judgement and common sense in a given situation.

Nonetheless, there exists the management need to provide archeological inventories of unsurveyed areas and establish National Register properties for the State of New Mexico. Our review of contracted archeological surveys (presented earlier in this chapter) has led us to the conclusion that methodological concerns are at least as important as specific research questions to the profession. These needs can be broken into five categories: impacts, inventory of unknown areas, resolution of classic problems in the literature of Southwestern archeology, research suggested by reformulations of traditional questions, and methodology. Each of these is discussed below.

1. IMPACTS

Priority according to the intensity of foreseeable land altering impacts is straightforward and not very controversial. In our terms, we merely need to project the likelihood of general developments in given portions of New Mexico for, let us say, the next three to five years, to have a usable scheme. It is first necessary to define broad areas where different kinds of development will arguably take place. These are defined as three orders of magnitude (or one to three) from little to moderate, then intense.

Little impact is taken here to mean that a given block of land is relatively inaccessible to pothunters, collectors and tourists, has few fast developing population nodes, little likelihood of immediate mineral exploration (oil, gas, coal, uranium, etc.), is moderately grazed and not subject to major timbering operations. Areas of this nature on the map include portions of the higher Sangre de Cristo, northernmost Rio Grande, the Sierra Blanca, the Jicarilla Reservation, etc.

Moderate impacts (2) is taken to mean areas of relatively easy access to tourists, pothunters, collectors, etc., and where substantial impacts in timbering, intensive grazing operations and widely spaced mineral exploration activities can be expected to take place. Substantial portions of the study area fall into this category. Widely spaced gas drilling and upcoming timber sales on the Jicarilla Reservation suggest reasonable examples. Obviously, areas subject to little commercial impact but which have a history of organized pothunting would fall here, such as the Mimbres area.

Intense impacts (3) is taken to mean areas of dramatic and protracted population increase, intensive mineral exploration and mining (strip mining coal) and other developments which will permanently destroy substantial portions of the original surface or subject the surface to intense and protracted but, in theory, reversible impact. Areas in the Grants uranium belt, the lower Chaco coal development areas, the Carlsbad gas fields, and population centers around Albuquerque, Santa Fe, Taos, Farmington, Gallup, Grants, Shiprock, Las Cruces, and El Paso are included.

Conditions or available information could change by the time this document is read, so adjustments may need to be made. Let us just keep this simple and based on common sense where federal agency studies fail to provide specific projections. The uranium and coal development studies by the BLM and NPS were used in part to derive these judgements.

2. SURVEY OF UNKNOWN AREAS

It is one major object of the next few years to begin to close some of the gaps in our understanding of lesser known areas. It is necessary to the SHPO's program and mandated in federal requirement that the state be inventory surveyed to identify properties eligible for nomination to the National Register of Historic Places. From the SHPO's perspective, this is the major source of inspiration for this project. It is a pleasant circumstance in archeology that our passion to hunt out the unknown should be a funded requirement of some agency. Let us make the most of it, without forgetting that the administrative need dictates that we accomodate the paperwork required to fill out nomination forms for the National Register and prepare statements on significance as backgrounds to determinations of eligibility.

In suggesting priorities here, we are focusing on three attributes — money, access and archeological unknowns. If someone later wishes to separate these, fine, but we consider them interrelated to the extent that a combined judgment makes good sense.

MONEY: It should certainly be an object to fund archeological projects that can be conducted in areas not previously fundable. Funds are most available for federal and certain Indian lands. Award a tentative 1 for low priority to federal and appropriate Indian lands (Navajo, for instance) on the assumption that the SHPO can make funds available which are not tied to specific impacts and other specific federal programs already in progress. Funds are less available for state lands — award a tentative 2. And funds are generally unavailable to survey private lands — award a 3, unless a major federally regulated project is forseeable on such lands.

ACCESS: The status of lands with regard to ownership or administration is an important factor to consider in making judgments about ease of access and planning surveys. For convenience, we have prepared tables which appear throughout the volume and summarize acreages and ownership/administration in each of the sub-units of New Mexico. Access has also been ranked from 1 to 3 (easiest access: most federal and state lands, therefore lesser priority; more difficult access: most private and Indian lands, therefore higher priority).

We are most fortunate in New Mexico that both federal archeologists and the State Archeologist have facilitated their colleagues' physical access to lands through permit procedures and have refused to become enmeshed in notions of professional territoriality, which have been problems elsewhere. It is reasonable to rate access to federal land as easy, assign a score of 1 (exceptions for certain military and security facilities — Kirtland AFB, areas at Los Alamos and White Sands Missile Range come to mind).

Indian lands generally present fewer opportunities for access (the Navajo Reservation is often an exception), but circumstances vary from reservation to reservation. There are relatively few archeological projects on Indian lands not tied to very specific development projects and their impacts. For surveys independent of specific impacts (the subject of this volume), most reservations should be considered difficult (2) to very difficult (3). We do not care to make specific comparisons among the pueblos, for instance. In any case, as mentioned in previous chapters, access depends heavily on the Governor, Tribal Council and the presentation of the archeologist seeking permission to survey.

Private lands, in general, should be considered difficult of access. And, again, the case rests on presentation to the owner. In practical terms, some surveys that we feel we ought to implement will be impossible, but opportunities to survey lands not generally accessible to archeologists should be pursued vigorously and, if they meet other criteria, funded whenever opportunity presents itself.

ARCHEOLOGICAL UNKNOWNS: Here archeologists will have few problems in making judgments. If an area has been subjected to many larger inventory surveys [NIIP (Elyea, Abbink and Eschman 1979), CGP (Reher 1977), Chaco Canyon - Starlake Surveys (Wait 1976) etc., Chuska Valley, Puerco (Irwin-Williams 1977, 1978), Abiquiu Reservoir (Schaafsma 1975, 1976), Mimbres Valley (LeBlanc, *et al.* 1979a, b), and so forth], then it is a low priority (1) in terms of gross unknowns and will not contribute currently unknown properties for National Register nominations. Here we are speaking explicitly in terms of general unknowns, not areas that require further investigation to resolve particular questions or research problems — these will be discussed later under Research Priorities.

Of higher priority will be areas that have been subjected to fewer, scattered surveys of smaller scale or are transected only by narrow, linear ones. Portions of the Jicarilla Reservation and the Chama drainage come immediately to mind, as do large portions of the Carson and Santa Fe National Forests. The Plains of southeastern New Mexico also come to mind. At the same time, some areas that have been subjected to larger surveys should fall in this category if such surveys were thematic in nature (that is, surveys which sought out one kind of archeological site to record, thereby excluding others from the inventory). For example, the recent *Chacoan Outlier Survey*, funded jointly by the SHPO's office and the Public Service Company of New Mexico (Marshall, Stein, Loose and Novotny 1979), recorded specific Chacoan architectural features but not all surrounding communities. There are important, if not compelling, reasons for conducting such projects (this is discussed later), but they should not be taken as inventory surveys, and the investigators do not intend that they be taken as such. Other examples include Judge and Dawson's Paleo-Indian surveys in the Albuquerque area (Judge and Dawson 1972; Judge 1973) which were based on the technique of *site pattern recognition*. Less explicitly thematic surveys have produced a situation elsewhere in which larger Gallina sites have been recorded to the general exclusion of the far more numerous (and perhaps, earlier) single pithouse occupations (Seaman 1976; Cordell 1979:102).

Of highest priority is investigation in essentially unsurveyed territory. It is quite difficult to keep track of current surveys in contract and academic research. Nonetheless, it is clear that areas above 7,500-8,000 feet (with exceptions in the Mount Taylor, Baca Geothermal, certain upland portions of the Gallina and Pajarito areas and portions of the Gila Forest) tend to be very little known in the literature. Most surveys at those altitudes fall into the category of general reconnaissance surveys (10% coverage or less). In addition, substantial upland areas east of Taos, the far northern Rio Grande drainage and portions of the San Juan Basin floor, which lie outside the mineral exploration areas, are substantially underrepresented in the literature. The Jornada del Muerto, Tularosa Basin, and southern portions of Hidalgo and Luna counties are others. A general block of territory in central New Mexico (see Chapter V) is the least surveyed. We have provided a map entitled Priority of Survey by unknowns in a subsequent section (Map IX.3), which outlines broad areas of survey coverage ranging from modest to intense. Those who prepare projects will wish to make more refined judgments than those based only on the broad areas outlined here.

In summarizing priority by unknowns, we have suggested that availability of funds, opportunities of access and relative intensity of archeological survey be considered in judging a given survey's practical utility. Here, the object is to identify kinds of surveys that would otherwise not be likely to take place. In many cases, fiscal subsidy depends on rather direct impacts on public lands, but the effects of generalized, indirect impacts are less often provided for. Thus, a moderately high priority survey might be on private or municipal lands in the general area of an expanding city, like Albuquerque, where it could be assumed that eventual development would take place. There have been surveys in the Albuquerque area, to be certain, but most have only been reported thematically (that is, an emphasis on early Basketmaker, or Paleo-Indian, or whatever) in the literature and were of a reconnaissance nature. On the basis of availability of funds, ease of access and the generally thematic nature of previous surveys, such a survey would rate an overall 2. It could be very competitive from a funding standpoint if conducted from an Albuquerque base, since logistic costs (travel, per diem, etc.) would be modest. Such a survey would also rate high on impacts, and though most archeologists consider it prosaic to survey their own backyards, would be an attractive investment from the planning perspective, particularly since it would lead to National Register determinations of eligibility on blocks of land that can someday be presumed subject to actual development.

A proposed survey on undeveloped lands of Taos Pueblo, for instance, would clearly be a high priority (3), though it is unlikely to occur. Many archeologists might respond that they would have no interest in surveying higher forested lands *since there is nothing up there anyway*. There are two points to be made. One of our express tasks in preparing this manuscript has been to generate interest in traditionally *uninteresting* areas. Second, planning needs should not be dictated purely by the research interests of individual archeologists. Thus, we are proposing that priority by Impacts and by Unknowns be primarily in the view of those administrators who fund these projects.

In the section entitled *A Plan for National Register Surveys*, specific step-by-step suggestions for statewide surveys are outlined.

By the same token, it is important that the archeological profession be free to exercise judgment in research. Thus, we propose that priority of research be established in the categories of 1) *Classic* Southwestern research problems, 2) reformulation of research questions, and 3) methodology.

3. CLASSIC SOUTHWESTERN RESEARCH PROBLEMS

In this category of research, we refer specifically to established questions in the literature which have resisted ultimate solution. Perhaps we all know what these are: refinement in application of the Pecos Classification; the linguistic, ceramic, architectural evidence for the Wendorf and Reed (1955) and Ford, Schroeder and Peckham (1972) reconstructions of Rio Grande Development; temporal control over local chronologies; the nature of Largo-Gallina culture, the Apache Creek Phase, the Late Glencoe, etc. and other alleged anomalies: the production sources of particular ceramic types; *in situ* population expansion vs. migration, the Meso American influence question; the explanation for abandonments and so on *ad infinitum*. The Cordell (1979) overview of the Rio Grande, the Tainter (1980) overview of Mt. Taylor, the Berman (1979) overview of the Socorro District, the LeBlanc and Whalen (1979) overview of southwestern New Mexico, Camilli and Allen (1979) of the southeast Plains, and the San Juan Basin overview (Magers, n.d.) summarize these and many additional problems and will be useful to readers less familiar with one or another area of the state.

We do not wish to be misunderstood, for scholars are touchy about how their research is labeled. The distinction suggested is not strictly between *new* and *old* archeology — it is not the distinction between one theoretical school of thought or another. Rather, the distinction is between whether one is attempting to address questions already raised or is creating substantially new ones. As a practical matter, many traditionalists direct their research to previously proposed classificatory schemes and many *avante garde* researchers address themselves to questions of how systems behave and care little for classificatory or chronological matters. In theory, however, there is no requirement that this be the case, for many traditional questions will ultimately be answered by unusual techniques and *vice versa* — but that falls in the category of methodology.

The reason we have selected this distinction as important, then, is not to differentiate between schools of thought but to recognize that many questions we have raised in the literature still beg for an answer, and that this is so for some that remain in a form which is inherently unanswerable. Our judgment, for instance, is that many questions about prehistoric social organization fall into the latter category (both those styled in *new* and *old* school paradigms).

As has been pointed out by Cordell (1979) and in the earlier review of contract literature here, problems of classification and chronology remain as overriding problems. In a recent paper on the subject, Merlan (in press) has indicated that judgments of significance can be made if an archeological site is classifiable. An exceedingly important object of future surveys, then, is to reduce the number of unclassified sites recorded during survey, and to permit site forms from currently unclassified sites to be re-evaluated. This is no modest problem, for as was indicated earlier, the recent San Juan Basin archeological data base (Wait, n.d.) indicates that there are over 2,200 undefined artifact scatters and that 34% of the recorded Anasazi sites (2,686) were of unknown affiliation (that is, undefined with regard to Chacoan or Mesa Verdean, Chuska, etc. materials). Moreover, the gross time period or the Pecos Classification was unknown for 1,440 sites. The sample at that time consisted of 8,300 sites. The specific situation in the Rio Grande is unknown, but it is reasonable to suppose that it is similar, based on the data presented for the Cochiti-Pajarito "control area" (see Chapter III). It appears also to be the case in the Mimbres and in the Jornada. The Plains sites, if anything, are even more elusive to classify or control chronologically.

Surveys designed to resolve problems of classification and chronology, particularly for the large class of unknown ceramic and lithic scatters, should be a primary focus in addressing research questions to the existing literature. Such surveys will undoubtedly require that some sites be identified for limited testing or taking samples of datable material. In our mind it is easy to rank priorities for research of this nature. Low priority is appropriate for research designs which promise to resolve only chronological/classificatory (and related) issues in one cultural stratum, or period, or only locally, whether in one or several cultural periods. The distribution and chronology of Rio Grande glazeware sites strikes us as a reasonable example, particularly since it can be related to Mera's early work and Warren's (1979) study, among others.

Of moderate priority (2) would be studies designed to resolve issues of a regional scope and in several time periods. Since Judge (cited in Magers n.d.) and subsequent survey and excavation during the NIIP (Elyea *et al.* 1979) project, have noted an intensive Archaic occupation in the Gallegos Canyon region, a survey might be designed to compare either these results or Irwin-Williams' (1973) data on the Archaic to Basketmaker shift in the Arroyo Cuervo region with new data from intensive survey in the far northern Rio Grande.

Of high priority (3) would be surveys designed to address questions about the relationship between developments in several major archeological regions and through several time periods. Obviously, there is great promise in a survey which might further define the nature of Chacoan and later Mesa Verdean occupation in the San Juan Basin, and also addressed the classificatory problem of distinctions among P-II, P-II—P-III Transitional, and P-III sites beyond the dimensions of current ceramic and architectural analysis. Is the P-III missing, generally, in lower, drier elevations (Chapter IV)? The focus is on general problems of Southwestern archeology. The relationships between Mimbres and the Animas/El Paso phase occupations also come to mind.

There are, of course, hundred of examples that could be offered, and these have no special significance other than that they were the first that came to mind. The object here is to encourage research which makes increasingly broad bodies of literature (including sites record forms on file at the Museum of New Mexico and the NPS computerized San Juan Data Base) more usable. A major portion of such research will inevitably have to focus on chronology and classification even if the research object is phrased in defining differing ecological adaptations, or some evolutionary-systemic approach. A second and equally important general goal will be to sort those questions which are currently in answerable form from those that are not. That is, we had better get on with the task of determining which portions of our literature (including contract reports) will not aid us in our quest for further understanding.

4. MAJOR REFORMULATIONS OF RESEARCH QUESTIONS

The kind of investigation suggested here involves posing research in terms of new or different questions or questions rephrased from previous form. Rephrasing of questions need not be very dramatic. Instead of asking how one might characterize the site settings of large and small Basketmaker II and III sites, one might ask: What is the range of site setting or apparent niche for all pithouse sites in the San Juan or upper Rio Grande? If one stratifies these according to altitude, major soil types, exposure and distance to a major ecotone, what shall one infer if it is discovered that in each natural set, there are sites of similar size but of different time periods and different cultural affiliation?

Posing the first question merely requires one to ignore for a moment the assumption that Basketmaker II and Basketmaker III are real categories. It is the second question which separates researchers into schools of thought. Some will, of course, try to refit the data to some scheme like the Pecos Classification. Migrations, acculturation, and supposed climatic events will often be posited to resolve the discrepancy. In essence, some may believe that history is more real than an ecological niche. Others may develop equally elaborate schemes about site size, ecological catchment, etc., and ignore the jumbled time periods. That is to say, some believe in ecology, but not history or temporal classifications derived from it. We are convinced that cultural evolution is the sum of both intertwining rhythms. Unfortunately, few anthropologists would agree, judging by current jargon.

As in the last section, it will be seen as a matter of practice that most archeologists who style their research as *progressive* or *reformulated*, will take the second response above. I think a comment made by Frank Hole (1979:619) in a recent book review is appropriate here. Hole complained that in a new work on archeological theory, "The authors' marked disinterest in archeology as a source of history and in the history of archeology as a source of ideas isolates them from most of their colleagues". The previous category of research addresses this complaint, since a survey must address some existing body of Southwestern archeological literature in its design. But both colleagueship and fairness require an extraction of equal benefit in this category of research. It is essential that questions be rephrased and old assumptions set aside, for new data sets are thus required. And just as every survey must offer the promise of making previous literature more usable, so must every survey provide for the systematic collection of data which is not currently available. This could be done through resurvey of areas notable for inconsistent data and subsequent revision of old site forms, or by generating new data sets altogether.

You see, it is not one's theoretical interpretation which seals the fate of a data set and renders it unusable. It is its inconsistency or lack of organization. Now, our basic need is not for exotic means of data collection or endless detail. Our need is to state a series of questions and specify the data required to answer them. In addition, common sense dictates that certain generalized data be collected for the benefit of colleagues. Several of the contract survey reports which were reviewed referred to sites in the San Juan Basin as having "Black-on-white series pottery". Others gave measurements for one or two room pueblos as 8 x 11 meters (improbable for a two-room P-II site, since room size is small), and many do not record elevations of sites or make reference to the nature of any material considered non-diagnostic. It is painfully obvious that many surveys are conducted without posing any explicit questions at all. This cannot go on.

At any rate, some reformulations will be minor and the investigator's main interest will be elsewhere. In other cases, reformulations will be substantial. In this volume, Chapter II and the overview of Chapter V might be examples. Again, priorities can be ranked simply, as follows:

Research designs which reformulate fundamental approaches to regional cultural development and several time periods are lower in priority (1). Though it is based on excavation, Timothy Seaman's (1976) excellent monograph on LA 11843 re-evaluates Gallina archeology in promising ways and would be a good example of such research.

Of higher priority (2) are reformulations which address Southwestern cultural development at large. The kinds of research questions suggested by Drs. Cordell and Plog in their recent *Antiquities* article (1979) entitled *Escaping the Confines of Normative Thought: A Re-evaluation of Puebloan Prehistory* come to mind. We would suggest the CGP Survey (Reher 1977) as another good example, for though it was more localized geographically, it addressed many issues broader than its survey area (Archaic site placement and vegetative diversity).

Of highest priority (3) are reformulations which address fundamental issues in archeology and anthropology and, though derived from investigations here in New Mexico, are not confined to Southwestern archeology in their application. Questions which promise to specify the conditions under which agriculture develops, the creation of stratified social systems, the relationships between population growth and technological change, or the relationship between genetic and cultural adaptation are all candidates for this priority of research. These are difficult goals, but they are attainable.

5. METHODOLOGY

The subject of methodology, like that of research, is complex, but has been commented on at some length and will be very briefly dealt with here.

The essential feature of methodology is that it imposes two unavoidable tasks. The first is that one pose questions and derive the means to collect those particular data necessary to answer them. The second is that one must determine that the data are collected in ways which will permit them to be analyzed without obscuring their original purpose. A research design, then, is not merely a statement of theoretical interest, but can be summarized as: *What question* is asked, *what data* will be collected, *how* will data be *collected, how* will *data* be *analyzed*, and how will failure or the need for refinement be provided for?

A research design, then, relates the specific methods of data recovery and analysis to specific forms of research questions posed. It will be seen from the sections on research that both traditional and innovative research questions must be posed in each survey (though the total research emphasis will likely bear more heavily on one or the other). In this way, the base of collected data will be broadened beyond that ordinary in current contract surveys.

Priorities are a simple matter to establish. No National Register survey should be implemented (priority 1) that does not pose specific research questions for which specific techniques of field methodology have been developed. For instance, if one asks whether the number of surface rooms (or cists) increases with the need for storage in Basketmaker sites, then the number of surface rooms (or the size) should increase with some measure of agricultural potential. One would need to record every surface room in each site carefully, making a clear distinction between *certain* and *possible* rooms and the size of each, making quite explicit the method for measuring. One would also need to record *certain* and *possible* pithouses. At the same time, it would be necessary to record altitude and exposure and to take soil samples both from within sites and from nearby presumed agricultural facilities, and to consult rainfall charts. Nearness to an ecotone, vegetational communities and hydrological features are also important. The presumption would be that the greatest storage potential and agricultural potential covary. The total square (preferably cubic) footage of storage facilities should, then, increase with length of growing season, increase in soil moisture retention characteristics, and so forth. If one does confirm that such storage facilities increase with agricultural potential, then chronological stratification of such sites should allow one to identify adaptive trajectories. One then needs to determine whether sites in certain time periods or of certain ranges of agricultural potential multiply storage capacity by increasing the size of storage units, or by increasing the number, for energetically, and therefore evolutionarily, these are fundamentally different adaptive responses, as we shall discuss later. Now, one might think this paragraph simplistic, and that all surveys pose such straightforward questions and collect these kinds of data and make explicit the means by which they were obtained. This is simply not the case, for perhaps only one-third to one-fourth of the contract reports that have been reviewed for portions of New Mexico are so structured. Besides, when does anyone recall a survey that related the on-the-ground spacing of crew members to the mean or average size, or diameter, of 70-90% of the kinds of sites that are presumed to occur in the survey area?

Laboratory analysis of all kinds rates second priority (2), with the reminder that field method is also required. In other words, unlike the scope of research questions, methodological priorities are additive rather than discrete. Laboratory analysis simply means that one relates laboratory method to field method in a way which permits the initial question to be informed upon. No ceramic analysis, whether statistically seriated, subjected to trace element analysis, or whatever, can be considered a firm basis for chronological seriation or other interpretation unless the size of the sample is known, the method for taking it is replicable, and something is known of the population sampled. Ten percent of the painted sherds from a site are ordinarily representative of only one class of ceramics, not of the total ceramic assemblage of a site. The common assumption that these are *diagnostic* remains, ordinarily is only an assumption.

How many surveys have you seen that took ceramic seriations from other surveys that were independently dated through C-14 (or other techniques) to compare with their own analyses? Though revised chronological controls supersede Breternitz's (1966) study for many ceramics, one seldom sees them referred to. A few do, to be certain, but most surveys are self-contained research efforts, and the quality of comparative ceramic (or other kinds) studies usually depends upon who is retained later to conduct ceramic analysis. That is, the quality of research often depends on the expertise of given individuals rather than the structure of the research itself, and such individuals are usually called in *after* field data are collected. They therefore seldom have practical input into the methodology of data collection upon which the attribute of sample representativeness in fact depends. These are major issues — not minor ones to be resolved through afterthought.

Of highest priority (3) are methodologies which are designed to provide systematically for error while projects are in process, are comparative, and/or provide for methodological refinement in future research. A staged research design created to control for error, such as the CGP transect (Reher 1977) approach, would qualify. See also Judge, Ebert and Hitchcock (1975) on staged research approaches. Now, it is not explicitly advocated here that high priority surveys be based on sophisticated sampling designs. In fact, our position is the reverse. The subject of sampling is still controversial, again less in theory than in practice. One major need now is inventory surveys of lesser known areas. Larger block or inventory surveys designed to subject site locational data to after-field analysis and to make explicit the techniques and physiographic stratification of a future sample survey, having a specified level of confidence (say 80-90%) for the number of sites in total and by site function and cultural period (site bias), would be very useful.

In addition, surveys which promised to refine survey and analytical techniques important in improving the accuracy, consistency and/or efficiency of archeological survey, in general, would be of high priority. These might be either experimental in nature or comparative (that is, compare results and methods in detail with surveys reported elsewhere). One might wish, for example, to compare models of site prediction based on ecological stratification by remote sensing techniques, with a model of site prediction based on field stratification by ecozone.

Who should propose? Any institution, individual or consortium of individuals who have the expertise and the means to conduct the proposed research, and for whom administrative arrangements can be made, should propose. It is our understanding that most of the funds that may become available for National Register surveys will be of the matching variety. Most universities are quite taken with the profit motive these days, and quality proposals will necessarily have to also be encouraged from individuals who may be willing to commit some of their own funds or accept half-rate for their labor in pursuing research.

Two additional conventions need to be established. First, not less than 300-500 copies of the reports for National Register survey projects should be published, and about half of those sent to libraries. Second, recipients should assume the obligation to present a paper summarizing their investigation, either to a journal for wider distribution, or before a professional convention. A provision to facilitate this goal is suggested in the final section of the chapter.

SPECIAL RESEARCH PROJECTS

Special research projects should be distinguished from priority inventory surveys. Some readers may have noticed that thematic surveys have been argued against in earlier sections. It is here that they belong.

Thematic surveys offer the possibility of contributing substantial knowledge on specific archeological subjects and of contributing blocks of nominations to the National Register. We are all aware of the important survey of *Chacoan outliers* (Marshall, Stein, Loose and Novotny 1979). If one were now to propose an additional survey which also recorded the surrounding *Hosta Butte Phase* communities in their entirety, we would benefit administratively and, as indicated in an earlier research section, benefit greatly in our knowledge of developmental processes in the Chacoan system.

We also have special expertise here in New Mexico. We have individuals who have made substantial careers in lithic analysis, ceramic analysis and in finding and accurately recording archeological sites. We also have some very creative minds. We have always been fascinated with William Allan's (1975) short analysis of sherd-sorting by weight on a slope. This little survey was budgeted at $500 or $600, and a substantial portion went to the overhead fund at UNM. More recently, Pat Beckett (SAR Symposium: Santa Fe, April 1979) described a series of interesting experiments in the effects of wind and dune erosion on the spatial distribution of artifacts sorted into classes of different size and shape. Another example of such experimental studies is entitled *The Mechanical and Chemical Effects of Inundation at Abiquiu Reservoir* (Schaafsma 1978a). You can do something with almost anything if you've an interesting question, curiosity and a method. We need more of this — much more!

It is possible to make many contributions through projects of specific and limited scope.

John Stein has recently reminded us of the many large unrecorded Mesa Verdean sites along portions of the San Juan River. Many field workers have pointed out recently, that in general it is the larger sites which are well excavated but poorly recorded, while the smaller ones are generally better recorded but sometimes less well excavated. This latter phenomenon often occurs when contracted mitigation excavations get behind schedule and hurried limited excavations are undertaken at modest sites to achieve the numerical quota for a sample size designated in some contract. We all realize that this is not just an ancedote. There are many possible thematic projects that could and should be conducted throughout New Mexico.

In addition, small experimental projects can be constructed that have tremendous impact on methodology. For instance, one could spread several classes (points and scrapers, for instance) of artifacts out randomly in a one or two-acre plot. Four surveyors could then walk straight transects 5, 10 and 15 meters apart, to see at which distance the percentage of spotted artifacts was highest. One could then do the same for four persons walking these so-called *zig-zag* patterns at roughly the same distances, the artifacts being recast each time and field crews not told the size of the sample. One could then evaluate *zig-zag* vs. straight and 5, 10 and 20 meter distances (or 1, 5 and 10 meter, whatever). If one did this in different plots having different percentage of vegetative cover as described in survey reports — say 20%, 50%, 80%, and then varied them by walking into, then away from, the sun, and finally, varied cadence by stopwatch from 3 mph (264 feet per minute) to 1½ mph (132 feet per minute) to ¾ mph (66 feet per minute), we would know a great deal more about levels of in-field data recovery, and in particular, about those levels as they applied to "lithic period" archeological remains. To walk all of these variables would only require coverage of 108 acres (if one acre plots). If one then varied artifact density from, say, one artifact per 100 sq. feet (440 artifacts) to one per 200, 400 and 800, or whatever, it would be reasonable to suppose that some curve of critical mass of artifact density to percent recorded would emerge. Now *that* would be nice to know in evaluating surveys in which many isolated artifacts were found or in designing techniques for high altitude surveys.

A crew of four, plus two to set up the experiment, could conduct the fieldwork in six or seven days. Three could analyze the data and write it up in another week or two. At an average wage of $75.00 per day (including fringe benefits), such a project would cost no more than $6,000 or $7,000, requiring only $3,000 to $3,500 in matching funds. It would give federal and state planners better ideas of how to evaluate proposed ground coverage designs in projects that come before them. It would give us all a clearer notion of time-money-coverage tradeoffs than we have now, and it would give those who conducted it a valuable article to offer for publication. Who would not agree to accept matching funds to pursue such a project? Since it could be conducted on a series of weekends, no overhead would have to be paid or permission gotten from supervisors. Let us do some of these things — they would be fun, improve the state of our craft and give us something other than the drearier aspects of contract archeology to talk about!

Institutions will want to propose such projects in the ordinary way, but individuals and small groups of individuals, in particular, should be encouraged to propose and conduct a variety of these thematic and experimental projects. These should not be block surveys themselves, but might, in cases, lead to developing the information and techniques needed to conduct larger block surveys later. While we conceive of a manageable block survey to be between 10 and 20 sq. miles (something that can be conducted and reported in roughly one calendar year) and costing $50,000 on the low end and perhaps $100,000 on the upper end (that is, requiring roughly $25,000 to $50,000 at a 50/50 match), we conceive of special projects as of six months to a year in duration with one to six people involved and requiring $2,000 (or less) to $20,000 in matching funds.

If individuals propose such projects, they ordinarily have to document their wage to establish the value of their labor. But the wage/labor structure of many of the contract institutions (university affiliates are the worst, generally) is both unfair and abusive. The labor of a principal investigator (or other administrator of record) is often valued at double or triple that of those who actually conduct such projects. Though this more often has to do with the heirarchical thinking of institutional personnel offices than with the ungenerosity of principal investigators, it is not proper to require it.

Individuals who propose should have the option of claiming a prevailing federal pay scale equivalent to their experience. Most of us are able to say whether we would qualify as a GS-7, GS-9, GS-11 or whatever. Others may earn more and wish to use their own salary schedule, but most in the profession would be pleased with use of the federal scale. We cannot dictate that this be done, but we feel compelled to suggest it. Thus, by our calculation, a person who qualified as a GS-7 would claim $15,000 (roughly, in Spring 1980) as base wage, the equivalent of fringe benefits (25%, we think), and overhead for use of his/her home, books, typewriter, car, etc. in conducting such research. If anyone decides to use this system, percent of overhead from the major contracting institutions in New Mexico should be used to determine an average figure to be used by all. We believe this figure would currently average 25% or 26% of total project costs. If a sponsor is found who provides facilities (and, we hope, funds), then this figure would not accrue to the individual. Using the senior author as an example, we would qualify for a GS-11 grade, use roughly $20,000 as a base figure and fringe benefits (@ 25%) = $5,000 + Overhead (@ 25%) = $6,250. The total basis for the annual value of his labor and use of his facilities on a project with no other sponsor would be $31,250. At a current matching basis of 50/50, the senior author could expect to be reimbursed $15,625 for a year-long project. Such a system could make it workable for individuals to submit proposals, and we do not feel it awkward to suggest that the government should be satisfied to pay half its own cost in award to a similarly qualified outsider.

To those of you who may read this document and not be involved with contract archeology, this discussion may seem odd, even out of place. But the fact is that, as we write this, there are more than 150 archeologists employed in New Mexico. Of these, something on the order of two-thirds do not enjoy the benefits of permanent employment, though many have worked for a given employer over the course of many years. Some of these individuals now have ten to fifteen years field experience, though their average income over five to ten years would not bring most above the poverty level. Some of these individuals are highly talented and very dedicated. The vagaries of the labor system have prevented some from conducting the excellent research of which they are capable. It is our intent in this document to suggest that innovative research ideas be coupled with craftsmanship in pursuit of research that also fills important planning and administrative needs. It will do little good to inspire such intentions if all the best talent here in New Mexico cannot be set free and rewarded to conduct such National Register surveys. The scheme we have set forth here may not, ultimately, be the appropriate one, but some vehicle must be constructed to overcome these difficulties.

We believe that one-third of all available National Register survey funds should be set aside for thematic surveys and other special projects. In establishing priorities, these projects should display the attributes of contributing substantially to National Register nominations, or be of such methodological benefit to federal and state planners that they contribute materially to evaluating reports, projects, planning needs, assessment of impacts, etc. In research, such projects should ordinarily be rated in only one category of priority. Sometimes the proposor will wish to develop the proposal in two categories.

These, then, are our conceptions of project-specific priorities. We have provided for administrative and planning needs, the old and the new, the broader and the more focused.

Let us turn, then, to a proposed 13 year National Register survey program in which these needs may be met in the State of New Mexico.

A PLAN FOR NATIONAL REGISTER SURVEYS – NEW MEXICO

In this section we focus, generally, on what has been done in surveys of the various overview areas of New Mexico, and how a general program to conduct National Register surveys and resolve major data problems might be structured. First, let us consider the comparative survey data and estimates of survey coverage for each portion of the State.

THE DATA

Please refer to Table IX.1 for comparative data on known sites and survey coverage in New Mexico. We should make our confidence in these data specific. Our poorest control over acreage actually surveyed is in the Socorro district and southeastern New Mexico, because the majority of these surveys have been casual, and computing acreage surveyed is reduced to a series of educated guesses. Our total acreage figures fall 466 sq. miles short of the published surface area of New Mexico (121,666 sq. mi.). We can't work out the discrepancy but, in any case, the error is less than 4/10ths of one percent. We are confident enough of our computations to state categorically that not less than 2,200 sq. mi. nor more than 2,800 sq. mi. have been subjected to intensive survey where 90% of all archeological remains in a given locality were recorded. We feel that 2% is as accurate a generalization as can be gotten from the literature and site forms produced prior to July 1, 1980.

Some investigators may object to these figures. We saw several characterizations in the literature which took the form of *we surveyed 1,500 km²* in our survey. A careful reading of such reports often disclosed a field season of 7-9 months and crews ranging from 6-12 persons. Over hundreds of surveys, the senior author has computed that an ordinary survey crew can get 90% or better data recovery averaging 40 acres per person per day. Now, the specifics do, indeed, depend on terrain, crew experience, fatigue, recording time, etc. Nonetheless, if we assume the 1,500 km² to be partly allegorical, and compute on 500 miles square as equivalent, then a crew of 10 working *every* day for 8 months (240 days) would have to cover 133 acres per person per day, *every* day. This suggests spectacular endurance for a crew of any size. When the claim of *100% inventory* is also offered, we just plain balk.

Though some prodigious feats of ground coverage at high levels of data recovery are well documented in the Southwest, these projects have several rather uniform characteristics: crews are *small*, i.e. 2-4 persons; terrain is open; site density is low and the sustained effort is short, typically several days to several weeks. In short, many such monumental claims for intensive inventory are exaggerated by two- or three-fold, whether one wishes to adjust the claim by percent of ground covered or by percent of artifactual clusters (sites) recorded. Thus, if all those who had made such claims banded together, they might conclude amongst themselves that our 2% figure was simply too small, since they, collectively, had surveyed a greater portion of the New Mexico landscape. When very carefully done surveys in adjacent areas are used as a balance, or yardstick, both in site density and in field time, the 2% figure offered here is quite reasonable.

Because thematic and *fast cruise* surveys (our term for above) generally do spot both high site concentrations and a higher percentage of the larger sites, and because many sites in the LA files were singly recorded (no real survey), we suggest that the 2% ground coverage in New Mexico reflects roughly 6-8% of the recordable site inventory. As we said earlier, we do not project a site population at 50 times the currently recorded sites, or *1,175,000* sites. We project the total site population at one-third to one-fourth that figure — as we said in Chapter V: a low of 2.5 and a high of 3.5 sites per square mile for the entire state. This again is 300,000 to 420,000 sites. We exclude single artifacts and single *pot drops* from this projection. In Chapter VII, we note that the placement of reservoir surveys in the northeastern Plains, for instance, may have inflated average site density when projected for the region by a factor of two or three.

Table IX.1

COMPARATIVE DATA: KNOWN SITES AND SURVEY COVERAGE IN NEW MEXICO

Text Table	Chapter	Overview Units BLM/U.S.F.S.	No. Known Sites	Total m² in Unit	% Survey Coverage	No. m² Surveyed
	Ch. 3	Northwestern New Mexico	13,314	27,500	3.0	1,050
III.12		*San Juan Basin, III NM[1]	9,614	15,000	5.0	750
III.13		Upper Rio Grande, II NM[2]	3,700	12,500	2.5	300
	Ch. 4	West Central New Mexico	3,539	19,200	2.0+	375
IV.6		**Mt. Taylor District[3], IV NM	2,119	6,700	3.0+	210
		Socorro District, V NM	1,420	12,500	1.4	165
	Ch. 5	Southwestern New Mexico	3,871	30,000	2.5	750
V.3		Mimbres District[5]	1,871	15,000	1.0+	150
		Jornada District[5] VII NM	2,000+	15,000	4.0	***600
VI.7	Ch. 6	†Southeastern New Mexico[6], VI NM	1,818	27,000	1.0+	280
VII.8	Ch. 7	Northeast New Mexico[7], I NM	1,000	15,700	.8	125
VII.11		Central New Mexico[7], I NM	106	3,456	.5	20
TOTALS		KNOWN NEW MEXICO SITES (As of 7/1980)	23,520	121,200	2.0>	2,580

* north of I-40
** south of I-40
*** Note: This figure influenced by 2 surveys south of Alamogordo. Though 100% survey is claimed, the time frame for these projects leaves us wondering about percentage of retrieved data.
† south of Vaughn

Sources:
1 SJBRUS File
2 Stuart (this volume) and Biella and Chapman (1977-79)
3 SJBRUS File, Wimberly and Eidenbach (1980), Hunter-Anderson (1978)
4 LA Files and Marshall (n.d.), Stuart's estimates (this volume)
5 Kelley (1966), Wimberly and Rogers (1977), LeBlanc and Whalen (1979), Wimberly and Eidenbach (1980)
6 Camilli and Allen (1979)
7 Gauthier (this volume), based on total count in LA Files and published sources

How secure are we with the *known sites* figured for each region? We feel there is good control for the northeast Plains, the southeast Plains, the Jornada, and the Mimbres. We had problems separating the San Juan Data Base sites from overlapping areas in Mt. Taylor and in the upper Rio Grande. Thus, it may be that the reapportionment of perhaps 500 sites will ultimately take place when all sites in the LA files are plotted by UTM coordinate. As for the total site inventory at June 1, 1980, we feel reasonably confident of less than 5% error for all known sites, including those not in the LA file (usually recorded in other states or buried in federal agency files). The LA files had approximately 21,500 sites at the time these data were prepared. The remaining 2,000 sites can be easily accounted for in files kept in Colorado, Texas and several federal agencies (BLM, BIA, Forest Service). If our error is larger, we err on the low side of site numbers. The SHPO for New Mexico and the State Archeologist for New Mexico should see to a more rapid processing of this *corpus* into the Laboratory of Anthropology series (*LA* numbered sites).

In Map IX.1 these data are summarized. The dotted lines indicate our computation base (see Chapters III, IV and VII for areas of the San Juan Basin and the division between northeast and southwest Plains).

It is obvious from this map that one cannot simply arrange each of the BLM/ Forest Service overview units from 1-8 on the basis of surveyed acreage and achieve logically ranked priorities for future survey. This is particularly true for the Jornada unit, where two federally funded surveys yield a high *raw* survey coverage, because 9/10ths of all sites have been recorded from a block (McGregor and Dona Ana ranges) equaling 1/6th of the region. Notably, those two block surveys yielded a relatively low site density. This sort of situation makes one very nervous about assigning an effective 4% survey coverage for the region.

To overcome the logical and practical liabilities imposed by the administrative boundaries of these study units, we impose a different general structure on the state and rank priorities in only three categories as follows (see Map IX.2).

The priorities suggested here are for the general *investment* of funds only. Specific survey proposals should be ranked as suggested in the previous section. Additionally, the San Juan Basin, Mt. Taylor district and portions of the upper Rio Grande are ranked at a lower priority for committment of National Register surveys. Though impacts (from mineral development and population expansion) will be high in this region (Plog, in press), other federal programs and environmental legislation will continue to be the impetus for intensive archeological investigation. National Register surveys should be planned, generally, to meet goals that are not achievable by other means.

A NATIONAL REGISTER SURVEY PROGRAM

A program of National Register surveys must address basic needs to be effective. 1) There must be a usable data base from which to define issues of significance, and major imbalances in our knowledge of the archeological record. 2) There must be a generally acceptable plan for assigning survey priorities based on research needs. 3) Surveys must be conducted where most needed, resources being finite, and their results must be both of enduring value and well distributed. 4) We require better chronological control over the archeological record to determine many issues of significance. 5) We require better classificatory/comparative control over large groups of sites to determine their significance (see Chapter VIII, this volume). Finally 6) We require increased methdological knowledge about the efficient conduct of archeological survey itself.

All these needs must be met in order to determine which sites, districts, localities and,

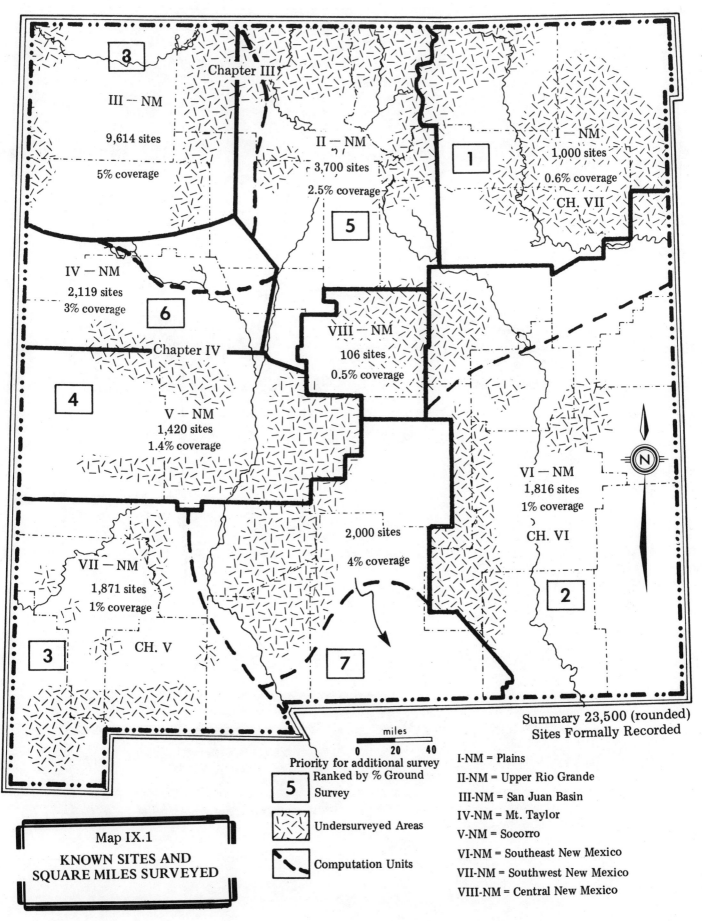

3

III — NM

9,614 sites

5% coverage

Chapter III

II — NM

3,700 sites

2.5% coverage

1

I — NM

1,000 sites

0.6% coverage

CH. VII

5

IV — NM

2,119 sites
3% coverage

6

Chapter IV

VIII — NM

106 sites

0.5% coverage

4

V — NM

1,420 sites

1.4% coverage

VI — NM

1,816 sites

1% coverage

CH. VI

2

2,000 sites

4% coverage

VII — NM

1,871 sites

1% coverage

3

CH. V

7

N

Summary 23,500 (rounded)
Sites Formally Recorded

miles

0   20   40

Priority for additional survey
Ranked by % Ground
5   Survey

Undersurveyed Areas

Computation Units

I-NM = Plains

II-NM = Upper Rio Grande

III-NM = San Juan Basin

IV-NM = Mt. Taylor

V-NM = Socorro

VI-NM = Southeast New Mexico

VII-NM = Southwest New Mexico

VIII-NM = Central New Mexico

Map IX.1

KNOWN SITES AND
SQUARE MILES SURVEYED

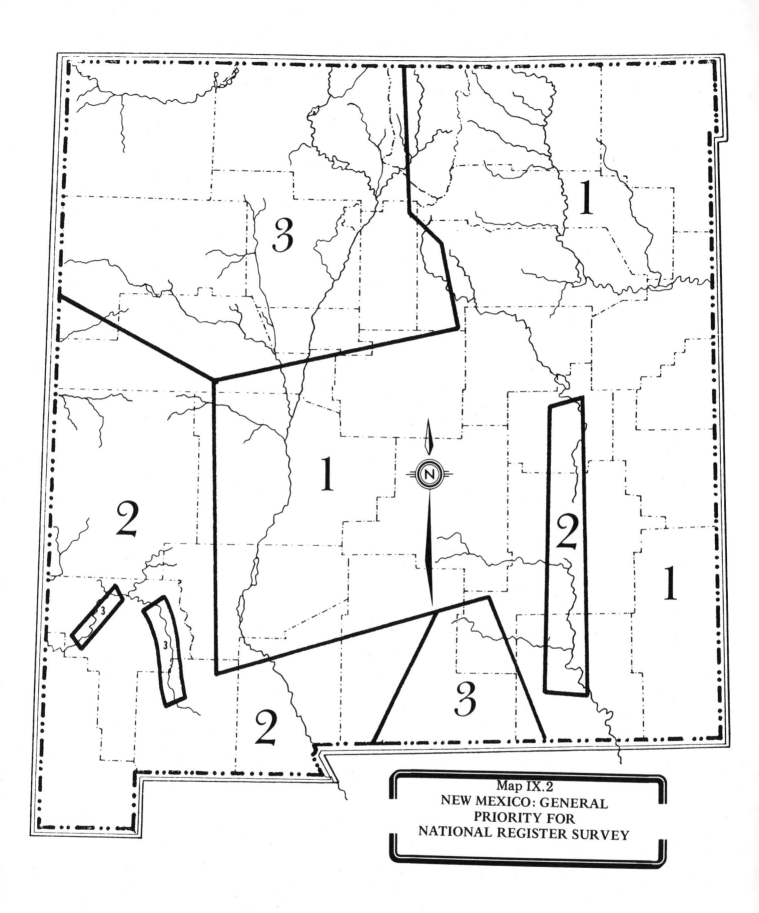

Map IX.2
NEW MEXICO: GENERAL
PRIORITY FOR
NATIONAL REGISTER SURVEY

perhaps most importantly, which *classes* of sites merit inclusion on the National Register of Historic Places. Below we propose an approach to each of these problems. It is our conception that a National Register program must provide a general professional and methodological matrix in which surveys can be conducted with maximum effectiveness.

STEP 1: THE REGIONAL SITE DATA BASE

PROBLEM: The most urgent task of a National Register survey program is to set the stage for the future conduct of effective surveys. The current program of the Laboratory of Anthropology to computerize its LA site file is the correct general approach, as is the development of the SJBRUS File (San Juan Data Base) by the National Park Service, Santa Fe. When these projects are completed they will be enormously valuable. Nonetheless, several more specific problems arise. These are: 1) timeliness in completing the computerizations, 2) availability of computer terminals at outlying institutions, 3) quality of the data for survey research design preparations.

SOLUTION: A solution to these problems can be achieved by pursuing the data retrieval strategies started by Gauthier (northeast Plains), Camilli and Allen (1980, southeast Plains); and for the Mimbres-Jornada (Whalen and LeBlanc 1979).

For each of the major regions of New Mexico, the site files can be gone through, by hand, to separate those sites where data are workably complete from those that are not. Additionally, attempts should be made to resolve the missing data by contacting original investigators and securing site forms filed in other states and agencies for the LA file. The data from these site forms should then be abstracted and printed up for distribution as regional data sets. Site data should be summarized to point out patterns of site distribution, ceramic assemblages, soil placement, elevation, general vegetative zone and the like. Appended to each data file, optimally, would be a list of dated archeological remains in that region and a short bibliography of major surveys in the region which summarize data for 50-100, or more, sites.

Since we have assigned the highest survey priorities to the northeast Plains, southeast Plains, southwestern New Mexico (excluding Dona Ana and McGregor ranges) and the Socorro-Torrance County area, the projects should proceed in roughly that order.

The object, then, is to prepare a regional survey data base of between 1,000 and 2,000 sites, for each portion of New Mexico. For the Plains, central New Mexico and southwestern New Mexico, such a data base would encompass most of the known survey remains. For the San Juan Basin, Mt. Taylor and the upper Rio Grande, about 20-50% of currently recorded sites might be represented. Sites represented should include those recorded from all areas of the study units and all archeological phases, that is, be broadly representative.

COST: Each of these regional projects could be conducted with one data coordinator and one research assistant within one year's time.

BUDGET: EACH AREA

Labor: Data Coordinator	$ 16,000	per annum
Assistant	12,000	per annum
	$ 27,000	
Phone	1,000	
Typing (1,000 pp. maximum, two drafts)	2,000	
Drafting (10 maps)	1,500	
Travel (30 days @ $40/day) and		
Gas for 3,000 miles (20 cents/mile)	1,800	
Xerox	1,800	
EACH AREA'S COST	$ 35,100	

($35,100 x 8 areas = 280,800 less 50% matching funds = $140,400)

TOTAL COST $140,400

Order of Priority:	Projected Data Set	Initiate Project
1) NE Plains	1,000 sites	1981
2) SE Plains	1,500 sites	1981
3) Jornada	1,500 sites	1981
4) Mimbres	1,500 sites	1982
5) Socorro District	1,500 sites	1982
6) Upper Rio Grande	1,500 sites	1982
7) Mt. Taylor	1,500 sites	1983
8) San Juan Basin	1,500 sites	1983
	11,500 sites	Complete 1984

Again, these regional projects would produce, not site forms, but brief tabular data for sites, plus appropriate summaries and maps. These data sets will provide a basis for preparing National Register survey proposals and will enormously promote the conduct of other research. The *resolved* data in these can be fed back to the Laboratory of Anthropology, along with retrieved and corrected site forms, for entry into their computerized bank.

STEP 2: GENERAL CHRONOLOGICAL CONTROL: STATEWIDE

PROBLEM: What is our actual chronological control on the archeological record? Though the tree-ring bulletins are highly useful, other dated remains are slow to find their way into the literature. Excavation reports are often published before all samples have been processed. No general summary of dated sites has appeared since Breternitz (1966).

SOLUTION: The simple solution is to draw together and summarize all dated archeological remains, by component, in New Mexico, with brief notes on the archeological context of dated samples. This compilation should be completed so that appropriate abstracts of dated materials can be supplied for each regional summary. The general compilation should be published and made available to the general literature of southwestern archeology.

COST: This project can be completed, as the above, with two persons for a maximum of one year's time.

BUDGET: NEW MEXICO

Labor: Data Coordinator	$16,000 per annum
Assistant	12,000 per annum
	$ 27,000
Phone	1,000
Typing	2,000
Drafting (10 maps)	1,500
Travel (1,000 miles @ 20 cents/mile)	200
Xerox	1,800
Publication	6,000
TOTAL	$ 38,000

($38,000 less 50% matching = $19,000)

The publication should be sold at cost and be in an inexpensive but sturdy format. Matching costs include recovery of publication costs, so that recipients of contracts do not have to fund publication in actual cost.

TIME: This project should be started in 1981 and be completed as soon as possible.

STEP 3: FORMALIZE AND UPDATE A STATE PLAN
FOR NATIONAL REGISTER SURVEYS

PROBLEM: The authors of this volume have set the stage for the process of consensus which will lead to a formal state plan for National Register surveys, and, though this volume should permit the first steps in a National Register program to be implemented, the process of consensus is not complete. Gaining a statewide consensus for research and survey priorities may never be possible.

SOLUTION: a) The National Register program should first present the contents of this volume to the profession at large and to the officers and members of the New Mexico Archeological Council and other interested archeological associations. At least two broad, open forums for the discussion of its contents should be publicly announced during the first half of 1981.

b) Thereafter, the needs and general priorities for survey, research, and kinds and categories should be discussed biannually in regional symposia open to interested scholars. Symposia similar to the one which produced the recent volume on *Jornada-Mogollon Archeology* are an appropriate vehicle to establish research consensus and produce a distributed record of that consensus to the profession and the public.

We suggest that six regional symposia would be sufficient to administer these needs. Perhaps these might be:

1) An Anasazi Symposium (San Juan Basin, Upper Rio Grande, Mt. Taylor)
2) A Central New Mexico Symposium
3) A Mogollon Mimbres Symposium
4) The Jornada-Mogollon Symposium
5) A Northeast Plains Symposium
6) A Southeast Plains Symposium

The general points are these. One should not be finicky with the geographic boundaries imposed on these symposia. Whether or not they met annually, their charge in discussing the National Register program would be biannual. Biannually, each such symposium would schedule an entire day's session to: hear the results of all National Register surveys conducted in that region during the previous two years. These would be presented as papers which summarized and abstracted site data along with theoretical conclusions, discuss in open forum, the remaining priorities for additional survey and research in the region, and conduct a short panel session to comment on the results of previous National Register surveys.

Finally, each such symposium would prepare, biannually, a formal publication which contained, in addition to the customary results of personal research, a) all those papers and data summaries presented from National Register surveys, b) a brief report on the proceedings of discussion on priorities (a titled section such as *Suggested Research Priorities in the Jornada Region* would be appropriate), c) a review, in standard book review format, of the report for each National Register survey conducted in the previous two years. Reviewers are *not* to include any who have had or expect to have any financial interest in the National Register survey program and otherwise have a relationship of review authority to that program. That is, all those, who have a formal or administrative or customary authority of review over the program and its implementation, should not also exercise a second vehicle for review. In professional terms, such individuals do not have the status of independent reviewers.

The editor of each biannual volume should be charged with including these necessary proceedings. Finally, as a matter of record, the volume should include a simple table of all sizeable surveys conducted in that region during the previous two years. This summary should include: name of institution, general map referents for survey, number of sites located, title and authors of survey report, and an address where it can be obtained. The judgment of what constitutes a *major* survey will be left to each editor, but we imagine that most would say a report that summarized information on 50 or more sites merited a place of record. Of course, smaller site inventories and projects may be considered notable for other reasons.

COST: The publication of each biannual volume and symposium could be funded at $10,000, the preparation time of all participating scholars to be taken into account to create the matching funds.

BUDGET: Three Symposia Annually @ $10,000 = $30,000 annually.
Not less than an edition of 500 volumes would be distributed at half-cost to the public and profession ($10 per volume, or less).
Actual Cost after Distribution of Publication = $15,000.

TIME: a) Schedule the Northeast Plains and Southeast Plains to coincide with the distribution of the first regional site data packets, late in 1981.

b) Schedule the Jornada and Mogollon Regions, funded symposia in late 1982, for the same reasons as above (The structures of existing regional symposia should be utilized where possible. It is merely that, biannually, they shall be asked to schedule a special session and volume in return for the provision to publish their proceedings.).

c) Schedule the Central New Mexico Symposium in early 1983 and the Anasazi Symposium late in 1983, for the same reasons as above.

STEP 4: IMPLEMENT THE NATIONAL REGISTER SURVEYS

PROBLEM: The problems that arise with the implementation of National Register surveys are multifaceted. Some of these problems are philosophical and theoretical, while others are practical. Our interest here is in the practical and the administrative. The practical problems are: *How much to survey? Where to survey? When to survey? What kind of surveys should be proposed? How are priorities assigned?*

SOLUTIONS: 1) How much should be surveyed? We propose that an equivalent of 1½% survey of the acreage in New Mexico be the minimum goal of the National Register surveys in New Mexico.

How much to survey? Since the state of New Mexico consists of 121,666 sq. miles, we propose that 1,800 sq. miles or: 1,152,000 acres be inventory surveyed during a 12 year period.

Where to Survey? Those who have special research interests in each area of the state, whether heavily surveyed or not, should be offered an opportunity to propose survey in under-surveyed localities within each region. Therefore, funds should be made available to conduct inventory survey of half of one percent (.5%) ground coverage *in each county of New Mexico* (that is a total of *600 square miles* or *384,000 acres*).

To balance the data base in generally undersurveyed regions of New Mexico, *an equal percent* ground coverage should be funded in:
      a) the Northeast Plains
      b) the Southeast Plains

c) Southwestern New Mexico: 1) North of U.S. 82/70 and east of the Rio Grande (Tularosa Basin, San Andres Mountains, southern Jornada del Muerto); 2) The portion of southwestern New Mexico south of I-10 and west of the Rio Grande (the Animas District).
        d) Socorro District, east of the Catron County line
        e) Central New Mexico -- Torrance County and adjacent undersurveyed areas.

Since this represents about half the acreage of New Mexico, an investment equal to the first would again be: *600* square *miles or 384,000* acres. This would approach a 1% sample of the ground surface in these regions. Added to the half percent investment in each county, the survey base would all be brought to between 2% (Northeast Plains) and 3% (the rest), representing a survey base similar to those we have today in the northwest quarter (San Juan Basin, Mt. Taylor, Upper Rio Grande) of New Mexico.

The equivalent in funds of ½% survey of the State of New Mexico should be invested in thematic surveys to relocate, rerecord and nominate sites and classes of sites to the National Register. The model of such a project should be that which produced the volume entitled *Anasazi Communities of the San Juan Basin* (Marshall, Stein, Loose and Novotny 1979). Such surveys are not computed in actual acreage. They should be unrestricted as to the region in which they are conducted (free of regional priorities) but subject to the specific priorities (review priorities — see earlier section, this chapter, entitled *Priorities*). Funds equivalent to inventory survey of 600 square miles or 384,000 acres are required.

COST OF SURVEY: The high bid for survey of 1,152,000 acres or 1,800 square miles in July 1, 1980 dollars is as follows:

HIGH RANGE BUDGET
NATIONAL REGISTER SURVEYS
(Labor valued at an average of $18,500/annum,
i.e., average of all federal employees as of 6/80)

A. Survey Time — 28,800 person days @ 40a. day
    Administrative Time for Above — 5,760 person days @ 20% of above
        SUBTOTAL — 34,560 person days

B. Laboratory and Write-up Time -- 86,400 person days @ 2.5 days x above
    Administrative Time for Above -- 8,640 person days @ 10% of above
        SUBTOTAL — 95,040 person days

Labor Time - Project Total = 129,600 person days (rounded = 130,000 person days x $77.08)

Direct Cost for Labor
(240 day work year @ $77.08/day) . . . . $ 10,020,400.00
Fringe Benefits @ 25% above 2,505,100.00
Per Diem @ $36.00/field day (x 34,560) 1,244,160.00
Mileage @ 20 cents/mile (100 miles x person days in survey) 691,200.00
                              SUBTOTAL $ 14,460,860.00
Materials and Services (10% of above) 1,446,086.00
                              SUBTOTAL $ 15,906,946.00
Institutional Overhead @ average of 25% total costs 3,976,736.00
                       TOTAL COST $19,883,682.00
                            (= $17.26 acre)

           Less 50% Matching = $ 9,941,184.00

The legitimate low range budget is as follows:

LOW RANGE BUDGET
NATIONAL REGISTER SURVEYS
(Labor valued at an average of $15,000/annum,
i.e., contract institution average)

A. Survey Time -- 19,200 person days @ 60a. day
    Administrative Time for above -- 2,880 person days @ 15% of above
        SUBTOTAL — 22,080 person days

B. Laboratory and Write-up Time -- 44,160 person days @ 2 days x above
    Administrative Time for Above — 4,416 person days @ 10% of above
        SUBTOTAL — 48,576 person days

Labor Time — Project Total = 70,656 person days (rounded = 71,000 person days x $62.50)

Direct Cost for Labor
(240 day work year @ $62.50/day) .... $ 4,437,500.00
Fringe Benefits @ 25% above 1,109,375.00
Per Diem @ $30.00/field day (x 22,080) 662,400.00
Mileage @ 20 cents/mile (100 miles x person days in survey) 441,600.00
                                           SUBTOTAL $ 6,650,875.00
Materials and Services @ 10% of above 665,087.00
                                           SUBTOTAL $ 7,315,962.00
Institutional Overhead @ 20% of above 1,463,192.00
                                       TOTAL COST $ 8,779,154.00
                                      (= $7.62/acre)
                            Less 50% Matching = $ 4,389,577.00

The estimated cost of the National Register survey program alone is the average of these two figures, or:

$$\begin{array}{c} \$\ 14,331,418.00 \\ \hline \$\ \ 7,165,709.00 \end{array} = \$12.44 \text{ acre}$$

less 50% matching

The survey cost per acre may seem high to many in contract archeology. Nonetheless, it is the case that many contract administrators have not properly provided for inflation the last several years. For instance, the CGP Survey budget (Reher 1977) came to $5.65 an acre in 1973 (the contract year). Those who worked for nothing to complete the project know that it was underfunded. Calculating 7 years of inflation at roughly 10% per annum, that budget would now (6/80) cost $9.60 per acre. The above figure of $12.44 an acre would adequately, but not lavishly, fund a top quality large survey project in 1980.

WHEN TO SURVEY. Thematic surveys may be conducted as soon as is convenient, regional data permitting. Inventory surveys should begin after professional consensus on research priorities has solidified and regional data packages are becoming available, about the beginning of 1982. Inventory National Register surveys should be conducted over a 12 year period. Inventory survey would include 1,200 square miles in total, the remainder of funds being invested in thematic surveys. That is, 100 square miles a year should be surveyed.

WHAT KIND OF SURVEYS. We strongly advocate that National Register surveys be conducted as block surveys (contiguous acreage) or in square mile sample quadrats. Recent survey (Wimberly and Eidenbach 1980) indicates that the majority of sites are not found *within* vegetational/physiographic strata but in the *contact zones between* such strata. Square mile units or larger can be more easily relocated, easily located to maximize environmental variability, and are cheaper to survey than small (40 acres is common) sample units. Moreover, once a section (640 acres) is surveyed in the National Register program, it should be recorded not needing additional survey. On theoretical grounds, many may disagree with this position. Be that as it may, it is a tenaciously held opinion, based on practicality.

The best value obtainable is from surveys of moderate size, employing small to moderate sized crews. The National Register Survey program should be cautious about administering to surveys which operate on the "cast of millions" principle. A survey of roughly 20 square miles, or 12,800 acres, which employs a crew of four will take about 80 field days, or four working months to complete. Writeup time for such a survey would take from 8-10 working months. Such surveys would cost from $100,000 to $150,000 and could be completed in a year; a *failure to perform* judgment, or clause, is reasonable at 18 months from award. Since these are matching funds, the optimal awards will range from $50,000 to $75,000 each. It is inadvisable for a single institution or individual to be involved in more than one survey at a time. We further suggest that no individual or institution be awarded more than three such surveys over the life of the program, whatever the merits of their proposals. In many cases, it may be that three awards are necessary to continue a large survey program over a 3-4 year period. The upper limit for a given award should probably be set at 40 square miles, the lower at 10.

For thematic surveys, awards should attempt to fall within the $50,000 to $100,000 range in matching funds, not more.

It is our opinion then, that the survey of 100 square miles per annum should involve 4 to 6 survey projects a year. Additionally, 2 to 4 thematic surveys a year would be conducted, these latter would total $398,095.00/annum in 1980 dollars, or $199,047.50 in matching funds.

The cost of survey apportioned over 12 years (12 ÷ $14,331,418) would be $1,194,285 per year, one-third of this in thematic surveys. At matching cost the *per annum basis is $597,142.50.*

STEP 5: SPECIAL PROJECTS

PROBLEMS: There are three remaining major problems in conducting National Register surveys. These involve a) chronological control over the archeological record (both in the totality of dated materials and in the identification of *non-diagnostic* artifactual remains), b) the consistent recording and identification of artifactual, architectural and ecological data, and c) the efficacy of survey methodology itself.

SOLUTIONS: a) CHRONOLOGY — Establish a *dating fund*. The National Register program should match the cost of processing and analyzing datable material for any project conducted by any professional archeologist in New Mexico where a legitimate effort to obtain other funds sufficient to cover those costs has been made first and failed. On entirely unfunded projects, an investigator's labor time in retrieving the samples may be used to create the match in kind. A limit of $3,000.00 in such funds for any individual or institution in a given year would be advisable.

COST: $30,000.00 per annum. Match to be made with labor in kind. Limit, $3,000.00 per individual or institution, annually.

For instance, Mr. Scott Andrea of La Plata, New Mexico proposed to collect additional tree-ring samples from Gobernador phase Navajo pueblitos, forked stick hogans and cut juniper stumps throughout the region before they disappeared as firewood in Farmington and Aztec homes (this is already happening). Such a project would make an excellent thematic survey, but even if it were not so funded, an individual could conduct his/her research and obtain dating analysis under this program. Perhaps we might find graduate students again conducting field excavations for thesis projects if some incentive were available.

Dateable materials observed on general (including contract) surveys could also be processed with fewer restraints. We believe this program could achieve a great deal for a moderate investment.

b) IDENTIFICATION OF MATERIAL REMAINS — The preparation of field manuals for archeological site recording and identification procedures is essential to generating a broadly useable site file data base.

These manuals should be prepared as simple, straightforward ring-binder type field booklets. These should, for instance, indicate standard artifact attributes, and techniques for field identification, and provide advice on which procedures require complex laboratory analysis. Artifact sketches and photographs are, of course, necessary and appropriate. These field manuals should be broadly regional, such as: the Mogollon area, the Jornada area, the Plains area and the Anasazi area.

*Four categories of booklet should be produced. These are:
1)   Field identification of ceramics
2)   Field identification of lithics
3)   Field identification of architectural and other features
4)   Field recording of environmental data
* Note: We do not include historic artifactual and architectural remains because these are not the subject of this volume.

These booklets should be produced by a select committee of several highly regarded experts in each subject area. They should be simple, straightforward and direct, the object being to achieve a level of consistency in recording materials that, though short of the most minute analysis, would broadly serve the profession in creating a consistent body of literature in the site data forms.

In ceramics, persons like Stewart Peckham , A.H. Warren, and Michael Marshall come to mind. We are not attempting to select a committee here, but by referring to well-known ceramic investigators, we are stating the appropriate level of expertise for inviting authorship.

Cost: $30,000.00 per booklet, including first small publication run to be sold at printing cost to the public. TOTAL COST $120,000.00 for 4 Booklets.

We suggest that approximately three senior persons work on each booklet and standardize their technique, insofar as is possible, among regions of the state. On the presumption that such persons will be otherwise employed, an honorarium for each of three authors at $5,000.00 or a total of $15,000.00, seems appropriate.

These individuals should have access to a research assistant, which accounts for $9,000 ($3,000 each in assistance). Additionally, $6,000 for drafting, typing and the first small print run of field booklets seems reasonable. If the length of these is permitted to exceed 75 or 100 pages, they will surely become too elaborate for general usage. Arrangements to produce these manuals should be made as soon as is practicable in 1981.

c) SURVEY METHODOLOGY — As mentioned in the section on *Project Specific Priorities*, certain advances in methodology are required to improve the efficiency of survey and, in some cases, to determine the quality of significance. These might include ground survey procedures, methods for *coring* pithouses, and techniques to identify the lithic assemblages that do not contain otherwise diagnostic procedures. Since many of these projects will be experimental in nature, it is proposed that initial financial investments in them be modest. Perhaps about 10% of these funds committed for thematic surveys annually (about $20,000) could be used to accomodate such projects. These should be considered as (or perhaps, if) promising proposals are received. Unless major methodological advancement can be demonstrated, no major funding is warranted.

SUMMARY: A PLAN FOR NATIONAL REGISTER SURVEYS

GENERAL PRIORITIES

The general priorities for survey and investment of funds should be the purview jointly of the SHPO, New Mexico, all those committees and/or authorities with whom he formally consults in the implementation of his programs and, biannually, open symposia where the profession at large makes its suggestions a matter of formal record. These general priorities should be guided by the intensity of survey coverage in the various overview regions of New Mexico as those various intensities of survey have been identified in this volume. The general priorities for balancing the kinds and categories of sites, districts, localities and classes of sites which should be sought out for nomination to the National Register may be guided, in part, by each of the discussions entitled *State and National Register Priorities* (Chapters III-VII) in this volume. In no case do we intend that a rigid or slavish adherence to these proposals be attempted.

THE SURVEY PROGRAM   14 years — 1981-1995 (13 years funded)

As a prelude to implementing National Register Inventory programs several background needs require attention. These are as follows:

	Full Cost	Matching
Step 1: The Regional Site Data Base: 8 regional site inventories to be produced between 1981 and 1984	$ 280,800	$ 140,400
Step 2: Summary of Chronological Information: 1 published summary of all dated components in New Mexico; to be produced between 1981 and 1982	$ 38,000	$ 19,000
Step 3: Formalize and Update A Statewide Plan for National Register Surveys: Conduct 6 regional symposia biannually and fund publication of record including survey results, review of survey reports, and priorities for additional survey Start symposia in LATE 1981	$ 360,000	$180,000

(return of half cost in sale of publication)

Step 4: Conduct National Register Surveys:

*A.   ½% ground coverage in every county
of New Mexico (1/3 survey funds)

*B.   1% additional ground coverage in
Priority 1 study areas of New Mexico
(1/3 funds)

* (Implement EARLY 1982 as Steps 1-3 are accomplished)

    C.   Thematic Surveys, unrestricted as to
general priorities, restricted as to
project specific priorities. Implement
as needed (1/3 survey funds)

    D.   Administration: 4-6 inventory surveys
to be conducted per annum. 2-4 thematic
surveys per annum. Awards and acreage
per survey to be kept moderate. 100 mi^2
to be inventoried annually for 12 years;
thematic surveys as required.

	Full Cost	Matching
COSTS OF SURVEY	$ 14,331,418	$ 7,165,709

ANNUAL SURVEY BUDGET $1,194,285 @ FULL COST, $597,142 MATCHING

Step 5: Special Projects:

		Full Cost	Matching
A.	*Dating Fund* to improve judgements of significance (implement late 1981)	$ 360,000	$ 360,000 (match in labor)
B.	Identification of Material Remains 4 field manuals. Implement ASAP, prior to bulk of surveys	$ 120,000	$ 120,000 (match in labor)
C.	Survey Methodology: As needed *set aside* of 4C above at 10% (i.e., $20,000/annum)	—	--

	Full Cost	Matching
TOTAL COST OF NATIONAL REGISTER PROGRAM, NEW MEXICO	$ 15,490,218	$ 7,985,109

Matching Cost in 1980 dollars: $7,985,109
Annual Budget Calendar Years 1981-93: $614,239.15 at 50% match in 1980 dollars.

The program proposed above should be taken to mean the conduct of surveys and necessary background research to meet National Register objectives in New Mexico for prehistoric archeological surveys. This program should not be taken to include any programs in progress, such as computerization of site files, etc.

This proposed National Register program, we believe, will meet the needs of the State of New Mexico in preserving archeological remains and expanding both the data base available and in providing for properly refined judgments on significance and eligibility for nomination to the National Register of Historic Places. While this may seem a costly program, it must be remembered that the State of New Mexico is a vast domain containing a remarkably rich and irreplaceable archeological heritage.

The cost of this program is, at 50% matching funds, precisely $5.04 per square mile per annum, or 0.00788 cents per acre, annually. Over the entire 13 year life of the program, the commitment in matching funds would equal one-tenth of one cent per acre. Viewed in these terms, it is a modest program, not grandiose in any sense. To place this program in an even more highly focused perspective, we may calculate on the basis of acreage for a State closer to those who reside in Washington. An identical program for the entire state of Maryland, which is 11.5 times smaller than New Mexico, would cost precisely $53,412.10 in annual matching funds.

Finally, it is fundamentally important that provision be made for the adequate long-term maintenance of site data files. Both computerized data and site survey forms themselves will provide much of the future basis for comparative research, and therefore for determinations of National Register significance. If the program suggested here is implemented, and archeologists learn how to conduct genuinely broad-scale research based on comparative site data, there will be an increasing demand for both computer printouts and physical access to the original data. Long-term provisions should be made to expand the role and the facilities of the survey room at the Museum of New Mexico's Laboratory of Anthropology in Santa Fe. The goals of the program presented here, when coupled with facilities at the Laboratory of Anthropology and augmented by continued contracted surveys, can place us on the frontier of a kind and scale of comparative research undreamed of twenty years ago. In the last few years we have, most of us, begun to conceive of how such research might be conducted. It is now time to develop precision in our concepts and to forge the essential tools of a new scale of observation.

PATTERNS OF PALEO-INDIAN SITE DISTRIBUTION

Map X.1

miles

0   20   40

(after Raisz, Landforms of the United States)

The Shiprock

Gallegos Wash

SAN JUAN RIVER

Suspected

Chuska Mts

Broilo's Peach Springs

CHACO RIVER

'aco Mesa

Nacimiento Mts

Sierra de Los Valles

CHAMA RIVER

Park Plateau

Trinidad Escarpment

Folsom Site

Los Vegas Plateau

Raton Plateau

Truchas Pk.

Cornudo Hills

Sangre de Cristo Mts.

Zuni Mts

Mt. Taylor

Mesa Chivato

Mesa Prieta

Jemez Mts

Santa Fe

Ocate Mesa

Escarpment

Canadian

Lava Fields

Cebolleta Mesa

Mesa Lucero

RIO PUERCO

Sandia Mts

Ortiz Mts

Glorieta Mesa

CANADIAN RIVER

SAN JO

E RIVER

Albuquerque

Manzano Mts

Estancia Valley

Pedernal Hills

San Jon Site

The Caprock

Cebolleta Mesa Sites

Gallo Mts

Bear Mts

Ladrone Mts

Datil Mts

los Pin

Magdal

austin

Pierg

Judge's Paleo Survey

nadera

Gallinas Mts

Jicarilla Mts

Lucy Site

Blackwater Draw

Llano Estacado

PECOS

Sierra Blanca

Capitan Mts

Mogollon Mts

inos Altos Range

GILA

Burro Mts

ores

RIO GRANDE

allos Mts

del

Fra

San Andres Mts

Jornada

White Sands

Sacramento

Roswell

Plain

PECOS RIVER

Mescalero Escarpment

Pyramid Mts

Animas Valley

Playas Valley

Cedar Mts

Hatchet Mts

Pyloncillo Mts

Tres Hermanos

Florida Mts

Deming

Sierra de Las Uvas

Organ Mts

Tularosa Bas

Guadalupe Mts

Hermits Cave

Chapter X
OVERVIEW: PATTERNS IN THE ARCHEOLOGICAL RECORD

In concluding this volume we have three goals. The first of these is to provide a brief sketch, of each major archeological period, that will point out patterns in the data which have not previously received complete attention. Secondly, several general phenomena will be discussed, such as shifts in altitude, episodes of abandonment, subsistence patterns, changes in room size, etc. Third, we present a very brief overview as it relates to the ideas of power and efficiency. None of these characterizations is intended to be complete in any way. Thus, they should not be taken as replacements for standard general characterizations of one time period or another. Rather, they focus on additional avenues of inquiry. With some adjustments, we use the basic Pecos Classification of periods here, but it is applied only to define temporal horizons statewide.

PALEO-INDIAN
(10,000 B.C. – 5,000 B.C.?)

We focused acutely on the Paleo-Indian period in Chapter III (Northwestern New Mexico) and in Chapter VII (Northeast Plains). We did this because the literature on Paleo-Indian is less well documented in the San Juan Basin [Judge's (1973) Rio Grande Survey on the eastern periphery being an exception] and in the Northeastern Plains than for southeastern New Mexico.

Several tentative, but very interesting patterns emerged. To a certain extent, Cordell's (1979) suggestion that the known distribution of Paleo-Indian remains is related to general patterns of erosion, statewide, seems well warranted. The Gallegos Wash area, the central Rio Grande and adjacent west mesa, the Plains of San Agustin, portions of the Estancia Basin and the Southeast Plains are all areas of substantial erosion and well-known localities of Paleo-Indian remains. It is therefore probably the case, that our general notions about the distribution of Paleo-Indian occupations have been more highly conditioned by post-depositional erosional process than had previously been suspected.

A second pattern has also emerged. Paleo-Indian remains have recently been recorded in some quantity along Cebolleta Mesa (Grants-Acoma area), to a lesser extent in the Gallup and Peach Springs area, in the Gallegos Wash area and, recently (Broster, personal communication) in modest quantities on the Jicarilla Indian Reservation. When these data are added to Judge's (1973) Rio Grande survey, it becomes obvious that the San Juan Basin is literally encircled (though the circle is yet incomplete) by Paleo-Indian remains. Characteristically, these localities are either near the base of, or on top of, major landforms. Additionally, many of these localities are being recorded at elevations (6,800-8,000 feet) not previously thought to be very rich in such materials. Third, the recent BIA surveys (Broster, personal communication) which have been recording many of these materials do not have the luxury of returning time and again to the same sample quadrat to record these Paleo-Indian materials, which are notably difficult to see (Judge 1973). Since numerous contracted archeological surveys in the same general areas of the Acoma and Jicarilla Reservations have not reported Paleo-Indian remains, we may assume the BIA surveys to be meticulous by contract archeology standards. Nonetheless, we may also assume that even the BIA surveys substantially understate the occurrence of Paleo-Indian remains when time/visibility constraints are considered.

To assume that the San Juan Basin was not much utilized during Paleo-Indian times appears to be an increasingly risky proposition. To be certain, the depositional context of some of these remains is questionable. That is to say that some materials may have been curated by later populations. Yet, it is equally possible that this is the case with many Paleo-Indian finds in southeastern New Mexico as well.

In Chapter VII, we tried to show graphically that Paleo-Indian materials are also found along major landforms in the Northeast Plains. More importantly, perhaps, these remains are generally found in areas also having later Apachean sites (tipi rings) where buffalo hunting is known to be the major means of subsistence. Though one may again raise the issue of secondary curation, the pattern of curation is at least consistent with basic large game hunting subsistence in both cases.

In Chapter III, we characterized the Paleo-Indian occupation as one in which buffalo *were pressed against the spine of the Rockies*. We should amplify that statement to characterize the basic Paleo-Indian hunting strategy as *pressing hunted game against the spine of any major landform*. In the San Juan Basin this strategy probably applied to deer and antelope more often than to buffalo. In southeastern New Mexico, game may also have been pursued along the Mescalero pediment.

It is almost certainly the case that we have not yet learned adequately to identify Paleo-Indian assemblages that do not occur in the hunting context, as has been suggested by Tainter (1980a) and Judge (in press).

There also appears to be a long term trend in Paleo-Indian point types toward both increased specialization and increasing diversity in point size. Judge has isolated a generalized (piercing and cutting functions) from a specialized (piercing) point series. It is clear that increasing specialization from Clovis-Folsom times is one general characteristic of the trends in lithic function. We point out that increasing specialization also involves increasing divergence among the size attributes of point types. We suggest that the Cody Complex involves both the greatest functional specialization and diversity in size attributes among tool types. The Paleo-Indian period terminates in general with succession to smaller point forms, and the entire nature of assemblage specialization increasingly shifts to classes of artifacts not considered points (that is, neither lances nor knives). Though the general pattern is fairly clear, the specific adaptive contexts of generalization as opposed to specialization are not yet known. Certainly they are knowable in the long term.

We ask, would additional survey along major landforms in southwestern New Mexico also turn up the Paleo-Indian remains as they are now known from the other three quadrants of the state? The suspicious scarcity (absence?) of Paleo-Indian materials from the west flank of the Sierra Blanca, Sacramento chain and the northern Tularosa Basin may, as we suggested in Chapter III, indicate a lesser degree of population compression as one moves away from the major highland land masses of Colorado-New Mexico. Of course, it may also be that bison had less access to the Tularosa Basin or that different erosional trends are at work. If, on the other hand, more Paleo-Indian remains are not eventually recorded in southwestern New Mexico, it would be surprising and perplexing. Just when the Paleo-Indian adaptations terminate is, in our minds, an open question. We question the alleged hiatus in occupation between the Cody Complex (roughly 6000 or 6500 B.C.) and the Jay period (roughly 5000 B.C.). Our suspicion is that early Jay and Cody materials are partially contemporaneous, though partly discontinuous geographically, while late Jay material (a.k.a. Bajada) more accurately represents the transition to an Archaic adaptation (perhaps 4000-5000 B.C.). Technological comparisons between accepted Paleo-Indian and Jay-Bajada materials are important areas for future research.

THE ARCHAIC
(5000 B.C. – 500 B.C. in some localities, A.D. 500 in others?)

The Archaic periods (roughly 5000 B.C. to the Christian era) are not nearly so well known from the adaptive standpoint as they ought to be. Archaic materials are not scarce, but the majority of suspected Archaic sites contain few diagnostic materials. Archaic assemblages are widespread throughout all altitude zones, but Judge (in press) has pointed out a concentration of these materials in the northeastern quadrant of the central San Juan Basin, an area where surprisingly few Puebloan remains have been recorded during recent surveys.

Many major problems remain in the interpretation of Archaic materials. The published *Oshara* sequence (Irwin-Williams 1973) has been widely cited, but can fairly be said to have raised as many questions as are supposed to have been answered. First, though often cited, there are few published data regarding evidence for the proposed chronology and subsistence attributes of each phase in the Oshara sequence. An entire generation of contract archeologists has tended to generalize from an archeological sequence in which the specific comparative data have neither been made widely available nor carefully reviewed. Since those data presumably would also include the specific assemblage attributes (reduction techniques, material types, edge angle analysis, etc.) which are known to have occurred with particular diagnostic point types, they should be made available to field investigators. We have still not learned to identify the specific temporal period of most Archaic sites from field survey when points are not located. Most do, however, assign a *middle to late* Archaic period to sites containing one-handed manos as a prominent feature of the assemblage.

Moreover, the Oshara terminology has tended to confuse readers who fail to recall that San Jose points and Pinto Basin points have a substantial classificatory overlap. The same is true of the Armijo point type and assemblages variously termed Lobo, Atrisco and Santa Ana. The transitional En Medio phase of the Oshara sequence is the BM-II period in other schemes. While these pseudonyms are presumably all well known to lithic specialists, they confused the senior author no end during the first months of this project. Perhaps a broader understanding of the period could be gained if the attributes of lithic assemblages were less often treated as *arcana principia*.

Nonetheless, several impressionistic statements can be made. Intriguingly, the Jay points (early and middle) are quite scarce in many areas when compared to the San Jose (Pinto Basin) types. Many Archaic remains co-occur with Paleo-Indian materials along the perimeters of basin areas, and in the San Juan Basin and Plains of San Agustin these are often found in the same settings (sometimes on the same sites, or localities) as the Paleo-Indian materials. Again the question of curation and secondary deposition arises, but it may be more to the point that, as with late Apachean sites, game hunting strategies might be similar.

Our reading of contract reports also suggests that proportionally more Archaic sites along major landforms and in higher elevations contain diagnostic points than do lithic scatters in many of the extensive dune settings. It may be that these two kinds of site locations reflect the collecting versus the hunting strategy, and are seasonally distinct assemblage sets of the same populations. In Chapter II we raised the point that successful intensification by some would make the continued pursuit of hunting strategies more possible by others. Since there is evidence both for and against the vegetative diversity hypothesis, this attribute of Archaic site selection may also vary with subsistence strategy. Again, are such assemblages the results merely of seasonal transhumance or are slightly heterogeneous subsistence traditions involved? Have we gone too far with the seasonality model? Contemporary ethnographic evidence suggests not, but we point out that there has been strong selective pressure on hunting-gathering populations in the last 10,000 years. To suppose that the survivors of this strategy have not had to modify land use to increase niche separation between themselves and more complex systems would be naive for any place in the world's mid latitudes.

Statewide, the distribution of Oshara and Cochise materials has been of substantial concern. The basic thesis underlying the Oshara tradition is that it represents an unbroken *in situ* development from early Archaic times into the Anasazi era, a development distinct from Archaic developments to the south and west (and perhaps east also — the Galisteo Basin). As Judge (in press) points out, the unbroken sequence from the Bajada to *San Jose* materials is not as well documented as it ought to be, considering the importance of the issue. The *San Jose* point materials appear to represent a very rapid and dramatic numerical increase over earlier Archaic periods in New Mexico.

It may be heresy, but we are increasingly suspicious of an unbroken, *in situ* developmental trajectory prior to the San Jose period (3000 B.C. — 1800 B.C. in the Oshara sequence). The *San Jose-Pinto Basin* point types represent a rather remarkable geographic distribution. Though we are *not* lithic experts, our untrained eyes see no difference between some points assigned to the Chiricahua phase (Cochise) from the Bat Cave excavations (Dick 1965) and *San Jose* points from the San Juan Basin. In fact, there are, to our eye, good *San Jose* points from the straits of Magellan sequence (see *Handbook of South American Indians*, Volume 1, Plate 10, bottom two rows; 6th plate following page 24)! With this kind of geographic distribution and time depth for at least those San Jose points which are also like Pinto Basin (perhaps 5 millenia throughout the geographic range — see Willey 1966:31, 57), how is it to be argued that the occurrence of such San Jose points bears at all on the cultural-linguistic or adaptive attributes that become distinctly Anasazi as opposed to Mogollon? Again, any case must be made on other assemblage attributes. Just when does the Oshara sequence become distinctive from the Cochise assemblages, and how would an ordinary survey crew be able to pinpoint those differences?

Until the enormous task of geographic plotting of known Archaic points by period is undertaken, and specific assemblage attributes are used to also plot, by phase, Archaic sites. having no diagnostic points, we will not know much more than we do now. Until survey crews prepare such data in their reports, such a program could not be undertaken for a wide region, in any case.

TERMINAL ARCHAIC — BM-II
(800 B.C. — A.D. 200+?)

It is clear that the Archaic traditions did not end simultaneously in all areas of New Mexico. There is little evidence for early sedentism in the Zuni highlands, the upper Rio Grande, the eastern chain of mountains extending from the Manzanos to near the Texas border and the eastern Plains. Whether this pattern is merely an appearance created by inadequate field investigation, or reflects the actual continuation of more mobile populations, is not yet known. Basketmaker II sites are often very ephemeral, even where structures are present. It would probably not be a drastic error to suppose some important distinctions between sites having fairly well formed storage pits or cists, but no habitation structures, and those that do have pithouses. While most scholars place primary emphasis on the first appearance of pithouse structures as indicating the degree of sedentism associated with the agricultural strategy, we are much more concerned with the appearance of storage facilities. We believe that well-formed storage facilities will provide the first consistent evidence (though indirect) of the potential for population disequilibrium that is outlined in Chapter II. It would be important to know whether sites having storage facilities, but lacking habitation structures, are always in areas where slightly later pithouse occupations occur.

The enormously developed storage facilities associated with the pithouses at Talus

Village near Durango, Colorado, again, suggest that such facilities are more highly diagnostic of a full agricultural transition than is the presence of ceramics. It is probably more important to date early storage facilities in the Mogollon and Anasazi regions, respectively, than to date ceramic occupations, if one wants to know whether the transition to agricultural dependency came earlier in one area than the other. What is curious is the inconsistent presence of storage facilities, ceramics and hearth features in pithouse occupations thought to be roughly contemporaneous and thought to represent the BM-II/BM-III transition. While some of this variability may be due simply to less attention on extramural test excavations in some regions, these variations are too common to be dismissed easily. Because of these differences, many propositions regarding seasonal use of late BM-II-early BM-III pithouses have appeared in the literature. However, the heavy labor investment in alleged summer season pithouses strikes us as hard to explain.

The temporality of the Archaic/BM-II shift is not at all clear. Recent excavations in the San Juan Basin (Harlan, personal communication) suggest a date as early as 800-900 B.C. for the BM-II period. In southwestern New Mexico, earlier San Pedro Cochise pithouses are known, though they are usually quite small. The evidence is not definitive, but maize may have appeared as much as a millenium earlier in southern New Mexico than in the north. For the moment, then, we are satisfied with our portrayal of an early agricultural strategy as fragile, sporadic, and determined by local population density. If the presence of substantial storage facilities was taken as the indicator of the Archaic/BM-II transition, we believe 500 B.C. would be a good round date in the western half of New Mexico for this transition.

In each area where BM-II occupations are notable (Chaco Canyon, Albuquerque area and its west mesa, Hueco Bolson, Durango, Colorado area; etc.) they are near, *but not in*, major mountainous areas. Most are near, but not immediately adjacent to, permanent streams (Durango area and Navajo Reservoir may be exceptions). We can discern no notable pattern of concentration on a given *general* soil type, or in areas of higher than average rainfall. A surprising number have a general exposure to the south and west, while many can also be characterized as having an open setting. Our sense of the matter is that these sites represent a temporal span, at the extreme, of about a millenium (800 B.C.?—A.D. 200?). Lack of sophistication in early site placement and changing climatic conditions undoubtedly create an overall data base that is dominated more by *noise* than by singular pattern. To this we add the cautions that many BM-II sites are probably identified as late Archaic in surface surveys, and that we have little evidence of a uniform move toward an agricultural strategy during BM-II times.

Since only about 200 of these sites in all are known, a major research effort to excavate and date more of them would be feasible. If, say, 50 were actually dated and clustered by setting attributes according to dates, a clearer pattern in adaptive shifts should emerge.

BM-III – "THE OLD PITHOUSE ADAPTATIONS" (A.D. 250-900) and P-I (A.D. 650/700-925?)

No, the above dates are not a typographical error. It is clear to us, even if to no one else, that many sites, identified from field survey as BM-III, completely overlap the P-I period, temporally, and may partly overlap the *very earliest* P-II.

About A.D. 250 the late BM-II pattern begins to expand rapidly. Small villages appear widely throughout the western half of the state. They may also occur to the east of the west flank of the central mountain chain, but the evidence is so far unconvincing. The vast majority of the earlier sites are along permanent streams. Between A.D. 250 and 500, the archeological attributes of BM-III become well-distributed in each of the general localities where sedentary occupation continues. These characteristics are: well-formed pithouses, fairly consistent presence of ceramics and introduction of the small points associated with the bow and arrow.

The Basketmaker III period is interesting in several respects. Throughout its history there are several major periods of florescence, and several significant shifts in settlement pattern. The first really major episode of notable village organization seems to occur between about A.D. 350 or 400 and about A.D. 550 or 600. In many areas of the state, villages of the A.D. 400-500 period are as large, or larger, than succeeding occupations *in the same specific locale*. Most of these early Basketmaker villages are small, but a few are sizeable (over 20 pithouses). Most of these occupations are in upland settings. In areas where basin floors run 4,000-5,000 feet in elevation (west central and southern New Mexico), these sites tend to cluster at roughly 6,000 feet (Pine Lawn Valley, for example). In northern New Mexico, where basin floors tend to be between 5,000-6,000 feet in elevation, these tend to cluster around 6,500+ feet (Chaco Canyon environs and Tohatchi environs are examples). From southern New Mexico to northern New Mexico there appears to be about a one hundred year temporal gradient in the occurrence of *larger* villages. Let us suggest roughly A.D. 450 in the south and perhaps A.D. 550 in the north.

In southern New Mexico, the A.D. 500-700 period (Martin and Plog 1973) is thought to represent an occupational hiatus in the Pine Lawn/Reserve district, while it is denied in the Mimbres (LeBlanc 1979). If there is a similar dislocation in northern New Mexico, it is not prominently discussed in the literature.

Somewhere between A.D. 550 and 650, the painted ceramics become fairly widespread (La Plata B/W and White Mound in the north; San Francisco Red and Mogollon R/B in the south) but do not occur on many sites of the period (they are not often found on the smallest). The P-I period in northern and north central New Mexico is usually noted on survey forms when Kana'a neck-banded wares are found. When painted wares are found with these, and surface storage units (slab-lined cists or jacals) are also found in association with pithouses, the P-I designation is almost certain. When the pithouses are deep, or prominent, depressions, and the proportion of painted wares is small and the Kana'a scarce (that is, there are few neck sherds to distinguish it from the Lino Gray) either a BM-III or BM-III/P-I transitional classification is made. These *BM-III/P-I* sites are usually small, occur often in areas where no large *Classic* BM-III villages are present and, most importantly, are in lower elevational settings (roughly 5,000-5,500 feet), often riverine (Recently surveyed sites in the lower Puerco drainage come to mind; see Wimberly and Eidenbach 1980. So do sites in the upper Rio Grande; see Chapter III). Ceramic assemblages on these are often modest, and pithouses often discernible only from surface stains. Allan (1975) describes several such sites in the Corrales area near Albuquerque. This trend may account for the scarcity of Georgetown phase occupation in the Reserve area (Mogollon). Perhaps this period is A.D. 550 or 600 — ca. A.D. 700 throughout western New Mexico and bears directly on Martin and Plog's (1973) suggestion of population decline. Perhaps population decline is a feature of the higher elevations.

Shortly after A.D. 750 there is, apparently, a second episode of village aggregation (Alkali Ridge and White Mound Village would be well known examples). This period would correspond to the Piedra phase at Mesa Verde (A.D. 700-900); the San Francisco phase in the Mogollon area, and the Kiatuthlanna phase in the Cebolleta Mesa area (A.D. 800-870), and the late Rosa phase at Navajo Reservoir. These are all full P-I phases (temporally), and they are primarily in relative upland settings — 6,000 to 7,000 feet. That is, they are characterized by the continued presence of at least some relatively deep pithouses during a period of alleged transition to surface construction.

This period terminates with the Ackmen phase at Mesa Verde (A.D. 900-1000), the Three Circle phase in the Mimbres (A.D. 850-975), the Piedra phase in Navajo Reservoir (roughly A.D. 850-950) and near the beginning of the Red Mesa phase (A.D. 870-900?) in the Acoma Culture area. The final surge in village size in these upland areas can be rather narrowly dated as an episode beginning about A.D. 850 and terminating by roughly A.D. 950 throughout New Mexico. This period properly marks the end of the pithouse *village* adaptations until the A.D. 1100's, irrespective of cultural district. In each of these areas, the terminal pithouse occupations are constructed very shallowly, the trend toward surface units being pronounced.

In summary, many BM-III sites cannot be distinguished from P-I during survey. The temporal range of the larger pithouse village adaptations spans the period from about A.D. 350-950. We see three episodes of *upland* village aggregation which, though not simultaneous throughout the western half of the state, nonetheless cluster broadly around A.D. 500, 750 and 850. The final episode of pithouse village construction about A.D. 850 is primarily one of very shallow pitrooms. We strongly suspect, but cannot yet formally confirm, a short constructional hiatus about A.D. 775 to 825 or 850 in these upland villages. At this point we can appeal only to the hiatus in construction dates in the Mimbres area from A.D. 750-850, that separates the San Francisco from Three Circle construction. These dates are from just a few sites. We present them as a plausible support, rather than as definitive.

In the *lower* elevations, the BM-III/P-I adaptations move into the early P-II period while the terminal upland building episodes take place (A.D. 850-900). We specifically suggest that the variance in BM-III/P-I architectural forms has more to do with buffering the effects of changing climate and elevation, than with any other *cultural* factors. Since many of the smaller sites appear to have only plainwares, while others also contain only miniscule quantities of painted wares that have, generally, long temporal spans, temporal control over BM-III/P-I sites from surface survey is often no better than half a millenium. We further predict that small sites, fairly deep (half meter?) pithouses, few surface structures and "BM-III" ceramic assemblages (let us say, for example, Lino Gray with either no painted wares or a few sherds of La Plata B/W) will eventually be excavated and found to date (C-14, dendro, archeomagnetic) to roughly A.D. 900. A certain degree of economic isolation and a fairly cold local setting (higher elevation, perhaps 6,500 feet, or northern exposure) are all that would be required to produce such a site.

In patterns of ceramic trade, the pithouse adaptations can be characterized as primarily an extensive upland/highland trade network. San Francisco Red ceramics, for instance, are widely traded throughout upland areas, except in the colder portions of the Rio Grande. Somewhere about A.D. 700-800 there also seems to be an episode of increasing trade between upland and basin areas.

In central and northern New Mexico, the BM-III and P-I stages of the Pecos classification need to be rethought, particularly as they are applied to surface survey. In southern New Mexico, more smaller sites need to be excavated to refine Mimbres/Mogollon chronology (see Chapter V).

P-II – "THE BASIN CLASSIC"
(A.D. 850 or 900 – 1140)

The late P-I, early P-II transition first took place in the drier basin settings in northern and west central New Mexico. Early P-II sites are characterized primarily by small roomblocks of above ground masonry architecture, metates having more grinding surface, and the introduction of pottery types such as Red Mesa B/W. In the Mimbres area, the transition to surface architecture is alleged not to have taken place until roughly A.D. 1000. This is a major distinction between the Mimbres area and the Anasazi region. Nonetheless, few very small Mimbres sites have been excavated anywhere, and practically none have been investigated that occur in the lower, more desertic settings of Hidalgo and Luna counties. We think the occurrence of jacal or adobe/cobble sites in such settings is still very much an open question. Such sites might now be reduced to large sherd scatters having Boldface B/W (perhaps also Three Circle R/W and San Francisco Red) and plainwares which included the Three Circle neck corrugated. The P-II time period in the Mimbres area includes the later Three Circle phase, the Mangus and the Classic Mimbres.

The P-II period represents several major shifts in settlement pattern. The earliest of these shifts is also contemporaneous with the final episode of pithouse architecture that we mentioned previously. Somewhere about A.D. 900 there is an initial upstream shift of riverine sites in many areas of the state. This has been noted in the Navajo Reservoir as settlement (Arboles phase) shifting upstream out of the Reservoir. The same phenomenon has been noted at about A.D. 900 in the Chuska Valley area (Peckham and Wilson, n.d.); and in the Sierra Blanca area (Early Glencoe phase). It is almost certainly the case in the Mimbres/Reserve areas. Wheat (1955) suggests dates for transition to the Three Circle phase in the Reserve area as A.D. 927 at Starkweather Ruin and A.D. 908 at Mogollon Village (see also discussion in Breternitz 1966:46). Thus, there appears to be a slight temporal gradient in Three Circle type ceramics and in construction between the middle Mimbres Valley (5,200 feet) and the Reserve area (about 6,100 feet) of 30-50 years. This, coupled with the suspected Mangus/Nantack phase dispersal (which was discussed in detail in Chapter V) leads us to characterize the P-I/P-II transition as a period of substantial settlement shifts — the first of these being a rapid, short, upstream (therefore uphill) dispersal.

By about A.D. 950 in many areas, and A.D. 1000 in nearly all areas, the upstream/uphill trend broke, and the essential characteristic of the P-II period emerged. At this time there was a major downhill shift in settlement, followed by increasing dispersal throughout the western basins. This dispersal spilled over into the eastern plains. Thus, this settlement shift was both rapid and forceful. It has been noted in the late Ackman and Mancos phases at Mesa Verde and the late Red Mesa and early Cebolleta phases in the Acoma culture area (about A.D. 925-1000). It is further confirmed by confinement of Classic Mimbres site development to below 6,000 feet, as a rule, and by the ensuing movement into the more desertic situations of the lower Mimbres drainage (Deming Plain).

Kelley's statement that the Lincoln phase started first in the lower elevations suggests that this basin shift also occurred on the east flank of Sierra Blanca. This basin floor movement is also confirmed for the Tularosa Basin (Wimberly and Rogers 1977). The elevation data presented in Chapters III and VII (Upper Rio Grande and Northeast Plains) also support the case, particularly for early to middle P-II sites. The near absence of "P-I" sites above 6,500 feet in the Cimarron area is notable. Though occupations are not confined entirely to the lower, drier, basin settings, at this time the primary focus of P-II occupation develops there.

By about A.D. 1050, dispersal was near its maximum, and substantial complexity in trade networks and local population aggregations is apparent. While a few pithouses are noted with very early "P-II" sites, the number of pithouses constructed between A.D. 950 and 1100 must be very few (the Flagstaff area in Arizona may be an exception after A.D. 1050-1075). Occupation in highland areas is notoriously hard to document for this period. Though many archeologists seem to be set against accepting a local occupational hiatus, there is little evidence for sedentary communities in many highland areas at this time. The Rosa-Piedra sequence in the Navajo Reservoir-Cuba area shows a general hiatus until Gallina occupation around A.D. 1100. The population at Mesa Verde (Wetherill Mesa) is lowest during the late P-II period (McElmo phase). There is an occupational hiatus at El Morro from roughly A.D. 950 or 1000 to perhaps A.D. 1250 (see Chapter IV). Finally, as a general architectural characteristic, P-II period room size (including Three Circle pithouses) declines from earlier Basketmaker periods.

By very late in the period (about A.D. 1100), there had already been substantial expansion into the Galisteo Basin and outward from the east slope of the Sangre de Cristos. In the

PUEBLO II EXPANSION
IN BLACK-ON-WHITE
CERAMIC DISTRIBUTION
Map X.2

San Juan Basin

Chaco II

Red Mesa B/W
Chaco II wares

Red Mesa B/W

Reserve B/W

Reserve/Gallup B/W

Reserve

Quemado

Mimbres B/W

Mimbres B/W

Mimbres B/W

Mimbres

miles
0   20   40

(after Raisz, Landforms of the United States)

south, there was expansion throughout the basin floors of the Jornada region, at least to the valley of the Pecos.

By A.D. 1100 an enormous, and extremely fragile, complexity was sustained as the Chacoan network assumed its final form. Though the economic and demographic network which underlay Chacoan development began to emerge at important agricultural localities as early as A.D. 900 or 950, the system assumed its ultimate complexity somewhere between A.D. 1080 and 1120. Perhaps this terminal complexity was, in part, induced by an already overstressed system. Systems of lesser complexity developed to the south (Mimbres, Reserve, etc.) and southeast.

The P-II development ended rapidly, the Classic Mimbres area, the San Juan Basin and the lower elevations of Socorro County being largely abandoned some time in the early A.D. 1100's. Many scholars have also suggested a temporary retreat from tentative Puebloan and Mogollon incursion into the west flank of the plains. It seems quite reasonable to accept such characterizations as accurate for the mid 12th century. No substantial agriculturally-based systems are yet documented as having reoccupied any of the major basin floors again. In southern New Mexico the subsistence basis for many allegedly later basin occupations is not well known, and chronology for both the post Mimbres and late Chacoan periods is scantily documented. The picture we now have of post P-II basin occupations may undergo substantial revision in the years ahead.

Economic patterns clearly illustrate the major shift in settlement during the P-II period. During the initial P-II transition there is dramatically increased trade in ceramic materials and in exotic goods of many kinds. There is, first, rapid development in ceramic styles in areas bordering the upland perimeters of basin areas. This is followed by a rapid extension of economic networks into the basins themselves. By the middle of the period (A.D. 1000) it appears that major adjustments in trading patterns had begun to take place. In the San Juan Basin, changing frequencies of ceramics from the Red Mesa Valley and the Chuska Valley come to mind. Late in the period there is a final major episode of changing production centers for ceramics, and the locus of economic activity again moves to the basin margins.

It is notable that only a moderate percentage of the ceramics occurring at Chaco Canyon between A.D. 900 and 1140 were made there. Imports came from production centers at the basin periphery (excluding, largely, the eastern periphery), but these centers shifted notably from the south to the west by the end of the period (Warren, n.d.).

Since temper and trace element analysis of ceramics to identify production centers has been conducted for relatively few major localities in New Mexico, the case is not so well known for P-II occupations outside the San Juan Basin.

Apparently substantial mixing between the economic networks of San Juan Basin and the Quemado-Reserve-Cebolleta Mesa margins of the San Agustin Plains occurred. The stylistic overlap between Gallup B/W and Reserve B/W is notable. The Gallup (Puerco of the west) and Zuni areas (Zuni-Pescado drainages) seem to have been both important economic nodes and continuous sources of interchange from at least sometime in the late P-I period onward. While a number of the denser and more durable P-II population centers were in localities having permanent streams, the bulk of P-II occupation was not similarly located.

There is another notable consequence of the downhill shift during P-II times. Populations which had earlier commingled in the old upland Basketmaker village settings were increasingly separated into adjacent basin systems. Thus, the Mimbres populations were increasingly isolated from those in the Pine Lawn-Reserve areas to the north. This led, of course, to increasingly heterogeneous traditions. We suspect the same for populations in the Rio Puerco

414

and Rio Grande corridor and those in the San Juan Basin, but the evidence is unclear now. This same heterogeneity increased for populations on the north and south slopes of the Zuni highlands (including Cebolleta Mesa). It is the case, then, that each regional system was focused on a major basin area. Populations from widely dispersed highland localities mingled in the basin interaction systems, creating a new mixture of trade and material characteristics, and a source of speculation for archeologists about the nature of interacting economic and demographic systems. Just as many archeologists doubt linguistic and genetic uniformity in the Anasazi/Mogollon contact zone of west central New Mexico, so do we also doubt it for the San Juan Basin. The Mimbres area may have enjoyed more internal homogeneity, if one accepts LeBlanc's (1979) view. Not all do.

The P-II period is notable for strong dependence on relatively large-cobbed corn and very small animals. This latter pattern is striking. Jelinek (1967) makes much of faunal remains including rabbit, jackrabbit, rodents and turtle spp. in the Middle Pecos Valley. LeBlanc (1979) notes that rabbit, gopher, and small bird species dominate faunal assemblages in the Classic Mimbres sites. Few excavation reports of P-II sites in the San Juan Basin indicate significant numbers of large game animals. This use of small species is a hallmark of most P-II basin faunal assemblages, and is useful as a basic diagnostic trait for the period.

The P-II period closes at A.D. 1140. We have chosen this date because Breternitz's data (1966:57) suggest a suspicious (and convenient) unconformity in dated archeological sites between A.D. 1140 and 1160 or 1165. In fact, the shift away from the basin adaptations begins about A.D. 1100 (Windes 1977). We characterize the Pueblo II period throughout the western two-thirds of New Mexico as *The Basin Classic*, since we feel that this is appropriate descriptively and adaptively, whatever the ethnic/linguistic affiliations of the participating populations.

P-III – "THE LITTLE HIGHLAND CLASSIC"
(A.D. 1125 or 1150 – 1290 or 1300?)

The Pueblo III period throughout New Mexico is enormously complex. While we do not pretend to understand this complexity in its entirety, there are nonetheless several patterns which have clearly emerged. Following the decline of the Chacoan system in the San Juan Basin, the Reserve phase in west central New Mexico and the Classic Mimbres in southwestern New Mexico, there is a rapid shift in settlement away from these basin areas. In general, the direction of movement in P-III settlement is into highland areas. We will discuss this more fully in a moment. The period is notable in other ways, for while there are few very large sites of the period until quite late (that is, in the late A.D. 1200's), there is also a tendency for site size to cluster around 10 to 15 rooms, unlike the previous P-II period. In general, room size increases statewide. In the Animas phase of southwestern New Mexico, room size increases dramatically over that of the Classic Mimbres period. In the upper Rio Grande we note that room size also increases from that of the smaller or Hosta Butte phase sites of the P-II period in the San Juan Basin. An exception to this trend toward increasing room size is discernible in the Mesa Verde reoccupation at a few of the larger Chacoan sites in the San Juan Basin. This reoccupation can be dated around A.D. 1250. In those large Chacoan sites which were characterized by relatively large room size for the period, the Mesa Verdean tendency is to divide these into smaller living units during the period of reoccupation.

During this period there is also a notable increase in architectural variety throughout the state. We again see the introduction of pithouse forms and increasing use of adobe architecture, sometimes alongside masonry construction. This increasing architectural variability, particularly that noted in kiva construction, has, of course, contributed substantially to speculations regarding the identity of historically known Puebloan populations. In general, the use of adobe as opposed to masonry seems to have a great deal to do with the local availability of materials with site setting. That is, there are relatively few adobe constructions in the wetter areas of P-III occupation. Nonetheless, throughout the areas of P-III occupation, there can be found increasing adobe construction near the terminus of the period as appears to also have been the case for the late P-II period. The P-III period can be characterized as one of intensified population shifts. The general sequence of events during the P-III period is somewhat obscure. It will be discussed briefly below.

The most notable harbinger of P-III occupation is the reintroduction of pithouse construction throughout the highlands of New Mexico. The pithouse occupations of the Gallinas highlands are numerous, notable and often cited in the literature. These have been dated from shortly after A.D. 1100 to roughly A.D. 1200. In the Sierra Blanca area, the late pithouse occupation is known as the late Glencoe phase. In the Reserve area of west central New Mexico, this pithouse occupation is known as the Apache Creek phase. While pithouse occupations in some other areas of New Mexico seem to be more limited, they are nonetheless common in the upper Rio Grande. Some are known in the Mesa Verde region. There is also a well known pithouse occupation in the Flagstaff area at roughly this period.

In each of these areas, pithouse construction is closely followed by the resurgence of above-ground masonry architecture. In the Sierra Blanca region, the masonry construction is known as the Lincoln phase. In the Reserve-Pine Lawn district, late masonry occupations were generally attributed to the Tularosa phase. In the upper Rio Grande, the masonry architecture is associated with the development of Santa Fe B/W. The precise temporal relationships between pithouse architecture and masonry construction in each of these areas remains a subject of speculation. In general, however, it seems clear that the pithouse forms generally precede masonry forms in each region. In several areas, however, the above-ground masonry construction seems to follow pithouse construction closely. In fact some pithouses and some surface units may have been occupied simultaneously in many areas of highland New Mexico.

Following the development of surface architecture in the highland areas, there is a relatively rapid population aggregation, and site size increases. The increase is most notable at the very terminus of the P-III period, and also involves a downhill shift in population. In areas such as the Galisteo Basin and Marianna Mesa, excavated sites indicate that occupations during this period are short and that construction is episodal. Both in the Galisteo Basin and at Marianna Mesa there seems to be a pattern involving three construction episodes. Whether this pattern is also documentable elsewhere is not yet known.

Major shifts in elevation are a common theme in the literature. At Mesa Verde, the Mesa Verde phase (A.D. 1150-1300) displays a threefold increase in the number of sites over the preceding McElmo phase. At this time there are probably more sites, and there are more rooms at Mesa Verde (that is, Wetherill Mesa), than at any other period. Nonetheless, Hayes (1964) feels that population is not quite so high as in earlier periods. In the upper Rio Grande, elevation data presented in Chapter III clearly indicates a striking tendency to occupation in the higher, wetter ecological zones. This same pattern is also suggested by the data on the Northeast plains, which appears in Chapter VII, though, in this case, the samples are too small for the case to be definitive. In the Zuni area (Marshall, n.d.), there is a clear move to higher elevations east of the Pescado drainage. From gross ceramic data, this seems to occur somewhere between A.D. 1150 and 1250. In the El Morro area (7,000 feet), there is a dramatic increase in population at about A.D. 1250. This occupation is known as the Scribe S Phase, and follows a roughly 200-year period of occupational hiatus in that upland locality. In the Gila Forest, the occupation in higher elevations is dense and notable. In the Acoma Culture area, Dittert (1959) notes that during the late Cebolleta phase around A.D. 1100, there is intense occupation of mountain meadows. In the following Pilares phase (A.D. 1100-1200), there is first less settlement in higher topographic divisions, followed by a shift to the higher flat-topped mesas at the end of the phase (that is, about A.D. 1150-1200). In the succeeding

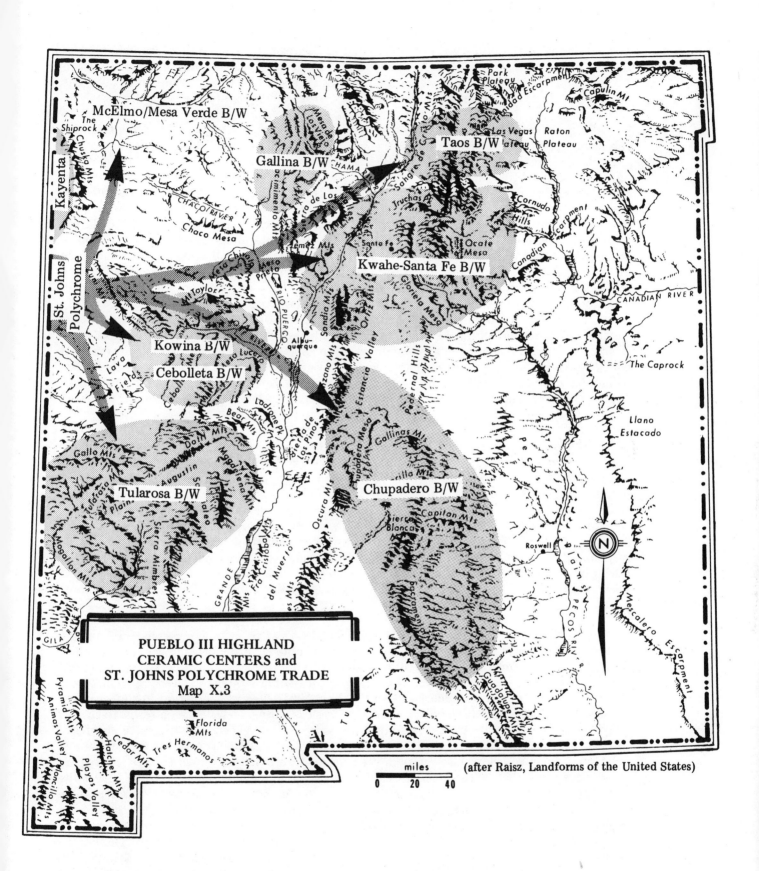

McElmo/Mesa Verde B/W

Kayenta

St. Johns Polychrome

Gallina B/W

Taos B/W

Kwahe-Santa Fe B/W

Kowina B/W

Cebolleta B/W

Tularosa B/W

Chupadero B/W

PUEBLO III HIGHLAND
CERAMIC CENTERS and
ST. JOHNS POLYCHROME TRADE
Map X.3

miles
0   20   40

(after Raisz, Landforms of the United States)

417

Kowina phase (A.D. 1200-1400), population first aggregated in large sites on high mesa or woodlands. It is irrefutably clear from thousands of site survey forms that the general pattern throughout New Mexico is one of shift to the highlands between A.D. 1100 and 1300. The specific pattern of settlement shift in each area, however, is very confusing.

In the Sierra Blanca area, few dated sites are known, so the picture is one of general uphill movement followed by downhill movement at roughly A.D. 1300. The same pattern seems demonstrable for the Chupadero Mesa area. In the upper Rio Grande we have noted a suspicious lack of tree-ring dates at roughly A.D. 1200. This suggests, but does not confirm, a temporary occupational hiatus in the middle of the P-III period. It is also notable that the Mesa Verdean reoccupation of the San Juan Basin involves a shift away from the wetter portions of Wetherill Mesa to the drier basin areas at sometime around A.D. 1200-1250. In the Acoma Culture area, it is clear that between the late Cebolleta phase and the earlier portion of the Kowina phase there is first an uphill shift, followed by a downhill shift, and followed again by reoccupation in the highest elevations. The pattern of settlement shift remains unclear in the Reserve area. Rice (1979) has noted that the late Tularosa phase occupation is lower in elevation than that of the preceding Reserve phase. The Reserve phase is dated very roughly from A.D. 1000 to approximately A.D. 1150. It is not clear to us at all whether the intense Reserve phase occupation in the Gila Forest and adjacent areas is from the earlier portion of this phase or from the later, and a ceramic seriation and additional excavation in the area must be undertaken. Our judgment is that future excavation of Reserve phase sites in the higher elevations will provide dates either very early or very late (that is, A.D. 975-1000 or A.D. 1125-1150) with few verified dates falling in between, these latter being constructed primarily in the lower margins of the San Agustin Plain during the A.D. 1000-1100 period.

We conclude, then, that the general P-III pattern of settlement shift involves a rapid uphill move between roughly A.D. 1125-50 and A.D. 1200, followed by a downhill trend from about A.D. 1275 to 1300. The specific pattern in several areas, however, seems to involve an uphill shift, followed by a hiatus in occupation in the highest elevations somewhere between A.D. 1200 to 1250, followed again by reoccupation in the higher elevations, and then rapid abandonment and movement again into the lower areas. There is currently a great deal of speculation about the P-III period as a refugee phenomenon in the higher elevations. This response in settlement shift is thought to be associated with drought conditions sometime during the 13th century. We are not convinced that this is the entire story. If it, indeed, became warmer and drier, as these studies suggest, why the labor investment in deep pithouse occupations at roughly A.D. 1150-1200?

The P-III period seems to represent a general retreat from major dependence on agriculture. In the Sierra Blanca area, Kelley (1966) has noted, both in assemblages and in faunal remains, evidence for a high degree of dependence on hunting and collecting. In the upper Rio Grande the case is less clear. In the Gallina area, substantial remains of deer are found, as in Sierra Blanca. The preponderance of deer in the Animas sites of the period in southwestern New Mexico is also notable when compared to Classic Mimbres subsistence patterns. In each of these areas, the generally high elevations (the Animas is an exception) suggest a shortened growing season, and it is for this reason that a number of scholars have suggested warmer, drier conditions which, in essence, permitted occupation based on an agricultural strategy at these elevations. That is, the growing season is thought to have lengthened. While this is possible, we have noted that in each area of the state, corn excavated from sites of this period has been characterized as either primitive (Chapalote-like) or immature. We have specifically suggested that the growing season may not have lengthened. Rather, a renewed dependence on specialized corn varieties, requiring a short growing season, may have occurred. Though the Animas sites excavated by McCluney (1962) are not in notably high elevations, it is important that corn there was also found to be, in many cases, "immature". More to the point, it would appear that several varieties of corn were carefully curated in different room units. This also seems to be the case in sites excavated at Marianna Mesa (McGimsey 1980). This indicates to us that caution was required to prevent the mixing of corn varieties which might quickly lose important adaptive qualities through careless cross-pollination. Why would one separately curate "stunted" corn for seed? The case for other areas is not so clear, but this pattern of careful curation of substantially different varieties of corn should attract more attention in excavation of sites from the P-III period.

In general, there seems to be a retrogression in the P-III period to much greater dependence upon hunting and collecting. We note that under such circumstances, populations would require substantially greater subsistence space than under intensive, highly productive agricultural strategies. It is perhaps for this reason that we also find so much evidence for *defensive* site location during this period, and the side effects of competition (violent deaths and burned structures or complete assemblages abandoned in place), whether interregionally or locally.

Patterns of ceramic trade tell the P-III story. Following the decline of the basin systems, we see a rapid transition to new ceramic styles. In the western highlands these are, from north to south, McElmo B/W (Mesa Verde variety), followed by Mesa Verde B/W at Wetherill Mesa, Cebolleta B/W, Kowina B/W in the Acoma Culture area and Tularosa B/W in the Reserve-Pine Lawn districts of west central New Mexico. In the eastern highlands, Taos B/W develops in the far north. In the Gallina highlands we see the development of Gallina B/W. In the Pajarito and Santa Fe districts we see the development first of Kwahee B/W (which may be P-II), followed by the more distinctive Santa Fe B/W. In the Chupadero Mesa and Sierra Blanca regions we see the development of Chupadero B/W. In every major highland area of New Mexico, then, we see the development at this time of either restyled or new ceramic styles in Black-on-White pottery. These western and eastern styles are widely traded up and down the eastern and western mountainous spines and adjacent foothills, respectively. We consider these, or conceive of these, as the two supports of a substantial economic ladder. The rungs of this ladder are formed by trading in such specialized items as St. Johns Polychrome bowls. Since the St. Johns Polychrome and several other similar specialized tradewares are little found in the intervening basin areas during the period (see Chapter IV for data from 1,300 sites), it is the eastern and western highland masses which are connected in trade during this period. The point is that a great and expansive highland trade network replaces the previous basin interaction patterns.

In general, then, we may characterize the P-III period statewide as one which also involves substantial economic and demographic shift to the highland areas and renewed pithouse construction, either contemporaneous with or followed closely by, surface unit construction. There is also a complex pattern of continual population movement throughout the period, and these shifts seem everywhere to involve major adjustments to altitudinal differences. The late P-III period involves substantial reaggregation into large communities, and at the same time an increasing tendency to downhill resettlement. Lastly, the complex highland trade pattern re-emerges late in the period, though the earlier portion of the P-III period was characterized by relative isolation in trade patterns. This isolation characterizes the Gallina occupation. It is also characteristic of the Pilares phase in the Acoma district, and may also be characteristic of the early Santa Fe B/W sites in the Pajarito Plateau. Because of the absence of Tularosa B/W from the Apache Creek pithouse sites, it also appears to be a feature of certain occupations in west central New Mexico. There is increasing evidence that this is also the case in the Sierra Blanca district.

For these reasons it is best to consider the P-III period as composed of two subphases. The first of these involves a dramatic uphill settlement shift between A.D. 1100-1200, the resurgence of pithouse architecture, relative isolation in trade statewide, and a notable resurgence in hunting and gathering subsistence strategies, coupled with the use of "primitive" corn varieties. The second of these involves a shift from highland to increasingly lowland and riverine settlements between A.D. 1200-1300, increasing village size, the resurgence of substantial masonry architecture and perhaps also the resurgence of dependence on maize agriculture at the very end of the period. This later phase, or downhill phase, of the P-III period is also that which sees the development of the great highland trade network. For these reasons, we have characterized the P-III period as the Little Highland Classic. It is in fact a period divided by two distinctive adaptive subphases. The A.D. 1200-1250 period is not yet well known. A plausible but speculative explanation for this pattern was offered in the Jornada section of Chapter V, and involves a shift in rainfall seasonality. For the moment, then, let us turn to the P-IV period.

P-IV, "THE RIVERINE PERIOD"
(A.D. 1300–1540)

The Pueblo IV period is traditionally considered to begin at around A.D. 1300, with the introduction of Rio Grande Glazes such as Los Padillas and Glaze A. It is a time when one also sees the introduction of Pinedale and Heshotauthla Polychromes. In fact, it is difficult to separate the terminal P-III from early P-IV occupations in several areas of New Mexico. This is particularly so in the upper Rio Grande, where the P-IV period is usually referred to as the Rio Grande Classic. In actuality, the trends culminating in P-IV adaptation start in most areas of New Mexico roughly at A.D. 1275. It is the termination of occupation in the higher, wetter woodland settings that signals the first onset of a new kind of adaptation. In general, the P-IV period can be characterized as one of riverine site setting for Puebloan occupations. Nonetheless, there are several other and major adaptive themes that emerge during this time. In the Hopi area (which is not in New Mexico), there develops a mixed strategy for agriculture which involves both wet and dry farming techniques. In the eastern plains it would appear that adaptation to buffalo hunting intensifies. For these "plains" occupations, even those which are characterized by late pithouse or small masonry and/or adobe unit constructions, it is not adequately known whether, in fact, actual Anasazi and Mogollon populations are involved. Let us consider each of these adaptations in turn.

The P-IV period sees a substantial readjustment in site setting for nearly all of the puebloan occupations, and those sites which occur early in this period are exclusively, or almost exclusively, in riverine settings[1]. While some occupation appears to occur along secondary streams, there is rather little occupational permanence except along perennial water courses. Occupation along the Rio Grande and its upper tributaries, that is, north of Albuquerque, appears to be heavy. To the west, the occupations in the Acoma area, which lead to the historic Acoma Pueblo along the Rio San Jose, are established. Further west yet than Acoma, there is substantial settlement along the Rio Pescado drainage in the Zuni area. There is apparently also occupation in the lower Rio Grande, but the facts are less clear for that region, since survey has been so limited along the lower Rio Grande itself.

In the eastern portions of New Mexico there is some late occupation in the Pecos drainage and in the Canadian drainage, but again, the data are limited when compared to other regions of New Mexico, and the actual subsistence base of these populations is not yet clearly understood. In southwestern New Mexico, in the former Classic Mimbres area, there is a modest Saladoan occupation in the upper Mimbres drainage which is not well documented, and a better documented occupation in the Cliff area of the Gila drainage. To the west, towards Arizona, this is the period of intense Saladoan occupation in the riverine settings of the Rio Salado and its tributaries.

Where archeologists have defined geographically localized *classic periods* throughout the Southwest, these are invariably along the major river settings at this time. There is also some P-IV occupation along the lower Puerco of the east, but it seems not to have endured for a long time. What we do not know is the specific situation along major portions of the San Juan

1 There is a second episode of upland settlement in several areas during the late P-IV period.

River, for the canyon country along the San Juan has not been adequately surveyed. Thus, there may well be an early P-IV occupation in the area, but it is not well recorded. Both logic and data obtained from the San Juan Data Base suggest that there is some occupation along the San Juan River in the early A.D. 1300's, but its extent, as we have said, is not known, and if there was such an occupation following the move out of the elevated portions of the Mesa Verde area, it may not have endured any length of time there, either. Additional survey along the San Juan River in the Four Corners district is a pressing need. We need to determine whether Mesa Verdean reoccupation of the San Juan Basin was a feature of the early to mid or late A.D. 1200's, or all three episodally.

In the upper Rio Grande, specifically the Santa Fe district, the period is characterized by substantial aggregation quite early into very large unit pueblos, often over 100 rooms in size and occasionally up to 500 rooms in size. It is notable, however, that the settlement pattern for the period suggests a rather remarkable differentiation between large and small sites. That is, the tendency in a given area is for one or two large unit pueblos to be surrounded throughout the locality by many one or two room so-called *fieldhouses*. It is also characteristic of the P-IV in the Rio Grande for room size to drop substantially from that of the preceding P-III period. We note, however, that this is not uniformly the case elsewhere in New Mexico.

The Saladoan occupation of southwestern New Mexico evidences both substantial increase in room size and remarkable uniformity in room size. The Saladoan occupations are characterized in the literature as consisting of thick-walled, massive adobe construction. These pueblos or "great houses" are usually enclosed compounds. Though a few small Saladoan sites are known, their characteristics seem not to have been much considered in the literature. It is also quite possible that the pattern of settlement with Saladoan occupations is for one or two large compound houses in a given area to be surrounded by many smaller, ephemeral farmsteads. This has been tentatively suggested (Martin and Plog 1973) but not adequately confirmed. Thus, it may be that the large room size which characterizes the Saladoan occupations of southwestern New Mexico (and Arizona) pertains only to the massive masonry construction. For this reason, our impressions may not be accurate for comparative purposes.

At this time, many previously occupied regions in New Mexico seem to have been vacated, many of them permanently. There is no further substantial occupation in the Mesa Verdean area. Most of the higher elevations of the upper Rio Grande, such as the Pajarito Plateau, are vacated. The El Morro area and most of Cebolleta Mesa area is permanently vacated, as are the forest areas in the Reserve-Pine Lawn districts. There is little evidence for occupation in the higher elevations of the Mimbres district. Further, there appears to be some occupation in the basin areas of southwestern New Mexico and the Tularosa Basin. These are suggested by the presence of many ceramic scatters in desertic areas which contain El Paso Polychrome, Ramos Polychrome, and the like. These alleged late occupations in the southern basins are nowhere adequately dated; rather, they are presumed to last as long as the final occupation, perhaps longer, of Casas Grandes in Chihuahua. Casas Grandes is said to have declined in the A.D. 1340's.

Whatever basin occupation may have existed at the onset of the P-IV period, it was quickly extinguished. For it is the case that few sites, grossly dated from either ceramics or other means of cross-dating, can be attributed to a period which postdates A.D. 1350 throughout the southern tier of New Mexico. There is little doubt that primary subsistence during this period involves the resurgence of maize agriculture, specifically varieties which come to be known as Puebloan. The only colder and wetter areas which appear to contain P-IV occupations are the upper Chama River and several of its larger tributaries. This P-IV occupation is not well documented .

421

The P-IV period also seems to be one which involved intense selective pressures. For it is the case that by A.D. 1450, many major areas of New Mexico were substantially unoccupied, and we suggest that the trend from A.D. 1300 to A.D. 1450 involved actual population decline throughout New Mexico. The P-IV period is also characterized by continual population movements in and out of local riverine areas. Only a few pueblos which survived into the historic period are known to have been founded and occupied continuously from this time. It is probable that, by A.D. 1450, Puebloan occupation was largely restricted to those areas documented for the early historic period (Schroeder 1979).

Patterns of ceramic trade are fascinating, particularly for the early P-IV period. With the introduction of Rio Grande glazewares, specifically Glaze A at the P-IV horizon, there develops a pattern of traded ceramics which is increasingly confined to a broad band centered on the Rio Grande from northern to southern New Mexico. By A.D. 1350 the distribution of trade in the Rio Grande Glazes appears to be restricted mainly to the Rio Grande drainage itself and east to the spine of the Rockies which separates the Plains province from western New Mexico, and extending from the southern end of Chupadero Mesa north no further than the Chama drainage. While it is not surprising that the Rio Grande glazewares should become increasingly restricted in their range through this 50 year period, it is interesting to note that at A.D. 1300, when the first Glaze A's are widely introduced, they are often found in association with traces of St. Johns Polychrome.

The Rio Grande Glaze A's are, in fact, a facsimile, or, rather, an attempt at facsimile, of the St. Johns Polychrome. We can presume, then, that somewhere between A.D. 1300 and 1325, the genuine St. Johns Polychrome was no longer available from trade with the western highlands. What is most interesting and most to the point is that sites containing ceramic assemblages characterized by small quantities of St. Johns Polychrome, Chupadero B/W and the initial Rio Grande glazes, evidence a geographic pattern which is a sort of *smear* to the east of the highland spine dividing New Mexico. That is, somewhere between A.D. 1275 and 1325 or 1335 there has been, not only a downhill shift from P-III to P-IV times, but one which moves eastward.

Chupadero B/W, for instance, is far more widely distributed to the east of Chupadero Mesa, both north and south, than it is to the west, for it seems to extend in association with the Rio Grande glazes, that is, no further west than the higher western margins of the Rio Grande drainage. It is also the case that, while ceramic assemblages containing Chupadero B/W, Santa Fe B/W, St. Johns Polychrome and the earliest Rio Grande glazes (also, usually, some brownwares) are known to occur east of the Rio Grande roughly between Mora and Springer, New Mexico, it is not the case that such assemblages, whether produced by trade or local manufacture, are commonly found to the west in the San Juan Basin. While we do not mean to imply that no P-IV period ceramics are found elsewhere in minute quantities, we do mean that the bulk of the trade network which focused on the Rio Grande at this time shows an eastward extension very early in the P-IV period.

This eastward focused tendency is then pretty much reversed by about A.D. 1350, and trade at least seems to become more confined to the Rio Grande drainage itself. Trade to the west with the Zuni area seems to be quickly re-emphasized. While it is a tricky business to attach dates to these events, the sequence of events is fairly clear. First, there is a partial disruption in the late P-III highland trade network. This is followed closely, or is perhaps simultaneous with, an extension of trade networks along the east slopes of the central highland spine. Then, the disrupted trade with western New Mexico is quickly reestablished, and the eastward trending trade network is reversed.

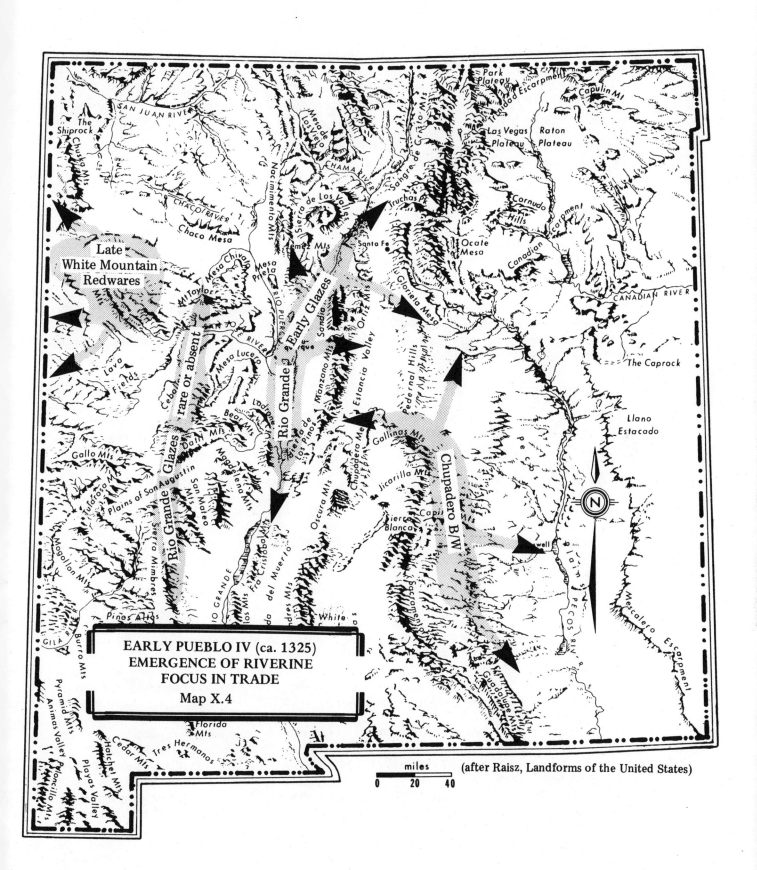

Late
White Mountain
Redwares

Early Glazes

Rio Grande

Rio Grande Glazes rare or absent

Chupadero B/W

**EARLY PUEBLO IV (ca. 1325)
EMERGENCE OF RIVERINE
FOCUS IN TRADE**

Map X.4

miles

0   20   40

(after Raisz, Landforms of the United States)

423

In the eastern plains, the P-IV period seems to involve the rapid development of buffalo hunting as at least a temporary subsistence focus. The data are not clear, for as we have said previously, few sites in the entire eastern half of New Mexico have been dated by independent means. Nonetheless, the evidence suggests that there were optimum grassland conditions during the A.D. 1200's, followed soon by sites which show evidence of substantial buffalo hunting. The rapid and notable increase of bison bones in sites along the northern Pecos and Canadian drainages is intriguing. It seems to be the case that these sites date to the Great Drought conditions which Antevs has documented for the late A.D. 1200's.

Reher (1977) has noted, however, that maximal buffalo populations *follow* climatic optimum conditions. Thus, we may presume that somewhere in the A.D. 1200's, perhaps prior to A.D. 1250, conditions favored increased grass production. Sometime thereafter, buffalo population temporarily peaked, and human populations in the eastern plains seemed to have taken substantial advantage of this increased resource. This episode appears to have been of relatively short duration. In the Fort Sumner area it is associated with the late McKenzie phase period, which lasted perhaps only fifty years. Thereafter, evidence for occupation in the eastern portions of New Mexico becomes much more ephemeral. We suggest that populations which had previously attempted an agricultural strategy in the very marginal regions, were attracted to the buffalo hunting strategy. It is in this context that an appeal to the principle of mimimum effort appears appropriate.

So it is necessary to raise the old questions about relationships between Puebloan and Plains populations. While we do not believe that all of the so-called puebloid occupations of the eastern plains and its margins in fact involved Puebloan racial stocks, we do believe that localized populations were drawn outward into more productive "tall grass" buffalo hunting areas to the east sometime after A.D. 1300. If this is in fact the case, then it appears logical to argue that between A.D. 1300 and roughly A.D. 1500-1600, there was an outward movement to the plains followed by an inward movement after the onset of the Little Ice Age which Reher discusses (1977). That is, a second optimum in buffalo population, occurring somewhere after A.D. 1500, brought returning bison populations along the eastern spine of highland New Mexico. These animals were followed by human populations which may once have been linguistically and/or socially tied into other *in situ* populations in central New Mexico. We thus raise the possibility that historical documents which indicate the influx of Apachean and other populations (Comanche and Ute) in the early historic period merely documented *a return* of such populations to the flanks of the central highlands.

It would almost certainly be, then, this second optimum in buffalo population which induced some remaining Puebloan groups to revert to a Plains-like hunting and gathering strategy. The period of greatest *temptation* then, we suggest, would have come in the early historic period, and not in the A.D. 1200-1300 period, which appeared to have been a rather limited episode. Thus, we characterize the dawn of the P-V period as one in which the pattern of raid and trade between Puebloan and Plains populations was intensified, and while this pattern may have been a feature of relationships between Plains and Puebloan populations throughout, we suggest that it was the characteristic feature of the early P-V period.

Though the historic period is not the subject of this volume, we will end our story here with one bit of speculation. We do not conclude, but we ask whether it is possible that the groups which became Navajo, and those that are associated with the other eastern Apachean groups, were separated, one group (Navajo and western Apache) to the west and one to the east, at between A.D. 1100 and 1300? The western groups could have moved into largely vacated basin environments first following the Chacoan collapse, then re-entered the western highland environments as well, which were abandoned during the late P-III period (A.D. 1275-1300), while some of the eastern groups (eastern Apache and perhaps some Towa) moved out into the plains, perhaps as far as the Texas border or a little further east about A.D. 1275-1350, then to return westward in numbers just two centuries later at the dawn of the historic period, when buffalo population again surged as a response to increased rainfall and cooler climatic conditions.

Though this scenario is speculative, it is at least as plausible as several others currently accepted in the literature. Let us return now, to our original theoretical discussion.

POWER AND EFFICIENCY

The nature of evolution in general, and cultural evolution in particular, has long been a major theme in the literature of archeology and anthropology. A century ago it was customarily argued that evolution proceeded in well-defined and successive stages. These have traditionally been ordered from the simple to the complex, the small to the large, and the homogeneous to the heterogenous. It has been a major idea in anthropology that evolution was a gradual process. It has therefore been difficult for anthropology to separate the processes of change from the fundamental processes of evolution. Hence, there has been substantial investment of thought in the question of what constitutes culture change as opposed to cultural evolution, and it is often asked at what point quantitative change also becomes qualitative.

The primary difficulty in creating these distinctions has been that anthropologists have confused the generally stable and gradualistic properties of the homeostatic drive in living systems with basic evolutionary process. This is not surprising, for the primary goal of systems in general, and human systems in particular, is the maintenance of stability. The practical difficulty arises, however, when it is understood that the world is in continual change and that variation in those external factors which condition adaptive responses is an unavoidable reality for any living system. The growing awareness of this reality has tended to refocus our notions regarding evolution on the concept of adaptation. While the concept of adaptation is, and will probably remain, fundamental to our understanding of evolutionary process, it is also the case that we have tended to look uncritically upon responses in human systems as, of necessity, well-adapted to particular circumstances.

In order to get at the underlying nature of adaptive process, contemporary archeology has begun to focus on maxims such as the principle of least effort. The principle of least effort assumes that a human population will serve its adaptive needs with the minimum possible investment of resources, labor or complexity. As we said previously, the principle of minimum effort, or of least cost, more than satisfactorily explains many human responses to short-term adaptive exigencies. But it specifically describes conditions under which one would expect homeostasis more often than dramatic change. More to the point, the principle of minimum effort describes a tendency to seek efficiency in adaptive response. Anthropologists often become so interested in the idea of efficiency that they tend to forget that at 100% efficiency a system is inert, since no energy is available to do work. As a creature, the common box turtle is enormously efficient, offering a living metaphor of the Principle of Minimum Effort. Yet neither turtles nor human systems which mimic their efficiency are good candidates for recurring episodes of rapid evolution. This is a point of importance in constructing theories of such transformations.

The other side of the evolutionary coin involves dramatic reorganization of a living system. It is now generally accepted in evolutionary biology that evolution proceeds in rapid episodal displays of such dramatic change. The explanation for such change, we have suggested here, is the power response. It is the power to displace — to overwhelm — and to out-reproduce, which is the essence of Darwinian evolution. It is not so much adaptive fitness which explains evolutionary change, it is power. But it is also the case that systems cannot indefinitely sustain remarkable power outputs and survive. It is therefore the case that every human system must balance its competitive requirements for power against its sustaining requirements for efficiency. It is this complex, internal mirroring of the structural ability to enlarge and amplify, coupled with the ability to contract and simplify, which permits us to penetrate the true processual structure of evolution.

It is the basic need, then, of human systems, to have both the capacity for power and the capacity for efficiency. These capacities are interwoven in a matrix whose ordinary goal is homeostasis. It is the case with simple, undifferentiated organisms, that they may be, at a given time, either powerful or efficient, but being nondifferentiated, they may not be both simultaneously. Thus in ecology we see, as a consequence, Gause's rule of competitive exclusion. The principle of competitive exclusion states that two organisms may not occupy the same niche, and in a petrie dish under laboratory conditions, it can be demonstrated that two competing strains of bacteria will not both survive. One will always displace the other. This displacement is generated primarily by reproductive power. The successful bacterium, once having displaced its competitor, is then presented with an entirely different problem. This problem is in not using up the resources of the culture medium in the petrie dish. Thus the bacterium's ability to survive, once its competitive edge is established, is directly proportional to its metabolic efficiency in the petrie dish. While this analogy may seem inappropriate in the context of archeology, it is the case that (unlike bacteria) human systems are, in fact, internally differentiated, even if in small ways. This differentiation, or heterogeneity in behavior, accounts for the facts of human evolution and cultural evolution.

When this internal differentiation is amplified to a point at which problems of observational scale do not confuse the issue, we speak of a stratified system in archeology. The entire point of cultural evolution is that a stratified system may be both simultaneously powerful and efficient, for it is the case that some subsystems, or specialized technological sets, or social organizational features, will be power-specialized, whereas others will be efficiency-specialized. While the case has been less clear to anthropologists for simple *egalitarian* hunting and gathering systems, it is a problem of observation rather than of theory, for such systems also display heterogeneous behavior when subjected to close observation. Evolution in general, then, and cultural evolution in particular, is that process wherein power-specialized structures are diverged and differentiated from efficiency specialized structures. Evolution is nothing less and it is most certainly nothing more.

The process of speciation itself is the separation of thermodynamically (therefore metabolically and/or reproductively) more powerful from more efficient organisms. As an appropriate example, we cite the case of the large *Bison antiquus*, which eventually became differentiated from smaller bison tending toward dwarfism or pigmy characteristics (Reher 1977). Ultimately, both these Pleistocene forms were displaced by *Bison bison*, an intermediate form in size, and therefore in thermodynamic characteristics. *Bison bison*, being the intermediate form, was in some sense the sum of the extremes, and therefore represents the homoeostatic drive in the genus *Bison*.

In the archeological record we have identified characteristics of what we have termed the power drive. These are: remarkable increase in the rate of population growth, increase in the rate and quantity of labor investment, increase in the rate of construction, and increase in general in the rate of creation of material goods of all kinds. These characteristics identify the archeologically powerful system. Archeologists have had no trouble in identifying these *classic* systems. The efficient systems, or those which are in an efficiency phase, tend to be less visible archeologically, and are characterized by low rates of technological and social change, and population growth, and relative stability in size and in the nature of basic adaptive responses. Systems which are in an extended efficiency phase have not generally been very difficult for archeologists to identify when problems of archeological visibility did not intrude. The case of Apachean occupation in New Mexico is one in which such factors have clearly intruded on archeological interpretation.

What has been generally impossible to identify is the system which is in the immediate process of dramatic change toward either an efficiency response or a power response. This is equivalent in archeology to discovery of the missing link in paleontology. The missing link is missing because, in fact, the energetic requirements of undergoing remarkable and rapid transformation occur at the cost of deleting the previously identified structure.

Until we, or others, learn to apply the concepts of power and efficiency in a more technical and less anecdotal way, it will be the basic patterns and rhythms of evolution that we will be most easily able to identify. One basic pattern we have identified in this volume is that the small tend to get larger. There is, then, increasing divergence between the large and the small, followed by rapid succession of the small (but not necessarily the very smallest). We have seen this in point types and in room size in the archeological record here in New Mexico. We again point to the case of *Bison* evolution as an example in the biological record. One attribute of the basic rhythm of evolution is that the power phase is of relatively short duration when compared to the efficiency phase in the history of any given system.

For these reasons, we caution that the tendency of archeologists to create temporally symmetrical series (as in 200 years per phase) of archeological phases may not accurately represent evolutionary development as we conceive it. Since the power phase or power drive of a system is followed either by extinction, or by an efficiency phase of longer duration, it cannot be the case that evenly spaced archeological phases permit us adequately to identify evolutionary process in a given region. While we acknowledge that there remains a great deal to be done with the analysis that we have suggested here, both in theoretical terms and in terms of practical application, we suggest that our sophistication in interpreting the archeological record depends on the degree to which we are able to tune our observations to the fundamental rhythms of evolution. These rhythms are the oscillations between power and efficiency.

SUMMARY STATEMENT

It is our conception that much about human history is to be understood, not through the view that history repeats itself, but, as we have said, that process repeats itself. It is these recurring patterns of evolutionary process which make possible the recurrence of the general outline of historical events. For example, we may note that our nation has been characterized in our lifetimes by conspicuous *per capita* utilization of energy. This has led to circumstances in which we can fairly be characterized as having been energetically and materially profligate. As a response both to availability of resources and to competition in a complex world-system, we have been in a remarkable power drive in this nation for most of the last 80 or 90 years. Now that the realities of resource availability have affixed the inevitable price to our profligacy, we are entering the predictable efficiency phase in the evolution of our society.

This phase will undoubtedly be characterized by increased competition among the social classes — that is, competition and conflict between those that are power specialized as opposed to those that are efficiency specialized. In order to reduce the cost of complexity and to attempt homeostasis, diversity of behavior, opinion, political and religious viewpoints may be restricted. The relative social/behavioral liberalism which is a characteristic of any system in power drive may be replaced by the relative conservatism of any system which is in an efficiency phase.

It is interesting to listen to the debate over whether the U.S. will maintain its position as "the number one power" in the world at this time. We are, and we sense that we are, on the verge of some fundamental and unalterable change in the nature of things. In 1980, we stand at the threshold of a forced divergence of power and efficiency. And we note that on the contemporary political scene, there are those who wish to return to the 65 or 70 miles-per-hour

427

speed limit, those who deny that the *American dream* of energetic profligacy and thermodynamic power has been aborted, and those who refuse to accept that fundamental change is upon us.

This longing for the way things were, or more accurately, are perceived to have been, is no more or less a revitalization movement than the Ghost Dance of the 1890's. In that case, you will recall, it was believed that all of the fallen warriors of the Indian nations would return to life, as would the long gone buffalo. The world would then return to its rightful condition for Indian people; that is, the demographic and subsistence power lost to conquest would be magically returned. This is familiar in the context of contemporary debate, as we have said, not because history repeats itself in its details, but because a process has recurred.

Truth and worth in archeology and anthropology may be approached by students who are able to incorporate history and process in an intelligible whole. If the ideas which we have advanced here persuade a few of our colleagues to pursue this object, we will take it that we have done something of value.

PHOTOGRAPHS

Photo 11: A.V. Kidder's crew posing in front of the work shack at Pecos Pueblo. Photo taken about 1917. Photograph courtesy of the Museum of New Mexico.

SAR and SAR-L = From the School of American Research collections in the Museum of New Mexico.
MNM = From the collections of the Museum of New Mexico.

Photo 12: Select pottery types dating from ca. A.D. 500 to A.D. 900. Top row (left to right): Kana'a neck-banded (SAR-L 8284/11); Three Circle R/W (MNN 20224/11); Lino B/G (SAR-L 8244/11). Bottom row (left to right): Kiatuthlanna B/W (MNM 19850/11); White Mound B/W (SAR-L 8235/11). Lino B/G vessel is 22 cm. high. Photo courtesy of Robin Gilmore.

Photo 13: Select pottery types dating from ca. A.D. 950 to A.D. 1200. Top: Gallup B/W (MNM 8842/11); Bottom row (left to right): Mimbres B/W (SAR 19929/11); Red Mesa B/W (SAR-L 8224/11). Red Mesa B/W bowl is 20 cm. in diameter. Photo courtesy of Robin Gilmore.

Photo 14: Select pottery types dating from ca. A.D. 1200 to A.D. 1325. Top row (left to right): Pueblo III Corrugated (MNM 20537/11); Tularosa B/W (MNM 49221/11). Bottom row (left to right): St. Johns Polychrome (MNM 8872/11); miniature Santa Fe B/W (MNM 21459/11); Mesa Verde B/W (SAR-L 18624/11). Pueblo III Corrugated vessel is 19 cm. tall. Photo courtesy of Robin Gilmore.

Photo 15: Select pottery types dating from ca. A.D. 1325 to A.D. 1600. Top row (left to right): Espinoso G/P (MNM 42948/11); Agua Fria G/R (MNM 21167/11). Bottom row (left to right): Bandelier B/G (MNM 16241/11); Puaray G-P (MNM 11516/11). Agua Fria G/R vessel is 28 cm. in diameter. Photo courtesy of Robin Gilmore.

431

Photo 16: A Los Pinos Phase cobble-ring structure in the Navajo Reservoir area. These sites, which are affiliated with the BM-II period, have been described by Eddy (1966). The cobble rings form a terrace or apron around many Los Pinos Phase wood structures and some cobbles were also incorporated into a low masonry wall leaned against the exterior of the wooden structure. Photograph courtesy of the Museum of New Mexico.

Photo 17: A shallow pithouse in the Chuska Valley near Littlewater. This BM-III pithouse yielded archeomagnetic dates at A.D. 600 ± 25. Photograph by G.S. Condon, courtesy of the Museum of New Mexico.

Photo 18: San Juan Mesa Ruin, LA 303. This large site is believed to have been occupied during the first three-quarters of the 17th century. Barbara Peckham is standing next to walls belonging to a late component. The archeology of the Jemez area is not well documented. There have been relatively few investigations in this area since World War II. Photograph by S.L. Peckham, courtesy of the Museum of New Mexico, Santa Fe.

Photo 19: Gallinas Springs Ruin near Magdalena, New Mexico. This is an extremely large P-III site with an estimated 500 to 600 ground floor rooms. Note the extreme mound height and the walls in the foreground exposed by erosion and vandalism. View is to the south. Photograph by S.L. Peckham, courtesy of the Museum of New Mexico, Santa Fe.

Photo 20: An aerial photograph of Sapawe, LA 306, located in the El Rito Valley. This site is probably the largest adobe pueblo in the American Southwest. The plaza with the large kiva depression in the foreground is approximately 95 yards long. Photograph by Charles Lindbergh, courtesy of the Museum of New Mexico, Santa Fe.

REFERENCES CITED

Agogino, G.A.
1968   Archeological excavations at Blackwater Draw Locality No. 1, New Mexico 1963-64. *National Geographic Society Research Reports on 1963 Projects* 1-7.

Agogino, G.A. and J. Hester
1953   The Santa Ana preceramic sites. *El Palacio* 60(4):131-140, Santa Fe.

Agogino, G.A., C. Smith and J. Runyan
1966   A progress report on a preceramic site at Rattlesnake Draw. *Plains Anthropologist* 11(34): 302-311.

Alexander, H.G. and P. Reiter
1935   Report on the excavation of Jemez Cave, New Mexico. *University of New Mexico Bulletin, Monograph Series* 1(3), Albuquerque.

Allan, W.C.
1975   Excavations at OCA:CGP:758, an Anasazi open campsite. In *Archeological Reports, Cultural Resource Management Projects* No. 1. Edited by F.J. Broilo and D.E. Stuart. Office of Contract Archeology, University of New Mexico, pp. 243-258.

1975a   An archeological survey of a floodwater retarding structure in the Corrales watershed. In *Archeological Reports, Cultural Resource Management Projects* No. 1. Edited by F.J. Broilo and D.E. Stuart. Office of Contract Archeology, University of New Mexico, pp. 145-158.

1977   Present and past climate. In *Settlement and subsistence along the lower Chaco River: The CGP survey*. Edited by C.A. Reher. University of New Mexico Press, Albuquerque, pp. 127-148.

Allan, W.C., A. Osborn, W.J. Chasko and D.E. Stuart
1975   An archeological survey: Road construction right-of-way Block II — Navajo Indian irrigation project. In *Archeological Reports, Cultural Resources Management Projects* No. 1. Edited by F.J. Broilo and D.E. Stuart. Office of Contract Archeology, University of New Mexico, pp. 91-143.

Allan, W.C., R.P. Gauthier, F.J. Broilo and R.W. Loose
1976   *An archeological survey near San Mateo, New Mexico: The Keradamex, Inc. lease.* Office of Contract Archeology, University of New Mexico, Albuquerque.

Anderson, A.B.
1975   "Least cost" strategy and limited activity site location, upper Dry Cimarron River Valley, northeastern New Mexico. Unpublished Ph.D. dissertation, Department of Anthropology, University of Colorado, Boulder.

Anyon, R.
1979   The late pithouse period. In *An archeological synthesis of south central and southwestern New Mexico*. Edited by S. LeBlanc and M. Whalen [BLM Draft Report], pp. 141-255.

Anyon, R., P.A. Gilman and S.A. LeBlanc
1980   *A reevaluation of the Mogollon-Mimbres archeological sequence.* A paper presented at the first annual Mogollon Conference, Las Cruces, New Mexico, April 1980.

Applegarth, S.M.
1976   Prehistoric utilization of the environment of the eastern slopes of the Guadalupe Mountains, southeastern New Mexico. Unpublished Ph.D. dissertation, University of Wisconsin, Madison.

Arnold, B.
1943   An archeological survey in the vicinity of the SU site. In The SU site, excavations at a Mogollon village (by Paul S. Martin). *Field Museum of Natural History Anthropological Series* 32(2): 252-265.

Baker, W.E. and T.N. Campbell
1960   Artifacts from preceramic sites in northeastern and southern New Mexico. *El Palacio* 67(3): 78-86.

Bannister, B.
1964   Tree-ring dating of the archeological sites in the Chaco Canyon region, New Mexico. *Southwest Parks and Monument Association Technical Series* 6, Part II, Globe, Arizona.

Basehart, H.W.
1973   Mescalero Apache subsistence patterns. In *Technical Manual: 1973 survey of the Tularosa Basin, the research design.* Human Systems Research, Albuquerque, pp. 145-181.

Beckes, M.R.
1977   Prehistoric cultural stability and change in the southern Tularosa Basin, New Mexico. Unpublished Ph.D. dissertation, Department of Anthropology, University of Pittsburgh.

Beckett, P.
1973   *Cochise culture sites in south central and north central New Mexico.* M.A. Thesis, Department of Anthropology, Eastern New Mexico State University, Portales.

1979   Hueco phase: Fact or fiction. In *Jornada Mogollon archeology.* Edited by P. Beckett and R.N. Wiseman. Historic Preservation Bureau, Santa Fe, pp. 223-225.

1980   *The Ake site: Collection and excavation of LA 13423, Catron County, New Mexico.* Department of Sociology and Anthropology, Cultural Resources Management Division, New Mexico State University, Las Cruces.

*Beckett, P.H. and R.N. Wiseman (Editors)
1979   *Jornada Mogollon archeology.* Historic Preservation Bureau, Santa Fe.

Berman, M.J.
1979   *Cultural resources overview, Socorro area, New Mexico.* USDA Forest Service and Bureau of Land Management, Albuquerque. Also, U.S. Superintendent of Documents, Washington, D.C.

Bez, E.
1979   Burial analysis. In *Studies in the prehistory of the Forestdale region.* Edited by S. Stafford and G. Rice. Arizona State University, Tempe [Draft Report], pp. 667-687.

Biella, J.V.
1979   Changing residential patterns among the Anasazi, A.D. 750-1525. In *Archeological investigations in Cochiti Reservoir, New Mexico* 4:103-144. Edited by J.V. Biella and R.C. Chapman. Office of Contract Archeology, University of New Mexico, Albuquerque.

Biella, J.V. and R.C. Chapman
1977   Significance of cultural resources in Cochiti Reservoir. In *Archeological investigations in Cochiti Reservoir, New Mexico* 1:295-316. Edited by J.V. Biella and R.C. Chapman. Office of Contract Archeology, University of New Mexico, Albuquerque.

1977-   *Archeological investigations in Cochiti Reservoir, New Mexico,* four volumes. Office of Con-
1979   tract Archeology, University of New Mexico, Albuquerque.

Binford, L.R.
1968   Post Pleistocene adaptation. In *New perspectives in archeology.* Edited by S.R. Binford and L.R. Binford. Aldine, Chicago, pp. 313-342.

Birdsell, J.B.
1968   Some predictions for the Pleistocene based upon equilibrium systems among recent hunters. In *Man the hunter.* Edited by R.B. Lee and I. DeVore. Aldine, Chicago, pp. 229-240.

Birkedal, T.G.
1976   Basketmaker III residence units: A study of prehistoric social organization in the Mesa Verde Archeological District. Unpublished Ph.D. dissertation, Department of Anthropology, University of Colorado, Boulder.

Bluhm, E.
1960   Mogollon settlement patterns in Pine Lawn Valley, New Mexico. *American Antiquity* 25(4): 538-546.

---

* References cited in the extensive quotation which appears on pp. 211-215 of this volume are not duplicated in this bibliography. Consult Beckett and Wiseman (1979).

Bolton, H.E.
  1949   *Coronado: Knight of Pueblos and Plains.* University of New Mexico Press, Albuquerque [1964 edition].

Boserup, E.
  1965   *The conditions of agricultural growth.* Aldine, Chicago.

Bradfield, W.
  1929   Cameron Creek Village: A site in the Mimbres area in Grant County, New Mexico. *Monographs of the School of American Research* 1, Santa Fe.

Breternitz, D.A.
  1959   Excavations at Nantack Village Point of Pines, Arizona. *Anthropological papers of the University of Arizona* No. 1, Tucson.

  1966   An appraisal of tree-ring dated pottery in the southwest. *Anthropological papers of the University of Arizona* No. 10, Tucson.

  1973   Tree-ring dated Basketmaker III and Pueblo I sites in Mesa Verde National Park. Ms. on file, Midwest Archeological Center, National Park Service, Lincoln, Nebraska.

Brody, J.
  1977   *Mimbres painted pottery.* School of American Research and University of New Mexico Press, Albuquerque.

Broilo, F.J.
  1971   An investigation of surface collected Clovis, Folsom, and Midland projectile points from Blackwater Draw and adjacent localities. Unpublished Masters Thesis, Department of Anthropology, Eastern New Mexico University, Portales.

  1973   Early human occupation of the Tularosa Basin: A model [unsigned]. In *Technical Manual: 1973 survey of the Tularosa Basin, the research design.* Human Systems Research, Albuquerque, pp. 221-225.

Brook, V.R.
  1979   An El Paso astronomical observatory. In *Jornada Mogollon archeology.* Edited by P. Beckett and R.N. Wiseman. Historic Preservation Bureau, Santa Fe, pp. 25-39.

Broster, J.B.
  1980   *Paleo-Indian occupation of the Cebolleta Mesa region, New Mexico.* Paper presented at the first annual meeting of the New Mexico Archeological Council, April 1980.

Brugge, D.M.
  1977   *A history of the Chaco Navajo.* Ms. circulated by Division of Chaco Research, National Park Service, University of New Mexico, Albuquerque.

  1977a   *Tsegai: An archeological ethnohistory of the Chaco region.* Ms. circulated by Division of Chaco Research, National Park Service, University of New Mexico, Albuquerque.

Bryan, K. and J.H. Toulouse, Jr.
  1943   The San Jose non-ceramic culture and its relation to puebloan culture in New Mexico. *American Antiquity* 8(3):269-290.

Bullard, W.R.
  1962   The Cerro Colorado site and pithouse architecture in the southwestern United States prior to A.D. 900. *Papers of the Peabody Museum* XLIV(2), Cambridge.

Bussey, *et al.*
  1976   LA 4921, Three Rivers, Otero County, New Mexico: A project of excavation, stabilization and interpretation of a prehistoric village. *Cultural Resources Management Division Report* 69, New Mexico State University, Las Cruces.

Callen, E.O.
1973   Dietary patterns in Mexico between 6500 B.P. and A.D. 1580. In *Man and his foods*. Edited by C.E. Smith, Jr. University of Alabama Press.

Camilli, E.L.
1979   Cultural resources overview of prehistoric periods. In *A cultural resources overview for the Bureau of Land Management, Roswell District*. E. Camilli and C. Allen (assemblers). Draft report, Office of Contract Archeology, University of New Mexico, Albuquerque.

Camilli, E.L. and C. Allen (Assemblers)
1979   *A cultural resources overview for the Bureau of Land Management, Roswell District*. Draft report, Office of Contract Archeology, University of New Mexico, Albuquerque.

Campbell, R.G.
1969   Prehistoric panhandle culture on the Chaquaqua Plateau, southeast Colorado. Unpublished Ph.D. dissertation, Department of Anthropology, University of Colorado, Boulder.

1976   The panhandle aspect of the Chaquaqua Plateau. *Texas Tech University Graduate Studies* 11. Lubbock.

Caperton, T.
n.d.   A surface reconnaissance of the Gran Quivira area. Manuscript on file at the Laboratory of Anthropology, Santa Fe.

Carlson, R.L.
1965   Eighteenth century fortresses of the Gobernador District (the Earl Morris Papers No. 2). University of Colorado *Series in Anthropology* 10, Boulder.

Carroll, C.H., *et al.*
1979   *An archeological survey of Ceboyeta Mesa, New Mexico*. Draft report circulated by Public Service Company of New Mexico, Albuquerque.

Casselberry, S.E.
1974   Further refinement of formulas for determining population from floor area. *World Archeology* 6(1):117-122.

Chapman, R.C.
1979   Archaic settlement and the vegetative diversity model. In *Archeological excavations in Cochiti Reservoir, New Mexico* 4:75-102. Edited by J.V. Biella and R.C. Chapman. Office of Contract Archeology, University of New Mexico, Albuquerque.

Chapman, R.C. and J.V. Biella
1979   A review of research results. In *Archeological investigations in Cochiti Reservoir, New Mexico* 4:385-406. Edited by J.V. Biella and R.C. Chapman. Office of Contract Archeology, University of New Mexico, Albuquerque.

Chapman, R.C., J.V. Biella and S. Bussey (Editors)
1977   *Archeological investigations of Cochiti Reservoir, New Mexico, volume 2: Excavation and analysis 1975 season*. Office of Contract Archeology, University of New Mexico, Albuquerque.

Clark, G.A.
1967   A preliminary analysis of burial clusters at the Grasshopper site, east-central Arizona. Unpublished M.A. Thesis, Department of Anthropology, University of Arizona, Tucson.

Clark, Graham
1969   *World prehistory: A new outline*. Cambridge University Press, Cambridge.

Cohen, M.N.
1977   *The food crisis in prehistory*. Yale University Press, New Haven.

Collins, M.B.
1968   The Andrews Lake locality: New archeological data from the southern Llano Estacado, Texas. Unpublished M.A. Thesis, Department of Anthropology, University of Texas, Austin.

Collins, M.B. (continued)
1971   A review of Llano Estacado archeology and ethnohistory. *Plains Anthropologist* 16(52):85-104.

Colton, H.S. and L.L. Hargrave
1937   Handbook of northern Arizona pottery wares. *Museum of Northern Arizona Bulletin* 11, Flagstaff.

Cordell, L.S.
1979   *A cultural resources overview of the middle Rio Grande Valley, New Mexico*. USDA Forest Service, Albuquerque, Superintendent of Documents, Washington, D.C.

1979a   Prehistory, eastern Anasazi. In *Handbook of North American Indians, Volume 9, Southwest*. Edited by A. Ortiz. Smithsonian Institution, Washington, D.C., pp. 131-151.

in press   The Pueblo period in the San Juan Basin: Overview and research problems. In *The past tomorrow: Planning for the preservation of archeological resources in the San Juan Basin* (tentative title). Edited by F. Plog. School of American Research, Santa Fe.

Cordell, L.S. and F. Plog
1979   Escaping the confines of normative thought: A reevaluation of puebloan prehistory. *American Antiquity* 44(3):405-429.

Corley, J.A.
1965   Proposed eastern extension of the Jornada branch of the Mogollon. In Transactions of the first regional archeological symposium for southeastern New Mexico and western Texas. *Lea County Archeological Society Bulletin* No. 1:30-36. Hobbs.

Corley, J.A. and R. Leslie
1960   The Boot Hill site. *Lea County Archeological Society Bulletin* No. 2, Hobbs.

Cosgrove, C.B.
1923   Two kivas at Treasure Hill. *El Palacio* 15(2):19-21.

1947   Caves of the upper Gila and Hueco areas in New Mexico and Texas. *Papers of the Peabody Museum, Harvard University* 24(2), Cambridge.

Cosgrove, H.S. and C.B. Cosgrove
1932   The Swarts Ruin, a typical Mimbres site in southwestern New Mexico. *Papers of the Peabody Museum of American Archeology and Ethnology* 15(1). Harvard University, Cambridge.

Cowgill, G.L.
1975   Population pressure as a non-explanation. In Population studies in archeology and biological anthropology: A symposium. Edited by A.C. Swedlund. *American Antiquity* 40(2), Part 2: 127-131.

Cutler, H. and M. Eickmeier
1962   Corn and other plant remains from four sites in Hidalgo County, New Mexico. In Clanton Draw and Box Canyon (by E. McCluney). *School of American Research Monograph* No. 26, Santa Fe, pp. 48-54.

Danson, E.B.
1957   An archeological survey of west central New Mexico and east central Arizona. *Papers of the Peabody Museum of Archeology and Ethnology* 44(1).

Davis, E.L. and J.H. Winkler
1962   *Progress report sites D 125 (LA 8931) and D 118 (LA 8932), Cibola National Forest, New Mexico*. Museum of New Mexico, Laboratory of Anthropology, Santa Fe.

Department of the Interior
1935   *Historic sites, buildings and Antiquities Act of 1935*. Pub. L. 74-292, 49 STAT 666, 16 USC 461-467.

1966   *National Historic Preservation Act of 1966*. Pub. L. 89-665, 80 STAT 915, 16 USC 470.

Department of the Interior, National Park Service
1971   *A master plan for proposed Zuni-Cibola National Cultural Park, New Mexico.*

1977a   *How to complete National Register forms.* National Register of Historic Places, Office of Archeology and Historic Preservation, National Park Service, Washington, D.C. (January).

1977b   *How to complete National Register thematic group nomination forms.* National Register of Historic Places, Office of Archeology and Historic Preservation, National Park Service, Washington, D.C.

1977c   *How to complete National Register multiple resource nomination forms.* National Register of Historic Places, Office of Archeology and Historic Preservation, National Park Service, Washington, D.C.

Dick, H.W.
1953   The Hodges site: Two rock shelters near Tucumcari, New Mexico. *Bureau of American Ethnology Bulletin* 154:267-284, Washington, D.C.

1965   Bat Cave. *School of American Research Monograph* No. 27, Santa Fe.

1976   Archeological excavations in the Llaves area, Santa Fe National Forest, New Mexico, 1972-1974. Part 1: Architecture. *Archeological Report* 13. U.S.D.A. Forest Service, Southwest Region, Albuquerque.

DiPeso, C.
1974   *Casas Grandes: A fallen trade center of the Gran Chichimeca* Vol. 2. The Amerind Foundation, Dragoon, Arizona.

Dittert, A.E.
1949   *The prehistoric population and architecture of the Cebolleta Mesa region, central western New Mexico.* M.A. Thesis, Department of Anthropology, University of New Mexico, Albuquerque.

1959   Culture change in the Cebolleta Mesa region, New Mexico. Unpublished Ph.D. dissertation, Department of Anthropology, University of Arizona, Tucson.

Dittert, A.E., Jr., J.J. Hester and F.W. Eddy
1961   An archeological survey of the Navajo Reservoir district, northwestern New Mexico. *School of American Research and Museum of New Mexico Monographs* 23, Santa Fe.

Douglass, A.E.
1942   Checking the date of Bluff Ruin, Forestdale: A study in technique. *Tree-ring Bulletin* 9(2):2-7.

Duggins, O.
1961   A study of human hair. In A survey and excavation of caves in Hidalgo County, New Mexico (by M. Lambert and J.R. Ambler). *School of American Research Monograph* No. 25:99-101, Santa Fe.

Dutton, B.
1964   Las Madres in light of Anasazi migrations. *American Antiquity* 29(4):449-454.

Eddy, F.W.
1966   Prehistory in the Navajo Reservoir district in northwestern New Mexico, Part I and Part II. *Museum of New Mexico Papers in Anthropology* No. 15, Santa Fe.

Eldredge, N. and S.J. Gould
1972   Punctuated equilibria: An alternative to phyletic gradualism. In *Models in paleobiology.* Edited by T.J.M. Schopf. Freeman, Cooper & Co., San Francisco, pp. 82-115.

Ellis, F.H.
1975   Preliminary report on the Turkey Springs sites. Unpublished manuscript, USDA Forest Service, Regional Office, Albuquerque.

n.d.   The background of Gallina culture and its development into that of Jemez Pueblo. Unpublished manuscript.

Ellis, F.H. and J.J. Brody
1964   Ceramic stratigraphy and tribal history at Taos Pueblo. *American Antiquity* 29(3):316-327.

Ellis, F.H. and L. Hammack
1968   Inner sanctum of Feather Cave, a Mogollon sun and earth shrine linking Mexico and the Southwest. *American Antiquity* 33(1):25-44.

Ely, A.G.
1935   The excavation and repair of Quarai Mission. *El Palacio* 39(25-26):133-144.

Elyea, J.M., E. Abbink and P.N. Eschman
1979   *Cultural resources of the N.I.I.P. Blocks 4 and 5 survey.* Navajo Tribal Cultural Resource Management Program, Window Rock.

Eidenbach, P.L.
1979   Wizard's Roost and Wally's Dome: Continuing investigations of prehistoric observatory sites in the Sacramento Mountains, New Mexico. In *Jornada Mogollon archeology.* Edited by P. Beckett and R.N. Wiseman. Historic Preservation Bureau, Santa Fe, pp. 103-105.

1980   *Along the dotted line — a re-examination of the Rio Salado.* A paper circulated by Human Systems Research, Inc., Tularosa, New Mexico.

Euler, R.C., *et al.*
1979   Colorado Plateaus: Cultural dynamics and paleoenvironment. *Science* 205(4411):1089-1101.

Fallon, D.
1979   An archeological investigation of the petroglyphs at the Waterflow site, LA 8970, San Juan County, New Mexico. *Laboratory of Anthropology Note* No. 135, Santa Fe.

Fanale, R. and D. Drager
in press   *Environmental mapping for cultural resource management: The Navajo Indian irrigation project.* National Park Service, Remote Sensing Division, Albuquerque.

Farwell, R.E.
1979   Roy North: Archeological clearance investigations along New Mexico State Road 39 and the haul road for Borrow Pit D, for NMSHD projects F-RF-044-1(2) and F-RF-044-1(3). *Laboratory of Anthropology Note* No. 188, Museum of New Mexico, Santa Fe.

Farwell, R.E. and Y.R. Oakes
n.d.   Pueblo III pithouse occupations in the Sierra Blanca region, New Mexico. In preparation.

Fenega, F.
1956   Excavations at site LA 2579, a Mogollon village near Gran Quivira, New Mexico. In *Pipeline archeology.* Edited by F. Wendorf, N. Fox and O. Lewis. Laboratory of Anthropology, Santa Fe and Museum of Northern Arizona, Flagstaff, pp. 226-233.

Fenega, F. and F. Wendorf
1956   Excavations at the Ignacio, Colorado field camp, site LA 2605. In *Pipeline archeology.* Edited by F. Wendorf, N. Fox and O. Lewis. Laboratory of Anthropology, Santa Fe, and Museum of Northern Arizona, Flagstaff.

Fergusson, M.
1933   Preliminary report on Tecolote Ruin. *El Palacio* 34:196-198.

Figgins, J.D.
1927   Antiquity of man in America. *Natural History* 27(3):229-239.

Fitting, J.E.
1973   An early Mogollon community: A preliminary report on the Winn Canyon site. *The Artifact* 11(1,2,3). El Paso Archeological Society, El Paso.

Flannery, K.V.
1969   Origins and ecological effects of early domestication in Iran and the Near East. In *The domestication and exploitation of plants and animals.* Edited by P.J. Ucko and G.W. Dimbleby. Aldine-Atherton, Chicago, pp. 73-100.

Fliedner, D.
1974   *Der Aufbauder vorspanischen Siedlungo — und Wirtschaftslandschaft im Kulturraum der Pueblo-Indianer.* Selbstverlag des Geographischen Instituts der Universitat des Saarlandes.

Ford, D.
1979   Testing and excavation of an early aceramic Navajo site in Carrizo Canyon. *New Mexico State University Report* 78SJC030, San Juan Campus, Farmington, N.M.

Ford, R.I., A.H. Schroeder and S.L. Peckham
1972   Three perspectives on puebloan prehistory. In *New perspectives on the pueblos.* School of American Research, and University of New Mexico Press, Albuquerque.

Gause, G.F.
1934   *The struggle for existence.* Williams and Wilkins, Baltimore.

Gebhard, D.
1958   Hidden Lakes pictographs. *El Palacio* 65(4):146-150.

Gilman, P.A.
1979   The classic Mimbres. In *An archeological synthesis of south central and southwestern New Mexico.* Edited by S. LeBlanc and M. Whalen [BLM Draft Report], pp. 256-343.

Gladwin, H.S.
1945   The Chaco branch, excavations at White Mound and in the Red Mesa Valley. *Medallion Papers* 33, Globe, Arizona.

Gladwin, W. and H.S. Gladwin
1934   A method for the designation of cultures and their variations. *Medallion Paper* 15, Gila Pueblo, Globe, Arizona.

Glassow, M.A.
1980   *Prehistoric agricultural developments in the northern southwest: A study in changing patterns of land use.* Ballena Press, Socorro.

Gould, S.H.
1977   *Ever since Darwin.* W.W. Norton & Co., New York.

1977a   *Ontogeny and phylogeny.* Harvard University Press, Cambridge.

Graybill, D.A.
1973   Prehistoric settlement pattern analysis in the Mimbres region, New Mexico. Unpublished Ph.D. dissertation, Department of Anthropology, University of Arizona, Tucson.

Green, E.
1955   Excavations near Gran Quivira, New Mexico. *Bulletin of the Texas Archeological Society* 26:182-185.

Gunnerson, J.H.
1959   Archeological survey in northeastern New Mexico. *El Palacio* 66(5):145-154.

1969   Apache archeology in northeastern New Mexico. *American Antiquity* 34(1):23-39.

1979   Southern Athapaskan archeology. In *Handbook of North American Indians*, Volume 9, pp. 162-169. Smithsonian Institution, Washington, D.C.

Hadlock, H.L.
1962   Surface surveys of lithic sites on the Gallegos Wash. *El Palacio* 69(3):174-184.

Hale, K. and D. Harris
1979   Historical linguistics and archeology. In *Handbook of North American Indians*, Volume 9, pp. 170-177. Smithsonian Institution, Washington, D.C.

Hall, E.T.
1938   Canadian River rock shelters. Manuscript on file, Laboratory of Anthropology, Museum of New Mexico, Santa Fe.

1944   Early stockaded settlements in the Governador, New Mexico. *Columbia studies in archeology and ethnology* 2(1). New York.

Hammack, L.C.
1965   Archeology of the Ute Dam and Reservoir. *Museum of New Mexico Papers in Anthropology* No. 14, Santa Fe.

Hammond, G.P. and A. Rey
1940   *Narratives of the Coronado expedition, 1540-1542.* University of New Mexico Press, Albuquerque.

Hannaford, C.A.
1979   Archeological survey and mitigation of three sites along State Road 203 in Guadalupe County, New Mexico. *Laboratory of Anthropology Note* No. 150, Santa Fe.

Harris, A.H., J. Schoenwetter and A.H. Warren
1967   An archeological survey of the Chuska Valley and the Chaco Plateau, Part I. *Museum of New Mexico Research Records* 4, Santa Fe.

Harris, D.R.
1969   Agricultural systems, ecosystems and the origins of agriculture. In *The domestication and exploitation of plants and animals.* Edited by P.J. Ucko and G.W. Dimbleby, Aldine-Atherton, Chicago, pp. 3-15.

Haury, E.W.
1936   The Mogollon culture of southwestern New Mexico. *Medallion Paper* 2. Gila Pueblo, Globe, Arizona.

Hawley, F.M.
1934   The significance of the dated prehistory of Chettro Ketl, Chaco Cañon, New Mexico. Monograph Series 1(1). *University of New Mexico Bulletin* 246, Albuquerque.

Hayes, A.C.
1964   The archeological survey of Wetherill Mesa. *National Park Service Archeological Research Series* 7-A, Washington, D.C.

1975   A survey of Chaco Canyon archeology. Unpublished Ms. No. 13, Chaco Center, National Park Service, University of New Mexico, Albuquerque.

Hayes, A.D. and J.A. Lancaster
1975   Badger House community, Mesa Verde National Park, Colorado. *National Park Service Archeological Research Series* 7-E. Washington, D.C.

Haynes, C.V.
1955   Evidence of early man in Torrance County, New Mexico. *Bulletin of the Texas Archeological Society* 26:144-164.

Henderson, M.
1976   An archeological inventory of Brantley Reservoir, New Mexico. *Southern Methodist University Contributions in Anthropology* No. 18, Dallas.

Hendron, J.W.
1940   Prehistory of El Rito de los Frijoles. *Southwestern Monuments Association Technical Series* 1.

Hester, J.
1962   Early Navajo migrations and acculturation in the southwest. *Museum of New Mexico Papers in Anthropology* 6, Santa Fe.

Hester, J. (continued)
1975   Paleoarcheology of the Llano Estacado. In Late Pleistocene environments of the southern high plains. Edited by F. Wendorf and J. Hester. *Fort Burgwin Research Center Publication* No. 9. Southern Methodist University, Dallas, pp. 247-256.

Hewett, E.L.
1906   Antiquities of the Jemez Plateau, New Mexico. *Bureau of American Ethnology Bulletin* 2, Smithsonian Institution, Washington, D.C.

1936   *The Chaco Canyon and its monuments.* University of New Mexico Press, Albuquerque.

1938   *The Pajarito Plateau and its ancient people.* University of New Mexico Press, Albuquerque.

Hibben, F.C.
1941   Evidences of early occupation of Sandia Cave, New Mexico and other sites in the Sandia-Manzano region. *Smithsonian Miscellaneous Collections* 99(23):1-44.

1955   Excavations at Pottery Mound, New Mexico. *American Antiquity* 21:179-180.

1975   *Kiva art of the Anasazi at Pottery Mound.* K.C. Publications, Las Vegas.

Hill, J.N.
1970   Broken K Pueblo: Prehistoric social organization in the American Southwest. *Anthropological Papers of the University of Arizona* 18, Tucson.

Hoebel, E.A.
1960   *The Cheyennes.* Holt, Rinehart and Winston.

Hoijer, H.
1956   The chronology of the Athapaskan languages. *International Journal of American Linguistics* 22(4):219-232.

Holden, W.C.
1930   The Canadian Valley expedition of March 1930. *Bulletin of the Texas Archeological and Paleontological Society* 2:21-32.

1931   Texas Tech archeological expedition, summer 1930. *Bulletin of the Texas Archeological and Paleontological Society* 3:43-52.

Hole, F.H.
1979   A review of Advances in archeological method and theory, volume 1 (by M.B. Schiffer). *American Scientist* 67(5):618-619.

Honea, K.H.
1964   A late Archaic horizon site near Folsom, New Mexico. Museum of New Mexico *Laboratory of Anthropology Notes* 3(29), Santa Fe.

1965   The Caballo Highway salvage project. *Laboratory of Anthropology Notes* 4(35). Museum of New Mexico, Santa Fe.

1969   The Rio Grande complex and the northern plains. *Plains Anthropologist* 14(43):57-70.

Human Systems Research, Inc.
1973   *Technical Manual: 1973 survey of the Tularosa Basin, the research design.* Albuquerque.

Hume, V.
1974   Preliminary report for the 1974 field season on Garrapata Ridge. Manuscript on file, USDA Forest Service, Southwestern Regional Office, Albuquerque.

Hunter-Anderson, R.L.
1978   *An archeological survey of the Yellowhouse Dam area.* Office of Contract Archeology, University of New Mexico, Albuquerque.

444

Hunter-Anderson, R.L. (continued)
1979   LA 13326, LA 13329, LA 13331, LA 13332 and LA 13333. In *Archeological investigations in Cochiti Reservoir, New Mexico, volume 3: 1976-1977 field seasons.* Edited by J.V. Biella. Office of Contract Archeology, University of New Mexico, Albuquerque, pp. 208-216.

1979a   Explaining residential aggregation in the northern Rio Grande: A competition reduction model. In *Archeological investigations in Cochiti Reservoir, New Mexico* 4:169-175. Edited by J.V. Biella and R.C. Chapman. Office of Contract Archeology, University of New Mexico, Albuquerque.

1979b   Observations on the changing role of small structural sites in the northern Rio Grande. In *Archeological investigations in Cochiti Reservoir, New Mexico* 4:177-186. Edited by J.V. Biella and R. C. Chapman. Office of Contract Archeology, University of New Mexico, Albuquerque.

Husted, W.M.
1965   Early occupation of the Colorado Front Range. *American Antiquity* 30(4):494-498.

Irwin-Williams, C.
1973   The Oshara tradition: Origins of Anasazi culture. *Eastern New Mexico University Contributions in Anthropology* 5(1). Eastern New Mexico University, Paleo-Indian Institute, Portales.

1977   Archeological investigations in the area of the middle Puerco River, New Mexico, May to December 1977. Ms. of progress report to the BLM, Albuquerque Area Office.

1978   Archeological investigations in the area of the middle Puerco River Valley, New Mexico, May to December 1978. Ms. of progress report to the BLM, Albuquerque Area Office.

1979   Post-Pleistocene archeology, 7,000 B.C. − 2,000 B.C. In *Handbook of North American Indians*, Volume 9, pp. 31-42. Smithsonian Institution, Washington, D.C.

Jeancon, J.A.
1923   Excavations in the Chama Valley. *Bureau of American Ethnology Bulletin* 81, Washington, D.C.

Jelinek, A.J.
1967   A prehistoric sequence in the middle Pecos Valley, New Mexico. *Anthropological Papers* No. 31, Museum of Anthropology, University of Michigan, Ann Arbor.

Johnson, L., Jr.
1967   Toward a statistical overview of the Archaic cultures of central and southwestern Texas. *Texas Memorial Museum Bulletin* No. 12.

Jorde, L.B.
1977   Precipitation cycles and cultural buffering in the prehistoric southwest. In *For theory building in archeology: Essays on faunal remains, aquatic resources, spatial analysis and systemic modeling.* Edited by L.R. Binford. Academic Press, New York, pp. 385-396.

Judd, N.M.
1954   The material culture of Pueblo Bonito. *Smithsonian Miscellaneous Collections* 124. Washington, D.C.

1959   Pueblo del Arroyo, Chaco Canyon, New Mexico. *Smithsonian Miscellaneous Collections* 38(1), Washington, D.C.

Judge, W.J.
1973   *The Paleo-Indian occupation of the central Rio Grande Valley, New Mexico.* University of New Mexico Press, Albuquerque.

1979   The development of a complex cultural ecosystem in the Chaco Basin, New Mexico. In *Scientific Research in the National Parks* II:901-905. Edited by Robert M. Linn. National Park Service, Washington, D.C.

n.d.   Early Man: Plains and Southwest. To appear in *Handbook of North American Indians*, volume 3. Edited by Wm. C. Sturtevant.

Judge, W.J. (continued)
  in press   Paleo-Indian Basketmaker: Overview and research problems. In *The past tomorrow: Planning for the preservation of the archeological resources in the San Juan Basin* (tentative title). Edited by F. Plog. School of American Research, Santa Fe.

Judge, W.J. and J. Dawson
  1972   Paleo-Indian settlement technology in New Mexico. *Science* 176:1210-1216.

Judge, W.J., J.I. Ebert and R.K. Hitchcock
  1975   Sampling in regional archeological survey. In *Sampling in archeology*. Edited by J.W. Mueller. The University of Arizona Press, Tucson, pp. 82-123.

Kelley, J.C.
  1952   Factors involved in the abandonment of certain peripheral southwestern settlements. *American Anthropologist* 54(3):356-387.

Kelley, J.H.
  1966   The archeology of the Sierra Blanca region of southeastern New Mexico. Unpublished Ph.D. dissertation, Harvard University, Cambridge.

  1979   The Sierra Blanca restudy project. In *Jornada Mogollon archeology*. Edited by P. Beckett and R.N. Wiseman. Historic Preservation Bureau, Santa Fe, pp. 107-132.

Kemrer, M.F.
  1974   The dynamics of western Navajo settlement, A.D. 1750-1900. Unpublished Ph.D. dissertation, Department of Anthropology, University of Arizona, Tucson.

Kenner, C.L.
  1969   *A history of New Mexican-Plains relations.* University of Oklahoma Press, Norman.

Keur, D.L.
  1941   Big Bead Mesa: An archeological study of Navajo acculturation, 1745-1812. *Memoirs of the Society of American Archeology* 1. Menasha, Wisconsin.

Kidder, A.V.
  1915   Pottery of the Pajarito Plateau and of some adjacent regions in New Mexico. *Memoirs of the American Anthropological Association* 2:407-462.

  1932   *The artifacts of Pecos.* Yale University Press, New Haven.

  1958   Pecos, New Mexico: Archeological notes. *Papers of the Robert S. Peabody Foundation for Archeology* 5. Phillips Academy, Andover.

Kidder, A.V. and C.A. Amsden
  1931   *The pottery of Pecos* 1. Yale University Press, New Haven.

Kidder, A.V. and A.O. Shepard
  1936   *The pottery of Pecos* 2. Yale University Press, New Haven.

Kidder, A.V., H.S. Cosgrove and C.B. Cosgrove
  1949   The Pendleton Ruin, Hidalgo County, New Mexico. *Contributions to American Anthropology and History* 50. Carnegie Institute of Washington, Publication 585.

Kirkpatrick, D.T.
  1976   Archeological investigations in the Cimarron district, northeastern New Mexico: 1929-1975. *Awanyu* 4(3):6-15.

Kirkpatrick, D.T. and R.I. Ford
  1977   Basketmaker food plants from the Cimarron district, northeastern New Mexico. *The Kiva* 42(3-4):257-269.

Koczan, S.
  n.d.   Las Vegas highway project excavations. Laboratory of Anthropology, Museum of New Mexico, Santa Fe. In preparation.

Krieger, A.D.
  1946   Cultural complexes and chronology in north Texas, with extensions of puebloan datings to the Mississippi Valley. *The University of Texas Publications* No. 4640, Austin.

Laboratory of Anthropology Site Survey Files, Santa Fe.

Lambe, J.M.
  1967   *Legislative history of the Historic Preservation Act of 1966.* National Park Service, Washington, D.C.

Lambert, M.
  1954   Paa-ko: archeological chronicle of an Indian village in north central New Mexico, Parts I-V. *School of American Research Monograph* 19, Santa Fe.

Lambert, M.F. and J.R. Ambler
  1961   A survey and excavation of caves in Hidalgo County, New Mexico. *School of American Research Monograph* No. 25, Santa Fe.

Lang, R.W.
  1977   Archeological survey of the upper San Cristobal arroyo drainage, Galisteo Basin, Santa Fe County, New Mexico. *The School of American Research Contract Program*, Santa Fe (Contract Report).

  1977a   The prehistoric pueblo cultural sequence in the northern Rio Grande. A paper presented at the fiftieth annual Pecos Conference, Pecos, New Mexico. August 1977.

  1978   *The archeology and culture history of the Conchas Dam and Reservoir area, San Miguel County, New Mexico.* School of American Research, Santa Fe.

Lange, C.H.
  1979   Relations of the southwest with the plains and great basin. In *Handbook of North American Indians* Volume 9, pp. 201-205. Smithsonian Institution, Washington, D.C.

LeBlanc, S.A.
  1976   Mimbres archeological center: Preliminary report of the second season, 1975. *Journal of New World Archeology* 1(6).

  1977   Preliminary report on the 1976 field season of the Mimbres Foundation in southwestern New Mexico. *Journal of New World Archeology* 2(2).

  1978   Settlement patterns in the El Morro Valley, New Mexico. In *Investigations of the southwestern anthropological research group: An experiment in archeological cooperation.* Edited by R. Euler and G. Gumerman. Museum of Northern Arizona, Flagstaff.

  1979   The early pithouse period. In *An archeological synthesis of southcentral and southwestern New Mexico.* Edited by S. LeBlanc and M. Whalen [BLM Draft Overview], Albuquerque, pp. 91-130.

LeBlanc, S.A. and D. Rugge
  1979   The late pueblo period: Animas. In *An archeological synthesis of southcentral and southwestern New Mexico.* Edited by S. LeBlanc and M. Whalen [BLM Draft Report], pp. 344-382.

LeBlanc, S.A. and M.E. Whalen (Editors)
  1979   *An archeological synthesis of southcentral and southwestern New Mexico* [BLM Draft Overview], Albuquerque.

Lee, R.B. and I. DeVore
  1968   *Man the hunter.* Aldine, Chicago.

Lehmer, D.
  1948   The Jornada branch of the Mogollon. *University of Arizona Social Science Bulletin* 17. University of Arizona Press, Tucson.

Lekson, S.
1978   Settlement patterns in the Redrock Valley, southwestern New Mexico. Unpublished M.A. thesis, Eastern New Mexico University, Portales.

Leslie, R.H.
1978   Projectile point types and sequence of the eastern Jornada-Mogollon. *Transactions of the 13th regional archeological symposium for southeastern New Mexico and west Texas*, pp. 81-157.

1979   The eastern Jornada Mogollon, extreme southwestern New Mexico. In *Jornada-Mogollon archeology*. Edited by P. Beckett and R.N. Wiseman. Historic Preservation Bureau, Santa Fe.

Levine, F. and C.M. Mobley
1976   Archeological resources at Los Esteros Lake, New Mexico. *Southern Methodist University Contributions in Anthropology* 17, Dallas.

Lintz, C.
1978   Architecture and radio-carbon dating of the Antelope Creek Focus: A test of Campbell's model. *Plains Anthropologist* 23(82, II):319-328.

Lipe, W.D.
1978   The southwest. In *Ancient Native Americans*. Edited by J. Jennings. W.H. Freeman & Co., San Francisco, pp. 327-402.

Lister, R.H.
1948   Notes on the archeology of the Watrous Valley, New Mexico. *El Palacio* 55(2):35-41.

Lister, R.H. and F.C. Lister
1968   *Earl Morris and southwestern archeology*. University of New Mexico Press, Albuquerque.

Longacre, W.A.
1970   Archeology as anthropology: A case study. *Anthropological Papers of the University of Arizona* 17, Tucson.

Loose, R.W. and T.R. Lyons
1976   The Chetro Ketl Field: A planned water control system in Chaco Canyon. Remote Sensing Experiments in Cultural Resource Studies. *Reports of the Chaco Center* No. 1. National Park Service, Albuquerque.

Lotka, A.J.
1922   Contributions to the energetics of evolution. *Proceedings of the National Academy of Science* 8:147-151.

Lummis, C.F.
1925   *The land of Poco Tiempo*. Charles Scribner's Sons, New York.

Lutes, E.
1959   A marginal prehistoric culture of northwestern New Mexico. *El Palacio* 66(2):59-68.

Lutz, B.J. and W.J. Hunt
1979   *Models for patterns and change in prehistoric settlement-subsistence systems of the Purgatoire and Apishapa highlands*. Office of Public and Contract Archeology, University of Northern Colorado, Greely.

Lyons, T.R.
1969   A study of Paleo-Indian and desert culture complexes of the Estancia Valley area, New Mexico. Unpublished Ph.D. dissertation, Department of Anthropology, University of New Mexico, Albuquerque.

Lyons, T.R. and R. Switzer
1975   Archeological excavations at Tillery Springs, Estancia, New Mexico. In Collected Papers in Honor of Florence Hawley Ellis. *Papers of the Archeological Society of New Mexico* No. 2, Santa Fe.

Mackey, J.C. and S.J. Holbrook
  1978   Environmental reconstruction and the abandonment of the Largo-Gallina area. *Journal of Field Archeology* 5(1):29-49.

Magers, P.C. (Editor)
  n.d.   Class I cultural resource inventory of the Chaco, San Juan and portions of the Cabezon planning unit. Draft report to BLM. *Cultural Resource Management Division Report* 289. New Mexico State University, Las Cruces.

Marshall, M.P.
  1973   Ceramic descriptions. In *Technical Manual: 1973 survey of the Tularosa Basin, the research design.* Human Systems Research, Albuquerque, pp. 326-373.

  1973a   Background information on the Jornada culture area. In *Technical Manual: 1973 survey of the Tularosa Basin, the research design.* Human Systems Research, Albuquerque, pp. 49-120.

  1978   Yellowhouse ceramic groups, phases, dates and ceramic complexes. In *An archeological survey of the Yellowhouse dam area* (by R.L. Hunter-Anderson). Office of Contract Archeology, University of New Mexico, Albuquerque, pp. 31-41.

  n.d.   An archeological survey of the upper Pescado drainage, Zuni Indian Reservation. Xeroxed report. Office of Contract Archeology, University of New Mexico, Albuquerque.

Marshall, M.P., J.R. Stein, R.W. Loose and J.E. Novotny
  1979   *Anasazi communities of the San Juan Basin.* Public Service Company of New Mexico, Albuquerque and Historic Preservation Bureau, Santa Fe.

Martin, P.S.
  1979   Prehistory: Mogollon. In *Handbook of North American Indians* Vol. 9, Southwest. Smithsonian Institution, Washington, D.C.

Martin, P.S. and F. Plog
  1973   *The archeology of Arizona.* Doubleday, New York.

Martin, P.S. *et al.*
  1952   Mogollon cultural continuity and change: The stratigraphic analysis of Tularosa and Cordova caves. *Fieldianna: Anthropology* 40. Chicago Natural History Museum.

Mason, J.A.
  1929   The Texas expedition. *Journal of the University of Pennsylvannia Museum* 22:318-338.

Maybury-Lewis, D.H.P.
  1967   *The Akwe-Shavante.* Clarendon Press, Oxford.

McCluney, E.B.
  1962   Clanton Draw and Box Canyon. *The School of American Research Monograph* No. 26, Santa Fe.

  n.d.   The excavation at the Joyce Well site, Hidalgo County, New Mexico. Ms. on file at the School of American Research, Santa Fe.

McGimsey, C.R., III
  1980   Marianna Mesa: Seven prehistoric settlements in west-central New Mexico. *Papers of the Peabody Museum of Archeology and Ethnology* 72. Harvard University, Cambridge.

McGregor, J.C.
  1965   *Southwestern archeology.* John Wiley and Sons, New York.

  1974   *Southwestern archeology.* University of Illinois Press, Urbana [revised edition].

McNitt, F.
  1957   *Richard Wetherill: Anasazi.* University of New Mexico Press, Albuquerque.

Mera, H.P.

1931   Chupadero Black-on-White. *Laboratory of Anthropology Technical Series Bulletin* No. 1. Santa Fe.

1938   Reconnaissance and excavation in southeastern New Mexico. *Memoirs of the American Anthropological Association* 51. Menasha.

1940   Population changes in the Rio Grande glaze paint area. *Laboratory of Anthropology Technical Series Bulletin* No. 9. Santa Fe.

1943   An outline of ceramic development in southern and southeastern New Mexico. *Laboratory of Anthropology Technical Series Bulletin* No. 11. Santa Fe.

1944   Jaritas rock shelter, northeastern New Mexico. *American Antiquity* 9(3):291-305.

Merlan, T.W.

in press   The quality of significance in National Register determinations. In *The past tomorrow: Planning for the preservation of archeological resources in the San Juan Basin* (tentative title). Edited by F. Plog. School of American Research, Santa Fe.

Minnis, P.

1979   Prehistoric population and settlement configuration in southwestern New Mexico. In *An archeological synthesis of southcentral and southwestern New Mexico.* Edited by S. LeBlanc and M. Whalen [BLM Draft Report], pp. 575-634.

Mobley, C.M. (Editor)

1978   Archeological research and management at Los Esteros Reservoir, New Mexico. *Archeological Research Program Research Report* 107. Southern Methodist University, Dallas.

1979   The terminal Archaic at Los Esteros: A late hunter-gatherer community on the Jornada Mogollon frontier. In *Jornada Mogollon archeology.* Edited by P.H. Beckett and R.N. Wiseman. Historic Preservation Bureau, Santa Fe.

Moorehead, W.K.

1931   *Archeology of the Arkansas River Valley.* Yale University Press, New Haven.

Morris, D.P.

1968   A preliminary report: A survey of Gila Cliff Dwellings National Monument and a portion of the Gila National Forest. Manuscript on file at Gila National Forest, Silver City, New Mexico.

Morris, E.H. and R.F. Burgh

1954   Basketmaker II sites near Durango, Colorado. *Carnegie Institution of Washington Publication* 604, Washington, D.C.

Nelson, N.C.

1914   Pueblo ruins of the Galisteo Basin, New Mexico. *Anthropological Papers of the American Museum of Natural History* 15(1). New York.

1916   Chronology of the Tano Ruins, New Mexico. *American Anthropologist* 18(2):159-180.

Oakes, Y.R.

1979   Cross L Ranch site: A study of plains adaptations. State Highway 325 east of Folsom, Union County, New Mexico. NMSHD Project BRS-1443(7). *Laboratory of Anthropology Notes* No. 164, Santa Fe.

Odum, H.T.

1971   *Environment power and society.* John Wiley & Sons, New York.

Ortiz, A. (Editor)

1979   *Handbook of North American Indians, Volume 9: The Southwest.* Smithsonian Institution, Washington, D.C.

Pattison, N.B.
1968   Nogales Cliff House: A Largo-Gallina site. Unpublished M.A. thesis, Department of Anthropology, University of New Mexico, Albuquerque.

Peckham, S.L.
1958   Hillside Pueblo: Early masonry architecture in the Reserve area, New Mexico. *El Palacio* 65(3): 81-94.

1967   Archeological salvage excavations along Interstate 40 near Laguna Pueblo, New Mexico. *Laboratory of Anthropology Notes* 17, Santa Fe.

1969   An archeological site inventory of New Mexico, Part 1. On file, Laboratory of Anthropology, Museum of New Mexico, Santa Fe.

1971   Unpublished site forms from survey on the Bernabe Montoya Land Grant. In the files of the Laboratory of Anthropology, Museum of New Mexico, Santa Fe.

Peckham, S.L. and E.K. Reed
1963   Three sites near Ranchos de Taos, New Mexico. *Highway Salvage Archeology* 4(3):1-30.

Peckham, S.L. and J. Wilson
n.d.   Chuska Valley ceramics. Manuscript on file at Museum of New Mexico, Santa Fe.

Pippin, L.C.
1978   The archeology and paleoecology of Guadalupe Ruin, Sandoval County, New Mexico. Unpublished Ph.D. dissertation, Department of Anthropology, Washington State University, Pullman.

Plog, F.
1974   *The study of prehistoric change.* Academic Press, New York.

Plog, S.
1969   Prehistoric population movements: Measurement and explanation. Unpublished manuscript, Field Museum of Natural History, Chicago.

Powell, N.
1978   An archeological clearance survey of two and one-half sections of land on La Jara Mesa west of Mt. Taylor, west-central New Mexico. *Cultural Resources Management Division Report* 263, New Mexico State University, Las Cruces.

Reed, A.S., J.A. Halasi, A.S. White and D.A. Breternitz
1979   *The archeology and stabilization of the Dominguez and Escalante Ruins.* Bureau of Land Management, Colorado State Office.

Reher, C.A.
1977   Adaptive process on the shortgrass plains. In *For theory building in archeology*, pp. 13-40. Edited by L.R. Binford. Academic Press, New York.

1977a   Settlement and subsistence along the lower Chaco River. In *Settlement and subsistence along the lower Chaco River: The CGP survey*, pp. 7-111. University of New Mexico Press, Albuquerque.

1977b   *Settlement and subsistence along the lower Chaco River: The CGP survey.* University of New
(Editor)   Mexico Press, Albuquerque.

Reher, C.A. and D.C. Witter
1977   Archaic settlement and vegetative diversity. In *Settlement and subsistence along the lower Chaco River: The CGP survey*, pp. 113-126. Edited by C.A. Reher. University of New Mexico Press, Albuquerque.

Reinhart, T.R.
1967   The Rio Rancho phase: A preliminary report on early Basketmaker culture in the Rio Grande Valley, New Mexico. *American Antiquity* 32(4):458-470.

Reinhart, T.R. (continued)
1968   Late Archaic cultures of the middle Rio Grande Valley, New Mexico. Unpublished Ph.D. dissertation, University of New Mexico, Albuquerque.

Reiter, P.
1938   The Jemez Pueblo of Unshagi, New Mexico with notes on earlier excavations at Amokiumqua and Guisewa, Parts 1 and 2. *School of American Research Monographs* 5 and 6. Santa Fe.

Renaud, E.T.
1929   Archeological research in northeastern New Mexico and western Oklahoma. *El Palacio* 27(23-24):276-279.

1930   Prehistoric cultures of the Cimarron Valley: Northeastern New Mexico and western Oklahoma. *Colorado Scientific Society Proceedings* 12(5):113-150. Denver.

1936   Archeological survey of the high western plains, pictographs and petroglyphs of the western plains. *Department of Antrhopology, University of Denver Archeological Series*, Eighth Paper. Denver.

1942   Reconnaissance work in the upper Rio Grande Valley, Colorado and New Mexico. *Department of Anthropology, University of Denver Archeological Series*, Third paper. Denver.

1942a   Indian stone enclosures of Colorado and New Mexico. *Department of Anthropology, University of Denver Archeological Series, Second Paper*. Denver.

1946   Archeology of the upper Rio Grande Basin in southern Colorado and northern New Mexico. *Department of Anthropology, University of Denver*, Sixth Paper. Denver.

Rice, G.E.
1975   A systematic explanation of Mogollon settlement pattern changes. Unpublished Ph.D. dissertation, Department of Anthropology, University of Washington.

1979   An analytical overview of the Mogollon tradition. In *Studies in the prehistory of the Forestdale region*. Edited by R. Stafford and G. Rice. Arizona State University, Tempe [Draft], pp. 14-90.

Richert, R.
1964   Excavation of a portion of the East Ruin, Aztec Ruins National Monument, New Mexico. *Southwest Parks and Monuments Association Technical Series* 4. Globe, Arizona.

Roberts, F.H.H., Jr.
1929   Shabik'eshehee Village, a late Basketmaker site in Chaco Canyon, New Mexico. *Bureau of American Ethnology Bulletin* 192, Washington, D.C.

1932   The village of the Great Kivas on the Zuni Reservation, New Mexico. *Bureau of American Ethnology Bulletin* No. 111, Washington, D.C.

1942   Archeological and geological investigations in the San Jon district, eastern New Mexico. *Smithsonian Miscellaneous Collections* 103(4).

Robinson, W., B. Harrill and R. Warren
1973   *Tree-ring dates from New Mexico J-K, P, V*. Laboratory of Tree-ring Research, University of Arizona, Tucson.

Robinson, W., J. Bruge, B. Harrill and R. Warren
1974   *Tree-ring dates from New Mexico B: Chaco-Gobernador area*. Laboratory of Tree-ring Research, Tucson.

Rohn, A. H.
1977   *Cultural change and continuity on Chapin Mesa*. The Regents Press, University of Kansas, Lawrence.

Roosa, W.B.
1956   Preliminary report on the Lucy site. *El Palacio* 63(2):36-49.

Rostow, W.W.
1980   *Why the poor get richer and the rich slow down: Essays in the Marshallian long period.* University of Texas Press, Austin.

Ruppe, R.J.
1953   *The Acoma culture province: An archeological concept.* Ph.D. dissertation, Department of Anthropology, Harvard University, Cambridge.

Ruppe, R.J. and A.E. Dittert
1952   The archeology of Cebolleta Mesa and Acoma Pueblo. *El Palacio* 59(7):191-217.

1953   Acoma archeology: A preliminary report of the final field season in the Cebolleta Mesa region, New Mexico. *El Palacio* 69(7):259-273.

Sahlins, M.D. and E.R. Service
1966   *Evolution and culture.* University of Michigan, Ann Arbor.

Sando, J.S.
1979   Jemez Pueblo. In *Handbook of North American Indians, Volume 9, Southwest.* Smithsonian Institution, Washington, D.C., pp. 418-429.

Schaafsma, C.F.
1976   *Archeological survey of maximum pool and Navajo excavations at Abiquiu Reservoir, Rio Arriba County, New Mexico.* School of American Research, Santa Fe.

1978   *A survey in the vicinity of Ambrosia Lake, McKinley County.* School of American Research, Santa Fe.

1978a   *The mechanical and chemical effects of inundation at Abiquiu Reservoir.* School of American Research, Santa Fe.

1979   The "El Paso Phase" and its relationship to the "Casas Grandes Phenomenon". In *Jornada Mogollon archeology.* Edited by P. Beckett and R.N. Wiseman. Historic Preservation Bureau, Santa Fe, pp. 383-388.

Schaafsma, P.
1972   *Rock art in New Mexico.* New Mexico State Planning Office, Santa Fe.

Schaafsma, P. and C.F. Schaafsma
1974   Evidence for the origins of the Pueblo Katchina cult as suggested by southwest rock art. *American Antiquity* 39(4):535-545.

Schelberg, J. D.
1980   Social complexity in Chaco Canyon. In *Scientific Research in the National Parks* Vol. 1:414-437. National Park Service, Washington, D.C.

Scholes, F.V. and H.P. Mera
1940   Some aspects of the Jumano problem. *Carnegie Institution of Washington Publication* No. 523. Washington, D.C.

Schoenwetter, J. and F. Eddy
1964   Alluvial and palynological reconstruction of environments, Navajo Reservoir district. *Museum of New Mexico Papers in Anthropology* 13, Santa Fe.

Schroeder, A.H.
1979   Pueblos abandoned in historic times. In *Handbook of North American Indians, Volume 9, Southwest.* Smithsonian Institution, Washington, D.C., pp. 236-254.

1979a   Pecos Pueblo. In *Handbook of North American Indians, Volume 9, Southwest.* Smithsonian Institution, Washington, D.C., pp. 430-437.

n.d.   A study of the Apache Indians, Part II. The Jicarilla Apaches. Manuscript, Santa Fe.

Seaman, T.J.
1976   Excavation of LA 11843: An early stockaded settlement of the Gallina phase. *Laboratory of Anthropology Note* No. 111g. Santa Fe.

n.d.   Archeological excavations at the S.M. Butcher and A.E. Wyatt homesteads, Tucumcari, New Mexico. Laboratory of Anthropology, Santa Fe (in preparation).

n.d.a   Archeological excavations of lithic sites near Tucumcari, New Mexico. Laboratory of Anthropology, Santa Fe (in preparation).

Shepard, A.O.
1965   Ceramics for the archeologist. *Carnegie Institution of Washington Publication* No. 609. Washington, D.C.

Simmons, M.
1979   History of Pueblo-Spanish relations to 1821. In *Handbook of North American Indians, Volume 9, Southwest.* Smithsonian Institution, Washington, D.C., pp. 178-193.

1979a   History of the pueblos since 1821. In *Handbook of North American Indians, Volume 9, Southwest.* Smithsonian Institution, Washington, D.C., pp. 206-223.

Skinner, S.A.
1965   The Sedillo site: A pithouse village in Albuquerque. *El Palacio* 72(1):5-24.

Smiley, N.K.
1979   Evidence for ceramic trade specialization in the southern Jornada branch. In *Jornada Mogollon archeology*. Edited by P. Beckett and R.N. Wiseman. Historic Preservation Bureau, Santa Fe, pp. 53-60.

Smiley, T.L., S.A. Stubbs and B. Bannister
1953   A foundation for the dating of some late archeological sites in the Rio Grande area, New Mexico: Based on studies in tree-ring methods and pottery analyses. *Laboratory of Tree-ring Research Bulletin* 6, University of Arizona, Tucson.

Smith, C.B., S.E. Smith and J.W. Runyan
1966   A preliminary investigation of the Rattlesnake Draw site. *The Lea County Archeological Society* Special Series 1. Hobbs.

Snow, D.H.
1974   The excavation of Saltbush Pueblo, Bandelier National Monument, New Mexico, 1971. *Laboratory of Anthropology Notes* 97, Santa Fe.

Speth, J.D.
1979   The Garnsey Bison Kill site, Chaves County, New Mexico. In *Jornada Mogollon archeology*. Edited by P. Beckett and R.N. Wiseman. Historic Preservation Bureau, Santa Fe, pp. 143-158.

Spier, L.
1917   Zuni chronology. *Proceedings of the National Academy of Sciences* 3(3):380-383.

Stafford, C.R.
1979   Subsistence-settlement systems in the Forestdale region. In *Studies in the prehistory of the Forestdale region*. Edited by R. Stafford and G. Rice. Arizona State University, Tempe, pp. 114-151 [Draft].

Stafford, C.R. and G. Rice (Editors)
1979   *Studies in the prehistory of the Forestdale region.* Three volumes. Office of Cultural Resource Management, Arizona State University, Tempe [Draft of a report prepared for National Park Service, Western Archeological Center, Tucson].

State Planning Office
1973   *The historic preservation program for New Mexico: The historical background* 1. Santa Fe.

Steen, C.R.
1955   The Pigeon Cliffs site: A preliminary report. *El Palacio* 62(5-6):174-180.

1976   Excavations at Pigeon Cliff. In Collected papers in honor of Marjorie Ferguson Lambert. *Papers of the Archeological Society of New Mexico* No. 3, Albuquerque.

1977   *Pajarito Plateau archeological survey and excavations.* Los Alamos Scientific Laboratory, Los Alamos.

Steward, J.H.
1955   *Theory of culture change: The methodology of multilinear evolution.* University of Illinois Press, Urbana.

Stickel, E.G.
1968   Status differentiation at the Rincon site. *UCLA Archeological Survey Annual Report* No. 10. Los Angeles.

Stuart, D.E.
1972   Band structure and ecological variability: The Ona and Yahgan of Tierra del Fuego. Unpublished Ph.D. dissertation, Department of Anthropology, University of New Mexico, Albuquerque.

1977   Seasonal phases in Ona subsistence, territorial distribution and organization: Implications for the archeological record. In *For theory building in archeology.* Edited by L.R. Binford. Academic Press, New York, pp. 251-283.

1978   *A proposed project design for the timber management program archeological surveys.* Bureau of Indian Affairs, Albuquerque.

1980   Kinship and social organization in Tierra del Fuego: Evolutionary consequences. In *The versatility of kinship.* Edited by L.S. Cordell and S.J. Beckerman. Academic Press, New York, pp. 269-284.

in press   Power and efficiency: Demographic behavior and energetic trajectories in cultural evolution. In *The past tomorrow: Planning for the preservation of archeological resources in the San Juan Basin* (tentative title). Edited by F. Plog. School of American Research, Santa Fe.

n.d.   Stratification of adaptive risks: An essay on cultural evolution and the archeological record. Manuscript in author's possession, Albuquerque.

Stubbs, S.A.
1959   "New" old churches found at Quarai and Tabira. *El Palacio* 66(5):162-169.

Stubbs, S.A. and W.S. Stallings
1953   The excavation of Pindi Pueblo, New Mexico. *Monographs of the School of American Research* 18, Santa Fe.

Suhm, D.A. and E.B. Jelks
1962   Handbook of Texas archeology: Type descriptions. *Texas Archeological Society* and the *Texas Memorial Museum*, Austin.

Suhm, D.A., A.D. Krieger and E.B. Jelks
1954   An introductory handbook to Texas archeology. *Bulletin of the Texas Archeological Society* 25, Austin.

Tainter, J.A.
1979   Cultural evolution in the Jornada Mogollon area. In *Jornada Mogollon archeology.* Edited by P. Beckett and R.N. Wiseman, pp. 377-382. New Mexico Historic Preservation Bureau, Santa Fe.

1980   Symbolism, interaction and cultural boundaries: The Anasazi-Mogollon transition zone in west-central New Mexico. A paper presented at the first annual Mogollon Conference, New Mexico State University, Las Cruces.

Tainter, J.A. (and D.A. Gillio)
1980a   *Cultural resources overview: Mount Taylor area, New Mexico.* USDA Forest Service and Bureau of Land Management, Albuquerque. U.S. Superintendent of Documents, Washington, D.C.

Thomas, D.H.
1975   Nonsite sampling in archeology: Up the creek without a site. In *Sampling in archeology.* Edited by J.W. Mueller. University of Arizona Press, Tucson, pp. 61-81.

Thoms, A.V.
1976   Review of northeastern New Mexico archeology. *Awanyu* 4(1):8-35.

Toll, H. W., T.C. Windes and P.J. McKenna
1980   Late ceramic patterns in Chaco Canyon: The pragmatics of modeling ceramic exchange. In *Models and methods in regional exchange.* Edited by Robert E. Fry. *SAA Papers* No. 1, Washington, D.C., pp. 95-117.

Toulouse, J.H.
1949   The mission of San Gregorio de Abo. *School of American Research Monograph* No. 13, Santa Fe.

Toulouse, J.H. and R.L. Stephenson
1960   Excavations at Pueblo Pardo. *The Museum of New Mexico Papers in Anthropology* No. 2, Santa Fe.

Turner, C.G., II
1977   Field report presented at the 50th Pecos conference. Pecos, New Mexico.

Van Valkenburgh, R.F.
1965   Report of the archeological survey of the Navajo-Hopi contact area. Manuscript on file at the Navajo Tribal Museum, Window Rock, Arizona.

Van Zeist, W.
1969   Reflections on prehistoric environments in the Near East. In *The domestication and exploitation of plants and animals.* Edited by P.J. Ucko and G.W. Dimbleby. Aldine-Atherton, Chicago, pp. 35-46.

Vivian, R.G.
1964   Gran Quivira: Excavations in a 17th-century Jumano pueblo. *Archeological Research Series* 8, National Park Service, U.S. Department of the Interior, Washington, D.C.

1965   The 3-C site: An early Pueblo II ruin in Chaco Canyon, New Mexico. *Publications in Anthropology* 13. University of New Mexico, Albuquerque.

Vivian, R. Gordon and T.W. Mathews
1965   Kin Kletso, a Pueblo II community in Chaco Canyon, New Mexico. *Southwestern Parks and Monuments Association Technical Series* 6(1). Globe, Arizona.

Vivian, R. Gordon and P. Reiter
1960   The Great Kivas of Chaco Canyon and their relationships. *Monographs of the School of American Research* 22, Santa Fe.

Vivian, R. Gwinn
1974   Conservation and diversion: Water control systems in the Anasazi southwest. In *Irrigation impact on society.* Edited by T.E. Downing and M. Gibson. *Anthropological Papers of the University of Arizona* 25, Tucson.

Vivian, R.Gwinn and N. Clendenen
1965   The Denison site: Four pithouses near Isleta, New Mexico. *El Palacio* 72(2):5-24.

Wade, W.D.
1970   Skeletal remains of a prehistoric population from the Puerco Valley, eastern Arizona. Ph.D. dissertation, Department of Anthropology, University of Colorado, Boulder.

Wait, W.
   in press   The development of a computerized cultural resource data base for assessing the impacts of
            uranium mining on the San Juan Basin, New Mexico. In *The past tomorrow: Planning for the
            preservation of archeological resources in the San Juan Basin* (tentative title). Edited by F. Plog.
            School of American Research, Santa Fe.

Walter, P.A.F.
   1916   The cities that died of fear. *School of American Research Paper* No. 35, Santa Fe.

Warren, A.H.
   1977   Appendix 1: New dimensions in the study of prehistoric pottery. In *Archeological investiga-
            tions in Cochiti Reservoir, New Mexico, volume 2: Excavation and analysis 1975 season.*
            Edited by R. Chapman and J.V. Biella. Office of Contract Archeology, University of New
            Mexico, Albuquerque, pp. 363-374.

   1979   The glaze paint wares of the upper Rio Grande. In *Archeological investigations in Cochiti
            Reservoir, New Mexico, volume 4: Adaptive change in the northern Rio Grande Valley.* Edited
            by J.V. Biella and R.C. Chapman. Office of Contract Archeology, University of New Mexico,
            Albuquerque, pp. 187-216.

   n.d.   Production and distribution of pottery in Chaco Canyon and northwestern New Mexico (un-
            dated spiral bound and xeroxed monograph; 95 pp. and appendix — copies in possession of
            the author), Albuquerque.

Watson, P.J., S.A. LeBlanc and C.L. Redman
   n.d.   Aspects of Zuni prehistory: A preliminary report on excavations and survey in the El Morro
            Valley of New Mexico. Unpublished Ms., Department of Anthropology, Washington University,
            St. Louis.

Way, K.L.
   1979   Early pueblo occupation in the southern Tularosa Basin, New Mexico. In *Jornada Mogollon
            archeology.* Edited by P. Beckett and R.N. Wiseman. Historic Preservation Bureau, Santa Fe,
            pp. 41-52.

Weaver, D.E.
   1978   Prehistoric population dynamics and environmental exploitation in the Manuelito Canyon
            district, northwestern New Mexico. Unpublished Ph.D. dissertation, Department of Anthro-
            pology, Arizona State University, Tempe.

Wendorf, F. (Assembler)
   1953   Salvage archeology in the Chama Valley, New Mexico. *Monographs of the School of American
            Research* No. 17, Santa Fe.

Wendorf, F.
   1954   A reconstruction of northern Rio Grande prehistory. *American Anthropologist* 56:200-227.

   1960   The archeology of northeastern New Mexico. *El Palacio* 67(2):55-65.

Wendorf, F. and J.P. Miller
   1959   Artifacts from high mountain sites in the Sangre de Cristo range, New Mexico. *El Palacio*
            66(2):37-52.

Wendorf, F. and E.K. Reed
   1955   An alternate reconstruction of northern Rio Grande prehistory. *El Palacio* 62(5 & 6):131-173.

Wetherington, R.K.
   1968   Excavations at Pot Creek Pueblo. *Fort Burgwin Research Center Report* 6, Taos.

Whalen, M.E.
   1977   Settlement patterns of the eastern Hueco Bolson. *Anthropological Paper* No. 4. El Paso Cen-
            tennial Museum, University of Texas at El Paso.

Whalen, M.E. (continued)

1978   Settlement patterns of the western Hueco Bolson. *Anthropological Paper* No. 6. El Paso Centennial Museum, University of Texas at El Paso.

1979   "The pithouse periods" and the "pueblo periods". In *An archeological synthesis of south-central and southwestern New Mexico*. Edited by S. LeBlanc and M. Whalen [BLM Draft Report], pp. 411-564.

1979a   Social organization and interaction during the pithouse period in the Jornada area. In *Jornada Mogollon archeology*. Edited by P. Beckett and R.N. Wiseman. Historic Preservation Bureau, Santa Fe, pp. 345-358.

Wheat, J.B.

1955   Mogollon culture prior to A.D. 1000. *Memoirs of the Society for American Archeology* No. 10, Salt Lake City.

Wilmsen, E.N.

1974   *Lindenmeier: A Pleistocene hunting society*. Harper and Row, New York.

White, L.A.

1959   *The evolution of culture*. McGraw Hill, New York.

Whittlesy, S.M.

1978   Status and death at Grasshopper Pueblo: Experiments toward an archeological theory of correlates. Unpublished Ph.D. dissertation, Department of Anthropology, University of Arizona, Tucson.

Willey, G.R.

1966   *An introduction to American archeology, volume 1: North America*. Prentice-Hall, Englewood.

Williams, J.L. and P.E. McAllister

1979   *New Mexico in maps*. Technology Application Center, the University of New Mexico, Albuquerque.

Wimberly, M. and P. Eidenbach

1977   *Inventory of the cultural resources: Sierra Blanca ski area land transfer*. BIA Contract No. MOOC14202478. Human Systems Research, Tularosa.

1980   *Reconnaissance study of the archaeological and related resources of the lower Puerco and Salado drainages, central New Mexico*. Human Systems Research, Tularosa.

1980a   *An archaeological reconnaissance in White Sands National Monument*. Human Systems Research, Tularosa.

Wimberly, M., P. Eidenbach, and J. Betancourt

1979   Canon del Perro, a history of Dog Canyon. Unpublished report for the Department of Natural Resources, New Mexico State Parks and Recreation Division. Human Systems Research, Tularosa.

Wimberly, M. and A. Rogers

1977   Archaeological survey: Three Rivers drainage, New Mexico. *The Artifact* 15. El Paso Archeological Society.

Windes, T.C.

1977   Typology and technology of Anasazi ceramics. In *Settlement and subsistence along the lower Chaco River: The CGP survey*. Edited by C. Reher. University of New Mexico Press, Albuquerque, pp. 269-370; 525-566.

Wiseman, R.N.

1975   Sitio Creston (LA 4939), A stone enclosure site near Las Vegas, New Mexico. *Plains Anthropologist* 20(68):81-104.

Wiseman, R.N. (continued)
1978   Eastern New Mexico archeology: A case example of interpretive potential. *Laboratory of Anthropology Note* No. 133, Santa Fe.

1979   Recent excavation and survey near Bent, Otero County, New Mexico. In *Jornada Mogollon archeology*. Edited by P. Beckett and R.N. Wiseman. Historic Preservation Bureau, Santa Fe, pp. 61-66.

Wiseman, R.N. and P. Beckett
1979   Comments and queries. In *Jornada Mogollon archeology*. Edited by P. Beckett and R.N. Wiseman. Historic Preservation Bureau, Santa Fe, pp. 397-401.

Wiseman, R.N., *et al.*
1976   Multi-disciplinary investigations at the Smokey Bear Ruin (LA 2112), Lincoln County, New Mexico. *COAS Publishing and Research Monograph* No. 4, Las Cruces.

Woodbury, R.B. and E.B.W. Zubrow
1979   Agricultural beginnings, 2000 B.C.—A.D. 500. In *Handbook of North American Indians, volume 9: Southwest.* Smithsonian Institution, Washington, D.C., pp. 43-60.

Worman, F.C.V.
1967   *Archeological salvage excavations on the Mesita del Buey, Los Alamos County, New Mexico.* Los Alamos Scientific Laboratory.

Wormington, H.M.
1947   *Prehistoric Indians of the southwest.* Denver Museum of Natural History, Denver.

1957   Ancient man in North America. *The Denver Museum of Natural History, Popular Series* No. 4, Denver.

Zubrow, E.B.W.
1971   Carrying capacity and dynamic equilibrium in the prehistoric southwest. *American Antiquity* 36(2):127-138.